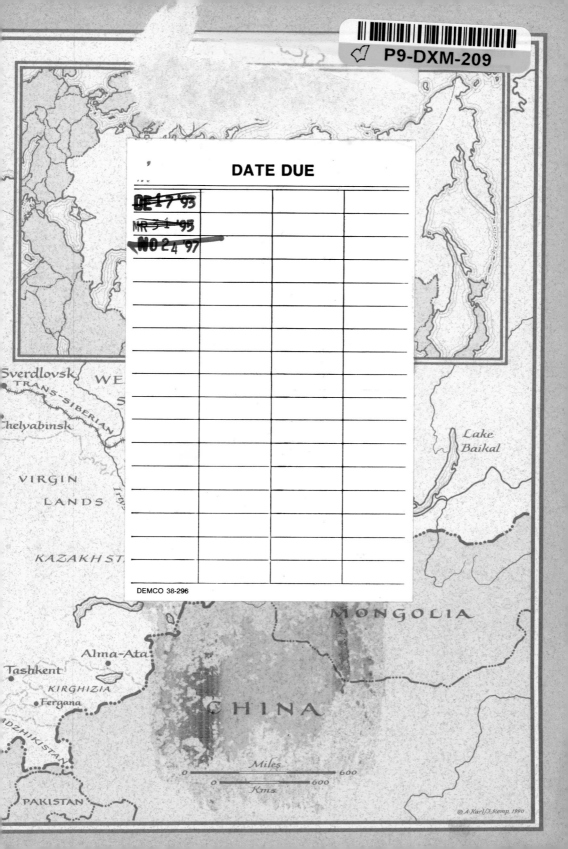

DATE DUE

THE NEW RUSSIANS

THE
NEW
RUSSIANS

HEDRICK SMITH

RANDOM HOUSE

NEW YORK

Grateful acknowledgment is made to the following for permission
to reprint previously published material:
Thurlbeck Productions, Inc.: Seven lines from the song "Revolution" by DDT.
Reprinted by permission of Thurlbeck Productions (DDT).

Library of Congress Cataloging-in-Publication Data

Smith, Hedrick.
  The new Russians.
  Includes index.
  1. Soviet Union—Social life and customs—1970–
2. Soviet Union—Social conditions—1970–
DK276.S527 1990   947.085   90-53127
ISBN 0-394-58190-3

Manufactured in the United States of America
First Edition

Book design by Jo Anne Metsch

To my children,
Laurie, Jenny, Scott, and Lesley

May you enjoy a lifetime
of genuine peace
and love

ACKNOWLEDGMENTS

Whatever the shortcomings of this book, they would have been much greater without the generous help, advice, and comments of many friends and colleagues.

Five people deserve special acknowledgment. My friend Greg Guroff, a Russian historian with a fund of knowledge and personal acquaintances in Moscow, not only opened the doors of his many friends for me but read the entire manuscript and infused each section with his understanding of Soviet society and Russian history. Bruce Parrott, director of Soviet Studies at the Johns Hopkins School of Advanced International Studies, also read the manuscript, sharing with me his insights and steering me from missteps in the world of Soviet high politics.

Anne Lawrence, my chief researcher and an accomplished student of Soviet society, provided me not only with organized, detailed chronologies of rapidly changing developments in many fields, but also with rich memoranda on many special events, people, and topics—all of which made the swift writing of this book not only easier but possible. Kate Medina, my editor at Random House, mingled her infectious and supportive enthusiasm with wise comments about its architecture and suggestions about making it more alive and accessible for the reader. With history literally in the making, she persuaded an entire publishing house to move with unusual speed so the reporting would be fresh to the reader. My wife, Susan, not only gave me her many acute observations and personal reflections during months of our traveling together, but then sat up into the wee hours many a morning, reading the new pages and offering her suggestions and, best of all, her encouragement.

I am indebted to two institutions: WGBH-TV in Boston, and in particular to Peter McGhee, manager for national productions, for backing my documentary series, *Inside Gorbachev's USSR with Hedrick Smith,* and putting me in the Soviet Union at the most fascinating period of change since the Russian Revolution. The commitment of WGBH made possible much of the reporting in this book; and the support of people at WGBH such as Marcia Storkerson and Paul Taylor made the effort more fruitful and more pleasant.

Each of the four series producers, Martin Smith, Sherry Jones, Marian Marzynski, and David Royle—and especially Martin Smith as executive producer—shared with me their reporting and their ideas; in the collaborative process of fashioning films and working out scripts with them, I honed many of my own concepts. I thank them for their help and tip my hat to them as first-class professionals. I gained much, too, from the knowledge and experience of Louis Menashe, professor of Soviet studies at Brooklyn's Polytechnic Institute, and from the reporting of Natasha Lance, who, with Louis Menashe, served as associate producer.

I am indebted as well to the Foreign Policy Institute of the Johns Hopkins University, to its president, Harold Brown, to executive director Simon Serfaty, and to George Packard, dean of the Johns Hopkins School of Advanced International Studies, for giving me an academic home and a congenial working atmosphere. I benefited particularly from the knowledge of three Johns Hopkins colleagues: Bruce Parrott and Charles Fairbanks, Jr., of the Foreign Policy Institute, and David Calleo, director of European studies, SAIS. Linda Carlson, the reference librarian at SAIS, provided invaluable assistance on innumerable occasions.

Scholars in the field of Soviet studies at other institutions were very generous. Two deserve special note for their highly regarded expertise and generosity: Ed Hewett, a specialist on the Soviet economy at the Brookings Institution, and Paul Goble, a specialist on Soviet nationality issues, formerly with the State Department and now with Radio Free Europe/ Radio Liberty.

I am also grateful for the assistance and advice of many other scholars, especially Stephen F. Cohen of Princeton University; Nancy Condee of the University of Pittsburgh; Murray Feshbach of Georgetown University; William Fierman of the University of Tennessee; Ken Gray, U.S. Department of Agriculture; Gregory Grossman, University of California at Berkeley; Nicholas Hayes of Hamline University; Jerry Hough of Duke University; Gail Lapidus of the University of California at Berkeley;

Robert Legvold of Columbia University; Ellen Mickiewicz of Emory University; Vladimir Padunov of Pittsburgh University; Peter Reddaway of George Washington University; Gertrude Schroeder of the University of Virginia; Anatole Shub of the United States Information Agency; Vladimir Treml of Duke University; Don Van Atta of Hamilton College; Josephine Wool of Howard University; and Steve Wegren of Duke University.

In the Soviet Union, three officials were unusually important in helping me gain wide access and in sharing their own life experiences and ideas: Leonid Dobrokhotov and Nikolai Shishlin of the Central Committee staff, and Valentin Lazutkin, deputy chairman of the State Committee for Television and Radio.

I could not have completed this book without the assistance of my research staff: not only Anne Lawrence, but those who worked with her so closely and devoted many long hours to my book—Louise Keefe, Jeffrey Lilley, and Sue Thornton. At the Library of Congress, I owe special thanks to Grant Harris of the European reading room; and at Radio Free Europe/Radio Liberty, to Jane Lester, Julie Moffett, and Brian Reed.

I owe thanks as well to my translators: Aleksei Levin, Julie Moffett, Moira Ratchford, Conrad Turner, Michele Berdy; to Randa Murphy, who transcribed many interviews; to Maryliss Bartlett, my secretary, who did countless chores; and to several interns—Jon Ballis, Paul Poletes, Christine Feig, Anastasia Urtz, Cynthia Kop.

At Random House, I am grateful to Amy Edelman for her painstaking copy editing of my manuscript and for keeping me from many missteps, and to Jon Karp for his shepherding of my work through the byways of Random House, often under considerable pressure but always with good cheer. And finally, my thanks to Julian Bach, my literary agent, who was enthusiastic about my writing about the Russians long ago, and to Ann Rittenberg, his associate, for their strong support.

Sovietologists will contend that this book should not be titled *The New Russians* because it is the Soviet peoples, all nationalities, and not just the ethnic Russians, who are engaged in massive transformation of their country. They will assert that with the Soviet Union now breaking up, readers should not mistakenly identify Russia with the whole Soviet Union.

That is correct, but I believe that Gorbachev, who set free the process of *perestroika,* is very much an ethnic Russian, not only in lineage but also in psychology, and that ultimately, success or failure of the process of reform will be decided by how it is handled by the Russians, who are the dominant people. Other nationalities, for example in the Baltics and in the Caucasus, were much more ready for reform, almost like the East Europeans. It is the Russians who have to remake their society and themselves. I have tried, as well, to make it clear to readers when I am talking specifically about Russians, and when about Soviets in general. And because of my earlier book, *The Russians,* I wanted to make explicit that *The New Russians* was a comparison of the same people and culture over time.

Finally, there are several systems of transliteration for Russian into English. I have adopted the practice of American newspapers, such as *The New York Times,* which generally follow accepted academic rules but make minor adaptations, for example, inserting the *y* before vowels (as in *Y*eltsin or *Y*evgeny) in personal names. My standard has been to make names and terms easier for the general reader.

HEDRICK SMITH
Chevy Chase, Maryland
September 6, 1990

CONTENTS

INTRODUCTION:
AFTER THE WALL CAME DOWN

When I left Russia and the Russians in December 1974, after three years as Moscow bureau chief for *The New York Times,* I thought that vast country and its people would never really change. As a people, they were so Russian, so different from people in the West.

Having lived since 1971 under the oppressive orthodoxy of Communist party leader Leonid Brezhnev, and having endured numerous personal scrapes with the chill and arrogance of Soviet officialdom, I had come to see authoritarian rule as something firmly embedded in Russian society and ingrained in the Russian psyche. A solid wall separated the rulers and the ruled. In 1956, Nikita Khrushchev had eased the raw despotism of Stalin, but he had left intact the granite citadel of power that was the self-perpetuating hierarchy of the Communist Party.

Five long centuries of absolutism—from Ivan the Terrible to the Soviet seventies—had left the Russian masses submissive. In their personal lives, I found them ingenious in beating the numbing inefficiency of the state economy. Their black market was so vast that it operated as a countereconomy, even to the extent of producing underground millionaires. But in the sphere of political action, grass-roots initiative was moribund.

In Russian history, tiny shoots of democracy had sprung up briefly from time to time, but none had taken root. Except for a handful of dissidents, most of the intellectuals I encountered in the seventies were politically passive: Fear had taught them to save cynical jokes for private company. Ordinary people might grumble about shortages or injustices, but they never took action. As I was told time and time again, Russians would choose stability over chaos, order over freedom.

The Chinese are known as a nation of traders and businessmen, but I learned firsthand that the Russians had little entrepreneurial know-how. Underground centers of illicit private enterprise were in the non-Russian republics of Georgia, Azerbaijan, and Uzbekistan, or in the more Western-oriented Baltic regions of Latvia or Lithuania. In places like Moscow or Leningrad, Jews or transplanted Georgians or Armenians showed more of a knack for commerce than most Russians did. The vast majority of Soviet people expected the state to take care of them—especially of their economic needs, however poorly—and to tell them what to do. For despite its revolutionary conceits, the Soviet Union was a profoundly conservative society. Most Russians were not driven by Western appetites for the new and trendy; they were held back by the dual weights of inertia and dogma.

I did know some intellectuals who were desperate for a bit of fresh air, some room to breathe, for a modest "thaw" such as the one initiated by Khrushchev in the late 1950s. But it seemed to me that even a modest reform would be long in coming. Like others who had lived among the Russians, sent children to their schools, studied their history and their institutions, come to know their ways and their mentality, I left Russia sixteen years ago thinking that fundamental change was impossible. And I wrote that in my book *The Russians*.

The decline and stagnation that sank into place for the next decade, into the mid-eighties, seemed to confirm this judgment. Soviet politics appeared as frozen as the Siberian tundra.

As it turned out, of course, I was wrong.

Never had I imagined that the Soviet Union would undergo the kind of seismic transformation that became apparent a couple of years after Mikhail Gorbachev came to power in March 1985.

In the name of reforms that would modernize, humanize, and ultimately save Soviet socialism, Gorbachev cracked open the wall between the rulers and the ruled and let loose massive popular discontent; he shook the very foundations of the system that Stalin had imposed from above. He provoked the Soviet people to begin taking their destinies in their own hands. He summoned a democratic spirit that aroused the slumbering giant of Russia and then swept across Eastern Europe, toppling Communist governments like a row of helpless toy soldiers—Poland, Hungary, East Germany, Czechoslovakia, Romania. When these puppet governments looked to the Kremlin for protection, they got none. Gorbachev let the tidal wave roll on, until it swept over the Berlin Wall and carried the Iron Curtain out to sea.

He called this vast undertaking *perestroika*. But like any shrewd political leader who is improvising strategy as he goes along, Gorbachev has kept manipulating the definition of that word to suit his purposes. In his hands, it is a slogan for the general urge for reform, and also a label for whatever measures he chooses to implement. Sometimes, when Gorbachev is on the offensive, his *perestroika* rings with what he loves to call "revolutionary" change; it harbors gossamer promises of democracy, of private enterprise—and it smacks of heresy to the Soviet power establishment. At other times, when Gorbachev is on the defensive, the term has more limited, cautious connotations—of modernization, of readapting Soviet socialism without dismantling the system founded by Lenin. Then, Gorbachev uses the term *perestroika* in ways that include protection of the establishment.

In talking with Gorbachev's colleagues and following his course closely, I have come to see Gorbachev not as a theorist with a pure vision of the future, but as a pragmatist, who pursues what works and is ready to junk what does not. *Perestroika* is a process, not a fixed and finite objective. Literally, it means "reconstruction" or "restructuring." But on a deeper level, it is the Reformation. Think of Gorbachev, then, as a kind of Martin Luther, setting out to cleanse, purify, and renew a corrupt and failing Socialist Church, but instead forever changing its nature and its destiny.

Because, in fact, *perestroika*, in its essence, represents a sweeping and profound change, far more extensive than a specific program of reforms. It is the catalyst for a wholesale societal transformation, analogous to the opening of Japan by Commodore Perry in 1854, or Bismarck's forging of the modern German state in the nineteenth century. It has parallels with Kemal Atatürk's disciplined drive to modernize the remnants of the Ottoman Empire and thrust Turkey into the twentieth century, and with Mahatma Gandhi's sounding the death knell of British colonialism with his nonviolent campaign to free India from Imperial England. These were not passing trends that flashed brightly for a few years and then disappeared. They were major bend points in the path of history. So, too, is Gorbachev's *perestroika*.

Initially, of course, many in the West were skeptical. For several years, people wondered: Was Gorbachev a Communist charlatan, a masterful media politician whose changes were cosmetic, but not cosmic, not real, whose "new thinking" was transitory, not fundamental? At first, both President Reagan and then President Bush were cautious, and careful not to embrace Gorbachev too hastily. But with the stunning collapse of

Communist power in Eastern Europe in the latter half of 1989, it became clear to almost everyone that the long, painful period of the Cold War was ending, and that the world was crossing an important historical divide.

Overnight, it seemed, the world order was transformed and our global agenda reshaped. The old structure based on East-West confrontation became obsolete. German reunification replaced the Cold War as the number one concern of the major powers. Subtly at first, but then very dramatically, the world was shifting from an era in which international affairs were driven by the arms race and the threat of a nuclear apocaplyse, to a new epoch in which the principal driving force of global affairs was economic competition.

In the American psyche, the threat of Soviet nuclear missiles was replaced by anxiety over the economic challenge from Japan and the fear that the United States could not compete well enough in the global marketplace. Gorbachev's *perestroika* did not create these trends, but it accelerated them. It vaulted us all into a new era.

What was so striking about Gorbachev's approach, when I finally had a chance to see it up close, was that he was daring to trust the people; and he was daring to disassemble the pyramid of power in the Soviet Union. His strategy represented a reversal of much of twentieth-century history, for this has been the century of totalitarian governments, epitomized by Adolf Hitler and Joseph Stalin. Dictators, parties, ideological movements, have single-mindedly set about accumulating power, concentrating power—total power—in their own hands. Yet now, near the century's end, both Gorbachev in the Soviet Union and Deng Xiaoping in China have tried to head in the opposite direction. Each has attempted the controlled dispersal of power, but when those attempts got out of control, as they were bound to, Deng pulled back; Gorbachev has kept going.

Once Gorbachev lifted the threat that Soviet tanks would roll out to suppress the democratic spirit in Eastern Europe, the pent-up rage of masses of people who took to the streets shattered dictatorships and converted the Berlin Wall from the world's ugliest barricade into a bandstand for the celebration of freedom.

In a less visible way, Gorbachev is responding to popular pressures at home. The sullen discontent and stubborn lethargy of millions of Soviet workers and a cynical, disenchanted Soviet intelligentsia have forced Gorbachev to embark on reform—to try to energize his people and revitalize his country. At each stage, when he has hesitated, popular pressures have impelled him forward. In his fifth year, for example, he was provoked to do what Khrushchev could not or would not do, and what he himself had hesitated to do—attack the Communist Party's lock on power.

In December 1989, he admonished the dissident physicist Andrei Sakharov for demanding a multiparty system, but within two months, after political uprisings in Lithuania and Azerbaijan that showed the Party's loss of authority, Gorbachev reversed his course. He summoned the Party bosses in early February 1990 and told them that the Party would have to change or it would perish; that it would have to give up its constitutionally guaranteed monopoly on power and prove itself in the competition of a multiparty system. On the eve of that Party session, in the largest spontaneous gathering in Moscow since the Bolshevik Revolution, nearly two hundred thousand people massed outside the Kremlin to demand that the party *apparatchiki* yield to popular will. *Perestroika* had come full circle. Gorbachev was being propelled forward by the very forces he had unleashed.

My personal introduction to this new world, the world of the New Russians, so different from the world I had known in the early 1970s, came at one of the high tides of *perestroika*, in May 1988, when I went to Moscow for President Reagan's summit meeting with Gorbachev.

For Americans, Reagan's venture to the Kremlin was big news. His strolls on Red Square with Gorbachev, his luncheon for Moscow dissidents, his speech to university students, all made great television soap opera: the old Cold Warrior playing in the heart of "the evil empire."

But the Russians I talked with then were blasé about the summit. They saw Reagan's visit as a sideshow; the much more compelling battle was the one within their own country, over internal change. Its outcome that May was most uncertain. The Russians knew that Reagan's coming was important for Soviet-American relations, but it stirred no real excitement. They were glad for his courtesy call, especially after all the harsh things he had said about them, and they were polite to the president for a few days. But they could hardly wait for him to get out of town, so they could get back to their own unfolding political brawl, a struggle over their national destiny.

That 1988 trip to Russia was my first to Moscow in nearly fourteen years, and the ferment and electricity astonished me. It began an adventure of discovery and rediscovery that would take me to the Soviet Union nine times in the next two years, to do the reporting for this book and to film a series of documentary programs for American public television, *Inside Gorbachev's USSR.*

On the way into Moscow from Sheremyetovo Airport that first visit back, I remember looking for immediate evidence of Gorbachev's supposed earthquake, but at first I couldn't see any. Along the main highway I saw the same massive, naked apartment buildings that I had remembered from the seventies, huge, impersonal, thirteen- and twenty-story tenement blocks that looked like a vast construction site, a sprawling, gargantuan Levittown, balconies aflutter with the wash, buildings crying out for paint, for trees, for shrubbery, for any tiny bit of decoration. These behemoths had been designed with one object in mind: to pack in as many people as possible, with little thought for individual convenience, human scale, or diversity. Along Gorky Street in Moscow proper were the same old concrete block constructions of the Khrushchev era, the same impersonal signs that I knew so well: MYASO (meat), APTEKA (drugstore), KHLYEB (bread). I searched in vain for signs of individuality—VANYA'S BAKERY or GORKY STREET GROCERY—something that would convey a new spirit of entrepreneurship; but there was none.

Later, with producer Martin Smith and writer Paul Taylor from WGBH-TV in Boston, I went up to the Old Arbat, a long strolling mall, hunting some more for evidence of material change. But in one state store after another, we found only a paltry selection of staples—potatoes, cabbages, cucumbers, a few carrots, and some sad-looking green oranges; in the meat store, one brand of fatty salami, one brand of fatty bologna, each at over $5 a pound. Otherwise, the meat counter was empty. Chances were that the state-store butchers were sneaking the better cuts of meat under the counter to sell for private profit, and, of course, for very steep prices, peasants were selling meat and produce at the farmers' market. Nevertheless, the food situation in the heart of Moscow looked no better than it had fourteen years earlier.

I was eager to talk with old friends, so I phoned Zinovy Yuryev, a science-fiction writer and for a long time deputy editor of *Krokodil,* the Soviet humor magazine. During the seventies, I had often visited Zinovy and his wife, Yelena Kornyevskaya. Following my old precautions, I did not call Zinovy from my hotel, where the lines might be bugged. Instead, I went to a pay phone on the street. Yelena was away, but Zinovy was eager to meet for dinner. He asked a question that caught me by surprise: "What restaurant shall we choose?"

I had never met with Zinovy and Yelena in public; always we had talked at their apartment, and often, when going there, I had taken precautions: I had used the metro or had driven my car partway there, then had parked some distance from their home and taken a taxi or a metro the rest of the way. In those days we foreign correspondents sometimes saw unmarked cars tailing us; one American reporter found a radio device under his car that sent out a signal, letting the KGB secret police know where his car was at all times. We had assumed such devices were planted somewhere on all our cars, so we did not drive directly to the homes of Soviet friends, unless they had official reasons for meeting us. Zinovy, as a Jew with a high-level press job subject to Communist Party oversight, had had to be careful about private contacts with foreigners.

So his willingness now to meet in a public place signaled a change in the political climate. Moreover, he suggested Kropotkinskaya 36, a new cooperative (privately owned) restaurant. This was a treat for me because I had not yet eaten at a Moscow cooperative, and the service and food turned out to be unusually good, the atmosphere quiet and intimate— unknown in the Moscow of my day—even if the prices rivaled those in Manhattan.

"Two years ago, I would not have been here and seen you in public like this," Zinovy told me after we greeted each other with warm Russian hugs and kisses.

Zinovy is a short, intense man in his early sixties, with thick graying hair and the energy of someone much younger. His English is excellent, his accent sharp and choppy. With me, he has never minced words. He is a satirical writer, ironic and sophisticated in conversation, but never indirect. He speaks in staccato bursts, either with great passion or with acid cynicism—and during the Brezhnev era he found ample cause to be cynical. He believed in nothing, trusted virtually no one, had little good to say about the leadership or the system. But now he was brimming with enthusiasm. He told me that he had left *Krokodil* and was trying his hand at writing movie scenarios as well as books.

"The director of Gorky Studio phones me and says, 'Zinovy, I'd like to see you. Come over,'" Zinovy reported. "To you, it's nothing. But to me it is as if Buddha were calling me—these bureaucrats never call anyone. So I go to see him and he says to me, 'I've looked at your script and it seems to me that it can be a good movie and it will make money.' To you, that's nothing. It's a natural idea. But to me, it's *astonishing* to think that this will be the standard—to make money. These idiots have produced so much rubbish over the years, never worrying a damn about wasting billions of rubles. Now suddenly they want to make money. If they really stick to this, it's a revolution."[1]

But Zinovy had an even more surprising story to tell about the revolution going on in his country. It involved his son Misha.

I remembered Misha as a boy of eleven, with large brown eyes and a mind that matched the intelligence of his parents. So brilliant was he, in fact, that he had later graduated from the Moscow State University biology department at nineteen, headed for a career as a geneticist—until he found himself in serious political trouble.

I knew from my earlier experience that many free-thinking Soviet intellectuals had faced a dilemma in raising their bright adolescent children. They could simply keep silent, hiding their honest beliefs and opinions from their children. This guaranteed that under the political pressures for conformity their children wouldn't be induced to expose the parents as hidden dissenters. This would spare their children from having to grow up living double lives—speaking their minds in the privacy of their families, and toeing the Party line in public. Or they could do what Zinovy did, be honest and open with his two sons, Yura and Misha. He had talked candidly with them and let them dip into his extensive personal library of contraband literature—modern American and British fiction and nonfiction as well as dissident Soviet writers like Solzhenitsyn, Sakharov, and others.

So it was only natural that Misha, working in 1986 as a young biologist in his early twenties, had borrowed his father's copy of Tom Clancy's novel *The Hunt for Red October* and taken it to his office at a prestigious scientific institute. Of course, as the story of a Soviet submarine captain defecting to the West, *Red October* is not a book on which Party watchdogs or security officers looked kindly. Unfortunately for Misha, he lent it to a friend, and either the friend or somebody else reported Misha to the KGB for possessing and disseminating anti-Soviet literature. The incident occurred in Gorbachev's early period, when his emphasis was not so much on reform as on work discipline and the drive against alcoholism and corruption. So the investigation blossomed and eventually led the KGB to Zinovy's private library of forbidden books.

One morning a KGB major and several workmen arrived in a truck to do an *obysk*—a search of Zinovy's apartment. When the KGB do an *obysk*, as Zinovy explained, they do it methodically, top to bottom, meticulously listing all the materials they confiscate for an investigation. This morning, they went through Zinovy's entire collection, not only his books but his Western videotapes and cassettes. They took everything, cataloging every single item, and they expanded their original investigation of Misha to include Zinovy as well.

Investigations such as this one have a way of dragging on, with all the various complications and interrogations. The family used what connections it had with Communist Party higher-ups to get the matter dismissed, but the situation looked grim for both father and son. Although formal charges had not been filed, Misha appeared headed for Siberia, and Zinovy likely to lose his job and perhaps worse.

Then suddenly, on December 17, 1986, Gorbachev called Andrei Sakharov at his enforced exile in the city of Gorky and invited the famous dissident to come back to Moscow and help enlist the intelligentsia for Gorbachev's reforms. That phone call was a dramatic harbinger of cultural liberalization to come, as Zinovy was soon to find out.

Within a few weeks, the KGB investigator in Zinovy's case telephoned Misha and said, "Why don't you write us a letter asking us to drop your case?" Misha, who had steadfastly refused to write or sign any paper for the KGB, balked at first, but eventually Zinovy persuaded him to go ahead and do it.

More weeks went by, and then a phone call came from the KGB telling Zinovy and Misha to be at their apartment on a certain morning. Once again, the KGB major appeared with the workmen in a gray truck—but this time they began to unload Zinovy's books and tapes, and then systematically put them back on the shelves. When they had finished, Zinovy noticed that the KGB had kept two of his videotapes.

"One was *Pretty Baby,* which they considered porno," Zinovy recalled with a chuckle. "Too dangerous, they evidently thought, for an old guy like me. And the other was *Aliens,* which they considered too violent."

All the books were returned, except one. "They said that was a mistake," Zinovy reported, "and they apologized!"

Zinovy sat there shaking his head in wonder and disbelief at this weird new KGB politesse. And at the somersault in his own family's fortunes.

"Imagine it, Rick," he said. "The KGB *apologized* to an ordinary citizen! Now you see why Gorbachev is the first Soviet leader I have believed in."

It seemed a fantastic story, worthy of Zinovy's satirical fiction, but this time it was true. And it conveyed a wider message about the mechanism of state terror and the climate of fear that had ruled Russia for seven decades of Communist power, and for centuries of Russian absolutism before that. For if the KGB were truly to be held in some check, and Gorbachev really to lift the threat of arbitrary arrest for the mere possession of liberal writings, then gradually ordinary people might gain the nerve to speak their minds in public.

On the day that President Reagan arrived for his summit meeting with Gorbachev, my colleagues from WGBH and I decided to try to talk to some ordinary Russians. We went out to the Great Stone Bridge, which crosses the Moscow River on the southern approach to the Kremlin, to mingle with the crowds along Reagan's motorcade route. As executive producer of our documentary series, Marty Smith had a minicamera and wanted to try out some man-in-the-street interviews. I wanted to see whether the Russian people would talk to us openly.

I was recalling my arrival in Moscow in 1971. During my first week, Nikita Khrushchev died an anonymous pensioner, and Western reporters had been tipped off within hours by friends of the Khrushchev family. Nothing appeared in the Soviet press for two days; obviously, Khrushchev's successors could not decide what to say about him, so they did not print even the news that he had died. Of course *The New York Times* had the story, and we wanted to get reactions from ordinary Russians.

So, fresh from Russian-language tutoring, I went to find out firsthand what the people had to say about old Nikita, the bumptious upstart peasant who had dared denounce Stalin, had put missiles into Cuba, and had banged his shoe on his desk at the United Nations.

No one would talk.

People scurried away when I mentioned Khrushchev's name. I managed to lure people into conversation by asking for telephone change, but when they got my drift, they fled with vague mumblings of "I'm not from around here," or "I don't know what you're talking about." Then I tried cornering vegetable vendors at stands in the farmers' market, but they, too, were full of evasions. "Poor old man," said one grandmother. A middle-aged man parried, "Where was he all this time?" But more typical was a ticket seller in a movie house. Eyeing me suspiciously, she demanded, "How do you know he died?" I realized that people were so wary that it was ridiculous to put together a story.

So with that memory still in mind in 1988, I headed out to the Great Stone Bridge, skeptical at our prospects for a genuine give-and-take. I figured the camera would be an extra handicap, more likely to attract police interference than talkative Muscovites.

But my experience from the seventies was a poor guide. As soon as I explained to people on the bridge that we were American public-television reporters here for Reagan's visit and eager to sample public opinion, they wanted to talk. The sight of the camera drew a crowd. Moscow suddenly seemed like New York or Los Angeles.

At first, their comments were safe and obvious, sentiments about wishing Reagan well. People said they were glad he was in Moscow; they hoped his visit would strengthen peace. It was far better, they said, to have our leaders talking than preparing for war. When I edged toward more controversial territory, such as questions about their personal lives, there was a moment's hesitation; then a wiry little man in a straw hat, with the almond-shaped eyes and Oriental face of a Tatar, started delivering a rapid-fire speech from the back of the crowd.

"We ought not to be talking about this—this is not what's number one on our minds," he declared. "What's number one is that our economy is in terrible shape. These people are *Moskvichy*, Muscovites—they're well taken care of compared to the rest of us. I come from near Kazan on the Volga River [six hundred miles east of Moscow], and our situation is a nightmare. We can't find sugar or tea in our shops. Coffee is hard to get. Housing is terrible. . . ."

And he went on. I kept expecting someone to object, or to put a hand in front of Marty's camera. That's what would have happened in the 1970s. Some Soviet patriot or some militia officer would have grabbed this little Tatar by the scruff of the neck, pulled him out of the crowd, and lectured him about washing dirty linen in front of foreigners. But instead, his tirade touched off a kvetching session. Others chimed in with pet peeves—the lack of meat, the shortage of baby clothes. One serious young man began to preach that there was too much materialism, that more people should turn to religion, now that Gorbachev was letting churches reopen. Suddenly, we were in the midst of a mini–Hyde Park. People were pushing and shoving to get to the camera to give America a piece of their minds.

Then a sturdy, middle-aged matron with black hair tied back severely in a bun pushed aggressively through the crowd and demanded to speak. She had the authoritarian aura of a school principal. Her iron back and steely eyes reminded me of a type I had encountered all too often in years gone by: the ideological vigilantes, self-appointed keepers of order. Her advance to the front rank signaled a moment of reckoning. There will be no more self-indulgent whimpering, I thought to myself; this woman will cuff the ears of any who would sully the honor of the motherland.

I was trying to figure out how to finesse her. "I don't think we need this one," I said to Marty Smith. "Let's just take a little bit," he replied; and so I asked her to state her problem, and her script began as I imagined.

All the others had spoken anonymously. But with the abrupt efficiency of a military officer giving name, rank, and serial number, this woman self-confidently reeled off her name, address, and occupation: "Tretyakova, Olga; Stavropol Territory; teacher, retired." For special effect, she emphasized that she came from the home province of Mikhail Sergeyevich, using Gorbachev's first name and patronymic, the normal Russian way. Obviously, not a lady to be trifled with.

Then, with stentorian oratory, she commenced to deliver a pitiful indictment of the Soviet health system. To my astonishment, she was speaking out not to defend the system but to drive a nail into its coffin. "Eleven years ago my only son died in a hospital," she began, "a victim of corruption." She was outraged not only at faulty diagnosis and bad treatment but also at the arrogance of one doctor who had demanded a bribe for treatment that was supposed to be free under Soviet socialism. When she took her case to a public prosecutor, she said, he, too, demanded a hefty bribe, of 1,600 rubles (practically a year's pay for her), and then disappeared with the money.

"Later, he was arrested and convicted," she said, apparently for other crimes. But the doctor, whom she condemned as "a killer in a white coat," was still unpunished because of a "cover-up" in the Stavropol prosecutor's office.

Initially, Olga Tretyakova's riveting story and commanding presence kept the others silent. Then people began to grumble. Several uniformed militia men at the fringe of our group pressed in closer to listen just as Mrs. Tretyakova was emphasizing that this scandal had taken place practically under Gorbachev's nose, in his home province.

"I have written the Communist Party Central Committee," she complained, "but they just pass the buck."

One onlooker cautioned her to be careful or she might get in trouble.

"Let them arrest me!" she blurted out.

I fully expected a militia officer's gray-uniformed arm to reach over the crowd and lead her away, but the police made no move. Eventually, she became frustrated that we, the Americans, would not promise to right the wrong and investigate the doctor; she reluctantly relinquished her hold on the camera and the crowd, and made her way out along the street—still a free woman, for as far as I could see.

In the end, it was we, not the Russians, who ended the dialogue.

For me, the episode was a revelation. In the 1970s, I had heard Russians gripe about terrible living conditions, but they had been wary of expressing individual criticism too freely in front of strangers, especially other Soviets. Indeed, as we strolled away that afternoon, a young blond workman in rumpled clothes tagged along after us. When the militia were out of sight, he approached me with a story of being fired from his job and blacklisted because his bosses condemned his complaints as a political protest. He was having trouble getting work; he wanted us to help him emigrate. His furtive contact was typical of my encounters in the 1970s, a symptom of a system of repression, some of the effects of which obviously still lingered on.

But the openness of the others, their willingness to voice their criticisms in public, on camera, was a striking change. In three and a half years of roaming the country in the 1970s, I had heard many candid and sordid stories from Soviet citizens, but if they had a negative message to deliver, they were usually careful to check that no one was eavesdropping and to protect themselves with anonymity. In a crowd, Big Brother was always assumed to be present. Fear had been palpable.

As we returned to our hotel that afternoon, I had to admit that even if the food selection was still grim and other material conditions had not improved three years after Gorbachev's ascent, people's psychology had changed. I found it remarkable that Russians, who have almost no tradition of tolerance for differing opinion, would let each other speak without shouting each other down, and without some Communist Party busybody stepping in to set the record straight or call a halt. The notion of public dialogue had obviously gained some legitimacy, but what impressed me most of all was that these people had lost much of their old fear. If Gorbachev had done nothing else, he had created a whole new world merely by lifting people's fear.

It is tempting for us in the West, especially Americans, to witness such sea changes in events and in people's psychology and then to interpret them through the prism of our own values, our own political framework. We assume we understand what is really going on inside the Soviet Union; we assume that as soon as Soviet people are given freedom, they will behave as we do. Our framework is capitalism and multiparty democracy; our way of life seems so natural, so right to us, that we take for granted that once dictatorship is removed, Russians will reflect and assert our same values.

When Gorbachev talks about democratization and greater freedoms, we mishear his rhetoric because few of us understand that Russian history has given those words different meanings for him and his people. We expect that people who have been politically inert for decades will immediately know how to operate democratic institutions, how to take charge of their destinies. We imagine that only an entrenched Old Guard is blocking them, that once a few "bad guys" at the top are removed, the world of the average Russian will look like ours. To us, Gorbachev's *perestroika,* or casting off of the old Stalinist dictatorship, makes so much sense that we cannot fathom how deeply embedded is the resistance to change among the vast majority of people, even those dissatisfied with the past.

The swiftness of political change in Eastern Europe only compounds our misperceptions of what is happening inside the Soviet Union. The governments of Poland, East Germany, Czechoslovakia, and Romania fell with such electrifying speed in the fall of 1989 that it fostered the illusion that tyranny can be replaced by democracy overnight. A banner waved aloft by exuberant street crowds in Romania on their most fateful day captured the lightning tempo with which the old world was being turned upside down. It read: POLAND—TEN YEARS. EAST GERMANY—TEN WEEKS. CZECHOSLOVAKIA—TEN DAYS. ROMANIA—?

On our television screens, we see the same massive street marches in Lithuania, Azerbaijan, and in Russian cities that we saw in Prague, Leipzig, and Bucharest, and we are tempted to assume the Soviets will transform their country as swiftly as East Europeans have.

But as the past five years have shown, the Soviet Union, and at its heart, Mother Russia, is different from its neighbors. As a society and a people, Russia is more difficult to change. Even the largest street demonstrations in Moscow have been nowhere near as large or universal as the demonstrating masses in the smaller capitals of Eastern Europe—a sign that Muscovites, indeed most Russians, are not as swept up by the magnetic attraction of a new way of life as are Poles, Germans, or Czechoslovaks.

Eastern Europe faces a torturous process in its move from socialism to capitalism and revival of working democracies, but at least in Eastern Europe there was a relatively recent tradition of democracy, within the memories of people now alive. As World War II began, governments in Eastern Europe included the institutions of democracy. But Russia has been ruled by czars and Communist dictators for five centuries, with only brief interludes of democratic reform.

What is more, the dictatorial brand of Soviet socialism had its roots in Russia. It was not imposed by an alien army, as the Soviet army imposed Communist dictatorships on Eastern Europe. It was fired and hardened in the crucible of war, famine, terror, and hard sacrifice, and it has its committed legions. Moreover, the Russians are a people who historically have needed a belief system, an ideology to live by, whether Communism or Russian Orthodoxy. Many are uneasy with a political system in which the guiding principles of public life are concerned with means, not ends.

When I have described our political ethic to Russians, many of them have said that they felt something was missing; they have been uncomfortable with our notion that while the wider society establishes process—the institutions of government, its legislatures, division of powers, and free press—the individual himself is left to develop philosophy, faith, and the meaning of life. That is not the Russian tradition. Most Russians look to the state and the ruler to provide an ideology and a purpose as well as law and order.

So the collapse of the wall—both the Berlin Wall and the wall in the Soviet Union between the rulers and the ruled—is not the whole story; it is just the beginning. The story now is what happens after the first massive political tremors; what happens after the wall comes down. That is the story which has fascinated me most, the human story, the story of personal transformations: how people cope with reform, some promoting it, others resisting it or mouthing its slogans but secretly sabotaging it, still others floating in uncertainty, voicing hope for change but unwilling to take risks to make it happen.

In pursuit of that story, I have spent nearly nine months in the Soviet Union over the past two years, traveling more than forty thousand miles, visiting twenty-five major cities and nine republics. I have ranged from Siberia to the Baltic republics, from Central Russia to Uzbekistan, from Armenia and Azerbaijan to the Ukraine. I have tried to probe the innards of Gorbachev's U.S.S.R., talking to coal miners, farmers, high school students, listening to city officials and industrial bosses, reformers and hard-liners, questioning taxi drivers and members of the Politburo. My own reactions to what was happening have passed through several stages of deepening awareness. My opinions of Gorbachev have changed several times.

What follows in this book are the stories of what it is like in the Soviet Union today; what it is like for individuals to live through a cultural convulsion, a wholesale change in their society and environment.

There is the story, for example, of a local Communist Party leader who for the first time stands for election in a genuine contest, and loses. There is the story of an industrial manager who is suddenly told, "Run your own business and make a profit"—but first he must struggle to extricate himself from the web of a state-run economy. There is the story of high school teachers who dutifully preached the dogma of the past, but are suddenly told the old textbook is full of lies and that they must invent a new version, using disclosures in the daily newspapers.

I write about students who have heard one orthodoxy from early childhood, taught by both teachers and parents, only to discover that, actually, their teachers believed one thing, their parents another. What is it like for a television producer to be given license by Gorbachev to tackle any topic, but then to discover she is being held back by the taboos of her own superiors? How do older people, who once worshiped Stalin and made sacrifices in his name, react when their idol is discredited—when their own lives are discredited? To whom does a mine worker turn if he shares Gorbachev's infectious dream but sees, after five years, there is still little food on the shelves? Or a farmer who would like to till his own land but cannot be sure that the state will not snatch it back from him if Gorbachev disappears tomorrow?

From afar, there's a tendency to see things in either utopian or apocalyptic terms: success or failure, stability or collapse, dictatorship or chaos, black or white. We don't necessarily see the shades and the fluctuating currents that swirl around ordinary people. The epic story of Russians today has been personalized around Gorbachev: Is he winning or losing? Will he survive or not?

But in truth, the struggle in the Soviet Union, and within individual Soviets, has become far more complex than that; change is operating on so many levels and in so many directions simultaneously. There is no single hero, no single plot line to follow. All too much of the time, our focus has been on Gorbachev and whether he will "make it"; but the most important questions reach beyond Gorbachev personally.

In fact, one of the most important things I hope this book will show is that whether Gorbachev "makes it" or not, the process of change has taken root in the Soviet Union. It may be halting, untidy, embattled, and its course unsteady and sometimes uncertain, but whether or not Gorbachev survives, reform has now acquired a momentum of its own, and it will carry on regardless of his individual fate.

The transformation of a society as large as the Soviet Union, and as enmeshed in the habits and traditions of authoritarian rule, will inevitably take so long to run its course that no single leader can hope to see the process to the end. The old dictatorial order of Soviet Communism has been broken, and the process of forging a new social and political order will be painful, turbulent, and prolonged. The battle will ebb and flow over two or three decades and more, for it is impossible to crack an entrenched dictatorship without peril and bloodshed. Some leaders, frightened by the powerful forces that Gorbachev has unleashed, have already tried to check or reverse the process, and at some point they may succeed for a while; but I believe that others, now maturing and learning the skills of democracy, will emerge to carry reform forward to another stage, further than Gorbachev himself either intended or was capable of realizing.

In time, we may come to see Gorbachev as a transitional figure, who uncorked the process and set the yeast of change to work in the Soviet body politic. In fact, as we shall see, fundamental change had been gestating within Soviet society for years before Gorbachev appeared. He fostered its birth, and now, finally, reform has taken on a life and dynamism of its own.

That fact comes through most clearly in the personal experiences of the people you will meet in this book.

Even from afar, the transformation now under way in the Soviet Union holds a special fascination for all of us, and not only because its success or failure affects our destiny, our survival, even the changing nature of our own society. What is happening there rivets our interest for a deeper reason: It is a modern enactment of one of the archetypal stories of human existence, that of the struggle from darkness to light, from poverty toward prosperity, from dictatorship toward democracy. It represents an affirmation of the relentless human struggle to break free from the bonds of hierarchy and dogma, to strive for a better life, for stronger, richer values. It is an affirmation of the human capacity for change, growth, renewal.

This book is about how that story of change began and what it is like to live through it today. And it is about what this change means for the New Russians, and for the rest of the world, in the 1990s and beyond.

PART ONE

ROOTS OF REFORM

For more than five years, events in the Soviet Union have raced past all of us so rapidly that we have hardly had time to absorb their long-term meaning.

We have noted certain milestones: the first elections offering choice in seventy years; the rise of the independence movements in the Baltic republics; coal miners in Siberia and the southern Ukraine staging the first mass strikes since the time of the Revolution.

We have watched Gorbachev force the Communist Party to renounce its constitutional monopoly on power and gradually shift to a new Soviet parliament and presidency. But what has been less noticeable is that city governments in Moscow, Leningrad, Gorky, and Sverdlovsk have been taken over by reformers, who are now quietly at work building the infrastructure of democracy.

We have followed the incredible political fall and redemption of the populist leader Boris Yeltsin, who defied Gorbachev once and lost his post in the Politburo, defied him a second time and won the leadership of the Russian republic. But we know little about political movements at the grass-roots level, movements that have forced the opening of churches, taken charge of neighborhoods, stopped the construction of half a dozen nuclear reactors since the accident at Chernobyl.

We have seen an inefficient, top-heavy economy convulsed in crisis, ordinary people in despair over chronic shortages and panic-shopping out of fear of higher prices. But it has been harder to catch sight of the new private sector, which now employs five million people, making textiles, developing inventions, building highways.

In short, the headlines of the week have so dominated our attention that it has been hard to fathom and comprehend the fundamental transformations that are taking place throughout Soviet society; to piece together what has really happened and why; to understand what is merely transitory and what trends will begin to define the future.

The purpose of this book is to look beneath the surface of events, to try to see how deep and wide the process of reform runs: how much of it is likely to endure, and who will be the carriers of reform in the future.

The seeds of that future were in fact germinating in the Soviet past, largely unseen. Before we can understand the New Russians and where they are heading, it is necessary to understand the roots of the present reforms, and the forces that have propelled change inexorably forward.

CHAPTER I
THE HIDDEN WELLSPRINGS OF REFORM

"Problems snowballed faster than
they were resolved. On the whole,
society was becoming increasingly
unmanageable. We only thought that
we were in the saddle. . . . The need
for change was brewing."[1]

—Gorbachev, 1987

"*Perestroika* is like a spring
bursting from the rocks in this
mountainside of ours. . . . It comes from
an underground stream flowing somewhere
beneath the surface of the soil."[2]

—Tatyana Zaslavskaya
Sociologist
September 1989

When Gorbachev burst upon the world stage to proclaim a Soviet New
Deal under the trumpet call of *perestroika,* it seemed as if he and his ideas
about reform had emerged from nowhere. But it is now clear that under
what seemed like the dark, still surface of Soviet life in the seventies,
wellsprings of reform were churning, and the vision of dramatic reform
slowly beginning to take shape.

Many Americans were tempted to think that Moscow had been forced into reform by Washington's policies. In this view, Ronald Reagan's toughness toward Brezhnev, Andropov, and Chernenko, the aging Kremlin leaders of the early 1980s, had compelled the Politburo to pick a younger leader, to change the Party line and scrap the Communist system.

But the evidence is overwhelming that Gorbachev's reforms blossomed forth from forces germinating within Russia itself. The impulse for change was homegrown. It took a generation for the forces favoring reform to gather and for a broad base of support to develop. Because of the secretive way in which Soviet society moved in the past, this process was almost entirely hidden from view. And so it took us all very much by surprise.

In fact, by the time Gorbachev became the top man in the Kremlin, reform had hidden constituencies at every level of Soviet society: mine workers and housewives incensed about and weary of chronic consumer shortages and the dismal quality of Soviet goods; farmers and teachers demoralized by rural decay; little people outraged by the arrogant, pervasive, Mafia-like corruption of ministers and high Party officials; others embittered by the rampant black market, and by underground millionaires profiting from the gaping inefficiency of Stalinist economics.

Scientists and engineers were worried about the Soviet Union's industrial stagnation and its growing technological inferiority to the West. Intellectuals and young military veterans were sickened by the futile war in Afghanistan. Army generals, intelligence chiefs, and civilian technocrats were alarmed by the Soviet inability to compete in the world market and by the prospect of becoming a fourth-rate power in the twenty-first century, outstripped not only by the United States, Western Europe, and Japan, but even by China. Cab drivers and poets alike were sick of the blatant hypocrisy of Soviet propaganda. There was a pervasive cynicism about the widening chasm between the pompous pretensions of Brezhnev and the bleak reality of a Russian's everyday life.

Still, these forces were dormant, inchoate, until Gorbachev set them free, galvanized them, and gave them direction and form. They were the tinder, he the match. The kind of astonishing political explosion that took place in the mid-eighties required both ingredients; until the match was struck, that undergrowth of social disenchantment lacked fire and force. But without a vast reserve of incendiary disaffection, the match could have been struck and the flame of reform would have flickered out and died.

Reform of the bold and sweeping nature attempted by Gorbachev was not inevitable; the changes could have been more modest—indeed, Gorbachev himself began modestly. Or reform could have been postponed.

But historically some thrust toward reform was overdue. For within Soviet history, there is an alternating rhythm, a pattern of repression-and-thaw that goes back centuries to the time of the czars, and then up through the Soviet era.

In 1989, a Soviet philosopher told me a bit of folk wisdom. According to an anecdote then making the rounds in Moscow, he said, the Soviet state oscillates between bald leaders and hairy ones—between reformers and conservative tyrants. He ticked off the pairs: Lenin, the bald revolutionary, was followed by Stalin, the tyrant with thick, bristling brush-cut hair and menacing mustache. Nikita Khrushchev, the peasant reformer, who was bald as a potato, gave way to Brezhnev, the conservative, whose bushy eyebrows and headful of hair were parodied by cartoonists in the East and West. Yuri Andropov, a wispy-haired puritan bent on modernism and efficiency, was succeeded by Konstantin Chernenko, a defender of the Old Guard, who even in senility had an abundant head of white hair. So it was only natural that Gorbachev, whose birthmark gleams from a naked pate, should usher in a new era of radical reform. And of course, the philosopher said, smiling, nervous liberals were already beginning to speculate about what hairy hard-liner would succeed Gorbachev.

In Russia, as elsewhere, history moves with a rough Newtonian logic—action and reaction, one generation reacting to the policies and practices of the previous generation. By Gorbachev's takeover in 1985, it had been nearly a quarter of a century since the heyday of the last major reformer, Nikita Khrushchev, who had dethroned Stalin and challenged the Communist Party apparatus. Khrushchev's successors had reacted against him; Brezhnev had largely restored Stalin and enthroned the Party hierarchy.

But now it was time for Khrushchev's political children to come to power and carry on from where he left off.

If America and the West played any role in provoking *perestroika,* it was not through any specific policy of the 1980s, but rather because of our long-term economic success. For contrary to Khrushchev's vain boasting of the early 1960s, the Russians did not "bury" us or even come close to catching up. The capitalist world did not falter and collapse as Marx and Lenin had predicted and scores of Soviet ideologists had dutifully echoed. Just the opposite had occurred. The West had leapfrogged ahead into the Information Age, so that by the early 1980s, the brightest people in the Soviet system could see the telling contrast between Soviet stagnation and Western progress. They could see that the world was passing them by—and that realization forced them to reexamine their own system, to try to find out what had failed and discover ways to shake their nation out of its despotic lethargy.

What has fooled so many Westerners is that this Soviet soul-searching and dissatisfaction had long remained intensely private. Open, incremental evolution—that we understand. Covert, subterranean shifts within the body politic of an authoritarian regime are much harder to detect and comprehend. When grumbling private discontent and dissent become audible, we wonder: Are these just black moods, which a dictator can hold in check? Or do they indicate a gathering storm of irresistible forces? And if so, when, if ever, will it break?

Of course, this is precisely the purpose of censorship—not only to block unwanted views, but to keep people who are unhappy from knowing how many millions of others share their unhappiness; to keep the dormant opposition from awakening to its own developing strength.

THE SAFE HAVENS OF HIDDEN DISSENT

One person who, in the seventies and early eighties, nursed the idea of reform and eventually broke through the veil of secrecy to awaken others to the need for dramatic economic and social change was sociologist Tatyana Zaslavskaya. Her analysis of the ills of Soviet socialism and her ideas for reviving the Soviet economy certainly influenced Gorbachev's thinking. She was among the first people, if not the very first one, actually to use the term *perestroika*.

"Perestroika," Zaslavskaya said years later, "is like a spring bursting from the rocks in this mountainside of ours. It comes shooting out of a specific spot, and you can tell where the water is coming from. It comes from an underground stream flowing somewhere beneath the surface of the soil. Then some kind of opening appears, a chance to burst out into freedom—and then suddenly out of nowhere, a spring emerges and turns into a river."

Zaslavskaya, herself an innovative iconoclast, had been part of that underground stream. She had graduated from the economics faculty at Moscow State University, having first studied physics, and in 1950 she began to do research in Moscow. Then, in 1963, restless and intrigued by the challenge, she had been lured to Akademgorodok, or the Academic City, outside the Siberian industrial center of Novosibirsk. The man who had lured her there was Abel Aganbegyan, just beginning to gain a reputation as a free-thinking economist with maverick ideas about the Soviet system.

The Academic City, a community of twenty-two scientific institutes, had been set up under Khrushchev in 1957. It was peopled largely by younger scholars and discontented free-thinkers prepared to give up the prestige and cultural attractions of Moscow and Leningrad for more opportunity and a bit of freedom, permissible because it was nearly two thousand miles from the Kremlin and because its scientific founder, the physicist Mikhail A. Lavrentyev, had been canny enough to locate it just far enough away from Novosibirsk proper that it did not fall constantly under the prying eyes of regional Party bosses. Akademgorodok was popular with those who had savored Khrushchev's cultural thaw in the 1960s and were gagging under Brezhnev's sterner rule. It had quickly gained a reputation within the Soviet Union as a place with some degree of intellectual freedom, with fairly lively discussion groups, Western rock and jazz, and the Soviet abstract art that its scientists hung in their homes.

But after the Soviet invasion of Czechoslovakia in 1968, the screws were tightened.

I visited Akademgorodok in 1972, and the mood there was no longer as heady as it had been in its early years. For example, Club Integral, a discussion group for university students and junior scholars, had been shut down for something as mild as organizing a concert featuring politically risqué songs by Aleksandr Galich, a playwright recently expelled from the Writers' Union.

Even so, for the Brezhnev years, Academic City was still a relatively safe haven for developing unorthodox ideas. Zaslavskaya, for example, had become a sociologist and was practicing that heretical science without excessive political interference. That was unusual. In most places, Brezhnev's ideologists had banned sociology as a "bourgeois pseudoscience," because its concepts of group interests and conflicts and its empirical methods were a challenge to orthodox ideology and the Party's monopoly on social information. During the Brezhnev crackdown, sociology departments had been shut down at universities in Moscow and Leningrad, and many academic institutes had been purged of sociologists. Yet in distant Siberia, Zaslavskaya had managed to keep on doing her research, but so invisibly that I had not even known then that she existed.

I had gone to Akademgorodok to search out the more independent political climate of Siberia and talk with such intellectuals as the economist Aganbegyan, then head of the Institute of Economics and Industrial Organization, and already known, even then, for having an independent-minded slant on the Soviet economy. Aganbegyan, an Armenian and a great bear of a man, was a maverick, a loyal socialist who nonetheless refused to bend economic facts to fit ideology. He had taught himself statistics and mathematical economics in defiance of Stalinist strictures; Stalin had not wanted people collecting hard economic data that could be used to challenge his claims.

I did not know it then, but years later, traveling with Aganbegyan in America after he had become an adviser to Gorbachev, I learned that he had incurred the wrath of the late Prime Minister Aleksei Kosygin in the early seventies. Aganbegyan had insisted at a private Kremlin conference that Kosygin's halfhearted reforms were failing, and that the country was suffering from hidden inflation, inflation that was disguised by official statistics on the economy. When Kosygin started to dress him down, Aganbegyan had sent cold shock through the room by having the nerve to assert: "Mr. Minister, I want you to take a pencil and paper and write these numbers down. It's my job to get these numbers. If you want to check them and they're wrong, you can fire me." To the astonishment of others, Kosygin had proceeded to take notes; Aganbegyan was not fired, but because of his open impertinence, Kosygin banished the outspoken Armenian from his group of outside consultants.[3]

Aganbegyan's diagnosis back then, refined over the years, was that the Soviet economy was not capable of continuing its rapid postwar growth through the old formula: massive investments and constant expansion of its labor force. Aganbegyan did not back down when Brezhnev or Kosygin blamed economic setbacks on bottlenecks in transportation, bad weather, poor use of new technology, or the ineptitude of individual managers. Long before Gorbachev's emergence, Aganbegyan saw fundamental flaws: straitjacket controls on industrial managers, the rigidity of central planning, low productivity caused by the abysmal morale of workers. In October 1981, for example, Aganbegyan had written in the official trade-union newspaper *Trud* that the main drag on the economy, a major cause of the alarming drop in Soviet economic growth rates, was "people's attitude toward their work." One crucial indicator, he said, was endemic alcoholism, including widespread drinking on the job.

But during my first interview with Aganbegyan back in 1972, he had kept his most heretical thinking to himself, shying away from any spectacular statements. I remember his brown eyes as impassive and wary. At that time, he had been more interesting than ideologues, but still cautious, careful not to go beyond what he had already said in published articles, which contained what I now know was only a fraction of what he really thought and knew. Aganbegyan clearly felt he had troubles enough without sounding off to *The New York Times*. Typical of many Soviet establishment figures in that day, he preferred to work through private channels, occasionally publishing troubling statistics in his institute's magazine, *Eko.*

Aganbegyan was one, almost invisible tip of what was actually an under-surface archipelago of the Soviet scientific and cultural intelligentsia, and his caution had kept me from penetrating the island of free thinking at Akademgorodok. But in Moscow, Leningrad, and elsewhere, I had become acquainted with others in that archipelago: writers, poets, and artists who had let me, like Alice, pass through the looking glass into their own private, underground worlds of discussions, readings, and other little gatherings.

During those years, I had learned that Russia was a split-level society, with an official public facade and another reality in private. I had come to understand that I could not judge someone by what he said in public. It was clear to me that after Stalin's death in 1953, and probably during Stalin's reign as well, the U.S.S.R. was not as monolithic as most people in the West assumed. Even the Communist Party was not as monolithic as I had once thought, though in the seventies it was still pretty opaque. Repression and fear, and the Party's siege mentality, its compulsion for secrecy toward external enemies, papered over the cracks.

In those years only a tiny band of courageous dissidents dared to shatter the pretense of unanimity in public—Andrei Sakharov, Aleksandr Solzhenitsyn, Roy and Zhores Medvedev, Vladimir Bukovsky, a few Ukrainian dissidents, Crimean Tatars, and Lithuanian Catholics. Or Jews such as Volodya Slepak and Aleksandr Lerner, who wanted to emigrate but were refused permission, and became known as *refuzniki.* Their voices were like bolts of lightning crackling against a darkened sky. Yet in a nation then numbering 220 million, these were an infinitesimal sliver of Soviet society.

I had sensed from my travels and contacts that there must be thousands upon thousands of other clandestine objectors, scattered pockets of malcontents who could not unite because they were afraid to expose their views. In the Brezhnev years, these people saved candor for their families and perhaps one or two trusted friends. Ever fearful of informers, they had pulled the curtains, turned on a radio, and locked the doors to bare their hearts. From Moscow to Siberia, from the Baltics to Georgia and Armenia, I had listened to such people share irreverent jokes about Brezhnev's chest full of medals and his slobbering peasant speech, or tell heartrending stories of how Stalin's terror had shattered their families. The most desperate and daring had huddled in small circles like conspirators to read Solzhenitsyn's contraband book about Stalin's camps, *The Gulag Archipelago,* typed secretly and laboriously, page by page, on onionskin paper. Sometimes they would read all night, passing pages from hand to hand, exhilarated and terrified by the risks they were taking.

Of course, many of these invisible dissenters were at the fringe of the system, but I knew from my acquaintances, or theirs, that there was ideological dry rot even in the pillars of the establishment; it affected editors, diplomats, established writers, scientists, actors, the children and grandchildren of the political elite. There were ideological defectors-in-place, who hid their real views and sold their souls to the Communist Party in order to get good jobs and bargain their way for trips to the outside (Western) world as diplomats, trade officials, physicists, econo-mists, regional leaders, university administrators, tour guides, ballerinas, poets, hockey players. Most of these philosophical defectors kept their heads down low, shying away from political activism.

One training ground for reform in the late 1970s was the environmental movement to save Siberia's world-famous Lake Baikal from industrial pollution. This was an issue on which some establishment liberals and conservatives could unite, and it was one that the Communist Party hierarchy, for some reason, did not find threatening—perhaps because the problem was localized and far from Moscow. Then, too, there were occasional daring snippets of poetry or theater, or politically salty songs by such underground balladiers as Vladimir Vysotsky, Aleksandr Galich, or Bulat Okudzhava. But basically, the Soviet intelligentsia had almost no safety valve, and things were at the bursting point when Gorbachev came along.

THE HUMAN FACTOR

By the late 1980s, when I finally met Tatyana Zaslavskaya, she was a tall, distinguished woman in her early sixties. In an odd way, she reminded me of a taller version of Winston Churchill, with white hair and without the jowls. Her large, alert, unblinking eyes gazed out over roundish Churchill-ian cheeks, and her high forehead and erect posture gave her the air of a British aristocrat. She wore a woman's black-and-white-checked business suit, and she carried a handsome imported briefcase. She was nearly six feet tall in sturdy two-inch heels, vigorous in stride and vigorous in conver-sation, chortling with a kind of lusty enjoyment at her scrapes with authority.

Zaslavskaya had achieved great distinction in the last few years, becom-ing one of a handful of women members of the Soviet Academy of Sciences, a consultant to Gorbachev, head of the Soviet Sociological

Association, and director of a center for the study of public opinion. But in the 1970s she had operated in the hidden archipelago, studying why young people left the countryside, why workers were so unmotivated. She was busy developing concepts of economic sociology. During what seemed like a decade of darkness, she was part of the gathering intellectual streams that Gorbachev would eventually tap into for *perestroika*.

Under Brezhnev, Zaslavskaya recalled matter-of-factly, there was harassment. Many intellectuals, she told me, had tasted the relative freedom under Khrushchev. But when Brezhnev clamped down, most adjusted and played along. Others, like herself, had been unwilling to conform. Unable to publish their most cherished work, they labored in private, developing new concepts invisibly, talking only among small groups of trusted colleagues.

"My colleagues at work constantly grappled with the fact that it was impossible to publish the results of their research in an original, unmodified form," she said. "Harsh censorship simply rooted out every stimulating idea. Any phrase that sounded in the least bit unusual would have the censor crossing it out, deleting it. . . . The censorship was quite thorough. But while censorship could, of course, prevent the release of certain materials, it could not prevent ideas from taking shape. And so, ideas continued to develop, and because of this people continued to discuss things among themselves, to get involved in debates, and to type lectures in five copies, to share with each other. The thought process did not stop."[4]

For the group of nearly fifty sociologists who eventually took refuge under Zaslavskaya's umbrella at Akademgorodok, the key was to *unlearn* many of the official teachings—the teachings of a lifetime—and learn anew about Soviet society, sifting fact from fiction. "Ideological propaganda tried to establish certain precepts: that we were building fully developed socialism, that nowhere else did people live better than we did in the Soviet Union, that in the West there existed widespread poverty," she said. "However, we *saw* what real life was like and naturally we drew our own conclusions. Still, it took time for people to free themselves from ideas that had accumulated over the course of many years and decades."

This little group of scholars quietly pursuing their research was hampered by the difficulty of exchanging views with others, of learning from academic work done elsewhere. The Novosibirsk group had heard that there were others doing serious work, the economist Gavril Popov at Moscow State University, Boris Kurashvili of the Institute of State and Law in Moscow, the sociologist Vladimir Yadov in Leningrad. But in the seventies, independent-minded scholars dared not speak out openly at large academic conferences, for instance, because they knew that among the participants were not only intellectual hacks but also informants who would take notes and report to Party watchdogs on anyone who deviated from the Party line.

Nonetheless, by 1981, the Aganbegyan-Zaslavskaya team felt confident enough of their work to launch a broad, interdisciplinary study of the Soviet economy. Over the course of the next two years, Zaslavskaya developed a searing indictment of the centralized Stalinist command system and an argument for major reforms. Her work was more advanced and heretical than what Aganbegyan had done previously, and in early 1983 she circulated a 150-page report to a limited number of like-minded economists, sociologists, and lawyers at ten major institutes in Moscow, Leningrad, Novosibirsk, and elsewhere.

By her account, about 150 scholars, each one hand-picked, came to Akademgorodok in April 1983 for a closed seminar at which Zaslavskaya's report, among others, was debated.

By another account, Zaslavskaya's reform-oriented paper also circulated to specialists in the economic departments of the Communist Party Central Committee, and in Gosplan, the state planning committee.[5]

Her paper, which became known as "The Novosibirsk Report," was leaked to Dusko Doder of *The Washington Post* by an official in Moscow close to the Politburo faction of Konstantin Chernenko, who was then number two in the Party. Doder waited four months before publishing a story about the report, but when his story did appear, high officials in Moscow denied there was any serious talk of reform and launched a KGB investigation to track down the leak.[6]

"There were deep reverberations [to the story] here," Zaslavskaya told me. "The KGB hunted down and confiscated every copy of that report, down to the last one."

"They conducted searches?" I asked.

"Well, not in people's homes, but at the institute," she replied. "They went through everything, because they were short two copies. They never found them. The documents had been published for official use, and each copy was numbered. So two copies were missing, and they found out how they ended up in the West. Many participants in the seminar experienced extremely unpleasant consequences as a result of the report."

When I read Zaslavskaya's report, I was struck by how much of its thinking was later reflected in Gorbachev's general approach. Zaslavskaya diplomatically disavowed any claim that she was an architect of Gorbachev's reforms, but she told me she had good reasons for believing that

Gorbachev and other Politburo leaders had read her paper after the *Washington Post* story appeared.

In her document, Zaslavskaya had depicted the Soviet economy as being at a dead end and headed for even worse disaster. She blamed the iron hand of the rigidly centralized Stalinist system for the economic mess; she asserted that the tinkering and piecemeal reforms of previous Soviet leaders had proven inadequate; and she called for "a serious reorganization of the system of state management of the economy. . . .

"It is impossible to improve the mechanism of economic management, arrived at years ago, by gradually replacing the more outmoded of its elements with more effective ones," she argued. Past reforms had failed, she said, because the system had not undergone what was needed—"a qualitative restructuring"—and her term for this restructuring was *perestroika.*

Although in 1983 Zaslavskaya had stopped short of explicitly advocating market economics, she had damned the Soviet system for its weak market relations and for putting prices on goods that "bear no relation to their social value." She had made no mention of political reforms; hers was an economic paper. But as a sociologist, her central thesis was that the Soviet economy was being crippled by what she called, and what Gorbachev would later emphasize as, the human factor—the laziness, incompetence, and apathy of masses of workers who were alienated from their jobs by a system that offered them no personal stake in or connection with the enterprises where they worked.

Zaslavskaya argued that the old Stalinist method of command might have been successful in the 1930s, with a work force that was obedient, passive, and poorly educated, but it no longer fit Soviet workers in the 1980s, who were more skilled, educated, mobile, and conscious of their interests and rights. It was in society's interest, she asserted, to give workers, and presumably managers too, a "wide margin of freedom of individual behavior" to make them more productive.

Zaslavskaya's report was prophetic in many ways. She warned that sweeping reforms "cannot run their course without conflict"; she predicted with precision that among the powerful forces that would oppose reforms would be central ministries and subagencies "that have grown like mushrooms in recent decades" and whose armies of bureaucrats occupy "numerous 'cosy niches' with ill-defined responsibilities, but thoroughly agreeable salaries." Surprisingly, she said nothing about the likely reaction of the Communist Party apparatus, either in Moscow or around the country. But she did forecast that important support for reform would come from the people, especially from the most qualified, energetic, and active workers and from the managerial staffs of industrial enterprises.7

Overall, as she said to me later, her message was that the Soviet economy was in "no small crisis, that it wasn't a matter of sewing arm patches on an old suit in order to extend its wearability. I argued that the suit was no longer usable, and that an entirely new one had to be purchased. But to obtain this new suit you needed a restructuring of ideas, the development of market forces, the economic independence of enterprises."8 In other words, and in her words, the country needed *perestroika*.

Her message reached a receptive audience, both among intellectuals and on high, and it was to have profound reverberations.

CHAPTER 2
THE BREZHNEV GENERATION: SLIDE INTO CYNICISM

The responses of three Soviet
leaders when the "train" of
Soviet Communism stalls:
  STALIN: Shoot the engineers.
Exile the crew. Get someone new.
  KHRUSHCHEV: Pardon the crew
and put them back to work.
  BREZHNEV: Pull down the shades
and pretend we're moving.
—Soviet political joke

Gorbachev's reform movement was successful not only because it tapped
into important and hidden intellectual wellsprings; it also struck a reso-
nant chord with millions of people in Soviet society. *Perestroika* has been
called "a revolution from above," but it is not a cabal mounted by a single
leader and a handful of disaffected intellectuals. Such a narrow group
could hardly have inspired the wave of popular upheavals that swept across
the country in the mid-1980s. For that populist response, Gorbachev's
reform needed a mass base.

This mass support had been gathering slowly for two decades, gestating
amid the mass discontent and developing with the social changes brought
by the process of modernization. Tatyana Zaslavskaya's report was one of

several pointing out that a transformation had occurred in Soviet society, providing not only fertile soil for change, but also an army of followers ready to respond when Gorbachev sounded the trumpet call of reform.

For in spite of all of the shortcomings of the Soviet economy and the stagnant inertia of the Brezhnev period, the Soviet Union had changed greatly in the decades since World War II. It was no longer a predominantly peasant society with a primitive work force comprised largely of unskilled manual laborers, and commanded by primitively undereducated political leaders. It had become a predominantly urban society, still dominated by smokestack industry but with a sizable middle class and a growing professional intelligentsia trained at the university level.

And while Soviet political culture was still at a very low level compared with the West, it had undergone a social sea change since the Stalin era. Millions of Soviet citizens were now more receptive to the politics of modernization.

Raw figures reveal an important part of the story. At the end of World War II, only 56.1 million people lived in cities; by 1987, that figure had more than tripled to 180 million. In Khrushchev's time, there were only three cities with a population of more than 1 million; in 1980, there were twenty-three. That massive shift from country to city has slowly worn away the peasant mentality that long characterized the Russian *narod,* or masses. In the early 1970s, this peasant mentality had been a prime source of the political passivity and fatalism of many Russians.

But during my recent travels, one provincial leader after another complained to me that large numbers of young people, especially those with some education and skills, had left dreary villages for big cities in search of better jobs, housing, clothes, stimulation—the latest movies, rock music. Such middle-class urges now made these younger urban transplants dissatisfied with the old, ossified ways of doing things; they were susceptible to the promise of change, impatient and ready to lash back when reforms failed to deliver a better life.

The reemergence of Solidarity, the Polish workers' movement, undoubtedly had an impact both on Soviet intellectuals, inside and outside of the Communist Party, and on the blue-collar proletariat. In her 1983 essay, Zaslavskaya pointed out that in the 1980s, Soviet blue-collar workers were no longer as obedient nor as moved by fear or Communist sloganeering as they had been under Stalin. The Soviet proletariat was now more skilled, more likely to have finished high school, more conscious of its own interests. And, in a distant, muffled echo of Solidarity, it was more assertive.

What is worth noting is that at least in some instances, fear of repression was not enough to check the economic disillusionment of the working class and their fury at the privileges of the Party and government elite—their cars and drivers, special stores, country *dachas,* special clinics, trips abroad. In sum, by the early eighties, even before Gorbachev took over, Soviet society was no longer as docile as it had been. Not only were people more open with their wisecracking jokes about Brezhnev and the regime, but workers as well as intellectuals were getting feedback from abroad, learning that workers in Eastern Europe were living much better than they were. That fed Soviet dissatisfaction and led to some acts of daring unheard-of during my earlier stay in Moscow, though only rarely did active mass dissatisfaction rumble to the surface.

During my Moscow tour from 1971 to 1974, I had not heard of a single serious labor strike. Fear had stifled what was in fact desperate economic discontent. But several years later, even with Brezhnev's repressive apparatus still in place, the situation had changed, inspired in part by Solidarity. In 1980 and 1981, there were wildcat strikes at auto and tractor plants in Gorky, Togliatti, Tartu, Cheboksary, and Naberezhnye Chelny; among coal miners at Vorkuta and Donetsk, where an illegal union was briefly formed; in industrial plants at Vyborg, Riga, and Krivoi Rog; and at three different factories around the Ukrainian capital of Kiev. This phenomenon spoke not only of widespread disaffection among blue-collar workers but also of a new activism, even in the face of possible arrest and punishment. This message cannot have been lost on reform-minded leaders in the Kremlin.[1]

But the most natural source of support for reform, in the late 1970s and early 1980s, was the growing, university-educated urban middle class. Fed up with Party exhortations in the face of obvious stagnation and decline, this growing stratum was eager for a better life, not only in material terms but also in terms of greater personal freedom and flexibility, of more respect and protection for the individual, of more openness and honesty in Soviet political and cultural life.

For years, Moscow and Leningrad intellectuals have charged the Soviet leadership with a deliberate decimation of the Russian intelligentsia and professional classes by cycles of violence, beginning with the Bolshevik Revolution, continuing through civil war, collectivization, the Stalinist purges, and on up through World War II. Then the Brezhnev crackdowns of the 1970s prompted new waves of a cultural diaspora to the West. All of this took a devastating toll on the most talented portion of the Russian population. Quite a few of my Russian friends said that it literally "depleted the Russian genetic stock," leaving the Soviet Union genetically inferior to the West. Even if the notion of genetic inferiority seems extreme, the national brain drain has been enormous. Some Russian intellectuals have begun to feel that only recently has their stock begun to be replenished.

The increase in the numbers of people getting a higher education is striking, even though the quality of that education is uneven. In 1950, there were 1.2 million university-level students in the Soviet Union; by the mid-1980s, that number had multiplied over four times to 5.4 million students being taught by half a million professors and instructors.

The Soviet Union now has one of the largest bodies of scientific researchers in the world: 1.5 million scientists and engineers doing research work.[2] In the past decade, new fields have gained acceptance—systems analysis, ecology, social psychology, mathematical economics, ethnicity, political science. Even though sociology was long under a cloud, there are now fifteen to twenty thousand sociologists, not only doing research and public-opinion polling, but also employed in factories across the country advising industrial managers on how to cope with their changing work force.[3]

Under Stalin, law had low status. In 1940, Soviet universities produced only fifty-seven hundred economists and lawyers a year. But by 1974 that figure had jumped to seventy thousand a year, enough to produce a million lawyers and economists since the mid-1970s. So much interest has developed in the law that the magazine *Chelovyek i Zakon (Man and Law)* has a monthly circulation of ten million.[4]

Gorbachev himself is part of this burgeoning educated middle class. He is the first university-educated Soviet leader since Lenin, born the son of peasants and, like Lenin, educated in the law. Despite Gorbachev's rural roots and his Party career, the intelligentsia see him as their champion. Some of his concerns—the rule of law, the rights of individuals, freer expression—match the concerns of professionals and the intelligentsia— individual self-expression, personal development, and impatience with the heavy-handed imposition of state morality. This group was a natural constituency for reform aimed at increasing citizen participation and decreasing the role of the state and an entrenched bureaucracy.

In the dynamics of change within the Soviet Union, the most important segment of the intelligentsia is the so-called Khrushchev generation—people who from 1953 to 1964 experienced the excitement of the political and cultural thaw under Nikita Khrushchev.

Some of these people are now in their fifties and early sixties; they were liberated from the heavy pall of Stalinism during their formative university years, and were given hope for greater cultural freedom and personal autonomy. And then they watched in horror as these changes were stolen away from them by the retrogression of the Brezhnev years.

Another stream of reformers are younger, now in their forties; they were schoolchildren under Khrushchev, but nevertheless were caught up in the optimism of that era.

For both groups, hope in the future and faith in Soviet socialism had soared in the years after the first Soviet sputnik in 1957 and of Yuri Gagarin's first manned space flight on April 12, 1961. Despite Khrushchev's bumptious saber-rattling, his shoe-pounding at the United Nations, millions of middle-aged Soviets believed him when he boasted that the Soviet Union would catch up with and then overtake the West, and Gagarin's orbital flight had marked the zenith of that feeling.

"I was in school. All the lessons ended. Even today I can remember that tremendous joy, literally the tears we all had in our eyes—because we were the first, because we were in space," recalled Leonid Dobrokhotov, later one of the most articulate, candid, and thoughtful followers of Gorbachev in the Communist Party Central Committee apparatus.

"We felt our power," he told me. "We felt that there were no limits, that all tasks would be accomplished, and so on. It's no wonder that in 1961 the third program of the Communist Party of the Soviet Union was published. That program stated that we would achieve Communism in twenty years. It was like President Johnson's Great Society program, which many Americans believed in. But here, almost *everyone* believed that in twenty years we would surpass the U.S. in every way—in living standards, in food production, housing, in meeting spiritual needs, in everything.

"We would become Country Number One in the world—and socialism would be utterly victorious. Almost everyone believed that. That was in 1961."[5]

THE POLITICS OF LIES

The heady optimism of this Khrushchev generation set them up for the crushing disillusionment of the long, painful decline under Brezhnev. The Brezhnev period had actually begun in 1964 with a certain optimism—attempts at managerial reform in the economy, slow but steady improvements in the general standard of living; communal apartments were slowly being replaced, and better clothing, washing machines, and refrigerators became available. But in Brezhnev's second decade, economic reform was dead, strangled by the party apparat; cultural controls tightened. In every sphere, reality fell short of people's expectations and public morale took a nosedive. This was true even among the most loyal and optimistic Communists, such as Leonid Dobrokhotov, people who were making their way up the ladder in the Communist Party.

Leonid's terse description of his own disenchantment is etched in my mind, his pale blue eyes locked on mine, his slender arms thrown out wide, his slender pianist's fingers gesticulating. A member of a theatrical family, Leonid is more expressive, and more sensitive to the moods of the intelligentsia, than most Communist Party officials. For many years, his job involved dealing with the Academy of Sciences, which put him in contact with the intellectual and scientific community. His recollections, therefore, reflect a wider perspective, both within the scientific intelligentsia and within a reformist element in the Communist Party apparatus.

I asked how Leonid felt at the end of the 1970s.

"It's the exact opposite of the feelings I described in 1961," he replied. "I wouldn't call it disenchantment with socialism, but it was certainly disenchantment with our country's leadership, and an understanding that the program to build Communism in twenty years was a total fiction. That that program had not been carried out at all, that it *couldn't* be carried out. That everything was very bad in the country. The economy was bad. There was no real provision for the population's needs. There was no democracy. The leadership was corrupt. And finally, there was Afghanistan."

But if segments of the intelligentsia were disillusioned by the early eighties, Leonid said the masses were not quite; they were more skeptical than disillusioned. "People saw that things were bad and that the system didn't work, but why it didn't work was unclear to the overwhelming majority of people. So it's true to say that almost everyone continued to believe in socialism, in the foundation of the system." What they didn't believe in was Brezhnev. "They simply thought that Brezhnev had not justified the hopes pinned on him. And that the people working with Brezhnev were not the right people. So they thought it would be rather easy to replace those people, and leave the mechanism essentially the same. Only an insignificant number of people understood that the system had to be radically changed—that it wasn't a matter of people, but rather of the system. I think that was understood only by a minority, mostly the intelligentsia."[6]

The majority view is in many ways understandable. In his eighteen years of power, Brezhnev had concentrated the country's efforts on a few high-priority areas, and had driven the Soviet Union to accumulate an enormous nuclear arsenal. The Soviet Union had surpassed the United States in such yardsticks of industrial might as steel output and oil production. And the living standards of Soviet people had actually improved during the first dozen years of Brezhnev's rule. However much the West was offended by the invasion of Czechoslovakia in 1968, most Russians were proud that Brezhnev had asserted Soviet power and kept the empire intact.

But sometime in the mid-seventies, the tide began to turn. By the end of the decade, the economy had quite clearly lost momentum. Four bad agricultural harvests, from 1979 through 1982, made food shortages endemic. There was rationing of meat and milk in some regions. Industrial sectors went into decline; labor productivity went flat. The free health-care system, a much-vaunted pride of Soviet socialism, had deteriorated so much that infant mortality rates rose while male life expectancy went down. The statistics were covered up, but people could experience for themselves the horrible inadequacies of the health system: shortages of medicine, unbearably long waits for treatment, serious infections picked up in hospitals, the bribery necessary to secure treatment. The press occasionally reported stories of corruption by middle-level officials. Moscow was full of unseemly rumors that reached into Brezhnev's own family and entourage. Later it turned out that even the army, Party officials, and the KGB, headed by Brezhnev's eventual successor, Yuri Andropov, were embarrassed and angered by the corruption and sloth of the Brezhnev era. The whole country was sliding into cynicism.[7]

"That was an awful time," recalled Roy Medvedev, the dissident Marxist historian who had dared, in the Brezhnev era, to write and publish in the West his devastating book on Stalin, *Let History Judge.* Roy, a Communist idealist whose father had been executed under Stalin and whose twin brother, Zhores, had gone into exile in London, had squirreled himself away in a cubbyhole writing den in his fifth-floor apartment. Basically isolated, he was nevertheless still fed information and documents for his archives by covert Khrushchev-style reformers within government institutes and the Party apparatus. I had known Roy in the early 1970s as one of a handful of outspoken dissidents; he told me how much worse things had gotten after I left.

"People did not believe in anything," Roy recalled. "Brezhnev was so cynical, his whole policies and politics were full of lies. Power was more important to him than ideals. He was a vain, stupid person. When people saw him come on the screen, they just switched off the TV. Not just when he became sick, but before he was sick. So you could say those years were lost for politics. People focused on their personal lives, because culture, politics, and art, especially social sciences, were not developing anymore. Nobody wanted to take part."[8]

The same was true in the economy. Workers, managers, everyone, went through the motions of working in the official economy, but when consumers really wanted something they turned to the black market, which was so massive that it really amounted to a countereconomy. People turned to this for meat, fresh vegetables, toothpaste, caviar, women's boots, baby clothes, rugs, wall lamps, ballet tickets, spare parts to fix the refrigerator or the car, medicine, tutoring for the kids, a decent apartment. Entire underground industries flourished, illegal factories within legal ones, operating with the same workers and the same raw materials, but this time efficiently because for private profit. There were underground millionaires managing wholesale production and marketing enterprises with links all over the country. This is where people's energies were going, where they were applying their ingenuity. Just as in academic life and the world of culture, progress did not stop. People pursued their own ends in private, underground, ignoring or eluding the regime's threats of prosecution. In fact, the practice was so much a part of everyone's daily life that most Russians I knew believed that Brezhnev and his cronies counted on the black market as a safety valve for people's frustrations.

The gap between real life and Communist dogma yawned ever wider. As the problems grew worse, the regime became more boastful. As official propaganda became more pretentious, as Brezhnev held ceremonies to have decorations pinned on his chest, ordinary Russians mocked him. I remember several jokes poking fun at the Brezhnev cult. The first lampooned the nation's immobility under Brezhnev; the second mocked his dim wit.

In the first joke, a train carrying Stalin, Khrushchev, and Brezhnev stalls somewhere in the steppes. People turn to Stalin, as the senior leader, to ask how to get the train moving. Without hesitation, he gives a characteristic command: "Shoot the engineers. Exile the crew. Get someone new." But a short while later, the train stalls again. This time, responsibility falls on Khrushchev, who pardons the crew members exiled by Stalin and puts them back on the job, and the train resumes its journey. Inevitably, it stalls a third time. This time Brezhnev has to deal with the problem. The others turn to him, he thinks a moment, and then orders: "Pull down the shades and pretend we're moving."

In the second anecdote, Brezhnev is congratulating some Soviet cosmonauts after a successful space flight. But conscious that the Americans have landed on the moon and are leading in the space race, he discloses that the Soviet Union intends to leap ahead with a special new mission. The Politburo, he announces, has voted to send out a Soviet cosmonaut team—to the sun!

"But, comrade leader," one cosmonaut protests, "we'll be burned alive."

"Do you think we understand nothing?" Brezhnev replies. "Don't worry. We have planned every detail. We have arranged for you to land at night."

By the early eighties, Brezhnev's senility had become an embarrassment. When I went to Vienna to cover President Carter's summit meeting with Brezhnev in 1979, I remembered the Brezhnev who had visited America six years earlier. He had been vigorous then, cavorting with husky Western movie star Chuck Connors, who had hoisted Brezhnev off the ground in a Russian bear hug. But in Vienna he seemed a walking corpse. He hobbled off the plane from Moscow, his gait unsteady, his face sallow and waxen. Then, when I followed him to a ceremony at a monument honoring the Soviet dead in Austria during World War II, I was even more shocked at his infirmities.

He was supposed to march past a gathering of Soviet officials and embassy families, make a right turn, take half a dozen steps, and then symbolically touch a huge green wreath that had been placed before the monument. I watched him approach, moving mechanically, like a windup doll. His feet shuffled in short little steps from the knees down, arms pinned to his sides, his hands flapping back and forth. His loyal lieutenant Konstantin Chernenko was a step behind, followed by other dignitaries.

Then, as I watched from fifteen feet away, Brezhnev missed the turning point and plowed helplessly into a group of onlookers. There was an audible gasp from the people around me, as Brezhnev was rescued by Chernenko, who pulled him back and manually steered him onto the correct path. The rest of the ceremony went all right, but I was left astonished by Brezhnev's obvious incapacity.

Nevertheless he stayed in office three more years, his geriatric decline a symbol of the general stagnation and drift that was afflicting his country.

THE HALF-LOST GENERATION

Periodically, Brezhnev—and the Kremlin—would lash out, as if to assert the regime's power, to ward off the developing urge for change. But these assertions of power only added to the growing hunger for reform. The

December 1979 invasion of Afghanistan was the most violent of these power moves, and it served to alienate a new generation, the young people of the 1980s.

"It was a shock for us, the Afghanistan invasion, an absolute shock," one of them told me. Sergei Stankevich was in his mid-twenties in 1979, teaching at Moscow Pedagogical Institute. "It was a very bad New Year— the invasion took place on the eve of the New Year. It was a time of mourning for us. In my circle, everyone was ironic about the official rhetoric—that we were 'invited' in by the Afghans. At the same time we were terrified, because we understood that when the war starts outside, the war also starts inside. The war against truth, openness, against liberals. We understood that it meant a long period of tightening the screws. Still, almost nobody had enough courage to protest openly—except Sakharov, of course. We heard about him by foreign radio. At that time, everybody listened to foreign radio. Our reaction was blaming: We blamed the whole system and Brezhnev personally. But blaming in the kitchen, a typical situation for us, kitchen blaming. There was absolute rejection of Brezhnev and all that he was doing."[9]

Stankevich and his friends confined their protests to the kitchen, because they knew that public protests over the Afghan war would result in a trip to Siberia and the end of their careers.

Stankevich had entered the university in 1972, at the dawning of détente between Nixon and Brezhnev. He and his classmates were hoping for a real opening to the world, and not just through government-to-government agreements. They were encouraged by the Helsinki Accords on human rights, signed in 1975. And they were devastated by Brezhnev's subsequent repression of human-rights activists, and by the invasion of Afghanistan.

"Afghanistan was a watershed for our generation," Stankevich told me. "It was the funeral of hope."

Stankevich turned thirty before Gorbachev came to power. He felt cheated out of freedom and out of the new opportunities his generation had expected from détente. He said that he and his friends felt that their lives had been half wasted under Brezhnev and his geriatric successors, Andropov and Chernenko.

"We are the half-lost generation," he said bitterly.

Still, Stankevich and his friends thought the war in Afghanistan might eventually work to their benefit. Remembering that the Crimean War in the 1850s had been the undoing of Czar Nicholas I, and the Russo-Japanese War of 1905 had begun the unraveling for Czar Nicholas II, they saw the Afghan war as a potentially fatal mistake for Brezhnev and company.

"It was a kind of sunset of the regime, because they were involved in such a bad business," Stankevich said. "[We thought,] 'They can never prevail in this war, and it can only aggravate the crisis.' We felt that sometime, sooner or later, radical changes would be inevitable."

"Really?" I asked. "You felt that even before Brezhnev died?"

"Even before Brezhnev died." Stankevich replied. "You know when the government of a regime in crisis goes to war, it's also an attempt to postpone the crash. But in practice it accelerates the crash."

FERMENT WITHIN THE PARTY

And so the intellectuals, in both the middle and younger generations, as well as consumers and workers, were disaffected by economic misery, but they were still politically inert. What about the hidden world of the Communist Party?

Contrary to the Western perception of the Soviet Communist Party as a monolith that operates with Nazi-like discipline, by the late 1970s feelings of grievance, failure, and the need for change had penetrated and fragmented the Party as well. Many Soviets have told me in recent years that the inner life of the Party reflects a range of popular moods. On basic economic issues, the views of rank-and-file Party members are likely to be fairly close to those of the public at large. The prevailing views of people in the Party apparatus are dominated by older, more conservative career-ists, including regional power barons and *apparatchiki* who have a vested interest in the status quo. But throughout the Brezhnev period, and certainly by the end of it, there were already several different tendencies within the Party: Old Guard conservatives like Brezhnev protecting the status quo; neo-Stalinists who wanted a return to a tougher line; Khrush-chevite reformers who wanted Stalin and Stalinism explicitly rejected; a growing stream of newer reformers; and a preponderance of opportunists feathering their own careers by going along with the Brezhnev line.

By 1980, many of the brightest people rising through the Party hierar-chy shared the disenchantment of non-Party intellectuals. Within the Party, morale was sagging and ideological cynicism was on the rise. Many were sickened by official corruption; others were fed up with the two laughable old fools Brezhnev and Chernenko. Although they dared not speak out publicly, they were deeply offended by the fatuous personality cult fostered by Brezhnev, reminiscent of Stalin, and by the false claims of the Brezhnev regime.

"The first three years of Brezhnev's rule had offered some hope," recalled Aleksandr Yakovlev. Now Gorbachev's closest political ally, Yakovlev was a powerful figure even back in the late 1960s, when he was acting chief of the Party's propaganda department. "Brezhnev said the right things; I didn't know he was speaking someone else's words. He seemed open to reforms, to fresh ideas. And then later it all turned out so obscenely. I remember that certain comrades in his entourage began to call me and ask why I wasn't promoting Brezhnev. That astounded me. It was simply impossible for me to do—it was physically unbearable."[10]

Yakovlev's refusal to play along with Brezhnev and his entourage on issues important to Brezhnev and his ideological attack on Russian nationalism, to which Brezhnev was sympathetic, cost Yakovlev his job. He was banished to Canada, as ambassador, in 1972; Gorbachev rescued him in 1983.

Other high-ranking officials, such as Andropov, the KGB boss whose intelligence role required him to study the West as well as manage internal security, and army marshals such as Chief of Staff Nikolai Ogarkov, who saw Western advances in modern technology, knew the U.S.S.R. was slipping badly. Internally, the Communist Party was full of ferment as the 1980s began.

"I can speak only for myself and my comrades, but at that time, we talked only politics," recalled Leonid Dobrokhotov, who at that time was a rising Moscow Party functionary in his mid-to-late thirties. "We argued. Everyone was dissatisfied. Everyone saw that the situation wasn't getting better, it was getting worse. We argued about what to do. The majority of us felt [our national crisis] was due to a lack of discipline, to insufficient demands, insufficient control over how people fulfilled various laws and decisions, because Brezhnev was not capable. His policy was too liberal. So we came to the conclusion that we had to make tougher demands, improve discipline. Of course, this was not truly deep, analytical thinking, and it did not uncover the real reasons for the country's problems. But that's the way the majority thought. Only a few understood that the fault was not the lack of formal discipline; the fault was the system—it didn't work, or it was working worse and worse all the time."[11]

Even very near the top, the spirit of reform was gestating. In Brezhnev's final year, agencies such as Gosplan (the State Planning Committee) and the Committee for Science and Technology set up study groups to look at the option of decentralized economic management. In 1983, Vadim Medvedev, rector of the Academy of Social Sciences, the main domestic think tank of the Communist Party Central Committee, published a book advocating new attempts at economic reform. Medvedev, an economist who would emerge as a member of Gorbachev's Politburo, praised Kosygin's reforms of 1965 but said they did not go far enough. He urged more autonomy for state enterprises, more material incentives for workers, letting consumers have more say in determining output, and introducing "commodity-money" relations (a code term for market economics).[12] His book was not as blunt and radical as Zaslavskaya's "Novosibirsk Report"; it was couched in vaguer, more technical wording. But it pointed in the same direction.

Some experimentation was already under way in Soviet Georgia, under Eduard Shevardnadze, the innovative Georgian Party boss who had been a close political friend of Gorbachev since the two were leaders of Komsomol youth organizations in the late 1950s. In the early 1970s, I had known of Shevardnadze as a Party puritan. He had purged the corrupt Georgian Party apparatus and sent scores of officials and businessmen to jail for illegal economic operations. But by 1979, he was known as a liberal who had set up a public-opinion center under the Georgian Party Central Committee and used public-opinion polls to help monitor the quality of state services and then fired high officials who got bad reports from the public. Later, Shevardnadze allowed experiments in enterprise self-management, in market-oriented pricing, in leasing small businesses to families, and in legalizing industrial black-market industries so as to tap their entrepreneurship.[13] Shevardnadze began by liberalizing controls over the arts, cinema, and the press.

Dobrokhotov, intrigued by an article about Shevardnadze's unorthodox approach, went to Georgia in 1979 for a firsthand look.

"In Georgia, I saw the *perestroika* that is now going on here," Dobrokhotov told me. "So that even during the worst period of stagnation in our country, democratization was going on in Tbilisi, Georgia. They were chasing out bureaucrats. The jails were filled with almost all of the former leaders of the republic—they were jailed for corruption and theft, for deception. There was a battle against bureaucracy. The press was extremely critical of these negative elements. I was inspired, awed by what I saw in Georgia. When I came home, I started to report about this to the leadership; I said that we should do what they were doing in Georgia. But my boss at the time was a rather shrewd leader, as I understand now, and he told me, 'Leonid, under no circumstances should you tell anyone about your impressions.' "[14]

In short, even if Shevardnadze was testing out a mild version of Gorbachev's future policy of *glasnost* in the provinces, it was not smart for a rising Party official like Dobrokhotov to risk his career by going out on a limb with the Brezhnev regime.

But times were changing. By the time Brezhnev died in November 1982 and Yuri Andropov took over, there was substantial sentiment for change within the Party as well as among the people.

Widely regarded as the smartest member of the Politburo, Andropov seemed aware of the country's paralysis and bent on restoring a national sense of purpose. He began like a man in a hurry, intent on breaking the economic logjams and stirring up an apathetic society. He immediately launched a purge of Brezhnevite corruption and a campaign for greater work discipline and more economic efficiency. He injected a sense of momentum. But essentially, his reforms were conservative—tightening rather than loosening control. And in just fifteen months, his rule was cut short by death.

Reformers' hopes were dashed, then, when Politburo conservatives proved powerful enough to impose as the new leader Konstantin Chernenko, Brezhnev's old lieutenant and a doddering apparatchik in his seventies. Chernenko was a throwback, his rule an embarrassment. He revived Brezhnev's personality cult, pomposity, inertia. The old Brezhnev jokes were recycled and applied to Chernenko. Everywhere lay the dead hand of the oppressive bureaucracy grown fat under Brezhnev. People were ashamed of the past, frustrated by the present, fearful for the future.

It was doubly painful for the older people, whose hopes were raised by Khrushchev in the 1950s and then dashed by Brezhnev, only to have that cycle repeated by the quicker up-and-down of Andropov and Chernenko.

By the time Chernenko died in March 1985, the gloom was pervasive, the pressure for reform explosive. Aleksandr Yakovlev, by then an adviser to Gorbachev, described to me the mood of that time:

"I had a sense of foreboding, like before a storm. That there was something brewing in people and there would be a time when they would say, 'That's it. We can't go on living like this. We can't. We need to redo everything.' "[15]

CHAPTER 3

GORBACHEV AND THE KHRUSHCHEV GENERATION

"The main social forces behind *perestroika* are people in that generation. Those are the people that we call the Children of the Twentieth Party Congress—Khrushchev's Congress, where he gave his secret speech denouncing Stalin. These were the people who came out of Khrushchev's thaw, which formed their mentality, and of course, he—Gorbachev— was part of that generation."[1]

—Vladimir Tikhonov
Economist
September 1989

While a political storm had been gathering, it took Gorbachev to unleash its fury. A new kind of Soviet leader was needed to pry the lid off and deal with decades of discontent, to legitimize protest, permit free expression, restrain the KGB and police from scooping up the first new demonstrators and starting to refill Stalin's old gulag. It took a political visionary, one who was both desperate and self-confident, to declare that it was impossible to rescue Soviet socialism and pump life back into its decrepit carcass without also injecting political freedoms and giving people, especially educated people, a voice and a stake in the Soviet system. It took Gorbachev, idealistic, bold, and supremely agile, to set the match to the fuse of political dynamite that had been building up. It took Gorbachev to proclaim the Grand Reformation of the Soviet system.

But where had this Mikhail Gorbachev come from?

How had such a daring innovator wriggled his way up through a bureaucracy that had put a premium on orthodoxy, had ground individuality out of its apparatchiks?

Once Gorbachev emerged as the leader, we began to see for ourselves some of the traits that led to his success: strong beliefs, strict candor about the failures within the system, intellectual curiosity and openness, an ebullience, and a penchant for change and experimentation. Gorbachev became a political trapeze artist who defied the normal laws of gravity. But how did such a risk taker get himself chosen by his Politburo peers to preside over a conservative, self-protective power pyramid that had habitually hidden behind lies, punished political deviation, and routinely quashed anything that smacked of intellectual independence?

What was the crucible that forged the steel in Gorbachev's character? Where had his notions of reform come from, and how had he struck such an exquisite balance between the need to conform and the need to be open enough to think anew? How had he been cunning enough to preserve a vital core of belief deep inside himself, while showing sufficient obedience to satisfy his superiors? What intellectual and biographical origins had shaped his inner mental world?

Many of Gorbachev's most important traits came from his family and took root in early childhood: his honesty and realism, his outspokenness, his tolerance for religion, his breathtaking self-assurance, his driving ambition, and most important, his astonishing resilience, his capacity to survive. At the pinnacle of power, Gorbachev stunned Westerners with his ability to ride over the turbulence of *perestroika,* to buck with confidence the waves of reaction. He seemed to thrive on crisis, as if crisis were his natural state.

The truth is that from the day of his birth, Mikhail Sergeyevich Gorbachev was tutored in the arts of biological and political survival in a hostile world. His life story evokes Abraham Lincoln's odyssey from log cabin to the White House, except that the death and famine from Stalin's farm collectivization, which engulfed the early years of Gorbachev's life, was far more devastating than anything Lincoln experienced growing up.

In 1931, the year Gorbachev was born in the village of Privolnoye, Stalin's terror and his collectivization reached a climax. Gorbachev's home was a little hut on a gentle rise in the open prairie, or steppe, of the Northern Caucasus, now called Stavropol Territory, or Krai. It is a place of broad expanses, like northern Texas, and the independent-minded people whom I met there speak of *prostor*, or space, the same way that Texans limn their romance with wide open spaces. The town's name, Privolnoye, means "free" or "spacious," alluding not only to the broad pastoral landscape stretching off in all directions, but also to a certain free-booter spirit among its people.

The land, lying nearly one thousand miles south of Moscow and stretching north from the Caucasus mountain range, is fertile, framed by the deltas of two great Russian rivers, the Volga and the Don. The soil is a rich ebony; with a kind of peasant reverence, the Russians call it *chernozem*, black earth. The long temperate growing season is a bit dry, but the favorable soil has made this one of the richest grain-producing areas in the entire country.

The people of this southern frontier region have a wilder, freer history than the more settled peasantry of central Russia. When they came to the region around the Don River in the sixteenth and seventeenth centuries, they became known as the Don cossacks, legendary as independent yeoman farmers and fierce horsemen, who settled the wild frontier and, as mercenaries, defended this southern outpost of the Russian Empire against Muslim peoples from the south. The cossacks were not ethnic stock but freedom seekers, runaways, even escaped criminals. A century later came the forebears of Gorbachev, peasants from central Russia and the Ukraine, again people escaping the yoke of serfdom and in search of better land and more freedom. Throughout the nineteenth century, the Northern Caucasus thrived on a tradition of independent homesteading, which was continued even by Lenin, only to be shattered by Stalin's violent collectivization of the land and his bloody repression of the kulaks (so-called wealthy peasants, even though their wealth might have consisted of no more than a home, a few acres, and a couple of cows).

In Privolnoye, the leader of collectivization was Gorbachev's maternal grandfather, Pantelei Yefimovich Gopkolo. By many accounts, he was the pivotal influence on Gorbachev's life. Family friends describe Grandfather Gopkolo as an active, dynamic Ukrainian, gregarious, persuasive, a good public speaker, with a self-confident manner, a masculine stride, and the presence of a natural leader. These qualities plus Grandfather Gopkolo's ability to swing pragmatically with the violent tides of history were an obvious model for Gorbachev.

Born in 1882, Gopkolo had to follow a zigzag course merely to survive to the age of seventy. On a trip to Great Britain in 1984, Gorbachev revealed that even though his grandfather was a Communist, his grandparents hid religious icons in their home behind portraits of Lenin and Stalin. This was hardly a unique experience; it was done in many families. But clearly, their way of secretly protecting something that was vital to them was an object lesson in political behavior that stuck in the mind of the grandson, and served as an example for his own dealings with higher authority.

As a young man, Grandfather Gopkolo had to adapt to the violent crosscurrents that swept through Privolnoye. As he moved into young adulthood, the region was benefiting from czarist land reforms of 1906 that legalized private farming. In the next few years, Russia become the world's number one exporter of grain, enriching the countryside. After the Bolshevik Revolution and during the civil war from 1918 to 1921, Privolnoye was caught in the crossfire between the Red Army and the counter-revolutionary Whites (many of them Don cossacks), who were battling for control of the region. Monuments to the civil-war dead, a few miles from Privolnoye, attest to the heavy toll in lives. When the Reds won, Grandfather Gopkolo cast his lot with the Communists. Lenin's New Economic Policy of the mid-1920s permitted the peasants to continue private farming.

By Gorbachev's later account, his family were not "wealthy" kulaks, but "middle peasants," who made a moderate but decent living. Yet when Stalin commanded collectivization, Grandfather Gopkolo was among the first to step forward.

The village elders told me that the peasantry were persuaded by roving Communist Party workers that collectives would be the most efficient way to work their modest plots of land. Some said that Gopkolo and others willing to form a new collective were offered the incentive of a few Ford and Caterpillar tractors, obtained from America.[2] Undoubtedly, some were also influenced by the ominous warnings dropped by Stalin's agents roaming the area. But according to Grigory Gorlov, a warm and craggy-faced old local Party leader who knew the Gorbachev family well, even before Stalin's campaign began in earnest in 1929, Gopkolo contributed his own land to what was initially a small farm cooperative of about twenty families.[3] As a respected figure in the village, someone to whom people turned for advice, Gopkolo actively went about recruiting others. Eventually, their cooperative became a full-fledged *kolkhoz*, or collective farm, of about three hundred families, with Gopkolo as its chairman.

The process was painful, Gorbachev's uncle Sergei Gopkolo told me. "Collectivization was a very hard time," he said. "Some people did not want to join, especially those who were 'rich.' "[4] What he meant was that many homesteaders, especially the cossacks, had to surrender not only their land, but often horses and other livestock and wagons. In many areas violence was used. But the village elders insisted to me that Gopkolo was a man of moderate temperament, opposed to using force and preferring "the course of persuasion."

If true, then Privolnoye was unusual and extremely fortunate, because the general devastation wrought by Stalin's policies was horrifying. In the Northern Caucasus, people are full of stories about terror against cossacks and peasants. Some Western experts have estimated from Soviet accounts that, during the forced collectivization, as many as six million peasant families disappeared nationwide between 1929 and 1934. The Northern Caucasus, with its cossack traditions of independence, was especially hard hit.[5]

What is more, the land and people were ravaged by what became known as the Great Famine. By the winter of 1932–33, Stavropol Krai had become a famine disaster zone. Conditions were harsher than during the American Great Depression. "The repressions of the 1930s hit the rural areas of the North Caucasus badly," wrote Zhores Medvedev, who grew up not far from Stavropol Territory. "Almost every family lost relatives, friends or neighbors during this period and Privolnoye was no exception."[6]

Each year, Stalin winched up his demands for ever more grain from the countryside, to feed urban factory workers—46 percent of the total harvest in 1930, 63 percent in 1931. Peasants were left without enough food for themselves. To survive, they went on grain strikes, hiding their grain from state procurement agents; yet Stalin tightened the vise of collectivization to capture every kernel. It was a vicious cycle. In Privolnoye, food virtually disappeared in the winter of 1932–33. People now claim that something like one third of the village's six thousand residents perished, some buried crudely in collective graves. A wizened old farm agronomist named Nikolai Lubenko told me, "The raw hunger was terrible."

This was the apocalypse into which Gorbachev was born, on March 2, 1931. His mother worked on Grandfather Gopkolo's *kolkhoz* as the leader of a team that raised vegetables. His father, Sergei Andreyevich, was a combine operator. Eventually he became the head of a tractor brigade of thirty workers at a machine tractor station, a Stalinist innovation that helped monitor all farm production.

On my two visits to Privolnoye with a television crew, I found a village of rough-hewn houses made of brick or wood, lined up on plots fifty feet wide behind weather-beaten wood fences. Only a few of the town's roads are paved. Today, Gorbachev's mother, now in her late seventies, lives on one of the paved roads in a brick house with a special telephone line to maintain contact with her son. The mother's house is under the watchful eye of security men and off limits to foreign visitors, at Gorbachev's personal request.

He has also obviously decreed that the town make no visible cult over its famous son. It is a very ordinary-looking village, in the center of which stands a Soviet "House of Culture." The whole scene looks like a village in Ohio or Wisconsin sixty years ago.

But back when Gorbachev was born, his family lived in a much more primitive, two-room hut made of mud bricks, dung, and straw, about three or four miles from the main village. Grigory Gorlov told me that the Gorbachevs had an outhouse, a small barn, a cow, a few pigs, and chickens and turkeys running around the yard. Next to the house was a grape arbor. Out back was a vegetable garden for growing potatoes, cucumbers, onions, and tomatoes; also there were some fruit trees—apricot, cherry, apple. The kitchen had a stove and table, but no running water. The main room had one big bed and heat, but the room given to young Misha (Gorbachev's Russian nickname) was unheated. It was his alone, until he was seventeen, when his brother, Aleksandr, was born.

The fierce deprivation he witnessed in the countryside left an indelible impression on Gorbachev. Years later, to fellow students at Moscow State University, he exposed the hypocrisy of Stalin's propaganda about the happy life on Soviet collective farms, recalling the forced labor and the meager meals of his own childhood. His family managed to endure the famine years, thanks to their backyard plot and to their favored standing at Grandfather Gopkolo's *kolkhoz*. But that experience hardened young Misha for the future. It taught him the basics of survival, while inculcating in him candor about the infirmities of the system that he had seen firsthand.

THE INSTINCT FOR CENTER STAGE

Misha Gorbachev was far from an average farm boy. His record, in and out of school, was impressive, but nothing that caused people to mark him as a future national leader. "He was not like a special person," his high school history teacher, Antonina Shcherbakova, told me. "He was just a regular guy. He liked games. He liked laughing. He liked soccer. He used to run barefoot in the grass. Even without pants, only in his shorts. He walked to school on foot."[7]

A hometown chum, Aleksandr Yakovenko, a combine operator with a twinkle in his eye who now looks a decade older than Gorbachev, recalled normal boyhood pursuits with Misha—splashing in a great wooden rain barrel, pulling the pigtails of the village girls, playing a Russian game like baseball called *lapta,* sitting on the bench outside his house singing folk songs while Misha played the stringed balalaika. As Yakovenko plucked one of those songs for me, "Bread First of All," tears welled up in his eyes. In those days, Yakovenko said, Misha loved munching on salted watermelon and gulping down cold *kvas,* a Russian peasant brew made by dripping water through burnt toast. Their boyhoods were hard, but not without pleasure, and Misha was known as a cheerful lad.

Still, by the time he finished high school, a discerning eye could pick out characteristics that would distinguish him later—his zeal for learning, his self-righteous contempt for alcohol, his ambition, his ability as a leader and organizer—and his instinct for center stage.

No one who has ever met Gorbachev comes away without mentioning his penetrating eyes. Gorbachev's gaze is commanding—his retinas sometimes a deep brown, sometimes a shining charcoal-black. These magnetic eyes radiate power, intensity, and energy—abnormal energy. I spoke with him briefly during his visit to Washington in December 1987, and I remember that his eyes were like lasers, locking onto mine, never shifting, never blinking. He was looking directly at me, yet through me. Family friends remember that Gorbachev's father had those same eyes, and in fact, that penetrating gaze stares out from beneath Misha's high forehead and over his round, fleshy cheeks in snapshots taken when he was only four years old.

Gorbachev's father, according to accounts given me, was a simple, practical, hardworking man, at home on his tractor in the fields, but rather shy. Like all the others in the family, he had no more than a few grades of education in a local village school. He was well regarded enough to be a trusted member of the Communist Party District Committee, but he intensely disliked making speeches, and would offer to work extra days in the fields if that would excuse him from making an oral report.

Young Misha took after his mother, old Gopkolo's daughter, Mariya Panteleyevna. She was—and is—a strong woman, sturdy, outspoken, self-confident, and self-righteous. People in the village know her as a religious believer who had young Misha baptized and probably inculcated in him tolerance of religion, although she did not make a believer out of him. But she did set a powerful example in speaking out. At district Party meetings, with her husband silently cringing beside her or trying to talk her out of making a fuss, she would rise to her feet and launch into a speech, bombarding her fellow farmers and local officials with questions and criticisms. She spoke at almost every meeting; no one was exempt from her tongue-lashings. Descriptions of her bring to mind the modern Gorbachev.

An aggressive teetotaler, "she would scold drunkards and people who worked badly," recalled Grigory Gorlov, the district Party secretary in those days. "She even argued with the chairman of the *kolkhoz* and the head of the machine tractor station. I recall one session vividly. There was a big fat farmhand named Kabakov, who had gotten drunk and left the barn door open. It was winter, and half of the *kolkhoz's* flock of poultry perished in the cold. Mariya Panteleyevna demanded: 'Why are all the poultry frozen to death and why didn't *you* freeze? I tell you why. You're not frozen because you were drunk, you were so full of alcohol!' "[8]

Temperance was the rule in the Gorbachev household. On holidays, the men might take one shot glass of vodka or cognac in celebration, no more. It's small wonder that, half a century later, Gorbachev would initiate, as one of his first priorities after taking power in March 1985, an anti-alcohol campaign combined with a drive to improve work discipline.

The hard life on the farm and the onset of World War II forced Misha to become an adult at an early age, gaining maturity and self-confidence. His father was called to the front in 1941; he served as a minelayer, from Smolensk to the end of the war in Prague, and was wounded three times. In 1942, when Nazi forces occupied the region around Privolnoye, Gorbachev, now the man of the house, left school for a year and went to work in the fields with the old folks and the women. He was then only eleven, having just passed the local rite of puberty—jumping off the rickety wooden bridge over the Yegorlyk River into the muddy waters fifteen feet below.

The Nazi occupation, part of Hitler's attempt to cut southern Russia off from the north and capture the important Soviet oil center at Baku on the Caspian Sea, lasted only five months, from August 5, 1942, to January 21, 1943. In Privolnoye, about three hundred Jews who had fled the German occupation of the nearby Ukraine were gathered up and deported by the Germans. Two or three local Jewish families, including a doctor and a teacher, were taken away and shot, according to Grigory Gorlov. But for most Ukrainians and Russians in the village, the German presence was not harsh. The local people were protected by a villager of German stock, whom the Germans used as a middleman; he ordered the Soviet peasants to turn over collective harvests of vegetables, corn, and sunflower seeds, used in making bread.

Grandfather Gopkolo, by then the village headman, tried to rally the peasants to passive resistance against the Germans, urging them to hide grain and refuse to cooperate. But most people thought they had little choice; even grandson Misha had to help supply the Germans. Practically every day, German soldiers would come through the village on motorcycles with sidecars, searching peasant homes, including Gorbachev's, and commandeering food for the troops.

"It was scary," Aleksandr Yakovenko recalled. "They took everything— meat, milk, eggs. Whether the family had kids or no kids, the Germans didn't care. There were two [German] pilots here. Their plane had crashed on our field. And this one pilot lived in our house for a couple of months."9

By the time Sergei Gorbachev returned from what Russians call the Great Patriotic War in 1946, his son was fifteen, a self-reliant young achiever who knew how to operate a Soviet S-80 harvester and seemed to thrive on a hard day's work in the fields. During the war years, curly-haired young Misha had grown in other ways. He had followed the course of the war in regional newspapers. Older people, only half-literate, brought Misha the papers so he could read aloud to them. He would figure out the various battles and explain the progress of the war. So Sergei returned to find a young man already developing an acquaintance with the world beyond Privolnoye.

Each summer, all summer long, the two worked together as a team. The father drove a harvester, and the son was assigned the dusty, dry, back-breaking work of pitchforking grain into the path of the combine. Years later, Gorbachev was to comment that "joint work with adults from a young age" had molded his inclination for hard work and taking responsibility.

The high point for the father and son came in 1948. Stalin wanted to recover from the severe drought and postwar hunger in Russia, and that whole summer, Misha and Aleksandr Yakovenko worked like slaves with their fathers, in a four-man harvest brigade. The wheat crop had been damaged by wind and rain. The stalks were bent over.

"We worked twenty to twenty-two hours a day, only stopping when the dew set on the grass," Yakovenko recalled, his face creased and red even today from working the fields. "We had only two hours of break, and then we had to clean the combines. If we slept at all, we'd dig holes in the haystacks and cover ourselves with straw. We didn't even have a place to wash our faces. We didn't have meat, just bread. For soup, we just had millet in water."10

The extraordinary effort paid off. The four-man brigade brought in a record yield, five or six times the average, and won national recognition. That fall, when national honors were passed out for outstanding work, both fathers and sons got the prestigious Order of the Red Banner of

Labor award. Normally, this award was given to veteran Party leaders, factory bosses, outstanding "shock workers," as the culmination of a lifetime career. It was unheard-of for a pair of teenage farm boys in Privolnoye to receive it. They were being held up to the nation as models.

They were decorated with medals at an official ceremony in Stavropol, the territorial capital one hundred miles away. Just going to Stavropol was an adventure for the two country boys.

"We didn't have a movie house here in Privolnoye, so we went to the movie in Stavropol just to celebrate," Yakovenko recalled. "Then, at the store, we told people we were going to be decorated and we wanted to have suits. The suits were too big and made of coarse wool, but we were still the best-looking guys in our village." Yakovenko stayed on in Privolnoye but, of course, Gorbachev did not.

If any single person fired Gorbachev's ambition, his drive to rise above the crowd and strike out beyond Privolnoye, even beyond Stavropol, it was Grandfather Gopkolo. Strange, perhaps, for a family in which no one had a formal education beyond fourth grade, but old Gopkolo constantly fueled young Misha's hunger for education. Understanding that for an ordinary peasant boy, education was the only ticket to a new life, he supplied Misha with books such as Pushkin's poetry, and Lermontov's novel *A Hero of Our Time.* He urged the boy to go on to high school when he finished the seven-grade school in Privolnoye.

"His grandfather practically forced him to learn," recalled a girl named Lyubov Grudchenko, the only other student from Privolnoye at that time to make it into the high school at the district town of Krasnogvardeisk, fifteen miles away. "Misha said, 'I don't have shoes.' And his grandfather said, 'Take these,' handing him a pair of boots. And Misha said, 'I don't have anything to wear.' And the grandfather said, 'Take this,' and gave him a shirt."[11]

Every week, spring, fall, winter, and spring, Misha and Lyubov walked to school, four or five hours across the open steppe, stopping halfway at the monument to the civil-war dead for a rest and a talk. During the school week, Gorbachev boarded with relatives or friends and returned to his village home for the weekend.

In school, Misha was always near the head of his class; he was diligent about his homework, a bit of a teacher's pet, a voracious reader who was always going to the dictionary. Even in first grade, he had won the biggest *yolka,* New Year's tree, for being the best student. Like all Soviet schoolchildren in the thirties and forties, he was drenched in propaganda about Stalin, who assumed grandiose titles such as the Benevolent Friend of All Children, the Mountain Eagle, the Leader and Teacher of the Workers of the World, the Greatest Genius of All Times. But Misha's boyhood hero was Lenin. When the high school principal ran an art contest, other youngsters drew portraits of literary figures, but Misha Gorbachev drew Lenin and won first prize. Teachers recall him as a natural mediator, a boy who broke up fights on the playground. Fellow students in primary school remember him as their intermediary with teachers when they had not finished their homework. He would get up and ask questions, stalling off a test on their behalf. Later, after the Nazi occupation, other students resisted learning German, seeing it as the language of the invader, but Misha was curious about the outside world and, after his year off from school, belatedly threw himself into studying German.

His grades were good. His teachers, now white-haired, proudly show off his high school report cards, a string of A's, except for a B in German, when his lost year put him behind. His record won him a silver medal, but not the coveted gold for straight A's, which his wife, Raisa, won at her high school. "He was gifted in history," his teacher Antonina Shcherbakova remembers. "Other students were learning material only from mark to mark, for tomorrow's lesson. He wanted more. He really wanted to understand. He was very curious to learn about life, and he did." Studying history in Soviet schools meant studying the Revolution, reading Marx and Lenin. Gorbachev pored over those texts, and Shcherbakova remembered him being especially taken with Lenin's slogan "One Step Forward, Two Steps Back"—justification for temporary retreat for the sake of the longer-term objective. In short, Gorbachev was absorbing Lenin's political pragmatism. Yet despite his diligence in class, it was not academics that set Misha Gorbachev apart. He was the Big Man on Campus, popular and active in everything—literary club, history club, drama club, political debates, the Komsomol youth organization.

"He was very interested in politics, in international affairs," recalled Mariya Grevtsova, former head of the high school teachers' union. "In those days, we had what we call *polboi*, political battles. The students divided up into teams to debate political questions. Mikhail Sergeyevich always gave very thorough answers. If some other student did not answer well, he would add something. One of his character traits was showing great respect for other people, older people. If there was some controversy, he did not force people to accept his opinion."[12]

If Gorbachev was a natural polemicist in high school debates, the drama club exposed his instincts for center stage, foreshadowing his future as a media politician. Teachers and fellow students remember his love of acting and how naturally he came to it. With his deep brown eyes, soft full lips, and commanding presence, he was a hit, playing the lead roles in Russian prerevolutionary classics. In a dashing czarist-era uniform with gold epaulets, he played the Grand Prince Arbenin in Lermontov's *Masquerade.* He was the lovelorn Mezgir in Ostrovsky's *Snow Maiden,* Chatsky in Griboyedov's *Woe from Wit.*

"When people watch Misha on television these days, they somehow think he is so natural, so self-confident," Gorbachev's high school sweetheart and fellow actor Yuliya Karagodina told David Remnick of *The Washington Post.* "Well, he was always that way, even forty years ago, when he was a handsome prince, wearing his fake mustache in our drama club. He had a kind of aura around him, the sort of person you just naturally listen to and even follow."[13]

But if the young Gorbachev had charm and charisma, he also had a hard edge. As a disciplinarian, he was a puritan who did not let friendship interfere with duty and the rules. Like his mother chastising errant farm workers, Lyubov Grudchenko told me, Misha would scold other high school students for not finishing their homework. One morning, she said, as leader of the morning calisthenics at school, he upbraided her and another girl for arriving late. "We thought that probably as a friend, he would disregard it," she recalled. "But he noticed it and said, 'Okay, we've done our morning exercises without them. Now let them do the exercises and we'll watch them. That will be a lesson to them. Next time, they'll be on time.' "

"He could be so cool and businesslike sometimes," added Yuliya Karagodina. "Once at a Komsomol meeting, in front of everyone at the local cinema house, he was angry with me for not finishing on time a little newspaper we put out. And despite our friendship, he reprimanded me in front of everyone, saying that I'd failed, that I was late. Then afterward, it was as if nothing had happened. He said, 'Let's go to the movies.' I was at a loss. I couldn't understand why he did what he did, and I said so. He said, 'My dear, one thing has nothing to do with another.' "[14]

Generally, however, he is given credit for having been diplomatic and skillful at handling people. In high school, he became the Soviet equivalent of senior-class president—secretary of the Komsomol, the Communist youth organization. And at nineteen, a very early age, he was chosen a candidate member of the Communist Party. The fact that he applied to join even before graduating from high school was a strong indication of his ambition.

Precisely how Gorbachev landed in the law faculty at Moscow State University is still a riddle. During the Stalin era, law was not a profession held in high esteem for a young achiever such as Gorbachev. Those who knew him well in school said history and international relations were obviously his first loves. "His dream was to be a diplomat," Ivan Manuilov, his high school geography teacher, told my television colleague Louis Menashe. By Manuilov's account, Gorbachev actually entered the faculty for international relations at Moscow State University and studied there for a year, but he had such a rough time, including a spell of severe headaches, that he fell back to the law faculty.[15] No one else with whom I talked confirmed that story. In retrospect, some who had known him speculated that he picked law because his hero Lenin had studied law and it was a good entrée to a political career.

Many years later, Gorbachev admitted that law had not been his first choice, saying that he preferred physics, or even mathematics, history, or literature, but "it was my weakness" to be a generalist and not enough of a specialist.[16] The clear implication was that he was not strong enough in science to be accepted into the physics faculty, and he had to fall back on law, along with a lot of returning Soviet war veterans who were preparing for political careers. As in Europe, Soviet universities are organized by faculties, or departments; competition for entrance is to each department, not to the university as a whole. Law was an easier faculty to enter than international relations, natural sciences, or his best subjects, history and literature. Because the quality of education at a small provincial high school was so modest, getting into Moscow State University— the nation's top university—was a very long shot even for a top rural student like Gorbachev.

Misha was understandably nervous as he headed off on the thirty-six-hour train ride to Moscow for the entrance examinations. According to his uncle Sergei, Grandfather Gopkolo gave the boy a pep talk.

"Don't be nervous," the grandfather coached. "You will pass all the exams. If you don't know something and you stumble, have confidence. Just keep going."

When Gorbachev came home, old man Gopkolo demanded the results: "How did you do?"

"I passed them all, thanks to your coaching," Misha replied.[17]

But the competition was so severe it was not enough merely to pass; Gorbachev was put on a waiting list.

Grandfather Gopkolo, having invested his dreams in his grandson, got impatient. As a veteran farm and Communist Party leader in Privolnoye, he put pressure on the Komsomol organization in Stavropol City to use its influence in Moscow, according to Grigory Gorlov, the old family friend. It was not just a matter of Gopkolo's pulling political strings. The Communist Party then, as now, was on the lookout for outstanding young people from humble beginnings and with the right political credentials.

In the university entrance competition, well-connected children whose parents were big-city officials had a built-in advantage, and quotas of university slots were set aside for proletarian youth. Gorbachev's agricultural medal and his work for the Komsomol, coupled with his academic record, marked him as an excellent candidate for one of these slots. That his parents and grandfather were longtime Party activists helped too.

"Why don't they take our guy?" Gopkolo demanded of the provincial higher-ups. "He was decorated with a silver medal in school and with the Order of the Red Banner of Labor for his farm work. Please take it up with the Central Committee of the Komsomol in Moscow." The top Komsomol youth officials in Stavropol took his advice, Gorlov said. "They called Moscow and the Komsomol in Moscow called the university."[18]

The odds against a farm boy from southern Russia making it into the nation's top university were tougher in 1950 than they would be for an American black from an urban ghetto getting into Harvard University in 1990. Gorbachev's making it not only testified to his personal success as a young man; it also put him into a politically sophisticated world that would reshape his outlook and serve as a springboard for his career.

"TELL ME, WHAT IS BALLET?"

The university years are a formative time in anyone's life, and in Gorbachev's case, that was especially true. For Gorbachev belongs to a special generation in Soviet history, the generation whose university careers roughly spanned the time of Stalin's death in March 1953 and Nikita Khrushchev's denunciation of Stalin, in a secret speech to the Twentieth Communist Party Congress in February 1956. Both events were watershed moments in the life of the nation and especially in the lives of impressionable young adults; they broke the iron grip of Stalinist tyranny and sowed the seeds of reform. They were earthquakes whose tremors are still being felt three decades later.

It is no accident that Gorbachev and other leaders of the *perestroika* reforms now under way come from a generation born between 1925 and 1935; they are people who are now fifty-five to sixty-five years old, not a typical age for reformers. But Khrushchev's secret speech was the seminal political event in their young lives; it jolted them out of their early belief in Stalin and the old dictatorial system, and opened up their minds to experimentation. Khrushchev's rule brought a cultural and political thaw that not only fostered intellectual ferment but also fired hopes for greater cultural freedom, economic flexibility, and social justice. Khrushchev himself was too disorganized, too impulsive, and too much the political loner to fulfill the expectations he raised. His attempts to break up the power of the Party apparatus helped provoke the political coup that ousted him in 1964. Still, the ideals of liberalization and democratization that he had inspired took root, and would resurface long after he was gone.

Those momentous events lay ahead for Misha Gorbachev when he arrived at Moscow State University in September 1950. He was a country hick, with one coarse, gray pin-striped wool suit that he would wear during all five years at the university. He was so tan from working in the fields that other students took him for a non-Russian, perhaps from one of the Caucasian hill tribes. His class was full of veterans returning from the war and gold-medal high school valedictorians. Perhaps hoping to be noticed, Gorbachev, following Soviet custom, wore his medal of the Red Banner of Labor on his suit. Some city sophisticates from Moscow and Leningrad snickered behind his back about his uncultured ways, and he worked terribly hard to catch up with them academically and culturally.

Conditions in Moscow then were primitive. The Soviet capital was still digging itself out of the devastation left by war. At the university, the monthly student stipend of 290 old rubles (29 current rubles, now worth less than $5) was barely enough to buy two meals a day in the student cafeteria, let alone clothes or luxuries. The diet in the canteen was spartan—on good days, dark bread, borscht or cabbage soup, and kasha, a buckwheat gruel, and very occasionally ground beef lost in watery stews. With other students from the provinces, Gorbachev shared a dorm room with no closets at the Stromynkha student hostel, a run-down building that had been a military barracks at the time of Peter the Great.[19]

"We were sixteen students in one room at Stromynkha—sixteen!" recalled Gorbachev's law classmate and roommate Rudolf Kulchanov, now deputy editor of the *Trud* newspaper. "Of course it was impossible to study there, but we had a reading room downstairs. This room was also too small for all of us, so we worked there in two shifts, one studying until nine. Misha was there pretty often until one or two A.M. We were poor, simply poor. At the end of each month we usually didn't even have enough money for dinner. We resorted to black bread and sweet tea, what people usually eat for breakfast. But that was all we got. Some used to get parcels from home. Sometimes I got potatoes. Misha received homemade salami. He used to put it on the mutual table and we all shared."[20]

Stalinism was omnipresent. Portraits of the leader hung in every room; his words were constantly quoted in the press, on the radio, in the lectures. The law faculty, like any other, had required courses on Soviet history and the classics of Marxism-Leninism, which included Stalin's speeches and writings. Typical of the time, one textbook, *A Course on Soviet Criminal Law* by Professors A. A. Piontovsky and V. D. Menshagin, presented the Stalinist show trials of the 1930s as true examples of "socialist legality."

There were a few broader courses in the humanities, taught by professors educated before the Bolshevik Revolution; they opened a window on a wider intellectual world. Several students spoke warmly—and said Gorbachev had also been an admirer—of Professor Stepan Kechekyan, one of the pre-Bolshevik lecturers. Kechekyan taught a two-year course in the history of political ideas (four lecture hours and four hours of tutorials each week). This course exposed the law students to such philosophers as Aristotle, Plato, Aquinas, Machiavelli, Hobbes, Montesquieu, Rousseau, and Hegel, and to concepts of international law from the Code of Hammurabi and Roman law to the American Constitution. Accounts differ on how free the discussion was, but there seems to have been more flexibility on writers before Marx because they were not censored if Marx himself had studied them.

"Speaking of this faculty of the 1950s, I wouldn't say that it gave a lot in terms of the understanding of law and the notion of law," commented Zdenek Mlynar, a classmate of Gorbachev. "Nevertheless, some remnants of the historical or economic approach did exist. They gave us a general picture of the significance of law in the life of civilized society, although at that time, law was totally superseded by politics."[21]

Mlynar, a gray-haired intellectual living in Vienna when I saw him in March 1989, was a particularly thoughtful observer of Gorbachev during their university years. Mlynar, who was Czech, had made it to Moscow as one of a small group of promising young East European Communists. He lived across the hall from Gorbachev. Taking a considerable risk at a time of Stalinist Cold War paranoia about spies and outside influences of any kind, Gorbachev formed a close friendship with Mlynar. They were often in the same classes and small study groups, and they spent hours talking together, comparing experiences. Mlynar, who would eventually become one of the leaders of the Prague Spring of 1968, was struck by Gorbachev's intellectual curiosity and openness.

"He was, of course, a country boy," Mlynar told me that balmy spring afternoon in a park outside Vienna. "What really separated him from the others, I felt, was that he was naturally intelligent, gifted, able to overcome all the limitations and barriers of a peasant boy coming to Moscow for the first time. He possessed a kind of open-mindedness, not merely an adaptability, but an openness.

"I remember, for instance, his asking somebody, 'What's ballet? Tell me, what is it about? Take me with you to see it. I've never seen it in my life.' He was not embarrassed to ask. I think that is characteristic of him until today. He is a person who is never embarrassed if he doesn't know something, but who always wants to know. When he learns something new, it gives him a sort of self-assurance. To some extent he has the mentality of what in English is called a self-made man. That was his mentality."

Other students, such as Nadezhda Mikhailova, who had a crush on Gorbachev at law school and is now a bubbly teacher of law, echo that assessment. They remember Gorbachev as always interested in improving his mind, asking them to take him along to symphony concerts or to art galleries. Soon Raisa Titorenko, who was in the philosophy faculty, had more polished ways, and came from a better social background, would take on the broadening of Misha's cultural horizons. They met at a dance in 1952. Gorbachev had gone along to make fun of a friend, an army veteran named Volodya Lieberman, who had been taking dancing lessons, but saw Raisa and was smitten with her at once. Two years later, they were married, and they celebrated with raucous singing and dancing in Gorbachev's dorm room. For their wedding night, Gorbachev's roommates cleared out, but the next day, everything went back to normal, and the two newlyweds lived separately for several months until they could get a room together in a residential hall for married students.

As time wore on, Gorbachev became known not only as a serious student, a workaholic with a phenomenal memory, but also as a young man of some intellectual independence and candor, who was willing to take risks for his own ideas about honesty and fairness. Fellow students remember his favorite saying, from Hegel, "Truth is always concrete," by which Gorbachev meant that truth had meaning in concrete situations. Many of those who knew him well retell the story of his violent reaction to the glossy Stalinist glorification of life in the countryside, in the movie *Cossacks of the Kuban*. The film showed peasants happily joining collective farms, their dinner tables groaning with plentiful harvests. This hypocritical whitewash of his own childhood experiences infuriated Gorbachev.

"We were big Communists with a capital *C*, but Gorbachev was always a person who saw the truth," Mlynar recalled. "When he saw that movie *Cossacks of the Kuban*, he spoke openly about the discrepancies, about miserable dinner tables rather than the depicted abundance. It was from Gorbachev that I learned that collective farm life didn't look the way it was depicted in movies or in propaganda. The reality was really frightening. People were forced into labor. He definitely didn't make any public statements, but he spoke to his friends pretty openly."

A cautious attitude was understandable; Stalin was still alive, and any deviation from the Stalinist line could be punished by expulsion, Siberian exile, even execution. During their study of the Stalinist purges, Mlynar recalled that Gorbachev pointed out to him privately that Lenin had allowed one foe, the Menshevik leader Julius Martov, to emigrate rather than be executed. The contrast with Stalin was implicit. Even though Gorbachev was speaking privately, Mlynar regarded it as risky, and highly unusual, for Gorbachev to confide such a critical view to a foreigner.

In 1952, his third year in law school, Gorbachev caused a scandal in class. A visiting professor arrived to deliver a special two-hour lecture on Stalin's new tome, *Economic Problems of Socialism in the U.S.S.R.* The students, already exhausted from the normal six hours of lectures, became furious at the visitor's droning on and on, merely reading aloud Stalin's numbing phrases, without comment or discussion. Gorbachev and Volodya Lieberman wrote an anonymous note of protest: "We are university students. We can read the material by ourselves. If you don't have anything to add, please take this into consideration."

The two upstarts, both active in Party and Komsomol work, hoped the visitor would simply stop lecturing, but instead he blew up and declared that the note showed hostility to Marxism-Leninism. The author, he said, was "un-Soviet." Who was it? he demanded.

First Gorbachev rose. Then Lieberman.

"I wrote it," Gorbachev said.

The lecturer stalked out, and within minutes, Gorbachev was summoned to the office of the university provost; Lieberman waited out in the corridor, as members of the Party committee for the university were summoned.

The other students were stunned, and quickly denounced the two renegades for criticizing a teacher.

"It was considered unethical to write such messages," Kulchanov recalled. "[Gorbachev] could easily have kept silent. But he stood up and admitted that he did it. I was scared. Nobody knew what would happen. Dismissal, perhaps."

After a while, Gorbachev emerged from the meeting to say, quite unexpectedly, that the Party committee had heard the students' complaint about the lecturer and had accepted it.

"Everything is all right," he said.

Gorbachev's stature suddenly rose in the eyes of the other students. According to Kulchanov, they were awed by his courage, his independence, and his ability to handle a tough situation, although several took the episode as evidence that his political conformity had limits.

"All of us, his schoolmates, had suddenly discovered that he was a brave guy," Kulchanov said. "We all began to respect him very much."[22]

Gorbachev's willingness to stick his neck out politically was even more dramatically demonstrated when, in the midst of a fever of Stalinist anti-Semitism, he defended his friend Lieberman, who was a Jew.

It was a dangerous time—February 1953, a month before Stalin's death. The press was full of fabricated accusations that Jewish doctors were plotting to kill Stalin. Arrests were being made, a witch-hunt was beginning, perhaps even a new purge. Party opportunists were speaking out against "the Judases of medicine" and "cosmopolitanism," a euphemism for Jewish influence.

As Lieberman tells the story, he and Gorbachev, as members of the Communist Party (Gorbachev had become a full member in 1952), were at a Party meeting at the university when a Communist named Balasayan suddenly launched a vicious personal attack on Lieberman, the only Jew in the room. Lieberman recalled that Balasayan "suddenly jumped on my neck, mentioning that in spite of my good marks I had lots of foibles, and in particular, I was talking too much." To others, there was no apparent reason for the attack other than the anti-Semitic campaign. Gorbachev broke in, scolded Balasayan, and denounced him as "a spineless animal" for stooping to such opportunism. His words were enough to deter others, and Lieberman was spared further harassment.[23] In Lieberman's eyes, Gorbachev's actions were a sign not only of personal loyalty but also of courage and willingness to stand behind the principles of honesty and fair play.

Over time, whether in class or in discussions back at the dorm, Gorbachev became known in his group for his rationality, logic, and skill at establishing group consensus. When arguments in the crowded dorm room became heated, especially when some of the older army veterans would take sharp positions, Gorbachev emerged as a kind of moderator. "He was a good listener," Kulchanov said, "and he tended to find some mutual background in our debates, to touch a mutual base, without giving up his principles. He was always looking for some consensus." In class, Lieberman recalled, "he used to say, 'This issue requires a dialectic approach. That is, first we have to consider one side, and then, on the other hand, we have to consider the opposite side.' "

Gradually, too, Gorbachev became a student leader. Many in his law-school group had their eyes on political careers. "We were all hand-picked cutters, so-called—people with a future," said Mlynar. "He is a man that always possessed an informal authority. You know, when there is a party of five people and he is one of them, everybody tends to listen to him, even though he has no formal position. He is persistent, single-minded, and he knows how to achieve. . . . Sometimes some of our schoolmates used to joke, 'Misha will someday make it big; he'll be at the top,' because they knew that we were all longing for politics. But I couldn't say I ever thought that in Stalin's place, we would get Gorbachev. It didn't seem possible at that time."[24]

There is a considerably less flattering side to Gorbachev's political ambitions and activities at the university—that of an officious disciplinarian, a Stalinist zealot in the university Komsomol organization. As a country boy in the fast world of Moscow, Misha seems to have lain low during his first year, but during his second year, 1951, he set out to become the Komsomol organizer, *komsorg*, for his class. He wanted the job so badly, according to a fellow activist, Fridrikh Neznansky, that he got the incumbent drunk one night and then denounced him the next day at a Komsomol meeting for behavior unworthy of a Communist youth leader.[25] Gorbachev got himself chosen Komsomol organizer for the law faculty as a whole, and served from 1952 to 1954. But in his senior year, the law faculty was merged with the Moscow Law Institute and he lost the top job to the Komsomol leader from the institute, a well-connected Muscovite.

Like Gorbachev's high school friends, some former law classmates recall his hard side, his martinet strictness as a Komsomol apparatchik. One law-faculty graduate outside Gorbachev's personal circle portrayed young Misha as a dogmatic defender of Stalinist orthodoxy who curried favor with Party higher-ups. "He was one of the boys with his colleagues, and he played up incredibly to those in authority," recalled Lev Yudovich, who later emigrated and became a teacher at the U.S. Army Russian Studies Institute in West Germany.[26] Yudovich, who graduated in 1953, two years ahead of Gorbachev, said that during the Stalin years, Gorbachev's ideological zeal was well enough known that Yudovich and his friends tried to steer clear of Gorbachev. Neznansky recalled Gorbachev's strict, formal reprimands for Komsomol members arriving late to meetings. Vivid in his memory was the "steely voice of the Komsomol secretary of the law faculty, Gorbachev, demanding expulsion from the Komsomol for the slightest offenses, from telling political anecdotes to shirking being sent to a *kolkhoz.*"

A dual portrait of Gorbachev seems inevitable, in part because friends saw Misha sympathetically, and he let them in on his doubts, his skepticism, whereas others saw him only from a distance, exercising an official role and toeing the Party line. Beyond that, Gorbachev had by then developed two sides to his character—a personal intellectual openness and an organizational conformity. He had split his life, public and private. Like his peers, including Neznansky and Yudovich, who served as hard-line prosecutors before emigrating to the West many years later, he had learned the need to conform and play by the rules of the Party's political game.

But most fundamentally, like everyone in his generation, he was a believer. He believed in Stalin and Stalinism. It was a religion ingested from birth and indoctrinated daily ever after.

"We were all Stalinists," Mlynar admitted to me, "all convinced of the necessity of the leading role of the Party led by Stalin. Stalin was the leader of the world proletariat."

Since Gorbachev had confided so much to this friend of his youth, I wanted to know: "Did Gorbachev have any doubts about Stalin during Stalin's lifetime?"

"I wouldn't say so," Mlynar replied. "During Stalin's life, we were dedicated Stalinists."

BREAKING FREE FROM STALINISM

That faith in Stalin, so all-enveloping, made the eventual break with Stalinism all the more shattering for true believers. The first blow fell powerfully, on March 5, 1953, with Stalin's death. For the overwhelming majority of Russians, that was a day of emotional trauma. It is hard for Americans, who see Stalin as an evil tyrant, to understand how differently Stalin was seen at that time by his own people.

Stalin's death was personally even more devastating for Russians than the assassination of John F. Kennedy was for many Americans a decade later. To this day, Russians can remember what they were doing when they heard Stalin had died, where they were standing, how they were feeling—as if it were yesterday. For most of them, Stalin was not the paranoid dictator of the purges, but their infallible leader, the Father of their country. Stalin had industrialized the country, had led them to victory in war. Millions had gone into battle shouting, "For the Mother-land, for Stalin!" He was the linchpin of their universe, their compass, their czar, the ruler who held life together and gave it meaning. His death shattered their national self-confidence, leaving them feeling bereaved and abandoned, vulnerable to external enemies, uncertain of a future without him. On the day of his funeral, millions stampeded in the center of Moscow in a frenzy of anxiety and grief.

When Stalin died, Gorbachev and his friends "were all gathered in one room and some of us were crying," recalled Nadezhda Mikhailova. "None of us really knew what to do next. We'd been brainwashed up to the level of idiocy. You have to understand. To us, yesterday's schoolchildren, he meant more than God. And we didn't really know how to survive after his death. So some of us were crying. Misha was silent."

"Yes, Misha remained silent," another classmate, Vladimir Kuzmin, added. "We didn't discuss it but we were thinking what would happen after Stalin's death."

"We were saying that now, after Stalin's death, the opportunists and careerists will take over," said Rudolf Kulchanov. "They will ruin socialism. We will forget our dreams about Communism. And I remember when we all went to see Stalin's body exposed in the Hall of Unions, there were tanks and troop carriers. I don't remember whether Misha managed to go. That was a terrible night. Lots of people died, crushed by the crowd."

"Here in the university, we had a memorial meeting," Mikhailova went on, "and somebody, I don't remember who, said that if all of his blood would be required in exchange for one hour of Stalin's life, he wouldn't think twice and would give all of his blood. And the same for me, you know; I would have given my blood in exchange for one hour of Stalin's life."[27]

Mlynar remembered standing next to Gorbachev at the time of Stalin's funeral. "There were two minutes of silence or something like that—and we thought of Stalin," he recalled. But shortly afterward, "when we discussed Stalin's death, we didn't really know what to do next. It was a real shock. Everything was just a big question mark."

"For Gorbachev too?" I asked.

"Yes, of course," Mlynar replied. "Yes, many people spoke that way. Nobody knew what would happen next, since God had died."[28]

Stalin's death occurred during Gorbachev's third year in the university. Gradually over the next two years, the atmosphere changed.

The charges against the Jewish doctors were found to be fabricated and the doctors released. By that first June, portraits of Lavrenti Beria, Stalin's feared secret-police chief, were taken down from prominent places in Moscow. In a power struggle with Khrushchev and others, Beria had been killed, and the bloody terror he had led exposed in documents circulated to Communist Party members. Privately, people began to suspect Stalin of involvement and to criticize him. Neznansky recalled that Gorbachev, as university Komsomol leader, spoke for the first time of injustices done to "middle peasants"—people who owned and farmed their own land—

during Stalin's brutal collectivization drive in the 1930s, and he even mentioned that one of his relatives had been arrested unjustly.[29]

"I knew that something had happened to his family," Mlynar told me. "But I don't think it happened to his father. Rather, to his grandfather. I didn't know any details. We never discussed family matters. But it was not that unusual for some member of a family to be repressed during the Stalinist purges in the early thirties."[30]

In later years, Gorbachev practically never mentioned that a relative had been repressed under Stalin, but with some bitterness he brought the matter up a few years ago at a small gathering of high Communist Party officials. "There were only about a hundred people present," Nikolai Shishlin, one of Gorbachev's speech writers, told me. "It was after he had become general secretary. When the Stalin period was being discussed, he told us, 'Although I was a child, I remember these times. I remember my *ded*, my grandfather, was arrested and taken away to the camps. And when he returned, he was silent, always sitting and thinking, and very sad.' "[31] According to Shishlin, Gorbachev said his grandfather Andrei Gorbachev had been arrested at the peak of the purges in 1937, when the secret police were headed by Nikolai Yezhov, and had been incredibly lucky to be released eighteen months later. As Shishlin reminded me, Lavrenti Beria had succeeded Yezhov as secret-police chief, had executed Yezhov and his sinister coterie, and then released some of those recently jailed by Yezhov, among them Gorbachev's grandfather.

The details of this incident are puzzling. There was little reason for a peasant to be arrested in 1937; by then, Stalin was going after high officials. By one published account, Gorbachev's paternal grandfather, Andrei Gorbachev, was arrested in 1931 and sentenced to nine years in the camps after an informer in the village of Privolnoye had accused him of hiding forty pounds of grain for his family, evading the Stalinist requisitions of grain. That timing sounds more appropriate for the arrest of a peasant, though the actual charges could easily have been a trumped-up pretext for his arrest.[32] Like Mlynar, Shishlin told me that Gorbachev had never cited the reason for the arrest. "It's impossible to say why. You know, it was Stalin!" Shishlin said emphatically, assuming that was sufficient explanation for any act of repression.

There is little question that the experience left a searing impression on Gorbachev and that he nursed a personal grievance against Stalin's mass repression of the peasantry—and he still does. In a major speech on November 2, 1987, the seventieth anniversary of the Revolution, Gorbachev sharply criticized Stalin's "excesses" against "middle peasants"—

average people, the group from which his own family came. Gorbachev extolled these people—the middle peasantry—who were given land under Lenin, who tilled their own modest plots, and whose lives were improving until Stalin's henchmen victimized many of them during the campaign against the kulaks, or rich peasants. "Gross violations of the principles of collectivization acquired a ubiquitous character," Gorbachev thundered. "The policy of struggle against the kulaks, which was in itself correct, was often interpreted so broadly that it also caught up a significant proportion of middle-level peasants."[33]

In short, Stalin's death allowed the young Gorbachev to draw on his own experience, and edge away from idolatry.

The real jolt to his thinking, however, came three years later, after Khrushchev bluntly denounced Stalin's mass terror at the Twentieth Party Congress on February 20, 1956. Khrushchev focused on Stalin's repression against high Party officials and on crimes that followed the murder of Leningrad Party leader Sergei Kirov in 1934, thereby excluding the crimes of collectivization and earlier political purges. Even so, the effect of his exposé was an enormous shock to the entire country, and especially to Gorbachev's generation.

Gorbachev, who by then had graduated from law school and gone back to his native Stavropol to begin a career in Komsomol and Party work in the provinces, would not have been a delegate to the Congress, but his future friend and Politburo colleague, his alter ego, Aleksandr Yakovlev, also a young Party worker in 1956, was at the Congress as a guest. He described to me the hall's stunned reaction to Khrushchev's speech. Particularly shocking, he said, was that Khrushchev talked not so much about mass terror, but about Stalin's arbitrary violence against the upper echelons of the Communist Party itself.

"There was a deathly silence," Yakovlev told me. "People stopped looking at each other."

Yakovlev was sitting on a couch a few feet from me during our on-camera interview in one of the private upstairs rooms of the Foreign Ministry's press center in Moscow. At first, he leaned back reflectively, talking of his boyhood, his childhood faith in Stalin, then some doubts arising when he was a teenager because of the mistreatment of an honest peasant in his village. Then later, his disapproval of Stalin for punishing returning Soviet prisoners of war. But his mother's admonition was: "Speaking ill of the czar is bad business." Then he recalled the fateful day when Khrushchev exposed Stalin. Leaning toward me to emphasize the details, he said:

"I remember I was sitting in the balcony, and when we went down, I heard just one word uttered by people around me: 'Yes.' Then after a while, 'Yes.' No conversation. People didn't even look at each other. They hung their heads, and left.

"That is, to hear what had happened, and understand, and accept it in full, after what had been! Yesterday like this, and today like this!" Yakovlev gestured first one way with both arms and then far in the other direction, illustrating the old lies about Stalin and the new truth. "It was very hard, especially for those who believed. For young people. And then to destroy it with that information, which would change radically the entire development of the society. It was, of course, very hard for every-one—emotionally very hard. And to make sense of it required much time, much time."

Yakovlev recalled the ideological body blow that he himself had felt. "I had thought of Stalin as a great man, a great intellectual, a profound thinker, and so on—and all that was destroyed. I had received some moral blow. . . . It gradually turned out that [what Khrushchev said] was the way it truly was. And it's right that it was destroyed.

"Gradually," he went on, "those convictions consolidated, the sense that many mistakes had been made. But after the Twentieth Congress, the process was very contradictory. It was like two trains, or two airplanes, or two carts—depending on the speed—traveling next to each other. One went the old way, and the other went in the direction of the maturing of civil consciousness."[34]

Again and again, I have heard Communists of Gorbachev's generation echo these sentiments. Khrushchev's speech was the seminal event in their young lives. Emotionally, it hit them as if they had been struck down by a train, shattering their beliefs to their very foundations, leaving them stunned at first but then, later on, open to new ways of thinking and more flexible than the generation that had preceded them, and even those that followed. So powerful and formative was the impact, on Gorbachev's generation, of Khrushchev's unmasking of Stalin in February 1956 that they became widely known as "the children of the Twentieth Party Congress."

"For those people, the Twentieth Congress was a shock because, you know, Stalin was like God to them," recalled Roy Medvedev, the historian whose disillusionment came earlier, after his father's arrest by Stalin. "It was as if they had lost their religion. You believe in Christ, or in Allah, or in Buddha, and all of a sudden something happens. Your whole life is changed and your beliefs are lost. And you are trying to look for something else to lean upon, some other foundation. So for the whole generation, this Twentieth Congress was such a blow I cannot describe it to you. Such a blow for them when they were very young people, just at the age of twenty to thirty."[35]

As a member of the Communist Party, Gorbachev was in the center of this ideological upheaval. He was summoned to a Party meeting where Khrushchev's speech was read aloud; then he had to take part in many discussions with Party members about Stalin's crimes, his prison gulag, his assault on the very apparatus of the Party itself.

"Gorbachev admired Khrushchev as an unbelievably courageous political leader," recalled Rudolf Kulchanov, who later saw Gorbachev on visits to Stavropol.[36] This was confirmed by Mlynar, who also went to Stavropol to see Gorbachev.

In short, Gorbachev's inner mental world had been reformed too. After the initial shock, he and his generation were caught up in the ferment and excitement of Khrushchev's early years—a time of hope and reform, of political and economic experimentation as well as cultural liberalization, even if far from real democratization. These were trends that not only appealed to some of Gorbachev's own youthful instincts, but also nurtured in him the desire for reform, for the dismantlement of the Stalinist system. These urges were to flower three decades later, with his final ascent to power and the beginnings of *perestroika*.

CHAPTER 4

How Did Gorbachev Make It to the Top?

"It's impossible to imagine
that Gorbachev would emerge at
the top of this system. There are so
many pitfalls he had to avoid, so many
traps he had to pass through,
so many obstacles to foil him.
One single little blemish could
have stopped him. How he made it
is one of those historical mysteries."[1]

—Zinovy Yuryev
Soviet Writer
June 1988

During the early seventies, neither I nor any of the Western specialists I knew spotted Mikhail Gorbachev as a future contender for national leadership.

By 1971, Gorbachev had become a member of the Communist Party Central Committee—one of the regional barons who comprise the backbone of the Party's power across the country. There are about 150 of them, reigning as Moscow's proconsuls over the nation's far-flung political fiefdoms.

But rarely does any individual in this powerful group stand out. While they all have power greater than governors of American states, they lack national visibility—if they are smart. For in traditional Soviet power politics, the route to the top is a quiet game of tough, inside politics, serving the apparat and fashioning alliances; it is more like old-fashioned American machine politics than modern American media politics, with its splashy speeches, telegenic style, and speculation about one's presidential intentions. Soviet politics are more covert, which makes it hard for outsiders to pick out the rising stars inside the system.

As Party boss of Stavropol Krai, Gorbachev was as far from the center of power as an American governor in South Carolina or Maine (those states are roughly the size of Stavropol Krai). But Gorbachev was blessed by fate. If he had come from Murmansk or Vladivostok, far off the beaten political track, he might have gotten lost in the crowd. But his home territory was more happily situated. For Stavropol Krai is not only one of the country's richest agricultural regions, but also contains the favorite health spas and mountain resorts of top national leaders. And so Stavropol's Party leaders have a chance to hobnob with the Politburo elite when they come for rest cures, a favorite vacation pastime of the Soviet elite. Not surprisingly, then, Stavropol, like Ohio, or Texas, or Massachusetts, is a promising springboard to national leadership. And some of Gorbachev's predecessors there had made the leap—no small advantage for a man who aspired to follow them.

In the twenty-three years Gorbachev spent in Stavropol, from his university graduation in 1955 to his selection for the upper reaches of Party power in 1978, he proved an intriguing amalgam—a loyal apparatchik who also nursed the germ of reform, an organization man with a streak of daring. He was both able and nimble. He could be an innovator or wear the veneer of the sycophant. As he climbed the Party ladder, Gorbachev maneuvered successfully through the twisting turns of policy, from the rambunctious reformism of Khrushchev to the gray conformity of Brezhnev and beyond.

People describe him in those years as being both a good political infighter who risked direct confrontations with powerful figures in Moscow and a canny master of the arts of flattery and concealment. He was able to cultivate high-level patrons from different factions. He was too intelligent, honest, and open to be a typical apparatchik of the corrupt Brezhnev era. He grew impatient, even alarmed, at the ineptitude and meddling of Moscow. But he never betrayed the radical urges of a maverick; he didn't upset the applecart.

Gorbachev's career in Stavropol also had a very fast start. He came home from law school and worked only a few months in the state prosecutor's office before shifting to political work in the Komsomol. Within a year, at twenty-six, he was named head of the Komsomol Communist youth organization for Stavropol City (population 123,000). Three years later, he had shot up to Komsomol chief for the entire Stavropol Krai (population 1.9 million). This put him in the inner cabinet of the regional Party boss in the late fifties, when Khrushchev was riding high.

Gorbachev rode the Khrushchev bandwagon, conveying to the young the leader's message of idealism and economic experimentation. Fellow Komsomol workers told me that in those years, Gorbachev promoted Khrushchev's line with a reformer's zeal.[2] As Komsomol chief of the krai, he had the singular honor of serving as one of the five thousand national delegates to the Twenty-second Communist Party Congress in 1961. Khrushchev, still feeling threatened by the Stalinist wing of the Party, played to Gorbachev and his generation as the hope of the future. In a highly symbolic gesture, the delegates—Gorbachev included—joined Khrushchev in a new act of de-Stalinization: They voted to remove Stalin's body from its honored place beside Lenin's in the mausoleum on Red Square.

Like many a rising young politician, Gorbachev found a political patron close to home. He hitched his wagon to the star of the Stavropol regional Party boss, then a veteran of Moscow infighting, Fyodor Kulakov, who would help Gorbachev climb the rungs of power. "He learned his lessons from Kulakov," old family friend Grigory Gorlov told me.[3] Kulakov had his eye on the top. To get there, he was intent on making Stavropol an agricultural showcase. In 1962, when Khrushchev launched a new agricultural experiment, setting up large regional farm units that embraced twenty-five to thirty collective farms, Kulakov persuaded Gorbachev to leave Komsomol work and step up into the Party hierarchy as one of the Party's sixteen new regional farm organizers in Stavropol Krai. From that post, Gorbachev began his climb up the Party's ranks.

And, in other ways, he followed Kulakov's pattern. Kulakov had gone to night school to get an agricultural degree, thereby boosting his career. In 1962, Gorbachev, to whom self-improvement came as second nature, signed up for a night-school degree at the local agricultural institute. Ironically, his wife, Raisa, was one of his instructors.

Raisa had come to Stavropol with her Moscow University degree in philosophy, a good cut above locally trained teachers. She quickly got an appointment at the local institute and plunged into the study of sociology, specializing in rural areas of Stavropol Krai. Eventually, she wrote the Soviet equivalent of a Ph.D. thesis on the problems, attitudes, and conditions of the peasantry—an unusual topic for a scholar in those days. Despite her schoolmarmish manner, her former colleagues respected her academically, and some spoke of her warmly as a person who took an interest in others. When I visited the institute in 1988, they proudly showed me her charts on the methodology of Marxism-Leninism, which were still hanging in her former classroom; her monographs were in the library.[4]

In class, Raisa proved herself Gorbachev's intellectual peer; she gave him no quarter. Grigory Gorlov, who was also in her seminar, recalled her correcting her students, including Gorbachev, if he strayed off the mark in some discussion of philosophy. "That's not correct," she would say. "You should understand it more like this." Gorlov said she was firm, without being a martinet. "She corrected us all in a comradely way," he told me.[5] Other instructors were equally demanding with Gorbachev, even though he was becoming an important local Party boss. Valentina Brelova, a fellow student, said Gorbachev asked for no special treatment, and he got none. She recalled one teacher eyeing him before an examination, and saying half in jest, "Ah, so you're the Party boss. Well, let's see. Let me check your brains."[6] It took him five years to get his degree; he finally received it in 1967.

That same year, the Gorbachevs had a visit from former law-school classmate Zdenek Mlynar, who had risen to become a member of the Czechoslovak Communist Party Politburo in the reformist government of Alexander Dubček. Mlynar flew into Mineralnye Vody, the heart of Stavropol's resort area. Gorbachev, then Party boss of Stavropol City— one notch above the mayor—met him at the airport.

"He had a fedora, you know, like these Soviet apparatchiks," Mlynar recalled, grinning at the thought of a pudgy Gorbachev in the baggy business suit and wide-brimmed hat that was the uniform of Soviet officials in that era. Even though Khrushchev was gone, Gorbachev looked like a mini-Khrushchev.

"The first thing I said to him was, 'Hey, Misha, you've got this fedora already.' And he said, 'Okay, forget it,' " Mlynar recalled. "He hadn't changed a lot.

"After that, we traveled across the steppe, and I enjoyed the landscape. You see, I had a hobby—I used to collect beetles, and I was collecting them during my meeting with him in the steppes. And he was helping me. He could even distinguish some basic species. 'After all,' he said, 'I am a graduate of the agricultural college.'

"We were talking all day long—lots of questions. As for politics, first and foremost, I asked him about Khrushchev's failure. It had been only [three] years since Khrushchev was dismissed. At that time, his opinion was that Brezhnev was just a transitional figure."

Mlynar was keen to get Gorbachev's assessment of Khrushchev because he was looking for reform ideas for Czechoslovakia. By his account, Gorbachev, then thirty-six, praised Khrushchev's anti-Stalin line but was impatient with his zigzagging agricultural policies and his interference in provincial affairs. In the end, Gorbachev had not been unhappy to see Khrushchev ousted. Mlynar told Gorbachev that the Czechs had considered Khrushchev a guarantor of their reform movement, and now, after his removal, they lacked a protector in Moscow. Mlynar complained that the Soviet Embassy in Prague was staffed with "ignoramuses who didn't understand one iota about Czech reality" and he feared they were sending Moscow reports "bad-mouthing our people.

"And Misha laughed and said, 'Okay, there are lots of idiotic bureaucrats. We have to take into consideration the local conditions for each socialist country.' " This remark foreshadowed Gorbachev's subsequent liberalism toward Eastern Europe. But it was heresy at a time when Brezhnev was trying to rein in Prague; within months he would launch an invasion to snuff out the reformist trends in Czechoslovakia.

"Today that sounds like a quotation of some legitimate central newspaper," Mlynar observed. "But at that time, it sounded almost revolutionary."

The two old schoolmates talked on and on into the night, arriving back at the Gorbachev apartment very late and a bit under the influence. Raisa was furious and bawled them out.

As they had talked, Mlynar had been struck by Gorbachev's interest in reform in Czechoslovakia. "Misha mentioned that things were possible in Czechoslovakia, but it would be quite different in the Soviet Union, though the Russians also need some changes," Mlynar recalled. "So I got the impression that not only he but his generation were against the stagnation then. They were looking for something newer. . . . I remember his wife, Raisa, was helping him do sociological research. He told me that she was visiting collective farmers and asking them questions. They were very surprised that anyone was actually asking peasants questions. Even at that time, you see, he was a person who tried to employ new methods."[7]

THE PRAGMATIC INNOVATOR

At that stage, Gorbachev was probably more candid with Mlynar than he was with Soviet colleagues about his reformist inclinations. For he was making his way up the ladder in traditional loyalist fashion; he wasn't making waves. His patron, Kulakov, had helped the plotters who threw out Khrushchev in 1964, and two years later was rewarded with an important job in Moscow as the Party's national chief for agriculture. From there, Kulakov could promote Gorbachev's career. Apparently, in 1970 he helped Gorbachev get Stavropol's top job—Party boss for the whole krai. This made him more powerful than an American governor—at the young age of thirty-nine.

During eight years in that job, Gorbachev established himself as a political leader of unusual integrity, and one with catholic intellectual tastes. By many accounts, he seems even then to have enjoyed lecturing journalists on economics or ideology and telling them to make their articles interesting. He was known for allowing several Russian Orthodox churches to operate in Stavropol and for mingling with visiting Moscow writers to discuss the latest books. According to Mikhail Novikov, a playwright and former theater director, Gorbachev was instrumental in opening a new cultural center. He and Raisa were regulars at Stavropol's Lermontov Drama Theater. They were fans of Shakespeare, of such American plays as Neil Simon's *Barefoot in the Park* and Tennessee Williams's *A Streetcar Named Desire,* and of the Russian classics that Gorbachev had played in in his own youth. Once, Novikov recalled, the company put on a controversial play, *Love, Jazz, and the Devil,* in which a playwright from the Baltics argued that young people should decide their own destiny. Some older people were offended and wanted the play banned. Gorbachev went to see it and was asked what should be done about it. According to Novikov, his reply was characteristic: "If this performance evokes arguments and makes people think about the problems of bringing up our children, then it should remain on stage."[8]

Unlike many provincial Party leaders who lived as feudal lords, aloof from ordinary people and protected by security men, Gorbachev was known as an approachable, populist-style leader. He enjoyed mixing with the people. As Party chief, he lived in a handsome old aristocrat's house, an ample residence down a side street lined with maples and poplars, about half a mile from his office in a massive Communist Party building. Valentin Mezin, a linguist, told me that Gorbachev used to jog and do exercises in the wooded park across the street from his house. He walked to work every day. He became well known for casual encounters with people on the street, who would accost him along his route, bringing him their problems directly rather than battling the bureaucratic apparatus.

"He was very open and free . . . and typical of the people of this region—he was dynamic and optimistic," Mezin told me as we strolled along Gorbachev's route. "I personally saw him walking to and from his office several times—no bodyguards. He was usually carrying his office folder and wearing a lamb's-wool *shapka* [hat]." Sometimes Gorbachev and Raisa would go shopping in the local department store just up the street from their house.[9]

As Party leader, Gorbachev's first priority was Stavropol's farm crop. Others now remember him for overseeing the installation of a major irrigation system to offset the dry climate, or battling Moscow ministries, convincing them not to impose inflated production quotas but settle for more realistic ones. He experimented with small work brigades and other measures to give farmers and factory workers greater incentives and more autonomy than the rigid Soviet planners usually allowed. Like an American governor, Gorbachev worked hard to diversify his region's economy, pushing Moscow higher-ups to invest in the construction of a huge chemical fertilizer plant and new electronics factories. He took a personal interest in stimulating local development—more along Western lines—of a massive broiler-chicken industry, the Stavropol Broiler Association.[10] Viktor Postnikov, the association's ruddy-faced, white-haired general director, credited Gorbachev with giving him, in the seventies, great autonomy as an industrial manager and then encouraging him to experiment with self-financing and profit-oriented business operations similar to those Gorbachev tried to introduce nationwide a decade later. Over the years Postnikov himself has come to act and talk more like a Western businessman than most Soviet managers.

Gorbachev was not a radical reformer in those years, Postnikov said. Rather, Gorbachev wanted what worked, and when one approach failed to produce results, he tried something new. He was a pragmatic innovator. In the early seventies, Gorbachev had taken trips to Italy, France, and Germany on various Communist Party delegations, once spending several weeks with Raisa motoring around France. That exposure to the West apparently opened him up to new ideas.

But he was also a canny politician, and a strong bureaucratic infighter. "He studied the bureaucracy well," observed Postnikov, with a knowing laugh. "He was always going to Moscow to get something. Often he would take me along. I could see he knew how the various ministers worked."[11]

Gorbachev's most celebrated fight with Moscow, recounted to me by Postnikov and others, came over his proposal that a portion of the territory's farmland should lie fallow every year. This ran counter to the policies of Brezhnev's agricultural advisers in Moscow, and of economic planners, who insisted on farming every acre for maximum output. On their advice, the Politburo had barred fallow lands. But Gorbachev, drawing on the experience of peasants working Stavropol's arid land, warned that constant planting was exhausting the soil. Productivity would rise,

Gorbachev said, if the land were allowed a periodic rest. He took the highly unusual—and risky—tack of appealing personally to Brezhnev, in effect putting his job on the line by openly bucking his Party superiors and the minister of agriculture.

"There was a standoff," Postnikov recalled. "The scientists demanded that we use the land every year; they said we'd have a better harvest. Those opinions were in conflict in the Politburo—two camps, the experts versus Gorbachev. . . . I remember how upset he was. I was in his office and he said, 'I don't know if I'm going to work today, or if I should look for a new job. I don't know if I'm going to be taken out of my job tomorrow for this.' But, fortunately, Brezhnev and his entourage allowed Gorbachev to carry out that experiment, and it has been tried on millions of acres since the seventies, and right now, the harvest has doubled. He started that surge."[12]

But at other times Gorbachev played along with Moscow, especially with Kulakov, and he benefited from his old patron's glory. In 1977, Kulakov decided to test a new method of harvesting winter wheat; he used a traveling armada—five combines, fifteen trucks, repair units, mobile homes, showers, and food services. This was a Soviet-style tactic—throwing big resources at a problem. Tapping his Stavropol connections, Kulakov decided to test the experiment in the Ipatovo District of Stavropol Krai. His approach became known as "the Ipatovsky method."

In July 1977, the method scored a great success—a harvest of two hundred thousand tons was completed in a record nine days. In Moscow, the Central Committee quickly passed a decree declaring that the Ipatovsky method should be copied nationwide. Kulakov was a hero—and so was Gorbachev. *Pravda* ran a front-page interview with Gorbachev, and the following March he was decorated with the Order of the October Revolution. Then, in May 1978, Mikhail Suslov, the Party's ideological chief and number three in the Kremlin hierarchy, came to Stavropol to award the city a special honor, and he spent several days traveling around the region with Gorbachev. There was talk that Kulakov, now sixty, might eventually be in line to replace Brezhnev. Actually, the success of the Ipatovsky method depended on favorable local conditions, and it never worked that well in much of the country. But it was a couple of years before this was apparent.

In July 1978, Kulakov died quite unexpectedly, seemingly in the peak of health. So odd was his death that some suspected suicide or foul play. Gorbachev, as his protégé and friend, flew to Moscow to give a eulogy at Kulakov's funeral, his first nationally televised speech. It was a pedestrian speech; more important was the fact that Kulakov's death left an opening in the Politburo, and in the Party secretariat, for a new agriculture secretary. It was a rare opportunity for someone to make a leap upward.

Gorbachev was a contender for the position, but he was not the most obvious one. Several Politburo members favored Agriculture Minister Valentin Mesyats, with whom Gorbachev had frequently crossed swords in bureaucratic infighting. Others in Brezhnev's circle suggested two Party bosses from southern Russia, Ivan Bondarenko and Sergei Medunov. Gorbachev had an excellent record, especially riding the publicity of the Ipatovo experiment, but his candid, teetotaling style did not fit in with the Brezhnev clique, with its reputation for partying and corruption.

Over the years, however, Gorbachev had carefully cultivated high-level connections. His honesty and intellectual style appealed to the spartan, puritanical, brainier members of the Politburo, such as Suslov, Prime Minister Aleksei Kosygin, and KGB Chief Yuri Andropov. All three of them had been regular visitors to the ornate hilltop sanitariums around Kislovodsk and Pyatigorsk in Stavropol. Suslov, as a former Party chief in Stavropol, took an interest in Gorbachev, especially revived by his visit that May. Andropov had been born and raised in Stavropol and had a *dacha* in Kislovodsk, where he enjoyed the pompous Stalinist architecture of the sanitariums, with their marbled baths and fountains. Kosygin, too, liked to take the Caucasian mountain air, and was so fond of his walks there that years later, one path was named "Kosygin's Walk," in his memory. As far back as 1971, Gorbachev been drawn to Andropov, who, despite his KGB job, was widely regarded as the brightest, most intellectual member of the Politburo. According to Postnikov, the two men often talked when Andropov came to Stavropol; they shared concern about the deteriorating economy and dissatisfactions with the corrupt, inflexible bureaucracy.

Back in May 1978, presumably emboldened by the Ipatovo success, Gorbachev had set out his thinking in a confidential twenty-page memo to Kulakov. With surprising bluntness, Gorbachev complained about the "incredible red tape" of overcentralized control; he said it was choking Soviet agriculture. "It takes the abilities of a gladiator to overcome the bureaucratic barriers standing in the way of resolving the smallest and most obvious questions," he groused.[13]

Typical of farmers and politicians from farm regions anywhere in the world, Gorbachev sounded the litany that farms were caught in a cost-price squeeze: Equipment prices were rising rapidly while the government's procurement prices for produce were fixed. Those prices had to be raised, he said. He also called for big new agro-industrial complexes that would bring the food-processing industry to the farms—an approach that Brezhnev later adopted.

But more intriguing is the fact that in 1978 Gorbachev was proposing reforms in agriculture that were a rough version of steps he would take in 1985–86, in the early phase of *perestroika*. He was applying the lessons of eight years as Stavropol Party boss, and while he paid lip service to the existing system of economic planning in Moscow, he asserted that there were too many output targets and quotas set by the centralized plans. "This discourages an increase in production," he said, "because people naturally spend all their time trying to reduce these excessive targets and shift responsibility." He called for more streamlined planning and decentralized economic management.

"In our opinion, we have to grant enterprises and associations greater independence in settling various questions of production and finance," Gorbachev wrote. "We must develop democratic principles, local initiative, free upper echelons from petty concerns, and maintain . . . flexibility in decision-making."[14]

Perhaps most characteristically, Gorbachev admitted there were many unprofitable farms, and he focused on what later would be called "the human factor" as the major reason for disaster in the farming sector. Presumably drawing on some of Raisa's research on the low morale and poverty of farm workers and the flight of young people from rural areas, Gorbachev asserted that material incentives and living conditions were insufficient to motivate farm workers.

This obviously very self-confident provincial chief told his superiors: "We must guarantee a growth in agricultural production not by administrative methods but rather by . . . a mechanism of material incentives and material-technical supply."[15] His language was stilted and bureaucratic, but his message was clear. If Moscow wanted better results from the farms, farm workers were going to have to be given better housing, better roads, better schools, and some decent health clinics ("material-technical supply") and investment was going to have to be increased to improve rural living standards.

Only Kremlin insiders can know how this memo affected Gorbachev's hopes for the Party's top national job in agriculture—or even whether anyone except Kulakov and his aides read it. Gorbachev's candor would hardly have gone over well with some members of Brezhnev's entourage, especially Agriculture Minister Mesyats, at whom Gorbachev was pointing an accusing finger. But the memo was the kind of constructive criticism that appealed to Andropov, who not only ran Moscow's spy operations and cracked down on dissidents, but also followed the Soviet Union's economy and built dossiers on the corruptive practices of the Brezhnev "mafia."

"Gorbachev talked with Andropov," Postnikov told me one morning as we sat in a park near the Kremlin walls. "And Andropov understood that [Gorbachev's] views were the same as his own. . . . Their views on what the Soviet Union needed were the same —two things: We need the country to be well fed and clothed, and we need defense. That's what Andropov said. Of course, [Gorbachev] was upset and dissatisfied [at the bad economic situation]. I think that was his view then. But he couldn't say publicly what he felt."[16]

Publicly, Gorbachev played along with Brezhnev, obliging him with the kind of flattery that the aging Party leader demanded as a political tithe from underlings all across the country. Brezhnev's later years were especially marked by vanity and fatuous self-glorification, as well as by the hyperbole of Soviet propaganda. Gorbachev bowed to the degrading necessity of delivering false hosannas to *The Little Land,* Brezhnev's ghostwritten war memoirs, which were published in 1978. "In terms of the profundity of its ideological content, the breadth of its generalizations, and the opinions expressed by the author, *The Little Land* has become a major event in public life," Gorbachev told an ideological conference in May, the same month that he wrote his blunt memo on economic mismanagement. "Communists and all the workers of Stavropol express limitless gratitude to Leonid Ilyich Brezhnev for this literary work."[17]

That September, the enfeebled Brezhnev made his way by train around southern Russia, meeting candidates for Kulakov's vacant post. When he arrived at the spas in Stavropol, Andropov was there, with Gorbachev, to endorse his candidacy. Later, back in Moscow, according to Kulakov's widow, the Politburo argued for three days over who would replace Kulakov in the Politburo and the Secretariat. Initially, the majority favored Mesyats, but Andropov pushed Gorbachev and gradually brought the others around.[18]

Years later, visiting Washington, Raisa Gorbacheva saw a picture of Andropov in the home of the late Ambassador Averell Harriman, and she remarked quietly, "Oh, yes, how much we owe him."

And so in November 1978, Gorbachev was summoned to Moscow. At forty-seven, he joined the national leadership as Party secretary for agriculture; two years later he became the youngest member by far of Brezhnev's geriatric Politburo. Gorbachev was an exception to the Brezhnev policy of keeping younger leaders down and replacing dead or retiring leaders with other officials who were just about as old, and this gave him an unusually long period to rise to the very top.

GATHERING A BRAIN TRUST

During the next seven years, Gorbachev developed his ideas for what Foreign Minister Eduard Shevardnadze would call the Soviet "New Deal," a program comparable to Franklin Delano Roosevelt's American model. Sweeping reforms were aimed not at scrapping the existing system, but at saving it. Gorbachev's style of work in these years, his leap over the final hurdles to supreme leadership, offer a rare glimpse into the inside workings of the upper reaches of the Communist Party hierarchy.

In those years, Gorbachev built a network of allies in his own generation of rising Party leaders, and recruited the intellectual brain trust that would help formulate his concepts for *perestroika*. For one of Gorbachev's trademarks throughout his career—and it is striking because it was then unusual for a Communist Party administrator—was his way of reaching out to scholars and academics for new ideas, and his obvious enjoyment of the company of Party intellectuals.

Reminiscent of his grandparents' hiding religious icons on the backs of portraits of Stalin and Lenin, Gorbachev let only a trusted inner circle of advisers and allies in on his thinking. The Moscow intelligentsia heard a few promising things about him, but during his first years in the capital they saw little external evidence that Gorbachev would become an extraordinary leader.

"Under Brezhnev, Gorbachev was a careful man, very careful—because at that time it was dangerous to be open and frank," I was told by Sasha Gelman, a well-known playwright who caught Gorbachev's favor and became a people's deputy during the later period of reform. "He always came to the theater to see the sharpest plays. He comes less now—he has no time. But he was a big fan of the theater. One nice thing about him was that—you know how these big shots come to a performance and say, 'It's good' or 'It's bad,' and everyone takes that as a big signal from on high. Well, the nice thing is Gorbachev would come and then leave without making any comment. That was the right thing to do."[19]

But a handful of Party insiders, those trusted by Gorbachev, quickly got a different picture of him. "When he arrived in Moscow, very soon it was clear that Gorbachev was really a new kind of person with a fresh look, with fresh ideas," recalled Nikolai Shishlin, who became a speech writer for Gorbachev and more recently a Soviet television commentator on world affairs. Shishlin has a deceptively sleepy-eyed, boyish look, but he is extremely bright, long a hidden reformer within the Central Committee apparatus.

"As I remember, our people began to say, 'He's too bold,' " Shishlin said, recalling Gorbachev circa 1980. "He had his own ideas on every problem—especially on agriculture and the economy. It was easy to talk with him because he knew life. He had seen in Stavropol that something was wrong. Everything at that time had to be decided through long discussions with Moscow, with different ministries, and that had bothered him. So he was interested in fresh ideas, in experiments in Hungary, in Bulgaria. He would travel there and bring back ideas. I liked reading notes of his conversations. They were real conversations with concrete ideas."[20]

At home, Gorbachev began to gather Soviet agricultural economists with innovative ideas and get them to formulate new approaches for coping with the nation's farm problems. One of those economists was Vladimir Tikhonov, who had been fighting the Brezhnev bureaucracy, unsuccessfully, for years. His view was that greater efficiency required that the massive state and collective farms be broken down into smaller work teams—"links," he called them—that would share the profit from their harvest, and thus have an incentive to produce more. Gorbachev had experimented with something similar—he called them "contract brigades"—in Stavropol Krai. The idea was that a brigade of workers would sign a contract with a state farm, take a plot of land, and promise to deliver so many tons of grain. If they could cut costs and manpower, or boost their yield per acre, they could increase their earnings, both as a group and individually. The idea was slowly catching on when Gorbachev left Stavropol. To reform-minded experts like Tikhonov, Gorbachev was a breath of fresh air in the Party hierarchy, especially when Gorbachev began seeking Tikhonov's advice in the early 1980s.

"We liked this young secretary of the Central Committee," the craggy-faced Tikhonov told me one morning as he chain-smoked in his book-lined study. "Because when he came here he manifested a clear, lively interest in economics, in social problems, in the development of rural areas and society as a whole. At that time, he rather frequently invited prominent economists home. And we got many instructions—directly from him—to carry out assignments, to study the most urgent, most essential, and most profound problems that the agrarian economy was suffering at the time."[21]

One of half a dozen economists whom Gorbachev assembled in April 1982 to prepare a new farm policy for Brezhnev was Tatyana Zaslavskaya, the sociologist from Novosibirsk, who was even then preparing her explosive report on the collapse of Soviet economic growth and the need for massive reform.[22] For Gorbachev, she became a bridge to Abel Aganbegyan, the maverick chief of the Novosibirsk Institute of Economics. And Zaslavskaya herself quickly became a favorite of Gorbachev because her outspoken ideas matched his private thinking.

How like-minded they were was evident from his behavior at a closed, high-level conference on agriculture in September 1982. The conference was sponsored by the Academy of Sciences and was attended by several Politburo members. In a fifteen-minute report to that session, Zaslavskaya gave a partial preview of the dynamite she was about to explode. Her key point was that Soviet agriculture could not be improved through technology, machinery, fertilizers, or administrative reorganizations, as the Party leadership had long contended. Rather, above all else, it would have to be improved by giving the peasant "an interest in his work . . . and normal living conditions." In short, she said, "everything depends on the people involved"—not on empty Party slogans.

Her analysis was candid and caustic enough that a senior Party official told others she had "overstepped the boundaries" of the permissible. In fact, when the full conference report was later published, her speech was so heavily censored that she found it unrecognizable.

Zaslavskaya's consolation was that the private audience of higher-ups was her primary target. Yet to her great disappointment, Gorbachev was called out of the room while she was speaking. For her, he was the most important person at the conference, and he had missed her report. What she did not know, and only learned later from Yuri Ovchinnikov, vice president of the academy, was that on his return, Gorbachev was given extensive notes on her analysis. "He read them, turned them over and read them a second time, got to the end, and then read them yet a third time," Ovchinnikov told her. "So I congratulate you. Even though he missed your presentation, I saw him read the entire thing three times."[23]

But if Zaslavskaya was frustrated to have missed a face-to-face exchange with Gorbachev on that occasion, Gorbachev's own frustration was even greater when Brezhnev and his Politburo rejected the reform program that Gorbachev had put together with her and the other agricultural economists.

Gorbachev's years as national agriculture secretary were not good ones. The grain harvests of the late 1970s and early 1980s were disastrous. Imports from the United States had been rising until President Carter's grain embargo of 1980. As Gorbachev's private memo indicated, he felt drastic steps were necessary. Brezhnev, who really made agriculture his own personal bailiwick, knew that food shortages were endemic and promised the people dramatic improvements. To great fanfare in May 1982, he announced his ten-year "food program," full of ambitious targets and high-sounding rhetoric.

With his team of agricultural economists, Gorbachev had tried to put together a comprehensive reform package. It promised less central planning, improved living standards for farm workers, plus more autonomy and more financial incentives for local units. In sum, he proposed liberalizing the farm sector. But the plan was shot down in the Politburo. They did not see the same urgency he did.

"He went up against strong opposition from Kosygin," Postnikov told me. "Kosygin had the view that agriculture was like a bottomless barrel: You put in a bunch of money at one end and you get nothing back. Kosygin was an industrialist. Industry was something else: Invest money and you get something back. . . . Gorbachev tried to prove to [Kosygin] that without food for people, you couldn't have anything—not defense, not industry. So he had a run-in with Kosygin and Brezhnev was constantly making peace between them."[24] Still, Brezhnev was no reformer at heart; that spring he was constantly sick, and too tired even to think of reform, let alone fight for it.

Gorbachev was flexible and pragmatic enough to try to get Politburo approval for individual proposals—the development of agro-industrial complexes, more investment in the rural infrastructure, some increases in state subsidies to farms and procurement prices. Some piecemeal measures were accepted. But the Brezhnev plan's targets were wildly unrealistic, and there was almost nothing of Gorbachev's ideas for real reform: no relaxation of centralized planning, no passing of decision-making to lower levels, no independence for individual farms, no real push for small, profit-oriented work brigades. Everything was still to be run top-down from Moscow and locked into the old inefficient superstructure left by Stalin.

Gorbachev gamely bit his tongue, even with his small team of advisers, but they sensed his deep disappointment at the Politburo's rejection. "It seemed to me that when they turned down that whole series of measures in this one very fundamental document, he was very upset," Tikhonov recalled. "In those high levels, leaders train themselves to be very reserved. But we saw his reaction, and we imagined what it was." Gorbachev's behavior betrayed his feelings. Brezhnev unveiled the plan and Gorbachev distanced himself from it. He seemed content not even to deliver a speech at the key Party meeting, although that was expected of him. Afterward, he always referred to it as Brezhnev's program.

"After Brezhnev's speech, no one was satisfied," Zaslavskaya recalled. "It was full of half measures rather than radical policies. But that was no longer Gorbachev's fault."

GROOMING FOR THE TOP

After Brezhnev died in November 1982 and Andropov took over, Gorbachev's star shot into ascendancy and his responsibilities suddenly mushroomed. He was then fifty-one and Andropov, sixty-eight and ill, began grooming him for the top job. Although Andropov also promoted a potential rival to Gorbachev, Leningrad Party boss Grigory Romanov, he made Gorbachev his deputy, gave him the ideological portfolio, expanded his mandate from agriculture to the entire economy, put science and technology under his wing, and had him oversee a purge of the Party apparatus to replace corrupt Brezhnev hacks with younger, more zealous, more honest leaders. Andropov was called a reformer, but his were traditional conservative reforms—demands for discipline and campaigns to fight corruption and inefficiency, to sweep deadwood out of the government, and to institute a crackdown against sloth and drinking among workers. In other words, no reforms of substance. He did not touch, let alone shake, the underlying structures of the Soviet system, as Gorbachev later would.

What served Gorbachev's development especially well was Andropov's decision to charge Gorbachev with developing a program for genuine reform of the management of the economy—a program that Andropov would not live long enough to begin to carry out. But its preparation enabled Gorbachev to surround himself with intellectual advisers and to expand his growing network of reformist allies within the Party hierarchy. Gorbachev's voracious appetite for intellectual input was reminiscent of the zeal for self-education evidenced by Peter the Great, who borrowed heavily from the West and used science to initiate a famous period of reform in czarist Russia.

In the field of economics, Zaslavskaya led Gorbachev to such new advisers as Aganbegyan, Leonid Abalkin, and Oleg Bogomolov, who generated more detailed critiques of the economy and began to discuss reform measures. Gorbachev's new responsibilities in science and technology brought him into contact with Yevgeny Velikhov, a specialist in computers and information technology and a vice president of the Academy of Sciences; and with Roald Sagdeyev, the outspoken, free-thinking head of the nation's space institute. As Sagdeyev said to me, "We scientists were being treated as very important people—and that would have been impossible without Gorbachev's personal interest. We talked to him about Reagan's 'Star Wars.' Our first written assessment was produced in August of 1983. We had a task force of ten or fifteen top people advising him."[25]

At the Academy of Sciences, a graceful old building constructed under Catherine the Great and still pale yellow, trimmed with white woodwork, Velikhov recalled Gorbachev's fascination with computers when Velikhov first showed him how they worked. "It was on a Saturday, a day off," Velikhov explained. "He was the agriculture secretary. I had called him and told him we were having this meeting that might interest him. He came over and then became very interested in how to promote systems analysis of agriculture. Later, he asked to see many scientists, not only me. He developed very rich relations with everybody. He does not want just a fifteen-minute protocol meeting, as with a lot of Party leaders. Gorbachev wants to understand, to go to the depths. Since that first meeting, I have met with him many times. We have discussed many issues, especially arms control. His grasp, his understanding, has steadily deepened."[26]

Within the Communist Party itself, Gorbachev developed another circle of advisers. He became a frequent visitor at the Party's Academy of Social Sciences, which was then headed by a political economist, Vadim Medvedev, whom Gorbachev eventually pulled into the Central Committee apparatus, and finally, the Politburo. Valentin Lazutkin, then an academy scholar and now deputy chief of the State Committee for Television and Radio, recalled that Gorbachev enjoyed giving a speech on some broad topic and inviting a sharp exchange with Party intellectuals at the academy. "He came there often in the early 1980s," Lazutkin said, "and seemed to thrive on lively debate of issues with us. He has a high regard for scholars, and a very analytical cast of mind."[27]

In 1983, Gorbachev traveled to Canada, his first exposure to the West in several years. There, he renewed his friendship with Aleksandr Yakovlev, who would become Gorbachev's alter ego in the Politburo. They had met in 1971, when Yakovlev had been a much more powerful figure than Gorbachev as chief of the propaganda department in the Central Committee. But Yakovlev had gotten in trouble for attacking Russian nationalism in a published article, and Brezhnev banished him to Canada in 1971 as ambassador. A decade in the West had made Yakovlev even more of a free-thinker than he had been in Moscow. When Gorbachev visited, their roles were reversed—this time Gorbachev was the big shot. Yakovlev told me they hit it off extremely well, talking late into the night about their country's problems. Others revealed that Yakovlev, looking over the main speech Gorbachev was going to give in Canada, advised Gorbachev that it would not go over well with a Western audience and wrote a new draft for Gorbachev overnight. Gorbachev liked Yakovlev's version so well, he delivered it and then recruited Yakovlev for his brain trust. He got Yakovlev reassigned as the head of Moscow's prestigious Institute on International Relations and World Economics, and moved him from there into a series of high Party posts.

"In Canada, we talked very, very candidly about everything," Yakovlev told me. When I asked whether Gorbachev was as critical of Brezhnev then as Yakovlev had been, Yakovlev sidestepped a direct answer. "Oh, I don't remember now what specifically he said, but the understanding that society should be changed and built on other principles—that was there."[28]

Gorbachev's visits to Canadian farmers were an eye-opener and added to his conviction that change in the U.S.S.R. was imperative. According to Canadian officials who accompanied him, Gorbachev was impressed by the initiative of the private Canadian farmers. At one stop, he tested one farmer: "Who makes you get up in the morning?" The farmer, non-plussed, said he got going on his own. At home, Gorbachev knew it would take the hounding of state farm supervisors and the threat of disciplinary action to get many farm workers on the job. In another encounter, he asked to see a farm's labor force, expecting the typical Soviet collective, and was taken aback when the farmer replied that he farmed several hundred acres with just his family and a few hired hands. Sharing his secret, the farmer showed Gorbachev his tractors and other modern farm machinery, close to $100,000 worth. "Do they trust you with all this?" Gorbachev asked, assuming that the equipment belonged to some government agency because he could not imagine a single farmer's owning such an expensive array of equipment. By the accounts of Canadian officials, Gorbachev walked away muttering, "We'll never have this for fifty years."

Gorbachev had good reason for more than a passing interest in the Canadian family farm. Back in Stavropol he had tried to stimulate individual initiative through a Soviet variation on family farming. His idea was not outright private ownership of the land, but a step in that direction— and a step away from massive collective farms. In his Stavropol experiments, a parcel of land was assigned to a small work "brigade," under a contract with the collective farm. If their harvest exceeded the contract, the family brigade could pocket the profit. This was known as the "brigade contract" or, when done by families, the "family brigade" system. In 1982, Gorbachev had tried to get this idea adopted as part of Brezhnev's food program, but he had failed. A year later, with Brezhnev out of the way and his patron Andropov in charge, Gorbachev won Politburo approval for it.

With Andropov's blessing, he was moving ahead on other fronts too, forming alliances with newcomers to the national Party leadership who had been promoted by Andropov. One who would become a significant figure in the Gorbachev era was Yegor Ligachev, a successful party boss in the big Siberian centers of Tomsk and Novosibirsk—whose streak of incorruptible puritanism appealed to the strict Andropov. A second was Nikolai Ryzhkov, a successful economic manager who had been chief of Uralmash, the huge heavy machine–building plant in the Ural Mountains city of Sverdlovsk. For Andropov, Ligachev was running the Central Committee's organization department, replacing the old Brezhnev mafia with new faces, while Ryzhkov was becoming the Party's top expert on the economy. Their roles in Andropov's regime foreshadowed the roles they would play in the future in Gorbachev's Politburo: Ligachev became number two to Gorbachev, and the Party watchdog, running the apparatus and serving as its pointman in the Politburo; Ryzhkov, the technocrat, became prime minister, running the economy and policing and protecting the ministries. In the late eighties they were often at odds with Gorbachev, but back in 1983 they were a team of rising reformers, impatient to shake off the corrupt lethargy left by Brezhnev.

Andropov fell so ill within a few months of his rise to the top that he had to abdicate much of his power and make Gorbachev his de facto deputy. As proxy, Gorbachev ran Politburo meetings and the Party Secretariat, relaying Andropov's orders and then reporting back to his chief. Andropov lay bedridden, tied to a kidney dialysis machine, either at his *dacha* in Usovo, west of Moscow, or at the Party elite's well-hidden hospital in the town of Kuntsevo. In addition to the day-to-day running of the country, Andropov assigned Gorbachev the crucial mandate: to begin preparing plans for revamping the system of economic management. Even better than Gorbachev, at first, Andropov understood that the whole economy was in a shambles, and that Russia was falling disastrously behind the West.

In what ultimately became essential preparation for his own future reforms, Gorbachev began to organize task forces. He drew on his widening circle of brain-trusters, in Soviet institutes and think tanks in Moscow, Leningrad, Novosibirsk, and other major cities. Working in tandem with Ryzhkov, he commissioned 110 different policy studies; he sought advisers on overall economic policy, experts in science and technology, computer scientists, agricultural specialists, labor sociologists, educators. Some of the topics covered were the space race, arms control, and foreign policy, but the bulk of them, by Gorbachev's account, were concerned with domestic affairs, especially the economy. Andropov's death in February 1984 did not interrupt that work, which continued until Gorbachev's ascension to power. More than once, Gorbachev has emphasized that the intellectual springboard for reform was prepared several years before he actually launched *perestroika*.

"[T]he appearance of the trends of restructuring," he would later recall, "was preceded by a specific period of analytical studies and moral assessments. All this was being prepared and was coming to a head within the Party, in science and culture, and in broad social circles. It has to be stated directly that a substantial reserve of fresh ideas was developed. We all sensed that it was impossible to live as before."[29]

Except, of course, for the Old Guard, which was powerful enough to impose Konstantin Chernenko, the doddering Brezhnev toady and life-long apparatchik, as Andropov's successor, in February 1984. Chernenko was even more of a geriatric embarrassment than Brezhnev had been. Gorbachev was formally named number two, the stand-in chairman at Politburo meetings and the Party Secretariat when Chernenko was too feeble to attend.

It was Gorbachev who went to London in December 1984, captivating the Britons as the leader of a new generation of Soviets and prompting Prime Minister Margaret Thatcher to gush, "We can work with him." It was Gorbachev that same month, in an astonishing speech to a Soviet ideological conference, who declared the need for openness (*glasnost*), for more self-management in the economy, for the use of such market levers as prices, profits, and credits, to make the system work. And it was Gorbachev who declared war on inertia and on the "moribund conceptions" of Party dogmatists—all reflecting the provocative work of his brain trusts.

It was also Gorbachev whom the outside world took to be the obvious heir apparent when Chernenko died after thirteen feeble months as general secretary. As Gorbachev's ally Aleksandr Yakovlev remarked to me, "It was historically logical" for the Kremlin to pass the torch to a new generation, and to signal the changing of the guard by anointing Gorbachev.

But as the Politburo met through the night of March 10, 1985, Gorbachev's prospects were touch and go. He had exposed his own beliefs more and more, dropping the double life he had carried on within the Party for so many years. Now, on the threshold of power, he faced the final obstacle. He was almost blocked by the aging, conservative Moscow Party leader

Viktor Grishin, whom Chernenko had tried to anoint before his death.

Ligachev, then a strong supporter of Gorbachev, has reported that the Politburo was closely divided on the critical choice, and passed "very anxious hours" that could have come out with very different people on top. I have been told by well-connected Party officials that Gorbachev's circle anticipated the close division as they watched Chernenko sink into a coma in the final days of his life and that Chernenko's vital life-support systems were pulled at a time when three Politburo conservatives were far from Moscow and unable to vote on the new leader. Vladimir Shcherbitsky, the Ukrainian Party leader, was in San Francisco; Vitaly Vorotnikov, future head of the Russian republic, was in Yugoslavia; and Dinmukhammed Kunyayev, the Kazakh Party leader, was in his capital of Alma-Ata, several hours away from Moscow by plane. Whether or not it is true that Chernenko's life support was removed at a politically propitious time, the fact that Shcherbitsky, Kunyayev, and Vorotnikov did not reach Moscow until March 11—after the Politburo had made its selection—unquestionably helped Gorbachev. By virtually all reckonings, at least two of them, if not all three, would have voted against him. Mikhail Shatrov, the playwright, has reported that the eight Politburo members voting that fateful night were evenly split until the deadlock was broken by threats from KGB Chief Viktor Chebrikov to expose corruption in Grishin's family. At the Central Committee meeting held to confirm the Politburo vote, the scales were tipped by former Foreign Minister Andrei Gromyko's stunning endorsement of Gorbachev as a skilled leader of the Politburo, nearly brilliant in foreign policy. Significantly, Gromyko did not review Gorbachev's record in agriculture, which was far from brilliant; in fact, Gorbachev had not been a good economic manager. But Gromyko praised his political finesse and hailed Gorbachev as a tough partisan, despite his nice smile—"a man with iron teeth."[30]

The moment for reform had arrived, and Gorbachev was unusually well prepared—by conviction, life experience, temperament, and the process of high-level analysis he had commissioned. He embarked, as he later said, with the understanding that "cosmetic repairs would not do; a major overhaul was required."[31]

Only the self-assurance that he had developed over a lifetime would have made him bold enough to tackle such a daunting task. If anything, his own success had made him overoptimistic about the chances for reform and overrational about how to go about it. "Gorbachev's main failing," one of his Party aides and admirers conceded to me privately, "is that he's too intellectual, too rational. He does not understand ordinary people well enough—what makes them tick." Gorbachev has, at times, been transparent in his own surprise at the difficulties. Nearly four years after taking power, in the midst of national turmoil, he admitted that "we are *only now* [emphasis added] truly understanding what *perestroika* is . . . the huge scale of the work to come."[32]

But if Gorbachev's failing would be political miscalculation and underestimation of the difficulties, his extraordinary talent as a political leader would be his capacity for survival, his ability to ride the tiger, to outflank his opposition, to sidestep catastrophe and improvise new solutions, to cast off policies that did not work and constantly to change the national agenda to make himself once again the vector of history—even if only long enough to keep the process of reform alive and deepen its hold on his society so that, if necessary, it could outlive him.

PART TWO

THE AWAKENING

A central element of Gorbachev's strategy to rebuild and modernize Soviet society was the marshaling of public opinion. For Gorbachev understood, if not initially, then by 1987, that to set in motion his economic and political reforms, he had to arouse his country from silence, to awaken his people and give them voice. Gorbachev could not hope to compete with the world in the twenty-first century—he could not hope to move his nation—without freeing up ideas and information.

For decades, orthodoxy had stifled initiative, had suppressed creativity in politics, the arts, the economy. For reform to flourish, the dead hand of dogma had to be lifted; the stimulus of intellectual ferment had to be fostered. In place of Party slogans, Gorbachev needed fresh thinking; in place of the Party line, a diversity of opinions; instead of a political monolith, pluralism.

Achieving these things required a political high-wire act.

Most Soviet leaders rise to the top on the power base of the Communist Party apparatus, and Gorbachev was no exception. Once he was installed, however, he had to reverse course; as the agent of change, he had to take action against the interests of the Party apparatus. In order to free up the creative energies of his people, he had to break the power monopoly of the very hierarchy that had chosen him.

To do this, he needed to create an army of supporters, to tap into the pent-up frustration of the masses. And so, very deliberately, he revived the people—especially the intelligentsia—from their slumber by liberating the press, television, the world of books and cinema.

CHAPTER 5

"WHAT DO YOU THINK?"

"Russia was deep in sleep and nothing was
happening. Then the people woke up
about two or two and a half years ago [1987]."[1]
—Yuri Levada
Sociologist
March 1990

"Before, I thought our people had
forgotten how to think. But our research
and the elections and campaigns have
shown that it just isn't so. Maybe
after all, we should trust our people more."[2]
—Leonid Sedov
Sociologist
September 1989

Yuri Levada does not look like a bomb thrower. He could be anybody's
friendly Dutch uncle—an ample, amiable man with engaging warmth, an
open manner, and an air of genial self-confidence. Given to wearing
turtleneck sweaters and zippered suede jackets rather than a coat and tie,
he looks like a French film director. In fact, Levada is a sociologist, and
that vocation puts him at the leading edge of Gorbachev's peaceful political revolution. Levada is one of the vital links between the leader and the

masses. His version of bomb throwing, suppressed in the 1970s, is political opinion polling.

His first mass experiment, a full-page questionnaire printed on February 1, 1989, in *Literaturnaya Gazeta (Literary Gazette),* the weekly of the Soviet Writers' Union, touched off an avalanche of responses, precisely the kind of popular reaction that Gorbachev needed to power his drive for reform. Levada's story, over the past quarter of a century, also illustrates how Soviet society has changed from the enforced orthodoxy of the Brezhnev era to Gorbachev's new openness.

In the late 1960s, Levada had created a stir by becoming the first Soviet scholar to teach sociology at Moscow State University. After Khrushchev's thaw in the early 1960s, sociology was no longer the forbidden territory it once had been, but it was still an academic black sheep; there was no sociology department at any Soviet university. But Levada, a philosopher by training who was always interested in "how people live" (as he put it), was permitted in 1966 to give lectures on sociology in the journalism faculty of the university. And at the Institute for Applied Social Research, he led a seminar in the theory and methods of sociology.

Levada's classes and seminars were immensely popular. Students flocked to him, attracted by his undogmatic thinking and his intellectual daring; he became a mentor to many. Testing the limits of the permissible, Levada had also dared to invite the American sociologist Talcott Parsons to lead some seminars in Moscow in 1967. Levada's own popularity grew to the point where the university published his lectures as a paperback book in 1969. But as the first thousand copies circulated, Levada found himself in trouble with the Party.

After the invasion of Czechoslovakia in August 1968, Brezhnev's line had hardened; the KGB was cracking down on dissidents and the Party was tightening up. Not that Levada was an open dissident like Andrei Sakharov or Aleksandr Solzhenitsyn; his political credentials were impeccable. He was an establishment scholar, a Communist Party member, and the ranking Communist in his institute—the secretary of the institute's Party committee.

Levada's sin was not personal; it was something more menacing— professional free-thinking, and the challenge to Soviet Party dogma inherent in sociology. His book was no flaming tract; it was a basic introduction to sociology, one that today's Soviet students find pretty tame. Yet in the Brezhnev era, another sociologist observed, simply by eschewing dogma, "Levada showed himself underneath as a real enemy of the system."[3]

Years before, Stalin's ideologists had branded sociology a "bourgeois pseudoscience." Their Marxist-Leninist argument was that historical materialism explained all reality and thus sociology was unnecessary. In practice, the danger for Communist ideology was that sociology presumed society was composed of competing interest groups, and the very idea of group antagonisms threatened the Communist Party's precious myth of the classless society living in monolithic harmony.

What is more, empirical sociology as practiced in the West sought data that inevitably challenged the Party's political claims. Indeed, Levada had cited some early, very limited opinion polls conducted by other Soviet sociologists such as Vladimir Shlyapentokh and Vladimir Shutkin, who had found that, contrary to the Party's boasts, few children of workers and peasants made it into decent universities; also that most readers of *Pravda* did not even bother to read its party-line editorials.

At bottom, of course, independent opinion polling posed too much of a threat to Kremlin leaders, who had rarely if ever worried about what the people thought. And after Czechoslovakia's spring of ferment, the Brezhnev leadership was pulling back from the risks of having to deal with public opinion at home.

Levada, whose impish candor rarely deserts him, compounded his problems with the wry comment, "You cannot solve ideological issues with the help of tanks." To the Kremlin, that remark, reprinted in his book, sounded like a slam on Moscow's military suppression of Czechoslovak liberalism. In reprisal, *Pravda* made Levada the first scapegoat of what became a broad purge of Soviet sociology. He was denounced at meetings at the Academy of Social Sciences and the Communist Party Central Committee. In the end, not only Levada but about two hundred other sociologists were fired from various institutes and universities in the early 1970s.[4]

By the time I arrived in Moscow in late 1971, Yuri Levada was something of a mystery man, beyond the reach of Western correspondents. He had become a symbolic target of the ideological hangmen of the Brezhnev era. Communist Party watchdogs had forced him off the faculty of Moscow State University and gotten him expelled from the Institute for Applied Social Research. He had slipped out of view and was lying low at another institute. Politically, he lived in a forbidden zone; and for close to fifteen years, he remained hidden in this way beneath the surface of Russian political and intellectual life.

Now, under Gorbachev, Levada has made a political and professional comeback. He is operating freely, though even now he is not easy to find. I found him, with considerable difficulty, tucked away in an unmarked room on the fourth floor of a third-class hotel, the Central House of Tourists, far from the center of Moscow. It was an unlikely place for an office, but apparently the only thing available with space so short in Moscow.

At sixty, with a white fringe of hair circling his head, Levada radiated vitality. In a system where senior academics are often formal and pretentious, Levada was relaxed and informal. He was born and brought up in the Ukraine, then went to Moscow State University. He comes by an intense interest in politics naturally: Both his parents were journalists and essayists. His mother was Russian, his father, Ukrainian. Of course, he speaks both those languages, but also Polish, French, and accented English. I knew in advance that he was considered a father figure by many young Soviet sociologists; when I met him, I could readily see why he was so popular with younger colleagues.

Six of them were clustered around Levada in what was once a skimpy double room; the Levada team was practicing sociology out of a garret. The place was crammed with old wooden school desks, file folders, piles of questionnaires, wall charts, and stacks of miscellaneous papers. Levada had the corner desk and his own chair; I'm not sure there were enough chairs to go around for all the others. Some of Levada's now middle-aged acolytes sat on their desks while we talked; the smokers spilled ash into cupped hands or onto the floor; someone made tea on a hot plate.

But there were no computers. Things were so tight financially and their operation so new that they had only a few computers, far too few to go around, and those were all three or four miles away, in the basement of an aristocrat's former mansion, which their technical department shared with several other agencies. Someday soon, they said, they hoped the whole operation would have new premises. I first visited them in April 1989, but a year later, their office situation had not improved.

Under the direction and political protection of Tatyana Zaslavskaya, Levada's group was now part of the All-Union Center for the Study of Public Opinion on Social and Economic Issues, with twenty-three suboffices scattered across the country to organize on-the-spot polling. When the center was set up in 1988, "politics" had been deliberately left out of its title and mandate, I was told, because Kremlin hard-liners mistrusted Zaslavskaya's radical tendencies; indeed, they were still making periodic attempts to remove her as the center's director. But, as she proudly told me, she was too well known to be knocked off easily.

THE UNEXPECTED AVALANCHE

Despite the inevitable obstacles, the Levada group exuded an ebullient sense of camaraderie and the enthusiasm of people finally doing what they had been forbidden to do for close to twenty years. Like excited children, they were sitting on the edge of history, watching a great democratic experiment unfold.

As Levada and two of his former students, the black-bearded, analytical Alex Levinson and close-cropped, sandy-haired, pragmatic Lev Gudkov, explained, the center had ignored the formal restrictions and plunged almost immediately into political polling. In the previous two decades, there had been some industrial polls on social and economic issues—jobs, education, problems in the workplace. But Levada's group was no longer content with dabbling. They wanted to get to the gut political questions. So they printed their full-page questionnaire in *Literaturnaya Gazeta* under the headline WHAT DO YOU THINK?

By American standards, the questionnaire was as daunting as a mortgage loan application: thirty-four questions, with many detailed, multiple-choice answers. Most Americans would have balked, refusing to devote more than half an hour to answering such a poll. But the Levada group hoped that by using a newspaper with six million subscribers, they could get enough responses for an adequate national sample. In the West, that would require roughly three thousand respondents.

Levada's team was wholly unprepared for the reaction: They received two hundred thousand responses in all!

When they told me the figure, I simply could not believe it. It was so incredible that we all broke out laughing.

In one stroke, the Soviet Union had gone from one voice to many, from orthodoxy to pluralism. The hold of dogma, long since weakened, had been destroyed.

Levada and his team had never in their wildest dreams imagined that their questionnaire would touch off such a Niagara. It was as if someone had thrown open the floodgates. Before, no one was sure whether there was even a trickle of public opinion to be measured. Now, overnight, a flood.

Levinson led me into the bathroom, where the tub was piled high with nine or ten huge mail sacks. The Levada group had carefully selected three thousand responses to tabulate, but they did not know what to do with the remaining mountains of replies. It was such a precious testament to the country's political awakening that it seemed criminal to throw the letters away. So they kept them, and a year later, when I peeped into the bathroom, those letter sacks were still there.

"Through the decades," Levinson remarked, "people have never been asked *anything*. All of a sudden their opinion is being counted—someone is seeking their answers. They feel this is some sign of trust toward them, a demonstration of their worth."

Gudkov added, "People write us: 'We see your questionnaire as a referendum' and the possibility of a referendum on major topics compels people to answer."

"People are saying things like, 'I have lived for eighty years and no one has ever wondered about my opinion. For the first time in my life I have experienced that moment,'" reported a third member of the group, Aleksandr Golov.[5]

Several times over the past year and a half, I have visited Levada and his group, and each time their wonder over that first poll, and its implications for the new world that Gorbachev is trying to open up, remained undiminished.

STUDYING A SOCIAL REVOLUTION FROM THE INSIDE

"Russia was deep in sleep and nothing was happening," Levada observed. "Then the people woke up about two or two and a half years ago."

As others have, Levada dated the real start of popular involvement in Gorbachev's reforms not from 1985, when Gorbachev first came to power, but 1987, when Gorbachev began to build toward a more open press and democratic reforms.

"It [the *Literaturnaya Gazeta* poll] was a tremendous event for us. For the first time we saw that our people are not only ready to answer a bold question but they actively want to speak out. The main result of *perestroika* is the disappearance of mass fear."

I suggested to Levada that this sudden eruption of public opinion must have seemed miraculous, a great discovery.

"Yes, yes," he said. "For the first time in history, we can study a social revolution from the inside. Because at the time of the American and French and other great revolutions, there were no sociologists out polling. But we . . ." He smiled broadly. "It's *verry* interesting."[6]

Even these maverick liberals were astonished that after decades of silence and repression, so many ordinary people were willing to risk political reprisal to express their views—something inconceivable even two or three years before.

"On the envelopes [mailing back questionnaires], people put their full names and addresses," Alex Levinson said. "And according to existing laws, these people could be brought to trial." What he did not say, but what I well understood, was that during the Brezhnev years, many dissidents had been sent off to Siberia, and in the Stalin years, many intellectuals had perished, for openly stating political opinions about the leadership. The great poet Osip Mandelstam had gone to his death in the mid-1930s for a fourteen-line poem that mocked Stalin's "cockroach whiskers leer" and his sycophantic circle of "fawning half-men for him to play with."[7] To underscore his point, Levinson fished out a letter.

"Here," he said, handing me a letter to inspect. "Someone writes something sharply critical about the Communist Party, about Gorbachev, about politics—and then he signs his full name and address. This could be used as evidence against him. So I think [this shows] the fear of the past has just disappeared. That's why, when our interviewers do their interviews, people speak very openly with them."

If this openness came as a surprise to free-thinking academics, it must have been even more of a shock to Communist Party higher-ups. I asked if Party officials had been interested in their findings, and they all nodded, adding that the poll results had gone to branches of the Central Committee.

"How does the Party apparatus react to all this?" I asked.

"Extremely negatively, of course," Gudkov replied.

The apparatchiks had of course ample cause for concern. The readers of *Literaturnaya Gazeta* were delivering a stinging indictment of the system and of the Party hierarchy. In answer to an open-ended question about the main reasons for the country's "current difficulties," the number one villain mentioned was the Party—government bureaucracy. With a choice of nineteen different reasons, plus a blank space to write in another explanation, responses broke down as follows:

63% cited the dominance of bureaucrats;
60% listed corruption, drunkenness, black-market speculation, and thievery from the state;
56% mentioned the country's technological backwardness;
45% cited a mistaken strategy of national development;
35% pointed to loss of faith in the ideals of socialism;
33% cited the consequences of Stalinism.[8]

What intrigued me especially was that only 1% chose a favorite whipping boy of Communist Party propaganda—the policies of "countries of imperialism"—that is, the West.

Of course, Levada and his group understood that the newspaper's subscribers were overwhelmingly intellectuals and the people who wrote in were self-selected; and so the poll was not entirely representative, no matter how many responses they received. It was not the kind of random or weighted sample that pollsters normally require. Indeed, the training and experience of Soviet sociologists and pollsters is a good deal less sophisticated than that in the West.

In the interests of greater accuracy than is possible in a reader's poll, the Levada group ran a second poll of forty-five hundred people, a sample of the general population that they selected to match the nation's various ages and social, economic, and demographic groups. In seventeen regions across the country, interviewers went door to door. In this poll, the number one villain cited was corruption and drunkenness (57%), closely followed by technical backwardness (42%) and the hated bureaucracy (41%). This more working-class-oriented sample was far less likely than the intellectuals to blame the country's ills on the wrong development strategy and popular loss of faith in the ideals of socialism. But surprisingly, even though there were plenty of workers polled, 28% blamed the nation's economic mess on the laziness or "shirking," as Russians say, of Soviet workers.

At the end of the national poll, I noticed figures about Soviet living standards that were stunning. Two thirds of the people reported that the per-capita income in their families was less than 125 rubles a month—about $200 at the official rate of exchange, but more like $20 on the free market. All but 3% made less than 250 rubles. Even allowing for some exaggeration, these were dismal living standards, and those of a Third World country, not of a superpower.

The two polls also confirmed an important divergence in attitudes between the intelligentsia and the working class. Differences cropped up on many questions, but most significantly on a question that asked people to choose ways to make "decisive changes for the better" in the nation's situation.

The national poll, which the Levada group saw as dominated by working-class opinion, showed little taste for reform. By far the largest number (50%) said the most important step was to restore *tvordy poryadok*— "strict order." In short, their cure for the current crisis was to run the nation like an army, show everybody a tough fist, impose discipline, and head back toward the Stalinist system. In a similar vein, they also wanted an improvement in central planning, rather than abandonment of it. Reforms came far down the list.

The intellectual readers of *Literaturnaya Gazeta* were on a different track. First of all, they said, give peasants the right to own land (66%) and cut army and military expenditures (55%). They also strongly favored breaking up the centralized power structure and giving more autonomy to minority republics and more authority to local governments. One third wanted a cutback in Soviet foreign aid and urged efforts to attract foreign capital investments in the U.S.S.R. In short, they had more appetite for reform than Gorbachev himself.

Rippling through the responses in both polls was what Gudkov called a civic rage over miserable living conditions—bad housing, a bad health system, shortages of all kinds—and a demoralizing sense of futility about the future.

The Levada group had touched the raw anger of the population, suppressed but accumulated over decades. As Levada observed, what the Russians call the *narod*, the masses, had finally awakened—and with a vengeance.

"They began to wake up with something of a hangover, not with a clear head," he explained to me. "The main form of consciousness, from what we can determine, is a wild hostility toward the apparat, which they feel fills its pockets, takes bribes, enjoys privileges. The main enemy is the corruption, the privileges of the apparat bureaucracy."

THE MAFIA

Everywhere I went in the Soviet Union, people simply called it the "mafia," not literally meaning organized crime in the Western sense but having that dark connotation. In Soviet parlance, the mafia is a stratum of society that includes powerful Party and government officials, economic managers, and criminal elements, an amorphous, privileged layer held in popular contempt for its corrupt life-style and evil tentacles that reach into all walks of life. The "mafia" is an epithet constantly on people's lips, but hard to get them to define with any precision; it almost always links political power and illicit economic advantages. When I tossed out names of political leaders who might be possible symbols of the mafia to the public, Levada rejected them all.

In 1990, the Levada group did a special survey to try to induce people to say more about what they meant by the term. "Let them put down anything they want—crime, the Party clique, retail trade," he said. "In general, it's hazy: some unclear powers-that-be. You know how Russians express themselves, as if there were some kind of sorcery, black magic. One third thinks the mafia is the main reason for all evil. This invisible, secret, universal, omnipresent mafia is considered responsible for whatever you please."

In subsequent polls conducted by the Levada group, some of which I witnessed, they found such mistrust among the people toward the bureaucracy and Party leadership that large majorities were demanding direct elections. Initially, Levada's team had been hesitant to ask people about a multiparty system. "It's not really necessary to ask such a question now," Lev Gudkov told me at our first meeting, in April 1989, when the Levada group was still feeling its way.[9] But within a few months, the idea of a multiparty system was no longer taboo. And once a choice was put to them and they had to answer a question asked by a poll taker, people started taking positions and then hungrily reading the results of the polls in which they had participated.

"We present a mirror for society," Gudkov remarked. "We show them what they are. And looking at that mirror, a person thinks about what he sees."

Leonid Sedov, one of Levada's longtime colleagues, who had paid for his own dissenting views in the Brezhnev era with a term of Siberian exile, remarked to me that the results of the new polls had changed his once-skeptical view of the Soviet people, whom he had always regarded as politically inert.

"Before, I had a much worse opinion about my countrymen," he said, stroking his weatherworn face and soft beard.

"I thought our people had forgotten how to think, how to want things, how to organize themselves, how to be active," he admitted a bit tensely, recalling his earlier disenchantment with others less radical than he. "But our research, and the elections and campaigns, have shown that this just isn't so. Maybe, after all, we should trust our people more—which is something that I'm going to do from now on."

What struck Alex Levinson especially forcefully was the synergy between polling and public opinion. The act of polling, he said, prompted people to think about issues they had long left to others; they had to formulate their own attitudes about elections, about relations among nationalities, about national priorities, and then to speak out. In short, polling stimulated what Gorbachev wanted—the formation of public opinion.

"We are needed first of all by the people who don't really know what they think until they find out what everybody else thinks," he observed.

"When someone knows that 'I'm not the only one who thinks this should be done; the whole country thinks that way,' this is extremely important.

"In a way," he concluded, "this [polling and publishing polls] is a quiet revolution."

The revolution, of course, is the emergence of a civil society—the very notion that society at large has legitimate interests and opinions, apart from the Communist Party's or the state's definition of what is good for society. In the nineteenth century, the appearance of this notion among the Russian intelligentsia was crucial for efforts to oppose and reform the czarist state. Granted legitimacy by Gorbachev, this same notion of the public's interests and opinions has reappeared—a foundation stone for a democratic society.

CHAPTER 6

GLASNOST: A MARRIAGE OF POLITICAL CONVENIENCE

"In short, comrades, what we are
talking about is a new role for
public opinion in the country. And
there is no need to fear the novel,
unconventional character of some
opinions. . . ."[1]
—Gorbachev, June 1988

"*Glasnost* comes from the Russian
word *glas,* or voice. So it literally
means voiceness, or speaking out."[2]
—Vladimir Pozner
TV Commentator
June 1988

In his assault on the existing Soviet power structure and the stultifying
effects of enforced ideological orthodoxy, Gorbachev did something unconventional for a Communist ruler: He reached out to form a political
alliance with the intelligentsia.

He was moving beyond his well-developed habit of tapping small academic brain trusts for private advice, to embark on open political warfare.
The marriage of political convenience he sought—engaging intellectuals
as his main allies against the Party hierarchy—required a much bolder

political stroke, and one not without risks, as Gorbachev later discovered.

Intellectuals were natural partisans of reform, far more so than the disgruntled masses. The most progressive of them were well ahead of Gorbachev and his circle in their desire for fundamental changes in the Soviet system. Broadly speaking, the liberal Soviet intelligentsia were united by a common revulsion toward Stalinism and its hallmarks: terror, censorship, the arbitrary *ukaz*—or dictatorship—of the state bureaucracy. More than other segments of Soviet society, they valued individual rights, freedom of expression, the rule of law. And since Khrushchev's demise in 1964, they had been a frustrated, latent political force.

No less a Communist icon than Karl Marx had put his finger on the reason for their disenchantment. "A censored press only serves to demoralize. That greatest of vices, hypocrisy, is inseparable from it," he had written back in 1842. "The government hears only its own voice while all the time deceiving itself, affecting to hear the voice of the people while demanding that they also support the pretense. And on their side, the people either partly succumb to political skepticism or completely turn away from public life and become a crowd of individuals, each living only his own private existence."[3]

Americans have often asked me, "Where were all these Gorbachev liberals before he appeared? Where did they all come from?" The answer is that they were hidden, an army of defectors-in-place. They were smirking at the sallies of poets and playwrights; they were desperately venting their anger to a few trusted friends. In the seventies, I had heard them describe how their fathers were carted away in the night by Stalin's henchmen; I had listened to their disapproval of the invasion of Czechoslovakia, laughed at their brutal lampoons of Brezhnev's slobbering speech. The ideological dry rot, extensive even then, indicated that Soviet society was not the monolith it appeared to be from afar. Among my personal acquaintances in those days, I could count poets, writers, artists, actors, journalists, musicians, scientists, historians, linguists, teachers, and university students. Their disaffection made them a veritable army, awaiting a new political moment, ready to be summoned into battle against the hated apparat.

Vladimir Pozner, the Soviet television commentator, told me a political anecdote that captured this cynicism and frustration. A man goes to a local health clinic and demands to see "the eye-ear doctor." The nurse explains there is no such thing—there is either a doctor who examines your eyes or a doctor who examines your ears and throat, but not one eye-ear doctor. But the patient is insistent. They argue, and finally the nurse says, "Well, there isn't one but if there were one, why would you want to see him?" The man replies, "Because I keep hearing one thing and seeing something very different."

Hypocrisy had bred disillusionment.

Gorbachev had another built-in advantage: The connection in Russia between the world of culture and the world of politics has long been much closer than it is in the United States. Americans generally regard culture as entertainment, a diversion, perhaps even a source of individual development; culture rarely plays a central role in national political life, except perhaps at times of mass protest, such as the Vietnam War. Not so in Russia. Through much of Russian history, culture has been a proxy battleground for politics. Russians have always turned to artists to reveal the truth behind official lies. Poetry and fables have served as Aesopian subterfuges when open political communication was impossible. So important was literature to Czar Nicholas I that he was Pushkin's personal censor; Dostoyevsky was exiled and faced a firing squad before being spared at the last minute by order of the czar. One reason the biting nineteenth-century satires of Nikolai Gogol and Mikhail Saltykov (Shchedrin) have played to enthusiastic modern audiences in Russia is that they mock the same political diktat and pretentious habits of rulers as modern underground balladiers do. Under dictators, life and thought do not cease; art becomes the substitute outlet for politics.

In the Khrushchev thaw of the 1960s, poets such as Andrei Voznesensky, Yevgeny Yevtushenko, and Bella Akhmadulina led the way. A decade later, underground balladiers such as Vladimir Vysotsky, Bulat Ozudzhava, and Aleksandr Galich stirred excitement with their off-color political songs and poetry. But this was esoteric politics, usually played behind closed doors for select audiences, rarely produced on an open stage. It was titillating to the cognoscenti, but it had no wide political impact. In the pre-Gorbachev period, the audience was very limited. The Party held the reins of control so tightly that disaffected Soviet intellectuals lacked any real notion of their strength.

Fear and suspicion kept most people from knowing the true opinions of their neighbors across the hall. Often, in the seventies, I found Russians more willing to talk candidly to me, a foreigner, than to each other, because they knew I would not inform on them to the secret police. My Russian friends taught me never to bring together in private company two Soviets who did not know each other well. In fact, they also taught me not to bring together two who *did know each other*—unless *they* initiated the idea. This was because there were so many informers that they could not afford to trust anyone but blood relatives and a few tested soul mates.

So they had no way of knowing how many millions of other people agreed with them.

In time, I concluded that the most important function of the Soviet press during the 1970s had been to keep these latent dissenters isolated and feeling impotent. Their disillusionment had progressed to the point where most university-educated big-city intellectuals were too cynical to be inspired by the endless outpouring of official ideology in the press, but the suffocating foam of the Party press kept them powerless. They plodded along obediently, out of inertia, fear of economic blacklisting or Siberian exile, and ignorance of their own numbers. The Party line numbed them, choked their voices, denied them the means of communicating with each other and thus of beginning to coalesce as an opposition opinion.

Gorbachev needed ways to activate this inchoate army, to summon the pressure of public opinion to help him break the power of the party apparat. Aleksandr Yakovlev, then the most philosophical and the most radical reformer in the Politburo, encouraged Gorbachev to open up the press and to recruit the intelligentsia as activists for reform.

Glasnost became Gorbachev's strategy for arousing his countrymen to action, but not *glasnost* meaning freedom of speech or freedom of the press, as we know it in the West. Despite Gorbachev's promise in early 1987 of a law guaranteeing the rights of the press, it was more than three years before such a law was passed, on June 12, 1990. It took relentless pressure from liberal reformers in the Supreme Soviet to draft and then push through a progressive piece of legislation lifting censorship and granting the right for individuals to start newspapers—the first law in the nation's history to provide guarantees for journalists. But in a society uneasy with the notion of journalistic freedom and lacking experience in libel law, high officials had trouble giving up the habit of control. Gorbachev himself was not immune. During the 1990 May Day parade, he was angered by catcalls and taunts from marchers; his response was to demand a tough law barring criticism of the Soviet president. Reformers toned it down so that punishment—up to six years in jail—could be imposed only for insulting the Soviet president "in an indecent way." The implication was obscenity, but the wording was so vague that no one could be sure that the new law did not bar political criticism as well.[4]

But even though *glasnost* does not connote the full freedoms that American newspapers and television networks take for granted, it has been a crucial and essential catalyst for Gorbachev's reforms. "*Glasnost* comes from the Russian word *glas*, or voice," to quote Vladimir Pozner. "So it literally means voiceness, or speaking out." And this speaking out, even with its imperfections, has broken down political taboos. It has given legitimacy to pent-up popular grievances, and stimulated that provocatively Western democratic notion called pluralism. It gave all those isolated critics a chance to build political networks. It made possible the watershed election of March 1989, which sent dozens of high regional Party officials into the shock of defeat. Without *glasnost,* the entire range of Gorbachev reforms would not have been possible.

In December 1984, even before he rose to supreme power, Gorbachev had called for *glasnost,* asserting the need for political candor and hinting at his future use of the media as a tool for reform. "Broad, timely, and frank information is testimony to trust in people, respect for their intelligence and feelings, their ability to interpret various events themselves," he told a conference on Communist ideology. "It raises the activeness of the toilers. *Glasnost* in the work of Party and state organs is an effective means of struggling against bureaucratic distortion. . . ."[5] In short, Gorbachev recognized the enormous gap between the dismal realities of Soviet life and the fatuous pretensions of Party propaganda, and recognized that he could not gain credibility until he had closed that gap.

Yet strangely, Gorbachev did not begin as boldly as he had foreshadowed. His reform program has gone through several stages. In the first of these, for most of 1985 and 1986, Gorbachev tried conservative reforms, picking up where his mentor Yuri Andropov had left off. In 1985, he launched a campaign against alcoholism, pushed for work discipline, purged corrupt Brezhnev hacks, and promoted progress in science and technology. In the economy, he began not by dispersing power or breaking up ministries but by creating new superministries and superagencies. In the media and in cultural life, there was a relaxation of controls. He and other political leaders spoke more openly about current problems and past mistakes. But these were very modest beginnings.

On April 26, 1986, a little more than a year after Gorbachev took over, the nuclear accident at Chernobyl showed that when a catastrophe occurred, the reflexive reaction of the Soviet leadership—Gorbachev included—was to hide behind a shroud of secrecy. Even with neighboring countries clamoring for information because of alarming rises in nuclear radiation and satellite photos of the damaged Chernobyl reactor, it was four full days after the reactor explosion before Moscow made a minimal acknowledgment that there had been a nuclear accident. In mid-May, Gorbachev spoke of the dead, but in a defensive, chauvinistic tone, he criticized Western reaction to the incident. It took time for the real story of Chernobyl, and the radiation hazards it released, to dribble out.

Even today, activists and experts in the surrounding areas complain, with good reason, that the Ministry of Health and other government agencies covered up their failures to evacuate people rapidly, and are still sitting on the terrible truth about radiation sickness among tens of thousands of people in the Ukraine and Byelorussia. On October 15, 1989, *Moscow News* ran a major story on the cover-ups at Chernobyl, headlined THE BIG LIE.

If nothing else, the embarrassment of the cover-up helped propel Gorbachev in late 1986 into a full-blown strategy of *glasnost.* In the fall, the Soviet press reported the sinking of a passenger ship on the Black Sea with the loss of some four hundred lives—an unprecedented admission for the Soviet government. In December, Gorbachev dismissed the state overlord of the movie industry, months after an upheaval in the cinematographers' union. Around the time of his October 1986 summit in Iceland with President Reagan, Gorbachev released a dissident poet, Irina Ratushinskaya. There were other partial gestures.

But the real signal of a major change in the works, and of Gorbachev's open political alliance with the intelligentsia against the Party bureaucracy, was his celebrated telephone call on December 16, 1986, to Andrei Sakharov, the dissident Soviet physicist and winner of the Nobel Peace Prize.

Sakharov had been banished to exile and political isolation in the city of Gorky for nearly seven years; KGB agents had grabbed him off a Moscow sidewalk, jammed him into a car, and shipped him out of town without a trial or a hearing. As the most vocal domestic critic of the Brezhnev leadership and, specifically, of Brezhnev's decision to send Soviet troops into Afghanistan, Sakharov was a genuine hero to the Soviet intelligentsia. He was revered as the country's most outspoken exponent of human rights and intellectual freedom. He spoke with such courage and integrity that even as a solitary individual, he was a moral force to be reckoned with.

Gorbachev's decision to lift the ban on Sakharov, his invitation to the physicist "to return to work for the public good" as a willing partner in *perestroika,* was a crucial symbolic gesture. In the West, this move was immediately seen as a sign of Gorbachev's liberalism. But it was more than that. It provided the Soviet leader with a bridge to the liberal, reformist wing of the intelligentsia and signaled a new phase in his move toward democratic reforms. The changes Gorbachev wrought in the political institutions of his country reached a crescendo in 1989 and 1990; but the ground was prepared by Sakharov's release and the acceleration of *glasnost* that took place in the winter of 1986–87.

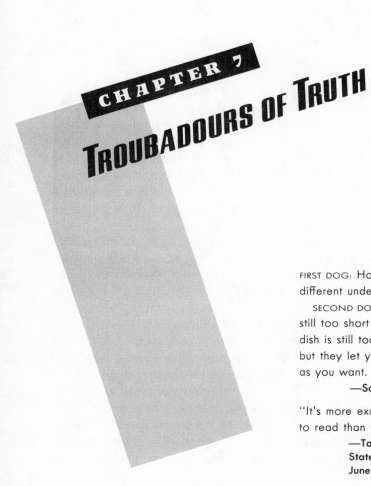

CHAPTER 7

TROUBADOURS OF TRUTH

FIRST DOG: How are things different under Gorbachev?

SECOND DOG: Well, the chain is still too short and the food dish is still too far away to reach, but they let you bark as loud as you want.

—Soviet political anecdote

"It's more exciting right now to read than to live."[1]

—Tankred Golenpolsky
State Publishing Committee
June 1988

When Gorbachev broke the dam with *glasnost,* he caused a deluge.

Suddenly, criticizing the Soviet past, the Soviet present, even the Soviet leadership, was not only tolerated, it was encouraged—in the press, books, theater, and films, and on television.

The press switched from being Party cheerleader to being Party watchdog. It was like a coiled spring suddenly released.

Especially from 1987 onward, newspapers and magazines blossomed forth with exposés about crime, prostitution, and high-level corruption.

The weekly magazine *Ogonek* ran confessions by former KGB investigators and prison guards. In the Party's theoretical journal, *Kommunist*, a senior KGB official conceded that political abuses of power had been caused in part by excessive secrecy. In mid-1989, the government admitted, after more than thirty years of denial, that the world's worst nuclear accident, an explosion of waste from the production of plutonium, had taken place in 1957 in the remote Ural Mountains, two thousand miles east of Moscow. The main military newspaper, *Krasnaya Zvezda*, revealed that in 1953, the Soviets had tested atomic bombs near some of their own military units, to check the psychological effects on combat troops.

Instead of promulgating false hosannas to Party leaders, television, too, began to carry candid political debates, live man-in-the-street interviews about such topics as housing conditions and whether to continue the military draft; they broadcast films of the Stalin show trials of the 1930s.

A number of movies long blocked by censors were released, among them *Scarecrow*, an allegory about Stalinist-style group persecution of an innocent schoolgirl by her classmates; *Rasputin*, a movie that depicted Czar Nicholas II not as a cardboard villain but as a well-meaning yet emotionally troubled and weak-willed man; *Commissar*, a sympathetic view of Jewish humanism and suffering, bottled up for twenty years; *Confession*, a chronicle of the bleak life of a Soviet drug addict; and *Is It Easy to Be Young?*, a documentary about Baltic youth who go on a rampage and the squalor of their lives.[2]

Books long banned by censors, such as George Orwell's *1984* and Boris Pasternak's *Doctor Zhivago*, started appearing in print.

In 1989, the literary event of the year was the serialization of *The Gulag Archipelago*, Aleksandr Solzhenitsyn's devastating record of prison-camp repression and cruelty, from Lenin and Stalin to Brezhnev. It took Sergei Zalygin, chief editor of the magazine *Novy Mir*, more than a year of relentless pressure to persuade the Politburo that under *glasnost*, the Soviet Union's most famous living author could not be ignored.

As recently as late 1988, Vadim Medvedev, then the Politburo's czar of press and culture, had declared that Solzhenitsyn would not be published. Many ranking Communist Party officials thoroughly detested Solzhenitsyn for his self-righteous defiance of the Kremlin from his exile in Vermont, as well as for his openly anti-Communist, monarchist views.

Of all Solzhenitsyn's works, *Gulag*, which explicitly blamed Lenin for the evil violence of Soviet dictatorship, was the hardest for Party leaders to swallow. In the early 1970s, mere possession of a few typescript pages of the book was enough to risk one's being sent to Siberia. Back in February 1974, Solzhenitsyn had released to me one then-unpublished portion, for an article, and he was arrested the next day and ejected from the country. But in the late 1980s, Solzhenitsyn was insisting that *Gulag* be the first of his banned works to be published in the U.S.S.R. and rebuffing suggestions that his novels *Cancer Ward* or *The First Circle* be published first, to break the ice. The argument raged on for months.

Ultimately, a Party official confirmed, it took Gorbachev's personal intervention for *Novy Mir* to begin publication of *Gulag*. And Party conservatives retaliated by holding up the magazine's paper supply in the spring of 1990, blocking publication of the March, April, and May issues.[3]

Other books hidden away by Soviet authors came off the shelves. In the dark years of heavy censorship, the most liberal novelists had written "for the drawer," as Soviets say, producing books they knew would never see the light of day and stashing them away in desk drawers. *Glasnost* brought them out into the daylight. One of the first was Anatoly Rybakov's novel about life during the Stalinist purges, *Children of the Arbat,* which the author kept in the drawer for twenty years. Even more politically shocking was the scathing portrait of Lenin, the most sacred icon in the Communist pantheon, in Vasily Grossman's *Forever Flowing,* written in 1963. In language previously unthinkable in Soviet literature, Grossman harshly portrayed Lenin's fanatic drive for power, his "intolerance . . . his contempt for freedom, his cruelty toward those who held different opinions and his capacity to wipe off the face of the earth, without trembling, not only fortresses but entire countries, districts and provinces that questioned his orthodox truth."[4] Just printing Grossman's short novel, starting with the November 1989 issue of the magazine *Oktyabr,* nearly cost chief editor Anatoly Anayev his job. Hard-liners went after his scalp, but he survived.

FRONT-LINE DISPATCHES FROM AFGHANISTAN

The liberal faction of the press was using Gorbachev's *glasnost* for an open assault on current policy—specifically, Soviet intervention in the Afghan war.

During a television roundtable in mid-June 1988, Fyodor Burlatsky, a former speech writer for Khrushchev, asserted that the Soviet intervention in Afghanistan had been a mistake. *Izvestia* columnist Aleksandr Bovin added that sending one hundred thousand troops into Afghanistan was typical of the excessive use of force in Soviet foreign policy.

Several months later, the weekly *Ogonek* ran an interview with General Valentin I. Varrenikov, for four years the Soviet commander in Kabul, who disclosed that the Soviet General Staff "did not support the idea of sending our troops into Afghanistan" until it was overruled by the Brezhnev Politburo.

This interview with General Varrenikov was the work of Artyom Borovik, one of the new breed of reporters, a jaunty twenty-eight-year-old who is impatient with the old-style Soviet propaganda-journalism formerly practiced by his father, Genrikh Borovik, and who even chafes at the limits of *glasnost.* In July 1987, Borovik had caused a sensation by filing the first honest, graphic dispatches from the front. He described how the flower of Soviet youth was dying, their boots oozing with blood, their stomachs pierced by bullet holes, their armored vehicles crumpled by land mines. "War tears the halo of secrecy away from death," Borovik wrote in his "Diary of a Reporter."

For the first time, the readers of *Ogonek* could see the war from the inside; they could sit in the foxholes, feel the fear and loneliness of Soviet troops dying far away from home. Borovik wrote about the cold terror of a night ambush, the gunfire, and the darkened sky lit up by tracers. He quoted from the diary of a dead helicopter pilot, who described how his flight suit had smelled for two days of charred flesh, from the corpses of three comrades he had recovered from the burned ruins of their downed helicopter.[5]

To get his unprecedented dispatches past the military censors, Borovik had hooked General Varrenikov himself into helping him.

Borovik told me that when the censors had balked at the pieces he had written, he had phoned the general and said: " 'Listen, I've written a big, big documentary and these guys in censorship won't let it go because they think you guys are, you know, staging a ballet in Afghanistan, raising flowers and nothing else. They don't want to show real life.'

"The general got angry," Borovik recalled, "because guys die there, they're risking their lives, and the press writes ridiculous things. So he helped me. He didn't read the articles. He just phoned them and said, 'Let Borovik publish what he saw, you know, the truth of what he saw.' Probably he wouldn't have made this call if I'd shown him the articles. But this is how I got the visa—we call it a visa—of approval from the military."[6]

Borovik's editor, Vitaly Korotich, told me that the whole project had even higher-level political approval—from Gorbachev himself.

"I have a hot-line phone—Gorbachev gave me this phone." Korotich is a chain-smoker whose flat, pudgy face looks as beaten as a prizefighter's but whose soft brown eyes betray his vulnerability. "I can call anyone on this phone," he bragged. "So I called Akhromeyev, chief of the General

Staff. I told him, 'I want to do a story on our boys in Afghanistan, a real story.' He said, 'Screw you and your journalists. They always want to make a story without taking any risks.' I told him, 'No, I want my boy to be in the front line with your boys.' He said, 'And if he gets killed, they'll all get angry at the army.' But I pushed him, and for the first time Akhromeyev gave me permission to send a reporter to the front. If he did not, he knew I would print that he refused. I understood that I must publish something about the end of this war to prepare the public. You see, it was already understood that the war must be finished."7

In short, he explained, Gorbachev, who had publicly lamented that the war in Afghanistan was "a bleeding wound," was using glasnost and specifically Korotich to prepare public opinion for the withdrawal of Soviet troops. The stream of articles on Afghanistan, just like articles criticizing Stalin, the Red Terror, and official secrecy, all suited Gorbachev's policy.

This interplay between the press and public opinion was a deliberate part of Gorbachev's new strategy of overturning old institutions as well as old policies. He was manipulating the press just as surely as American presidents do—but in ways that Soviets were unaccustomed to.

This pressure on public opinion continued for several years, turning the troop withdrawal from a political blow to Gorbachev into a public-relations triumph. In May 1988, Tass, the official Soviet news agency, revealed for the first time official Soviet casualty figures in Afghanistan—13,310 killed in action, 35,478 wounded, and 311 missing in action. To see such figures printed in the Soviet press, which in the seventies could not even reveal the number of traffic deaths in Moscow, was almost unbelievable—not only for me, but for Russians as well. Each new press revelation set people abuzz. Back in the seventies, people used to buy official newspapers to use as toilet paper; they were cheap, only three cents apiece. Now people were lining up to read the latest editions, displayed on billboards and walls, because there was so much news.

When I arrived in May 1988, I found it difficult to reach people by phone; friends told me it was because they were all so busy calling each other with the latest disclosures. One acquaintance, Tankred Golenpolsky of the State Publishing Committee, said exuberantly: "It's more exciting right now to read than to live! The oxygen of democracy is intoxicating and contagious."

There was a joke making the rounds those days about the newspaper Moscow News (Moskovskiye Novosti), which had gone from a pap and propaganda sheet for tourists to one of the hottest newspapers of glasnost, full of juicy items and hard to find before it sold out. In the anecdote, one Muscovite calls a friend to ask if he has managed to buy the latest issue.

"Yes, I got it," answers the friend, with a certain pride.

"What's in it?" the first man inquires.

The second man pauses, obviously thinking things over, and then replies: "Can't talk about it on the telephone."

Russians love that story because it is so rich with irony about their old fear of saying anything controversial or revealing on the telephone, for fear of listening devices. They were amused that those same old habits lingered on in the new era, even though the press was printing things they had previously not dared to mention on the phone.

The public hunger for news had generated a genuine competition among the press for readers. The hot new liberal publications that were pushing the limits of *glasnost* gained readers, while the circulation of orthodox, Party-line outlets fell. From 1985 to 1989, *Izvestia*'s circulation nearly doubled from 5.7 to 10.1 million, while *Pravda*'s stayed steady at about 9.6 million, and was always slow to sell at newsstands. *Komsomolskaya Pravda*, which went after younger readers with a liberal slant on the news, jumped from 12.8 to 17.5 million; the radical weekly magazine *Ogonek* shot up from 596,000 subscribers to more than 3 million; and the weekly *Argumenty i Fakty* skyrocketed from 1.4 to 20.4 million within four years. At the same time, the army newspaper, *Krasnaya Zvezda (Red Star)* drifted down from 1.6 to 1.4 million. People shunned the propaganda peddlers; they were drawn to real news.[8]

All of this was a remarkable change; fifteen years earlier it had taken a microscopic search to find and decipher nuggets of interest in the Soviet press; *Pravda* and *Izvestia* had left intellectuals numbed with boredom. I was stunned now to read about thousands of people marching in the streets of Tomsk, Omsk, and Irkutsk, defying Party leaders deep in the Soviet heartland, and to see pictures as well. In the seventies, protests never were written about in the Soviet press. Now *Izvestia,* the government paper, was reporting that in Sakhalin, on the Pacific coast, popular protests had become so strong that a regional Party boss had been forced to resign. The news described hundreds of thousands of people demonstrating in the capitals of Armenia and Azerbaijan, where violence had broken out over control of the mountainous region of Nagorno-Karabakh, an Armenian enclave turned over to Azerbaijan by Stalin. Party leaders in both republics had been fired. The Baltic republics were also exploding with unrest—"the singing revolution" in Estonia, the stunning rise of the national front Sajudis in Lithuania.

In Moscow, it was reported that the Supreme Soviet, for seven decades one of the most supine legislative bodies in the world, had taken the unprecedented step of refusing to rubber-stamp a law proposed by the government. A handful of delegates had the temerity to protest that the 90 percent tax rate proposed by ministry bureaucrats for economic cooperatives was strangling the new private sector. The government, evidently surprised by the opposition, backed off and promised to rewrite the law.

Reading *Pravda* one morning at breakfast, I laughed out loud at the impertinence of one letter to the editor. Gorbachev had been lecturing Communist Party officials to stop interfering in the day-to-day operation of the economy and government. Now one reader suggested that Gorbachev (who was not mentioned by name) follow his own advice and that the Politburo, holy of holies, pinnacle of Soviet power, stop poking its nose into other people's business.

More sweeping in its implications was the sudden announcement that all across the country, history examinations for high school seniors were being canceled because the old textbooks were so full of lies about Stalin, Brezhnev, and the Soviet past.

Russians were suddenly catching up with their own history, and learning what we in the West had known for decades. It was a time warp; the papers were bringing out daily disclosures about Stalin's tyranny and the Red Terror, debating how many millions had perished, urging the rehabilitation of Stalin's old rival Nikolai Bukharin, an advocate of a mixed economy.

Television, too, carried scenes never shown before to a mass Soviet audience. The talk of Moscow was a documentary called *Protsess (Trial)* that included segments of Stalin's show trials, depicting the insanity of the Stalinist purges of the 1930s. There on the screen was prosecutor Andrei Vishinsky, looking like a speeded-up Charlie Chaplin figure, sending old Bolsheviks to certain death based on trumped-up charges or on confessions extracted by torture. There, suddenly, mingling with Lenin and the others, were Trotsky and Bukharin, one murdered by Stalin, the other purged, and both nonpersons for sixty years now. The new *glasnost* television had people glued to their sets.

More bombshells exploded in leading literary magazines. A small group of intellectuals were pushing the limits of *glasnost* beyond officially encouraged attacks on Stalin, questioning the very legitimacy of Soviet Communism by tracing the roots of Stalinist tyranny back to Lenin and Marx. In the May 1988 issue of *Novy Mir*, an economic writer named Vasily Selyunin was the first to implicate Lenin for justifying the systematic use of state terror. "First, it was used to suppress opponents of the

Revolution, then it shifted to potential opponents, and finally it became a means of solving purely economic tasks," Selyunin wrote.[9] In a daring bit of ideological heresy, Selyunin suggested that Stalin's despotism was not accidental, but virtually inevitable under the Soviet system. Any system that concentrates all power in a single party and where the state owns all means of production, he argued, has a tendency to produce despots.

This seditious logic was carried another step by Aleksandr Tsipko, a philosopher and former Central Committee staff official, who suggested that Marxist theory was the root cause of Stalinism. "Stalin didn't just create his kingdom and strengthen his own one-man rule," Tsipko wrote in a scholarly journal. "He built socialism in accordance with prescriptive theories." Pointing his finger at Marx, Tsipko asserted, "When cracks appear in the walls of a new building," it is time to reexamine the foundations and the architecture. "We must doubtless begin . . . at the beginning, with the word, the blueprint, with our theoretical principles."[10]

GLASNOST OF THE STREETS

Even on the streets of Moscow, I could feel the ferment of glasnost. Pushkin Square, right outside the offices of Moscow News, had become the Soviet equivalent of London's Hyde Park. In the 1970s, a handful of dissidents used to gather there on Human Rights Day, December 5, but back then there were usually more foreign correspondents than dissidents—and both groups were outnumbered by plainclothes police agents. A dissident speaker would begin to read a statement, his colleagues would unfurl a banner, and usually before the banner was completely unfolded, KGB agents would have grabbed the demonstrators and hustled them off to jail.

But in 1988, the sidewalks in the square were jammed with people: They were reading the latest editions of Moscow News, buying and selling all sorts of unofficial—and previously underground—newspapers. Occasionally, the Old Guard still showed its muscle; the militia would swoop in to make some arrests. But this no longer seemed to intimidate the dissidents, or the crowd of people debating every conceivable issue—from how to fix the economy to the right of minority republics to secede from the Soviet Union.

Elsewhere in the city, the atmosphere on the streets was palpably more relaxed. On the strolling mall of the Old Arbat, crowds flocked around young groups with guitars, singing songs that mocked the political elite, the Afghan war, or the love affair Westerners were having with Gorbachev. "Perestroika, perestroika," sang Nikita Dzhigurda, a husky-throated youth. *"Our new* GenSek *[Party Leader], powerful or not, goes from one unfinished* stroika *[construction site] to another. The dumbfounded foreigners are naïve about him, my brothers. The foreign serenaders sing and toast to Russia."*

What struck even deeper resonance was an old favorite, an illicit song from the seventies by the late writer Aleksandr Galich, but always sung clandestinely back then. Now here it was out on the streets, this song about the life of the elite in their luxurious country *dachas* outside Moscow:

> *Grass is green there*
> *And Stalin's eagles*
> *Eat shish kebab and fine chocolates*
> *Behind seven fences.*
> *Bodyguards and informants*
> *Protect them from the people.*
> *They make us watch films*
> *About factories and collective farms*
> *And at night, they watch imported films about whores,*
> *And they like Marilyn Monroe.*

The bitter truth of that song got a laugh—and a grimace—from the crowd.

In the hotels, I found that both foreigners and Soviets had become less suspicious of each other. In the old days, we always assumed that the "key ladies" on each floor of Soviet hotels, who insisted on holding our keys whenever we left our rooms, kept a close eye on us and opened our rooms to allow the KGB to search whenever we were out. On walks, we would look over our shoulders to see if people were following us. At the National Hotel one day, my colleague Louis Menashe was talking with the maid about what differences she noticed now. "Oh, the Americans are much less nervous now," she said. "They are not looking over their shoulders all the time." Nor were the key ladies any longer demanding our keys.

Strolling in the wild, wooded meadows of Izmailovo Park, I noticed other changes. Not long after I had left Moscow at the end of 1974, underground artists had tried to hold an exhibition of forbidden paintings in the park; the KGB had used bulldozers to break it up. Now the park was a giant flea market, its pathways jammed with once-forbidden items—easel after easel of abstract and irreverent paintings, religious icons, old czarist medals and emblems, miniature statues of Christ on the cross, of Gorbachev as the Statue of Liberty. There were political buttons poking fun at the KGB, at Yegor Ligachev—then the Politburo's number two figure—at Raisa Gorbacheva, at Gorbachev's reforms (*Perestroika:* 2 + 2 = 5), playing on an old line of Dostoyevsky's, mocking the dreamy Russian notion that the world is what you want it to be. Favored items, at 25 rubles (officially $42), were rubber masks lampooning the faces of Brezhnev and other former Soviet leaders. Foster Wiley, one of the cameramen for our television series, caught a mask maker peeling off a series of masks—Brezhnev, Khrushchev, and Stalin, each with a punch line mocking Stalin's contempt for the people: BROTHERS AND SISTERS, GO TO HELL!

I found that, as always, Muscovites told wry jokes about their predicament; in fact, their lives had not improved under Gorbachev, even though they now were freer to speak out about it. One old political joke, revived with a new twist, was about a Soviet dog, back from a long trip. The dog asks an older, wiser mutt how life is different under Gorbachev.

"Well," says the old-timer, "the chain is still too short and the food dish is still too far away to reach, but they let you bark as loud as you want."

Even out in the provinces, different regions had their own symbols of *glasnost.* One of my favorites, pointed out to me by Pavel Nikitin, a newspaper correspondent in Yaroslavl, concerned the bells of the ancient city of Rostov, a rich musical chorus that ranged in size from modest to massive and required a team of ringers.

Bells have great symbolic importance in Russian history. As Greg Guroff, a friend and Russian historian, observed, historically bells have been used to summon Russians—to worship in their churches, to gather in town meetings, or to defend their cities against fire, or invaders. The famous Russian émigré writer Aleksandr Herzen named his nineteenth-century democratic newspaper *The Bell.* In the 1930s, Stalin ordered that thousands of churches all over the Soviet Union be closed, and their bells destroyed or their clangers removed. Among those silenced were the famous bells of Rostov.

In silencing those bells, Stalin was metaphorically silencing the people of Russia.

Not until Gorbachev's clarion call of *glasnost* did the bells of Rostov ring out freely once again.

Pavel Nikitin smiled as he remembered the ringing of the bells of Rostov in 1987—for the first time in more than half a century. "That," he told me, "is the sound of *glasnost.*"

THE PIED PIPERS OF THE CINEMA

If the primary vehicle of Gorbachev's drive to awaken his people was the mass media, movies and television were in the forefront.

During Khrushchev's cultural thaw, plays or novels such as Solzhenitsyn's *One Day in the Life of Ivan Denisovich* were the primary signs of new freedom. Young poets, especially Yevtushenko and Voznesensky, were the pied pipers of intellectual excitement, their poetry readings at times bringing out five or ten thousand people, filling soccer stadiums. But in the 1980s, Gorbachev had to reach audiences in the *millions* to create the kind of wide popular upheaval he needed.

Moreover, in terms of the media's power and influence, life inside the Soviet Union was becoming more like the rest of the world. The tube and the screen had the biggest impact; movies could draw audiences of eighty million, national television 150 million. Gorbachev needed to tap into that power.

If there was one movie that changed the climate and the popular political mind, it was *Repentance,* a powerful surrealist allegory of Stalinist terror and the cult of Stalin, produced in Soviet Georgia by Tengiz Abuladze. Its appearance in late 1986 caused a political earthquake. *Repentance* became the cinematic flagship of *glasnost.*

Tens of millions of people flocked to see the film. They broke into applause at the parody dictator who looks fat (Mussolini) and has a brush mustache (Hitler), but is modeled on Stalin and his last secret-police chief, Lavrenti Beria. They wept at the terror. Gorbachev himself, I heard, had cried on seeing the film, perhaps remembering his own grandfather's arrest.

One poignant scene portrayed the pitiful efforts of families hunting for scraps of news about loved ones sent off to Stalin's forced-labor camps. In the movie, a mother and daughter scramble frantically among logs that have floated downriver from the gulag. Prisoners have carved their initials on the logs, and these two women search frantically for some sign that their husband and father is still alive; but they search in vain.

The making of *Repentance* is revealing about Soviet cultural politics at the dawn of the Gorbachev era. The film had been written in the early 1980s, and was produced by 1984—a year *before* Gorbachev came to power. It had the political blessing of Gorbachev's close friend Eduard Shevardnadze, who was Georgia's Communist Party leader until Gorbachev appointed him foreign minister.

Shevardnadze told me that in 1982, while Brezhnev was still alive, Moscow censors had rejected the script as unacceptable for nationwide production and distribution in the Russian language. But Shevardnadze, who read the script himself three times, decided to permit the film to go into production in the Georgian language and for Georgian television—a domain under his control.[11] At least, he indicated, that was the pretext under which the film was permitted. Production took place while Andropov was in power, and things were starting to open up a bit. But by 1984, when production was completed, Andropov had died, and the winds from the Kremlin had turned chillier. As a result, *Repentance* was not released after its completion; in fact, it wasn't until eighteen months after Gorbachev came to power that the movie was finally shown in Georgia, and distributed, with Russian voice-overs, across the nation.

Another body blow to the old taboos was dealt by *Little Vera*, a box-office sensation that included nude scenes and explicit sex. Its twenty-eight-year-old director, Vasily Pichul, has a dark, gypsy-like face and a *dolce vita* air. I thought at first that he seemed like one of the petulant young offspring of the Soviet elite, derisively nicknamed the "golden youth" by others. But it turned out that Pichul was the son of a blue-collar worker from Mariupol, an industrial wasteland far from Moscow and more desolate and depressing than the South Side of Chicago. The real power of *Little Vera*, released in the West after it was seen by more than forty million Soviets, is its candid portrayal of the caldron of frustration and rage among Soviet workers. The father in the movie family is driven to uncontrollable drinking bouts and domestic violence, and the daughter, Little Vera, sleeps around and lives such a morally bankrupt, aimless existence that she winds up taking an overdose of pills.

Pichul's wife, María, whose Spanish ancestors came to Moscow after the Spanish Civil War, wrote the screenplay as a biting indictment of the misery to which the "heroic proletariat" was consigned by the Soviet leadership. When Pichul went home for the premiere, he was expecting a hero's welcome: He had shattered the hypocritical pretenses, promulgated by Soviet propaganda, that Mariupol was a model city; he had presented the unvarnished truth on behalf of the workers in his hometown. But he found instead that his parents and other workers were furious, resentful at what they took to be an exposé of the tawdry emptiness of their lives.

"My parents were insulted!" Pichul told me. "My mother said, 'You have insulted us. You have put our family's whole life up on the screen in front of the whole Soviet Union.' When my parents walked down the street, people pointed at them. One woman pointed at my mother and said, 'Is your family life really such a nightmare? Is your daughter so awful?' My mother couldn't handle it."[12]

I later learned that this reaction was typical of the response that Gorbachev's reforms produced among many people, especially blue-collar workers. In theory, these people were demanding change—they were fed up with the degrading misery of their lives, or they were infuriated with having to work for dictatorial bosses in inefficient factories. But when someone came along and offered them a chance to go out and work on their own, or exposed their misery in order to reform it, they recoiled, denouncing those who spoke the truth. They recoiled from change, preferring the old, familiar hell.

"Of course, this film is *not* about my own family," Pichul said, and it sounded as if he'd repeated this hundreds of times to his relatives and friends. "But I know this life. I am not a stranger from America, or a man from Mars. I have put in this movie what I have seen with my own eyes, and reflected about. Everybody knows this life; they recognize it in my film. Some people just don't like to *see* it up there on the screen. But *Little Vera* is very popular. Millions and millions go to see it. So you see, most people are sick of lies and half-truths."

Little Vera represented an important breakthrough for both artistic freedom and economic reform, and it was powerful because it was so close to real life. For in the unending trench warfare that Gorbachev's policies have triggered between radical advocates of change and Old Guard hardliners, documentaries have generally become more effective weapons than feature films. Once Gorbachev brought the political battle out in the open, fact had more persuasive force than fiction—especially after so many decades of censorship. The mere admission of reality had shock effect; it changed the nature of public dialogue.

In terms of the Afghan war, for example, the most powerful stories, aside from Artyom Borovik's front-line dispatches, were moving documentaries such as *Pain* and *Homecoming.* One portrayed the palpable grief of parents who had lost their sons; the other showed legless and armless veterans being helped off troop transports, and then later living as civilians, enraged by their country's indifference and ingratitude for their sacrifice in a distant and ugly war. The harsh atrocities of the gulag were dramatically brought home by documentaries such as *Greater Light* and *Solovetsky Power.* These films were pieced together from archives and from the bitter remembrances of onetime true believers, still incredulous and pained by having been unjustly jailed and by having seen so many comrades go to their deaths.

Documentaries became powerful weapons, too, in shaping reactions to current events. Reformers used them to expose the repressive instincts of Party hard-liners seeking to stem the tide of change.

When Soviet troops used poison gas and pick shovels to crush a peaceful demonstration in Tbilisi, Georgia, in April 1989, killing at least sixteen people, Georgian filmmakers put together footage of the brutality and made the army's excessive use of force a national cause célèbre. Eldar Shingalaya, head of the Georgian Filmmakers' Union, showed the documentary to Western correspondents and to deputies in the Congress of People's Deputies, creating a political storm and bringing about an investigation.

When Gorbachev sent massive forces to occupy the city of Baku in Azerbaijan in January 1990, killing more than one hundred civilians, the Azerbaijanis made their case against the Kremlin with gruesome films of the fighting and the dead.

In both these cases, films that were at first circulated privately became part of the national political debate. When the national press was giving skimpy or slanted coverage of events in the minority republics and Soviet authorities were denying that they used excessive violence, the films undercut their credibility and exposed the truth.

One filmmaker who has seized on the opening of *glasnost* to produce several politically potent, journalistic-style documentaries is Arkady Ruderman. Before Gorbachev, the richly bearded, forty-two-year-old Byelorussian was a quiet-spoken, laconic, rather conventional director at the Byelorussian studios; he had never attracted attention for political daring, nor was he known as a fighter by nature. But since 1987, Ruderman has come out with three striking films. One, developed from footage and interviews, told the real story of the Soviet invasion of Czechoslovakia, months before the Kremlin was prepared to admit that the incursion had been a brutal suppression of Prague's experiment in democracy. Eventually the official line embraced that view, and the Ruderman film has now played successfully in official Soviet theaters.

But the fate of two other Ruderman films has been more problematic.

One film concerned the violent suppression of a peaceful demonstration in Minsk by hard-line Byelorussian authorities. In October 1988, police were sent out with billy clubs to break up a peaceful rally calling for a memorial to local victims of Stalinist mass killings. At considerable risk, three local cameramen shot pictures, on amateur video cameras, of the police brutality, and Ruderman put their material together, along with sequences of a court battle over charges and countercharges about Stalin's actions and role in history. That documentary was called *Counter-Suit.*

Ruderman's second film, *Theater in the Time of* Glasnost *and* Perestroika, also made the case that neo-Stalinists were still running Byelorussia, describing the repression of the works and life story of the artist Marc Chagall, a native Byelorussian. The film detailed how authorities had blocked an exhibit of Chagall's paintings and fired an editor of the Byelorussian encyclopedia because she approved a favorable article about the painter. According to Ruderman, a top Communist Party official in Minsk claimed that Chagall was part of a "subversive intrigue," and the encyclopedia wound up printing a tendentious attack on Chagall.

I was interested not only by what Ruderman was reporting and his difficulties in trying to get the films shown, but also by what his experience illustrates about the difficulties of carrying out Gorbachev's policies at the local level. I was told in Moscow and Minsk that both films offended Byelorussian authorities, and that they were blocked by censors there. Even under *glasnost,* this was enough to keep the films from being circulated to regular movie houses through the state-run distribution system. But Ruderman got some help from powerful reformists at the national level.

Even in 1988, Byelorussian film studios, obviously under political pressure, had refused to do technical work on Ruderman's films, so he had shifted to a more sympathetic studio in Leningrad; he managed this with the help of a famous, well-established filmmaker, Aleksei Gherman, whose own film of life in Stalinist times, *My Friend, Ivan Lapshin,* was kept under wraps from 1971 to 1987, when it was finally shown. Andrei Smirnov, then leader of the national Cinematographers' Union, told me that he had personally taken Ruderman's film about the Chagall episode and shown it at a Soviet film festival in Sverdlovsk, where it caused a great stir. Smirnov also helped Ruderman enter *Counter-Suit,* the other film, in the 1989 Leningrad film festival, where it won a prize, although it had still not been officially released by the censors.[13]

Ruderman also became his own distributor, like other documentary filmmakers I met around the country. When censors stop them, they become traveling minstrels of the cinema, troubadours of truth going from city to city, republic to republic, with their contraband films hidden in their luggage. They show the films to film clubs, reformist groups, or sympathetic political activists—small but usually enthusiastic and influential audiences. This is done primarily for exposure, not profit. Sherry Jones, one producer of our American documentary series *Inside Gorbachev's USSR,* found Ruderman showing his movie *Counter-Suit* to an unofficial film club in Yaroslavl, a city north of Moscow, and about six hundred miles from Minsk. These people had seen no press coverage of the events Ruderman portrayed, and they were fascinated both by the news of the Byelorussian demonstration and its suppression and by the ways in which Ruderman had managed to gather his material. He described to them how the three cameramen had taken pictures, trying to keep their amateur cameras hidden from the police. He said the boldest of the three had been spotted by the police and arrested—and he had managed to keep his camera operating all the while, so that he filmed his own arrest. The police took away his cassette, but then, inexplicably, gave it back to him without destroying the film.

Ruderman also entertained the film club with a story of how he had outwitted the censors. When he had submitted *Counter-Suit* to the Leningrad film festival, he had left in a segment where the poet Yevgeny Yevtushenko was moving his lips but saying nothing, because the censor, a woman whose face had turned white at Yevtushenko's words, had banned that one piece of script. Instead of removing the picture, Ruderman had just cut out the words. Journalists covering the film festival had asked about the missing words, anticipating some stunning disclosure, but Ruderman told them Yevtushenko was only talking about a famous Russian writer whose name begins with *S.* He knew everyone would immediately realize that he meant Aleksandr Solzhenitsyn. Typical of the confused situation in the Soviet Union today, approval had been given for Solzhenitsyn to be published in Moscow, while censors in Leningrad were still excising the mere mention of his name!

Even stranger was the fact that press coverage of the episode won Ruderman an appointment at the office of *glavlit*, the chief censor of Leningrad, where he could argue for release of his film.

"The head censor turned out to be the most pleasant and well-mannered person," Ruderman told the film club. "He told me that my profession was an absolutely wonderful profession, but these journalists are scoundrels: They care only about hot facts and sensational news; they are always hired to attack the censors!"

Ruderman went on to describe their dialogue:

"He looked at the piece in the script and said, 'I don't see anything special about it.'

"I said, 'I don't see anything special about it either.'

"He said, 'It was a mistake. I'll give an order. Don't worry. Everything will be all right.'

"I said that I would work on the film and that I thought this scene was a bit too long and that I would make it shorter.

"Then he said, 'Yes, I think the film is much too long. Why don't you cut it here, here, and here.' "[14]

The audience roared with laughter, because they could see from the version Ruderman had just shown them that he had not cut it at all—and that Yevtushenko was heard to utter the forbidden name, Solzhenitsyn.

"I think that the Soviet Union is now an interesting place for documentary filmmakers because everything is moving, everything is bubbling," Ruderman remarked later. "People are turned on to politics because they finally realize that politics is not an abstract understanding of something far from their personal lives. All of a sudden we understand that politics is our life, that politics decides how we are going to live."[15]

As Ruderman explained it, *glasnost* had given his documentary filmmaking a new purpose—to present object lessons to people. It was his view that if his film on the 1968 Soviet invasion of Czechoslovakia had appeared in the early 1970s, it might have prevented the Soviet invasion of Afghanistan in 1979. And, had his film on the brutal suppression of the demonstration in Minsk in October 1988 gone on television right away, it might have prevented the bloody events of Tbilisi in April 1989. Ruderman now saw himself not only as a filmmaker but as an active participant in politics—and in the formation of public opinion.

A CLASSROOM IN DEMOCRACY

Gorbachev, of course, was the prime exponent of using the media to give object lessons in the new politics. Among his most sensational object lessons for the Soviet people were the nationally televised sessions of the most remarkable Communist Party meeting in seven decades—the Nineteenth All-Union Conference of the Communist Party of the Soviet Union, a truly open debate about the country's future.

For the first time since the Bolshevik Revolution in 1917, the nation was getting from Gorbachev the chance for mass participation in politics—both in the election of delegates to that conference and in its debates. The conservative Party apparat blocked many reformers from becoming delegates, but enough made it into the conference to cause confrontations entirely new to a public session of the Communist Party.

The conference lasted four solid days and became, for the Soviet people, an astonishing classroom in democracy. Occurring relatively early in Gorbachev's sequence of major political reforms (June 1988), it set the stage for the country's first contested elections in March 1989 and the beginnings of a real parliamentary system in the summer of 1989.

Gorbachev called the conference to win a mandate for political reforms, and he got from it formal backing for a two-term limit for government executives and Communist Party leaders; separation between the work of the Party apparatus and the government; mandatory retirement age of seventy for the Party's Old Guard; elections with multiple candidates.

In the West, a two-term limit for political office-holders might seem natural enough, but it was unprecedented in Russia, where for centuries czars and dictators either died in office or were removed by a coup d'état.

In addition, the concept of multicandidate elections was a crucial breakthrough toward democracy.

But beyond these steps, the major achievement of the conference may have been its impact on the public, thanks to television. People were riveted to their sets, incredulous at what they were seeing. They drank in the spectacle of their leaders' meeting in the open and engaging in fractious debate and disagreement. They had never seen this process in their lifetimes, and that they should do so was central to the entire thrust of what Gorbachev was trying to achieve.

Even before the conference convened, people were consumed with preliminary skirmishes over reform. Gorbachev's proposals were not enough to satisfy popular demands, and the press was bursting with more radical proposals that, under previous Soviet rulers, would have earned their authors a long term in frozen Siberia: abolish the Stalinist system of internal Soviet passports; control the KGB with legislative watchdogs; publish the Communist Party's secret budget; have the prime minister do a regular radio call-in show; eliminate the privileges of the Party elite, the nomenklatura, hand-picked, self-appointed, and self-perpetuating inner core of the Party at all levels; allow new political organizations to compete with the Party.

"Last January, I would not have dreamed that this May such things would be happening, that change would be taking place so fast," Genrikh Borovik, a longtime Soviet press commentator, remarked to me.

The conference was full of shockers, a political circus. It was like a massive, freewheeling town meeting, a laboratory for Gorbachev's new politics. Philip Taubman, then New York Times Moscow bureau chief, described the atmosphere as a cross between a revivalist gathering, a graduate-school seminar in politics, and a national catharsis.[16] Gorbachev began by admitting that in the first three years of his rule, his reforms had not achieved many tangible results. Then he bluntly told the nation: "Perestroika is not manna from heaven. Instead of waiting for it to be brought in from somewhere, it must be brought about by the people— themselves."[17]

The delegates, taking him literally, grabbed the microphone and re-wrote the traditional script for Party gatherings. For decades, the hallmark of Communist Party meetings had been harmony; they were famous for their leaden monotony, for droning, turgid speeches filled with sycophan-tic adulation for the leader and endless paeans to unity. But this time, no sooner had Gorbachev surrendered the lectern than the session turned into a political free-for-all.

With an entire nation watching in awe, Leonid Abalkin, normally a scholarly, mild-mannered academic economist, publicly shattered taboos by having the temerity to criticize Gorbachev for proposing to serve as head of the Communist Party and head of the government simulta-neously. He questioned whether democratic reforms could be achieved under a one-party system.

Then Vitaly Korotich, editor of *Ogonek,* announced he had evidence that four conference deputies from Uzbekistan were criminals. Amid conservative catcalls aimed at the media, filmmaker Yuri Bondarev lashed out at the press, especially *Ogonek,* for excessive negativism. Mikhail A. Ulyanov, an actor made famous for playing Lenin, retorted with a demand for increased protection of the press from censorship. Gorbachev, wagging his finger like a schoolmarm, granted the press its freedom, but rasped that freedom required responsibility too.

For a public accustomed to the facade of Party unity, such a political brawl was grand entertainment. There were shockers every day. Vladimir Kabaidze, head of a huge machine-building plant and one of the country's most successful industrial leaders, delivered a blistering speech against government economic ministries, and called for their abolition. "To tell you the truth, we don't need ministries," Kabaidze declared, to the delight of millions of viewers. "We earn our own feed. We earn our own hard currency. What can they give us? Nothing. . . . Let the ministries catch the mice. If they don't, they don't eat. . . . I can't stand this proliferation of paperwork. It's useless to fight the forms; you've got to kill the people who produce them. . . . I'll probably catch hell from them for saying this."[18]

An even more astonishing moment came when Vladimir Melnikov, a regional Party leader from Siberia, stood at the dais, just a few feet away from Soviet President Andrei Gromyko, and called for his ouster as well as those of three other high Party figures—Politburo member Mikhail Solomentsev, *Pravda* editor Viktor Afanasyev, and Georgy Arbatov, direc-tor of the Institute of the U.S.A. and Canada. Russians talked about Melnikov's audacity for months afterward.

But the climax came with verbal fireworks between Boris Yeltsin (the radical reformer and former Party boss of Moscow, who had been ousted from the Politburo several months earlier) and his Politburo nemesis Yegor Ligachev (then leader of the conservative faction). They had clashed the previous fall in the secrecy of closed Party sessions at the Kremlin, and rumors had continued to circulate of their rivalry after Yeltsin was fired from the Politburo. Suddenly, their political blood feud exploded on the tube.

On the final morning of the conference, Yeltsin, tall, husky, and silver-haired, strode to the podium to cry out for political rehabilitation. Unrepentant, he renewed his assault on the slow pace of reform, and once again fingered Ligachev, another white-haired veteran, who had begun the Gorbachev era as a reformer but then slid to the right, the chief villain.

In an angry rebuttal, his voice thick with anger, Ligachev savaged Yeltsin. He denounced the fallen leader as "a destructive force," who had implied "that the work of the Party and the people is in vain" and was "playing into the hands of our enemies." Wrapping himself in Party loyalty and solidarity, Ligachev—and eventually the conference delegates—spurned Yeltsin's appeal to have his honor restored by the Party.

The television broadcast of their clash was delayed for six hours, but people all across the country stayed awake into the wee hours to watch it.

As he closed the conference, Gorbachev himself was moved to remark that "nothing of the kind has occurred in this country for nearly six decades." In short, not since Stalin had consolidated his control over the Party in the 1920s had the nation seen such a tumultuous Party gathering. Gorbachev had thrown the door of debate wide open.

The example was there for all to see, and to follow in their own cities and provinces. The image of Yeltsin and Ligachev trading body blows was etched in the Soviet public's mind. Wherever I traveled over the next two years, people had fixed those two figures in their minds as champions of rival forces—Yeltsin the avant-garde, Ligachev the Old Guard. What struck me as especially significant was that Ligachev retained the formal power of a commanding Politburo position, but Yeltsin was the one who had forged a populist bond with the man in the street.

In this era of media politics, the televising of that conference is a classic lesson in the power of television to change the political dynamics of a society and alter the mind-set of a nation. It is a case study in the interaction between the media and public opinion. For that conference not only formed public opinion, it also opened up the country to debate, and ultimately to breaking the power monopoly of the Communist Party, though it would take nearly two more years to achieve that revolutionary step.

CHAPTER 8

STALINISM:
THE OPEN WOUND

"I agree with Solzhenitsyn that
without repentance, we cannot change
ourselves or our society. We must
feel responsibility for our history.
Who was it who made Stalin's terror?
It was we—our fathers—and we must
now pay for our fathers. But this is
repulsive to most people. They want to blame
others. They accuse Jews or someone else.
They do not want to accept responsibility."[1]

—Andrei Smirnov
Film Director
March 1990

"At Kuropaty, even the trees cry."[2]

—Nina Soboleva
TV Producer
April 1989

Kuropaty does not look like Auschwitz. At Auschwitz, the ovens remain
ugly carcasses, standing as grisly testimony to the Holocaust. But the
killing ground at Kuropaty, about five miles northeast of Minsk, capital
of the Slavic republic of Byelorussia, is a forest of tall pines sighing
peacefully in the wind. It looks deceptively ordinary and tranquil. From

the road, on a spring afternoon, it looks like the kind of place where people go picnicking or pause to play with their children or take a nap under the trees, soothed by a woodpecker tapping out his tattoo. A chance visitor might pass by, pine needles gently rustling underfoot, and not understand what happened here.

But go deeper under the trees, and the silence grows eerie; there is a feeling of desolation, of emptiness. Then, as the eye adjusts to the darkness, graves come into view—scar upon scar upon scar, gouged into the earth. These graves are not mounds, but unmarked hollows, as if a giant had clawed out enormous scoops of loam and left the face of the earth scarred by some hideous, deadly pox. These are not normal graves; they are great gaping holes, sagging like hammocks with weatherworn edges. They are huge graves—each one large enough for 50 or 100 or 250 corpses, stacked layer upon layer.

These malevolent hollows stretch in all directions, as far as the eye can see, for half a mile this way and hundreds of yards that way, acre after acre of graves, all hidden from view by the woods.

"Over the course of four and a half years, they shot people here every day. Literally every day. When people were driven to the graves, the pits were already dug. They were very deep—up to ten feet deep—and about ten feet wide by ten feet long, sometimes fifteen feet or even thirty feet long. People were taken out of the trucks. Their hands were untied. NKVD (secret police) officers stood around the pits, revolvers ready so that no one could run away. Pairs were led up to the pits and shot in the back of the head. Usually, people, when they were untied, understood that they had been brought to be killed. They threw themselves on their knees and usually began to ask why they were being killed, what they were guilty of. They appealed to God, prayed, remembered their families."[3]

My guide was Zenon Poznyak, a tall, gaunt Byelorussian archaeologist. His brown eyes blazed, his jaw was set, his voice was brimming with hatred for the killers who decimated his people. In a knee-length smock and a blue beret, Poznyak looked disarmingly like an artist loping across the countryside in search of some quiet spot to set up his easel. But Poznyak is a fighter, one of those dissenters who spring up miraculously under dictatorships: a moralist, daring, uncompromising, and forever challenging the authorities because his independent spirit will not be quelled.

"Around Kuropaty," Poznyak said, "there was a tall wooden fence, over ten feet high, and on top of that fence was barbed wire. Over beyond the fence there were guards and dogs, and the gates were tightly shut. They brought prisoners in the morning and at night, after dinner. So the people in the villages—it's less than a mile to the nearest village—they constantly heard those who were being shot, the screams, the shrieks of the women, men, young people, 'Oh, God, why?' 'We're innocent.' 'Please help us.' Every day for five years people living in the villages heard these shots, heard these screams. In the evening, they would walk outside. It was quiet, and they could hear everything—how the people were being murdered.[4]

"Two hundred people who saw and heard these shootings are alive— more than two hundred. All their accounts are recorded. Several villagers said they counted up to sixteen truckloads a day. The shootings continued over four and a half years, from 1937 to 1941, to the very beginning of the war [in Minsk]—July twenty-third. When the German planes had begun bombing the city, they [Stalin's men] were still shooting people. . . .

"Farmers were annihilated. The intelligentsia were annihilated. People who graduated from the university in Prague or some other place abroad were annihilated. People who had earlier belonged to some party or some movement were annihilated. People who protected Byelorussian culture were annihilated. They annihilated the believers—Russian Orthodox, Catholics. They annihilated priests. They annihilated ordinary people when it was necessary to fulfill their quota. And many people were annihilated simply under this system of secret informers or denunciations. . . .

"Every investigator was given a quota: One or two people per day should be unmasked as 'enemies of the people.' If he did not expose 'enemies,' he himself was killed. . . . And as far as the 'seksot'—the secret informer—was concerned, he would go get paid on the very day that he wrote the denunciation of an 'enemy'—one hundred and fifty rubles in old money. That is, around fifteen rubles today. This was the price of a human life.

"They shot about two hundred fifty thousand people here, a quarter of a million," Poznyak said to me. "People were shot like flies."[5]

Crisscrossing the Soviet Union, I encountered a handful of people like Poznyak, militants whose zeal, even fanaticism, to expose Stalin's terror, has emboldened millions of others. In Byelorussia, Poznyak led a team of archaeologists and a network of activists who were investigating the horrors of Stalinism. They called themselves Martyrologists, *Martyrolog* in Byelorussian. Later, Poznyak was chosen leader of the Byelorussian Popular Front, which was openly challenging the Communist Party hierarchy. By the elections in March 1990, Poznyak had won a sufficient following to be elected to the Byelorussian parliament.

I suspect that Poznyak is a restless soul by nature. Forty-six and unmarried, he has no family except his mother; he has adopted the descendants of Stalin's victims as his family. Some of them almost worship him for what he has dared to expose. He is married to their cause, has made it his personal crusade, and he pursues it with fierce passion and the single-minded commitment of a Jesuit.

I could not help wondering whether Poznyak's vibrant anti-Stalinism sprang from the sufferings of his own family.

"What happened to your family?" I asked him. "Did they perish here?"

"My mother is alive, but my father was killed by the Nazis," Poznyak replied matter-of-factly. Then his face hardened, and he said, "The Bolsheviks killed my father's father. He was the editor of a newspaper, a true intellectual, and they were trying to destroy the intelligentsia. So they shot him."

As a devout Catholic, Poznyak has never forgiven the Bolsheviks either for murdering his grandfather or for their desecration of Christianity, and he took up his grandfather's cause, defending Byelorussia against the alien anti-Christ. In 1962, when he was a college freshman studying acting in the drama faculty of the Byelorussian Central Institute of Art, he was expelled for criticizing Khrushchev. Somehow he wangled his way back into the institute, but in a different faculty, and he was expelled again in a post-Khrushchev purge of liberals. He became an archaeologist as a last resort, and eventually unearthed the terrible evidence of the slaughter at Kuropaty.

Mass murders were conducted not only at Kuropaty, but all over Byelorussia. In April 1989, when we met, Poznyak took me to Kuropaty, but when I returned to Minsk that fall, he told me there were other killing grounds, a ring of eight of them in the countryside surrounding Minsk. Despite dreadful weather, Poznyak, the missionary, led me and our film crew out in the chill rain to all eight gravesites—four in various forests, one in a swamp, one now plowed under a highway cloverleaf, another in a ravine asphalted over for a parking lot, and the last in a popular Minsk park.

With us was Maya Klishtornaya, a soft-spoken architect, whose father, beloved Byelorussian poet Todor Klishtorny, had been arrested during the Stalinist purges and "liquidated," as the Soviets say, at the age of thirty-two. After all these years, she still seemed incredulous at her father's fate.

"He saw everything through rose-colored glasses," Maya recalled. "He was surprised when he was arrested. He could not understand why, and they never told him. . . . He wanted only good things, pure things. That was the Revolution for him. . . . My mother literally ripped out her hair. She had long black hair, in braids. My mother went everywhere, tried to get through, asked questions. But nobody could explain anything to her, except one thing—your husband is an enemy, an enemy. This word didn't fit him, didn't, no way. . . . I was born when my father was already gone. He was in prison."[6]

Maya is a small, gentle, attractive woman gray beyond her years. She never saw her father. With her mother, she spent the first seventeen years of her life in exile in Kazakhstan and Siberia, in concentration camps for relatives of "enemies of the people." She never knew her father's precise fate, but she is convinced that he was shot at Kuropaty. And so now she makes a pilgrimage there every week, often planting red and white roses by the anonymous graves.

As I walked with her through the woods of Kuropaty, I noticed that at one grave someone had put up a crude wooden frame bearing a wreath and a handwritten note, now faded from the rain. It said something Maya herself might have written:

> Mother and Father,
>
> I have searched for you since your disappearance in 1937. At last, after 52 years, I have found you.
>
> Galya

Nearby, close to other graves, there were crosses, handmade from small stones laid out on the earth, and farther on, the simple legend REMEMBER FOREVER.

By then we were barely noticing the terrible weather. It seemed fitting that raindrops were falling from the branches of the pines; and I was reminded of something a TV producer in Moscow had said to me: "At Kuropaty, even the trees cry."

After Kuropaty, Poznyak took us to another cemetery, where the graves are marked, some with expensively cut stones. Here, Maya came face-to-face with a truth that millions of other Soviets now confront: The evil that killed their families was not the work of an invader; it was inflicted from within. Some of the people buried in this cemetery took part in the Stalinist murders.

Poznyak showed us one gravestone on which had been etched the almost photographic likeness of a youthful, square-jawed military officer with a crew cut—the stereotypical Soviet hero. This man's widow had recently admitted that in 1937 and 1938 her husband had been an NKVD officer and had participated in the Stalinist killings.

"Imagine this life-style," Poznyak said, drawing on a description he'd heard from another NKVD wife. "This person comes home from work every night, very late. He's tired, very drunk. The wife meets him. She is disgusted, of course. He smells like blood. And how do the kids react to that—'Daddy, how many did you kill today? Seventy or eighty?' It's hellish, surrealism. It's a nightmare that these people have lived in, destroying our society, destroying our people. . . . You know, maybe this person has killed Maya's father."[7]

Maya was in a state of shock, her face revealing unbearable pain. She looked as if she wanted to scream, but she spoke only in a murmur.

"They shouldn't have buried this one so close to the other graves," she said. "They shouldn't put him in a common cemetery."

Others like this man, Poznyak observed, are still alive.

"What do you think should be done with them?" I asked.

"We should investigate and start criminal cases against them," he replied, "and if their guilt is determined, we should judge them. We should start a criminal case and prove their guilt. Otherwise, it will be the same kind of killing all over again."

The threat of this kind of retribution paralyzes Soviet society, and so far those in power will not permit any such investigation to take place.

Poznyak emphasized that most important is the moral judgment of guilt so that historical truth can be established.

By his own reckoning, the Stalinist massacre in Byelorussia—"genocide," he calls it—took 2 million lives. The census counted 12 million Byelorussians in 1920, but only 9.8 million in 1940, before the war, and Poznyak blames Stalin and the Bolsheviks for those who vanished. If death from Stalin's violent collectivization of the farmlands and the famine that ensued is included along with the actual police killings, Poznyak may be right.

"I want to tell you, Hedrick," he said, "that a normal, civilized person cannot comprehend deliberate, cold-blooded, mass extermination of innocent people on a national scale. Stalin, after all, was a criminal. His psychology, his mentality, was criminal. There has never been anything like it."

"Even Hitler?" I asked.

"Even Hitler," he answered. "No comparison. If you compare the victims—fifty million lives in the U.S.S.R. annihilated by Stalin—that's an enormous number. Also, Hitler fought basically with external enemies." The greater horror of Stalin, in Poznyak's view, was that he had devoured his own people.

BITTER TRUTHS, COMFORTABLE LIES

Zenon Poznyak's campaign to dig up the truth about Kuropaty represents much more than a local struggle of Byelorussians to seek justice for the violence perpetrated against them. Poznyak's unearthing of the corpses at Kuropaty is a metaphor for the entire process of *glasnost*—for Gorbachev has been digging up the past and forcing Soviet society to confront the political skeletons in its history.

Sadly, Kuropaty and the ring of killing grounds around Minsk are far from unique. I have been taken to other mass graves, in forests outside of Kiev and Moscow, and there are many more, from Leningrad in the west all the way across Russia and Siberia to the Pacific. These have been unearthed in the past two or three years under the stimulus of Gorbachev's new openness and under his political protection.

Gorbachev understood that before his people could begin to define and build their future, transform the Soviet system, they had to consciously reject the legacy of Stalin, to confront the nature of the society that Stalin had created. Khrushchev had begun the task in 1956 when he dethroned Stalin personally, exposing the raw terror of his reign. But Gorbachev had a larger target: not just Stalin the person, but Stalinism, the entire Stalinist system. He was intent on digging deeper, on uprooting and casting off the Stalinist system by discrediting it morally, especially among generations in their middle and younger years.

Gorbachev and his liberal allies in the leadership, principally Eduard Shevardnadze and Aleksandr Yakovlev, encouraged Poznyak and other political radicals to come forward with the bitter truths that unmasked the long-held lies. This not only provided an outlet for pent-up grievances, but also helped legitimize the break with the Soviet past that Gorbachev needed; putting Stalin's terror and authoritarian rule under fire also served to discredit Stalin's militaristic management of the economy, and his one-man political rule. So the zealous anti-Stalinism of people like Zenon Poznyak served Gorbachev's broader reform movement in several different ways.

Nevertheless, there were formidable obstacles, and perhaps more in Byelorussia than elsewhere. That republic is widely known as a bastion of the hard-line Old Guard, much as Alabama and Mississippi were known as hard-core segregationist states during the American civil rights movement of the 1960s. Like the Ukraine and much of western Russia, Byelorussia was occupied by the German army during World War II, so Soviet authorities in these regions could blame all mass killings and mass grave sites on the Nazis. The Minsk park that Poznyak took us to, for example, has a monument to the victims of Nazi occupation, but Poznyak, and many others, dismiss this as "a mock monument" because by their reckoning German killings were minor compared to the slaughter inflicted by the Soviets themselves. Yet Byelorussian authorities refused to recognize that with a new monument to the innocent victims of Stalinism.

Another obstacle has been fear—a fear so keen that Poznyak himself was intimidated for many years. He confessed to me that he had first learned about Kuropaty about fifteen years ago, from the villagers. But he kept silent until 1988, doing nothing to publicize the horrible secret.

"Why did it take so long to come out?" I asked. "You had the opportunity to open this up."

We were standing only a foot or two apart, and I could see that his breathing was heavy. I sensed his anger and tension over my pressing him on this point. He fixed me with a stare.

"It was impossible to say anything out loud," he said finally. "In order to understand me, you need to live in this society, under Communism. Then you will understand everything. It was an absolutely impossible situation—to know everything but not be able to say anything. You can go mad, but still not say anything. The whole ideology, the whole press, the whole information—it's all in *their* hands. If a person comes out with that type of information, nobody's going to listen to him, or worse yet, they pronounce him crazy, or they take him to prison, or kill him. And they just say that he's stupid, he's crazy, he just made it all up, and that's how evil he is. This is how millions of people were destroyed."[8]

Beyond that, after the war the NKVD, forerunner of today's KGB, tried to cover up their crime—and nearly succeeded. According to what the villagers told Poznyak, NKVD troops came back to Kuropaty, dug up the graves, and carried away tens of thousands of corpses and dumped them somewhere else. That is why the mass graves at Kuropaty all sag like hammocks. Bodies have been removed and there is not enough earth to make the graves level. Eventually, Poznyak was able to confirm the villagers' story through archaeological detective work. The NKVD had done a sloppy job, leaving traces not only of the original crime but of the cover-up as well. Initially, however, the NKVD cover-up foiled Poznyak's efforts.

"We did the excavation, dug to about five feet, and not one bone— empty graves," he told me. "We discovered the corpses only by chance. Some children dug deeper in one pit than we had, to about six or seven feet, and they came upon the corpses. Then everything fell into place. Digging to the lower levels of the graves, we found bones, human skulls shot in the back of the head—every skull in the back of the head."

What apparently happened, he said, was that the original graves had been constructed in layers—first bodies, then a layer of earth and lime, then more bodies and another layer of earth, for several layers. When the NKVD came after the war, they dug down only to the normal depth of a grave, and removed the top layer or two, especially in the center of the graves, thus leaving the lower layers intact. Poznyak's investigations turned up those lower levels, confirming the villagers' stories.

But when Poznyak tried to go public with his findings on Kuropaty, the Byelorussian Communist Party Central Committee forbade all newspapers and magazines from printing his article. Only one Byelorussian magazine, *Literatura i Mastačtva (Literature and Art)*, was brave enough to try. Its editors warned Party officials that if the article was not printed, they would write a collective protest to the Nineteenth Communist Party Conference in Moscow. Even then, only by agreeing to cut about 20 percent of the article were they able to publish "Kuropaty—Road to Death," on June 3, 1988.

Poznyak is convinced the Party bosses relented only because this was the high tide of *glasnost,* during the buildup to the Party conference, and Byelorussian authorities were afraid to be caught too far out of step with Gorbachev's line.

"Our authorities did not know what to expect from the Party conference," he told me. "If they had not been so busy with the conference, they would have crushed this article. If it had been after the conference, they would have crushed it. Timing saved it, and it was a bombshell, because it became clear to people what a genocide had taken place."[9]

The Party leadership tried to discredit Poznyak personally, and to blame the Nazis for the Kuropaty killings. One Party activist claimed that thirty-eight thousand German officers had been shot after the war, so outlandish a story that it had no credibility. A rising public outcry forced the formation of a government commission to study Poznyak's charges. Some of the younger investigators took the charges seriously enough to dig up six graves, with the help of Poznyak's archaeological specialists. The evidence, as Poznyak knew it would be, was devastating.

"We found shells from Soviet revolvers—Nogam brand," Poznyak recalled. "We found bullets, homemade high boots, rubber galoshes from Soviet factories—Red Hero, Red Triangle, truck hubcaps, lights.[10]

"We found a lot of rubber boots—all made in '37, '38. Our population was pretty poor and at least half of them wore rubber rain boots. We found combs, little mugs. Some graves had toothbrushes, glasses, women's hair, remnants of clothes. We found wallets, a little bit of metal money made in the thirties. Then we found leather jackets, neatly folded, and inside them there were women's shoes, slippers, wrapped up. They even found chicken bones. Do you understand what happened? A person took some chicken and didn't have time to eat; he was shot and thrown into the grave, and the chicken bones were left over. When you make this analysis, you realize that these people were very poor, mostly farmers, locals, because all of the articles were local . . . basically people just taken in the middle of the night."[11]

The investigation confirmed the thrust of Poznyak's story, but officials then disputed his figures. He calculated the death toll at 250,000, having measured out that there were 250 corpses in each of the 1,000 graves that he estimated filled the fenced-in area at Kuropaty. The authorities put the figure at 30,000 because only 510 specific graves had been located; moreover, they only counted actual bodies found in the lower layers—excluding the larger numbers that had been removed from above.

To verify the death toll and help people learn the fate of their relatives, Poznyak and his organization Martyrolog demanded that the KGB open its files; the KGB insisted there were no documents because all files had been destroyed in the war. "All lies," Poznyak retorted. "There are people who clearly know that their parents were shot here, and these people applied in 1959 to the Minsk KGB for [political] rehabilitation of their parents. The documents were there, and they received rehabilitation. Aside from that, all documents on the shootings in the 1930s existed in four copies—two for Moscow and two for Byelorussia."

The Minsk press knows less about the details than Poznyak and Martyrolog, and Party leaders refuse to talk about the mass killings. I made repeated efforts to see them, but they completely stonewalled my requests; I did not encounter such total avoidance anywhere else in the Soviet Union.

To Americans, who have known of Stalin's Red Terror for decades, Poznyak's determination to pry out every last historical fact may seem obsessive. But to Soviets, Stalinism is a burning issue today because for the first time in their lives they can finally talk about it. Moreover, in fighting over the past, Poznyak and his allies see themselves as locked in battle with the neo-Stalinists of Byelorussia today.

"Stalinism will be dealt a mortal blow only when all the documents are revealed," Poznyak contended. "What we now relate, based on people's recollections—they can claim it was not so, that it is invented, it is a personal opinion, subjective. Even now, Stalinism still clamors for the right to exist. So one of the most important issues in dispute is whether to publish all documents about the crimes of Stalinism. *They* understand the importance of this. The system itself understands that the publication of these documents, and the unmasking of Stalinism, is the unmasking of that same system now."[12]

STALIN—DEMON OR DEMIGOD?

Half a century after the purges, Stalinism is still an open wound. No other issue cleaves Soviet society quite the same way. It defines the political spectrum. It lies at the heart of the country's struggle to recover its soul—a struggle that reaches deep into the personal lives of almost every adult over forty, testing the beliefs of a lifetime. Gorbachev's new openness may liberate some people, but it points the finger at others. Because tens of millions of people alive today enthusiastically supported or reluctantly collaborated with Stalinism, the painful questions being raised are about *their* responsibility and guilt, *their* pride or shame.

And what makes Stalinism still such a vibrant issue is that its influences continue to permeate Soviet life, shaping and coloring the mentality of most people. I saw this, and heard it, all over the country, from many thoughtful people, including Yuri Solomonov, a senior editor at the weekly newspaper *Sovetskaya Kultura.*

"Why do we have such arguments about Stalinism?" Solomonov echoed my question. "Because all the institutions of our society were created at that time. When we argue about Stalin, it's not just about the past, it's about the present. We have a part of Stalin in all of us. Stalinism is the living past, and the worst poison is here," he said, pointing at his head.[13]

From an eminent and elderly Soviet physicist, Andrei Borovik-Romanov, I heard how it felt to reflect on one's own role in the Stalinist period, after Khrushchev's revelations about Stalin.

"That was for me a very difficult moment," he said. "I felt guilty. All honest people have problems with this guilt. Every citizen is responsible. I knew innocent people were arrested. I knew at the time that my friend"—he paused, but gave no name—"who was arrested, was innocent, that it was a mistake. But you think that the others who were arrested were actually guilty. Most of the people in the thirties were interested in building a new world. What we need now is to formulate new policies. But it is much easier to criticize the past."[14]

People's views of Stalin are a touchstone for their political loyalties and their attitudes toward the Soviet future. For if there are millions like Zenon Poznyak who believe that Stalin was a demon, there still are millions of others who revere him as a demigod.

It was Stalin, they declare, who built the Soviet Union into a super-power. It was Stalin who industrialized a peasant country, took it from wooden plows to atomic weapons, thrust it into the twentieth century, and made the West tremble at the might of Russia. Above all, it was Stalin who won the war, destroyed Hitler, beat the Germans. As they talk of Stalin, his admirers romanticize the exploits of their own youth, when, with Stalin at the helm, they were building a Brave New World. And now, amid the disarray of Gorbachev's *perestroika,* they long nostalgically for the order and discipline imposed by the strong boss in the Kremlin. Those were times, they assert, when factories worked—and so did workers—unlike today!

The battle over Stalin and his legacy rages in virtually every level of society, and between two ideologically opposed camps—from the higher reaches of the Communist Party to factories and neighborhoods. In the Soviet Writers' Union, the neo-Stalinist Right battles the anti-Stalinist Left for control of the union and the editorship of major newspapers. In the streets on March 5, the anniversary of Stalin's death, rival demonstrations of the anti-Stalinist popular movement Memorial and the pro-Stalinist right-wing group Pamyat ("Memory") have ended in shouting matches and fisticuffs.

In the corridors of power, Memorial, which seeks to rehabilitate the victims of Stalinist repression and establish memorials at eight mass graves across the nation, including Kuropaty, has been waging a struggle for more than two years to be legally registered with the government and thereby be allowed an office, a bank account, and normal organizational facilities and rights. But it has been blocked, some of its leaders fear, by Stalin's defenders in the bureaucracy, who want to keep popular anti-Stalinism in check. Memorial's top priority is erecting a monument to Stalin's victims on Red Square; it has raised large funds from private donations to do this. It has even publicly exhibited the scores of designs submitted for the monument, only to have its unregistered bank account frozen by the Ministry of Culture.

Angered by a stream of articles on Stalinist repression, former Stalinist officials have gone to court, their chests lined with medals, to file lawsuits against Stalin's accusers. In September 1988, a retired prosecutor named Ivan Shekhovtsov created a sensation by charging the prominent writer Ales Adamovich with slandering Stalin and his henchmen by calling them "butchers" in a newspaper article. Among other things, Adamovich had accused Stalin of deliberately organizing the famine of 1930–31, in which millions died. Shekhovtsov retorted that this was illegal defamation because Stalin had never been found guilty by a legal tribunal. His case was dismissed, but when Moscow television ran a documentary on the trial, its producer, Nina Soboleva, received seventy-five hundred letters supporting Shekhovtsov.[15]

"It's a battle for power," Alla Nikitina, the editor of a monthly magazine for teenagers, asserted. "There's not just an effort to rehabilitate the victims of Stalin, but there is the battle [of reformers] against the Stalinists of today, the people who still use Stalinist methods. If they did not consider themselves Stalinists, they would not worry about that old society. But these people see a real danger to themselves."[16]

As Poznyak suggested, the most rigid and unyielding neo-Stalinists are people still in power who feel threatened by the drive to expose Stalinism. There are also the true believers, who are still in the grip of dogma, and the superpatriots, who take any criticism as a slur on the nation. There are the zealots of law and order, for whom crime, prostitution, gaudy television, rock music, and the loose ways of modern Soviet youth are evidence of decadent Western influence. The numbers are legion, especially among the older generation, who are defensive about their own lives, both what they did and what they did not do.

"Many people don't want to know the criminal things about Stalin because it means they have fought for a lost cause," observed Genrikh Borovik, a veteran news commentator.[17]

And there are those who simply find it too hard to change and who do not like the confusion of democracy. "Many people like a totalitarian regime," was the comment of Andrei Borovik-Romanov, the physicist. "You don't have to think about anything. You don't have to be responsible for anything. It is like being in the military. It's an easier life."

Soviet opinion polls indicate that Stalin's critics significantly outnumber his defenders. A December 1988 telephone survey done in five major Soviet cities by Moscow's Institute of Sociology found 65 percent had an unfavorable view of Stalin and only 10 percent were willing to state a favorable view. Another 20 percent had mixed feelings about him, or were unsure.[18] However, Vadim Andreyenkov, a sociologist at the institute, suggested that Stalin was probably viewed more favorably nationwide than this poll indicated. The reason, he said, is that this poll and others like it either leave out rural areas or underrepresent the elderly, two groups among whom sociologists have found that political conservativism—and approval of Stalin—runs higher than average.[19]

Stalin's most celebrated grass-roots defender is Nina Andreyeva, for years an ordinary chemistry teacher at the Leningrad Technological Institute, who sent political chills through the ranks of reformers in early 1988 with a bold defense of Stalin and an attack on Gorbachev's *glasnost* policy. Panic rose among anti-Stalinist liberals when Andreyeva's forty-five-hundred-word letter was printed in the newspaper *Sovetskaya Rossiya,* a conservative stronghold, and when it was warmly endorsed by Yegor Ligachev, then number two behind Gorbachev in the Politburo. It is a well-known maneuver in Kremlin infighting to use the views of an ordinary person—a real or fictitious letter-writer to a newspaper—as a proxy to promote the cause of one Politburo faction against another, so for days, many of the most daring liberal editors interpreted the publication of Nina Andreyeva's letter as a signal that a right-wing power play against Gorbachev was under way and that their own days might be numbered.

In her letter-essay, titled "I Cannot Forsake Principles," Andreyeva voiced alarm that her students had been plunged into "ideological confusion" and "nihilist views" by the press and by liberal writers. She chastised these groups for debunking Stalin and "falsifying" Soviet history, contending that Stalinist "repression has become excessively magnified" and that some writers sounded like "the professional anti-Communists in the West, who long ago chose the supposedly democratic slogan of 'anti-Stalinism.'

"Too many things have turned up that I cannot accept, that I cannot agree with—the constant harping on 'terrorism,' 'the people's political servility,' 'our spiritual slavery,' 'the entrenched rule of louts,' " she wrote. "Take the question of the position of J. V. Stalin in our country's history. . . . Industrialization, collectivization, and the cultural revolution, which brought our country into the ranks of the great world powers . . . all these things are being questioned."[20]

While paying obligatory lip service to the existing Party line, Andreyeva took issue with it. She challenged the tendencies of "leftist liberal dilettantish socialist" reformers—Gorbachev seemed implied but was not named—to abandon the "class struggle" against the West and indulge in heretical preaching about the superiority of capitalism over Soviet socialism. In frustration, she declared: "Against proletarian collectivism, the adherents of this trend put up 'the intrinsic worth of the individual'—with modernistic quests in the field of culture, God-seeking tendencies, technocratic idols, the preaching of the 'democratic' charms of present-day capitalism and fawning over its achievements, real and imagined. [They] assert that we have built the wrong kind of socialism. . . ."[21]

KTO KOGO—WHO WINS?

When Nina Andreyeva's bombshell landed in the press, Gorbachev was in Yugoslavia, and his close Politburo ally Aleksandr Yakovlev in Mongolia. Ligachev, the Politburo's leading conservative, who was acting as Gorbachev's temporary replacement, moved into the power vacuum.

On March 14, the day after *Sovetskaya Rossiya* printed the letter, Ligachev summoned leading newspaper editors to a meeting, excluding some important liberals. According to Valentin Chikin, chief editor of *Sovetskaya Rossiya*, Ligachev drew attention to the Andreyeva letter as something to be emulated. By Chikin's account, Ligachev merely said: "Undoubtedly, you did not read *Sovetskaya Rossiya*, but I saw a very interesting article there by Nina Andreyeva." That was enough to start a stampede. Ligachev's move was read by many editors as a dramatic reversal of Gorbachev's line.[22]

Tass, the official news agency, sent regional papers an advisory note, "authorizing"—that is, virtually instructing—them to reprint it; many did so. In closed lectures to Party activists, a common way the Party line is transmitted, speakers began citing the Andreyeva article approvingly. This was also done in military channels.[23]

Within days, there were reports that Ligachev and his staff actually had drafted the Andreyeva letter and planted it. I heard from Yuri Solomonov of *Sovetskaya Kultura* that his paper had received a copy of an original, fifty- to sixty-page version, directly from Nina Andreyeva. The published version, he said, was shorter and better written, showing extensive rewriting.[24] Chikin said his staff had contacted Andreyeva before publishing the letter, and although he tried to minimize their role, two other journalists, one on Chikin's staff, told me the letter had been largely reworked by Chikin's editors, including Vladimir Denisov, who had close links to Ligachev. Denisov had gotten to know Ligachev during four years as a correspondent in the Siberian city of Tomsk, where Ligachev had been the regional Party boss in the early 1980s.

Once Gorbachev and Yakovlev returned to Moscow, it took them several days to react to Ligachev's challenge. They did not immediately issue a high-level repudiation of the Andreyeva letter, despite strong appeals from liberals. For three weeks, the situation dragged on, delay fueling the reformers' sense of danger. Vitaly Korotich, whose magazine had been publishing revelations about Stalinism, told me that he became so worried there would be a conservative crackdown and he would be exiled to Siberia, that he actually made preparations for his own arrest. "We understood that an article like this is a sign to prepare a satchel of clothes for a long trip," he told me months later, with his boyish, crescent-moon grin. "We understood that if we lost our power and lost *perestroika*, it would be a catastrophe, for the government and for us personally."[25]

By the end of March, Politburo member Aleksandr Yakovlev and his staff had created a strong reply to the letter, and word was passed to leading editors that an authoritative Party statement would run in *Pravda* on March 31. But it did not appear that day, or the next, or the next.

Several months later, Roy Medvedev, who as a dissident in the 1970s had written the devastating history of Stalin *Let History Judge,* told me the Politburo had been split on publishing an answer to Andreyeva. Medvedev learned from his high-level Party contacts that Gorbachev had pushed hard, first lobbying Politburo members individually and then summoning the Politburo into session, in the first days of April. His difficulties indicated that there was resistance from Ligachev and others. I was told that Gorbachev broke the deadlock by playing his trump card: He warned the others that he could not continue to lead if they did not back him on this issue, and he stalked out of the Politburo meeting, going off to his *dacha* to await their verdict.[26]

On April 5, with Politburo approval, *Pravda* printed a stinging six-thousand-word rebuttal to Nina Andreyeva and her high-level backers. It denounced her letter as "an ideological platform and manifesto of anti-*perestroika* forces," namely "the conservative resistance to restructuring," which does not accept "the very idea of renewal." It mocked their view of history as "a nostalgia for the past when some people laid down the law and others were supposed to carry out orders without a murmur." It declared that "the guilt of Stalin and his immediate entourage . . . for the mass repressions and lawlessness they committed is enormous and unforgivable." In uncompromising language, it insisted that "those who defend Stalin are thereby advocating the preservation in our life and practice today of the methods he devised for 'resolving' debatable questions . . . but most important, they are defending the right of arbitrary action." It dismissed Andreyeva's letter as the work of a "blind diehard dogmatist" who confuses patriotism with "jingoism." As for the "nihilism" of today's youth, *Pravda* declared, "its roots go back into the past."[27]

This was one of those telltale moments in what Russians call the endless Kremlin struggle of *Kto kogo,* literally "Who is over whom?" Put more simply: "Who wins?" Gorbachev had forced Ligachev to back down.

The crisis was over—but the debate was not. Within ten days, Chikin had reprinted the *Pravda* article, along with his own editorial conceding that running the Andreyeva letter had been a mistake. In Stalinist times, Andreyeva would have vanished in a trice for crossing the Party leader so brashly. But no steps were taken against her, and within a month other letter writers, even those who disagreed with her, were defending her right to be heard under Gorbachev's policy of "socialist pluralism of opinions." A year later, in April 1989, I was told that Chikin was boasting to his hard-line staff at *Sovetskaya Rossiya* that they had brought Nina Andreyeva to five million readers "and the heavens opened up on us. The terrorists [evidently Gorbachev and Yakovlev] bombarded us. But that didn't dampen our spirits."

Far from being chastened by *Pravda*'s verbal caning, Nina Andreyeva became more outspoken. She was a national celebrity by the time I went to see her in September 1989. A hero, a symbol and rallying point for hard-line Stalinist and Russian nationalists, she was now the leader of a mass movement called Edinstvo—"Unity."

I found her and her husband, Vladimir Klushin, in a modest one-room apartment. They were swamped with mail—seven thousand letters, she said. A constant stream of Stalin loyalists made pilgrimages to her home. Only the day before, there had been someone from Tashkent, she said; and now there was an American television crew.

Andreyeva looked less like the nation's most notorious street-corner polemicist than a stocky, chubby-cheeked matron in her fifties. I had seen hundreds of women who resembled her, standing as self-important sentries at the entrances of government buildings, warily checking visitors. More stylish than they, she was decked out in tight-fitting slacks, platform heels, a short, upswept hairdo. She had a small mouth that was given to laughter as well as to smug little grins at the expense of her enemies—and she had them, for, as Moscow Party officials told me, she had been expelled from the Communist Party unit in her institute some years back for writing anonymous denunciations of colleagues and pretending they were written by students. With me, she was full of righteous talk about defending the working class, even though she and Klushin displayed distinctly bourgeois tastes: lacquered cabinets, cut crystal, and ten-year-old Georgian cognac, which they served along with a modest lunch of cold cuts and eggplant pâté.

Their apartment was only a few hundred yards away from the battlefield that marked the deepest penetration of German forces during the nine-hundred-day blockade of Leningrad in World War II. She and Klushin took me through a war memorial and to a nearby park, where he described the fighting and recalled that Russians had gone to their deaths shouting, "For the Motherland! For Stalin!"

Andreyeva had lost her father and brother in the war, but Klushin revealed that his father had been arrested, interrogated at the Lubyanka (the KGB headquarters prison), and sent to the gulag after being pressured into signing a false confession that he was part of a gang plotting against Stalin. Actually, Klushin said, his father was arrested because, as an officer, he had absentmindedly taken some classified data out of a secret room. When I asked Klushin his reaction to the false confession, he evaded my question, saying that, after all, his father had been guilty of something and had himself "felt they were correct to imprison him." But later, in another context, Klushin said his father's investigator had not been honest and he disclosed triumphantly that during the shadowy postwar intrigues of secret-police chief Lavrenti Beria, the investigator and, in fact, "all four who were on my father's case, were shot—deservedly, absolutely deservedly, shot!"[28]

Nonetheless, his father's fate had left Klushin strangely unaffected, his devotion to Stalin undimmed. Now beefy and white-haired, he has pursued a career as an instructor in Marxism-Leninism, one of several hundred thousand ideological instructors nationwide. This group is widely regarded as among the most simple-minded dogmatists in the system. Like an overgrown puppy, he would offer his comments whenever his wife permitted.

Andreyeva, now expert at her own public relations, was on her best behavior for our filming. Her original letter had included some anti-Semitic remarks about Trotsky. In a subsequent interview with David Remnick of *The Washington Post*, she had openly attacked what she regarded as excessive Jewish influence in Soviet life. "Why is the Academy of Sciences, in all its branches, and the prestigious professions and posts in culture, music, law—why are they almost all Jews?" she had complained, though exaggerating the facts. "Look at the essayists and the journalists—Jews mostly?" She had also fumed about the corrupting influence of rock and roll, especially about a male singer named Yuri Shevchuk, who performed with his shirt unbuttoned, his chest and belly button showing, "and down below his male dignity was protruding . . . in front of all those young girls."[29]

With the camera running, she was careful how she put things. But she made it plain that her famous letter had been provoked by a sense that the country was disintegrating. In the months since, with all the strikes, political movements, nationalist demonstrations, and violence, she saw the nation sliding into the abyss of anarchism.

"Now, what's the worst thing?" she demanded rhetorically. "Disorder! Disorder! It's in everything. You've noticed. It's everywhere. And to imagine that a state can exist in conditions of anarchy, that's ridiculous. Even take capitalists—they get profits because everything is well organized. We need to learn labor discipline from capitalism . . . discipline that we unfortunately don't have."

"There wasn't such disorder under Stalin or even under Khrushchev, and to some degree even during Brezhnev's time," Klushin chimed in. "Real disorder has come now. People have become irresponsible."

Both now saw a political division that was sharper and more open than at the time of Andreyeva's original letter. The differences of the spring of 1988 had become "irreconcilable contradictions," which were now being fought out at all levels, top to bottom, Klushin said. "We don't accept the switch to the capitalist economic system," Andreyeva proclaimed. "And no matter what the leaders of *perestroika* do to pull us in that direction, it still won't work. It's bad. Of course, there's only one solution out of this crisis, only one in the interest of the worker, if you examine our society. It is to stop the current ruinous economic reforms. . . . Only one path is acceptable—the path of further socialist development, our development as a socialist power."

Andreyeva dismissed *Pravda*'s reply to her letter as the work of the intelligentsia, whom she derisively termed "the superintendents of *perestroika.*" But I pointed out that the letter was in the Party newspaper, written by Politburo member Aleksandr Yakovlev. She waved me off. "It wasn't his style," she sniffed. Her cocky self-assurance indicated she still had powerful support from higher-ups as well as from the masses.

Both she and Klushin repeatedly criticized the press for picking on Stalin. "Such stupid things they publish now," she fumed. She ridiculed articles that said Stalin had "grabbed everything for his own good," saying that one of Stalin's KGB bodyguards had told her that the dictator did not even have shoes for his own funeral. But their pet peeve was the ever-mounting Stalinist death toll cited by their hated rivals.

"Khrushchev spoke of eight hundred thousand—Khrushchev, who directly knew about these issues," Andreyeva insisted to me. "Now in the period of *glasnost* and democracy, these eight hundred seventy-five thousand, it seems, have turned first into ten million, then twenty million, then thirty million. Everyone is trying to shock the listener, the reader, with these wild numbers."

"What about Stalin himself?" I asked. "As Khrushchev, and even Gorbachev said, Stalin gave the orders [for the killings] himself."

"You understand, the thing is there were no such orders," she shot back. "And there couldn't have been because this stupid thing that the press is saying now, that Stalin destroyed his own people, this prejudiced juggling of the facts, it's disinformation which is aimed at our very impressionable man in the street."

She raced on.

"If you say that all those generations that enthusiastically built our society, that they were all slaves, dehumanized, understood nothing, and that task number one is to rid yourself of this slavish part, drop by drop, what does this say? That all our past generations didn't understand what they were doing? It's criminal, just criminal. People lived a hard life. We didn't have a lot of material things, but the society which we created in 1917, it was building itself. It was hard. It was difficult. But with each day, people lived better, no matter what. The quantity of consumer goods increased, prices decreased, the problem of housing was solved, for we built huge amounts in the civilian sector. So to spit on all this, it's immoral."

The press was to blame, she said, for one-sided sensationalism. "*Glasnost* for the sake of *glasnost* isn't worth anything," she asserted. "It's a direction that leads to the collapse of society. If you accept that everyone can, excuse me, blather anything he wants, then we can say that psychiatric hospitals are the clearest example of *glasnost*. That would be utterly absurd."

"Is this the cost of freedom?" I asked.

"No," Klushin shot back. "It's the ugly face of freedom."[30]

TEACHING THE NEXT GENERATION

Some Russians say, "It's easier to live with comfortable lies than face the bitter truth." There are the comfortable lies of Andreyeva, the bitter truths of Poznyak. The choice ultimately lies with the next generation, teenagers now in high school. And what they are taught will be crucial in shaping their outlook ten or twenty years down the road. Then, they will be influencing the Soviet future.

One of Gorbachev's most far-reaching reforms—and one that is the least noticed in the West—is the dramatic change being made in the history that these Soviet high school students are taught. In what struck me as an incredibly daring step, because it was so visible and so sweeping, the government canceled history exams for Soviet high school students in May 1988. As *Izvestia* put it, the current textbook was "full of lies" and students should not be tested on that version of history. The textbook was out of sync with what the press was now writing about Stalinist repressions; there were gaping holes in Soviet history. A new textbook was needed. In the spirit of *glasnost,* Gorbachev's supporters in the Ministry of Education came up with the unusual idea of having rival teams of historians produce competitive versions of a new textbook; they would publish not one version, but two.

"We're talking about reeducating the teachers themselves, as well as the writers and historians." This according to Galina Klokova, a member of one team that is developing a text for high school seniors. She is a historian and former teacher.

"It is extremely difficult for a new approach to make headway, even on a personal level," she said. "The saddest thing of all is that a large portion of the teachers and students don't think for themselves. They have not been taught to analyze or to compare. They just accept. If they get a textbook, *any* textbook, they will teach whatever is in it. Unfortunately, teachers sometimes still try to work the old way, because it is more comfortable."[31]

I found it hard to imagine a Russian better suited to rewriting Soviet history than Mrs. Klokova. Or rather, she would be trying to write it honestly for the first time. For Mrs. Klokova is both a charming, gentle-spoken, white-haired woman of fifty-eight, with ruddy cheeks and a warm smile, and a scholar who combines intellectual rigor with a streak of tolerance and an instinctive feel for democracy, unusual among Russians. So many Soviets have grown accustomed to orthodoxy that they demand the single-textbook solution and get upset when it is not fed to them.

Galina Klokova is not only undogmatic, she is also untroubled by historical uncertainties and ambiguities.

"Dogma distorts history," she said simply. "It is important that history be opened clearly, vividly, to bring people into history. History should help to create a free person."

Her sentiments were echoed in principle by one of her textbook-writing colleagues, Oleg Voloboyev, an intense fifty-year-old who had long been an instructor at a citadel of historical orthodoxy, the Higher Communist Party School. Even so, he was willing to say that the teaching of Soviet history had suffered from excessive "mythologizing" (he meant hyperbole), and from dependence on one history book—the infamous *Short Course,* Stalin's own version of people and events.[32]

The problem was that textbook writing was to be a collective endeavor, and before they could write their textbook, Klokova, Voloboyev, and the rest of their team had to agree on the truth. I quickly discovered, however, that even these two could not see eye to eye on the fundamentals—for example, how many people had died at Stalin's hands.

"What will you tell your students?" I asked. "I've heard nine million, twenty million, forty million."

"I don't think we will ever be able to calculate those figures," answered Voloboyev. "We can only approximate."

Klokova had a far different notion. "Even forty million may be short of the mark," she said, "if you take figures connected with the civil war, the destruction of the countryside in the 1920s, the famine, the poverty. The figure forty million could include deaths from the Great Patriotic War [World War II]."

Voloboyev immediately objected: "You shouldn't lump together the civil-war dead with Stalin's repression. They are totally different things."

They got into a squabble. She held Stalin responsible for the millions who died from the rural famine, the millions of minority people who were forcibly relocated by Stalin, as well as those who were shot at places like Kuropaty or perished in forced-labor camps.

"These are all victims of Stalin's repression," she asserted.

"No, no, no," he interjected.[33]

They disagreed, too, over whether to teach high school students that the Red Terror had started in 1918; that meant not only Stalin, but Lenin, too, was culpable. Klokova believed that was true; Voloboyev adamantly objected.

Their argument was instructive not only because of their clashing views but also in terms of the problem historians have rewriting history. The press was far quicker than the historians in breaking new ground on Soviet history; the professional historians were already in print with books and articles that were now being discredited. They had a vested interest in the old orthodoxy, so they were slower to make amends than publicists or poets. Moreover, textbooks are always subject to political pressure when there is a monopoly customer—the state educational system. Decades of experience had schooled the professional textbook writers in political orthodoxy; the new freedoms were baffling for them.

Yet while the historians argue, teaching goes on, and the teachers who venture into the classroom every day, with history literally changing before their eyes, need immediate help.

For two years now, teachers have been sent periodic history bulletins for their courses through a teachers' magazine put out by the Ministry of Education. These instruct teachers how to deal with what Soviets call "the white spaces" in their history: Stalin's purges, the secret protocols of the 1939 Hitler-Stalin pact, the invasion of Czechoslovakia. Many teachers also clip newspaper and magazine articles to use in class, just to keep pace with what their students are reading or hearing at home. For many old-time teachers, the process of adjustment is painful.

In Yaroslavl, a city of half a million people about two hundred miles north of Moscow, I visited a provincial school that reminded me of the one my children attended in Moscow in the early seventies. Neither the uniforms nor the rules seemed to have changed much in fifteen years. The boys were still wearing navy-blue suits, the girls' uniforms consisting of dark brown sweaters and black skirts that I was told dated back to czarist times.

When I arrived in Yaroslavl, Viktoriya Kulikova, a heavy-set teacher with dyed red hair, was running her class with the order and formality of a German gymnasium. She lectured and the children stood to recite. She told me she felt it important to instill habits of work and discipline. Kulikova has been teaching for thirty years, and has been a member of the Communist Party all her adult life. She was trying to be tolerant of the changes, but they clearly made her uncomfortable.

"Indoctrination in citizenship—that's my most important task," she told me. "Basically that means, despite all our problems, love your motherland and its people, and respect their achievements."[34]

After class, several students, boys and girls of sixteen and seventeen, said that Kulikova's teaching was tame and orthodox compared to the candid, freewheeling discussions in their own homes. Their family talk revolved around revelations in the press and sometimes drew on personal recollections of older people in the community who were victims of Stalinist repression. Though Viktoriya Kulikova knew all this was going on, she was protective of the past. She spoke in terms of the students, but I think she was really speaking about herself.

"The kids suffer," she said. "Of course, I can't speak for all children, but I know in our school the children suffer from such recollections. They suffer because it seems to them that the history of their homeland should be just so, should be beautiful. . . . My position is this: We should show everything about our history, the bad and the good, the very bad and the very good. But nevertheless, we should try to instill in young people an image of something positive. . . . Too much criticism is dangerous. That's my opinion."[35]

At School No. 45 in Moscow, I met an educator with a very different cast of mind. For thirty years, Leonid Milgram has been the principal there. To see the energy of the kids running and talking in the corridors is to sense an unusually democratic school for the Soviet Union, despite the large gold profile head of Lenin with the slogan LENIN EVEN NOW IS MORE ALIVE THAN ALL THE LIVING.

Milgram is in his sixties, balding, potbellied; he looks as casual and approachable as the sleeveless sweaters he wears. Serious math and science students come into his office with schemes for computer hookups with high schools in Los Angeles. Younger children run up to him in the hall to show off their Michael Jackson buttons.

When I asked Milgram how things were going with the new teaching about Stalin and the purges, he admitted great problems. "The old teachers were indoctrinated with one textbook. You know the one," he said. "They can't reorient themselves and they don't want to. They respond well to Nina Andreyeva—to her views. They reflect those views. That's one problem. Others, the younger ones, are so far from that period that they don't know much and they didn't study the new history. They don't know how to study."[36]

Like Kulikova, Milgram is a lifelong Communist. He is still a believer in the socialist ideal of a humane society in which the goal is not profit but people. But he has been sorely disillusioned by how much has gone wrong, and above all, by the tyranny of Stalin. His own father was shot in 1937, at the peak of the purges; Milgram's disillusionment came two decades later.

"I don't trust people who say they always understood what Stalin was," he told me.

"I believed," he said. "I believed. You know, I'm not alone. In the class where I studied, thirteen of us ended up without parents. And still everybody believed. No one took it into his mind to say anything against Stalin. The tragedy is that we blindly believed Stalin, and even more painful was that we kept believing. That's where the tragedy is.

"I can say one thing: I never lied to the kids. Never. On the other hand, I was also mixed up in certain ways. Although I said what I thought, I might not have been correct. But I never intentionally lied. I could say, 'I don't know.' But I could never lie. It seemed to me that one could—and had to—remain a decent man.

"We need *perestroika* because we must create a new person—a person, I would say, with straight shoulders. Here for decades a person was taught to believe that if there's someone giving orders, you should obey them. Russia only touched democracy for several months in 1917, from February to October. Both before that and afterward, our politics always had the style of command. Command was its essence."

Milgram let that sink in, and then went on.

"To deny the beliefs that we grew up with is very difficult," he said. "So now we have to try to democratize society and to raise democrats anew. It's a hard road."[37]

Milgram has a natural talent for getting young people to think for themselves. He had wanted to take a class of his oldest students to Mikhail Shatrov's play *Dictatorship of Conscience*, a searing indictment of the development of the Communist Revolution that puts no less a figure than Lenin on trial. But Milgram could not get tickets, so our film crew videotaped the production and then took the film and a VCR to his class. Milgram used Shatrov's play to provoke thoughtful debate among his seniors. They were not typical—an unusually bright group, mostly from professional families. Nonetheless their reactions gave me an insight into the thinking of Soviet teenagers.

"The fact that Stalin appeared, this kind of tyrant, was it natural or wasn't it?" asked a pretty girl in a purple turtleneck named Marina. "That is, if it weren't Stalin, would it have been someone else? It's a very important question."

"And how do you answer it?" prodded Milgram.

"I don't know," said Marina. "It's a tough one."

A hand went up, and Milgram pointed to Masha, a girl with long blond hair. "It seems to me that Stalin was a product of the system," she suggested. "The system presupposed tyranny at that time."

"Generally, we must not say whether Stalin's coming to power is either natural or unnatural," added Alex, a dark-haired boy in a blue uniform. "When any man concentrates an unlimited amount of power in his hands, when there are no controls on him, he gradually of his own accord turns into a tyrant. Sooner or later, being intoxicated with power and having no controls, this is what happens."

Milgram put in his own word: "Haven't you noticed there's something dramatically opposed to this, which we're going through right now—being intoxicated by freedom?"

"It's not yet clear what that can lead to," young Alex replied. "It's pretty understandable that people like Sakharov and Yeltsin are concerned about what Gorbachev has concentrated in his own hands. He has taken for himself the key powers and in general has concentrated power in his hands."

A curly-haired boy named Boris saw historical parallels. "It seems to me the coming to power of Stalin was completely natural," he said. "The October [1917] Revolution was basically the first revolution in which power passed not to the middle class but to the very lowest class, and the lower class was not ready for this power. And right when people were unprepared for democracy, that's when, according to any law of history, some man of steel must appear to bring order. Right now, we can see approximately the same thing. Now, a kind of freedom has appeared. Most people use this freedom the wrong way. And now, once more we hear voices saying that we need another dictatorship, we need another firm hand."

"Criticism is crucial," Milgram advised. "Without that, without criticism, without external influence on those who are in power, there can be no movement forward. . . . Democratization leads to greater responsibility on the part of each individual. Otherwise, there will be anarchy."

"A dictatorship is in our future," said a dark-haired girl in the back. "Dictatorship is inevitable."

"We are pessimists," Marina, in the turtleneck, commented. "If we believe that everything that awaits us is terrible, if we really believe that, we should either leave this country or go and shoot ourselves. Why go on living if you think like that?"

Andrei, a thoughtful boy with glasses, wanted to go back to Shatrov's play and to history. "At the time when the country was being led by Lenin, was he guilty for all this?" he asked. "If he was guilty, then the whole foundation is destroyed."

"I would like to say that there's a famous saying, 'Create no idols,' " said a girl with a ponytail. "I think the followers of Lenin should have understood not only Lenin, not just believed in him blindly, but also understood his ideas."

Outspoken Boris had a response. "With Lenin's separation of the Church from the State, he removed all thinking people—except those who backed him," he asserted. "In this sense, he was very close to Stalin."

"You're out of bounds here," Milgram interjected, still defensive of Lenin, "because you don't know anything about Lenin, and you're confusing Stalin with Lenin and grouping them together. You should study both Stalin and Lenin."

"About Lenin, we should know more and study more," offered a pigtailed girl. "Not just about Lenin. We should generally just know more. And if there were mistakes in the past, they should not be repeated today."

"That's what school is for, right?" Milgram said.

Turning to the class as a whole, he went on. "This was a very interesting conversation," he said. "But one thing depresses me a little bit. You have very little optimism. That's tough; that depresses me. You know, my friends, future society depends on your optimism or pessimism. It's very serious.

"You know, there is socialism and there is socialism. What is socialism? From the point of view of an economic system, socialism is a system in which there is no private ownership. From the point of view of everyday socialism in society, in which there is a maximum of democracy and satisfying the demands of people, that kind of socialism is possible. Something else—command socialism—can also be. But we shouldn't allow it.

"The choice depends not on me, because I'm old, but on you," he said. "Therefore, it's very important that you understand everything correctly and look at things correctly. . . ."[38]

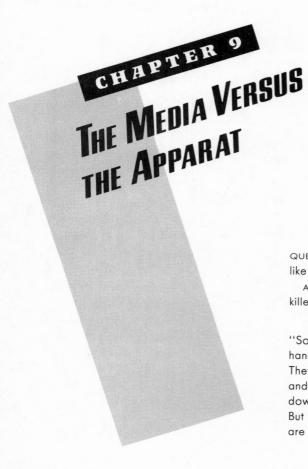

CHAPTER 9
THE MEDIA VERSUS THE APPARAT

QUESTION: Why is a minister like a fly?

ANSWER: Because both can be killed by a newspaper.

—Soviet riddle

"So far, *glasnost* is in the hands of the Party apparatchiks. They set limits for what we can and cannot do. We try to break down the walls they have erected. But no matter what we think, we are not completely free."[1]

—Bella Kurkova
Leningrad TV
September 1989

Bella Kurkova has the feisty, rebellious temper of a Bolshevik—especially when she is fighting Bolsheviks.

Bella is executive editor of *Fifth Wheel (Pyatoye Koleso)*, Leningrad's most daring television program, and when I first saw her in April 1989, she had just announced her candidacy for the Congress of People's Deputies in Moscow.

Having taken on the Leningrad Communist Party apparatus on the tube, she was now taking them on at the ballot box.

She bustled into her office, shaking hands all around, looking less like a radical than like a suburbanite. In her late forties, she has a soft, open face, her bleached blond hair done in a modified bouffant. With traditional Russian femininity, Bella was all dolled up in a pale peach blouse with a huge bow at the throat—yet she radiated the hyperkinetic energy of a short-order cook at lunchtime rush. She was about to have a campaign photograph taken, but even so, she headed for her desk, and without sitting down began to give instructions to assistants, answer the phone— all the while conversing with me and my companions, Martin Smith and Louis Menashe. Primping for the photographer, she motioned him into position with one half-free hand.

I decided to start right in on my questions. "Isn't it a conflict of interest for a journalist to be an elected member of Congress at the same time?" I asked.

"Excuse me . . . the photographer," Bella said, and she posed primly, before turning to my question. "Before, I never would have thought about this—about becoming a candidate. I'm doing it to defend my program and to defend *glasnost* for journalists in general. If everything were going smoothly for *Fifth Wheel*, I would never have gotten into this. But we cannot work normally. And so I have to take the risk."[2]

She was referring to the fact that in the first round of the elections on March 26, 1989, the Communist Party hierarchy in Leningrad had been savaged—and Party apparatchiks were blaming the media, specifically *Fifth Wheel*, for the fact that seven top figures in the provincial and city leadership had been rejected by the voters. "Certain press organs joined with anti-Marxist forces," one speaker complained at a Party meeting. Another accused Leningrad television of "gaining popularity on the cheap by pandering to the narrow-mindedness of the man in the street." He zeroed in on the culprits: "We can point to many shows, including *Fifth Wheel*. There are many instances where they behave in a truly ugly fashion."[3]

The media clearly were functioning at the forefront of political opposition to the Communist Party hierarchy.

No organized political force had yet emerged to galvanize mass support. And so muckrakers in the media, especially those on television who had a mass following, were leading the challenge against the Party apparat. They were exposing official corruption, the privileges of the elite, and the inept mismanagement of the economy, as well as giving vent to public grievances.

Party conservatives were now lashing back, trying to stifle the media. They were demanding that Bella be fired, and *Fifth Wheel* shut down.

To fight back, Bella felt that going to the public as a candidate would be the strongest tactic. According to Soviet law, she was allowed to become a second-round candidate in districts where no one had won the election in the first round. And so she had happily cast herself as a foe of the apparatus, even though she was a Communist Party member and held a *nomenklatura* appointment—meaning that she had been picked for her job by the ideological department of the Leningrad Province Party Committee, the very same officials she was now fighting.

As a print and television journalist, for twenty years Bella had been boiling with indignation at the tactics of her Party overlords. "I want to kick the apparatchiks out of the Communist Party," she declared. "We live for the day when the apparatchiks don't boss us around."[4] Years of chafing at ideological control now mingled with bitterness at the miseries of everyday living and fueled her protest.

"Every day I give thanks to our government for our terrible transportation system," she told me, barely containing her fury. "It takes me an hour to get to work—first on the bus, then on the subway, and finally on the trolley. And I live pretty close to the center of the city. But I have three transfers, so it's a terrible struggle. I never find a seat. But I thank God, because it puts me into a fighting mood. You can't make great art if you are completely satisfied. You only get great art when there's a sense of crisis. We always have that sense of crisis.

"And it's not just a matter of transportation. My pay is great—eight hundred rubles a month[5]—from my salary as chief editor, plus extra fees for my own scripts and appearances. But what can I do with the money? I can't find the books I love. I can't buy good-quality records. I can live without sugar or meat or vegetables, or a car, but I can't live without food for my mind. I love Italian culture and I want to get good books or subscriptions to Italian magazines. I can't do it. It's hard to get good tickets to the theater—I can't simply go to the box office and get them. I'm an executive editor so I have ways of getting tickets, but it's a struggle. If I could go to Italy or Spain or wherever I want, then everything else would be tolerable. Once, for six days, I got to Italy on a delegation from Leningrad. We shot twenty-four hours of videotape in six days. Imagine how intense that was. I saw it as a unique opportunity, so I worked eighteen hours a day. But I can't get out now."[6]

There was an explosive excitement among the team at *Fifth Wheel*. Bursting with ideas, they had the wild enthusiasm of an American university campus in the 1960s. To be with them was like being at Berkeley—a swarm of producers and reporters milling about in their jeans, with the hair of flower children. Rebellion was in the air.

Bella and her crew knew which side they were on: They were the "antis"—the people against the "power structure." Their programs amounted to unabashed advocacy journalism. Long suppressed, they had a sudden sense of power, having just shaken up the Party establishment, yet they also had a sense of vulnerability. Fear of retaliation was palpable; in the darkened hallway of her television studio, Bella told me the Party was after her scalp. "The situation is dangerous," she said.

While that danger was partly romantic, it was also realistic. The new muckrakers of Gorbachev's *perestroika* had known life under a repressive dictatorship. Until the spring of 1988, when *Fifth Wheel* began, they were hidden away in the interstices of safe programs on the Hermitage Museum or czarist palaces, on filming theatrical classics, doing shows for children or a few risqué programs—Western jazz, features for young people. They had fresh memories of hiding in the shadows, recalled one wine-filled Russian evening at the apartment of a producer named Natasha Sereva.

"The most important thing is to get rid of the feeling of fear," said Sasha Krivonos, a rumpled, chain-smoking producer, still infectiously boyish after twenty years in television.

"It's important to heal the soul inside us," he went on. "It's a terrible feeling—this horrible fear which makes you turn back now and then to make sure you are not being followed. No matter how we behave, the feeling of fear is deep in our souls. We are trying to overcome it. We try to argue with our superiors. We tell them, 'We don't give a damn about you. We will air our show.' But we still have this feeling of fear. Each of us has this censor inside, which prevents us from doing many things. We ask ourselves, 'Can we do it or can't we do it? Will it be allowed or not?' "

"Oh, Sasha, speak for yourself—not everybody's afraid," blurted out Tatyana Smorodinskaya, a slender reporter with long thin hair, sharp eyes, and a tense face. "We are absolutely not afraid. We have an opportunity to make basic changes, to try to change the political system and to get new laws."

But what had they all been doing and thinking before Gorbachev came to power?

"No matter how we are suppressed by the ideologists, they haven't yet invented a way to ban thinking," replied the hostess, Sereva, a strong-looking woman with dark hair. "They can't forbid us to think. Even before, it was possible to use one's brains."

"You had to resort to all kinds of tricks," chirped Zoya Belyayeva, an aggressive young reporter. "The more they banned, the more tricks we invented. Remember how, when we gave them our scripts to approve, we would drop phrases they could object to, and then we would use them during the shooting?"

"Do you think that we didn't understand what was going on ten years ago, twenty years ago?" Natasha Sereva asked. "We were no different ten years ago than we are today. We were exactly the same. But we lived, then, in the atmosphere of a concentration camp. We could take a step in this direction, but we could not take a step in that direction. They set limits for us. We *always* wanted to work the way we do today."

"Then, everybody was silent," Sasha Krivonos added. "Now, more things are made public. If they stop it tomorrow, it will be terrible."

"Five years ago, I lost my job," Zoya Belyayeva said.

"Yes," Natasha said, "Zoya lost her job because she did a show about an American musician. I don't remember who—was it Bob Dylan?"

"No—it was B. B. King," Zoya corrected her. "He came to Leningrad."

The reporter Tatyana Smorodinskaya grew philosophical. "It would be difficult for you to understand what it means to be a stranger in your own country," she said. "That's how many of the intelligentsia existed, as 'internal exiles.' "

It was a phrase that I had often heard in the seventies, for intellectuals who had withdrawn from involvement in public life because they rejected the system.

"To tell you the truth," Smorodinskaya added, "the only purpose of our lives then was not to turn into mutants—into deformed people." And she went on to explain how "the system," with its pressures to conform, had divided people into two groups.

In one group there were in every field the "careerists—those who wanted to serve the regime and be rewarded. They gave something, and they got something for themselves—and they were morally destroyed. Those who lived according to this pattern turned into mutants."

Then there was another group. "The people you are talking to here went out of their way not to become mutants. It was hard. You had to keep your behavior under control constantly. You had to maintain a very delicate sense of ethics. A great number of people did not turn into mutants, thank God. But the rest did. It's a terrible drama—a terrible historic drama."

"Now [on TV] we can cover more themes," Natasha Sereva said, "but the symbol of our time is still struggle—struggle, just as before. Freedom is still limited. Our leaders tell us, *This* you can do and *this* you cannot. The general structure hasn't changed. They only expanded the range of subjects and themes we're allowed to cover."

It was a thought that sobered everyone.

Natasha began to talk about Soviet intellectuals who had emigrated to the West during years of repression.

"All of us here could have emigrated to your homeland and lived very well there. We stayed here. We're not fanatics, we're not idiots. We stayed here because we must tell people the truth."

"The flow of truth is powerful," Sasha Krivonos observed, "so powerful that it knocked a lot of people off their feet."[7]

"A CLASS STRUGGLE AGAINST *GLASNOST*"

Leningrad is a natural battleground for the struggle between the media and the apparat. Its rich cultural tradition and its large intelligentsia have made it a city with pretensions to cultural leadership of the entire nation. The fact that it is now Russia's second city gives it an inferiority complex, and this has spurred its radicals to cause a splash that would outdo Moscow.

Arrayed against those cultural forces and ambitions is a powerful, hidebound Old Guard political leadership, one of the most autocratic in the Soviet system.

So sparks were bound to fly in Leningrad when Gorbachev kindled the ferment of *glasnost.*

The Party kept control of the main newspaper, *Leningradskaya Pravda,* but the film studios and the television station became hotbeds of radicalism.

Fifth Wheel is one of three major television programs that are on the cutting edge of new media freedoms. These programs play to an audience of twenty million people in and around Leningrad, northwest Russia, and the Baltic republics.

The most widely watched program is the nightly *600 Seconds (Shestsot Sekunduv),* a graphic, ten-minute news kaleidoscope, featuring crime, corruption, and sensation. Its anchor, Aleksandr Nevzorov, was once a movie stuntman and singer in a church choir. Now, at thirty-one years old, he is a full-tilt ambulance chaser. He can cover thirteen news bits in ten minutes. His topics range from how rotting meat is ground into sausages at a Leningrad factory, to how radioactivity emanates from old Soviet helicopters in a children's park, to a trip to the morgue to report on the tragic suicide leap of a woman and her two small children. The reporting is aggressive, if skimpy, and the camera work looks like an amateur imitation of *60 Minutes.*

Nevzorov, whose brash disclosures and leather-jacketed cockiness have made him the best-known figure in Leningrad, brags that he once did a piece from a hospital, about a man whose dog bit off his genitals after the man had tried to bugger the dog.[8] People with grievances to air insist that Nevzorov shakes news free and gets action. "He names names," one youthful admirer said. "One line from Nevzorov will kill three apparatchiks."

But critics suggest that he may be the unwitting tool, or secret ally, of hard-liners among the police who want to oppose *perestroika:* His steady drumbeat of bad news feeds popular pessimism.

The second program in the Leningrad TV troika is *Public Opinion (Obshchestvennoye Mneniye),* a three-hour call-in show that combines debates among experts on topical issues, live man-in-the-street interviews, and a running poll of call-ins on the issue of the night. Its anchor is Tamara Maksimova, who comes on like "Miss Gollywood" (the Russians, having no *H* in their alphabet, use *G* instead); she wears almond-shaped dark glasses and thick black leather slacks. Her husband, Vladimir, more modest and self-contained, is the producer. Their show, which went on the air in early 1987, has discussed the death penalty, alcoholism, the economy, the terrible pollution of Leningrad's water system, and *perestroika.*

On one show, Soviets and Yugoslavs debated whether it was better to live in Yugoslavia, where the stores had plenty of goods but inflation was so bad that many people could not afford to shop, or in the Soviet Union, where many people had cash but the stores were so empty there was little worth buying.

In another show, "Blackboard of Democracy," people were invited to write their own political slogans on a huge board in downtown Leningrad. Among those that appeared were: DOWN WITH LIGACHEV; AFGHANISTAN IS OUR SHAME; and GIVE US A MULTIPARTY SYSTEM.

Some Party progressives had backed *Public Opinion* as a way of monitoring the general mood, but they went into shock one night when a listener mockingly asked how there could be *perestroika* if Gorbachev and Politburo colleagues like Yegor Ligachev could not agree on what the word meant. Any mention of breaches at the top was beyond the tolerance of even progressive Party members. Tamara Maksimova saved her career by smothering the question, and the program became a bit more cautious after that.[9]

Fifth Wheel was different from the other two programs in the way it used investigative documentaries to discuss both current issues and Soviet history. First aired in the spring of 1988, it soon built a popular following; its twice-a-week, two-hour shows were penetrating, in-depth reports. The name *Fifth Wheel* symbolized the supposedly superfluous people in Leningrad television who covertly created the first show and then persuaded their bosses to run it.

In one short year, *Fifth Wheel* ran shows on the problems of returning Afghan veterans; the maltreatment of children at an orphanage run by the police; dangers posed by a nuclear-power station near Leningrad; the problems of poor, disabled, and lonely people; the battles of rebel artists; communal tensions in Soviet Georgia; the execution of Czar Nicholas II and his family; recollections of Stalinist purge victims; unprecedented footage on the destruction by Stalin of the famous Church of Christ the Redeemer in Moscow; and Arkady Ruderman's interview with former Czechoslovak leader Alexander Dubček.

In one of *Fifth Wheel*'s most unforgettable scenes, Bella Kurkova and Sasha Krivonos tracked down a former Stalinist executioner, who was living in the cramped poverty of old age. Sasha persuaded him to show, on camera, how he shot people.

"Tell me, Andrei Ivanovich," Sasha coaxed the former gulag guard, "from what distance were people shot?"

The bald old man moved around behind Sasha and raised his arm, not quite straight. He made a gun with his hand and pointed his index finger at the back of Sasha's head.

"Bang in the head," he said, eyes staring wildly. "At approximately this distance."

"At the distance of an outstretched arm?" Sasha asked.

"No," the former executioner replied. "Arm slightly bent. You can't shoot with a straight arm."

Then he described how guards later stripped the corpses of jewelry and gold fillings.

"You'd put some sort of spirit, alcohol, on the gums, and the teeth came out easier," he said.

Later in the program, as the camera panned the smokestack of the crematorium at Moscow's Donskoi Monastery, Bella Kurkova took up the narrative, telling viewers that in the dark of night, "trucks with crates marked MEAT or VEGETABLES or FURNITURE would pull up to the crematorium and dump the bodies in the fire. The place where they finally buried the bones and ashes was paved over a few years ago."[10]

Politically, the most explosive broadcasts were a series of three programs on the privileges of the Leningrad Communist Party elite. The first, focusing on Party leaders' exclusive, well-furbished *dachas* in the wooded areas of Stone Island near Leningrad, was called "Silent Walls," for the seven-foot-high walls and fences built to hide these opulent residences from public view. Some of the estates had separate housing for servants. Zoya Belyayeva, the reporter fired for doing the program on B. B. King, climbed the walls with a cameraman to show the lavish mansions that Party leaders had built for themselves, while nearby, a hospital and a historic home of Pushkin's languished in disrepair, for lack of funds.

Stung by the public outcry, Party leaders lashed back at *Fifth Wheel.* They denounced it in the press, and set up an ideological commission to investigate it. A battle royal was on, the Party trying to silence Bella while she made more accusations, more appeals to the public, on her show; and the public egged her on. The first broadcast in December 1988 was followed by two more, on official graft; each was cut by censors, but they were still powerful. The third one ran on March 17, and nine days later was the fateful election in which seven Party bigwigs lost. In the Soviet system, it takes at least 50 percent of eligible votes to win, so there were lots of runoffs that spring.

Fighting for her life and for the survival of *Fifth Wheel* in the second round of the election, Bella Kurkova became a political candidate and carried the battle directly to Yuri Solovyov, the top Party boss in Leningrad and a junior member of the Politburo in Moscow. During a televised debate, Bella attacked Solovyov, who was not present. "I criticized him severely for interfering in our work," she recalled. "I spoke about the fact that when he takes part in an event in town, we are stripped of all the good equipment—cameras, cutting rooms, everything—because the authorities require other crews to shoot him with three cameras." Bella told me she had seized the candidate debate to criticize Solovyov, even in his absence, because she assumed he would never agree to see her.[11]

In the elections, Bella Kurkova was beaten by an even more outspoken foe of the Party apparat, a criminal prosecutor pursuing official corruption named Nikolai Ivanov.

On May 16, two days after the election, Solovyov sent an official car to bring Bella to Party headquarters; the Party was demanding a written explanation for her criticism of him. She refused to go, advised by Anatoly

Sobchak, a lawyer and people's deputy, that her campaign statements were protected by law. But the heat was on, and the campaign to strangle *Fifth Wheel* resumed. Leningrad Mayor Vladimir Khodyrev, who had lost in the election, declared Bella Kurkova and *Fifth Wheel* his personal enemies.

"Can you imagine—who he is and who I am?" Bella said, sharing her astonishment with me. "*We* are dangerous for *him*? The man who is in charge of TV in the Obkom Province Party Committee told me that in the committee offices they jump every time they hear my name. They are afraid of us! The humor is in the fact that *they* are afraid of *us*."[12]

Despite that fear—or because of it—Bella was told that the provincial Party committee had decided to shut down *Fifth Wheel* and fire her. At a closed Party meeting, she was informed, sixteen of twenty-two speakers had come out against the program; only one defended it. "My colleagues tried to console me but the situation was really serious," she told me later. "I remember May twenty-fourth, twenty-fifth, before the opening of the People's Congress [in Moscow]. It looked like our program could be banned."

She went on: "It's a real class struggle against *glasnost.* The apparatchiks think the press is given too much freedom. They don't want the public to learn about their doings. For seventy years, they have been so used to giving orders which are fulfilled. Now the time has come when their orders are ignored. They can't take it. . . . They fan up hatred toward Jews. To divert people's hatred from the Party bureaucrats, they blame Jews. I'm Russian but I am considered a Jew because I think that all nationalities are equal. I receive letters in which they call me a kike."

During the campaign, Party hard-liners had tried to whip up the anger of workers against the intelligentsia, and specifically the media, as a force for liberalization. Neo-Stalinist conservatives, joined by Russian nationalists from the right-wing Pamyat, meaning "Memory," organized a rally near television headquarters, attacking the most aggressive programs— and *Fifth Wheel* was a prime target. Placards declared: THE KGB AND MINISTRY OF INTERNAL AFFAIRS ARE THE STRONGHOLDS OF DEMOCRACY; DOWN WITH *FIFTH WHEEL*; DOWN WITH THE RUSSOPHOBES FROM *FIFTH WHEEL.*

Fifth Wheel put out the word that it was to be closed down.

The public response was overwhelming. Liberal cultural organizations called a counterrally in support of the program. "Many, many people came to that rally," Bella recalled. "The whole square was filled with people. The apparatchiks saw that we were stronger than they were. And that is why they hate us." Other protest meetings were held at institutions and factories. One huge plant sent a telegram to Party leaders: IF YOU TOUCH *FIFTH WHEEL* AND KURKOVA, WE WILL GO ON STRIKE.

Not only did *Fifth Wheel* escape the guillotine, Bella told me triumphantly, but its bête noire, Leningrad Party boss Yuri Solovyov, was removed by Gorbachev for being so out of step with Gorbachev's own policies and, as the elections had shown, with the public.

"I always said either he would outlast us or we would outlast him," Bella said. "Thank God we're the ones who lasted."

"You're a politician, Bella, not just a journalist," I observed.

"I don't think I'm a politician," she replied. "But today, any honest journalist is a politician. Because if you want to restore justice, if you want the life in your country changed, it's necessary," she answered. "Each of us has only one life. It's necessary not to waste it. A decent journalist cannot avoid hot issues. . . .

"We are rather amateurish politicians at *Fifth Wheel*. We tried to stay away from politics. We didn't think it was our business. Then, after our first show was broadcast, politics burst into the life of every person [involved in the show]. In the last year and a half, politics has become almost everyone's concern in the country. There are no indifferent people left."[13]

THE LIMITS OF *GLASNOST*

If Party hard-liners could not close down *Fifth Wheel*, they tried, covertly, to squeeze the life out of it by working through Bella's bosses and employers, and through the Leningrad branch of the State Committee for Television and Radio. Bella's staff was cut by one third. *Fifth Wheel* was reduced from two shows a week to one. It was denied financing and good equipment.

Censorship was tightened through a system that was multilayered: military censors, literary censors with their lists of taboo names and topics, and most important, political censors from the Party apparat and the television administration. The first two were the official censors; the last group were not officially called censors, but they were in fact the most important and most controlling.

In *Fifth Wheel*'s first eighteen months, Bella told me, about twenty segments of various programs had been banned outright by censors before the Party's outright effort to shut it down. Included among them were one on the mass graves at Minsk, an interview with a people's deputy who quoted private statements by Gorbachev that were at odds with his public positions, and a program about the repression of a Soviet choreographer named Roman Yakobson. Twenty more programs had been heavily censored, including the program about the Leningrad nuclear-power station and those on the privileges of the Party elite. Still other programs had been delayed for weeks and months—especially several that dealt with tensions among Soviet nationalities.

In September 1989, Bella fought for approval of a powerful documentary on the Leningrad boss of the NKVD (Stalin's KGB). The man was named Litvin, and he had allegedly ordered the murders of twenty thousand people in 1937, and then committed suicide just as he himself was about to be killed. According to Bella, the new head of Leningrad television, Viktor Senin, had been blocking this film for a couple of months, presumably on orders from Party headquarters. On the script, he had written, "Specify the actions of Litvin." Bella had hopes of bringing Senin around because he was a former *Pravda* correspondent, and better to deal with than the ideological watchdogs the Party usually put in such posts. She urged me, and our camera crew, to go with her to Senin's office.

It was huge, with a polished table long enough for twenty people. Senin, a trim, well-dressed man in his mid-forties with a self-confident jut to his chin, greeted us at his desk. We had asked to see him at that very hour, but our arrival with Bella caught him by surprise. Still, he was polite and agile. On that day, with our cameras rolling, Senin cast himself in the role of a man caught in the middle, forced to serve as agent of the Party hierarchy above him but sympathetic to the journalists and people below.

It was instantly apparent that he was no longer going to block *Fifth Wheel*'s exposé of the NKVD. Without even sitting down, he signed off on what had been a suspect script. Bella winked at me, pleased that her ploy had worked.

"This is the first time we have covered this theme—a machine of extermination," Senin bragged to me. "You see we are giving an inside story about the KGB."

Eager to reinstate his liberal credentials, Senin reported how he had recently championed a program on the controversial people's deputy Boris Yeltsin, over the objections of Party apparatchiks for whom Yeltsin was a mortal enemy.

"I signed off a week before the show and they were trying to ban it up to the last moment," Senin said. "An official from the provincial Party committee was sitting right here, in my office, right on top of my head, telling me, 'You should not,' and I was telling him we should."

"What kind of *glasnost* is this, if they are sitting on top of your head?" I asked.

"There are people who dream of the time when it will be possible to go back to the old methods," he replied. "But we have a TV audience today that can't be shut down by any bureaucrats. They can fire me, they can kick me out of this chair, but they can't silence the audience."

"Can they fire her?" I asked, gesturing to Bella. We were all three still standing around his large desk.

"Sure they can," Senin said, then reconsidered. "No, it's more difficult to fire her. It's a very popular program. That's why we have meetings . . . to think what can be done to preserve this program."

That was enough to launch Bella into a diatribe—for her, a relatively mild one—against the whole process of censorship.

"Above him, on the staircase of power, there are many steps which interfere with his work," she said. "Here in journalism a bureaucratic machine has been created which doesn't care to make journalism exciting and interesting for readers and listeners."

She thrust the script about the NKVD chief at me, showing how the censors were holding her responsible for every single word.

"Each line of the script is checked and double-checked," she protested. Then, riffling through it page by page, she raced on: "I must sign every page. Here is my signature. Let me show you how many times I signed. Thirty-one times. Thirty-second time here, and thirty-third on the back. What's next? Then the censor at the city literary censorship office will have to sign. There is a chance that he won't sign because the show is about the KGB. He can send me to the censor of the KGB. They also have a censor."

She was describing a system stuck in inertia, which, out of habits bred over decades, squashed independent-minded journalists and ignored Gorbachev's dictates for greater openness. This system had a reflexive instinct for self-preservation, a natural suspicion of anything new. The state monopoly of broadcasting, which Gorbachev had retained, made Senin's office a natural choke point.

"Bella is right when she says we have too many people who are not responsible for anything but who have a right to ban things," Senin said. "That's how they earn their salaries."

"But what's the reason for it?" I asked.

"Well, they have to do *something*," Senin sputtered. "They aren't qualified to do anything else. They have to demonstrate they are working hard, that they are zealous. If they forbid a lot of things, it means they're doing their job. They can show their superiors at the Party committee that they are zealous, because they censor things."

"How many people are there?" I asked. "Ten?"

"Oh no. About a hundred and fifty, and all over the country about eighteen million," Senin replied, using the figure Gorbachev gave for the entire national bureaucratic apparatus. "I am talking about our provincial committee staff. They must be responsible for something. They must pretend they are working. Do you expect them to show up and say, 'Viktor, go ahead, air the show'? They'll die from fear."

"How often do they visit you?" I asked.

"Every day," he said. "Every day."

"But Gorbachev said there should be more openness," I reminded him.

"For whom?"

"For everyone."

"Excuse me." Senin straightened up. "Gorbachev himself is not quite free to do what he wants. He is tied hand and foot. Even *he* cannot control things."[14]

HOW THEY PORTRAY US

The brawl between *Fifth Wheel* and the Leningrad Party apparat illustrates how the media have become both an instrument of change and a prime political battleground. This is true all across the country. The revolution in the Soviet media, their coverage of the West as well as of domestic affairs, has played a vital role in reshaping public attitudes and in driving the political agenda of *perestroika* in ways that Gorbachev did not anticipate.

In the summer of 1988, nationalist movements in the Baltic republics of Lithuania, Estonia, and Latvia were practically born on local television-discussion shows. In Georgia, Armenia, Azerbaijan, and elsewhere, the spark of nationalism was spread by regional television. In mid-1989, striking coal miners in Siberia and the southern Ukraine forced their demands on Gorbachev and Prime Minister Nikolai Ryzhkov through the visibility and political leverage given them by local and national television.

At Kemerovo, in western Siberia, Aleksandr Melnikov, the regional Party boss, complained to me that the media, especially television, were hounding him, publicizing the grievances of workers and criticizing him.[15] A senior television official, Gennady Metyakhin, openly disagreed with the Party leadership over the sources and cures of trouble in the coal mines. They clashed as well over the proper function of state television: As Party boss, Melnikov wanted his regional television to help mobilize factory workers to go out into rural areas and bring in the harvest; Metyakhin refused to be the Party's mouthpiece, asserting that this would merely perpetuate an inefficient farm system, rather than bring a reform of Stalin's collectivized farm system.

"We don't want to help the bureaucracy," he said, "because if the harvest is brought in that way, then once again the Party will claim, 'Thanks to our leadership, the people are well fed and happy.' "[16]

In Yaroslavl, four young journalists told me how Aleksandr Tsvetkov, a gutsy local television reporter, had battled his skittish TV bosses and forced them to let him broadcast a series that exposed a major construction scandal. The mayor was forced to resign and a slew of Party officials were punished.[17]

What is astonishing is that this fresh breeze is blowing through one of the stalest, most centralized monopolies of the Soviet state—Gosteleradio—the State Committee for Television and Radio. Back in the seventies, Soviet national television was leaden and immobile; it was the most politically orthodox of all the media because the Kremlin worried about the impact of any whimper of dissonance on the immense national television audience. On the stage and occasionally in books, little heresies were allowed to slip through. But not on television.

Only two channels broadcast nationwide across the eleven time zones, from Vladivostok on the Pacific to Kaliningrad near Poland: the First Program, for the most important news and cultural events, and the Second Program, for less important shows. Moscow had two other channels, for several hours a day, one for adult education and another for sports. Minority republics and important regional centers like Leningrad or Novosibirsk were allowed for a few hours a week to broadcast local programming, which was usually heavy on folklore and native costumes. In other words, it was a dull wasteland in the early 1970s, so insufferably dull that a Soviet diplomat, back home after a stint in Washington, admitted to me that his eleven-year-old son, having become accustomed to American TV, was bored out of his wits with Soviet programming and had become practically unmanageable.

The Soviet news, carried coast to coast to what was then estimated to be 100 million viewers (it's now 150 million), was literally read to viewers by announcers who were more notable for buttoned-up reliability than for their ease on camera. Flat and formal, the shows were also heavily censored. *Vremya (The Times),* the one evening news show, which came on at 9 P.M., was long on official Soviet communiqués, gray bureaucrats in wooden ceremonies, Foreign Minister Andrei Gromyko shaking hands with visiting delegations, and foreign footage of violence in America, protest marchers in Germany or Britain, bloodshed in Vietnam. Interspersed were paeans to Soviet economic achievements, statistics, films of

Soviet harvesters in formation as they swept across fields of waving wheat, blast furnaces belching mightily for the Socialist Cause. Children's programs, sports events, and concerts or ballets provided some relief, but even so the camera work was monotonous.

An anecdote mocked these programs: A viewer tuned in to find, on the First Program, Brezhnev delivering a windy speech. He switched to the Second Program: again, Brezhnev droning on. On the Third Program, a uniformed officer pointed a gun at the viewer and ordered: "Comrade, go back to Channel One."

Today, there are startling changes in form, style, and content. While much of the old wooden programming persists, a host of new shows offer live programming, Western-style visuals and graphics, a sprinkling of ads, and some out-and-out entertainment. Rock music and MTV have arrived with a vengeance. Even the morning news is spiced every few minutes with splashy, non-sequitur cutaways to Soviet rock groups or pop singers in spangly costumes and voluptuous poses. In the old days, women on Soviet TV were dowdy or costumed. Now, willowy young women lead aerobics classes or do suggestive dances in skintight leotards, and on news shows, the anchorwomen dress more stylishly. *Vremya* is still pretty tame, but even it has more on-the-spot reporting and a quotient of controversial material. The rest of the TV programming includes topical talk shows, fashion parades, game shows, film clips of Western stars from the Beatles to Bruce Springsteen, and even an occasional beauty contest.

The hard edges of the old Cold War stereotypes have been rounded off. Just as the American media have found plenty that is positive in the Gorbachev-*perestroika* story, the Soviet media no longer portray the West as a hostile armed camp seething with social tensions and anti-Soviet cabals. For one thing, Soviet television has given its viewer direct, uncensored access to Americans, from former Secretary of State George Shultz or Moscow-based American correspondents, to live satellite telecasts of citizen exchanges between cities like Seattle and Leningrad, or arguments between American senators and Soviet legislators.

What is more, the image of America itself is changing, as coverage becomes more balanced and varied. Typical of the new attitude was the public confessional I heard, in Tbilisi in September 1988, from Melor Sturua, a veteran Washington correspondent for *Izvestia*. Sturua acknowledged that his reporting on America had been deliberately negative, meant to reinforce ideological stereotypes. He voiced personal shame and promised to turn over a new leaf. Later, Valentin Lazutkin, deputy chairman and chief of foreign relations for Gosteleradio, wanted to be sure I took notice of the shift from the bad old days.

"Our picture of capitalist countries used to be very negative," he admitted. "We emphasized the poor and the homeless. From our correspondents in America, we used to order stories such as who is sleeping under the Brooklyn Bridge [an actual report in 1985]. We knew, especially those of us who traveled to the West, that this was a one-sided picture. Now we don't order such stories anymore—although like you we assert our right to cover anything and everything. But we try now to give a more balanced and accurate picture of life in the West."[18]

By the late 1980s, the Soviet press had a flow of favorable stories, especially about how well the American economy was working. Soviet television did admiring portraits of the McDonald's fast-food service, the efficiency of construction projects in Seattle, a well-run American family farm in Iowa, and even the way American political conventions operate. In a three-part documentary series on American farming, Soviet viewers got an impressive look at the modern technology used by family farmers, from tractors to computers—not to mention what to Russians would be an incredible network of businesses serving the farmer. In a report on traffic congestion in New York City, Soviet TV also ran flattering shots of the interstate highway system—light-years ahead of the rutted, gutted Soviet roads. Another documentary took a close look at Congress, showing its inner workings, almost textbook-style, for Soviet newcomers to the world of parliamentary politics. Policy differences on issues such as the American invasion of Panama or the war in Nicaragua have been pointed out, but without the vitriol of the coverage during the Cold War. And, wonder of wonders, given the traditional Soviet treatment of sports, Moscow television has run advertisements showing American athletes winning gold medals at the 1988 Olympics.

Ordinary Soviets have an enormous appetite for realistic pictures of the outside world, both out of curiosity and out of a desire for a standard by which to measure their own lives. At a grass-roots level, I have found them to be far more curious about us than we as a nation have been about them, and their greater interest shows up in the media. Academic specialists have found, for example, that Soviet television has given more coverage to foreign news than American networks have.[19] As Sturua and Lazutkin conceded in the past, the coverage has fit the paradigms of Soviet ideology.

With *glasnost,* and especially with the crumbling of Communist regimes in Eastern Europe in the fall of 1989, Soviet viewers got a fresh slant on events abroad. The breaching of the Berlin Wall, for example, was given timely and candid coverage. Sakharov's widow, Yelena Bonner, compared the opening of the Wall to the capture of the Bastille during the French Revolution. "Our TV showed all of this," she said. "We saw the same things you saw—those people on top of the wall."[20] Tass, the official Soviet press agency, was quick to assure Russians that the collapse of the Wall—and the collapse of the old hard-line regime—did not mean any change in the postwar borders, a sensitive issue for Russians. Before long, their focus, like ours, shifted to Bucharest, and the bloody Romanian revolt, the overthrow of Nicolae Ceauşescu, was played out on Soviet television.

It intrigued me that throughout the tumultuous events of 1989 and 1990, Moscow television was more candid about the political upheavals in Eastern Europe than it was about the nationalist tensions within its own borders. The Moscow media, especially television and its flagship, *Vremya,* have either ignored or given tendentious accounts of the violent suppression of the peaceful demonstrations in Georgia in April 1989, the bloody occupation of Azerbaijan in January 1990, the Lithuanian drive toward secession in the spring of 1990. Despite such omissions, *Vremya* remains the most-watched program in the nation, helped by its monopoly on the evening news. But cautious coverage of the most ticklish domestic developments has cost it some credibility. To most people, it is no longer the premier pacesetter of Soviet television.

THE FRIDAY-NIGHT RITUAL

The most popular program—the one that epitomizes the new trendiness and daring—is a brassy weekly magazine show that is like a combination of *Nightline, 60 Minutes,* and MTV. It is called *Vzglyad*—meaning "Glance" or "View." My pollster friends say that it is at least six or seven times more popular than any other program, especially with the under-thirty-five crowd. For modish young Muscovites, *Vzglyad* serves up a blend of cool informality, hot rock, and the most modern video gimmickry on Soviet TV. In bastions of conservatism like Minsk, Kiev, or Ivanovo in the Russian heartland, *Vzglyad* is a shot of adrenaline to advocates of change. Even its detractors have to watch it, to be in on what's new and controversial. *Vzglyad* never fails to stir reactions—enough to receive fifteen thousand letters a month and to get the national chief of Soviet television fired.

Shock is its trademark. Since it began on October 2, 1987, *Vzglyad* has broken more taboos and more exclusives than any other show on television. It has interviewed Gorbachev and Nina Andreyeva, presented Western rock stars such as Pink Floyd and Bon Jovi, and examined both the

Soviet and American armies. If *Fifth Wheel* is made up primarily of documentaries, *Vzglyad* consists of sharp talk and fast-paced movie segments. In an hour and a half to two hours, it rarely lingers with one segment for more than six or seven minutes. Watching it on Friday night has become a ritual all across the country. From Moscow to Yaroslavl, Sverdlovsk to Tallinn, I have watched parties and conversations stop dead in their tracks at 10 P.M. Friday, when *Vzglyad* comes on.

The show on the eve of the March 1990 elections was typical of *Vzglyad*'s kaleidoscopic pace. It opened with quick little sound bites of people telling why they believed in the Communist Party or why they were fed up with it. Cut to the Soviet rock group Nautilus Pompilius, singing, *"We're all soldered together, like pieces of a chain."* Then, over shots of Stalin in pompous poses, a historian asserts that Soviet tyranny began not with Stalin but with Lenin. Cut to a report from Bulgaria about moves toward a multiparty system. Switch to a montage on life in the West, from Michael Jackson to Americans hiking in the forests, scenes of pro football, and Carneval in Rio. Cut to a piece on a would-be Soviet Madonna, a singer named Laima Vaikal, with a throaty voice, high cheekbones, liquid hips, and blond Scandinavian beauty. Switch to mothers in Byelorussia sobbing about the radiation sickness their children suffered in the Chernobyl nuclear accident. Cut to a joint interview—rare for Soviet television—with Moscow Communist Party boss Yuri Prokofyev and former gulag dissident Sergei Kovolev. Cut to an economist urging the formation of private banks. Segue to a sequence from an upcoming movie about a lovers' tryst on a train. And finally, a tongue-in-cheek recitation of great moments in Soviet history on March 2: 1930—Stalin proclaiming the success of collectivization; 1931—Gorbachev born; 1957—Khrushchev saying America could never catch up with the Soviets in space.

To Anatoly Lysenko, *Vzglyad*'s producer and a canny old television hand, this program resembles an original idea of his from the 1970s. He had wanted to create a television show that was as candid and unpredictable as kitchen-table conversation. He dubbed it *In Your Kitchen*, which is where Russians had usually let their hair down. But this was the Brezhnev era, and the television watchdogs were not buying experiments. "We didn't find a common language with the leadership of television at that time," is how Lysenko tactfully put it to me. "Without *glasnost*, this show couldn't have happened."[21]

When Lysenko finally got the go-ahead, he roped in three young comers from Moscow radio, Dmitri Zakharov, Sasha Lyubimov, and Vladislav Listyev, live wires, but inexperienced in television. They became instant anchors, with nothing but a few hours of coaching from a circus clown on how to behave in front of the camera. It worked, Lysenko felt, partly because people were stunned to see a live talk show led by anchors slouching in easy chairs and dressed in jeans and windbreakers rather than sitting at desks in coats and ties.

"I don't like the news so much," observed Zakharov, obviously putting down *Vremya*. "They write a script. It's read. And then it's thrown into a wastebasket. That's too close to life itself."

Zakharov, at thirty-one, is the central figure of the three and the most iconoclastic. He is a wiry, slender intellectual, with a lively sense of the absurd, alert brown eyes, an artful way of staying laid back while he draws people out—and then pouncing on them. He stands in a permanent slouch, his silhouette forming a question mark. It should be forming an exclamation point, for he is given to sudden, dartlike pronouncements. Walking to a coatrack one day, he casually remarked to me: "This is a country of fading fascism, like Spain and Portugal were, only it is fading here later than in those other countries." When I asked about Communism, he mockingly shot back, "Oh, Communism and all that? . . . I don't know what socialism is." While others like Bella Kurkova work at exposing Stalin's Red Terror, Zakharov sees the roots of Soviet violence in Lenin. For him, the execution of Czar Nicholas II and his family was unnecessary. "It made all the later killing possible, if not inevitable," he said.[22]

Zakharov, who graduated from the Maurice Thorez Institute of Foreign Languages, is an avid fan of Monty Python and Alec Guinness. He studied hundreds of hours of Western TV footage to develop concepts for *Vzglyad*. But, he advised me, "you must take into account the Russian mentality."

"What do you mean?" I asked.

"This is a country of poor people, with a distorted psychology, who for seventy years have been deceived and pumped full of ideology."

"So what do you do?" I asked.

"You have to explain everything very simply to them—this was this and that was that," he replied. "I want to have a program showing people that the Revolution was not made for them. This is all very painful. When you tell them that they have been deceived, they don't believe you. It turns out many of them prefer to be fooled rather than to know the truth."

In shattering old myths and stereotypes, *Vzglyad* has used hard-hitting reporting on problems that Soviet propaganda used to relegate to the capitalist West—prostitution, police corruption, and drug addiction. When Soviet forces killed nineteen people while suppressing a peaceful demonstration in Tbilisi, Georgia, on April 9, 1989, *Vzglyad* was the first national television program to run film showing the bloodshed and tying it to the army and security forces. The following January, when a violent right-wing group raided a meeting at the Writers' Union in Moscow, shouting anti-Semitic slogans, *Vzglyad* broke the story. Months before the Soviet government was prepared to admit that Stalin's NKVD had slaughtered thousands of Polish army officers at Katyn, in Byelorussia, at the end of the war, *Vzglyad* presented the evidence. Nikolai Travkin, a people's deputy, suggested on *Vzglyad* that Prime Minister Nikolai Ryzhkov's wife give up the special stores for the Party elite and get a taste of shortages and standing in line with ordinary folks at the regular state stores.

Vzglyad pioneered one arena after another. In 1987 and 1988, it put more Soviet rock on television than any other program, giving mass exposure to Soviet heavy-metal groups such as Akvarium, DDT, and Brigada S. Their stark, sarcastic lyrics often brought delays from the censors. In "Revolution," DDT sings:

> *Two fingers held high—that's victory.*
> *But it's really a poke in the eye . . .*
> *But, Revolution, you've taught us to believe*
> *That good can be perverted.*
> *How many worlds do we burn up in an hour*
> *In the name of your sacred flame? . . .*
> *How many Afghanis does death cost?*[23]

Vzglyad was the first to report on AIDS in the Soviet Union, revealing that there were eighty-one cases of children with the virus in the provincial cities of Elista and Volgograd and pointing the finger at hospitals. Yevgeniya Albatso, a reporter for *Moscow News*, declared on *Vzglyad*: "No mother in the Soviet Union today can be guaranteed that her child will not be infected with AIDS. . . . You see our maternity hospitals are simply made for AIDS to spread uncontrollably. There is filth, lack of disposable medical products, one toilet for a postnatal ward of seventy women. Eighty percent of the maternity hospitals in Moscow are infected with staphylococcus. . . . In our country, however blasphemous it may sound, the main source of AIDS infection is health-care organizations and their polyclinics and hospitals."[24]

While Soviet troops were still in Afghanistan, *Vzglyad* ran powerful footage on the carnage. In one sequence, there was an audio track of a Soviet pilot whose helicopter had been hit. It was plunging out of control, and his words, barely intelligible, became panicked and hysterical, rising to a high-pitched squeal. Then, at the final second, the audience heard his last transmission: "Farewell. Farewell." Then a crash, and a lingering silence.[25]

The military has been one of *Vzglyad*'s spiciest targets, in part because the show caters to a young audience, for whom the draft, the Afghan war, and military spending are hot topics. One program featured the novelist Yuri Polyakov, whose book *One Hundred Days Before Mustering Out* described the violent hazing, gang rapes, and psychological browbeating of raw recruits by older soldiers. *Vzglyad*'s exposés of this often interethnic brutality, known as *dedovshchina;* its repeated critiques of the draft; and its pressures for a professional army so nettled Defense Minister Dmitri Yazov that he summoned Zakharov for a sharp dressing-down. Other military officers accused the program of "slandering the army" and fanning hostility toward career officers. *Vzglyad*'s anchors replied that all three had served in the military, and some of their staff had been in Afghanistan. Zakharov told me that he pursued military stories because it had "dawned on me one day in school that these guys could kill us all someday because they have the button, and I thought they should be under control."

But *Vzglyad*'s biggest political bombshell was its broadcast of the blasphemous proposal that the central shrine of Soviet Communism, the Lenin mausoleum, be removed from Red Square and that Lenin be given a normal burial in Leningrad with his wife, Nadezhda Krupskaya. That bolt of political lightning was hurled not by *Vzglyad*'s anchors but by a guest, Mark Zakharov (no relation to Dmitri Zakharov), director of the Leninsky Komsomol Theater. The mausoleum had been not Lenin's idea but Stalin's—he intended to immortalize Lenin and thereby build the cult of the Party and its leader. Mark Zakharov suggested this was immoral and that the mausoleum was tacky. "No matter how much we hate a person, no matter how much we love him," he asserted, "we do not have the right to deprive a person of burial."

That outrageously seditious suggestion touched off an absolute storm at the Communist Party Central Committee meeting on April 25, 1989, just four days after the broadcast. Party leaders were on a rampage against the press and media after the humiliating defeats many of them had suffered in the March 1989 elections, and *Vzglyad* became the lightning rod for their general fury. The chairman of Gosteleradio, a senior Party veteran named Aleksandr Aksenov, joined in the general condemnation, obviously trying to save his own neck. The suggestion to move Lenin was "rude," Aksenov declared, adding that on television, "political mistakes are especially inadmissible."[26]

A few days later, Vadim Medvedev, the Politburo's chief for press and ideology, paid a visit to Gosteleradio for a two-hour session with the major figures at *Vzglyad,* presumably to roll some heads. Dmitri Zakharov, ever the history buff and quick to live by his wits, was well prepared. "We had a discussion about our program and its influence, and [Medvedev] said, 'By the way, about Lenin . . .' " Zakharov recalled with a wry grin. "I had found some documents from Krupskaya which spoke of Lenin's desire for a normal burial and not to have a mausoleum. And Medvedev couldn't really argue with Lenin."

Somehow the ax did not fall on Mark Zakharov either; Gorbachev seemed to be friendly and approving toward him a few days later at a large reception. It was Aksenov, the head of Gosteleradio, who took the fall. Within a month he was fired, the prime casualty of *Vzglyad*'s irreverence toward the sacrosanct figure of Lenin.

Nonetheless, as with *Fifth Wheel,* the noose has tightened on *Vzglyad.* As the months wore on, fewer and fewer of its segments went on live and unrehearsed, leaving fewer chances to slip things past the censors. A white phone was put on the anchors' table, amid phones used for viewer call-ins; this was the line by which management told the anchors, while they were on the air, to get off some sensitive theme. Here and there, Gosteleradio bosses have sheared away offensive material. An interview with historian Vyacheslav Kondratev, which was highly critical of Lenin, was trimmed back sharply. An interview with former Czechoslovak leader Alexander Dubček was stalled six months. Zakharov produced a probing film on the execution of Czar Nicholas II and his family, but the new boss of Gosteleradio, Mikhail Nenashev, refused to let it go on the air. When *Vzglyad* got documents showing that Stalin's NKVD had cooperated with Nazi forces invading Poland, helping them to locate military targets with radio signals, it broadcast that revelation on its first transmissions to the Soviet Far East. But the censors banned it from later broadcasts to central Russia, the Ukraine, Byelorussia, and the Baltics, the regions neighboring Poland. On the same show, September 1, 1989, *Vzglyad*'s censor barred an impersonation of Gorbachev by the comedian Mikhail Grushevsky.[27]

But the sharpest blow was the seizure of the tape for *Vzglyad*'s year-end show for 1989. Scheduled for broadcast on December 29, it was full of New Year's Eve–style black humor. It opened with a serious segment on the life and funeral of Andrei Sakharov, the physicist who had become the moral leader of the democratic opposition and who had died shortly before. Another segment, more offensive to the television hierarchy, was a parody of a *Vremya* broadcast of government ministers seeking a solution to the nation's economic problems. "In it, I had a discussion with a wizard and a prophet about *perestroika* and the fate of the economy,"

Zakharov told me. "As the discussion ended, a huge spider ran across the stage, and I said, 'We can't put our faith in wizards and prophets. We have to believe in the further development of democracy in our country.'"

The final segment was a melancholy allegory about the ultimate fate of *perestroika*, reflecting the pessimism of the Moscow intelligentsia in the winter of 1989–90. It played out the liberals' nightmare ending for the current era of reform. In this scene the three anchors were sitting around a fictional campfire of the future, representing three advocates of more aggressive reform—deputies Boris Yeltsin and Yuri Afanasyev, and Vitaly Korotich, editor of *Ogonek*. They were deep in the woods, wearing the uniforms of gulag prisoners and mulling over the past. "Once upon a time," they said, "there was *perestroika*. But the president was too kind to take steps against the right-wing extremists." With that, a gulag guard with a submachine gun arrived to order them "back to the barracks"—a symbolic slogan for Stalinism.

"A lot of elements in this program bothered the authorities. So they sent a fat old woman to get the cassette," Zakharov told me. "She was trembling. She said, 'I'm very sorry, but I have to take this.' It was astounding to us. That had never happened before. One of us destroyed the master tape, out of fear of more serious actions being taken. They had seized the show tape the day before the program. The next day, they returned it—we don't know why. But by then, we decided that we did not want to air the program. We felt, 'They did this thing. Let them live with the consequences.' So the program didn't run and Nenashev had to give a press conference to explain why. He said the program was bad, dull, poorly put together."[28]

For the bulk of the Party hierarchy *Vzglyad* represents the worst of the Pandora's box that Gorbachev has opened. As they began their reforms, they accepted Gorbachev's logic that modernizing the country meant allowing greater intellectual freedom for scientists, industry, even the arts, and requiring greater honesty about the past. But the ways of democracy have clearly been more provocative and unruly than they anticipated, and they have fought back.

What is more, Gorbachev himself has been quixotic, sometimes urging the press on and other times warning it not to overstep some vague line. In October 1989, for example, Gorbachev went after Vladislav Starkov, chief editor of *Argumenty i Fakty*. He had published a readers' poll about attitudes toward members of the Supreme Soviet that made Gorbachev look bad. At a closed meeting of senior editors, Gorbachev thundered that Starkov's poll was "divisive" and intolerable and Starkov should quit. In the old days, that would have finished Starkov's career. But in the spirit of the new politics, Starkov stood his ground, backed by his staff and a readership of twenty-six million, the highest circulation in the country. It was ironic that Gorbachev had picked on him, because Starkov, while assertive, was not among the most provocative editors. In the end, Gorbachev relented.

Vzglyad's survival, given its more persistently provocative record, is harder to understand without some appreciation for the factional infighting within the upper reaches of the Communist Party. In Leningrad, the Party apparatus is relatively unified and conservative. That deprived Bella Kurkova of high-level patrons for *Fifth Wheel*. In Moscow, there are Party radicals and progressives in high posts as well as hard-liners. Obviously, *Vzglyad* has had its well-placed protectors. I suggested to Zakharov and Lyubimov that *Vzglyad*'s main patron was Aleksandr Yakovlev, Gorbachev's close ally and the guiding spirit behind *glasnost*. They did not want to say. But others connected with the show privately agreed, pointing as well to influential reformers in the Central Committee apparatus a level or two below Yakovlev, officials who might not have liked the jab about reburying Lenin, but were still ready to protect *Vzglyad* so that it could keep stoking the fires of reform. In other words, *Vzglyad* benefited from the splintering of power that Gorbachev set free, but it has suffered from his failure, or unwillingness, to break the grip of the old system.

Vzglyad's mixture of sensational popular success and unending difficulty with the powers-that-be tells a great deal about how far reform in the media has come and how far it still has to go. New freedoms are there for the bold to grasp and fight for, but they are not complete. Nor are they guaranteed. In 1987, as he was gearing up *glasnost*, Gorbachev promised to provide a law guaranteeing the rights of the press and media. But three years later, editors and broadcasters were still waiting for that law. One quite progressive piece of legislation I was shown provided for the end of censorship and took control of the media away from the Communist Party by allowing any group or individual to operate a publication or a television outlet. That bill was drafted by liberal deputies in the Supreme Soviet and approved by the Committee on Glasnost. But months later, the bill was still bottled up by Party bureaucrats who were keeping it from coming to a public vote under the ruse of having it studied by experts. Even without the press law, efforts were under way to establish an independent television network and outlets—another method of assuring greater freedom and less control. But Gosteleradio was fighting tooth and nail to hang on to its monopoly.

Without legal protection and alternatives to state ownership, the media can be neither free nor secure. As Bella Kurkova said to me, "I don't dismiss the idea we may finish in a prison camp," like the three characters in *Vzglyad*'s banned program. But each new truth the public learns is itself an irreversible step, a small but important widening of the borders of the permissible and a shrinking of the forbidden domain controlled by censors. Ultimately, of course, public opinion—what the public demands and expects—has been and will be the greatest protection and guarantee for ground-breaking programs like *Fifth Wheel* and *Vzglyad* and their counterparts in the print media, such as the weeklies *Ogonek* and *Moscow News*.

"What people are finding out today about the past is the first and greatest guarantee that they will not want to return to that past," was how Yegor Yakovlev, chief editor of *Moscow News*, put it. "The thing is we can adopt any law or decree, and easily change it later. The single guarantee is public opinion. Public opinion has found out so much that only a suicidal person could return to the past. And that's the most important thing."[29]

PART THREE

LOOKING FOR PERESTROIKA

*T*he economy was the real reason for Mikhail Gorbachev's rise to power. It will be the ultimate test of his success.

The economy that Gorbachev inherited was in desperate straits: Growth rates were tumbling, consumer shortages were endemic, the farms were not feeding the Soviet people, smokestack industry was old-fashioned, rigid, inefficient. The Information Age was passing the Russians by.

World competition was a goad, and a challenge. Not only Gorbachev, but his scientists, economists, Politburo colleagues, even his generals, understood that, as a superpower, the Soviet Union was slipping because its economy could not keep pace with the world.

Soviet prospects in the twenty-first century were bleak—unless something dramatic was done. In stark language, Gorbachev spelled out the stakes and the nation's mission to his countrymen: "Only an intensive, highly developed economy can safeguard our country's position on the international stage and allow her to enter the new millennium with dignity as a great and flourishing power."[1]

And yet the messianic Gorbachev set off on his bold effort to modernize the Soviet economy and to catch up with the West without a blueprint, without a model, without even an overall economic strategy. On *glasnost,* Gorbachev's strategy was clear; on economics, he improvised, deferring often to Prime Minister Nikolai Ryzhkov. He proceeded by trial and error.

In his first months, Gorbachev sailed under the banner of *uskoreniye*—

acceleration—intending mainly to tap science and technology to lift the Soviet economy out of its morass. To improve performance, he created new bureaucracies, one of them a huge new agency to enforce quality control. To sharpen work discipline, he launched a drive against alcoholism. To energize the government, he fired old Brezhnev hacks and promoted their deputies.

Only belatedly, when *uskoreniye* failed to produce what he wanted, did Gorbachev turn to structural reform, to *perestroika;* only then did he declare that generating new dynamism would require "scope for the initiative and creativity of the masses and for genuine revolutionary transformations."[2]

Even *perestroika,* however, was a vision, not a program with well-thought-out phases. It was a move away from the old, but Gorbachev never clearly defined the new. By declaring it as his goal, he launched his own search for *perestroika.*

That was enough to stir a battle royal within the Soviet system. On the offensive in 1987 and 1988, Gorbachev tackled one sector after another: promulgating new rules and laws; declaring his desire to tame the massive, centralized superstructure that commanded the Soviet economy; promising new freedom to industrial managers, farmers, even private entrepreneurs. But he quickly discovered that economic change is much more of a test than turning loose the press or declaring elections.

At every inch, his economic measures met resistance and opposition—from ministers, bureaucrats, and Party bigwigs (even from Ryzhkov), who saw their power threatened; from ordinary people, skeptical of yet another leader's promises of a better life and wary of the risks of a genuinely free market; from advisers, who warned of a popular backlash, even civil violence, if state prices were raised; from radical reformers, who pushed for bolder, more sweeping changes.

For Gorbachev, the temptation was powerful to try incremental change, to settle for half measures, to compromise. But this, too, had its risks.

CHAPTER 10

THE CULTURE OF ENVY

One Saturday evening in the autumn of 1989, when I was working late, alone, in a Moscow office loaned to my film group by an American friend, I heard a knock at the office door. I couldn't imagine who it might be.

It was sometime after ten, and even when I had come in at around six, the building had been so deserted that I could hear my footsteps echoing in the corridor. The *dezhurnaya,* an elderly Russian woman working as the twenty-four-hour watchman, had had to unlock the front door for me. She had emerged from the *dezhurnaya*'s room, no bigger than a closet, in which was crammed a cot, a small desk, clothes hooks, a hot plate. Each day, a different *dezhurnaya* was on duty; I'd never seen this woman before.

In Moscow, unexpected knocks at the door can bear ill tidings. I wondered who would be interrupting me at that hour in a locked office in a locked building.

When I opened the door, there stood the *dezhurnaya,* a rather tall woman in her sixties, erect and businesslike. I asked if there was some problem.

"No," she said, "no problem." She paused, then said, "You've been working hard for a long time. You must be hungry. Would you like me to fix you a cup of tea?"

I was startled, not only because she and I were total strangers but also because I have encountered many a *dezhurnaya,* and most have the mentality of a sentry—gruff, suspicious of aliens, protective of turf, and accustomed to reducing human commerce to the inspection of a permit. I mumbled something like: "It's really not necessary. I hadn't realized it had gotten so late. I'll be leaving soon."

She could see my papers spread out, could reckon that I would be there for some time. *"Seichas, prinesu,"* she said—"I'll bring it in a moment."

I was deep into my work again and had almost forgotten her when she returned, not just with a cup of tea but with a whole tray of things, including four small open-faced sandwiches, bologna topped by a slice of cucumber, plus a packet of tasty Polish biscuits. She said in clear but unpracticed English, "I put some strawberry preserves in your tea. We do it that way. Is that right? Is that how you say it, 'strawberry preserves'?"

Understanding that she must have sacrificed part of her own nighttime rations, I thanked her, invited her to sit down, and said her English was quite correct. Not wanting to intrude, she stood by the doorway of our inner office as we talked.

I learned that she was a retired teacher, supplementing her tiny pension. To pass the hours, she was reading *Mezhdunarodnayazhizn (International Life),* a Soviet magazine in which the man whose office I was using, Simon Chilewich, had an article. The magazine also happened to include an excerpt from *The Power Game,* my book on Washington, D.C.

"Oh, I'll look for it," she said. "But I don't even know your name."

When I told her and asked her name, she said, "My name is Anna Ivanovna." Only then did we shake hands, as properly acquainted. In return for her generosity, I gave her a book and some magazines to practice her English, and after that, when I saw her, we would swap stories, comments, little gifts.

That first late-night encounter illustrates an endearing quality of the Russians—their extraordinarily warm hospitality, their love of bestowing gifts on each other and on people whom they choose to befriend, especially foreign visitors. I have often encountered this touching generosity. For example, one night when my wife, Susan, and I were leaving Minsk on a late train for Moscow, two new Soviet acquaintances surprised us by showing up at the station to say good-bye. One, Galina Laskova, arrived with a huge bouquet of flowers for Susan—they must have cost her 10–15 rubles, more than a day's pay. The other, Maya Klishtornaya, presented Susan with a book of Byelorussian recipes, now out of print and a rare treasure, which probably came from her own library.

Flowers are a special hallmark of hospitality in the Soviet Union. Once, a slender, gracious schoolteacher named Nana Batashvili struck up an acquaintance with Susan during a Soviet-American conference in Tbilisi, Georgia, and she subsequently invited us home. She lived in a cramped apartment with six other members of her family—her mother, sister, sister's husband, and their three children. Their furniture was tasteful but limited. The floors were bare. What sticks out in my memory is a shelf stuffed with books. Both teachers, the sisters were surely underpaid. The brother-in-law had been disabled by a heart attack, and disability pensions are below Soviet poverty levels. So their family means were severely limited. Nonetheless, the brother-in-law immediately bought Susan an immense bouquet of roses. The next day, after feasting us on a traditional Georgian meal, Nana pulled two books of illustrated Georgian folk tales from their bookshelf as a gift, and her brother-in-law produced four bottles of Mukuzani, one of Georgia's best red wines. These were gifts the family could ill afford, but when I tried to take no more than one bottle of wine, they sneaked the other bottles into our taxi.

Often, the poorer a person's circumstances, the more generous his or her instincts. One morning, as we entered a government building in Sverdlovsk, about two thousand miles east of Moscow, our talking in English drew the attention of an old woman washing the floors. While the guard checked our credentials, she disappeared, and soon she re-emerged with a container of milk, which she handed Susan. We knew that getting that milk had cost this woman a long wait in line in the early hours of the morning. We tried to deflect her gift, but she insisted. Having spotted us as Americans, she wanted to make this gesture. "Please, take it," she told Susan. "It's fresh. It is very good for you, our milk."

To American travelers who have found Russians on the street to be brusque and impersonal, who have found Soviet officials cold and rigid, and Soviet waiters exasperating in their imperious and surly indifference, this generous side of the Russian character often comes as a surprise. But the Russian character is made up of both coldness and warmth.

Over the years, I have found Russians generally to be a warm and sentimental people, more like the Irish or the Italians than like most Americans. One reason many Russians don't especially like the Baltic peoples—Estonians, Lithuanians, and Latvians—is that they find them too cool and reserved, too self-contained, too Nordic. Russians are more emotional, more likely to strike deep friendships, less superficially gregarious. They make great sacrifices for those within their trusted circle, and they expect real sacrifices in return. Their willingness, indeed their eagerness, to engage at a personal level makes private life in Russia both enormously rich and incredibly entangling. Close emotional bonds are part of Russia's enchantment and also its complexity. It complicates Gorbachev's drive to set up a law-governed state, for example, because people are more readily moved by the partisanship of personal loyalties than by belief in individual rights and a sense of fair play. Within the trusted tribal ring, the bonds are strong, but outside it, the frictions are abrasive and the mistrust corrosive. This often plays havoc with the most obvious steps toward raising the Soviet economy out of its morass.

"THEY PRETEND TO PAY US AND WE PRETEND TO WORK"

While the kindhearted impulses of Russians and most other Soviet nationalities make private life tolerable, there are other less positive and less charitable qualities in the Russian character that tend to make public life intractable and pose formidable obstacles to Gorbachev's drive for reform: their escapism, their impracticality, their lackadaisical attitude toward work, and their vicious envy of people who try to get ahead.

Westerners know, because Gorbachev has made it an issue, that an entrenched bureaucracy of Party and government officials—eighteen million strong, by Gorbachev's count—have been blocking and sabotaging many reforms, clinging to power and privilege. What is far less understood in the West is that the mind-set of ordinary people is an equally forbidding obstacle. My intellectual friends would tell me, "We Russians are long on debating, arguing, philosophizing, or reciting poetry; we are good at feasting, drinking, toasting, and at talking deep into the night; but we have no head for business."

"Russian mentality is not based on common sense. It has nothing to do with common sense," the writer Tatyana Tolstaya told David Royle, one of our producers. "Our thinking is not orderly, logical. We do not have a linear consciousness. . . . In Western culture, European culture maybe, emotions are considered to be on a lower level than reason. But in Russia, no. . . . It is bad to be rational, to be smart, clever, intelligent, and so on. And to be emotional, warm, lovable, maybe spiritual, in the full meaning of that word—that is good."[2]

"It is the Russian soul," the poet Andrei Voznesensky told me one afternoon, as we sat on a park bench talking in a light snowfall. "In Russia, I think we have a love of literature, a so-called spiritual life. We can talk all day and all night long about all kinds of questions, immortal questions. That is the Russian style of thinking.

"I want our economy to be the same as in the West. I want our people to have a good quality of life, a good level, the same as in America, and technology as in Japan and America. But I am afraid to lose this Russian part of our soul, to lose our love of literature and . . . how to put it . . . our impractical character. Maybe too lazy, it is a minus, but it is a plus too."[3]

In this view, which I have heard echoed time and again, Russians are prone to escapism, whether it be the "lazy, dreamy" philosophizing of the intelligentsia, as Tolstaya has put it, or the brutal, destructive, and often self-destructive mass alcoholism of workers and peasants. "We just ruin everything we touch," Tolstaya lamented, contending that Communism had given vent to that destructive streak in the Russian character. Under the hardships of the Soviet era, she said sadly, "people are very cruel with each other, more cruel than I ever encountered anywhere else."

It is only natural, I suppose, for writers and poets to assert the importance of the inner life over pragmatism and creature comforts. As Tolstaya said, it is "better to be poor, unhappy, and suffering" than rich and successful, because such a life is purer. For writers, philosophers, and religious figures, this is true—perhaps.

But among the rank and file, I found that people are fed up with suffering. They are demanding a minimal standard of material well-being. Even among the affluent, such as world-traveled writers Voznesensky and Tolstaya, materialism is thriving. People indulge in reckless bursts of conspicuous consumption, such as blowing a month's salary on a lavish birthday party, living for the moment instead of planning, saving, building for the long term. Soviet people live this way largely because that is just about all the system offers. The shortage of goods is demoralizing; grim prospects for the economy foster hedonism, the search for immediate gratification.

Such escapist habits, however understandable, are powerful handicaps in Gorbachev's drive to energize his people and galvanize them into purposeful initiative.

It is true that over the decades, the Soviet system has turned out regiments of result-oriented engineers, something of a counterpart to Western businessmen. They now fill echelons of the Soviet government and Communist Party, running city councils and Party organizations at all levels. Yet even allowing for this group, Voznesensky and Tolstaya are correct in suggesting that by contrast with people in the West, Russians are not a career-driven people; their primary touchstones are not success, getting ahead, making deals, accumulating material possessions.

In fact, one of the most notable traits in the Soviet Union is the lax national work ethic. Tolstaya's comments about the lazy, dreamy side of the Russian soul made me think of Oblomov, the famous character in the nineteenth-century Russian novel of the same name by Ivan Goncharov. Oblomov is an anti-hero who hates work and is incapable of discipline and effort. It takes him an entire chapter to get out of bed. He is a symbol and paradigm for those Russians who prefer to dream and plan rather than work and take action. Although that literary portrait derives from the slack gentry of a bygone era, even today, a century later, Russians recognize in Oblomov the embodiment of an important facet of their national character.

It is ironic that this should be so, given the extensive Soviet propaganda aimed at inculcating work and discipline as national values. Even so, industriousness, discipline, efficiency do not rank high with most Soviets, whether they be blue-collar workers, peasants, or white-collar bureaucrats.

During my first tour as a correspondent in Moscow, I remember a government economist describing where work stood on the Russian scale of values. "A man can be a good worker, but work is just a *thing,*" he told me. "What really matters is his spirit, his relationship to others. If he is too scrupulous, too cold, people will dislike him. We have a word for that, *sukovaly*—dryish—but *sukhoi*—dry—is even worse. And finally *sukhar,* which means dry like a bread crust—no human touch at all—that is the worst."

Such admiration for human warmth is understandable and appealing, but the problem is that Russians tend to slip over the line, turning commendable traits into a justification for avoiding responsibility and initiative, for a slack attitude toward work. If, as psychologists have suggested, America is dominated by workaholic Type-A personalities, the Soviet Union is mired in hard-to-motivate Type B's—no small problem for a leader such as Gorbachev, who is bent on thrusting his people bodily into the twenty-first century.

For decades, the mass output of the Soviet system, especially its concentration on military might and production, masked the inefficiencies of the system. The Stalinist command economy could concentrate enormous national resources on showpiece targets—huge hydroelectric dams spanning great rivers, massive steel plants, machine-tool factories that turned out tanks for the Soviet army in World War II—all built at the cost of enormous sacrifices by the people. During the early Stalinist years, the masses were motivated by the romance of building a New World. Then the war against the Nazi invader summoned Russian workers to a great patriotic effort. Finally, the fear of a demonic dictator drove the people. But once Stalin was gone, and as the postwar years rolled by, the Soviet work force sagged into a now legendary pattern of sloth and shirking.

"Our unemployment is the highest in the world," leading reform economist Pavel Bunich quipped, watching for my astonishment; officially the Soviets admit to less than 1 percent unemployment. "But unfortunately," he quickly added, "all our unemployed get salaries."[4]

FREELOADING SOCIALISM

Stories about the monumental inefficiencies of Soviet workers are legion. In early 1988, I was introduced to Vladimir Kabaidze, long one of the most energetic Soviet industrial managers; at that time he ran a huge plant in Ivanovo, 250 miles northeast of Moscow. A slender, wiry, chain-smoking, canny Georgian, Kabaidze was presented to me by Soviet Party officials as a model Soviet manager, someone able to get much more work out of his people than most supervisors. Given his reputation, I was especially struck by Kabaidze's blunt comments in a speech he made to the Nineteenth Communist Party Conference a few weeks after we met. He spoke about the appalling incompetence of Soviet construction workers and their reckless disregard for deadlines—ironic in a planned economy.

"We think it's normal to take fifteen to twenty years to build a factory," Kabaidze said. "As general director of the Ivanovo–North Korea Machine Building Works [a Soviet/Korean joint venture], I can tell you how they build things in North Korea. The shell is built the same way as ours, and it takes nine months to build a fifty-thousand-square-meter building. Nine months! Our [factory's] project is one of twenty-seven important projects in the country, and it has been under construction for eight years already. I'm afraid they'll still be writing up change-orders when I'm carried out feet first."[5]

The Party delegates broke into laughter, amused that someone of Kabaidze's stature had suffered from the same unbearable delays that they all knew from personal experience, and that he had dared to make fun of them at a nationally televised Party conference.

Economists and political thinkers like Tatyana Zaslavskaya, the sociologist who gained fame from her Novosibirsk report, blame the Stalinist command economy and rigid central control for molding an obedient, passive labor force, a labor force plagued by heavy absenteeism, idleness on the job, poor quality of work, low morale, and serious alcoholism. As Zaslavskaya put it, Stalin's system turned workers into robots. "People were consistently regarded as 'cogs' in the mechanism of the national economy—and they behaved themselves just as obediently (and passively) as machines and materials," she wrote.[6]

"Apathy, indifference, pilfering, and a lack of respect for honest work have become rampant," added the reform economist Nikolai Shmelyov, "as has aggressive envy of those who earn a lot, even if they earn it honestly. There are signs of an almost physical degradation of a considerable part of the population as a result of drunkenness and sloth."[7]

The Kremlin's two would-be modernizers over the past decade, Yuri Andropov and Mikhail Gorbachev, recognized the slack Soviet work ethic as a national Achilles' heel, and they attacked it the moment they took office. Each began his tenure with a loudly trumpeted campaign to tighten work discipline and fight both the indolent torpor of the Soviet working class and its companion disease, mass alcoholism. Andropov, the former KGB chief, closed down liquor stores during working hours and even had his police agents raid the *banyas*, the communal Russian baths, which are notorious hideouts for workers playing hooky. In the *banyas*, people not only bathe, but also drink beer and eat salted fish and play cards or just while away the hours talking. Despite Andropov's attack on such behavior and Gorbachev's even more ambitious battle against vodka drinking, neither one was able to make much of a change in Soviet productivity, primarily because there was no significant change in the attitude of the Soviet proletariat toward their jobs.

Soviet workers themselves have an ironic saying that expresses their open cynicism toward their "social contract" with the so-called workers' state: "They pretend to pay us and we pretend to work."

Cynicism is understandable. The state has conditioned people to perform badly, having given them little incentive to work harder. Soviet workers have faced neither the threat of being fired nor the reward of higher pay for good work. And so they have drifted along—secure, but feeling little or no connection between their performance and their wages. That applies up and down the line throughout the economy, among professionals as well as the proletariat.

Dima Mamedov, one of Moscow television's leading young producers of youth programs, burst out in frustration one night, complaining about his pitiful salary. We were at a private rehearsal of the American rock group Bon Jovi and the Soviet group Gorky Park. Dima was wearing an Italian-made cotton sport jacket, which he said had cost 350 rubles (nearly $600). Either the jacket was a gift from his father, a senior editor on the nightly newscast *Vremya*, or Dima had bought it with extra money made moonlighting for foreign firms. His regular pay from *Good Evening, Moscow*, one of Moscow television's more popular shows, could not support such expensive tastes.

"Even if I don't work hard at it, for my job they pay me one hundred seventy rubles [about $285] a month," he groused. "If the show is no good—boring—they pay me one hundred seventy rubles. If I work hard and kill myself and the show is very popular, they still pay me the same measly one hundred seventy rubles. Does that make sense?"

Lots of Soviet workers make up for such poor pay by stealing from the state. The common saying is, "What belongs to everyone, belongs to no one, so why shouldn't it be mine?" Sometimes, Soviets indulge merely in petty purloining or quick cadging of state equipment where they work.

Late one afternoon at a lumber mill outside Novgorod, a huge industrial truck mounted with a crane came lumbering into the muddy parking area outside the front gate. No one was around. Out of the truck cab spilled a workman, a couple of children, and a mother carrying string bags full of what looked like picnic leftovers. Sure enough, overhearing their talk, we could tell they had filched the lumberyard's crane truck to go off picnicking.

Sometimes, however, the hijacking is on a grander scale. Underground industries have operated on millions of rubles' worth of pirated textile goods, entire warehouses of construction materials and equipment, fresh fruits and vegetables, lockers of meat. So endemic is larceny of state supplies that the Ministry of Internal Affairs has set up a special police force to combat petty pilfering and big-time swindling. Soviets joke openly about fooling the state inspectors.

One of my favorite anecdotes is about a worker who leaves his factory one afternoon with a wheelbarrow covered with a piece of cloth. The guard at the gate lifts the cloth, looks underneath it, and, finding the wheelbarrow empty, waves the worker on. The next day, the worker shows up again with a wheelbarrow covered with a cloth. Again the guard checks. Nothing underneath the cloth, so he lets the worker pass. A third day, it happens again—the wheelbarrow is still empty.

Finally, the guard bursts out, in utter frustration: "Look, comrade, you must be stealing something. What is it?"

"Wheelbarrows," the worker replies.

Another facet of the cynicism about work is the historic collusion of industrial managers and local Party officials to deceive higher-ups about the real levels of output on the farm or in the factory. When Gorbachev came into power, it was clear that practically everyone from the bottom up was cooking the books. In Uzbekistan, for example, investigators found that every year the entire republic had reported to Moscow one million tons of phantom cotton harvest; massive bribery kept officials quiet. Ever since Count Potemkin built fake villages in the eighteenth century to impress the Empress Catherine the Great on her visit to the Crimea, Potemkinizing has become a Russian national pastime. Gogol's famous Inspector General faced the same shenanigans from the locals.

Upon visiting Soviet farms, factories, schools, and institutes, I have often been shown freshly painted buildings, phony statistics, new equipment borrowed for display; I have encountered not typical citizens, but model ones. The modern expression is *pokazukha*—show—that is, putting on a show, a bogus veneer to impress outsiders who are not in the know.

This penchant for falsifying reality can easily be translated into subverting Gorbachev's ambitious reforms. Inevitably, Russians have jokes about how people pretend to reform. In one, a flock of birds is roosting on a tree. Along comes a man with a stick, and he begins banging the branches. The birds all fly off and the man walks away. Back come the birds to their old perches, announcing with satisfaction: "We have 'restructured' ourselves."

In another Soviet anecdote, one man is demonstrating to a second man the meaning of *perestroika*. The man has two pails. One pail is empty and the other is full of potatoes. He pours the potatoes from one pail into the other, very satisfied with what he is doing.

"But nothing has changed," objects the second man.

"Ah, yes," agrees the first, "but think what a noise it creates."

PERESTROIKA IN THE MIND

People are looking for some external transformation to take place, but *perestroika* is first of all internal. *"Perestroika* has to happen in the mind," my friend Vladimir Pozner, the television commentator, remarked to me. "For it to work, people's outlooks have to change, and that happens as society changes. It's a push-pull, gradual process. It cannot be decreed."[8]

Old habits die hard, even among supposedly reform-minded intellectuals. I recall a visit one Tuesday morning to Vladimir Yadov, director of the Institute of Sociology, reputedly one of the more active academic institutes in Moscow. The place was almost deserted, and as I sat down to talk with Yadov, I commented on the absence of people on a normal workday. Yadov, a sympathetic figure with a craggy, Robert Frost face, is a scholar who, like sociologist Yuri Levada, had nurtured his craft in hiding during the dark years of Brezhnev.

With his wry humor, he said, "This is what my driver calls 'bath day.' " He grinned, assuming I knew that people hid from work in the baths. "No one is around our institute except the director," he went on, pointing to himself, "and a few of my assistants. Everyone else is away. No one is at work. Theoretically, this is library day, when they are all supposed to be at the library." He shrugged, again assuming I understood that this was fiction. "Do you remember what Maksim Gorky told Lenin when Lenin asked Gorky why he did not want to come back from living abroad to work in Russia?" When I shook my head, he went on. "Gorky told Lenin, 'You know, Vladimir Ilyich, at home in Russia they all go around and shake each other's hands and talk all the time and swap anecdotes. No one really works.' Well, that's how it is here on 'bath day.' They all go around and shake each other's hands and swap anecdotes. That's how it is—just what Gorky said."[9]

Occasionally I ran into middle-aged officials and intellectuals who had begun to think that the Soviets' casual attitude toward work took root during their youth, especially among the educated middle class, which allowed its children to develop an easy dependence on their parents and, later, on the state. In short, they observed, self-reliance comes slowly among the very class of people that in Western societies show the greatest spark of responsibility and initiative. Russians are soft on their children; they spoil them all through childhood, trying to protect them from hardship. They readily make considerable sacrifices for their children's education without demanding that their children earn money; they keep them living at home after the university and often support them financially during those years. This is partly out of necessity: Housing is almost impossible to find, Soviet society provides few part-time jobs, and in a society where there is little to inherit, education is the road to opportunity and therefore an extremely high priority. In short, reality reinforces cultural traits.

The contrast with American young people is so striking that Soviet writers and journalists, reporting on travels across America, have been moved to send home detailed descriptions of the summer jobs taken by American college students. Soviet parents are both horrified and impressed to read about how middle-class American young people take jobs waiting tables, pumping gasoline, baby-sitting, digging ditches, serving fast food. They have told me that they are horrified that well-heeled American parents can be so cold toward their own children as to force them to work to make money. To many Russians, that smacks of exploiting child labor. And they are impressed, I was told, that American teenagers show so much initiative and self-reliance.

Either way, Soviet parents are extremely curious about the American experience. On an all-day car trip through the farming regions of Yaroslavl Province, a senior provincial Party official named Igor Beshev fired questions at me about the jobs my children had taken, the money they had earned, and how I had persuaded them to go out and work.

"I just tell them they have to contribute a part of the cost of their college education," I said.

Beshev approved of their *delavoi*—businesslike—attitude, but he reminded me that Soviet university students got stipends from the state, leaving them with no tuition to pay.

"What about meals, clothing, and other costs?" I asked.

Beshev nodded, but said little, looking uncomfortable. Like many a Russian parent, he seemed to be taken aback at the notion that parents would ask their children to pay for such things.

"Well, our kids earn their own spending money," I said suggestively.

Beshev warmed to that idea. His twenty-year-old son was a university student, but he had never had a job. Like other Soviet young people, he had taken part in various work projects organized by the Komsomol, the youth wing of the Communist Party. Those activities, however, were not a step toward financial self-sufficiency. Beshev was concerned that so far his son had no practical sense of money.

"He's dependent on me," Beshev said. "He never earns any money. Of course, I expect he will have a good career when he finishes university. But I do not think he knows how to take care of himself. And I would like to see him get some preparation now, the way your children have. I'm trying to get him to find some job. But that's a big change, and it's very hard for him, for all of us."[10]

With variations, it was a story I had heard often. Sometimes the young people were eager to find jobs and the older generation was disapproving, saying that children should be cared for and protected.

Of course, total dependence on parents is a prelude to dependence on the state, which the Soviet system encourages. After graduation, univer-

sity students are assigned jobs called *raspradeleniye*—literally, the "distribution"—which they must accept as a way of repaying the state for their
education. Often out of inertia or limited possibilities, they stick with
those assigned jobs for many years, sometimes for the rest of their lives.
They often get housing through their employer, and big factories have
their own health clinics. In the countryside, villages are like old-fashioned
company towns, dominated by the local state or collective farm. The
individual fits into the local hierarchy, which both supports him and
checks his initiative. Dependence is the routine.

Dependence is also nurtured by subsidies for essentials like housing,
food, health care, education. Soviet apartments are spartan and dreary by
Western standards, but they are cheap. The rent for a one-room apartment can be as little as 15 rubles a month, not much more than the cost
of those big bouquets of flowers Susan was given. Even a good-sized
apartment of three rooms may be no more than 25 or 30 rubles a month,
two or three days' pay, a pittance by Western standards. Health care is
poor, but it's free—except for the bribes that people have to pay to get
service. Education, even at the university level, is free. Dietary staples—
bread, milk, potatoes, cheese—are all subsidized. For years, a small but
tasty loaf of Soviet brown bread has cost about 25 kopecks (35 cents). The
state buys potatoes from farmers at 30 kopecks a kilo and sells them to
city dwellers for 20 kopecks a kilo (about 15 cents a pound). The result
is enormous food subsidies, running about 96 billion rubles—about $155
billion—in 1990.[11]

The majority of Soviet workers clamor for greater efficiency, for more
consumer goods, but they react violently to any proposal suggesting that
overall economic improvement means floating prices and an end to state
subsidies on consumer essentials. That is a potent element in the new
politics of public opinion in the Soviet Union. For five years this mass
dependence on subsidized socialism has been a deterrent to Gorbachev's
move toward a free market; and each time he has approached it, he has
backed off or watered down his plans. His caution is in dramatic contrast
to the boldness of the new Polish leaders, who have plunged headlong into
free-market reforms, allowing price inflation.

"The Poles prefer high prices to empty counters," was the response of
Nikolai Petrakov, Gorbachev's personal economic adviser. "In this country, all the opinion polls show quite the opposite. People accept rationing
coupons and standing in line—especially during work time—but not price
increases."[12]

"We all shout in unison—including those who otherwise favor the
market: 'Do not touch prices!' " observed a reform-minded economist,

Otto Latsis. "This is the kind of 'market' we have imagined. Like a rose without thorns. But such a plant does not exist in nature. The market is a rose with thorns. . . . Ours is the only country in the world where there are strong 'anti-market' feelings."

Then he added sarcastically, "Perhaps Albania has them too."[13]

In line with this attitude is a widespread aversion among Soviets to risk taking. As a people, they are economically cautious and conservative. In a society built on job security, the specter of unemployment is terrifying, and Soviet society has little experience and no infrastructure for dealing with it. By government estimates, roughly three million people were thrown out of work by state ministries, agencies, and enterprises from 1985 to 1989, and about fifteen million more jobs will be eliminated by the end of the century.[14] New jobs, of course, are developing in other sectors, including private enterprise hiding behind the euphemistic title of "cooperatives"—that is, group-owned businesses. The more daring workers, especially younger people, are giving this sector a try, but that is still a small minority.

Most Soviet workers are reluctant to make changes. I have been told this countless times, by workers as well as by economic specialists. The vast majority have grown accustomed to leaning on the state. They would rather settle for a meager wage and miserable living standards—and continue to complain about these shortcomings—than quit their jobs and take the chance of shifting to a cooperative with an uncertain future. They would rather pass up higher pay than take the risk of a cooperative's failure, or face the certain knowledge that they will have to work harder. Risk and uncertainty are things most Soviets habitually avoid like the plague.

"The masses expect change to come from the top," my friend Andrei Smirnov, the filmmaker, remarked to me over dinner one night in the Writers' Union dining hall. "They do not understand that real democracy, or real changes in the economy, must come from below. They resist the idea that we must change ourselves."[15]

Dependence on the state and resistance to taking chances reaches far beyond the blue-collar proletariat. It exists at all levels of Soviet society, affecting creative professionals, scholars, and industrial managers as well. Smirnov, head of the Filmmakers' Union for two critical years of adjustment in the late 1980s, described his union as a microcosm of Soviet responses to greater economic freedom.

"Everyone was enthusiastic about overthrowing the old dictatorial system," he told me, "but our directors and producers are fearful of the new system of competition. If we have a choice between the free market and a guaranteed salary, the majority will pick a guaranteed salary. Those who can't compete on the market are unhappy at the prospect of being unemployed. Others who are more talented are unhappy because they think that studio directors will pick friends and favorites to make films, not the qualified people. They want the union to protect them and to go after the studio directors. The really good ones, who can work well in any situation, are unhappy with our poor technology and the bad system of financing in the country."[16]

Rair Simonyan, an adviser to the Council of Ministers and a specialist on industrial management at Moscow's prestigious Institute of International Relations and World Economics, reported similar reactions among industrial managers and even his own efficiency experts.

"Everybody can tell you about the necessity for change, but when it relates to them, it's different," he told me. "As director of the Department of Industrial Economics, I had trouble with my own people. Everybody said we need radical reforms. The first thing I tried to do was to cut our staff—sixty researchers is too many. But people were upset. They told me, 'You can't arrange these jobs purely on the basis of efficiency. You have to balance efficiency and social security. You cannot fire a man in his fifties with no job prospects or a woman with two children. . . . Even our industrial managers, to whom we are trying to give more autonomy from the state to decide their own production—they want the old system of being guaranteed their supplies. Often they will tell us, 'We need one hundred percent state orders, so we will have no problem with material supplies.' "[17]

Leonid Abalkin, deputy premier and Gorbachev's top adviser on economic reform, notes the contradictions even among the advocates of reform at the Supreme Soviet, where new laws and policies are being debated and formulated.

"All the speakers were demanding independence, abolition of the dictate of ministries and departments, reduction of the percentage of state orders," Abalkin said. "I often sat alongside [Prime Minister] Ryzhkov and . . . dozens of deputies would come up to him with written and oral requests to guarantee deliveries, to guarantee material and technological supply, and so on. Although they should have all understood that as soon as you have been victorious in taking from the government [the power to issue] state orders, by which it assembles resources, you no longer have the right to demand supplies from the state."

As Abalkin said, "No one wants to notice the contradictions" between the demand for freedom from state control and the lingering desire to be protected and supplied by the state. They all want to "exert pressure on the government, extort from it supplies, benefits, and resources," he said, "as though the government were the head of a patriarchal commune—a strong, good, and wise father. Just ask and he will make a present to you from his bounty."[18]

Aleksandr Yakovlev, who has a well-deserved reputation as an even more radical proponent of reform than Gorbachev himself, calls this mind-set "freeloading socialism," and cites it as the most debilitating obstacle to Gorbachev's reform program. In Yakovlev's view, this mentality entails not just economic dependence on the state but a broader psychological dependence on state paternalism in general—a mass inertia, unless there are orders from on high.

"Society is accustomed to freeloading, and not only in the material sense," Yakovlev explained to me during a long conversation one afternoon. "A person wants to be sure he'll get paid, even if he doesn't work. But also in politics, he wants to be sure that he'll be given instructions, orders, that people will explain, will show him what to do. In every sphere, this is a society of freeloading—of freeloading socialism.

"If we don't break through that, if a person doesn't accept some inner freedom and initiative and responsibility, if there is no self-governance, in society, in outlying districts, then nothing will happen."

"That means people taking real responsibility themselves," I interjected.

"And people don't feel like taking responsibility," he shot back. " 'Let someone else answer, but not me.' That's also freeloading. And it has eaten into our pores and our life."[19]

THE INDIVIDUAL IS NOTHING

This passive mentality stalls the engine of reform. But this habit of mind, of course, is of the Soviet state's own making. As sociologist Tatyana Zaslavskaya observed, the Stalinist system turned the Soviet worker into a robot. In many ways, the psychic termites of statism have eaten away at the foundations of individual self-esteem and initiative; it is the latter that Gorbachev, Yakovlev, and others now so desperately want to revive. For decades, the all-powerful state has literally dwarfed the individual, and given ordinary people a sense of their own insignificance.

Soviet ideology, of course, exalts the "collective" over the individual. In the 1970s, our *New York Times* Moscow office had two American correspondents and three Soviets. The Russians talked about our office group as the *kollektiv,* as if it had some mystical significance beyond the five individuals involved. One of the high-priest poets of Soviet socialism, Vladimir Mayakovsky, captured the Soviet mind-set when he framed the line *edinitsa nul'*, variously translatable as "the single unit is zero" or "the individual is nothing." In a paean to Lenin, he wrote:

> The Individual: who needs him?
> The voice of one man is weaker than a squeak.
> Who will listen to it? Not even a wife. . . .
> The Party is the all-encompassing hurricane, fused from voices, soft and
>   quiet. . . .
> Misfortune befalls a man when he's alone.
> Grief comes to one man, for one alone is not a warrior.
> Every pair is his master,
> Whether sturdy, or even weak. . . .
> The individual is nonsense,
> The individual is nothing. . . .'[20]

Every time I visited the Soviet Union, I saw this disdain for the individual. It is reflected in the very architecture of Moscow, with acre upon acre of massive, cheerless tenement apartments; twelve-lane boulevards so broad that pedestrians are forced into underpasses; pompous state offices like so many somber banks; and cavernous stores with empty shelves. The Kremlin is mighty too, handsome and historic; it was once a fortress, and the golden domes of its churches lend it beauty and grace. But the rest of the city, especially seven skyscrapers built by Stalin, which look like massive drip castles—the Foreign Ministry, Moscow State University, the Ukraine Hotel, and four others—is simply huge and overwhelming. With a fetish for gigantism, Stalin sought to impress, even intimidate, his people by the sheer magnitude and volume of the awesome structures he had built. Unfortunately, Khrushchev and his successors perpetuated Stalin's tendency toward gigantism in architecture in even more vulgar ways.

"We lost the proper scale in our city," Aleksandr Kuzmin, a Moscow city architect, lamented to me one afternoon as we were looking at models of urban development. "It has lost the feel of a city in many places. It has an inhuman scale."

"All these huge tenement buildings look mass-produced," I observed, and Kuzmin nodded. "And in some places the neighborhoods are so barren, the buildings look as if they had been dropped on the face of the moon."

"You see," Kuzmin said, "Stalin had a plan in 1935. He told the people,

'We are building the world's first Capital of Socialism.' So he destroyed some of the most charming old sections of Moscow and replaced them with these huge new structures. Now we are trying to save the few old areas that remain."

"The individual gets lost in the leader's dreams of glory," I suggested.

"I think it's worse in the new development areas," Kuzmin said, referring to the rows of dreary apartment blocks. "The scale there is especially inhuman. That comes from our desire to get the maximum floor space for the minimum cost. We have this notion of equality of housing, which means we have to build these massive buildings which depress people."[21]

There are other ways the individual gets lost in the Soviet system. Soviet hotels and restaurants are set up to serve groups, not individuals. In Moscow and Leningrad, the better tourist hotels have caught on to the idea of the individual self-serve breakfast, but the Miner Hotel in the coal-mining city of Donetsk in the southern Ukraine is more typical of the country. The majority of foreign visitors there are East German tour groups, Polish schoolchildren, and Bulgarian basketball teams, and the dining room cannot cope with individual tourists for breakfast. One morning, Susan and I appeared and were told by a waitress that there was no breakfast, despite the fact that she was at that very moment setting out breakfast dishes for twenty-five to thirty people. I pointed out the inconsistency to her.

"Oh, but this is for a group," she explained. "Are you a group?"

"Well, we are three Americans," I answered, referring to Susan, Marian Marzynski, and me.

"That's not a group!" she sniffed, turning away.

"But we need breakfast and we are staying in your hotel," I protested. "Where can we get something to eat?"

The waitress shrugged and went back to setting out meals for the group.

Another waitress overheard the end of our conversation and advised us to try a little buffet elsewhere in the hotel. It offered some terrible coffee, tea, cold hot dogs, and cookies. No cereal, eggs, or anything else resembling normal breakfast food. We settled for tea and a very dry cookie, while the group of tourists in the dining room were served pancakes, little *blinis* with cheese, as well as a selection of breads, jams, rolls, and fruit.

The attitude of that first hotel waitress epitomized the attitude of the Soviet state toward customers in general, and the approach of Soviet sales clerks toward shoppers. The Soviet economy is a command economy, not a demand economy. It is run by and for producers, not for customers. Marketing is unheard of. For decades, volume of output has been the yardstick of success; never mind quality or a selection that consumers may want. Tens of millions of tons of potatoes or other vegetables rot in the fields, railroad cars, or warehouses because the Soviet distribution system is abysmally run and central plans and pay bonuses are based on output, not on delivery. Millions of pairs of shoes can be produced, but they sit on shelves unwanted, because the quality is awful or the sizes do not match those of the population. Once again, the state's interest over the individual's.

Even when efforts are made to cater to the individual, the Soviet system is long on form and short on function. For years, Moscow's Sheremyetovo Airport had no pushcarts for luggage inside the customs area. Apparently, Soviet officials were so besieged by complaints that they finally allowed a cooperative firm to bring in luggage carts. But there was a catch. The co-op, being a Soviet firm, was not allowed to accept hard currency as payment, only Soviet rubles. By Soviet law, however, arriving tourists were not allowed either to bring Soviet currency into the country or to exchange money in the customs area. So they had no rubles to pay for the carts. Human ingenuity eventually developed a barter in cigarettes; it took several months before Soviet officials realized the need for a hard-currency cashier to rent the carts.

In another gesture, theoretically designed to spare some tourists from the tedious delays of customs inspections, the Soviets copied other countries by setting up two customs lanes—a red lane for detailed inspections and a green lane for people with no imports to declare. Once again, catch-22. Any foreigners arriving with $50 or more in any foreign currency had to declare it and go through the red lane. So, of course, no one got to use the green lane. It was a nice *pokazukha*, for appearances, but not much use.

Service is not an ingrained notion in the Soviet system. Foreigners quickly discover that many waiters, drivers, and desk clerks working for Intourist hotels are uncaring, petty tyrants. My own encounters with their imperiousness and rigidity would fill a book. Drivers refuse to deviate a couple of blocks from normal routes, even for extra pay, if it is not written on their job tickets. Once, in Baku, I approached a hotel cashier, urgently needing to change a 10-ruble note. "I don't change money," he replied haughtily, motioning me to another, identical cashier's desk three feet away. That cashier was on a long break. I waited for several minutes. The man who had refused to serve me dipped into the cash drawer in front of me to do several transactions. But no appeal from me would get him to change my bill.

Meals often involve a tedious hassle. The pet peeve of Scott Breindel, our sound man, was getting breakfast served in the National Hotel. The dining room had a faded baroque elegance, with a huge wall mirror and gilt molding, but service was nonexistent. After the first round of diners, the tables lay littered with dishes and bread crumbs. Waiters would stand around talking with each other or looking bored, ignoring newcomers at the tables. The menu was fixed, so people were spared the complication of ordering, but it took repeated appeals to break through their indolence and get bread, coffee, one third of a cup of juice (evidently they were saving on juice), and a cold boiled egg.

Dinner at the National Hotel was my Waterloo. Even as a guest in the hotel, it was almost impossible to get a table. Reservations mattered little, except in the hard-currency dining room. One day, when I had invited a Soviet couple to dinner, I took the precaution of ordering a table early in the day. No seats were available in the hard-currency dining room, so I approached the maître d'hôtel in the salon marked for hotel guests and "payment in rubles." But for a table he wanted to blackmail me into paying in dollars or into ordering *zakuski*, Russian hors d'oeuvres, in advance, for 100 rubles. I refused and it took me about ten minutes to get him to quit glaring at me and write down my name. That evening, we were left standing for fifteen or twenty minutes, even though there were free tables in the room. Once seated, we were ignored for another forty-five minutes. When we finally ordered—we chose hot dishes—there was another long wait. Our Soviet guests were mortified by the wretched service, saying that is why they never went out for meals. Finally, in desperation, I demanded, "Bring us anything cold, just bring us something." Out came the *zakuski* for, you guessed it, about 100 rubles. We never got our hot dishes, but we did get ice cream.

Soviet store clerks treat Soviet customers with a similar arrogant indifference. There is simply no culture of service, no tradition of greeting customers by asking, "Can I help you?" or saying, as they depart, "Thank you, come back again." In part, the haughtiness comes from the economics of supply and demand. Chronic shortages make the Soviet Union a seller's market; the buyer is a mere supplicant. The sales clerk is besieged by more customers than she—it always seems to be women in these jobs—can ever hope to satisfy. She feels overwhelmed, harassed, and helpless. Moreover, she is in the driver's seat, empowered by the state and its shortages either to cut down her customers with a crippling *"Nyet,* we don't have any," or to whisper a demand for a fancy under-the-counter bribe for an item in short supply.

There is another reason for the Soviet aversion to service. In the context of socialist equality, one person does not serve another, because that puts the server into a lower social status. It smacks of capitalist exploitation.

Soviet intellectuals are smart enough to realize the hypocrisy of this attitude in a system where state planners grasp all the power of decision-making and relegate the citizenry to economic serfdom. They still relish a joke I heard in the 1970s. One person asks, "What's the difference between communism and capitalism?" The other answers, "Capitalism is the exploitation of man by man, and communism is the reverse."

Humor aside, the haughty disdain of Soviet salespeople for their customers can be exasperating. To me, one of the classic examples is the *pereriv,* or lunch break. In the buffets and cafeterias at Soviet hotels or airports, the staff are fond of taking their break just when most customers want to buy a meal. I cannot begin to count how often that has happened to me. Soviets have simply surrendered to it, and no longer protest. Once, our group had a short layover in Voroshilovgrad during a six-hour trip from Yerevan to Vilnius. We had taken off at 6:00 A.M., been given no food on the plane, and were quite hungry by the time we landed at Voroshilovgrad at 8:30—a normal breakfast time. But the only airport restaurant had a chair in the doorway, blocking the entrance, and a sign announcing CLOSED FOR A BREAK. We had nothing to eat until we landed in Lithuania at noon.

"EQUAL POVERTY FOR ALL"

For the great mass of Soviet people, the years of unrelieved struggle against shortages of goods to meet the most elementary of human needs have bred still other habits and attitudes that go against the grain of reform. Illicit profiteering is as pervasive as crabgrass in a summer lawn; it's an almost universal defense mechanism that has been operating sub rosa for many years. Think of the worker stealing wheelbarrows and multiply him by a million. This pilfering causes many Soviets, even though they regularly benefit from underhanded dealings, to look on anyone who makes a profit as an illicit operator.

Beyond that, the competitive combat that shopping has become has fed a meanspirited streak in the Soviet soul. For if Russians are justly known for their warmth within a trusted circle, and for their hospitality toward guests, they often show an abrasiveness, a churlish spite, toward people outside their circle; the natural breeding ground for this attitude is the floating anger engendered by wretched circumstances. The Russians are long-suffering people who can bear the pain of their misery, so long as they see that others are sharing it. The collective jealousy can be fierce against those who rise above the crowd.

Traveling around the country, I came to see the great mass of Soviets as protagonists in what I call the culture of envy. In this culture, corrosive animosity took root under the czars in the deep-seated collectivism in Russian life and then was cultivated by Leninist ideology. Now it has turned rancid under the misery of everyday living.

On a plane from Sverdlovsk to Moscow, our producer Marian Marzynski struck up a conversation with the young woman next to him, an attractive, jovial person who was full of consumer woes. Her name was Galya Zhirnova, and she was a buyer for the central trade agency of the city of Sverdlovsk; this agency supplied all the state department stores and consumer outlets in her city. Galya was going to a trade fair in Moscow, with a budget of 10 million rubles. She was going to meet with manufacturers to try to contract for shipments of television sets, radios, cameras, records, cassettes, electronic games, sports equipment, and other recreational goods for her city's one and a half million people. The budget did not sound too bad—until I did the arithmetic. It worked out to 7 rubles a head, a little over $10 per person for the entire year 1990. A pitiful amount.

"We have no television sets to sell," she said. "We could sell a railroad car full of TV sets in an hour. Bed linens are impossible to find in our stores. We have people who signed up to buy furniture fifteen years ago and they are still waiting. We could have bought one hundred twenty million rubles of furniture for next year, but they only allotted us twenty million rubles' worth. And we don't have enough storage space for that. So it sits in railroad cars—millions of rubles' worth—because we have no warehouses."[22]

When we landed at Domodyedovo Airport, nearly an hour's drive south of downtown Moscow, the number of taxis was far from adequate. Great droves of people stood in a drizzle waiting for buses. Galya laughed bitterly at the human disarray. "That's Russia," she snorted. "Things don't work. If they worked well, it would be America."

Galya, with her bourgeois tastes, sneered at the poor quality of Soviet products—but she could afford to. Her job put her in an enviable position between suppliers and consumers, an ideal place for skimming off choice items for herself and, if she chose (as any Russian would assume), for a profitable under-the-counter trade. I don't know whether she indulged in graft, but from her conversation, she seemed already to be, at thirty, a canny operator, and her wardrobe hinted at an access to goods far beyond the reach of ordinary Russians. She was wearing a smart black Yugoslav raincoat and a stylish woman's suit. Before we parted, she proudly informed me, "Everything I'm wearing is *importny*—imported."

My driver the next day, Volodya Konoplanikov, commented, "Of course the sales clerks engage in speculation, because there are never enough goods to go around. You go to a sports shop and they have nothing. Then they toss out on the table a hundred pairs of athletic shoes. What's that—nothing! So people speculate. The clerks hold things back. People do business for themselves."

Volodya himself was a repairman at the State Optical Factory, which makes high-quality optical lenses for the Soviet space program. He was moonlighting as a driver on his days off, for extra pay. I was amazed that he had a brand-new Zhiguli, a Soviet variant of the Fiat. He told me that his mother had had to wait nearly twenty years for the car, and only got it through a special allotment to her factory, where she had worked for forty-three years.

Volodya's tone turned to anger. "Everyone knows you can't buy anything," he said. "I want a warmup suit, one of those sports outfits. I can't get one. Really! I should live thirty-five years and still I won't get a warmup suit! People don't want to work—the ruble has lost so much value, there's no point in working. I've put in ten, twelve hours today, for good money, but why should I care? I can't buy anything with my money. Everywhere there are shortages—sugar, soap, tea, shoes. Such a great country, and it's a real problem to buy shoes. Is it really true that with all this space, we cannot grow enough leather for shoes? It is to our shame."

Like many Muscovites, Volodya was working himself up into a virulent sulk, pouring out one old grievance after another. He kept turning around to make sure I got his point—I had to motion to him to keep his eyes on the road!

"You know they turn off the hot-water system in Moscow for two months every summer," he fumed. "What are you going to wash in—cold water? This has been going on for the past twenty-five years, ever since they set up a centralized hot-water system."

Then Volodya turned his venom against the elite, the people on top, or as the Russians call them, the *vertushka*.

"People see how the *vertushka* live—not one *dacha*, but two!" he sputtered. "All kinds of medicines. We can't get such medicines. But *they* get them from you in the West. Why don't they get them for everyone? Why only for the elite? They have much more housing space than ordinary people do. My kitchen is only six feet by six feet. Two people get in there and you can't even turn around. It's like a closet. But *they*—they get three- and four-room apartments with kitchens three times the size of mine. These bureaucrats 'sit' on our backs. They produce nothing. Everywhere there are extra people in those jobs. People get hired because their papa or some political friends protect them. They are incompetent. We have to get rid of them. We have to get rid of those high mucky-muck bureaucrats. And the only way is revolution."[23]

As Volodya built up to his crescendo, my mind flashed to sociologist Yuri Levada, and his description of the popular rage against the "political mafia." This was the rage tapped into by Boris Yeltsin, the renegade Moscow Communist Party boss ousted by Gorbachev and the conservatives in 1987. In the elections of March 1989, the Party apparat had tried to discredit Yeltsin, but Yeltsin, with his brash outspokenness and populist instincts, had gone to rally after rally, savaging the political elite for its privileges. It was a monumentally successful strategy—more than five million Muscovites had voted for him. Yeltsin had provided an outlet for the boiling anger of the masses.

The Soviet ruling class, with their cushy cars, clinics, and country homes, are a natural enough target for the wrath of the little people. But what is ominous for Gorbachev's reforms is that this free-floating anger, the jealousy of the rank and file, often lights on anyone who rises above the crowd—anyone who works harder, gets ahead, and becomes better off, even if his gains are honestly earned. This hostility is a serious danger to the new entrepreneurs whom Gorbachev is trying to nurture. It is a deterrent to even modest initiative among ordinary people in factories or on farms. It freezes the vast majority into the immobility of conforming to the group.

Valentin Bereshkov, a former Soviet diplomat, told me of a farmer he knew in a town outside of Moscow whose horse and few cows were set free and whose barn was set afire by neighboring farm workers who were jealous of his modest prosperity. The Soviet press is full of stories about attacks on privately owned cooperative restaurants and other small service shops, the perpetrators people who resent seeing others do well. In the debates at the Supreme Soviet, the most potent arguments, the ones with the strongest resonance among the general populace, are the passionate accusations that the free market will yield speculators getting rich from profiteering and exploiting the working class.

Such antagonisms, of course, bear witness to the powerful influence of decades of Leninist indoctrination. For great masses of Soviet people, capitalism is still a dirty word, and the fact that someone earns more, gets more, is a violation of the egalitarian ideal of socialism. Tens of millions of Soviets deeply mistrust the market, fearing they will be cheated and outsmarted. They see the profit motive as immoral. After all, Lenin wrote in 1918, "We consider the land to be common property. But if I take a piece . . . for myself, cultivate twice as much grain as I need and sell the excess at a profit . . . am I really behaving like a Communist? No. I am behaving like an exploiter, like a proprietor."[24] That mind-set is strongly entrenched, despite the efforts of Gorbachev and the reformers to uproot it.

But there is more than ideology at work here. There are class and collective instincts, born in the countryside of prerevolutionary Russia, embedded in the peasant psyche, and often carried from the farm to the factory when peasants have migrated to the cities. This hostility toward those who rise above the herd reflects the collective ethic of the *obshchina,* the commune of villagers who in czarist times lived in a small huddle of homes, close by one another, not in single homesteads dotted independently across the open plains. After serfdom was abolished in 1861, the peasantry banded together, working the land together. There is good evidence that the czarist bureaucracy, before the Soviet state, encouraged collective farming because it feared there would be anarchy once the power of the rural lords was suddenly taken away by emancipation.

The peasant commune apportioned to each family strips of land to work, in different fields, some near the village, some off by the forest, distributed so that each family was assigned some good land and some not-so-good land. The *obshchina* decided when they would all plant, when they would all harvest, and often how they would all work the fields. The villagers shared the bad weather. They planted the same crops. They grew accustomed to a common fate. And they reacted warily against anyone who tried to advance beyond his peers. Because the commune members were collectively responsible for paying the "redemption" costs of their emancipation, the elders did not want young people leaving for the cities; they either charged high fees or refused to let them leave the *obshchina.* So the commune imposed a harsh order and maintained a social leveling.[25]

In my travels, villagers have told me more than once: Remember—the tallest blade of grass is the first to be cut down by the scythe. The lesson? Do not try to stand above the crowd, the collective.

Felicity Barringer, a former *New York Times* correspondent in Moscow, put that sentiment into language that drives home the point. At a Soviet-American conference, she made the shrewd observation that "in America, it's a sin to be a loser, but if there's one sin in Soviet society, it's being a winner."[26]

Dmitri Zakharov, the anchor of the Friday-night television show *Vzglyad,* said:

"In the West, if an American sees someone on TV with a shiny new car, he will think, 'Oh, maybe I can get that someday for myself.' But if a Russian sees that, he will think, 'This bastard with his car. I would like to kill him for living better than I do.' When Russians see a cooperative where people make a lot of money, they ask angrily, 'Why do those people make so much money?' They do not ask, 'Why does the state pay me so little?' Instead of making an effort to raise their own incomes, they want to close down the cooperative."[27]

I heard another slant on that from Anatoly Sobchak, a reformist deputy in the Supreme Soviet. "Our people cannot endure seeing someone else earn more than they do," he told me one night in Leningrad, where he had come for a television interview with *Fifth Wheel.* "Our people want equal distribution of money, whether that means wealth or poverty. They are so jealous of other people that they want others to be worse off, if need be, to keep things equal. We have a story that describes this trait. God comes to a lucky Russian peasant one day and offers him any wish in the world. The peasant is excited and starts dreaming his fantasies. 'Just remember,' God says, 'whatever you choose, I will do twice as much for your neighbor as I do for you.' The peasant is stumped because he cannot bear to think of his neighbor being so much better off than he is, no matter how well off he becomes. Finally, he is struck by an idea and he tells God, 'Strike out one of my eyes and take out both eyes of my neighbor.' "

Sobchak paused. I was stunned by the implications of this terrible story, which I later heard repeated in several variations by others.

"Changing that psychology is the hardest part of our economic reform," Sobchak resumed. "That psychology of intolerance toward others who make more money, no matter why, no matter whether they work harder, longer, or better—that psychology is blocking economic reform on the collective and state farms. Peasants actually smash the machinery and burn the barns of other peasants who try to work their own land to make a better living."[28]

Not only that, but—not surprisingly—successful people try to hide their light under a bushel. Vladimir Pozner put a new twist on something I had noticed among Russians: the built-in caution of their daily greeting. "When two Americans meet, they ask each other, 'How are things?' and they tell each other 'Fine,' " Pozner said. "An American will say 'Fine,' even if his mother died yesterday. After a while, a Russian will conclude, 'Americans are hypocrites. They have problems. Why don't they admit it?' By contrast, when two Soviets meet and ask each other how they are, they will say, 'Normal,' or 'So-so.' Even if things are good—especially if things are good! You don't want to tempt the devil. You don't want people to think things are great. Because they might be envious. And if they're envious, there's no telling what they might do."[29]

This impulse for leveling the fate of all, for sharing misfortune and spreading misery rather than letting anyone get ahead, is what radical economic reformer Nikolai Shmelyov has called the syndrome of "equal poverty for all."[30]

"The blind, burning envy of your neighbor's success . . . has become the most powerful brake on the ideas and practice of *perestroika*," Shmelyov asserted in an important analysis of the Soviet economy in the magazine *Novy Mir.* "Until we at least damp down this envy, the success of *perestroika* will always be in jeopardy."[31]

No less a figure than Gorbachev himself has picked up this theme. In April 1990, stumping for a new phase of economic reform, Gorbachev bowed to popular resistance to raising prices on consumer essentials. But simultaneously, he upbraided Soviet workers for lacking "a sense of responsibility" and for resisting wage reforms that would reward good work. Specifically, he warned that the culture of envy would snuff out any spark of initiative and daring and cripple hopes of real economic progress.

"If we do not break out of this foolish system of wage leveling," he declared, "we will ruin everything that's alive in our people. We shall suffocate."[32]

CHAPTER II

WHY THE RELUCTANT FARMERS?

"As a peasant might say, our field grew too thick with the weeds and thistles of bureaucratism, mismanagement, social apathy, and irresponsibility. And weeding alone won't suffice."[1]

—Gorbachev, April 1988

"It's the fifth year of *perestroika,* and our people should be confident but they're not. Our people do not believe in tomorrow. . . . [They have] never owned the land. . . . They are afraid of it. It has become alien to them."[2]

—Dmitri Starodubtsev
State Farm Director
September 1989

When I returned to the Soviet Union in 1988, I expected that on the economy Gorbachev would follow the pattern set by China. As a correspondent, I had visited China when President Reagan went there in 1984, and that trip gave me not only my first look at that country, but also firsthand impressions of its daring new economic reforms. That was nearly a year before Gorbachev took over the Kremlin, and China's resilient, canny, innovative leader, Deng Xiaoping, was already blazing a path away from orthodox Communist economics.

For five years, Deng had been decollectivizing agriculture—dismantling China's infamous peasant communes and turning over land to individual peasant households to farm on their own. After delivering a set quota to local governments, peasants were allowed to sell the rest of their crops for personal profit. To heighten incentive, Deng had raised the prices for farm produce.

A sudden, stunning explosion had taken place in the Chinese countryside. Most of China's roughly three hundred million peasants had seized the opportunity, and generated a great leap ahead in production and living standards. Since 1978, grain output had shot up 33 percent—from 305 million to 407 million metric tons. Overall, the farm sector was rolling along at 7 percent growth a year—certainly enviable in Moscow, and unheard of not only in other Communist countries but almost anywhere in the world. New cottage industries had sprung up all over the countryside—small service shops, little textile mills, and the like—creating an economic boom in rural China: 52.9 percent growth in 1984 alone. Close to seventy million people were now at work in that sector, and the Chinese press carried stories of new millionaire-entrepreneurs in the hinterlands.

Marxism seemed turned on its ideological head.

On a bus trip through the countryside around Shanxi, I had been struck by what seemed like a thriving hive of activity—swarms of Chinese farmers on their bicycles, pushing carts, or on foot, toting produce to market, choking the roadways. Squawking chickens tied by their legs were draped over the handlebars by some cyclists; others had little crates of produce precariously perched on their bikes. The energy and commotion were overwhelming. Those who had studied China or knew it from earlier visits, such as my friend China scholar Doak Barnett, were even more stunned than I by the dynamism of rural China.

"I found the countryside unrecognizable," Doak said. He had returned to China in the late 1980s after an absence of seventeen years. "The physical changes were really impressive. In towns and villages along the Yangtse and Pearl River valleys, there were little shops and township industries. The peasants had all built themselves new houses. Their earnings had doubled and tripled in just a few short years. The whole countryside of east China, and much of west China, too, looked vastly different from what I had seen before."[3]

In Beijing and Shanghai, middle-class urban Chinese—government officials, journalists, and intellectuals—told me how Deng's reforms had changed their everyday lives. Food, of course, was the big change; it was much fresher, more varied, more plentiful. Industrial reform had begun, but essentially Deng was propelling his nation forward with a peaceful revolution in the countryside. At that stage, he had struck together two combustible elements—food and profit—to forge a huge constituency for reform, both among villagers, who were reaping profits, and among the urban middle class, which was enjoying the food.

Four years later, returning to the Soviet Union, I anticipated that Gorbachev would use Deng's example and begin his economic reform by harnessing the energies of tens of millions of farm workers; that he would liberate them from the Procrustean Stalinist regimen of collectivized agriculture. After all, before the Bolshevik Revolution there had been something like seventeen million private farmsteads in Russia; under Lenin's New Economic Policy, the number had risen to twenty-five million. And then Stalin's ax had fallen.[4]

Moreover, Gorbachev had a natural base to build on, smaller in scale than what was going on in China, but a base nonetheless. Back in the 1970s, I had been impressed by the success of farmworkers who cultivated little quarter-acre kitchen gardens and half-acre private plots. The state owned the land, but the *kolkhozniki*—the collective-farm workers— farmed little plots next to their log-cabin homes to feed themselves and make some money by selling their surplus at farmers' markets in the big cities. In the heartland of Russia proper, the *kolkhozniki* raised potatoes, carrots, and cabbages, and tended tiny orchards of apple trees. In the warmer southern climates of Georgia, Azerbaijan, and Uzbekistan, they raised grapes, pears, and citrus fruits. Driving through the Russian countryside, I had often seen several chickens pecking around peasant homes, and here and there a pig; and in Central Asia, goats and sheep.

In a land that falsely trumpeted "the heroic success of socialized agriculture," the government grudgingly let private plots exist, but played down their importance. They were a pragmatic necessity, but an ideological embarrassment. In 1977, Brezhnev increased the legal size of the plots to one acre; typically, local Party bosses kept the actual size much smaller. Nonetheless, by 1985, there were thirty-five million private plots with an average size of half an acre.[5] The private plot was a well-established staple of Soviet agriculture, a throwback, I was told, to the little gardens allowed serfs in czarist times. Farmers' markets functioned everywhere, from Siberia to Moldavia.

The truth was that Brezhnev could not have fed his people unless he allowed in his system this one legal vestige of private enterprise. And the same was true for Gorbachev, of course.

In terms of market value, the private-plot system Gorbachev inherited in 1985 produced 60 percent of the nation's potatoes, 32 percent of other vegetables and meat, 30 percent of the eggs, and 29 percent of the milk.[6] And all this on about 1.6 percent of the Soviet Union's agricultural lands.

Theoretically, that meant that as Gorbachev came into office, private plots were at least twenty-five times as efficient as land farmed collectively.[7] The figures were somewhat misleading because peasants simply stole seed, fertilizer, transport, and other equipment from their state and collective farms, rather than having to buy or rent these items; often, when they could get away with it, they cheated on their collective work time. Even allowing for this mass rip-off of the state, private plots were indisputably the most productive sector of Soviet agriculture.

Many city people, especially the educated middle class, could not live without the farmers' markets. In the 1970s, we had gone to those markets all the time to bargain with fat, nubby-fingered Russian peasant women who offered their dusty carrots and cucumbers beside wiry, swarthy Georgians or Azerbaijanis, who had flown north to Moscow with sweet-smelling suitcases full of ripening grapes or pears and fresh-cut flowers. Prices were steep but it was a relief to find better produce and better cuts of meat, and more of both than were available in the state stores—testimony to the basic marketing ingenuity of cash-crop farmers, with personal profit as an incentive.

By contrast, what Gorbachev inherited on the official side—the collectivized side of Soviet agriculture—was all too palpable, visible in the dismal disintegration of rural life in the core provinces around Moscow, the heartland of central Russia. In the late eighties, it looked much the same as it had in the early seventies. Traveling to such ancient tourist sites as Rostov, Vladimir, Suzdal, and Yaroslavl, I would stop to photograph the colorful carved woodwork of the peasant log cabins, only to be shocked by the primitive living conditions: the absence of indoor plumbing, necessitating freezing trips to the outhouse in the depth of the Russian winter; the peasant women trudging along with two pails of water from the village well hanging from a shoulder yoke; the poor schools; bad health care; empty stores; rutted roads; and the scarred faces of the peasants, as weatherworn as a lighthouse beaten constantly by gale and lightning. This area of Russia is known as the "non–black earth zone," because it lacks the chocolate earth of the more fertile farmlands to the south, such as in Gorbachev's home region of Stavropol. In central Russia, farmers scratch a subsistence from the gritty brown soil. Their life is grimmer than in American Appalachia.

The people of this region looked to Gorbachev for a better life.

During the Brezhnev years, the spirit and vitality had been sucked out of the Russian heartland. There had been the mass exodus of the young, millions of whom—the brighter and more energetic ones—had fled the countryside for the cities. Especially in northern Russia, whole villages had become ghost towns. If a few hardy souls hung on, local authorities eventually came and transferred them to larger towns with tacky dormitories for farm workers. But still the hemorrhaging had continued, a clear sign of the failing agricultural policy. Brezhnev, unlike Deng in China, had never recognized the problem for what it was—the system's failure to motivate its people. The blame was always placed on the weather, the soil, or occasionally backward technology or incompetent local leaders. The system itself was never found to be at fault.

Paradoxically, Brezhnev's sympathies were with the core constituency of the Russian heartland. As a Russian loyalist, he had tried to prop up this huge region with vast infusions of money—for roads, buildings, village administrators, hundreds of thousands of new tractors and combines. He had mounted campaigns, drives, programs, all run from the top down by phalanxes of bureaucrats and Party officials. He had somewhat liberalized the rules for private gardening and the raising of livestock, but lack of grain kept the peasants from developing any decent herds. In the main, Brezhnev's strategy was to throw money at the farm problem, to the exasperation of his prime minister, Aleksei Kosygin, who saw (so Gorbachev's colleagues told me) the farm sector as a rat hole. One Soviet economist reported that the non–black earth heartland received 474,000 new tractors and combines between 1976 and 1980; by 1980, more than two thirds—322,000—were written off as unusable.[8] Kosygin had been right; the funds spent on the farm sector had been sucked up and had disappeared almost without a trace.

By the time Gorbachev took over, the farm sector was a stagnant quagmire, a symbol par excellence of what was wrong with Soviet economic policies. Before the Bolzhevik Revolution, czarist Russia had been an exporter of grain. By the mid-eighties, it was importing from the United States fifty-one million tons of grain annually. As the Chinese grain harvest began to skyrocket upward in the late seventies and early eighties, the Soviet grain harvests were sagging. The most demoralizing failure, however, was not simply the harvest, but the stunning losses in the Soviet storage, transportation, and distribution system. It was so bad that Gorbachev himself estimated that 20–30 percent of the annual harvest never reached consumers; others put the figure at closer to 40 percent.[9] Great volumes of crops were—and are—left in the ground or else rotted in storage or in transit.

What is more, the gross inefficiencies of the farm sector had been perpetuated by government policy. Literally thousands of unprofitable collective and state farms were kept afloat in the Brezhnev era by rising subsidies. Brezhnev had fueled a vicious cycle; the more he propped up failing farms with larger subsidies, the less efficient they became and the more dependent on the state. For example, in 1982, Gorbachev and his colleagues in Moscow had determined that literally half of the fifty thousand state and collective farms in the country were operating at a loss.[10] In 1983, Moscow approved massive new subsidies of 55 billion rubles (about $90 billion) on top of the already inflated state procurement prices—just to keep failing farms from going bankrupt.[11] By the late 1980s, the failing farms were disguised by newer, higher price supports; only two thousand farms were officially listed as unprofitable. But one of Gorbachev's aides, Georgy Shakhnazarov, estimated to me that roughly 40 percent of the nation's farms were actually losing money.[12]

In sum, Gorbachev himself was moved to comment: "As a peasant might say, our field grew too thick with the weeds and thistles of bureaucratism, mismanagement, social apathy, and irresponsibility. And weeding alone won't suffice here."[13]

To me, all these elements—China's new leap forward, the success of Soviet private-plot farmers, and the disaster in the collective farm sector—seemed to give Gorbachev compelling reasons to launch his economic reforms with radical changes on the farm, and specifically to promote private farming.

FIVE "RULES" OF ECONOMIC REFORM

Strangely, that is not what Gorbachev did. For all his liberal, reformist reputation, Gorbachev began his farm reform not at the bottom, with the farmer, as Deng Xiaoping had done, but at the top, with the bureaucracy.

After all those years as Brezhnev's lieutenant for agriculture, Gorbachev took power without any clear-cut economic strategy beyond a drive to accelerate output and demand more discipline. Even as he attacked Brezhnev's old ways, he continued them.

His first big step in farming was to create a superministry—the State Committee for Agroindustry—which swallowed up five other ministries. It was supposed to break bureaucratic deadlocks, but still, this was the tenth—the *tenth*—time the agricultural bureaucracy had been reorganized since World War II. Gorbachev offered one difference from Brezhnev's periodic shakeups: He cut thousands of bureaucratic jobs when he combined the five ministries.

Gorbachev's aim was to integrate farm production and food processing under one umbrella. Back in 1982, he had wanted to create "a unified economic mechanism" for agriculture, but Brezhnev and the Politburo had blocked him.[14] Now, as number one, he could impose his own plan.

The difficulty was that Gorbachev's plan did not address the fundamental problem of motivating farmers at the grass-roots level. It perpetuated the command mentality, and farms continued to get their output plans from the top.

To make matters worse, Gorbachev put in charge an old Stavropol crony, Vyacheslav Murakhovsky, who was stiff, pompous, and not up to the job. In speeches, Gorbachev and Murakhovsky tossed out talk about markets and more flexible wholesale trade, but nothing happened. The Party apparat kept right on giving out detailed orders to farms on sowing and harvesting. Gorbachev's superministry only seemed to deepen the farm mess, not cure it.

For a supposed innovator who advocated decentralization when he was in Stavropol, this was not an impressive beginning. He gambled on administrative readjustments and modifications rather than going for structural reforms.

Irreverent Russian humorists inevitably mocked Gorbachev's bureaucratic white elephant, which was known as Gosagroprom, drawn from its Soviet title, Gosudarstvenni Agropromyishlenni Komitet.

In one joke, a Soviet spy and an American spy get together after retirement for a few drinks. Eventually, Boris, the Soviet, turns to his new American friend and says, "Come on, John, you can tell me now. The CIA caused terrible disasters in our country. You were responsible for Chernobyl, right?"

"No," answers the CIA man modestly, "but we did something much worse. We invented Gosagroprom." Then both men laugh.

The one departure from big collectivized farming that Gorbachev did champion—indeed, which he had pushed as Stavropol leader and as Party secretary for agriculture in Moscow—were "contract brigades." These were small teams who, together, worked a section of land, leased equipment, brought in the harvest, and shared earnings. As Vladimir Tikhonov, a reform economist, told me, Gorbachev "understood very well that these small groups of peasants . . . could give new oxygen to agriculture."[15] This approach had the kernel of reform, but it was applied experimentally and not very widely, it was modest in thrust, and it was easily subverted by Party and agricultural leaders who disliked giving up their control. Most important, the work team did not get control of a specific section of land for a period of several years, so the people in it could not begin even to simulate the pride and profit of private land ownership.

In short, instead of hitting it at the outset, as Deng had done in China, Gorbachev's program put off real agricultural reform. In early 1988, after Gorbachev had been in command for three years, industry and the new privately owned service cooperatives had new laws on the books offering them autonomy, but there was no new Magna Charta for farmers.

Puzzled by this, I put the question to Abel Aganbegyan, the reform economist, who had become one of Gorbachev's senior advisers and was visiting America in 1988; I was writing an article about him and Soviet economic reform for *The New York Times Magazine.* I asked why Gorbachev's economic reform had not begun with agriculture, and why Moscow had not copied China's approach.

At first, he tried to put me off with an all-purpose joke: "You know, everything, every sector in our country, is in crisis, and we have a five-step strategy for dealing with a crisis. The first thing we do is make the mess even worse, to intensify the crisis. Second, we look for an outside enemy to blame. Third, we punish the innocents by firing some bureaucrats. Fourth, we pass out medals and awards to all of our leaders. And fifth, we finally recognize the problem."

"Okay," I said, "so it's easy to make fun of Brezhnev and his style of operating. But this is now the time of Gorbachev and *perestroika;* you are doing things differently. Why haven't you tried the Chinese approach?"

Then Aganbegyan said, "Chinese farmers are different from Russian farmers. They have not lived as long under state capitalism and a command economy as our people have. The Chinese still have the habit of private farming. They are natural traders. So they are suited to private farming. But our people have lost that habit. They have lived under the Stalinist system for nearly seven decades and they cannot adapt as quickly as the Chinese farmers did. It does not make sense for us."[16]

Only a couple of years later, Aganbegyan was singing a different tune, conceding that it had been a great mistake not to push private farming at the start of *perestroika.* But his answer to me in 1988 was typical of what I heard for the next couple of years. And of course, as we will see, there was some truth in his comment about the attitudes and aptitudes of Soviet farm workers. But his answer masked the larger, more powerful reasons for resistance to private farming in the Soviet Union.

First, there is an army of officials and bureaucrats, at least three million of them, who have a vested interest in the collectivized system. There are farm chairmen, directors, staffs of technicians, assistants, accountants, and agronomists, not to mention a parallel structure of Party organizations concerned with agriculture in every province capital, district town, and village.

More than one reformer has accused this powerful pyramid of blocking a shift toward private farming. "Some people who are strong and powerful fear our autonomy, because then we ourselves become strong and powerful within the confines of our economic territory," asserted a reform-minded collective-farm leader. "So who is it? Look and see where the decision adopted at the Party Congress and subsequent Central Committee plenums become bogged down, where they are devalued, and there you will find the answer to that question."[17]

I have met many of these obstructionists, but none who was more personally striking than Valery Romanov, a rugged, good-looking outdoorsman of fifty, who was the agricultural secretary for the important province of Sverdlovsk, in the heart of the Ural Mountains. Poised and self-confident, Romanov was unusual for a Party bureaucrat—when he met me on a Saturday morning in his gleaming, modernistic office, he was dressed in a khaki work shirt and slacks, rather than the normal bureaucrat's gray suit. Romanov had a gruff, masculine charm; clearly he relished the opportunity for verbal jousting with someone he saw as a representative of the capitalist world. His open manner was appealing, but I quickly discovered he was dogmatic when it came to policy.

When the Soviet farm performance had been repeatedly raked over the coals by Gorbachev each year, Romanov admitted to me that he had felt the sting of criticism, which was echoed by the masses. "I take that kind of criticism painfully," he admitted. "I've poured half of my life into agricultural work and when people say that the whole system of agriculture is a mess, of course it's an insult. I don't sleep well at night."[18]

Nonetheless, his own views had not changed. He had no use for market economics. He did not want to shift farmland from state farms to private operators, except for the private plots they already worked. He did not want to raise prices on potatoes or cut subsidies to the farms. He was furious and frustrated that Gorbachev's industrial reforms had taken away from him several thousand workers who, in years past, had helped bring in the fall harvest. The depleted countryside was short of labor.

Under the old system, Romanov had been able to requisition regiments of free labor. As a senior provincial Party leader, he had had the clout to call up local factory managers and give them orders on how many workers to send to the farms for field work during the key harvesting drive in the fall. Now Gorbachev's reforms had deprived Party bosses of that power and lifted that obligation from the factories. Romanov had been left desperately short of manpower, which risked the loss of part of the harvest.

Romanov's solution to the poor productivity of Soviet farms was to import fancy new harvesters and tractors from Holland, and to reimpose the factory corvée labor force for the harvest.

But, I reminded him, there was still the problem of lazy, unproductive workers and inefficient farm management.

"How do you solve that problem?" I asked.

"The old way—with the fist," he asserted, raising a fist in front of my face, an unmistakably neo-Stalinist answer.

Another deterrent to radical change in Soviet agriculture is the brooding fear among the peasants—a fear that the parasitic apparatus of officials and Party workers shrewdly manipulates—that free-market economics will cause thousands of state and collective farms to fail, throwing the mass of peasants into chaos, and leaving them in even worse poverty than they are today.

Yevgeny Sokolov, Byelorussia's top Communist Party leader and a staunch foe of private farming, promoted the stark view in *Izvestia* that: "Breaking up the land into plots is a quick road to nowhere. Not only economically, but also socially. For the peasant himself, it means total slavery!"[19]

The specter of chaos, of being left at the mercy of the unpredictable gyrations of some unknown market, is something that Soviets, especially Russian peasants, desperately fear—and given the violent upheavals of their history, this is understandable. And so, as Aganbegyan implied, they cling to the only structure they know—the state and collective farm system.

LOSING IDEOLOGICAL VIRGINITY

One final source of psychic resistance to farm reform lies in the Leninist stereotypes embedded in the peasant mind—specifically, the stigma attached to the successful peasant farmer as a plush bourgeois, a covert capitalist. Lenin and Stalin created an ideological demon in the countryside: the class of kulaks, about five million individual homesteaders, usually modestly prosperous, hardworking, middle-class farmers, who were forever portrayed in Communist propaganda—often falsely—as rapacious landowners, as opposed to the masses, whose lives revolved around traditional peasant communes.[20]

Lenin, in his militant, postrevolutionary phase, was quick to accentuate class divisions. "The proletariat," he said, "must separate, demarcate the working peasant from the peasant owner, the peasant worker from the peasant huckster, the peasant who labors from the peasant who profiteers. In this demarcation lies the whole essence of socialism."[21]

Having rhetorically sharpened the knives of class warfare, Lenin then issued the call to battle, which was eventually waged by Stalin when he carried out the "liquidation" of the kulak class. Stalin deliberately crushed the private farmers, and in the process he destroyed the most productive elements of the peasantry, with devastating impact on Soviet agriculture for decades to come. He was carrying out Lenin's shrill command: "Kulaks are rabid enemies of the Soviet regime. . . . There can be no doubt at all that [either] the kulaks will cut down an infinite number of workers, or the workers will mercilessly cut down . . . the robbing kulak minority."[22]

Oddly enough, later Lenin had second thoughts; by 1922, he was not only more tolerant toward private farming, but he embraced it as part of his New Economic Policy. Sixty years later, however, his biting attacks on kulaks are more widely remembered. And they are easy for hard-liners to manipulate for their own ends: to ostracize would-be private farmers and intimidate others into keeping their heads down.

A celebrated case, brought to my attention soon after my arrival in Moscow in May 1988, was that of a peasant, or *muzhik*, from Arkhangelsk, a region in the northern tundra that raises only half the meat necessary for its inhabitants. This peasant, an unusually daring small-time farm entrepreneur named Nikolai Sivkov, was lionized in a documentary film called *Arkhangelsky Muzhik* made by Marina Goldovskaya. He was also vilified as a base profiteer by Communist diehards and apparatchiks.

This *muzhik*'s crime, in the eyes of local Party bosses, was that he used initiative and his own cow shed to breed a herd of bulls belonging to the state farm where he worked. He turned a nice profit—not only for himself but for the state farm too. He hacked a grazing area out of the forests and swamps, and gradually he built up a herd of sixty bulls, plus some cows and calves. Economists calculated that, single-handedly, Sivkov accounted for nearly 10 percent of the entire livestock herd of a huge state farm of several hundred people.[23] Thanks in good part to his hard work, his state farm was about the only one in the region that showed a profit.

Sivkov was doing what Gorbachev's program of "contract brigades" envisioned, except that Sivkov was operating alone as what he called a "one-man cooperative." This was not strictly legal, because no one else joined his co-op. But instead of rewarding Sivkov and helping him expand, or holding him up as a model to others, local Party and farm officials, angered by his independent spirit, harassed him and fought him every step of the way.

"For many years, people on the state farm, in the district Party committee, and in regional organs looked at me with suspicion," Sivkov glumly reported. "At first for feeding state-farm bulls in my own cow shed, then for my demands to be given land, and then for my aspiration to set up a cooperative. I heard lots of words—'kulak,' 'money-grubber,' 'capitalist dregs.' . . . I tried to explain that a peasant needs his own arable land, meadows for grazing and hay, his own agricultural machinery, and the unlimited right to buy or sell his output. . . . I failed to convince the [regional Party] secretary; he decided that I'd become a man of property, sort of an owner.

"Since 1982, they have not let me get on my feet," Sivkov complained. "With the greatest difficulty, I managed to get ten calves to fatten. In the district town, they do not want to deal with me. They also turn me down for loans. We are paupers."[24]

In Moscow, I was told that the harassment of Sivkov intensified after the documentary about him ran on nationwide television. Sivkov himself told reporters that local authorities actively intimidated other farmers from joining him in a farm cooperative.

Sivkov sometimes turned the glare of *glasnost* to his advantage. Once, when a French television crew came to film him, he used their presence to press for a loan to build a new house.

"I filled out the form and said quietly: 'Give me eight thousand rubles right away, or else I will tear up the document right in front of the camera,' " he recalled. "I knew that once the French left I would get nothing. The local officials were afraid of an international disgrace, and they gave me the loan. Recently, I filed a petition to lease a tract of woods. They turned me down. Must I wait for the French again?"[25]

The hard-liners showed no sympathy for his appeal. Wherever they detected economic initiative on the farm, they used the conservative wing of the press to attack what they called profiteering. One collective-farm chairman attacked Moscow for backing Sivkov and cried crocodile tears for Sivkov himself, mocking him as an uncouth bumpkin who worked so hard that he didn't "even have leisure time to straighten his hat."[26]

Ultimately, the documentary about Sivkov seemed to cut two ways. Among radical reformers in the big cities, it made him a cause célèbre. But among peasants, his unending problems were an object lesson in the apparat's capacity to victimize peasants who stepped out of line. It was also evidence of the dangers of Gorbachev's timid half measures.

This second message was understood by some of the more radical reformers, among them the sharp, iconoclastic, market-oriented economist Nikolai Shmelyov.

I met Shemlyov at the Institute for the U.S.A. and Canada—a think tank for studying North America—but Shmelyov was not looking overseas; his focus was on the domestic economic mess within Russia. A stocky scholar in his fifties, he spoke with appealing candor and a nasal twang. He was Nikita Khrushchev's son-in-law, which had given him access to high circles early in life and probably reinforced his natural self-confidence. He was an unabashed advocate of family farming. Shortly before our talk, he had laid out his views in a hard-hitting article, a copy of which he gave me.

"Family contracts and leasing [land] may be the only salvation for many farms that have long been 'unworked,' " Shmelyov declared. "How is one to justify the fact that a virtual campaign against personal farming has broken out again in the press? How is one to understand signs that . . . a new pogrom is brewing against personal orchards and hothouse operations, and against breeding personal livestock?

"We must decide finally once and for all what is more important to us: whether to have an abundance of food, or eternally to indulge . . . irresponsible loudmouths and proponents of equality in poverty. We need to call stupidity, incompetence, and active Stalinism by their proper names. We need to do whatever it takes to ensure an ample supply of foodstuffs. . . .

"We need to do these things even if it means losing our ideological virginity. . . ."27

GORBACHEV'S TURNAROUND

Late in the game—more than three years after he took power—Gorbachev finally heeded the logic of the reformers and turned his agricultural policy around. Lenin had made "Land to the Peasants" a revolutionary slogan; now, finally, Gorbachev appropriated it as his slogan too.

This move appealed to political progressives, who believed that turning land over to individual farmers was one way to reduce the power of the Party apparatus and bureaucracy, and thereby to promote economic—and hence political—independence among an important segment of the population. Returning "land to the peasants" also appealed to Russian nationalists, mainly conservatives, who saw it as a policy that could revive the dying Russian countryside. And it appealed to reform economists as a way to put food into the shops.

Also, they felt desperate to have Gorbachev's reform program show some tangible results, because the masses were getting restive.

The cornerstone of Gorbachev's new policy, first floated in June 1988, was a proposal to grant fifty-year leases of land to small "lease teams." It was a measure that stopped well short of outright peasant ownership of the land, and short of individual private farming, but it moved significantly in that direction.

Gorbachev's first serious push for long-term leases came at a Communist Party Central Committee meeting in October 1988. After three and a half years of defending the collectivized farm system, Gorbachev seemed finally to agree with such reform economists as Nikolai Shmelyov and Vladimir Tikhonov: The farm sector would never really improve until individual peasants were given strong incentives to produce, over a long period of time, on sections of land they could come to think of as their own.

"Much depends on giving the farmer a greater stake," Gorbachev told the Party conference in June. "Everything depends on how quickly we can interest the people . . . in leasing. We must overcome the estrangement between the farmer and the soil. We must make the farmer sovereign master, protect him against command methods and fundamentally change the conditions of life in the villages."[28]

Under Gorbachev's new proposal, Soviet farmers, like the Chinese under Deng Xiaoping, would get lease contracts on land, be given annual procurement targets, and then be allowed to sell any surpluses above their targets. The "lease team" would run its own business, decide what feed, seed grain, fertilizer, and machinery it needed, and buy or lease it from state and collective farms.

This still-relatively-modest approach was fraught with opportunities for sabotage by bureaucrats; and it met powerful resistance from Party conservatives who saw it as the first step toward dismantling the state- and collective-farm system.

By now, Gorbachev was growing impatient with conservative footdragging. There was nothing wrong with making money, he argued, and some incentives were needed to galvanize the peasantry. In the past, Gorbachev said, "the people have been alienated from the soil and the means of production" and turned into mere "wage-earners." To the doubting hard-liners, he declared: "People's desire to take possession of land and facilities, and to set up their own family livestock units, does not contradict socialism, comrades. This kind of owner would be operating on land that is the property of the whole people."[29] Then Gorbachev went on the offensive, denouncing Party and government organizations for resisting reform and "playing a waiting game."

It was typical of the relentless trench warfare that has gone on over the reform program that Gorbachev was unable immediately to carry the day for his new fifty-year-lease proposal, let alone for outright private owner- ship of the land. His new progressive push landed him in a hot battle with Communist Party dogmatists such as Yegor Ligachev, second-ranking figure in the Party, the conservative champion of collectivized farming and the foe of privately owned property. Gorbachev and Ligachev had begun in 1985 as allies for reform, but as Gorbachev became more progressive, Ligachev grew more outspoken and more resistant, all the while making a pretense of unity with Gorbachev's overall policies. As the March 1989 elections approached—the first Soviet elections in seven decades to offer a choice of candidates—their debate took on the aspect of an American political campaign, charge and countercharge, except that neither side used the other's name.

Barnstorming through the Ukraine in late February, Gorbachev declared: "We have to move on to new forms of life and organization of work. A revolution in our mentality is the most important thing. Vast social energy is needed to overcome the force of inertia and the resistance of the old, to smash braking mechanisms and shift society onto the path of intensive development."[30] Referring to Ligachev's two main areas of responsibility, agriculture and ideology, Gorbachev said that "stereotypes and dogmas" should be put aside. Specifically, he proposed that unproductive farms and other unproductive state-run enterprises should be dissolved in favor of new forms of land leasing and free-market cooperatives.

A few days later, Ligachev voiced his opposition, during a speech to the Party faithful in the Siberian city of Omsk. Ligachev backed leasing and farmers' cooperatives in principle, but not when they threatened the system of state and collective farms, which he insisted be maintained. In what looked like a planted question, Ligachev was asked how he felt about disbanding just the *unprofitable* farms, and he dug in his heels against Gorbachev. "You and I did not establish Soviet power so as to treat people and work collectives so shamelessly," he retorted. "We must find other ways."[31]

During the buildup to an important Central Committee meeting on farm policy in mid-March, Ligachev stepped up his advocacy of the traditional approach, asserting that the Party and government should bolster state and collective farms with large new infusions of money. During a visit to Czechoslovakia, he lavishly praised collective farming in that country and questioned Gorbachev's reform plan. Soviet television showed him walking through shops in Prague with well-stocked shelves and then, as if to offer a lesson for home audiences, Ligachev told the camera: "For all these years there has been no deviation from the Czechoslovak policy in the agrarian sector."[32] In other words, experience in Prague shows, comrades, that no dramatic changes are needed back in the Soviet Union.

On his side, Gorbachev stepped up the rhetoric. Finally, he said what the experts had been saying all along: that decades of experience showed that massive investments in collective farming had not paid off. "Analysis of history and experience of the past few years offer compelling evidence that if we opt for this as the mainstay of agricultural policy, it will be a serious mistake," Gorbachev declared. What is more, he took note of the conservative tactic of pretending to go along with his reforms while secretly sabotaging them, and he denounced sham lease contracts that assigned land but in practice gave farmers little real freedom—an echo of the nightmare problems of Nikolai Sivkov, the *Arkhangelsky Muzhik.*

At a Party meeting on March 15, Gorbachev called for the dismantling of the huge new superministry he had set up in 1985, and a gradual transition to a new market system that would give farmers "complete freedom" to choose how to market their products. Edging ever closer to outright advocacy of private property, Gorbachev outlined a new principle of "individual ownership" of farmland. In the first major shift in Soviet farm policy since Stalin's collectivization drive in the late 1920s, the Communist Party Central Committee bowed to Gorbachev's pressure and agreed to lifetime leases for farmers, with the right to pass on land to their children. In a burst of optimism, Gorbachev envisioned a gradual transformation of the existing huge state and collective farms into much looser amalgams of smaller independent farm units run by families and small groups of farmers. He argued that this would be a radical turning point, making it possible for the peasant once again to be the master of the land. Anything less, he said, would not work.

Ligachev had the last word. On the issue of long-term leasing, he had been beaten, but at a press conference he emphasized that the collective- and state-farm system remained the keystone of Soviet agriculture and that there should be strict limits on the implementation of Gorbachev's concept of "individual ownership."

In sum, Ligachev, the voice of the Party apparat, asserted: "I want to stress that everything will still be based on the principle of common ownership and common property."[33] His stand left a large question mark over the fate of private farming.

THE HALFWAY HOUSE OF REFORM

A few months after this celebrated clash among the leadership, I went out with my film crew to see how Gorbachev's new policy was faring in the grain-growing regions of the Russian heartland north of Moscow.

In the fall of 1989, a golden Indian-summer sunshine played over the meadows of ripened grain in central Russia, the kind of weather that should bring a bountiful harvest. But Vladimir Dorofeyev, the Communist Party's agricultural chief for Yaroslavl Province, conceded to me that the grain harvest in his domain was "very low" (sixty-five to seventy bushels per acre), barely half of a good Soviet harvest. Dorofeyev told me he was puzzled by the poor showing, but several others, including one state-farm chairman, said much of the grain had been lost in the fields because there were not enough farmhands to harvest it.

On individual farming, Dorofeyev mouthed the new Party line, and even had some astonishing things to say when I tested him by asking his view of the kulaks, so hated by Lenin and Stalin.

"I think they were real good owners of the land," he answered. "The old attitude did a lot of damage. I think that was wrong. Because the people who really farmed the land, who did such a great job on the land, who did it with their own backs, their sweat and blood, so to speak—they were doing a lot, they were dying for that land."[34]

Almost as an afterthought, he confessed under his breath: "I am the grandson of a kulak."

That a Party agriculture secretary would make such a confession was a mark of the changing times; under Brezhnev, this revelation could have cost him his job, and under Stalin, a trip to Siberia.

Dorofeyev gamely tried to walk the new line but inevitably betrayed the attitudes of an apparatchik. Under the new Party policy, he was supposed to promote individual farming, but when I suggested that this would soon eliminate the need for his own job, indeed for any role in agriculture for Party officials, he recoiled.

"The role of the Party is such that the peasant is always under the control of the Party," he said, bristling. "Everything here goes through the Communist Party."

Others in Yaroslavl, a city of half a million about two hundred miles northeast of Moscow, told me the man to see was Dmitri Starodubtsev, director of the nearby Dzerzhinsky State Farm, a man in the Gorbachev mold, one of the new breed of farm managers who was applying progressive methods.

Starodubtsev was a non-Party man, a favorite of the Popular Front reform movement in Yaroslavl, and an outspoken exponent of the new political freedoms. So well known was he as an independent-minded maverick that when he first announced his candidacy for the national parliament in the elections of March 1989, the Communist Party hierarchy in Yaroslavl had tried to torpedo him. Undaunted, Starodubtsev had cast himself as the champion of the little people and had easily beaten a Communist Party regular for a seat in the Congress of People's Deputies. His election had added to his local mystique and prestige.

When I first met Starodubtsev, it was not long after his election, and I quickly understood why he had won. He was a tough little bantamweight, short, strong in the arms, a tireless, kinetic, fifty-five-year-old bachelor with a flair for heroics and a taste for Georgian brandy. For years, he had lived—usually successfully—at the borders of the permissible. He earned an economics degree in night school, served as a jurist in the army, became a farm expert, and then got into trouble, lost his Party membership, and went to jail.

Back in the late seventies, Starodubtsev ran afoul of the system by being too entrepreneurial. The Brezhnev crowd, especially the Party boss where Starodubtsev was working, did not appreciate innovation. He and his two brothers, Vasily and Fyodor, were running a network of collective farms near Tula, south of Moscow; they had their own trading system and set their own prices, different from the fixed state prices. This infuriated the regional Party bosses, especially when Dmitri made deals to obtain farm supplies from outside the region. Dmitri was eventually accused, one of his allies told me, of spending farm funds lavishly to entertain visitors and to help a high Gosplan (state-planning) official repair his country home, in return for a kickback of feed for the cattle on Dmitri's farm. This kind of thing is typical of Soviet mutual back-scratching, and it's notable that it was not for private profit on his part. Starodubtsev insisted the case against him was a frame-up, and he mustered two hundred witnesses in his defense. Nonetheless, he went to jail for two years, from 1980 to 1982, because, he said, the Party bosses wanted him put away—"That's how it was done then." He's still pushing for an official pardon.[35]

After Starodubtsev had returned to normal life and held a couple of regular jobs, the Gorbachev reforms gave him a new chance—he was given control of Dzerzhinsky State Farm. Today, he bounces around his twenty-thousand-acre domain in the Soviet equivalent of a Jeep, barking orders to his office through an old-fashioned walkie-talkie radiophone, inspecting fields of wheat or potatoes, or stopping in to check on some of the farm's two thousand head of cattle. He is equally at home churning on foot through the mud, in his gray fedora hat, coat, and tie, half covered by an open windbreaker.

Starodubtsev is a hard-driving, no-frills, no-nonsense farm manager. Over the past three years, he has begun to turn handsome profits, Soviet-style, at a farm as big as a Texas cattle ranch, a farm that, despite its size, had been stumbling along in the red before he arrived. About six hundred people work on the farm, one of Stalin's creations, which is organized like a factory. The state organizes the farming, the workers punch the clock. Often, entire families are on the payroll. Housing and most of the food are provided.

The workers seem to like Starodubtsev, but they also fear him. He conveys power, and he doesn't mince words. He has won loyalty by being more humane and more concerned with his people's welfare than previous managers have been, building new housing and recreational facilities, offering more pay for good work, and using his political clout to hound local agencies into providing his farm with things it needs. On his farm, the new benefits he has offered have stopped the horrible flight into the cities of the best workers—mechanics, engineers, and other skilled laborers.

By Soviet standards, Starodubtsev runs a good shop. The obstacles for any Soviet farm director are daunting: from terrible roads, inadequate supplies, and shortage of labor to machinery that is antiquated and always breaking down. There are never any spare parts on the market. Many farms have to triple their manpower to compensate; Starodubtsev gets by with doubling it. He has brought in East German tractors and cut back the waste of his potato crop to 10 percent, although his potatoes are still low-grade. He is experimenting with improved strains of cattle and wheat to increase productivity, and he begged us to provide him with a real Idaho potato to upgrade his stock.

For all his drive for modernization, Starodubtsev's state farm is, at best, only a halfway house of reform. Clearly, he has improved efficiency through effective management, but even as a self-proclaimed reformer, he has not yet fulfilled Gorbachev's goal of creating a new body of self-reliant individual farmers. In principle, Starodubtsev supports the idea, but he's also something of a dictator who has difficulty letting real power slip away; he's reluctant to give his farm workers genuine independence.

When I asked Starodubtsev for a progress report on Gorbachev's new approach to individual farming, he said he had put the leasing idea to some of his best workers. He introduced me to the family who had been most successful raising cattle. Lydiya Popova and her teenage son, Sasha, were in the cattle shed that afternoon, feeding 220 head of cattle. Typical of Soviet farm workers, Starodubtsev said, this family had no money to buy cattle, so his idea was to lease livestock to the Popovs, let them fatten up the cattle, turn the cattle back to the state farm at a heavier weight, and make their money from the gain in weight. Or Starodubtsev had milk cows to offer, at about 1,000 rubles ($1,650) a head, and capable of producing 2,000 rubles' worth of milk a year.

"You find me someone to buy a hundred cows and I'll sell," he kidded me.

There was a catch, which Lydiya pointed out.

"I would like to take the cattle, but not the land," she said. "To lease land means I have to work it myself. But if the weather is nasty or something, how will I manage? It's impossible for us to grow enough. We're just three people in our family. What if I do not have enough feed for my cows?"

At the mention of cattle fodder, Starodubtsev was nodding his head.

"We're very short of cattle feed," Lydiya Popova went on. "It's impossible to buy cattle feed."

"Everyone wants to buy grain, but nobody wants to sell it," Starodubtsev agreed. "Everyone in this region grows rye. What they want to buy from us is wheat. We have a problem. We cannot give it to them free. We cannot even sell it to them."

"It's too big a risk for us to take the cattle if we cannot get the feed," Lydiya said.

Clearly, she preferred leaving the risk and the headaches to Starodubtsev, while she continued to draw her 200-ruble-a-month salary from the state farm.

"Too risky even to try?" I asked.

She nodded. "Too risky."[36]

REAL FARMING OR SHARECROPPING?

Starodubtsev had an even better candidate for a leasing deal, Aleksandr Orlov, the head of his twelve-man potato brigade, which worked five hundred acres of land and produced about five thousand tons of potatoes. Orlov had eight children, four of them married and working at the state farm, so he had a strong nucleus for a family farm. He had been farming in this region since 1943, when he was only a teenager. He was so outstanding as a worker that he had been officially designated a Hero of Socialist Labor, a rare distinction for a rank-and-file farm worker, won only by a few hundred farm workers nationwide.

"Orlov—he's a good professional who knows the machinery and how to grow and harvest potatoes," Starodubtsev told me. "I made him an offer: 'Comrade Orlov, lease the land and the machinery. We will give you the seeds and fertilizers. Grow potatoes and sell them to us.' He tells me, 'I'll think about it.' "

I found Orlov in the potato fields, driving a harvest combine. He was a nice-looking man with silver hair, deep-blue eyes, and a strong face, weatherbeaten from long days in the sun. He wore the costume of a field hand—flat visored cap, a faded padded jacket, high rubber boots. As the camera crew and I approached, he climbed off the combine. The September wind whipped around us as we talked among the hardened furrows of earth under a fading sky. It was early evening, and Orlov had been working for close to twelve hours.

"There's great excitement in the Soviet Union, in Moscow, about leasing land to the peasants," I said to him. "What do you say? Are you ready to take the land?"

"No, I'm not ready to take it yet," he replied cautiously. "I don't have a good enough head for it. You have to have a real good head on your shoulders to do that. Of course, it would be nice to be a farmer, to have my own place. I would take good care of everything. I'd get rid of all this stuff—no junk, none of these stones." He kicked his boot at some small rocks.

"I would live here on my own plot of land," he said, chewing over that idea, beginning to relish it. "That would be nice. I would like to buy land, but I don't have enough money. I could make an arrangement with the state somehow, but I'm afraid of it. I'm really afraid."

"Afraid of what?" I asked.

"Well, I'm afraid of . . . everything," he admitted. "I've never seen anyone lease land in my region. I'd like to go someplace and have a look, see how people do it."

"Is it such a huge risk?" I asked.

"Yes, it's a risk," he answered.

"What conditions would you need to make it work?" I asked.

"What conditions?" he echoed. "Conditions that would help me grow more and sell the produce at better prices."[37]

To lease or not to lease was a question for Orlov's entire family. He invited me home to hear their views. He was the patriarch but, at sixty-three, close to retirement. At dinner with Orlov and his wife, Katya, were his two daughters, Natasha and Lida, and their husbands, plus his son, Yuri, a tractor driver, and his wife—all employees of the farm.

"What I don't like," Orlov began, "is that there's no law about leasing yet. It's not written on paper. What if I start farming and then lose the land? . . . We saw on TV and heard on the radio that people leased some land from a collective farm and then the collective farm took it back."

Natasha, his energetic and outspoken older daughter, pointed out the problem of low prices in state stores. "The state people would tell us, 'You must sell your potatoes cheap,' and that won't be profitable to us." she said. "We want our profits."

"But there are great shortages," I pointed out. "Everybody knows you could sell produce that is in short supply."

"Where would I sell it—to the store?" Orlov asked skeptically. "They won't take it. So I'll have to bring everything I produce back home. That's no good. I don't have a warehouse to store it."

Orlov's wife did not want the headache. "I don't want him to work so hard anymore," she said. "In two more years, he goes on retirement. I can't wait until he enjoys himself, sitting on the sofa next to me."

The younger generation were full of practical questions about how they could operate amid a state-run economy, accustomed as they were to orders from above. They all assumed, as did Starodubtsev, that they would have to sell their produce to the state farm.

"Say we decide to grow beets," Natasha suggested. "The state farm may say, 'We don't want you to grow beets. We need potatoes.' But beets are more profitable for us, right? Well, they could say, 'If you don't want to do things our way, okay, we'll just take back the land.' What kind of lease is that?"

I fished for pragmatic motivation: "Wouldn't you like to earn more money so you could, say, buy a car?"

"We have already been on the waiting list for a car for five years," groused Yuri. "My father is not able to buy a car."

"A Hero Worker with no car!" Katya chirped sarcastically.

That phrase echoed around the table; it was obviously a sore point with Orlov's family. Supposedly his distinction as a Hero of Socialist Labor entitled Orlov to some privileges. In practice, however, Orlov had seen none, and that empty promise left his family wary of new promises from the state.

The larger message for Lida was the difficulty of getting farm equipment. "It's impossible to lease a tractor," she said. "When the state farm is short of tractors, they would never lease one to us. So where would we get one?"

As with tractors, so with other machinery, fertilizer, seeds, feed grain.

In an economy of constant shortages, they all took it for granted that the state farm would take care of its own needs first, leaving the family farmer out in the cold. If forced to turn outside their own state farm to try to obtain machinery and supplies, they were even more pessimistic about their chances with the state distribution network. Besides, Orlov pointed out, there was no system of financial credit to help independent farmers buy machinery over time.

Their fundamental worry was that they would wind up too dependent on the state farm and, therefore, not truly the masters of their own land.

"The director would be in the yard every day checking in every pail," said Natasha, "and if you wanted to sell something in the market, on the side, he would never let you. He would be in charge of everything the leasers produce. It wouldn't be like real leasing. It would be like half leasing."

"We have a saying in Russia—'Two bears can't live in one den,'" Orlov concluded. "You can't have two masters for one piece of land. I say, No leasing. Just give it all to us. We'll do everything. We'll farm it. We'll sell it. It's my own property. What I want to do, I do. That would be for real. If I want to grow beets or cabbages, this is my thing. It's just a tiny household but it's mine. I own it."[38]

The next morning I went to see Starodubtsev in his office, to ask why experienced and able farmers like Orlov didn't trust the new Gorbachev plan and didn't trust Starodubtsev himself.

"They don't trust me simply because during so many years of collective agriculture, the peasants have been lied to," he replied candidly. "As a result, they've developed a general mistrust, and they don't trust me because they see me connected to the system of collectivized farming. I'm telling them, 'We'll help you,' and they're afraid. They say, 'Today, Gorbachev is governing the country, and tomorrow he may disappear and there will be another man and a different attitude toward leasing land.' It's the fifth year of *perestroika* and our people should be confident, but they're not. Our people do not believe in tomorrow."

"How about yourself?" I asked. "As someone who was put in jail, do you believe in the system?"

"All my life I believed that there would someday be democracy in our country, democracy based on deeds, not slogans. And that laws would be used not against the people, but for them," Starodubtsev replied. "I believe such times have come. As an elected representative, I will try to fight for laws that promote truth and trust among the people. I believe that in the future we will have laws that will not cheat the peasants or other working people, and gradually people will come to believe in them too."

Starodubtsev's notion was to pit privately run family farms and small-lease cooperatives against the big state-run farms, "and we'll see who is better."

But even in his eyes, the eyes of a proponent of reform, the competition would be stacked in favor of the big farms, with their equipment and other advantages. The new family farmers not only had to overcome the inbred peasant caution against breaking out of the pack and standing out as individuals, but they would have to operate without firm assurances of necessary financing, marketing, and material support.

As for the Orlovs' worries about getting seeds and equipment, or marketing their crops, Starodubtsev said he would help as much as he could, but that as a state-farm director, he was "tied with all kinds of regulations and instructions." He could not, for example, sell the Orlovs tractors and machinery outright. If they turned to the state, he added, they would have to pay very steep prices, twice as much as a state farm pays.

"Your people feel this is all an enormous risk," I observed. "Knowing how the system works, would you be confident?"

"Well, they are afraid of something new and different, because they have grown accustomed to working as employees," Starodubtsev replied. "Now, Orlov works very well and he gets very good pay. Whether the harvest is good or bad, he draws his salary. And he says to me, 'If I lease the land and work hard, and there is no rain, or too much rain, then I lose my harvest, and I go broke.' That's what's worrying him."

Was that the "essence of the problem," I asked, the real reason Gorbachev's leasing plan was not taking hold?

Starodubtsev grew thoughtful.

"You see," he said, "the land was confiscated from the peasants in the thirties, even in the twenties. Sixty years ago. So the new generation never owned the land. They are not used to the land. They are afraid of it. It has become alien to them. The livestock they are willing to take. To breed animals, that's okay. But the land, they're afraid of it. Our people have lost the feeling of being masters of the land."[39]

Starodubtsev's views are shared by many, especially among government officials and leaders of collective and state farms. They put the primary blame for minimal progress in agricultural reform on the farm workers, their mentality and their habits. From what I saw and heard, the farm workers' reluctance is a critical obstacle. As the conversation around the Orlovs' dinner table illustrated, it is very hard to break the habit of dependency.

Even so, in spite of all the problems, some have dared to take the plunge. In Yaroslavl Province, the Ukraine, Siberia, and certainly the Baltic republics, I heard of individual farmers who were working the land on their own or in small cooperatives. Lithuanian and Estonian officials were aggressively trying to return farms to families who had owned the land before the Soviet occupation in 1940 and postwar collectivization. But the Baltics were exceptional in many ways, because individual farming had flourished there so recently and because the new reform governments were not hung up ideologically on keeping land under common state ownership.

Periodically, Gorbachev himself would cite encouraging examples of new farming ventures around the country. In one speech, he pointed with pride to the formation of thirty-three small "primary cooperatives" of three to five people each at the Krutishinsky State Farm not far from the Siberian city of Novosibirsk. Four of these cooperatives were growing grain, four growing feed, six producing milk, a dozen providing services, still others raising fur-bearing animals—all doing things that people on Starodubtsev's farm were not willing to try on their own.[40]

In the Russian heartland, I met some farm workers who had signed "lease contracts" with their parent state farms. The farther north and the more desperate the farming conditions, the more likely local Communist Party leaders were to promote experiments in leasing as a last desperate way of trying to hold younger workers on the land and to keep them from drifting off to the cities.

Yet the more I talked with these "lease teams," the more I came to see them not as the Soviet equivalent of independent homesteaders, but as tenant farmers working at the direction—and at the mercy—of state farms, which were reaping what profit there was. One of the staunchest advocates of private farming in the Communist Party Central Committee called these lease teams "not proprietors in the full sense, but halfway proprietors, or perhaps not even that."[41]

To me, they were simply sharecroppers.

As time wore on, it seemed to me that the fundamental failure was not the mind-set of the farmers but the failure of the reformers, from Staro-dubtsev up to Gorbachev, to provide attractive and viable conditions for private farming on anything larger than the kitchen-garden scale. The Orlovs had many legitimate worries that the reformers were dismissing all too lightly. Successful farm directors such as Starodubtsev were not eager to encourage real independence for their best farm workers, for fear of undercutting their own success. What is more, Gorbachev's plan failed to make provisions for the equipment, credit, service industry, and marketing support necessary for independent farming, and needed to spur farm workers on to make the leap of faith that Gorbachev proclaimed he wanted.

It puzzled me why Gorbachev and the reformers did not begin simply by increasing the size of the private plots, year by year, and letting the existing network of farmers' markets gradually expand. The main objection was that prices at farmers' markets were so high that few ordinary city dwellers could afford them; they were mainly for foreigners and more affluent Soviets. The ideologues were outraged by what they foresaw as profiteering. Still, gradual expansion of this sector might slowly bring down prices and encourage the development of the service industry that the farmers so badly needed.

The reluctance of the Orlovs was typical. Millions of other farm workers were watching and waiting too. Without greater assurances of support, only a small minority were intrigued by Gorbachev's offer of long-term land leasing. An opinion survey conducted by the government newspaper *Izvestia* in early 1990 found that roughly 40 percent of the rural people polled were willing to "take the land," but closer questioning revealed that only 10–14 percent were actually ready to organize personal farms—and then, *only* if a land law were passed.[42]

Finally, in late February 1990, the Supreme Soviet passed a land law. At Gorbachev's prompting, the new law allowed not merely small cooperative farms but "individual" landholdings—an important addition; it also allowed the right to lease land for life and to pass it on to inheritors.

Significantly, however, the legislation did not permit land to be bought, sold, or owned outright. For despite the urgings of some reformers, the government balked at accepting the concept of private property—an issue on which *Izvestia*'s poll found public opinion almost evenly divided. But it was an issue on which the conservative majority in the Supreme Soviet refused to budge; they gagged at even using the term *private property*.

"We are all children born during a time of meaningless political incantations, of meaningless fetishes, meaningless words, disinformation, and double standards," moaned one disappointed reform economist, Aleksandr Vladislavlev. "When I hear the words 'private property,' I will always be reminded of the helpless expression on the face of [Prime Minister] Nikolai Ivanovich Ryzhkov. He was so shocked by the sound of the words 'private property' being uttered within the walls of the

Supreme Soviet. 'Have you asked the people if they want this?' he asked. What is the point of asking the people when for seventy years the people were told things which had absolutely nothing in common with reality? . . .

"[Public opinion] will have to be remolded. . . . Private property . . . is the only way to achieve the highest work productivity, and this is the task which now faces our society."[43]

This was a minority view at the Supreme Soviet, a view that was rejected. Once again, the spirit of Ligachev and collective property prevailed. Gorbachev himself was either unwilling or not ready to assault the entrenched governmental resistance to genuine private farming, and he settled yet again for a weak compromise.

Over time, this law may persuade some farm workers—the 10 percent found in the *Izvestia* poll who were waiting for legal protection—to take the risk of setting up their own farms. Even 10 percent would mark some progress; but it would leave the vast majority of Soviet farming unchanged. Through the growing season of 1990, the political uncertainties and the resistance of officialdom persisted; so the Gorbachev policy brought no significant change to the face and structure of Soviet agriculture.

Gorbachev's half measures thus fell short of creating the kind of bandwagon surge in enthusiasm, production, and living standards that Deng Xiaoping had produced more than a decade earlier in China.

CHAPTER 12

THE CAPTIVE CAPTAINS OF SOVIET INDUSTRY

"What are we doing, talking about
catching up [with the West] when
we're two hundred years behind? And we sit
and wait, and our bosses sit on
their butts, doing nothing."[1]
—Soviet Worker
September 1989

"Extricating our economy from the
precrisis state necessitates truly
revolutionary transformations."[2]
—Gorbachev, June 1987

"Economic reforms are impossible
in Communist systems. What is
possible are political reforms
that have economic consequences."[3]
—President Tito, Yugoslavia

In March 1988, the government newspaper *Izvestia* reported the startling news that a Soviet enterprise had refused to accept the economic production plan given to it by the State Planning Committee and the Ministry of Heavy Machine–Building in Moscow. That news caught the eye of anyone familiar with the traditional workings of the Soviet economy. Here was a singular act of industrial rebellion: An enterprise out in the provinces was boldly challenging the central hierarchy, daring to threaten the nerve center of the state-run economy.

For six decades, ever since Stalin had imposed the command economy, armies of bureaucrats in Moscow had been drafting annual production plans for every single economic unit in the country: forty-six thousand industrial enterprises, fifty thousand state and collective farms, thirty-two thousand construction associations, plus several hundred thousand other miscellaneous economic units—warehouses, stores, retail outlets, repair shops, distribution centers, and the like.[4]

This herculean undertaking was mounted under the aegis of Gosplan, the State Planning Committee. Throughout the Stalin era, and then under Khrushchev and Brezhnev, the very word *Gosplan* acquired a mystique that conveyed power, authority, gospel. In the eyes of Soviet Marxists, the "Plan" exemplified the scientific, rational organization of the nation's might. It was the formula for achieving maximum growth, for overtaking the capitalist West; it was the unerring mechanism for marshaling the manpower and the resources of a sprawling empire; it was the Utopian device for assuring the coordinated functioning of the world's second-largest economy. The Plan embodied Soviet socialism.

In the highly centralized Stalinist system, the Plan came close to being the fundamental law of the land.

After Stalin initiated the first Five-Year Plans in 1928, each subsequent one became the compass by which the nation was steered, and "fulfilling the Plan" became a national incantation. It was endlessly intoned in speeches, in the press, on television. Back in the 1970s, I was told that it was the whole concept of central planning, epitomized by Stalin's Five-Year Plans, that had multiplied Soviet output manyfold, from 1928 to 1973, had built the backbone of Soviet industry and lifted Russia from backwardness up to superpower status.

The national Plan emanated from the Olympus of Gosplan. It was passed down to various ministries, was expanded and embellished by echelons of ministerial bureaucracies, and then was transmitted to huge industrial conglomerates, or associations. It was then sent further out, to subdivisions or enterprises, and so on down in hierarchical fashion. In short, Gosplan's word was law.

Soviet industrial executives told me that the Plan would arrive at an enterprise in the form of huge books—as large, as thick, and as full of fine print as the Manhattan telephone directory. The Plan spelled out every last detail of what the entire enterprise should produce, and at what cost, made from what materials, for what price, for which customers, on what time schedule, with how many workers, at what wages, and so on. There was both a production plan and a supply plan, one for output, the other for where the enterprise would get its supplies. These fat books, with their sweeping instructions and their picayune detail, were the embodiment of the Stalinist economic system.

Now here, suddenly, was the spectacle of a Soviet enterprise irreverently opposing the system: mailing its set of fat planning books back to Moscow, unopened. As *Izvestia* reported, the Ministry of Heavy Machine–Building saw the episode as "a socially dangerous phenomenon"; they tried to avoid discussing it with reporters, and most desperately tried to get the entire matter hushed up and kept out of the press.

First Deputy Minister R. Arutunyov asked the *Izvestia* reporter directly: "What do we have to do to ensure that your article doesn't appear in print?"

"It was something that had never happened before, and something that it did not seem ever *could* happen," the *Izvestia* reporter commented in his story, with a certain wry amusement at the bold defiance of the enterprise and at the discomfort of the central planners.

"In the view of those we spoke with [at the Ministry], this could plunge not only the industry but the entire economy into chaos. . . . The ministry painted us a downright apocalyptic picture of enterprises refusing en masse to obey orders from Moscow."[5]

This upstart industrial David that was challenging the Gosplan Goliath was no economic pip-squeak. It was Uralmash, one of the mightiest of Soviet industrial giants, a titan of the machine-building industry. What Uralmash was objecting to was one of the basic yardsticks of Soviet central planning, the gross-output target—that is, the total value of production the government was requiring it to turn out in the coming year.

Under Gosplan's supervision, the Ministry of Heavy Machine–Building had assigned Uralmash a 1988 output target of 610 billion rubles, or just a bit more than $1 billion worth of machinery. Uralmash had refused to accept that production target, and it had raised other objections to the ministry's plan. Not only were the overall figures too high, Uralmash argued, but it made no sense to require it to produce items that customers had rejected in the past. Furthermore, Uralmash would not be able to obtain sufficient component parts to produce the items, nor did it have the necessary machinery to do so.

A spokesman for the management and workers of the huge enterprise called the government orders an "unrealistic plan" typical of the old "arbitrary planning" methods of the Brezhnev era, and "at odds" with the new Gorbachev approach. As reported in *Izvestia*, "Uralmash called for realism: Don't succumb to a plan that is obviously impossible."[6] To Uralmash, realism meant cutting its overall output target by about 50 million rubles (about $85 million)—or about two weeks' output for Uralmash. It also proposed various other changes in the ministry's plan.[7]

In years past, enterprise managers had indulged in behind-the-scenes bargaining to try to shave down their output quotas and thus ease their work load. But the kind of open confrontation initiated by Uralmash was economic and political heresy. By going to the press and going public with its complaint, Uralmash was breaking the old rules of the Soviet economic game. Ministry and Gosplan bureaucrats were determined to crush this act of industrial insurrection before the example spread. In fact, seventeen other enterprises tried the same tactic within the ensuing weeks, but they were blocked. Only Uralmash had enough clout to win revision of its plan—and then only after an investigation by a neutral economic commission. What is more, the bureaucrats had their vengeance on other captains of industry: They transferred quotas initially imposed on Uralmash to more obedient enterprises in the automotive industry.

It was a victory—a very rare one; and it happened only because Uralmash shrewdly based its actions on the new bill of rights that Gorbachev and his *perestroika* had promised industrial managers nationwide.

GORBACHEV'S ECONOMIC MANIFESTO

In June 1987, two years after taking over supreme power, Gorbachev issued his major economic manifesto: a stinging indictment of the rigid, Stalinist command economy that he had inherited, and a call for "revolutionary transformations" that would move the Soviet system away from centralized controls and military structure toward freer, more flexible market economics. Gorbachev himself later claimed this was "the most important and radical program for economic reform our country has had since Lenin introduced his New Economic Policy in 1921."[8]

In a speech to the Communist Party Central Committee that rang with talk about efficiency, profit and loss, "real competition," and bankruptcy for losers, Gorbachev raised the banner of "more democracy" in the functioning of the Soviet economy. He offered to industrial enterprises new independence in the form of "economic accountability and self-management." He made it clear that he was bent on shattering the stifling inertia of top-down economics and on unshackling initiative at the enterprise level, and would effect this by curbing the power of the central

bureaucracy and guaranteeing greater autonomy and flexibility to industrial managers all across the country. Yet radical as he was, Gorbachev was
not ready to abandon centralized economic planning; nor was he ready,
by any means, to embrace capitalism.

"We are looking within socialism rather than outside it, for the answers
to all the questions that arise," Gorbachev later explained. "We assess our
successes and errors alike by socialist standards. Those who hope that we
shall move away from the socialist path will be greatly disappointed."9

Even so, this new economic program was a major turning point for
Gorbachev. He had been pursuing a conservative economic policy, trying
to tighten up the old system by firing incompetent people, holdovers from
Brezhnev, and by reshuffling ministries, instituting quality controls, fighting alcoholism, and pressing for greater discipline. Under the slogan of
uskoreniye—acceleration—he had left the old system in place and largely
undisturbed. Now he was talking about serious changes in its operation,
about breaking the iron grip of the central bureaucracy.

Far more candidly than any previous Soviet leader, Gorbachev used his
June speech to lay out the anatomy of the Soviet economic crisis. His
critique of existing practices was unusually sharp—focused first of all on
the micromanagement of all Soviet industry and agriculture. On previous
occasions, Gorbachev had chastised the central ministries for their "petty
tutelage" of industry, for "striving to embrace everything down to trifles."
Now his rhetorical blows were more sweeping against the pretense of
omniscience and omnipotence on the part of central planners. "It is an
illusion," he declared, "to think that everything can be foreseen from the
center within the framework of such a huge economy as ours."10 Overall
strategy, yes, he said; detailed direction, no.

In language more reminiscent of a Western market analyst than a
Communist leader, Gorbachev attacked another sacred cow: the system
of fixed prices, set by the central planners for more than two hundred
thousand individual commodities, from gargantuan earth movers to tiny
nails, a system that he said had produced inflated and wholly artificial
notions of profit throughout the Soviet economy.

"Economically unjustified approaches to price formation have led to
the emergence and rapid growth of subsidies for the production and sale
of a wide variety of products and services," he said. "For many types of
output, an unjustifiably high level of profitability has evolved, one that
bears no relationship whatsoever to efficiency in production. . . . Those
who make products for which prices are unjustifiably low have no incentive to increase their production, and those who obtain surplus profits due
to overstated [excessive] prices have no incentive to reduce outlays and

increase efficiency. In this situation, normal economic relations are simply impossible."[11]

From there, Gorbachev ticked off a long list of sins of what reformers were now calling the Stalinist "administrative-command system": its encouragement of massive waste, equally massive industrial hoarding, featherbedding, keeping unprofitable enterprises afloat. A few days later, Prime Minister Nikolai Ryzhkov reported that, even allowing for massive subsidies, 13 percent of all Soviet industrial enterprises were operating at a loss, and the government was bailing them out.[12]

Gorbachev's pet peeve, one to which he returned again and again in later speeches, was the mindless "cranking out of large amounts of gross output" to make production figures look good and to fulfill the numerical targets set by Gosplan, regardless of the quality of goods and whether customers really needed or wanted the items. "It is intolerable that enterprises are compelled to produce goods that no one wants just for gross output targets," Gorbachev later declared. Or again: "We don't need tons of oil and cubic meters of natural gas or tons of ore for their own sake. We don't need cubic meters of timber and tons of iron, steel, and so on for their own sake. We need them so that in the end, we have a higher national income, which we could use for improving every walk of life of our society, of our people."[13]

What Gorbachev all but said, and what some radical reform economists wanted him to make explicit, was that the fundamental cause of the nation's economic problems was the entire system of centralized planning to which Gorbachev and the Soviet leadership still clung. Their hang-up was ideological; but more than that, they looked back at what they saw as important gains in decades past from this centralized system. Most of the rest of the Politburo was more cautious than Gorbachev. But he was ambivalent too, even as he launched this ebullient new phase of reform. He wanted something new, but he was not ready to scrap the old.

Gorbachev's generation, for all their disenchantment with Stalin, were now in their late fifties and could remember how this militarized command economy had focused the nation's energies on a few top priorities—arms, space, certain elements of heavy industry—and lifted Soviet Russia from its role as a backward bit player in the game of nations after World War I to a nuclear-armed superpower in the 1980s. In the "Great Patriotic War"—what the West calls World War II—Stalin's economy, run with military urgency, had equipped an army that staved off and then defeated the technologically more sophisticated Germans. After the war, Stalin had set out to surpass the world in steel, oil, machine tools; and the Soviets took great pride when, in terms of raw volume, they had gotten out front in those areas. Centralized planning had worked in a few high-priority areas and in sectors where quantity was a useful yardstick of success, such as in electricity, crude oil, gas, iron ore, tonnage of steel. But unfortunately for Moscow, these were industrial raw materials, not finished products; they were the output of a developing economy, not the sophisticated wares of a modern industrialized nation.

As the years wore on and the running of a modern economy became increasingly complex, the anomalies and drawbacks of the Soviet system became starkly evident. A smokestack economy could not keep up with the Information Age. In 1987, when the United States had 25 million personal computers, the Soviet Union had about 150,000, according to a top Soviet computer expert.[14] The explosion of electronics, not to mention the millions of varieties of modern products, made it ludicrous to think of drafting a single economic master plan and honing it down to the last detail. The planning apparatus had subdivided into many baronies and fiefdoms, often working at cross purposes. Gorbachev himself noted the bottlenecks when one sector, one ministry, intersected with another. Nikolai Federenko, one of Moscow's most respected economists, reckoned only half in jest that even using computers, it would take thirty thousand years to draft a thoroughly calculated, balanced economic plan.

The very notion of producing a single blueprint for a continental-sized national economy was a reflection of the Utopian impracticality of Soviet socialism. As reform economist Nikolai Shmelyov observed, "From the very outset this entire system was marked by economic romanticism, heavily larded with economic incompetence."[15]

Moreover, since "fulfilling the Plan" meant using quantitative yardsticks—not profits—as the measures of economic success, this system often produced ridiculous results. It provided tens of thousands of tractors and harvesters without spare parts; millions of pairs of shoes that were left on the shelves because the sizes did not match up with the population's; television sets that self-destructed, literally blew up. The irrational worship of raw numbers ignored quality and bred inefficiency. For example, construction firms worked to fulfill mandatory quotas that reckoned their volume in terms of their total costs; that gave both labor and management every incentive to jack up wages and costs, rather than try to build things more cheaply. Transportation plans reckoned in ton-kilometers (how many tons of goods were transported over how many kilometers) encouraged both truckers and their customers to ship heavy items over long distances, rather than keep weight down and distances minimal. This "more the merrier" approach tightened national transportation bottlenecks.[16] Health care reckoned in numbers of hospital beds did not work to reduce abnormally high infant mortality or to extend life expectancy of Soviet males, which actually grew shorter during the Brezhnev period.

In industry, the "Plan mentality" discouraged modernization, because interrupting production to install new machinery inevitably meant falling behind prescribed quotas. Inventions and innovations of any kind disrupted the drive toward fulfilling the Plan, so innovation became a nuisance instead of an advance. Another anomaly was that in the Soviet economy, massive waste and enormous shortages existed side by side. For the Plan not only set production quotas but also allocated raw materials and components. Because of perennial shortages, smart industrial managers stocked up on needed parts and components. This led to colossal hoarding, making the shortages still worse, a vicious cycle. Beyond that, it was to everyone's advantage to play the game dishonestly and cover up their real results and activities. Planners won favor with political leaders by setting ambitious economic goals—Nikolai Shmelyov calls them "fantasy plan-targets."[17] And since enterprise managers and their workers were paid bonuses on the basis of fulfilling these targets, they turned to false reporting and outright lying about their actual results. Deception was endemic to the system.

Obviously, one central element of Gorbachev's new economic program was to shock the system into realism through a sharp dose of candor from the top. But in his economic manifesto of June 1987, Gorbachev declared his intentions to make vital changes in four areas: the rights of enterprises, the powers of central agencies, the role of prices, and the development of a wholesale market. The cornerstone of his new policy was the promise of more freedom from bureaucratic control for farms, enterprises, and industrial associations (large Soviet corporate conglomerates).

"The main thing that we should achieve by introducing the new mechanism is to give broad rights to enterprises and to ensure real economic independence for them, on the basis of full economic accountability," Gorbachev declared. "The enterprise itself, proceeding from the real requirements of society, draws up a plan for the production and sale of its output. The plan should not be based on a multitude of detailed plan assignments set in the form of directives by higher-level agencies. . . ."[18]

In order to cut back ministerial interference, Gorbachev said the ministries "must be relieved of their day-to-day management functions" and their staffs cut back. Even though central organs would continue to give "target figures" to enterprises, Gorbachev envisioned that these would be guidelines, not iron laws. These target figures, he said, "should not serve as directives and should not shackle the [enterprise] in drafting its plan but should leave it plenty of room for maneuver in making decisions and choosing partners when signing economic agreements."[19]

In perhaps his most daring declaration, given the universal Soviet dependency on subsidized prices, Gorbachev asserted that price reform was an essential element of the entire process, and he promised early action by 1990, so that a new pricing system would be working by the start of the new Five-Year Plan, for 1991–95.

"A radical reform in the formulation of prices is a very important component of the restructuring of economic management," Gorbachev asserted. In words that would come back to haunt him year after year, he added: "Without this, a complete changeover to the new mechanism is impossible. Prices should play an important incentive role in improving the use of resources, reducing outlays, increasing output quality, accelerating scientific and technical progress, and in rationalizing the entire system of distribution and consumption."[20]

Finally, he advocated moving away from the system of centralized allocation of raw materials and components by the powerful agency known as Gossnab, the State Committee for Material and Technical Supply; and to the establishment of a wholesale market where enterprises could simply buy what they needed from each other. Prime Minister Ryzhkov revealed that as of mid-1987, only 5 percent of industrial supplies were covered by genuine wholesale trade contracts between enterprises; Gorbachev's target was to boost that level sharply, to 60 percent by 1990, and to 100 percent by 1992.[21]

"The quicker we switch to direct ties and wholesale trade, the quicker we will get rid of shortages and of surplus stocks of goods," Gorbachev said enthusiastically. "And this is no armchair talk."[22]

To industrial managers, this was an impressive vision, a far-bolder-sounding mandate than had been attempted in the earlier economic reforms of Nikita Khrushchev in the late 1950s, and of former Prime Minister Aleksei Kosygin in 1965. Gorbachev was telling industrial managers: Be your own bosses, run your own businesses, do your own investments, keep your profits, and make your plants efficient.

There were, nonetheless, some troubling inconsistencies in Gorbachev's outline of the "new mechanism." Central planning would continue, mainly to plot longer-term national economic goals; its targets for various industries would be "nonbinding" guidelines rather than immutable decrees. Ministries could issue "state orders"—*goszakazy*—for the most essential goods and services. The ministries were to be responsible for ensuring that the nation's needs were met in every sector, and for

checking cost and price inflation among the enterprises under their jurisdiction. Beyond that, the basic priorities and levels of large industrial
investments would still be set in Moscow. Such were the terms that Prime
Minister Ryzhkov, as the principal figure in economic policy-making and
the prime protector of the ministerial bureaucracy, had extracted from
Gorbachev. Ryzhkov had come from Gosplan; he believed the central
machinery of planning was essential to keep the nation's needs and outputs in balance.[23]

Gorbachev himself, moreover, was wary of alarming the blue-collar
proletariat with his ideas of reform. While he drummed on the theme that
Soviet workers had to work and produce more and that managers had to
cut unnecessary staff, he also promised Soviet workers that his new economic mechanism would not cause unemployment. And to prevent catas-
trophes from befalling firms that operated in the red, the fine print in the
new economic scheme instructed ministries to build up reserve funds to
support these losers—by imposing special levies on profitable enterprises.

In short, Gorbachev's rhetoric was bold and dramatic, but in practice
he was actually straddling: He was embracing two contradictory economic
logics—the logic of market economics and the logic of central planning.
He was endorsing the power of two rival forces—the enterprises and the
ministries.

The real test was how this new scheme would work out in practice. If
there was one place where reform would stand a good chance, I figured
it would be at Uralmash, the upstart giant that had taken Gorbachev at
his word in early 1988—and gotten Gorbachev's minions to back its
challenge to Gosplan.

OPENING A "CLOSED CITY"

Getting to Uralmash was not simple. It is located in Sverdlovsk, the main
city in the Ural Mountains, about two thousand miles east of Moscow on
the western fringe of Siberia. A brawny industrial region, the Urals are
rich in iron, coal, and other minerals, and Sverdlovsk, now a city of 1.6
million people, is a kind of Soviet Pittsburgh. It was also the place where
Bolshevik militants had executed Czar Nicholas II and his family during
the Russian civil war.

For seven decades Sverdlovsk had been a "closed city"—closed, that
is, to foreigners. It is packed with huge defense plants, and it is in a region
of prison gulags, within one hundred miles of the site of the Soviet
Union's—and probably the world's—most disastrous nuclear accident,

which Soviet authorities tried to hush up for three decades. In 1957, the government now admits, an explosion of plutonium waste at a major nuclear-weapons plant, known as Chelyabinsk-40, released massive radiation. From personal contacts and after extensive research, Zhores Medvedev, a Soviet scientist now living in London, disclosed that radiation contaminated hundreds of square miles with strontium 90; hundreds of people were killed, and thousands more hospitalized.[24] For many years, road signs along the 150-mile stretch from Sverdlovsk to the city of Chelyabinsk warned of radioactivity; drivers of state vehicles were instructed to go at top speed and never to leave their vehicles on the highway.

Given Sverdlovsk's "closed" status, people were very surprised to see our film unit when we showed up there.

"Who do you know?" asked Nikolai Antonov, the regional television chief, in some amazement. "Must be someone important."

Antonov told me that only one other American party had ever visited Sverdlovsk: Vice President Richard Nixon, on a swift, three-hour stopover in 1959.

"But Mr. Nixon never spent the night," Antonov said. "You are the first Americans to spend the night here."

Actually, I later found out, some American arms-control inspectors had more recently visited Sverdlovsk to check on a plant that had previously made SS-20 missiles, the ones banned by the Reagan-Gorbachev arms-control agreement of 1987.

Getting permission for us to go to Sverdlovsk had taken six months of my prodding the government and Party Central Committee. In the end, my request had to go up to the office of Prime Minister Nikolai Ryzhkov. He had worked for years at Uralmash, once serving as its general director, and had taken an interest in our going there, thanks to a push from his press aide, Lev Voznesensky, and from Valentin Lazutkin of the State Television Committee.

Once the door opened a crack, it swung open wide. We got VIP treatment. As a closed city, Sverdlovsk lacked one of the standard facilities of most Soviet cities: an official Intourist hotel for foreigners. Our hosts considered the normal Soviet domestic hotels too shabby, so they put us up in the best facility available—the Communist Party hotel. We shared it with Party workers, government officials, and military officers on assignment.

This elite hotel was a handsome, well-built, five-story brick building on a tree-lined side street, with no markings to disclose its function to the unwitting passerby. You had to know in advance what it was and why you were going there. The only clues to its special nature were the black Volgas with gray curtains, a favorite of Soviet bigwigs, that occasionally were parked in the driveway. The rooms were nicely furnished and well maintained, and the service personnel more pleasant than usual; but the sauna did not work, and the food was no better than in our other hotels.

One feature was striking: the phones. They worked flawlessly, better than anywhere else I ever stayed in the Soviet Union. For example, it had taken me days to get a call through to the United States from Tashkent or Kiev; even getting through to Moscow was an ordeal that required several hours. From the Party hotel in Sverdlovsk, we got through with a snap of the fingers, and the line was crystal clear, rather than crippled by static. I attributed the speed of service to the almost military obedience of Sverdlovsk and Moscow operators when a call came from the Party's October Hotel. And I assumed the lines were so clear because they hooked into the military circuits serving Sverdlovsk's defense industry.

Uralmash, literally the Ural Heavy Machine–Building Works, is an industrial showcase, part of what earned Sverdlovsk its special place in the heroic saga of Soviet industrialization.

Uralmash is an industrial giant, literally built from scratch, which went into operation in 1933, a time when throwing up massive plants far from Moscow was a hallmark of Soviet socialism. It became a prime model of the Stalinist command economy: heavy industry built at the expense of ordinary people who were called upon to sacrifice for the might of the state.

In the pantheon of Soviet socialism, agriculture has always been something of a neglected stepchild, but heavy industry, symbolized by enterprises like Uralmash, has been celebrated not only in the ideological cheerleading of the nation's leaders, but quite literally in popular song and legend. Uralmash has its own factory song, and its own two-story museum. In fact, one of the first obligatory stops at Uralmash is the factory museum. Beside models of Uralmash products and displays of "hero workers" in Uralmash history were photos of such Bolshevik leaders as Ordzhonidkize and Sverdlov (for whom the city was named) and large mural-photos of crowds cheering as Uralmash rolled out tanks for the war against the Nazi invaders, and cheering again for victory in the Great Patriotic War.

Today, Uralmash is an industrial behemoth, a kind of Soviet General Motors, with a work force of fifty thousand. It has huge blast furnaces, 180-ton metal presses, blooming mills, rolling mills, slab-casting machines—shop after shop after shop stretching over five square miles on one side of Sverdlovsk. It is not one factory but many; more than one hundred in all, not counting several subsidiary plants at other locations, plus its own state farm. Its internal railroad spurs add up to more than one hundred miles of track. In short, Uralmash epitomizes the Soviet industrial romance with size.

Uralmash also epitomizes the current Soviet economic crisis. It is the embodiment of old-fashioned smokestack industry: an aging plant with antiquated equipment and a style of operation that is way out of date. The brute methods of high Stalinism, which worked in the first years of industrialization and the war, are now too rigid. They have stifled innovation and left the workers unmotivated.

My first strong impression of Uralmash was that the world had passed it by. The whole feel of the place was old: a 1950s factory operating with 1930s equipment. There was astonishingly little activity in some of the shops, which were as cavernous as airport hangars. Others were busy with activity, overhead cranes swinging huge pieces of cast metal into place, massive orange-hot ingots of steel being slammed into shape by metal presses, automated lathes and filers shaving steel parts down to specification. But other shops were as dusty, grimy, and idle as abandoned warehouses, piled high with rusted ingots or iron reinforcing rods bent in so many loops like metal noodles. Here and there, a black-overalled worker manned a blowtorch or a lathe, but others wandered about aimlessly. Smoking on the shop floor was common. Despite the enormous potential for disastrous accidents, safety lanes were rarely marked on the floor. A handful of safety signs reminded workers to wear safety glasses or to ground electrical equipment before using it, but I didn't notice many workers following these rules. It was unusual, too, to see them wearing hard hats, despite all the heavy metal carried overhead by cranes. Even though the plant had obviously been spruced up for our filming, the atmosphere was lax; plant officials who had been abroad knew their whole operation had fallen behind standards even in India, Brazil, or Czechoslovakia, let alone in the West or Japan.

WHERE ARE THE "HERO WORKERS"?

The man with the mandate to bring *perestroika* to Uralmash is Igor Ivanovich Stroganov, a captain of Soviet industry. He was only forty-two when he became general director of the enterprise—comparable to an American CEO—in 1985, the year Gorbachev took power. Just two years later, he had the nerve to face down Gosplan and the Ministry of Heavy Machine–Building.

Stroganov easily fits the image of a Soviet power player. He looks like a tough Irish cop—about five feet eleven and 240 pounds, with a lion-sized head and beefy hands. He speaks with a low, throaty growl and moves with the slow, athletic tread of a weight lifter. His bushy gray curls have been cultivated into a fifties style pompadour.

Despite his overpowering physical presence, I found Stroganov open and gregarious, quick to laugh, unusually willing (for a Soviet manager) to let his subordinates speak, and very friendly toward the United States. At lunch one day, he winced while his chief engineer told stories about drugs and crime in America. Stroganov quickly cut in to mock Russians who believed, as the Soviet press had reported, that there was a murder every fifty seconds in Manhattan. "I was there for two weeks," he said, "and I never saw one."

Like Prime Minister Ryzhkov, Stroganov had started his Uralmash career at the bottom. After army service, he became a welder, went to night school at Sverdlovsk Mining Institute, worked his way up to shift foreman and shop boss, and then, after ideological training, rose to Communist Party secretary at Uralmash, his last post before becoming general director. The Party job is a big one; at places such as Uralmash, the Party secretary hand-picks or has a voice in all high appointments, helps the management run production campaigns, and deals with worker morale. And Uralmash has one of the biggest Party units in Sverdlovsk—eight thousand members.

As boss of Uralmash, Stroganov has one of the largest offices I saw in the Soviet Union, as large as a deputy prime minister's, with a desk the size of a double bed, and a conference table long enough to seat twenty-two aides, whom he assembled for our arrival.

After the preliminaries, it became clear that in applying Gorbachev's economic manifesto, Stroganov had two major problems: people—retaining and motivating his work force; and power—gaining the freedom to pick his own products, set his own prices, choose his own customers.

After my visits to Soviet industry in the seventies, when it was like pulling teeth to get the barest admission of a tiny problem, I was surprised by Stroganov's candor. On the two visits I made to Sverdlovsk—each time for several days—he let me move around the plant with our film crew, to see the operation for ourselves and then ask questions.

Indelibly etched in my memory is a message playfully painted on some iron struts by the workers in Shop No. 15, the metalwork shop. To the customer, they wrote: HAPPY NEW YEAR 1989. These struts had been completed in 1988, in time for the New Year, but here it was July 1989, and they were still there, sitting in the shop. In September, I noticed they were still there. Looking around, I saw great piles of grids, rings, and parts of all kinds, waiting to be shipped.

Perestroika obviously was not working the way it was supposed to. I remembered from the old days that the Soviets divide the month into "decades"—three ten-day work periods. They are nicknamed *spyachka, goryachka,* and *likhoradka,* meaning sleepy time, hot time, and fever, to indicate the pace of work in Soviet factories. The first ten days of the month are pretty slow, the middle of the month things heat up, and the final ten days are a frenzy, as the factory races to complete its production quota, often resorting to "black Saturdays," extra weekend workdays *without* extra pay. The bosses and the Party have to whip the workers into a high tempo. Obviously, Stroganov still had to resort to these old methods, working like a cheerleader to mobilize workers to fulfill quotas. Deliveries were running late. Output was stacking up.

"What's the problem?" I asked Stroganov.

"This is what we call 'unfinished production,' " he said with a snort. "The less time this stuff lies around here and the quicker it is delivered to the customer, the more profit for us."

"How come this happens?" I asked. "What are your main problems?"

He looked at me for a moment, his huge head nodding in acknowledgment of his difficulties.

"We have *billions* of problems," he growled. "First and foremost, shortage of manpower. Look, this is his second shift," he said, gesturing to the shop boss standing nearby. "He now has only enough workers to man forty percent of the available machine tools." To the shop boss, he said, "The third shift has even fewer workers, right?"

"That's right," said the shop boss. "Ten percent of our machinery does not run at full capacity because there are not enough orders from customers. About sixty percent of the machinery cannot be used because there's a shortage of qualified workers. The rest works normally."[25]

In short, Uralmash was bleeding.

As Marian Marzynski, my producer on the economics film, quipped: "The era of the 'Hero Worker' is long gone." The new generation of workers are no longer willing to sacrifice for the state. They want better pay, better housing, better working conditions, and more modern equipment. Dissatisfied, they are looking for greener pastures. According to Georgy Pospelov, a plant sociologist who studies labor relations, Uralmash lost 10 percent of its work force—five thousand people—in a period of eighteen months, a staggering defection.

I ran into many indications that blue-collar morale was poor. In the smelting shop, the workers were threatening a strike for higher pensions and higher pay for night work. There was a brief test of power, then Moscow intervened; the ministry, panicked at the thought of a strike and having granted similar increases at other factories, told Stroganov to agree. But it was his problem to come up with money for the whopping 20 percent and 40 percent differentials, for night pay and other benefits.

Stroganov was trying to apply Gorbachev's reforms by putting each of his large shops on a more independent footing, responsible for its own output, work schedule, pay roster, and costs. As part of this self-management, his economists and supervisors had encouraged workers to organize small production teams and had offered them profit sharing as an incentive to boost production. In a few shops, this approach had begun to work, producing modest increases in output and wages. He had even managed to lease one unprofitable and distant subsidiary to a newly formed industrial cooperative. But in most of his empire, the *perestroika* approach was giving rise to more questions than answers.

"I was told we were getting rid of some bosses here," one dark-haired young metalworker shouted at a management aide. "Shouldn't we get rid of a few apparatchiks up there in Moscow?"

Other workers raised all kinds of dilemmas: What kind of self-management was it when prices were still fixed by the state? Why did the factory still need a central administration if each shop became independent? How could they catch up with the West?

"What are we doing, talking about catching up with them," jeered an older man, "when we're two hundred years behind? And we sit and wait, and our bosses sit on their butts, doing nothing."

The steady departure of dissatisfied workers has become such a serious problem that Uralmash conducts exit interviews with every one of them. The personnel officers who conduct the interviews call themselves "life savers" for Uralmash, because they rescue about one third of those who, as required by Soviet law, file departure notices.

I watched the personnel manager try to keep one young woman by offering her a raise, but after five years at Uralmash she was determined to leave. The manager put her through routine questions about her pay, work, the housing provided by Uralmash, and then came to the jackpot question.

"Have you got a new job yet?" he asked.

"Yes, I go to work for a private cooperative," she replied.

"Private co-op," he repeated distastefully. Then, typical for an official at a state enterprise, he tried to cast aspersions on this new rival economic sector. "Do you think the private cooperative movement will survive?"

Pospelov, the sociologist, objected.

"Wait a minute," he told the personnel manager. "You shouldn't put the question that way."

Then turning to the young woman, Pospelov asked a revealing question: "Are you going to have a very flexible work schedule at the new job, or not very flexible?"

"Well, at that place, it all depends on my productivity," she replied. "The more I do, the more I make."

"So that means it is very flexible," Pospelov said.[26]

Pospelov told me that 12 percent of the departing workers cited low wages as their reason for leaving; 20 percent cited bad working conditions; 40 percent inadequate housing.[27]

In the Soviet system, Uralmash and other big enterprises are expected to provide low-rent housing for their workers—an example of paternalism, Soviet-style. Uralmash was known as "the father of Soviet machine-building," and like a good father, it had financed the construction of an entire region of the city of Sverdlovsk. In recent years, however, the father had not kept pace with demand, and was now being cursed. Stroganov told me that twelve thousand Uralmash workers now lived in substandard housing.

On a Saturday morning, he took us around to see six- and seven-story worker dormitories. Typical of the situation was a family of four living in one room and sharing a bathroom and kitchen with other families. The two children, who were lucky to have a homemade double-decker bed, said it was pretty hard to do homework while their parents were watching television; and the parents never got any privacy. The daytime couch became their bed at night, a situation I saw repeated scores of times.

"How long have you been waiting for a separate apartment?" Stroganov asked the wife.

"Since 1981," she said. Eight years.

"What's your number on the waiting list?"

"Two thousand eight hundred forty-four."

"Well, after three years you'll get a separate apartment," he tried to assure her.

"That's a long time to live in these conditions," she replied.[28]

I could tell Stroganov was embarrassed and disturbed by the housing problem. It gnawed at him, especially since it was a major reason that his work force was draining away. To stem their departure, Stroganov was ready to spend some of his profits to build new housing, schools, and clinics.

But there was a catch. In the Soviet system, money is not enough to build a building. Stroganov did not have his own construction crews; he had to turn to state-owned enterprises, and they were under the thumb of the Sverdlovsk provincial government. So the government controlled all resources for local construction—manpower, equipment, bricks and mortar—and had veto power over every big construction request.

While we were in Stroganov's office, his construction manager delivered the bad news that the regional government had cut two thirds of his $50 million housing proposal.

I could feel Stroganov's frustration. He tried to call his Party connections, to get the decision reversed. The next day was the deadline for final appeals; his best contact was out. Another call; still no luck. Stroganov was chain-smoking, his fingers drumming the table.

"There is no logic to their action," he burst out. "All our problems today are related to the low level of social services for our workers: housing and daily provisions. I can understand the reduction of our industrial construction budget, in the light of recent national decisions. But to deny our request for housing? That makes no sense at all!"[29]

BIG DOESN'T MAKE A PROFIT

The other major problem for Stroganov, and hundreds of industrial managers like him, is how to get control of their own operations so they can turn a profit, modernize their factories, and compete on the world market—Gorbachev's proclaimed goal.

At first glance, Uralmash looks to be in an enviable position. It monopolizes the manufacture of most essential heavy machinery in the Soviet Union: giant mining excavators; deep oil-drilling rigs; turbines for power stations; cranes; struts and spans for bridges; iron wheels for steam engines; ore crushers; huge hydraulic metal presses; and industrial centrifuges—not to mention consumer items such as prefab kitchen cabinets and washing machines. As I wandered through the plant, everything except the consumer items seemed big. The annual volume at Uralmash was big too—over $1 billion.

The problem is that bigness does not equal profit; most of the big items are not making money.

If Stroganov had his way with *perestroika*, he would give up most of the big equipment, change his product mix, and go after the export trade.

He gave me chapter and verse on how the old ways of doing business were hurting Uralmash. Every kitchen-cabinet console, he said, cost him $135 more to produce than he got from the Ministry of Trade, which sold them to consumers through its network of retail outlets. The oil ministry, he said, was buying drilling rigs from Romania for $5 million, but paying Uralmash only 1 million rubles (about $1.6 million) for similar rigs; and it had refused his appeal to raise his price to 2 million rubles ($3.2 million).[30]

The most exasperating, Stroganov said, were the mining excavators. For strip mining, the ministry of coal mining had a passion for a massive mobile excavator with an arm one hundred meters long (just over one hundred yards long) and a scoop with a volume of one hundred cubic meters. The scoop alone was twice as big as a living room. Stroganov told me 250 schoolchildren could fit into it. There was a model of the excavator at the Uralmash museum. The cab was ten stories high; beside it, a human being was dwarfed. Uralmash finished seven of these mechanical dinosaurs each year; it took three years to build just one. And since nobody ever gets rich on the state's fixed prices, Uralmash earned not a single kopeck from their production.

"I won't lie to you—the price only covers our expenses," Stroganov confessed. "We don't make any profit on them."[31]

Stroganov suspected that he might make money if he could market them abroad. Recently, he said, Uralmash had sold a giant excavator to the Kemerovo Coal Combine in western Siberia for 11.5 million rubles (just under $20 million). On a trip to Canada, he had seen a similar one, perhaps a bit more sophisticated, made in America, that had sold for $86 million.

Still, the big ones were an enormous headache. Stroganov wanted to stop making them and, instead, make many more smaller ones (with a five-cubic-meter scoop—the size of a Volkswagen Beetle). Those were popular with foreign customers, in Spain, Austria, and West Germany, as well as in India, Algeria, Iran, and Eastern Europe. For Soviet customers, the fixed price was 190,000 rubles, but abroad they went for no less than 500,000 rubles apiece, according to Stroganov. Uralmash was already exporting sixty a year; he wanted to triple that figure.

"If we could produce another hundred of those smaller excavators and if we could sell them abroad," he said, puffing proudly on a filter tip, "that would be remarkable."

Yet he could not do what he wanted to do; in each case, ministries were blocking him. They said other Soviet industries would collapse without equipment made by Uralmash and unavailable elsewhere.

That was Stroganov's catch-22.

He could not get permission to export oil rigs because the oil ministry said Soviet oil fields would go dry without Uralmash rigs. The ministry would not let him charge more on the domestic market, on the grounds that Soviet prices were set according to technical calculations and could not be increased except for significant modifications.

And then, each ruble had to be justified in excruciating detail. A similar story with the excavators: The coal ministry had him in a bind, insisting on a continuing flow of giant machines, refusing to let him make more small ones for export. Even the Ministry of Trade insisted that Uralmash was obliged to keep making kitchen cabinets, at a loss, because of Gorbachev's drive for more consumer goods.

Where, I wanted to know, were Gorbachev's promises of more autonomy? How could the ministries tie his hands?

First, he explained, Uralmash was a monopoly producer and so it had to accept *goszakazy,* mandatory state orders from the ministries. Each ministry claimed it was following Gorbachev's decree that ministries fill the nation's needs. That was the massive loophole that the bureaucracy won from Gorbachev when he was promising industrial managers their independence.

"So how much do state orders account for?" I asked.

"One hundred percent of our big excavators," grunted Stroganov, "ninety-five percent of our cast-metal products, seventy-eight percent of our rolling equipment, one hundred percent of our consumer goods."[32]

"I thought Gorbachev had promised to cut the Plan," I observed. "Didn't they cut back anywhere?"

"Small excavators," he said. "Only thirty percent state orders."

I searched for a smile, some sign of satisfaction.

"So you can do what you want," I suggested, "produce more small excavators and export them?"

Stroganov shook his head.

Catch-22 again.

To produce what he wanted, Stroganov needed raw materials in great quantities, but only the state could supply them—so he had to produce what the state wanted. Uralmash was caught in the interlocking web of the Soviet economy, still controlled from the top.

The bureaucrats in Moscow were using a gimmick called *limity*—limited or rationed goods allocated by Gossnab, the State Committee for Material and Technical Supply. Under Gorbachev's blueprint, Gossnab was supposed to be fading away by late 1990, but Stroganov said it was as powerful as ever; now, it was even more powerful than Gosplan.

"They gave us freedom, but then through Gossnab they took it away from us," he sighed. "Instead of the Plan, they substitute state orders and state supply. One way or another, they decide ninety-five percent of our output, and we decide only five percent.

"We told them, 'You have to let us sell our production, using direct contracts between us and other companies,' and they told us, 'Yes, you can do it—sometime,' " Stroganov reported. "But at this point they have not permitted us to do that."[33]

The question on my mind, and on Stroganov's mind too, was what had happened to the wholesale market that Gorbachev promised would be working by this time, in late 1989.

"It's very hard for you Americans to understand the specifics of our production," Stroganov explained. "In your country, normal economic relations exist, meaning you have money, the free market exists, you purchase your raw materials, any kind of resources, and you solve any kind of problem. We, on the other hand, in the era of *perestroika*, have to learn from you and introduce this mechanism here. At this point, we don't have the means to develop factories and enterprises. I cannot solve all my problems, because the old mechanism is still in place. I cannot peacefully go and buy the things that I need . . . because, to put it mildly, the open market is very limited."

As Stroganov talked, he became more irked by the trap he was in. He had often clashed with the Moscow hierarchy over these same issues— perhaps one reason, as he later told me, that he had not been given annual pay bonuses above his regular salary of 600 rubles ($1,000) a month. The ministry decided which directors got bonuses.

"I always speak my mind about this situation," he said. "I do not hide my thoughts from anybody."[34]

The next afternoon, I learned of another place where the shoe of central control still pinched, in spite of Gorbachev's promises of autonomy. Stroganov met with some of his economic advisers. Vladislav Grammatin, head of the Uralmash subsidiary for foreign trade, blurted out his frustration at Moscow's stop-and-go policies. Grammatin was responsible for marketing nearly $150 million in exports annually.

"There was the new law saying that we have full independence to do what we want," Grammatin recalled. "They opened the gates wide and we happily entered. And then they slammed the gates shut right in our face. They said, 'Controls and licensing. You have to get a license from the State Committee on Foreign Relations. And they will decide whether each trade is profitable or not.' I said, 'If you trust us to work in this area, trust us all the way. Let them check me once a year and if I break the law, I will answer for that. . . .' But we are not a small firm with a hundred, a hundred and fifty employees. We are not a seedy enterprise, but a serious business with a huge inventory and customers in forty-two countries. Our turnover is so big that we deserve to be trusted and given special worldwide trade permission. At least seventy-five percent of our hard currency from modernization should be left with us."[35]

The point about hard currency was probably the sorest of all. Uralmash was working hard to develop new markets in the West, to earn dollars, yen, and deutsche marks in order to buy state-of-the-art equipment. The issue was more than just buying Western equipment; it was managerial freedom. Uralmash, like many Soviet factories and organizations, had accumulated rubles but it could not spend them on new technology, except by going through the state supply system. Foreign currency gave Uralmash freedom to bypass the clogged state apparatus. But on every foreign deal, Moscow was raking off more than half of Uralmash's hard currency, and then tying strings on the rest.

Stroganov had just lived through a particularly painful example: a promising partnership deal with the Japanese. In 1987, Kobe Steel of Japan had begun discussing a joint venture with Uralmash. The Japanese were prepared to invest $80 million in redesigning and modernizing the main metallurgical shops at Uralmash, with the latest computerized equipment for working cold metal. Uralmash had wanted to modernize that shop in the early 1970s, but the central planners vetoed it. Now, the shops desperately needed updating.

To make the Japanese deal work, Uralmash had to match the Japanese money with a combination of Soviet rubles and hard currency. Stroganov did not have enough hard currency in Uralmash accounts, so he had to ask the Soviet State Bank for a loan. This, in turn, required approval from Gosplan.

Catch-22 again.

The central planners did not want to spend their currency this way, even though Uralmash would have had enough if Moscow had let it keep all of its earnings in the first place. But that was not how Moscow played the game. So Stroganov had to let the Japanese deal slip through his fingers.

The final blow, I found out, was that Moscow's bureaucracy was undercutting Gorbachev's goal of promoting industrial efficiency by draining off most of Uralmash's profits.

According to Stroganov and his top financial deputy, this is how it worked: After all expenses, including the normal ones of Western firms, plus housing construction and reinvestment, Uralmash had a pretax income of $125 million. Its tax bill came to a paltry $13 million. But the bureaucrats had added one more item: *otchisleniye*, literally "the deduction"—a whopping $83 million that Uralmash had to contribute to the state budget and to the Ministry of Heavy Machine–Building. For some reason, no one—neither the bureaucrats nor Stroganov—called this an additional tax, though that's what it amounted to.[36]

What astonished me was that this money was earmarked to help subsidize other industries and companies operating in the red! Not only were the losers being kept afloat, but Uralmash was being punished, rather than rewarded, for its efficiency.

As we stopped by Stroganov's apartment to bid farewell over Russian tea and a thick chocolate cake prepared by his wife, Svetlana, Stroganov tried to put a good face on things.

"I must tell you that lately we have more freedom to decide," he said. "There is some movement forward, so when we start the next Five-Year Plan, we'll discuss all these issues and they will give more independence to the enterprises. But so far, the major issues are decided only through Moscow. Moscow is the master."[37]

It was a gentler echo of his frustration over the restrictions imposed by state orders and state supply.

"This is a very old disease in our country," he said then. "But now we have so much to do, so many problems to solve. So this situation really creates a lot of dissatisfaction."[38]

THE KREMLIN: BEWARE THE SWAMP

After talking with Stroganov and others around the country, I returned to Moscow to talk with top policy-makers, to find out what had gone wrong with Gorbachev's industrial blueprint. The man I saw at the Kremlin was Deputy Prime Minister Leonid Abalkin, chief economic adviser to Gorbachev and Prime Minister Nikolai Ryzhkov. Abalkin is a learned scholar, head of the Institute of Economics, with a reputation in the West as a moderate reformer. A thoughtful, professorial type nearing sixty, Abalkin is cautious in manner, but at times he has been very outspoken, startling Gorbachev. He has had quite a number of fresh ideas, such as paying hard currency to farmers to stimulate Soviet grain production, rather than buying from the West.

Nonetheless, I found him a classic case of the outsider who makes radical pronouncements from the academy, but becomes more moderate once he is invested with responsibility. He was brought into government to inject new thinking and push market-style reforms, but he had to adjust to the inside politics of the Gorbachev leadership, and he seemed to have become a captive of the system; Prime Minister Ryzhkov's resistance to radical measures tempered him more than he was able to spur Ryzhkov.

In addition, like all his economist colleagues, Abalkin has never had the headaches of meeting a payroll, so he is more at home with theory than with practice.

I told Abalkin about the various complaints that I had heard, specifically those from Stroganov, and he retorted quickly that Stroganov was exaggerating his limitations.

"You have to take into consideration the attitude of the Soviet people—we're criticizing everything now," he said. "Nowadays, everybody is complaining they are not in charge. They're saying, 'What can I do? I'm a little man.' "

I offered a specific: "Stroganov at Uralmash says they want to produce for the foreign market and it would be very profitable, but they are not allowed."

"So who would produce for the Russian market then?" Abalkin countered. "Maybe we should make the prices profitable for him, so he would like to deal with our local market."

"If you give him the opportunity to do business, he'll do it," I said. "But if he is not really a free person, he cannot do it."

"Yes, this is really a dead-end situation," Abalkin conceded. "But it cannot all be changed overnight."

He insisted managers had more freedom today than they had a year or two ago: "It's not the government that's tying our hands, it's the shortage of resources. It's deficits of all kinds, including our state budget deficit of one hundred twenty billion rubles."[39]

I was a little surprised at Abalkin's tack. I had met with him in July 1989, about four months earlier, soon after he had come into the government. At that point, he was saying that one major imperative of economic reform was the step-by-step elimination of "production ministries," that is, the very agencies that were tying Stroganov's hands and micromanaging his business.[40] Now Abalkin seemed to be defending the central agencies, or at least defending their current method of operating, which blocked any genuine autonomy for industry.

"What is the major problem?" I persisted.

"The major problem of *perestroika* is that there are some people who want *perestroika,* and there are some people who combat *perestroika,* who want to keep things the old way," Abalkin replied. "And the powers are almost equal. Today, one side is getting the upper hand. Tomorrow, the other side. So we call *perestroika* a revolution. It's a revolutionary fight. It's like the fight of two powers; it's not so simple."

Our discussion got interrupted because Abalkin had to meet with three young economists who were helping him prepare options for a new reform program for Gorbachev and the leadership. The group sat around his huge conference table; Abalkin let me listen in.

"We see very limited time for changes," Grigory Yarlinsky said, breaking the ice. "We should consider the experience of the small socialist countries of Eastern Europe. They've been doing their reforms slowly. In Hungary, it took twenty years, in Yugoslavia thirty years, in Poland ten years. And we see what happened, what mistakes they made. Why should we repeat their history step by step? Look at the Yugoslavs, for instance. They have a new concept. They know what they want to do now. Understanding why the slow pace failed, they have brought to their parliament a new, accelerated concept of reform."[41]

"We really have to organize all the different forms of ownership—state enterprises, cooperatives, individual, and the rest," suggested an Armenian economist, Gennady Melikyan. "We don't want to slip backward."

"It is impossible to provide all economic spheres with the same opportunities at the same time," cautioned Abalkin's aide, Yuri Ivanovich. "But in the area of finance, which is the lifeblood of the entire economy, we need a more radical approach."

They debated markets, freer prices, and measures that would help enterprises like Uralmash and the growing sphere of cooperatives. No one mentioned Sweden, but as they talked that seemed the kind of mixed economy that they wanted to head toward, and Abalkin confirmed later that Sweden was his model.

Urgency was the mood of the younger three. They saw the country in crisis, inflation growing, sharpening people's frustration with consumer shortages, provoking strikes and street demonstrations. One adviser proposed launching a major new reform effort in 1991, but the others, worried about public impatience, pushed Abalkin to act sooner.

"I have just heard your young economists saying that you have to take large steps forward at once," I said to Abalkin as we resumed our interview. "Are you going to do that?"

"Yes, I think we have to go forward rapidly, we have to break the barriers and obstacles that are blocking our way now," he said. "But maybe because I am older than they are, I think that we should make these steps cautiously. When I enter an unknown territory and take my first steps, I must first make one step, feel the solid ground under my foot, and make sure that I am not in the swamp or in the marshes. Only then, after I am sure that I won't slip into the swamp, I'll take my second step. When my foot feels solid again, I'll take my third step."

He was sitting across a table from me. As he spoke, Abalkin did a pantomime—using his hands—of an elephant treading very slowly, very carefully. He advanced one hand, fingers spread, and put it down, palm down, slowly, ponderously, as if the elephant were checking the ground to see if it would bear its weight. Slowly, Abalkin moved up his other hand, again checking the table beneath it carefully, and so on. His slow pantomime, more expressive than his words, was an apt metaphor for the pace of economic *perestroika.*

"We are living now in a highly charged social situation," Abalkin reminded me. "We have no right to make a mistake. Our society won't tolerate a government which makes mistakes."

"Haven't mistakes already been made?" I asked.

"Well, that's why I was transferred from academic life to government—so that there will not be more mistakes," he went on. "You can provoke social unrest and strikes by careless actions. Social disturbances don't come out of a void. They may be the result of ill-conceived decisions."

"But if you walk very slowly, it could also be a mistake," I suggested. "Some people are very dissatisfied with the slow pace of *perestroika.*"

"Everyone wants fast changes now, but you do not promise your people something you cannot do," he countered. "I would say in another year, year and a half, it will improve. But now we have to stop the worsening process. The market is deteriorating. The economy is going downhill. So what we have to do now is slow things down and stop this process."

"What specifically do you want to stop?" I asked.

"Stop the worsening of the economic situation, stop the budget deficit, stop the imbalance in the consumer market," he said. "That's what must be stopped . . . the economic downturn. We cannot let it go the wrong way. We must stop the process of decline."[42]

Abalkin had framed Gorbachev's dilemma.

Here was Gorbachev—roughly five years in office—with the urge to shake up the economic system and free up his most able managers, but the bureaucracy and its protectors in the Politburo, principally Prime Minister Nikolai Ryzhkov, had blocked him. The bold ambitions of the 1987 economic manifesto had been blunted, paralyzed, even sabotaged by the iron resistance of Gossnab, Gosplan, and the ministries, which had no intention of relinquishing power.

As an experienced politician, Gorbachev should have anticipated their resistance: A liberalizing reform, by definition, reduces the power of the bureaucracy and is therefore opposed by the bureaucracy. So Gorbachev had failed to carry through on the single most crucial step for successful economic reform: breaking the power of the bureaucracy by delivering real power to industrial managers such as Igor Stroganov, and by establishing a wholesale market with a system of free industrial prices. Only these conditions would let the better enterprises be rewarded and improve production and quality.

In late 1989, bright young government economists were urging a daring plunge, and even older, wiser heads like Abalkin knew, intellectually, that this course made sense. Within a few weeks of our encounter, Abalkin put before the political leadership a proposal to introduce a market economy—including unregulated prices—by the end of 1991. But arrayed against him was not only the ministerial bureaucracy headed by Ryzhkov, instinctively resistant as a matter of their survival, but also public opinion.

The hopes of Gorbachev's early years had given way to popular disenchantment. Gorbachev had squandered his precious period of initial popularity by settling for conservative economic measures and by failing to carry through on the few progressive measures he had adopted. By the end of 1989, as Abalkin said, the acute economic situation had raised the dangers of a public backlash and popular unrest, should Gorbachev finally get up his nerve to crack state controls and monopolies, and to set markets and prices free, giving Stroganov and his peers the conditions they needed to revitalize their enterprises, and laying the foundations of a new economic system.

Once again, Ryzhkov prevailed in the private Kremlin maneuvering, and on December 13, 1989, he announced an economic program that imposed austerity and centralized control for three more years; a market economy was not to be attempted before 1993.[43]

That, however, did not end the policy fight.

On March 15, 1990, after Gorbachev was elected to the newly established office of the presidency, he promised radical economic reforms. Economists such as Stanislav Shatalin and Nikolai Petrakov, two new advisers to Gorbachev, mounted a campaign to persuade Gorbachev, Ryzhkov, and Gorbachev's new Presidential Council to go for broke, to administer strong medicine: They urged the Kremlin to copy Poland's instant plunge into market economics. In the lingo of the private, high-level Soviet debate, the Polish formula became known as "shock therapy" for the Soviet economy. For weeks, working groups that included sixty economists, lawyers, and government officials debated drafts, options, and proposals in the government *dachas* west of Moscow.[44]

In the end, Gorbachev rejected the most radical proposals, revealing his decision in a series of campaign-style speeches through the Ural Mountains region at the end of April. He told his people that he had rejected "shock therapy" and the radical plans of "impatient" market enthusiasts:

"They want to gamble: 'We must move faster and do everything decisively, opting irrevocably for a market economy. Let everything be thrown open tomorrow. Let market conditions be put in place everywhere. Let's have free enterprise and give the green light to all forms of ownership, private ownership. Let everything be private. Let us sell the land, everything.' I cannot support such ideas, no matter how decisive and revolutionary they might appear. These are irresponsible ideas, irresponsible."[45]

Even so, Gorbachev was brutal in his diagnosis of the economy, in decrying how "the old structures were holding back reforms," and in declaring the need for urgent action: "We cannot wait." At his side, in Sverdlovsk and at Uralmash, was Igor Stroganov, obviously confronting Gorbachev with the same demands for greater economic freedom that I had heard. Gorbachev reported: "The Ural people are all asking for oxygen: 'Give us room to show initiative and enterprise both inside our country and abroad. We are prepared to assume this sort of responsibility.' "[46]

A month later, on May 23, yet another economic program was unveiled by the government; in the hyperole of his initial enthusiasm, Gorbachev called it a historic shift "equal to the October [1917] Revolution."[47]

Indeed, it had a near-revolutionary impact on the people, for what hit them hardest was the announcement that on July 1 the price of bread—stable for three decades—would triple; and come January 1, 1991, there would be 30–130 percent increases in the prices of other food products, clothes, and consumer goods. That news touched off a wave of panic buying and hoarding, which, in the first forty-eight hours, sopped up three fourths of Moscow's food supplies for an entire month. The new Moscow City Council barred sales to anyone from out of town; other regions as far away as Uzbekistan retaliated by imposing similar restrictions on their goods. In Kiev, the Ukrainian prime minister declared his "firm opposition" to the new package. In the Supreme Soviet, dissatisfied reformers clamored for a vote of no-confidence in Prime Minister Ryzhkov, the plan's primary sponsor. Deputy Prime Minister Yuri Maslyukov, a principal architect of the package, said that if it failed, the Ryzhkov cabinet should resign.

Amid the furor, Gorbachev appealed to the public not to "give way to panic," but he distanced himself from the package—leaving Ryzhkov as the scapegoat.

As with previous measures on the economy, this package bore Ryzhkov's fingerprints: He called it a gradual transition to a "regulated market economy," but his emphasis was on the gradualness, and, especially in the early phases, on regulation. He had some progressive-sounding phrases, but for an economy in deep trouble, his pace was a crawl. On prices, Ryzhkov emphasized increases rather than reform. In 1991, for example, his package kept 85 percent of all prices under state control, and left only 15 percent to supply and demand. His plan spoke of converting state enterprises into stock companies, but the shares would initially be held by the government. Only in the mid-1990s, he promised, would there be a major effort to break up administrative controls and to ensure real competition. Overall, Ryzhkov seemed more intent on closing the budget deficit than on reforming the economy.[48]

Not only was the Ryzhkov plan an economic failure, it was a political disaster. In economic terms, it failed to make a genuine shift to a market economy; politically, it caused a massive backlash against Gorbachev from all sides. By beginning with the bombshell of tripled bread prices, Ryzhkov ensured the program would be torn to shreds in the Supreme Soviet, and it was; the deputies flatly rejected the price increases, tinkered with some other elements, and blocked the rest. Gorbachev was finding out what Western politicians have had to contend with: The more democratic he made the Soviet political system, the harder it became to muster a majority for unpopular economic measures.

Gorbachev left Ryzhkov to defend the plan publicly, but even his own advisers admitted later, in somewhat veiled language, that Gorbachev had to shoulder blame because the plan had been so politically inept.[49] Yuri Prokofyev, the Moscow Party chief, was furious because Gorbachev gave him no advance warning to cushion the public shock; he accused Gorbachev and Ryzhkov of arrogantly assuming that people would accept whatever they offered.[50] The problem was that except for the harsh medicine of price increases, it was too timid a program to have been worth risking a public upheaval. Once again, Gorbachev had fallen short. As reform economist and Supreme Soviet deputy Pavel Bunich put it, the Ryzhkov formula offered the worst of all worlds: "shock without therapy."[51]

Gorbachev was thrown back on his heels. Not until the fall of 1990 was he ready to try again on economic reform. This time, he tried teaming up with his old nemesis the resilient Boris Yeltsin. As head of the Russian republic, Yeltsin won Gorbachev's consent for a five-hundred-day transition plan to a market economy, yet again Prime Minister Ryzhkov was resisting, applying the brakes, urging a preliminary six-month stabilization period. But the Soviet people had grown wary of plans and promises. With Moscow suffering bread shortages for the first time under *perestroika*, the people were tired of talk. They were impatient for results.

CHAPTER 13

THE NEW ENTREPRENEURS: TRYING OUT CAPITALISM

"A cooperative is private enterprise in a state economy. That's like a newspaper in a prison: It cannot operate freely."[1]
—Oleg Smirnoff
Soviet Businessman
April 1989

"The cooperative creates a different . . . mentality. . . . Working for a cooperative makes people independent, free. . . . [But the] whole system is built on dependence. . . . That's what the bureaucrats don't want to see change."[2]
—Gleb Orlikhovsky
Co-op Manager
March 1990

With the heavy-handed state bureaucracy still manacling industrial managers such as Igor Stroganov, Gorbachev tried to inject dynamism into the Soviet economy by inviting a new set of players into the economic game: private entrepreneurs.

Gorbachev was not directly invoking Adam Smith as a guiding spirit for running the Soviet economy, but he was taking the first important step away from state socialism and toward a mixed economy. So that this new element of Soviet economic life did not sound too capitalistic, too heretical to socialist believers, even to Gorbachev himself, the new enterprises were officially designated "cooperatives," a term that maintained the principle of collective property. Some cooperatives actually operated as group-owned businesses in which the workers all shared equally as owners and employees; in others, the cooperative label was merely an ideological veneer to make thinly disguised capitalism—businesses in which private owners hire workers and that run counter to the socialist ethic—seem acceptable.

No other element of Gorbachev's economic *perestroika* has proven so controversial as the cooperatives. Almost as sharply as Stalinism, the new privatized sector of the economy has divided public opinion and kindled passionate disputes. For the cooperative facade neither fooled nor pacified dogmatic Communists.

Spekulatsiya is a catch-all Soviet epithet for virtually any profitable private business, and for three years, the press has been filled with criticism of "profiteering" and "speculation" by cooperatives. Horror stories also abound about mafialike shakedowns and firebombings of cooperative-run restaurants and other establishments of private enterprise. Time and time again, Gorbachev has watched the Supreme Soviet explode into emotional debates over cooperatives. The new entrepreneurs and their defenders accuse the state bureaucracy of trying to strangle infant initiative in its cradle with taxes and harassment; the diehard Communists fling about accusations that Gorbachev has legalized "the plunder of the working class" by infamous capitalists; they demand the excision of this "malignant tumor" from the supposedly healthy body of Soviet socialism.

To one group, the cooperatives are the nation's best hope for economic revival. To the other, cooperatives are a fatal affliction, a mortal threat to their cherished system of command economics and social egalitarianism.

Given all the pain and furor—and the very real obstacles—it is remarkable that in three short years, the cooperative movement has mushroomed so rapidly that Aleksandr Yakovlev, Gorbachev's Politburo ally, has said that the future for the Soviet economy lies in "cooperative socialism."[3]

Gorbachev has not gone that far, but he has thrown his weight strongly behind helping cooperatives develop throughout the economy, even as he has warned against abuses by private operators. In 1986 and 1987, Gorbachev made piecemeal attempts at legalizing limited individual enterprise. Then, evidently not satisfied, in 1988 he moved forcefully to embrace cooperatives as a central element of his economic reforms and as a key to Soviet competition in the world market.[4]

Lashing out at "the scornful attitude" toward cooperatives of some officials, Gorbachev bluntly told one major national gathering: "We need highly efficient and technically well-equipped cooperatives, which are capable of providing commodities and services of the highest quality and of competing with domestic and foreign enterprises."[5]

Under *perestroika,* he said, cooperatives have "a truly golden opportunity to organize their operations." He envisioned that huge collective farms would be broken down into small units, each a cooperative, and that eventually each big farm would become "a cooperative of cooperatives." Technically speaking, the collective farms, or *kolkhozi,* were already cooperatives of farmers who shared property and income and elected their own chairmen, but in fact, practice had rendered this a fiction. The *kolkhozi* actually were run top-down, like factories; the chairmen and officials were selected by the local Communist Party organs, and their workers drew salaries (not profit shares), just like the workers at state farms, or *sovkhozi.* Gorbachev now wanted to inject reality back into this fiction, to make collective farms into genuine cooperatives.

In the consumer sector, Gorbachev was looking to small, flexible, market-oriented cooperatives to fill the gaps in the state economy and to compensate for its lumbering waste and inefficiency. "The potential of cooperatives and the need for them is especially great, not only on collective farms but also on state farms," he said. "And in all spheres—production, technical services, supply, the marketing and processing of products and consumer services."[6] The success of cooperatives, he suggested, would be a boon to local governments, which could collect taxes from co-ops. He subsequently made clear that he felt cooperatives should play an important role in city life too.

In late May 1988, Gorbachev's ideas were embodied in the Law on Cooperatives, the first legal charter for private enterprise in the Soviet Union since the 1920s. It permitted cooperatives to operate in almost all areas of the economy and conspicuously placed no ceiling on the number of members in a cooperative, or on the size of their assets. Both Gorbachev and Prime Minister Ryzhkov suggested that a vigorous, profit-oriented cooperative sector might not only improve the lot of Soviet consumers, but also, through competition, jab some life into the lethargic state sector.

For a conservative Communist country just beginning to edge away from ossified Stalinist command economics, this was a surprisingly liberal law. Cooperatives were legally entitled to set up banks, to sell stocks and bonds, to engage in foreign trade, and to obtain raw materials either from the state supply system—in which case their prices would be set by the state—or through the open market, if they could find one—in which case they could set their own prices.

Before 1988, the Soviet system had modest cooperative housing units and retail outlets, but they were very tightly controlled by state bodies; as commercial operations, they were emasculated. Gorbachev's new law offered cooperatives substantial rights: self-management, self-financing, price setting, the ability simply to go into business when three people agreed to form a co-op. With an eye to past practice of Party and government officials, the law shrewdly instructed local authorities not to interfere with cooperatives, and specifically not to prohibit them. Supposedly registration was unnecessary, although in practice, registering with local authorities became a requirement to get office space, which was controlled by each local government.

And in a remarkable departure from past Soviet practice, the new law gave cooperatives the right of ownership—not of land, but of machinery and equipment used in production.

Other significant changes were the rights given to cooperatives to hire part-time workers on contract, and for co-op members to own different-sized shares in the enterprise, based on their financial investments and on their amount of work.[7]

This was not the first time that Bolshevism had made a virtue out of necessity. As Gorbachev recalled, an early Soviet cooperative movement had helped the nation dig out of the devastation and famine brought on by the civil war in 1918–21; it put people to work, supplied the countryside, provided markets for farmers, and restored financial soundness to an economy racked by war.[8] In this period, Gorbachev recalled, Lenin had equated the growth of cooperatives with the growth of socialism.

In short, for his break with Soviet economic orthodoxy, Gorbachev found precedent and legitimacy in the policies of no less hallowed a figure than Lenin, whose New Economic Policy (NEP), starting in 1921, had leaned heavily on small private enterprise. After a period of nationalization and intense concentration of economic power in the state—known as War Communism—from 1917 to 1921, Lenin reversed direction and established a mixed economy, with small-scale private manufacturing, legalized private trade, and an overwhelmingly private agriculture. By 1923, three fourths of all retail trade was in private hands; the number of private farms rose from seventeen million before the Bolshevik Revolution to twenty-five million in 1927; and there was a handicraft and small-industry sector that employed 2.3 million people.[9] Lenin's example was obviously the model that Gorbachev had in mind.

THE SHADOW ECONOMY

Gorbachev was doing more than borrowing from Lenin; he was bowing to reality. For in a society of chronic and universal shortages, and under a rigid, inefficient state economy, the Soviet people had gone underground to meet their needs. During the Brezhnev period, illegal private trade had grown to enormous proportions; it was no longer merely a black market, but rather a full-fledged shadow economy, and one on which the nation depended. The Russians called it, colloquially, shopping *na levo,* literally "on the left" or "on the side"—under the table. In the early seventies, the physicist Andrei Sakharov estimated that the shadow economy accounted for at least 10 percent of the entire national output. Through the seventies, it kept expanding. An American team, professors Gregory Grossman of the University of California at Berkeley and Vladimir Treml of Duke University, surveyed Soviet émigrés and concluded that as much as 50 percent of the population's personal income in the later part of that decade came from private economic operations outside the state sector.[10]

Soviet estimates, made soon after Gorbachev took over, were almost as stunning and even more detailed. Reform economist Nikolai Shmelyov cited one official estimate that as many as twenty million people provided services through "underground business," mostly moonlighting from their state jobs. Further, that the volume of service business done under the table was 14–16 billion rubles, roughly 30 percent of the state service sector. "In some spheres [previously illegal] private enterprise outdoes the government," Shmelyov wrote. "In 1986, people working *na levo* in repair and construction earned nearly two times more than the state agencies offering those services."[11]

Shmelyov and other Soviet specialists estimated that in major cities, private operators—or *chastniki*—accounted for roughly half of all shoe repairs, nearly half of all apartment repairs, 40 percent of repairs on private automobiles, 40 percent of tailoring, 33 percent of repairs to household appliances.

Private operators also accounted for at least half of all illegal abortions. Shmelyov reported that "every year 4–8 million illegal abortions are performed, for which people pay several hundred million rubles. The entire 'gray market' of medical services is a 2.5–3-billion-ruble business. The black market trades almost 10,000 video titles, while the state market offers fewer than 1,000. Although there are virtually no government construction organizations that make contracts with individuals, 16 to 17 million square meters of private living space (about 15 percent of all the housing built in the country)—private garages, dachas, and other buildings—are built by this sector."[12]

Shmelyov and others sought to draw a distinction between the "gray" and "black" markets—"gray" often meaning the part-time moonlighting of state employees, using state supplies, rather than operations that were wholly illegal, or "black." It was legal but unofficial—"gray"—to buy and sell private cars at fixed state prices; but the real prices were far higher, therefore illegal, and "black."

In the early seventies, construction was a particularly lucrative field for private operators—for floating brigades of construction workers, known as *shabashniki*. As I traveled through Siberia, I was frequently told how local industries and governments were turning to migrant construction teams to complete crash projects. The *shabashniki*, who were in effect little private companies, journeyed from regions where there was excess labor, such as Central Asia or the Caucasus, to labor-short regions such as Siberia. They would sign short-term work contracts with tight deadlines, and their fast, hard work earned them what was colloquially termed "the long ruble"—double or triple the normal pay. By some accounts, as many as three hundred thousand workers were part of this floating construction pool. Their legal status was never quite clear, because they did not belong to official enterprises, yet they were employed openly.[13] Their use inevitably caused friction with regular state construction workers, who resented the fact that the *shabashniki* received higher pay. Early on, the Gorbachev regime tried to limit the *shabashniki* by imposing legal restrictions on them.

Almost every illegal private operation depended on graft and embezzlement from the state, which became such an endemic problem that there was a special branch of the militia to cope with it; in the most serious cases, the death penalty was imposed. In the seventies the press publicized huge operations, such as a ring that had stolen 260,000 rubles' worth of textiles and fabrics in Lithuania; another that had illegally marketed 650,000 rubles' worth of fruit juice in Azerbaijan; a third that had swiped 700,000 rubles' worth of gems from a Moscow diamond-cutting enterprise.[14] However sensationalized, these were not the most sophisticated operations—they were engaged merely in theft and resale.

Far more elaborate were factories-within-factories. One example was textile entrepreneurs who siphoned off raw cotton or wool from state enterprises, and then used these materials to manufacture shirts, dresses, sweaters, sheets, linens. They marketed their goods through illicit retail networks in other parts of the country. In some cases, these enterprises operated right within existing state factories; the same workers and managers worked part of the day legally, part of the day illegally—and they worked slowly for the state and rapidly for themselves.

These operations combined all the ingredients of the shadow economy—from thieving and phony bookkeeping on through manufacturing, sales, and distribution. Occasionally, the Soviet press would expose them—a plant in Bashkiria making plastic goods, tablecloths, women's summer shoes; a gang operating an illegal fur factory in Odessa; whole slews of factories in Soviet Georgia, eventually exposed by Gorbachev's longtime friend, Eduard Shevardnadze, who became the republic's leader after fighting economic crime and political corruption.[15]

I had read about various isolated cases in the seventies, but had not appreciated how extensive were the networks of illegal entrepreneurs until I read *U.S.S.R.: The Corrupt Society,* a book written by Konstantin Simis, a Soviet émigré lawyer who had worked for the Soviet Ministry of Justice and had later become a defense lawyer for some Soviet underground millionaires.

Simis identified Moscow, Leningrad, Riga, Vilnius, Odessa, Tbilisi, Baku, and Tashkent as the centers of illegal private enterprise. In Riga alone, he said, there were seventy to one hundred illegal operations. Nationwide, he estimated there were tens of thousands of modest underground factories, turning out knitwear, shoes, sunglasses, handbags, hosiery, sporting goods, recordings of Western popular music. In virtually every case, he said, they operated with the collusion of local, city, regional, and even national government officials who were on the take, known in Russian as *vzyatka.* His picture of Soviet society, pre-Gorbachev, made Tammany Hall bribery and corruption look small-time.

What upset Simis the most was the interconnection between illegal enterprises and the political apparat of the Communist Party, from the local or district level working up to Politburo members:

> Massive and ubiquitous corruption at the district level of the Party-state apparatus has forged such close ties between it and the criminal world that . . . a system of organized crime has come into existence in the Soviet Union, a system that has permeated the political power centers of the districts as well as the administrative apparat, the legal system, and key economic positions. Although not conceived as such by its creators, this Soviet variety of organized crime naturally is derived from and has become an organic part of the dictatorship of the apparat of the Soviet Union. Organized crime in the Soviet union bears the stamp of the Soviet political system. . . .

The paradox lies in the fact that the underworld is not made up of gangsters, drug peddlers, or white slavers. The criminal world of [the Soviet system] includes store and restaurant managers and directors of state enterprises, institutions, and collective and state farms. They are all members of this ruling monopoly—the Communist Party—and their principal professional activities are absolutely legal and aboveboard. . . . [It is] characteristic of the system that the ruling district elite acts in the name of the Party as racketeers and extortionists of tribute, and that it is the criminal world *per se* who must pay through the nose to the district apparat. Thus it happens that the system of organized regional crime combines with the political regime and the economic system of the country and becomes an inseparable component of them.[16]

Gorbachev, of course, knew all this well enough and had a reputation for honesty and incorruptibility. Several others in the Politburo were also economic puritans, from Yegor Ligachev on the ideological right to Boris Yeltsin on the progressive left and Prime Minister Nikolai Ryzhkov, just right of center. So it was only natural that they combine forces to try to clean up a system riddled with corruption. One strategy was to fire corrupt Brezhnev holdovers and to press ahead with criminal investigations begun in 1983 under Yuri Andropov. Eventually, these exposed massive corruption, most dramatically in Uzbekistan, in a scandal that led to the indictment and conviction of Brezhnev's son-in-law, Yuri Churbanov, for bribes taken when he was first deputy minister of the interior.

Gorbachev had an additional strategy: to tap all this underground business acumen, energy, and entrepreneurship and make it work for *perestroika*. It was with this in mind that he and some of his Politburo colleagues decided to legalize private enterprise in the form of cooperatives. In effect, Gorbachev set out to co-opt the illegal operators, to turn them from law evaders into taxpayers, to reduce demoralizing corruption and bribe taking, and turn its perpetrators into partners in Soviet socialism.

KEEP OUT THE PARTY CELLS

The new strategy worked with surprising speed. Entrepreneurs came out of the woodwork, especially in the Baltic republics, in Soviet Georgia, and in big cities such as Moscow and Leningrad, where illegal enterprises had been concentrated. In late 1987, after only a modest nudge from the Gorbachev regime, there had been 8,000 known cooperatives, with about

88,000 employees; but by the spring of 1989, just eighteen months later, the economist Abel Aganbegyan told me, the number had shot up to 75,000 co-ops with 1.5 million members and employees.[17]

For me, the change from the seventies was stunning.

Now I encountered cooperatives everywhere: a number of new restaurants, with far better food and service than in state restaurants—and some with prices that rivaled those in Manhattan; interpreters and translation services; copying co-ops with Xerox machines; beauty salons and little boutiques; and co-op bathrooms, in railroad stations or on Moscow streets, which charged just 15 kopecks, and which replaced some of the horrendously filthy public lavatories with relatively clean ones.

I met Soviets who were working in co-ops providing a wide variety of services: advertising co-ops beginning to edge into the world of modern marketing; biology co-ops, in which bright young Soviet scientists were inventing and marketing industrial and agricultural chemicals; banking co-ops engaged in financing new business ventures; information co-ops, such as Koop Fakt, engaged in instructing others on how to organize co-ops, or on where to get services from other co-ops; computer co-ops such as Micro-Contour, which was operated by the computer whiz Stefan Pachikov, whose team of twenty-five young computer programmers was developing software for Soviet industrial enterprises. Even striking coal miners whom I met in the Siberian mining town of Prokopyevsk wanted to form a cooperative to take over their mines.

"The driving force for me was to get away from the state system," said Sergei Vladov, a linguist from Kiev who is in his mid-thirties. Sergei, who speaks flawless English, joined five other linguists to form a language co-op that provides translation services and language instruction in Ukrainian, Russian, and several Western languages.

"I taught for the state system for ten years—literature, Russian as a foreign language, and English," he told me. "I did not make a decent salary—I had to supplement it with odd jobs. So when *perestroika* came along, I got together with a few friends and we set up a school to teach foreign languages. At the start, six of us broke away from the state language institute. Then our co-op got popular. Lawyers joined us. Computer experts. In all we have eighty people in six offices, not only in Kiev but in Minsk. Soon we will have branches in Leningrad and in Kishinev [Moldavia].

"For us, this co-op is not just for the money we make," Sergei explained. "It has meant freedom. For the first time, we are managing our own lives. One young woman told me that the first six months in the co-op was the best time of her life. She felt she had grown up, she had a sense of her own individuality. You know, a lot of people get their salary from a regular state job, but they get no sense of individuality from that job. The main group of people who went into co-ops at the start were people who wanted that, people who had done jobs *na levo* under the old system, people who had learned to rely on themselves."[18]

Almost inevitably, the change in economic life-style affects a person's whole life. Sergei told me about a Communist Party member who had been working part-time under contract for the co-op and wanted to work full-time. "We had two Communist Party members in our co-op already and we could not afford to have a third because [of the Party rule that] three Communists means they have to form a cell," he explained. "And we didn't need a Party organization in our co-op. So we told him, 'You can continue to work for us on a contract basis, or, if you want to be full-time, then you have to quit the Party.' The next day, we got a call from him saying, 'I'm on my way to the Raikom, the district Party Committee, to quit the Party.'"

Vladov's cooperative sprang out of nowhere, but many new cooperatives are the unprofitable subsidiaries of major state enterprises that the enterprise managers want to spin off. Ministries will not permit closing down these economic losers, but large factories have learned they can get rid of deadweight divisions by leasing their buildings and equipment to cooperatives. At Uralmash, Igor Stroganov told me that he was preparing to lease the Red Guard Crane Factory, a subsidiary about one hundred miles to the north, to a new cooperative being formed by fifteen of the factory's senior staff who wanted to fire their incompetent manager.

"We think that factory will work better with a new cooperative running it under a leasing arrangement from Uralmash," Stroganov told me. "That factory is working badly. It would simply die without some reorganization."[19]

When I visited the Red Guard Crane Factory, I could see why Stroganov was so willing to unload it. It was a mess. The buildings were old and decaying; mounds of scrap were piled outdoors, rusting in the rain; a new structure begun four years before was still no more than an empty shell of four exterior walls; next to it stood the hull of another shop, badly damaged by fire. Two large metalworking shops were busy, but their equipment was old; by comparison, the main factories at Uralmash looked modern. It took state subsidies to keep this plant operating.

The self-proclaimed spark plug of the new cooperative that was going to run the Red Guard Crane Factory was a toothy, potbellied, tired-looking forty-five-year-old engineer named Stanislav Dailitko. After fifteen years at this factory, Stanislav was now its deputy director, and he had ideas for making it more efficient. First, he planned to fire about 150 of its 870 workers, mainly in the overstaffed administration. When I tried out that idea on the women in the accounting office, they protested that it would be unfair to let older women go after years of loyal service, or to fire young mothers raising children. Like all the workers at the plant, they were people from the local villages, and they saw no other job prospects in the area. Several workmen in the machine shop, who agreed with Stanislav about the need for cuts, were skeptical that he could go through with firings in a such a small community.

Stanislav also imagined that the new cooperative could wriggle free of state orders for 20 percent of its output and instead sell that directly to other Soviet enterprises for a profit. But he acknowledged resistance among the workers to the cooperative idea. "At first, people were very cautious," he said. "But they were partly appeased when they heard that the highest authority would be the general assembly of the cooperative, and that the workers themselves would decide how to divide the profits—how much for reinvestment, how much for pay bonuses, how much for social funds."

How would he get people to work harder?

"We need to change the psychology of people," he said, mouthing the standard patter of *perestroika;* it was hard to tell if he really understood what he was saying. "We have to get people to see that to live better, you've got to work better. I think it will take about two years before we can see clear results."[20]

Neither Stanislav nor his factory inspired great confidence about the future of the Red Guard cooperative. If he did not succeed, it would be a real test of Gorbachev's policy: Would the state or Uralmash keep this loser factory afloat, or would they let the workers go unemployed and force them to find work elsewhere?

"THIS—THIS IS LIFE!"

Aleksandr Smolensky is a type whom many Americans would recognize: a quiet-spoken, fast-moving loan shark with golden hair, a golden mustache, a pocket calculator, leather jacket, and a wry view of the life and times of *perestroika.*

"My pay is twice Gorbachev's—I get twenty-five hundred rubles a month, he gets twelve hundred as a Politburo member, maybe some more as president," Smolensky quipped. His own financial success at the ripe young age of thirty-five amused him, but there were frustrations. "My ruble is not Gorbachev's ruble. I can't buy anything with my rubles. In our country, we have a sea of money, but a famine of goods."[21]

Still, Sasha Smolensky likes to make money—and fast. He and his cooperative, the Moscow Capital Bank, which only began operating in February 1989, move on a fast financial track. They have no tellers, computers, deposit windows, or cash machines. In fact, their cooperative doesn't look like a bank. The only physical hint that this is a bank is an old green safe stuck in the corner of one of the bare, high-ceilinged offices. Smolensky opened the safe to riffle through a couple of hundred thousand rubles in tightly wrapped packets of ten-ruble notes just to prove to me that they had money there.

I saw other evidence of this. Smolensky made a 1-million-ruble loan in about half an hour, and he charged 130 percent interest. His customers were from the All-Union Council of the Interbranch Association of Industrial Construction. They needed the 1.32 million rubles in a hurry, to finance the purchase of forty fax machines from a Soviet middleman who had imported them somehow from Singapore and was now reselling them at 33,000 rubles apiece ($55,000 at the official rate of exchange). Fax machines are practically unheard of in the Soviet Union; hence the sky-high price. In effect, the price acknowledged an exchange rate of about 60 rubles to the dollar, one hundred times the official rate.

When I asked how the deal to buy and then sell the faxes would work, Igor Karminsky, head of the group, explained: "We buy forty faxes, sell thirty-eight to our member enterprises, and keep two faxes for ourselves."

"So you make big money selling those thirty-eight faxes?" I asked.

"No, not on this deal," he replied. "But we have an urgent need for two faxes. That's what we get out of it." They wanted the two machines, not the money made in selling off the others.

And since they were reselling those thirty-eight faxes immediately, they did not need to borrow the money for long—only for two weeks.

Smolensky said he would charge 5 percent interest and, pulling out his calculator, reckoned that the loan would cost 66,000 rubles; the fine for late payment would be double the interest rate. Since the 5 percent was being charged for only two weeks, I privately calculated that this worked out to 130 percent annual rate of interest.

"That's a lot of interest," I said to Smolensky after his customers had left. "Wouldn't a state bank charge much less? Why didn't they go to the state bank?"

Smolensky allowed a smile to curl his golden mustache. "Because it would take them about six months just to do the paperwork at the state bank, and they needed the money right away or they would lose the deal."

The day before, Aleksandr Friedman, one of Smolensky's deputies, had explained that all their loans were very short-term: six months or nine months at most, preferably less. Quite a few loans are to help new cooperatives get started. "Six months is usually enough," Friedman said. "All cooperatives are based on quick profit. If it takes them five or ten years to be profitable, they'll never make it in our system."[22]

I got a quick lesson in why speed was so important. In the middle of the loan bargaining, Smolensky had gotten a call from Moscow City Hall telling him that his bank was being evicted from its offices—at once. Actually, Moscow Capital Bank had leased its office space from a state enterprise, but Lev Zaikov, then Moscow Party boss, had slammed cooperatives at a Party gathering and, according to Smolensky, Party functionaries were now trying to prove their loyalty by harassing co-ops. Smolensky sought protection from the city council, where he had many contacts because he had worked for years in reconstructing city buildings; in fact, initially he had run a construction co-op for building renovation, but, not finding that profitable enough, had switched to banking. Now he had to drop the loan business for several days to search for new office space and thus avoid being thrown out on the street.

Smolensky took it all in stride. It was a nuisance, but it was par for the course, not an overwhelming catastrophe. The bank had been formed by five cooperatives that had put up about 10 million rubles in capital; it had another 3 million rubles from about fifty large private depositors; and using that as collateral for credit from a state bank, Smolensky said his cooperative could loan up to twelve times its assets. It already had branches operating in distant cities such as Kharkov, Novgorod, Ryazan, Kiev, and Lvov—all cities where Smolensky saw promise for private commerce, and not too much risk of political interference from overzealous Party bosses. He had shied away from the Baltic republics, Georgia, and Armenia, he said, "because one fine day we'll need visas to get to those places." In short, they were expected to secede from the Soviet Union.

Over an expensive lunch of caviar, smoked salmon, and other hard-to-get delicacies, Smolensky told me and my colleagues Marian Marzynski and Natasha Lance of his ambitions. He had recently been approached for two very sizable loans (about 50 million rubles) from some generals at a defense factory that produced equipment for chemical weapons. Now, he said, they wanted to convert to making equipment for environmental protection for both Soviet and foreign markets.[23]

Foreign deals intrigued Smolensky, but he had discovered they involved more obstacles than domestic transactions did. An Austrian firm had signed a contract with the Soviet Ministry of Energy to deliver ten thousand computers for 500 million rubles and deposit the proceeds in Smolensky's bank. "The Austrians have a joint-venture enterprise in Simferopol and they want to set up an ice cream factory and other facilities," Smolensky said. "The whole deal got to the Ministry of Finance and . . ." He rapped the table, meaning it got killed. "They found a 1937 law passed under Stalin that a foreign firm cannot open a bank account in a Soviet bank without the agreement of the Ministry of Finance."

I had trouble understanding why the ministry would object; here the Ministry of Energy was getting badly needed Western computers, and the Austrian firm was willing to take payment in Soviet rubles rather than insisting on hard currency. It looked like a good deal for Moscow. When I saw Deputy Prime Minister Leonid Abalkin, I raised the question, and he agreed that the deal worked to Soviet advantage; he wrote down the details and said he would look into it. As I was leaving his office, Valentin Pavlov, the minister of finance, appeared, so I put the matter to him. With a crew cut and built like a tank, Pavlov was not to be outtalked, even by a deputy premier who was nominally his superior. He asserted that the deal could not be approved because that would give the Austrians power to decide where and how new investments would be made in the Soviet Union, something that central planners had to control; in short, it was a bad precedent.

Abalkin argued for the deal, pointing out the need for flexibility, but Pavlov sternly rebuffed him, insisting on central control.[24]

Nonetheless, Smolensky was undeterred. He was involved in a 1.2-billion-ruble liquid gas deal; he was drafting papers and making contacts with the ministries.

"What do you want for yourself out of all this?" I asked.

"I want to live normally," he said. "I want other people to live normally. For two years, I've tried to buy my apartment. Always there are excuses: 'We have to give it to invalids,' or whatever. So I say, 'Give me another apartment, a bigger one. I'll pay more; let it cost twenty thousand rubles or sixty thousand rubles.' And for my bank, I want equal rights with state banks. Now, we don't have them. They are always giving us trouble."

"Is it worth all the trouble?" I asked.

We were a couple of feet apart, leaning our elbows on a mantlepiece in the anteroom of his office. He looked at me, shaking his head, as if I had simply not understood what really made him tick.

"In spite of the headaches, the past two years have been the best in my life," he said.

"Why?"

"Because I worked for years inside the state system and that work is absolutely boring. I got sick of sitting in meetings with my eyes closed, sleeping.

"But *this*." He smiled triumphantly. "This is life!"[25]

THE "CIVILIZED" CAPITALIST

Mark Masarsky is Gorbachev's model for managing cooperatives. He combines socialist idealism with the business know-how and self-reliance of a capitalist. If Gorbachev's gamble on private enterprise is going to pay off, it will hinge on entrepreneurs like Masarsky.

He is not a speculator, making money off high interest rates or buying up goods in short supply and then marketing them for a fast profit. He runs what Gorbachev's entourage approvingly calls a "production cooperative"—that is, he produces things that are in short supply: roads and houses. He deftly walks a tightrope, doing business with the state, keeping favor with the local authorities, and yet preserving enough autonomy to manage his own business and turn a handsome profit, which he shares with his workers.

Masarsky, who has the close-cropped, clean-cut zeal of an Eagle Scout, calls his cooperative "socialist capitalism." He likes to quote Lenin, who said at the time of his New Economic Policy that socialism is a society of "civilized cooperators." Masarsky considers it "civilized" that his salary is only two and a half times the pay of his average worker. In short, he is a capitalist who sparkles with good citizenship.

For Masarsky, running a cooperative is a family tradition—after a gap of sixty years. In the 1920s, his grandfather ran a small cooperative that made building materials. The cooperative was liquidated in 1928, and Masarsky's grandfather was forced into a collective farm. In the Khrushchev era, Masarsky himself tried to make capitalism live side by side with socialism; he belonged to an experimental group that collectively operated a Siberian gold mine. But that experiment was shut down by Brezhnev. Gorbachev has given him a new opportunity.

Running a cooperative is also a function of Masarsky's disillusionment with the system.

As a boy, he was a Stalinist zealot, so caught up with ideological fervor that he became a local hero for catching a "spy." It was 1951, at the peak of the Cold War, and the Stalinist press, having fomented spy mania, told loyal Soviet citizens to look out for suspicious strangers dressed in trench coats with turned-up collars and taking notes. As a boy of eleven, young Mark spotted such a character outside his school, summoned his classmates, and they all surrounded the intruder until he could be marched off to custody by a militia officer. Masarsky was then drawn into a high political ritual of Stalinist times: The youthful informer was called to a regional meeting to receive a special award as the region's most outstanding Young Pioneer. As he approached the stage, he was stunned to see his "spy" about to give him the award. The man was a senior education official; he had been outside the school making an inspection on the day that Masarsky caught him "spying."

"I remembered him, but apparently he did not remember me because I had been in a crowd of children that day," Masarsky recalled. "I was in a state of shock. I took the award and left. I then understood that the adults had fooled us all. I no longer accepted everything they told me as the absolute truth."[26]

Masarsky's next shock was the shock of his generation: Khrushchev's denunciation of Stalin in 1956. Born in 1940, Masarsky marks Khrushchev's secret speech as his "political birthday," the moment when his eyes really opened. Paradoxically, as a philosophy student at Moscow State University in 1962, he ran afoul of Khrushchev. Masarsky had taken too literally Khrushchev's talk of pluralism of opinions; he did not understand that this did not include criticizing Khrushchev himself. He was expelled from the university for organizing a freewheeling discussion of the famous art exhibition at the Manezh Gallery, at which Khrushchev exploded against abstract paintings. Two years later, after Khrushchev was ousted, Masarsky was reinstated at the university; by then, he had worked in a factory and learned to fend for himself in the tough Soviet economy.

Masarsky is a born leader. He is not physically imposing, but rather short, trim, and compact. Nor is he charismatic; he speaks without flair or humor. He is very serious, a sort of Soviet Jimmy Carter: a manager, an organizer, a technocrat; well intentioned and quick to smile, but a bit pedantic. He can walk into a room of his own employees without attracting special attention, or demanding it. But it is a mistake to underestimate him: He has the ingenuity, drive, and tenacity to get what he wants.

Money is not the key to Masarsky's business, as it was in the case of Smolensky's bank. In addition to Masarsky's knowledge of how to get things done in the Soviet system, the keys are bricks and politics.

For example, Masarsky not only has high-level connections in Moscow, but he nurses close relations with the regional political leaders in Novgorod, the city southeast of Leningrad where Masarsky's cooperative is headquartered. People proposed that Masarsky run for people's deputy from Novgorod—against the regional Communist Party boss; but he chose not to, for fear he would win and alienate the local political hierarchy. In fact, the deputy chief of the Novgorod regional government, Vladimir Kondratev, had given Masarsky his big business break: the chance to buy a brick factory and to receive a 1-million-ruble loan from a state bank to get his business started.

The site of Masarsky's cooperative was a former prison factory at which three hundred inmates used to turn out about twelve million bricks a year. The prison population dwindled and the state turned the place over to Masarsky in December 1987. His deal was to deliver twelve million bricks to the state; any surplus was his to sell. So he brought in new machinery, hired ninety workers at good pay, and within two years, he had doubled the production. His political connections paid off.

So did the bricks, which, I learned, are not a simple commodity in the Soviet economy. Picking up a brick outside his plant, Masarsky instructed me on how cooperatives do business under Gorbachev's *perestroika.*

Bricks are in terribly short supply, so if Masarsky wanted to, he could charge steep prices for them and make a quick profit. But if he took that option, the state would make him pay heavy taxes and disqualify his cooperative from receiving certain state supplies. Masarsky preferred to pay lower taxes, keep on good terms with state suppliers, and charge the state's fixed, low prices.

"But how can you build a business that way?" I asked.

"This is *valuta,* hard currency," replied Masarsky, gesturing with his brick. "Bricks are better than money. I can use them to barter for whatever I need to build up my co-op. I sell four million bricks to the Volsky Automobile Factory for the fixed state price, and I make it part of the deal that they must sell me trucks, earth movers, and other equipment that I cannot get from the state. I pay them, of course, but that is how I get the machinery that I need. I sell a million bricks to the Leningrad Gas Enterprise and they promise to deliver me nine million cubic meters of gas above what I already get, and they grant me a credit of three hundred thousand rubles for five years. So I can add another line of brick ovens and be guaranteed enough gas to operate them."[27]

"We began two years ago with no moving equipment," said Yuri Kaplan, Masarsky's chief engineer. "Now we have one hundred twenty pieces—trucks, bulldozers, cranes, excavators. When I look at all that, I am amazed. Two years ago, the most private property you could own was a motorbike or a car. Now we have all this."[28]

For Masarsky, the brick factory is the foundation of a larger business. Already he has launched a road-building operation, with its own asphalt and cement factories; he gets good contracts from the regional government. He also gets contracts to build houses for a Soviet ministry. In two years, his output jumped from 8 million to 24 million rubles; he now has 750 workers, some building houses, some building roads, others making bricks. They have come from all over Russia, lured by high pay: an average of 1,000 rubles a month, roughly five times the normal factory worker's pay in state enterprises. They have left their families behind, and live in former prison dormitories as temporary quarters. Masarsky has promised to build them homes of their own, telling them what a good investment real estate is. As an appetizer, he turned the prison's former maximum-security section into a health club, with saunas and a small pool.

OWN YOUR OWN HOME

Masarsky's dream is to use his bricks to build private housing in a program that he calls Own Your Own Home. Construction is a particularly fertile field for cooperatives, because the housing shortage is so acute and because the former housing minister, Yuri Batalin, decided in 1989 that 40 percent of all construction should be done by cooperatives. Since then, Masarsky has been studying photographs of model homes in Western architectural magazines.

For all his ingenuity, Masarsky is stymied because he cannot obtain a steady supply of lumber to make his dream houses. All the lumber in Novgorod is controlled by the regional lumber trust; its deputy director is Aleksandr Bokhan, a veteran of the state sector. For several months, Masarsky tried leasing and operating one of Bokhan's lumber mills, but it did not pan out. The state demanded all but a tiny fraction of the output, leaving no lumber for Masarsky. So he gave the lumber mill back to Bokhan. A few months later, in September 1989, when I was in Novgorod, Masarsky was trying to arrange a partnership with Bokhan, and he took me along.

"At the moment we are limited by state orders, so there is no solution for Masarsky's situation," Bokhan explained to me. "They will fire me if I do not fulfill the state plan. I have no other way except doing what I am told. In order to give him lumber, I would have to produce more, but I don't have the resources to do that."[29]

"But this is *perestroika*," I said, prodding Bokhan. "Gorbachev says things are supposed to be worked out at the local level. Can't you work something out?"

Bokhan laughed.

"Yes, of course, everything is possible—*if* Moscow will untie my hands."

"So it's not possible," I said. "You can't solve it without Moscow."

"You are right," he nodded. "So far it is impossible. He [Masarsky] wants lots of wood. In the quantities he needs, it is impossible."

Masarsky took me out to the lumberyard. We found only about fifteen workmen; there had been nearly one hundred when Masarsky was running the place. It was a huge yard with great stacks of timber and a sawmill beside a railroad track. As I looked around, I found it hard to understand how Bokhan could claim that he lacked the resources to increase his output and supply Masarsky.

"The state is a monopolist, not capable of taking advantage of its wealth because nobody wants to work hard for it," Masarsky commented. "We have workers. If we combined his resources and my skills, we could have a treasure here. Leasing is not a solution—we should own this business. This lumber should find its way into the marketplace. Owned by the state, it lies dormant; it belongs to everybody and nobody."

We were standing on a platform overlooking a sea of timber. As he talked about the unused wealth in the lumberyard, Masarsky began doing a pantomime.

"The state and I, we are like two fighters," he said. "His feet are stable. He stands firmly on the ground, he has resources. But his hands are tied."

Masarsky pantomimed the state, feet planted solidly and securely, but his body immobile, arms hugged around his torso.

Then, suddenly, he switched to standing on one leg, wobbling all about, flapping his arms, mimicking himself and his co-op.

"I can do with my hands whatever I want," he said, "but I stand on only one leg. But I need two: One is brick, the other is lumber. With only one, I can't make it."[30]

Without the lumber, Masarsky cannot build houses his own way for his own customers. He has to build them for the state, according to the state's orders, at the state's fixed prices, and using inferior materials supplied by the state. He took me out to see some houses that were under construction in Grigorevo, a village not far from Novgorod. Yuri Kaplan, the chief engineer, pointed out some problems.

"The construction elements are soaking wet and soggy," he said. "We have nothing to cover them with because the roofing material never comes on time. The window frames arrive, made of raw, green wood, so they warp as they dry. It's hard to put in the glass. It takes a lot of effort to make the window right, a lot of manual labor."

Next, we went to see some finished homes paid for by the Ministry of Irrigation, which rents them cheaply to its local workers. They were a row of ten little cracker boxes made of gray bricks. These were brand-new houses, but there was a hitch. Masarsky explained that his builders could do no more than rough-finish them. The shortage of building materials was so severe that even a powerful ministry could not obtain what was needed for its own project. The solution: Give the tenant a token sum of 200 rubles and let him finish the job.

We walked into several homes; they were shells, far from ready for occupants—rough, ugly walls, primitive floors, no fixtures. In one, we found a young blond Russian, tools in hand, at work in his kitchen, the rough walls plastered with newspapers. Everywhere there was work to be done. Clearly, 200 rubles would not finish the job—*even if* he could get the necessary materials.

"The ceilings are a disaster," the tenant, whose name was Volodya, told me. "When you walk around in the attic, you feel them wobble. As for painting, before we could do it properly, my wife and I had to smooth the walls by gluing newspapers on them."

"How about the floors?" I asked.

"The floor doesn't seem very sturdy either," Volodya replied. "Unfortunately, I can't open the basement now to show you. Fungus is growing under the floors in the basement. It's very wet there. How long will this house last? I don't know."

Masarsky, who was listening, was terribly embarrassed. All his frustration with the state-run economy burst out.

"We won't build these homes anymore," he said. "We have refused to continue working on this kind of project, although it seems very easy to do. The house is made of prefab sections. A year ago, we were tempted by the simplicity of this design, but then we realized. . . ."

He interrupted himself and gestured at the hapless tenant. "Look, he's not my customer," Masarsky went on. "I never met him before. My customer is the state. The state ordered this house. The state approved it. And the state is pleased! We could have continued this arrangement with the state, but we don't want to work for the government anymore. It's not even profitable for us. Standing in front of a customer, we are ashamed. The bureaucrat who approved the project doesn't live in this house."

"Do you think you could build better houses—let's say for him directly?" I asked.

"If he pays me, of course," Masarsky replied.

Masarsky was moving out the front door. "Nobody is happy with this," he muttered. "I'm not happy, the renter is not happy. And I am saying the state should not be happy, but—"

"I say the state is happy, all right," interjected Volodya. "They have decided that before the year 2000, each of their workers here gets either an apartment or a house. So here"—he gestured at the row of houses— "ten families got housing. But the state doesn't care whether the families are happy or not. They made a check, filled a square."

We were outside the house now, and Volodya's brother Viktor joined the conversation. "Volodya used to live in one room with a family of three. He didn't have any choice. He was given this house and he took it."

"So we have to change the customer," insisted Masarsky. "It should not be the state, but an individual home owner, a paying customer. Why shouldn't the state give him a mortgage, let's say for fifty years?"

"Let there be capitalism," said Viktor. "Sort of socialist capitalism. But still . . . capitalism."

Masarsky nodded as he left the site, troubled but undaunted. He could not go on building these shoddy houses, and if Bokhan would not supply him with lumber, he had another idea. He was already negotiating with the head of a major electronics factory in Novgorod to build five hundred homes, and he knew the factory had enough clout with the regional government to obtain lumber. He was endlessly inventive, working out a joint venture for foreign sales of construction materials with Yugoslav and Austrian partners; already lobbying local authorities to try to get Novgorod declared a free-trade zone to stimulate foreign trade and investment; working with other leaders in the cooperative movement to strengthen their influence with the national government in Moscow.

I asked him if the risks were not too great in a Communist state to achieve his dreams. He agreed there were hurdles: first, getting workers to see themselves as both employees and shareholders and therefore to have a personal stake in making the cooperative a success; then the obvious risks of trying to develop "a free market inside an economy without a market" and run by people like Bokhan.

The biggest risk, he said, "is the social and political one: Some people do not believe in *perestroika*. But for me, it's the only chance. After this, I won't have another chance. I'm nearly fifty. This is my swan song."[31]

THE BATTLE ROYAL

Mark Masarsky put his finger on the heart of the cooperatives' problem. They have become the focus of a social and political battle royal that will decide the future direction of the Soviet economy. Masarsky and his compatriots are fighting to preserve and expand the opportunity Gorbachev has given them. Their foes see them as the dawning specter of a capitalist revival. In fact, people like Nina Andreyeva, the neo-Stalinist, speak derisively of "the restoration"—meaning the restoration of capitalism and the old conservative order in Russia. So the fate of cooperatives has political as well as economic ramifications.

From a tiny base, cooperatives have grown since 1987 at a stunning rate. And that remarkable success has made them a focus of controversy. The figures tell the story: at the end of 1989, there were 193,000 cooperatives; they employed 4.9 million people, produced 40.4 billion rubles' worth of goods and services, and accounted for roughly 10 percent of the country's retail trade.[32] And they kept expanding through 1990. Despite the fact that most cooperatives were still in the start-up phase in 1989, collectively they paid the state 1.6 billion rubles in taxes that year, and, sensitive to accusations that they were mere profit-mongers with no social conscience, they made charitable contributions worth 226 million rubles.[33]

In cooperatives, the average pay was 528 rubles a month, more than double what average state-factory workers were making.[34] The profile of the average co-op member was striking: young, well educated, and highly skilled—a natural risk taker. According to one survey, roughly three quarters of those in co-ops were under forty-five; two thirds had completed higher education; and three fourths had previously held managerial jobs in state industry, such as shop superintendents, department heads, or restaurant directors, or had worked as engineers and technicians.[35]

In its short history, the shape of the co-op movement has changed, the size and importance of its enterprises has grown. The mom-and-pop restaurants, bakeries, and repair shops that appeared when Gorbachev first eased conditions are now overshadowed by more substantial endeavors. Construction co-ops like Masarsky's have become the most numerous and financially the most important. Textile and consumer-goods manufacturing have joined the consumer-service industry, along with a surge of cooperatives doing scientific research and development and providing technical goods and services.

Entire factories, each with several hundred workers, have broken off from major industrial enterprises to form cooperatives that lease their plants and machinery from the parent firm with the intention of buying out their facilities within five years. By one government estimate, 60 percent of the Soviet cooperatives operate this way, a trend that has been gathering momentum.[36] Typical of more recent developments, I was told by Andrei Smirnov, secretary of the Cinematographers' Union, that sixty new independent film studios have been formed in the past two years, most of them cooperatives. Smirnov, who got Prime Minister Ryzhkov to sign off on regulations to protect them, predicted that by 1993 these independent studios would be making more films than the established state studios.[37]

Tankred Golenpolsky, who in 1988 left the State Publishing Committee to organize an information and book-marketing cooperative, spoke for many when he declared: "Give us five more years of this and you won't recognize this country—it will have gone beyond the point of no return."[38]

Despite their success, or rather because of it, the cooperative movement and the new breed of Soviet entrepreneur are constantly under fire, plagued by official obstructionism and the target of virulent political attacks. Many government officials regard cooperatives with deep suspicion, seeing them as vehicles for thieves and embezzlers of the Brezhnev era who want to launder money from illicit gains. Of course, there have been abuses by new cooperatives, although the fuzzy legal situation makes it hard for anyone to know for sure that he is following the rules.

The national government, split internally over whether cooperatives are good or bad, has zigzagged between promoting and blocking co-ops. In March 1988, just as Gorbachev was about to sanction cooperatives legally, the Ministry of Finance pushed through a 90 percent tax rate. After some Supreme Soviet deputies warned that this would kill Gorbachev's experiment before it got started, the government withdrew the tax law; later, the maximum tax rate was set at 35 percent. In December 1988, the Council of Ministers pushed through another law, barring cooperatives from a slew of activities—running private schools, making or marketing videos, running broadcast networks, manufacturing weapons or ammunition, making alcohol, narcotics, or jewelry from precious metals, and providing medical care for cancer, drug addiction, or any kind of surgery.

Medical co-ops were the prime victims of these new restrictions. They had rapidly become one of the most widely used forms of cooperatives, but the new restrictions were so tight that forty-five hundred medical co-ops went out of business in the wake of the new law.[39] Health Minister Yevgeny Chazov was their outspoken foe. "They produce nothing new, they work in our institutions, use our equipment, use our staff after hours, and they drain away our best specialists," he told me angrily one afternoon. "We don't need them. If they continue, the service to nonpaying patients will deteriorate. . . . Besides, they're unmanageable."[40] Despite Gorbachev's preferences, Chazov's position had great sway with the cabinet and the Supreme Soviet.

In conservative political strongholds, regional governments have carried out campaigns. In Uzbekistan, nearly two thousand cooperatives were shut down by the authorities in that republic; more than twenty-three hundred were closed in Kazakhstan; another thousand in Krasnodar Territory, not far from Gorbachev's home region of Stavropol, where two hundred were closed.[41] Even where officials did not formally decide to shut down co-ops, they applied the squeeze: They refused to register new ones or dragged out the process, denying them space to operate, harassing them with inspections and petty intrusions.

"There is no tradition of law in this country, so some powerful official can strangle a cooperative in five minutes—there are sixty-four thousand ways to do it," said a friend of mine, Oleg Smirnoff, a Soviet representative of Pepsi-Cola. "A cooperative is private enterprise in a state economy. That's like a newspaper inside a prison: It cannot operate freely."[42]

By accounts too numerous to cite, state enterprises and Gossnab, the State Committee for Material and Technical Supply, have not delivered raw materials and supplies to cooperatives that abide by the state pricing system, something they are legally required to do. The press is full of stories about cooperatives paying off local officials—an almost inevitable consequence of the uncertain rights of cooperatives and the petty bureaucrats' life-and-death power over the co-ops' fate. Oleg Smirnoff told me about one cooperative that had built a swimming pool in a district of Moscow under a 1-million-ruble contract, only to have the district government decide to expropriate the pool. The government promised to repay the million rubles, but Smirnoff said the cooperative, including some people whom he knew, simply lost another million rubles that they had paid in bribes to officials, contractors, and suppliers to get the job done. Another friend, a tall slender Russian who worked for an advertising cooperative, said that in Moscow to get office space "takes a bribe of three hundred rubles per square meter."

Cooperatives have also become primary targets of criminal-protection rackets. A rash of incidents were reported in the Soviet press in early 1989—the firebombing of the Come In and Try It restaurant; the torture of the manager of the Sokol Cooperative, coupled with a death threat unless he paid 50,000 rubles in protection money; similar threats to private taxi drivers at Moscow airports. Moscow's police have been hard pressed to keep up with the anti–co-op mafia.[43] Scores of Moscow co-ops united to form an association to combat racketeers, but I was told that plenty still make protection payments to be free of violent harassment.

"THE HONEST MILLIONAIRE"

However menacing, the new organized crime in the Soviet Union is a less serious long-term problem for cooperatives than popular and official hostility. A poll done by *Izvestia* in early 1990 illustrates the cloud under which cooperatives operate: Only 15 percent were strongly in favor of co-ops; twice that many were hostile, with the rest in between or uncertain.[44] From my experience, that in-between group includes many people who are still quite uneasy with private entrepreneurs.

At the Communist Party Central Committee, Leonid Dobrokhotov defined the opposition to cooperatives as ideological, economic, and personal.[45]

The ideological opposition hates cooperatives because it regards them as the start of a dangerous, immoral slide toward capitalism and exploitation, and toward abandonment of a socialist system that has protected the little people. These feelings are especially strong among older Communists, from high Party officials like Yegor Ligachev to members of the rank and file like Nina Andreyeva; they are also strong among the United Front of Russian Workers, a conservative Russian nationalist group, and among trade-union officials, who are trying to stay in office by playing on blue-collar workers' fears that their subsidized socialist welfare is about to disappear in the jungle of the marketplace.

Economic opposition is moved primarily by outrage over what is seen as unbridled greed on the part of some cooperatives. People gave me examples from personal experience or the press: co-ops that corner the market in ordinary T-shirts, print on them little slogans or designs, and then jack up the price five- or tenfold; trading co-ops that buy fruits and vegetables cheap in Uzbekistan and sell them at sky-high prices in Russia; others that wangle a way to import Western computers and reap enormous profits.

State enterprises, angry at the competition from more efficient cooperatives, also feed the economic opposition to co-ops. But more than vested interests and Communist prejudices are at work; dislike of profiteering predates the Bolshevik Revolution. In czarist times, the landed aristocracy and the peasantry showed a disdain for the Russian merchant class as *gryazny*—tainted by the pursuit of profit. Nowadays, pervasive shortages make for enormous profits, and they fuel widespread public anger at the profiteers.

A classic case in point for many Soviets was the self-proclaimed "honest millionaire," an experienced scientific researcher and inventor-turned-entrepreneur named Artyom Tarasov. In early 1989, he confessed on Soviet television that he had paid 90,000 rubles in Communist Party dues, which, since dues are 3 percent of earnings, meant that he had earned 3 million rubles the previous year. The public's shock and horror were enormous, especially when the details came out. His cooperative, Tekhnika, which was comprised of a team of scientists, inventors, and computer programmers, managed to export usable industrial waste and Soviet-built trucks, earning $10 million in the West, and then used that money to import thirty-five hundred computers that it sold for 184 million rubles.[46] When Tarasov revealed himself, the Ministry of Interior launched an investigation to uncover stolen state property. Tarasov contended that everything had been done aboveboard, according to Soviet law, and that his computer prices were 60 percent less than what state import monopolies charged. No wrongdoing was ever proven, but Tekhnika's assets were frozen for more than a year by the Ministry of Finance, and Tarasov had to let more than one hundred employees go. It was as if Tarasov had to be punished for having made all that money.[47]

The personal opposition to cooperatives mentioned by Dobrokhotov—and obviously felt by Tarasov—derives from sheer envy. People cannot stand to see anyone doing much better than they are, so instead of joining up, they blame co-ops for everything: "There's no sugar, because cooperatives bought it all"; "You can't find meat—it's all in the cooperative restaurants"; "Prices are going up because of the cooperatives"; "The co-ops are messing up the whole system." Never mind that cooperatives are still a small fraction (about 3 percent) of the Soviet economy, or that all these problems existed before cooperatives took hold. The envy factor makes cooperatives convenient scapegoats, and some Communist Party officials are only too happy to deflect the rage of the masses away from the apparat and onto the cooperatives.

That suggests a fourth basic opposition to cooperatives—the political hostility of Party and government officials. The issue, perhaps not obvious at first glance, is power. Cooperatives are clearly a threat to state planners and state enterprises; their very essence is a challenge to the old economic system. But cooperatives are also a threat to the political hierarchy, and Gorbachev's aides have suggested that he intended that. As Dobrokhotov put it, cooperatives represent democratization of the economy, and that promotes democratization of the political system.

Gleb Orlikhovsky, business manager for the cooperative film studio Fora Film, talked about this threat, and the political schizophrenia of the apparat, which is caught between Gorbachev's orders and its own survival.

"The authorities are crazy, illogical," Gleb fumed to me one evening. "They want the economy to grow, and the cooperative movement is the only way to get this economy moving, but they resist it."

"Why?" I asked.

"Because they are against the whole style of work in cooperatives," he said. "The cooperative creates a different psychology, a different mentality in people. Working for a cooperative makes people independent, free. They feel they can stand on their own. This changes their lives. They quit the Party. They think, 'What do I need this swamp for?' And that's not what the system wants. The whole system is built on dependence—not independence. It's built on people's dependence on government agencies. That's what the bureaucrats don't want to see change. If it changes, then the bureaucrats and the Party lose power."[48]

Probably the most aggressive public foe of cooperatives has been Ivan Polozkov, former regional Party boss in Krasnodar Territory, and now Party chief for the whole Russian republic.

"Cooperatives are a social evil, a malignant tumor—let us combat this evil in a united front," Polozkov declared at a major regional meeting, a tape of which was later shown on local television. He was prepared to override Gorbachev's Law on Cooperatives: "We can't simply do nothing when people are protesting against this vandalism and shamelessness. We must hold public meetings and rallies a thousand strong to resolve this question. . . . We must base our actions on reality, not on the law."[49]

Polozkov was on a rampage. He publicly scolded the director of a state farm who sold five tons of meat to a cooperative, which then made sausages out of the meat and sold them in other regions. He rapped the knuckles of the director of a state enterprise for buying batteries from a cooperative. He reprimanded judges for sticking to the letter of the law and demanding proof of concrete crimes by cooperatives before closing them down. Hard on the heels of Polozkov's diatribe, the regional soviet shut down, by fiat, 322 cooperatives.

When *Moscow News* sent a reporter to investigate how local authorities could ignore the law, one senior official, Nikolai Kharchenko, shot back: "What has the law to do with it? We are acting in the interests of the people." Polozkov's number two, the head of the regional government's executive committee, Nikolai Kondratenko, defended the old economic system. "At this stage, we won't survive without command methods," he said. "Sometimes I tell myself, all right, I will no longer use pressures, but when I see that things go amiss, I am ready to push aside any cooperative, relying in this on people's support."

The *Moscow News* reporter pointed out the enormous inefficiencies of the local state and collective farms: Seventy-eight thousand head of cattle worth 51 million rubles perished; 40 million rubles lost due to substandard production; annual losses from 320,000 tons to 390,000 tons of fruits and vegetables through spoilage in the fields. He questioned the vague charges of bribery and corruption against the cooperatives who were buying produce from the state and collective farms.

"Enough of this empty talk—we are on the offensive," boomed Kondratenko. "My people have the right to know who is robbing them. As long as I live, I'll show no mercy to speculators and grabbers. I want my children to come to my grave, when I die, without any feeling of shame."[50]

In the fall of 1989, Polozkov and other conservatives in the Supreme Soviet moved to kill the entire cooperative movement. For several days, the national parliament debated the issue, with such government officials as Deputy Premier Leonid Abalkin vigorously defending cooperatives, but conceding the need for better regulation. In the end, the Supreme Soviet banned "trading cooperatives" that did no more than buy items and resell them without adding in any way to their value. The rest of the cooperative movement was left untouched. In March 1990, at the Congress of People's Deputies, Polozkov was back with another assault on the cooperatives, calling them "a mafia . . . [who] compare with Brezhnev's extortioners." He implied there was a cabal, made up of cooperative millionaires and the liberal Soviet media, that was protecting co-ops and helping them plunder the state. And he made a surprisingly bold attack on Gorbachev's *perestroika:* "The dirt appearing now will be as bad as that during the period of [Brezhnev's] stagnation."[51]

The cooperatives have fought back politically and in the courts, an unusual new development of the Gorbachev era. During that same March 1990 session of the Congress of People's Deputies, Vladimir Tikhonov, a deputy and also president of the All-Union Association of Cooperatives, told me that the cooperatives had recently won two important legal cases, including one against Polozkov. The state procurator for the Russian republic had ruled that the regional government under Polozkov had to pay 30–40 million rubles in damages to cooperatives that had been illegally shut down. In the other case, brought by the "honest millionaire" Artyom Tarasov, the prosecutor's office ruled that the state had to return 108 million rubles in frozen assets to his cooperative, Tekhnika, which was still seeking another 200 million rubles in damages from the Ministry of Finance, the state bank, and the Ministry of Justice, for forcing the co-op out of business without legal cause.

"Bit by bit," Tikhonov said, "laws are beginning to work. Thank God.

These Party bosses have accused the cooperatives of being a mafia that is sowing social discord and plundering the people. We say *they* are the ones who are causing discord and robbing the people. Now, finally, we can show that they are committing crimes, and we have official bodies stating that. This is a very important development for us."[52]

Tikhonov, whose association has set up a management school and now publishes a monthly newspaper, *Kommersant,* has great ambitions for the cooperative movement, in tourism, in scientific and technical enterprises, and in the foreign sale of products now cast off as waste by Soviet state industry and agriculture—for example, he said, more than three hundred thousand tons of petrochemicals, eighty-nine million animal hides, half of the nation's cut timber. Tikhonov, an early adviser to Gorbachev on agricultural economics, but now impatient with the cautious pace of Gorbachev's reforms, spearheads a group of Supreme Soviet deputies who push cooperative interests in the parliament and with the cabinet.

At the top, cooperatives have had important backing from Gorbachev, Prime Minister Ryzhkov, Aleksandr Yakovlev, and Vadim Medvedev. The Politburo faction that opposed them, including Yegor Ligachev, Viktor Chebrikov, and Mikhail Solomentsev, were gradually eased out, Ligachev being the last to leave, by retirement, in July 1990. The new Politburo included Ivan Polozkov, an outspoken foe of cooperatives. Nonetheless, the legal and administrative climate improved for private entrepreneurs during 1990.

In early March, the Supreme Soviet granted individual citizens the right to own small-scale factories for the first time since Lenin's New Economic Policy in the 1920s. The law did not use the words "private property," still a taboo in Soviet socialism, but it revoked what had been a constitutional ban on individuals owning "means of production." It specifically authorized "individual labor"—in addition to cooperatives—in farming, handicrafts, and the service sector, and, in an especially important departure from past practices, it allowed small factory owners to hire a small number of workers. The new law also cleared the way for wide use of stock plans so that workers could purchase state enterprises, and for the first time it provided legal protection for private property against confiscation by the state.[53]

Two months later, in late May, Gorbachev issued a presidential decree to promote private construction, ownership, and sale of housing. For the first time in six decades, individuals were permitted "to own, use, dispose of, and inherit land plots with buildings."[54] Previously, individuals could own a single apartment or house, but the land belonged to the state; any resale was under the control of local authorities. Gorbachev's decree was an obvious effort not only to reduce the backlog of at least fourteen million people on waiting lists for better housing, but also to sop up billions of rubles of private savings by selling off state apartments. Gorbachev ordered the Council of Ministers by September 1, 1990, to draft measures to encourage a private housing market. He specifically ordered arrangements for the sale of state apartments, for bank loans, and for the rental of state construction equipment to individuals and small businesses, to promote private construction.[55]

Experience showed that issuing decrees was no guarantee of reform. But the takeover of city governments in Moscow, Leningrad, and more than a dozen other key cities by democratic reformers in the spring of 1990 led to the easing of local restrictions on cooperatives. Gorbachev, moreover, was undeterred by vocal right-wing opposition to them, and seemed determined to help the growing private sector expand.

Back in mid-1988, after the original Law on Cooperatives was passed, economist Leonid Abalkin had predicted privately that by the end of the century there would be thirty million people working in the cooperative sector, producing close to 20 percent of the nation's overall output.[56] It was a highly ambitious goal, but two years later, Gorbachev was still on track—one of the few areas of economic reform where he was following up his bold rhetoric with action. That is true, in good measure, because in this sphere he was backed by Prime Minister Ryzhkov, who had dragged his heels on liberalization in industry and agriculture. Aleksandr Yakovlev, Gorbachev's alter ego in the leadership, was another formidable supporter; "cooperative socialism" was his slogan for moving toward a mixed economy like Sweden's.

During a crescendo of conservative attacks on cooperatives in October 1989, Yakovlev was optimistic about the expanding role of the private sector.

"We're increasing private and cooperative construction," he said, adding prophetically: "That will progress; it's just a question of time. As for food, I think we'll move more quickly on leasing land and individual farming. There are very serious obstacles facing cooperatives. . . . People criticize 'speculative cooperatives'; they have created a bad impression for the entire cooperative movement. But the cooperative movement must develop. We won't move ahead without it."[57]

PART FOUR

THE EMPIRE
TEARING APART

*G*orbachev inherited not only a country that was failing economically but one that was fragmented, a country whose embittered peoples had been secretly seething with national tensions.

For seven decades, one of the major conceits of Communist propaganda was the indissoluble unity of more than one hundred different Soviet nationalities. Lenin had asserted that under the unifying bonds of Communism, nationalism would wither away as a force. But he had allowed a contradiction in Communist policy: He sought cultural assimilation, but he allowed cultural pluralism. Over time, intellectuals in various republics found meaning in their own national cultures and traditions; the Soviet Union was not a melting pot.

It is often true that a system that has been under pressure for a long time, such as the Soviet empire has, bursts at its weakest points when that pressure is abruptly released. That is what happened when Gorbachev suddenly relaxed the system of political repression, introduced the ferment of *glasnost,* invited a new grass-roots activism from the Soviet peoples, and assaulted old ideological canons.

Minority nationalities began exploding: ethnic civil war between Armenians and Azerbaijanis; the "singing revolutions," which became drives for political independence, in the Baltic republics of Lithuania, Estonia, and Latvia; bold nationalist movements in Moldavia, Georgia, and later, in the Ukraine; much slower-moving nationalism coupled with sporadic interethnic violence in Uzbekistan, Kazakhstan, Tadzhikistan.

All of this nationalist hatred and turmoil caught Gorbachev off guard. In fact, his initial outlines for reform had not even included the issue of nationalities or anticipated the ethnic ramifications of political change, though others had years ago spotted interethnic tension as the Achilles' heel of the Soviet empire.

To make matters worse, Gorbachev's political experience left him ill prepared for dealing with nationalist upheavals. His career had been narrower than those of Brezhnev or Khrushchev, who had done political work in minority republics. Except for his years in Moscow, Gorbachev had spent his entire career in Stavropol, a region dominated by Russians and Russo-Ukrainians, with only a smattering of highland tribes. So Gorbachev had risen to the top without being forced to learn ethnic politics.

Out of inexperience, then, he made simple political mistakes that fed hard feelings in Armenia, in Uzbekistan, in the Ukraine. More important, he did not grasp how deeply felt and powerful were nationalist feelings and protests, until it was too late. Sometimes he did not differentiate much between peaceful and popular political change, and ethnic violence, often taking nationalism as a challenge to his power.

"As a matter of self-criticism," he said finally, after five years in power, "one has to admit that we underestimated the forces of nationalism and separatism that were hidden deep within our system . . . creating a socially explosive mixture."[1]

For us, as well as for Gorbachev, it is important not to oversimplify, not to assume that turmoil in one republic signals an urge to secede, or that one secession inevitably will bring fifteen. National awareness and the drive for self-determination differ from one region to another: The Baltics have been far ahead of Central Asia in seeking to leave the Russian sphere; violence in the Caucasus and the Islamic regions has been against other nationalities, not the Russians. And Russia, late to erupt with nationalist demands, has now forced the reshaping of the entire union to the top of Gorbachev's agenda.

CHAPTER 14

UZBEKISTAN: "OUR LANGUAGE IS OUR HEART AND OUR SOUL"

"You know, in Russian the term
for cotton worker is cotton *rabochy—rab*
for short. Well, there is another Russian
word *rab,* which means slave. So a
cotton worker is a cotton slave."[1]
　　　　　　　　　—Abdur Rahim Pulatov
　　　　　　　　　Uzbek Nationalist Leader
　　　　　　　　　October 1989

"This is our rage, our protest. . . .
We want to arouse our authorities
and our people, . . . to make them rise up
and say, 'We can't live like this anymore!' "[2]
　　　　　　　　　—Shukhrat Makhmudov
　　　　　　　　　Filmmaker
　　　　　　　　　October 1989

Tashkent, Sunday morning, October 1, 1989—I hear that Birlik, the nationalist popular front of Uzbekistan in Soviet Central Asia, is planning an unauthorized rally in Lenin Square, the huge, hallowed parade ground of the Uzbek Communist Party.

As my film crew and I circle the area, we see busload after busload of gray-uniformed Soviet riot police, armed with shields, helmets, and nightsticks. There are easily several hundred police—an overwhelming force.

The Uzbek authorities, plenty of Brezhnev-style Old Guard leaders among them, are tough and nervous. They are clearly in no mood to brook trouble from the popular front, a new grass-roots movement of Uzbek intellectuals and young people.

Several weeks earlier, more than one hundred people were killed and another thousand wounded in a terrible interethnic bloodbath in the nearby Fergana Valley. Uzbeks went on a two-week rampage against Meshkhetians, a Turkic people whom Stalin had exiled decades ago from Soviet Georgia to the Central Asian Republic of Uzbekistan, twenty-five hundred miles southeast of Moscow and just north of Afghanistan.

As we drive toward the square, we are stopped by a cordon of police; I can see the crowd from there. This is the first time that our crew has been physically barred from filming a public meeting. The barriers heighten my suspicions about what is about to happen, and my urge to see the confrontion between the new nationalists and the old order.

I walk up to the officer in charge, a big burly Uzbek police major, and explain that we are from American public television, and that we are filming a documentary on the impact of Gorbachev's reforms on the Soviet people.

"This square is closed," he snaps.

"But you've got people in there—it's your people," I protest. "This is *glasnost.* It's democratization. It's what Gorbachev says is supposed to go on in this country. Why can't we go in?"

"Look—the square's closed," he repeats. "You can go there in an hour. You can't go there now."

"But we're in your country at the invitation of the Communist Party Central Committee in Moscow," I continue. "They told us it's an open country. We're not interested in anything secret. Why can't we go in and cover it?"

"Go over and talk to the big boss," he says, pointing to another approach route to the square, several blocks away.

It's an obvious stall, but we have no choice. We follow his directions and take our van near a large park, where there are even more police buses. In the square, I can see the police massing around the demonstrators. They do not seem to notice us, so we climb over some small barricades and walk toward the crowd.

The mood is turning ugly. The glint I see in the eyes of the police-unit commanders says they are itching to give these young political rebels a thrashing. Lines of khaki-uniformed troops and gray-uniformed riot police are closing, like a vise, around the demonstrators, about to make mass arrests. It is October, but the sun beats down as if it were July in New

York. The 90-degree heat simmers off the pavement, parching throats and fueling the tension.

As we move toward the crowd, I can barely see the dark hair of student demonstrators somewhere in the center of the tightening ring of police helmets. The scene makes my stomach churn: In years of reporting, I have seen police close in on peaceful demonstrators from Birmingham, Alabama, to Cairo, to Saigon, to Paris. I brace for the sounds of billy clubs cracking young Uzbek heads.

Our crew splits up: Producers David Royle and Oren Jacoby head off with Rustam Initiatov, our guide from Uzbek television, to get permission for our filming; cameraman Jean de Segonzac, sound man Scott Breindel, and I begin filming, working our way toward the speakers, who are standing on the steps of a gigantic statue of Lenin. Somehow we climb up on the pedestal of the Lenin statue before anyone can stop us.

Jean gets a few shots of the crowd and of a police officer harassing an Uzbek cameraman and his wife before the police catch sight of our crew. They turn on us, ordering us off the platform. As we retreat, Jean keeps filming; out of nowhere a plainclothes police agent slaps his hand on the camera lens. I demand to know who he is and why he is interfering. He shows me credentials: Major Lipshchak, Ministry of Internal Affairs.

"We have a city decree against unsanctioned meetings and this is an unsanctioned meeting," he says testily. "You have to get out of here. You are violating state order and discipline."

We do not move, and Lipshchak becomes aggressive, grabbing me by the arm and demanding our film. I wrestle free, then argue with him, trying to divert his attention and give the camera crew time to change film and hide the roll Jean has shot. Royle and Jacoby reappear, but Rustam is nowhere to be seen. We are surrounded by police. Lipshchak is still after our film, which is now hidden under Scott Breindel's jacket. The police threaten us with arrest. They form a tight wedge around us and start removing us from the square.

As we are being ejected, fresh detachments of troops rush past us. I glance at a twenty-story state office building overlooking the square, and notice huge red banners bearing the portraits of Marx and Lenin; from windows and balconies, a few people peer down on the melee. We are now a couple of hundred yards from the square, dragging our feet, hoping for a break.

Suddenly, without explanation, the tension eases; the police ring around us melts away. Some unseen chief has given a signal; the plainclothes agent who had blocked our camera and the head of the police detachment walk away, leaving us alone. Turning back toward the square, we sense that the authorities have decided to let Birlik go through with the rally. Regiments of troops and police still surround the square, but they make no mass arrests; they hold their positions, in formation, but do not interfere. Shields and billy clubs are lowered.

We make our way slowly back into the square, threading a path through a crowd of four or five thousand demonstrators now sitting on the asphalt, listening to speakers who are using a bullhorn from a spot just beneath Lenin's feet. For Uzbekistan, it is a good-sized demonstration, but by comparison with those in other republics, it is pretty small. Most of the demonstrators are university students or young workers in their shirt-sleeves.

Paradoxically, the powers-that-be have given the nationalist speakers from Birlik a second audience: the rank-and-file Uzbek soldiers and police-men who, except for their uniforms, look identical to the young demon-strators. I am fascinated to see hundreds of young police caught up in the speakers' appeals for a new national consciousness among the Uzbeks, long one of the most politically docile Soviet national minorities. The speeches are hardly inflammatory; Birlik's demands are modest. *Birlik* means unity, and its simple act of calling the Uzbeks to speak out and act in their own interests threatens Communist leaders accustomed to giving orders to the masses.

"Comrades, we appeal to you: Unite and consolidate," declares a mid-dle-aged man with a fringe beard, Abdur Rahim Pulatov, the head of Birlik. "We have come together to struggle for democracy, for a better future. The Uzbek people must finally take control of its own land. We must feel that we are the true masters."[3]

Other speakers protest the economic rape of Uzbekistan, Moscow's demands for ever-larger outputs of raw cotton—cotton that activists say has swallowed up Uzbekistan's precious water, distorted its farm economy, ruined its ecology, and left the people and the land impoverished.

"The Communist Party Central Committee has wasted all our trea-sures and keeps taking away all the fruits of our land," protests a vibrant young woman. "A future generation is going to ask us: 'What were you doing at that time? What were you thinking about? How did you get us into this situation? Where's our wealth?' And what will we answer them? How could we look them in the eye?"

Our Uzbek guide, Rustam, who had reappeared after we were seated, whispers to me: "Look at the militia. Look at how intensely they are listening. What she is saying is going right into their hearts. You can see it in their faces."

BLACKLISTING BIRLIK NATIONALISTS

At the core of Birlik's protest that day, its second in a fortnight, and at the heart of its effort to rouse the Uzbek people, is a very simple but significant demand: Restore Uzbek as the official state language.

After seven decades of Soviet rule and previous decades of domination by czarist Russia, the long-obedient, subservient Uzbeks are finally rebelling against Russification—Russian on their television screens, Russian in their schools, Russian in their newspapers, Russian in their government and commerce, Russian on the street signs—even in small villages where many people speak only Uzbek—Russian as the language of science or necessary in making a career, the teaching of great Russian writers of the nineteenth century at the expense of writers from the Uzbeks' own past.

Linguistic discrimination is a tender issue in Uzbekistan, a region larger than both Germanies put together, with a population of twenty million people. (In numbers, Uzbeks rank third, behind Russians and Ukrainians, among the more than one hundred recognized nationalities of the Soviet Union.) So when Birlik appeared out of nowhere in November 1988, encouraged by Gorbachev's new freedoms, it was a language protest by six hundred students from Tashkent University that galvanized it.

Uzbek intellectuals have a long list of language grievances. A writer named Nuraly Kabul told me angrily that Uzbekistan has far fewer children's books in its native language than do other major Soviet nationalities.[4] Shukhrat Makhmudov, the Uzbek cameraman whom we saw filming the Birlik rally, revealed that film scripts for Uzbek movies must be submitted in Russian, in part to accommodate Russian censors.[5] Uzbek medical students complained that their studies are all in Russian, even though many go work in villages where the peasants speak only Uzbek. So much advanced education in Uzbekistan is taught in Russian that its rural students are handicapped in the competition for admission, because training in Russian is weaker in the countryside than in the cities. Mohammed Salikh, an Uzbek poet, told me Uzbek graduate students doing doctoral work on Uzbek language and culture must submit their theses in Russian and defend their theses before a panel of Uzbek scholars—in Russian![6] From many people I heard that it is impossible to buy a typewriter in the Uzbek language; Uzbeks have to buy Russian typewriters and then spend 50 or 60 rubles to have the keys modified for Uzbek.

So it was little wonder that the Birlik demonstrators that day were carrying red-and-white banners declaring: UZBEK LANGUAGE FOR THE RE-PUBLIC; ATTENTION TO LANGUAGE IS ATTENTION TO OUR STATE; and OUR LANGUAGE IS OUR HEART AND OUR SOUL. On one banner, someone had

crossed out a Communist Party boilerplate slogan THE PLANS OF THE
PARTY ARE THE PLANS OF THE PEOPLE, and substituted a popular-front
slogan: NO, THE DEMANDS OF THE PEOPLE MUST BE THE PLANS OF THE
PARTY.

The banners were all written in Arabic script, because Uzbeks are a
Turkic people, whose religion over the centuries was Islam and whose
written script was Arabic. Fifty years ago, under Stalin, the Uzbek language was Russified, literally transcribed into the Russian Cyrillic alphabet, which was used in so-called Uzbek-language newspapers.

Birlik was now pressuring the government of the Republic of Uzbekistan to take two steps: restore the primacy of Uzbek over Russian, and
return Uzbek to its original, pre-Stalin form.

Although such steps had been taken in other minority republics, in
some cases years ago, Uzbekistan's political leaders were resisting; they
were old-fashioned Party loyalists used to taking orders from Moscow.
Their efforts to suppress that morning's demonstration were typical of
their resentment toward the new democratic forces released by Gorbachev. In the end, they had acquiesced, perhaps because we foreigners were
filming, or, more likely, because some Party official had been smart enough
to see that a bloody crackdown would serve Birlik's cause by making its
leaders popular martyrs.

That did not mean, however, that the Communist Party rulers of
Uzbekistan were bending to Birlik's will or even accepting the existence
of a grass-roots popular-front movement. Several hours after the rally,
Abdur Rahim Pulatov told me how hard it had been to get Uzbeks, long
a politically docile people, to stand up in the face of repressive measures
by the authorities.

That morning, he said, police had attacked the first wave of demonstrators arriving at Lenin Square: Several people were arrested; others were
clubbed and wounded. Pulatov himself, a slender forty-four-year-old
scholar who worked at the Institute of Cybernetics in Tashkent, had left
the fracas limping. But in spite of injuries, he had been determined to
reach Lenin Square, what he called "the sacred turf" of Communist
power in the Uzbek capital of Tashkent, to show the authorities that the
movement could not be shut down. In his eyes, simply to have held that
demonstration was a psychological victory.

Pulatov described a campaign of official harassment against Birlik.
Activists had been denounced in the press by high officials, and economi-
cally blacklisted. Rafik Nishanov, installed by Gorbachev as Uzbekistan
Party leader from January 1988 to September 1989, had attacked the new
Uzbek nationalists for promoting a non-Communist political and cultural

renaissance and for pressing economic and ecological protests. In one broadside, he declared: "Deformations revealed under *glasnost* and democratization have seriously disrupted social equilibrium and stability."[7] On other occasions, Nishanov accused liberal Uzbek intellectuals specifically of "linguistic chauvinism," of needlessly whipping up hysteria and public passions about the Uzbek economy and ecology, and of flirting with pan-Turkism, an ominous potential rival for Communist ideology.[8]

With such accusations, Pulatov said, the authorities were trying to intimidate people, to keep them from joining Birlik by painting it as extremist.

"The authorities," he said, "try to create the stereotype that we are fighting the whole [Soviet] system. Our people are very scared of being labeled 'anti-Soviet' or 'anti-Party.' They are even more fearful when somebody calls them 'nationalists.' In the past, any movement for national self-awareness has always been suppressed as 'nationalistic.' At my institute, they had meetings where I was criticized by my colleagues for my actions. We know some others who were fired, lost their jobs, were given a hard time at work. So the pressure is really strong against our members. Popular fear of the political leadership is very strong, you see, because the government has been our only employer. We have had no private sector. If somebody was fired, he remained on the street with no means of survival. So fear is great."[9]

As a result, Birlik set its first priority, not simply to address the most pressing Uzbek problems, but to rouse Uzbeks from political passivity into new, self-conscious nationalism.

"The main goal of our movement is to educate people, to raise their social consciousness and their political activism," Pulatov explained. "Only the people themselves can stand up for their own rights. . . . Our movement will be virtually powerless if the people keep on hibernating politically. So our main goal is to awaken the people, to turn our people into a politically active society."

DEMOGRAPHIC TIME BOMB

This is precisely what worries Moscow: the danger that the great slumbering giant of fifty million Muslim people in Central Asia is awakening, and stretching against the bonds—and the bondage—of empire.

Three things, above all, trouble the men in the Kremlin and ordinary Russians: the explosive population growth in Central Asia; the influence of Islam; and the difficulty of melding this huge region, still strange,

Oriental, and underdeveloped in its economic and political life, with the relatively more advanced world of European Russia, the Ukraine, and the Baltic republics.

To outsiders, Uzbekistan and its oasis cities—Samarkand, Bukhara, Khiva, and Tashkent—evoke the legendary Silk Route to the Orient, the famous caravan highway of Marco Polo. Uzbekistan is a region rich in history and exotica: traces of man found near Samarkand that date back one hundred thousand years; excavations of an ancient urban settlement at Khiva that is five thousand years old; the site near Tashkent of the Battle of Talas, where, in 751, the Arabs stopped an invasion by the Chinese and marked the outer frontier of Arab civilization; the treasures of Islamic art and architecture dating back six centuries.

Samarkand, located 170 miles southwest of Tashkent, is such a natural crossroads on the Eurasian landmass that it has been a plum choice for conquerors throughout the ages. It was captured in 329 B.C. by Alexander the Great; it was sacked in A.D. 1220 by Genghis Khan and the Mongolian Golden Horde; and then it was resurrected 150 years later by Tamerlane, the great warrior-king, who made Samarkand the prosperous capital of his sprawling Central Asian realm of towering mountains, long rivers, inland seas, and trackless wastes. Tamerlane's grandson, the scholar-astronomer Ulun-Beg, built a famous observatory at Samarkand, and made the oasis city the center of Muslim civilization in all of Central Asia.

Even today, behind the drab, cookie-cutter look of Soviet urban construction, Uzbekistan and the rest of Central Asia are a world apart from the European regions of the U.S.S.R. The peoples are of Turkic origin: Their copper-colored skin, almond-shaped eyes, and dark hair make them look as though they have stepped out of Mongolia, Iran, Afghanistan, or northwest China. Despite the efforts of Stalin and his successors to uproot the Muslim religion, these people still find their roots in Islamic culture. Their open bazaars are afire with dazzling colors and alive with the pungent aroma of fresh spices. Their territory is immense—more than one sixth of the Soviet landmass, an entire subcontinent as large as all of Western Europe, and comprised of five of the fifteen Soviet republics: Uzbekistan, Kazakhstan, Kirghizia, Tadzhikistan, and Turkmenistan.

And their population is multiplying at what Muscovites consider alarming rates. Some call Central Asia a demographic time bomb. The deep anxiety of Russians is that they are close to becoming a minority in their own country (145 million out of a total population of 285 million). When the issue arises in the intimate talk around kitchen tables or in restaurants in Moscow, Leningrad, Yaroslavl, or Sverdlovsk, Russians will say with bitterness that they can only afford, and can only find apartment space for, one child, whereas Uzbeks, Tadzhiks, Kazakhs, and other Central Asians commonly have four, five, eight, even ten children. Russians say too many children put a drag on living standards, and they widely resort to multiple abortions; Uzbeks glory in many children, as a supposed symbol of fertility and wealth, and they largely shun abortions. The absolute population figures still favor the Russians, but the trends are running against them. Between 1979 and 1989, the population of the Russian republic grew 7.2 percent, from 138 million to 147 million; the population of the five Central Asian republics grew more than three times as fast (23 percent), from 40 million to nearly 50 million.[10]

Each year, as the Soviet army takes in its draft recruits, the complement of young Central Asians grows. I have heard Uzbeks complain that they are bearing too much of a burden and that their boys were sent first to die in Afghanistan; I have heard the Russians reply that the Uzbek troops were too friendly with their fellow Muslims the Afghans, and had to be replaced by more reliable Russian boys; I have heard the parents of young draftees from Lithuania and Estonia say that the dark-haired, dark-skinned Uzbeks form gangs inside the army and beat up the blond, fair-skinned, Scandinavian-looking recruits from the Baltic republics.

Although Communist ideology was supposed to render national differences irrelevant and, through the solidarity of the international proletariat, make nationalist feelings wither away, in Central Asia it has not worked out that way. The people may not be rebellious, but they have practiced cultural passive resistance; they have clung to their customs in spite of all the official efforts to uproot traditions and homogenize the Soviet peoples.

Each time I visited Soviet Central Asia during my years as a Moscow correspondent in the early seventies, I was struck by how much more this region resembled countries to the south, from the Arab world to Persia, rather than the Soviet heartland. Arriving in Uzbekistan, I felt that I was stepping out of a European culture into the underdeveloped Third World; Uzbekistan was less like a subdivision of a modern superpower than like a foreign colony.

In Central Asia more than anywhere else in the Soviet Union, I had a sense of Imperial Russia. The regional capitals were the outposts of empire: They were as obviously under the political heel and economic diktat of a powerful, distant culture as Gaul had been under the heel of Rome, or as India and Egypt had been under the sway of the British Raj—until, in the years after World War II, Gandhi and Nasser liberated them, psychologically and politically. Like the British in Delhi, the Russians had put down a strong beachhead in Tashkent: In the seventies, the city's population was 40 percent Russian, and Russians outnumbered Uzbeks. Nonetheless, the pull of traditional culture was strong.

Most striking, perhaps, was the subdued but tenacious hold of Islam. All but a token handful of mosques had been closed, but Islamic customs had hung on, including arranged marriages, extravagant dowries, ritual animal slaughter, periodic fasting, unabashed male supremacy, elaborate family and tribal networks, the tendency of prominent Communist officials to insist on a traditional Islamic burial with a mullah chanting prayers at their funerals. When I visited Uzbekistan in 1972 and 1974, I found young people who observed the monthlong Islamic fast of Ramadan followed by the feast of Bairam. On great feast days, thousands of people would show up at shrines, such as the tomb of Tamerlane in Samarkand. The Soviet campaign to provide education had largely wiped out illiteracy, but a comparable ideological drive had fallen so far short of squelching Islam that former Uzbek Communist Party leader Sharaf Rashidov constantly called for greater efforts to "overcome religious survivals."[11]

In the early eighties, Moscow's worries were compounded by the rise of Islamic fundamentalism in Iran under the Ayatollah Khomeini. Muslims in Central Asia did not share the radical Shiite faith of Iran; they were from the Sunni sect. Even so, Moscow feared the pull of Islam on its people. After the Soviet invasion of Afghanistan, Brezhnev defended the action on grounds of a supposed threat to the Soviet Union's southern regions, and his spokesman railed against the radio propaganda of "reactionary Islamic organizations abroad."[12]

The underlying political danger for the Kremlin is that somehow Islam can become a vehicle for uniting the diverse peoples of Central Asia in some form of pan-Turkism. Under the czars, the whole region was known as Turkestan. In the early twentieth century, there was a pan-Turkic movement, a force for modernization that at one point rivaled Communism. In the late twenties and thirties, Stalin subdued nationalistic rebels and hill tribes by force and controlled the entire region with the classic imperialistic divide-and-conquer strategy. He split Turkestan into separate republics, none of which had ever been an independent nation before, including Uzbekistan. Even Gorbachev's proconsuls have shown alarm at even the slightest flicker of pan-Turkism in Central Asia today. Rafik Nishanov, for nearly two years Uzbekistan's Communist boss, attacked Uzbek intellectuals for glorifying figures whom he derided as "apologists for pan-Turkism and national narrow-mindedness."[13]

COTTON COLONIALISM

When I returned to Uzbekistan fifteen years later, in 1989, not much had visibly changed. It still seemed an exotic, backward province. With its immense cotton fields and their plantation culture, with its relentless sun, its backbreaking labor, its dry, dusty roads, its terrible sickness, its desperate rural poverty, its feudal political system, Uzbekistan reminded me of the Egypt I had known in the mid-sixties. The one new element was a tiny, budding cultural revival. I sensed a people trying to return to their own roots, a colony struggling to lift the burden of alien rule.

To Uzbek activists, the chief villain was King Cotton—what the Russians call "the white gold of Uzbekistan." Under Moscow's relentless pressure, Uzbekistan's cotton output had increased tenfold in the seven decades since 1917; by the mid-1980s, it totaled something like 5.5 million tons, two thirds of the entire Soviet cotton crop.

The Uzbek nationalists, with their social-science lingo, argued that the "cotton monoculture" had ravaged their land, destroyed their normal agriculture, ruined their ecology, left their soil so leached with salt that hundreds of thousands of peasants fell sick from drinking polluted, saline water. Uzbeks blamed what poet Mohammed Salikh called Moscow's "cotton colonialism" for corrupting their whole society.

In truth, under Brezhnev's crony Sharaf Rashidov, who ruled the republic like a feudal lord for a quarter of a century until his death in 1984, wholesale political corruption became the plague of Uzbekistan, infecting every pore of society, every crevice of the economy, every political echelon from the village to the district, to the city, to the region, to the republic, to the ministries in Moscow, to the Politburo (Rashidov and possibly others), and into Brezhnev's family.

"There was a pyramid of corruption, a whole criminal mechanism that developed over the last twenty years."[14] This according to Telman Gdlyan, the jaunty, arrogant, relentless investigator put on the case in 1983 by Yuri Andropov, the former KGB chief who became national Party leader.

Gdlyan's exposé became the most sensational criminal prosecution of the eighties. In early 1989, a tribunal in Moscow sent a slew of high officials to jail, including the number two figure in the national police, Brezhnev's son-in-law Yuri Churbanov, the first deputy minister of internal affairs. Gdlyan accused Churbanov of taking 657,000 rubles in bribes to cover up corruption at lower levels; the court sentenced Churbanov to twelve years in the gulag.[15] Uzbek kingpin Rashidov escaped into the grave, but Gdlyan nailed his successor, Inamshon Usmankhodzhayev, who had supposedly been brought in as Party boss to clean house. Gdlyan got him fired and convicted of bribe taking and coverups.

On a rainy Saturday afternoon, while forty thousand of his supporters staged a mass rally just outside the Kremlin walls, Gdlyan laid out for me the inner workings of the Uzbek cotton scam. He paced around his office, as if fancying himself a Soviet Humphrey Bogart, smoking slowly, deliberately, talking with tight-lipped confidentiality through the smoke, his tone laconic, understated; but he was more dapper than Bogart in his well-tailored, olive-tone suit and vest.

"Moscow provoked this situation, this crime—namely, Brezhnev and his clique in the Politburo," he said. "They simply imposed on Uzbekistan a totally unrealistic cotton quota—a quota of six million tons. They simply took this number out of nowhere, frivolously. One of our records describes the [Party] plenum at which Rashidov was promising to produce five and a half million tons of cotton. Brezhnev whispers his name—he says, 'Sharafchik [Rashidov's most intimate nickname], please, round it up. Add half a million more.' Rashidov, being a political prostitute rather than a leader, immediately answers, 'Yes, yes, Comrade General Secretary. We in Uzbekistan will produce six million tons of cotton.' That was the way it was done—'voluntarily,' as we used to say."[16]

Brezhnev's quota, impossible to fulfill in reality, spawned phantom crops, phony records, false bookkeeping, a pyramid of lies, thievery, bribes.

"If the promises were made at the top level without any material basis, false reports became inevitable. And false reports, you understand"— Gdlyan pantomimed with his palm out—"means a 'fast ruble,' bribery. So this massive mechanism of crime starts working from the very bottom and goes straight to the top. . . . The plan quotas are handed down by the government—totally unrealistic numbers. Equally unrealistic reports of fulfilling the quota come back immediately. There is no cotton, but government money is paid for it anyway. A part of the money goes into this one's pocket, a part of it goes to his boss, and his boss is paying his boss, and that's how it goes—all the way up to Moscow. So these false reports pushed people into making a fast ruble.

"They were even hiding hundreds of thousands of acres of cotton fields—never registered anywhere. Whole cotton fields were hidden and cotton harvested from them was also sold to the government for money. This sort of thing requires a total mechanism of crime, including the state authorities, starting with the local farm chairman, the local government collector, and ending in the office of the first Party secretary of Uzbekistan. Layer by layer, people were dragged into this criminal activity. There were hundreds of thousands involved in this crime—a scale that terrified us."

One state prosecutor who handled Gdlyan's cases estimated that between 1978 and 1983, Brezhnev's final five years, the state paid more than 1 billion rubles for cotton that was never produced.[17]

Gdlyan, who is given to hyperbole, may have exaggerated how many people were guilty of lining their pockets in this massive scam, but the clannish nature of Uzbek society, with its personal networks and informal ways of doing business, was fertile soil for mass corruption. By less self-serving reports than Gdlyan's, so many people were involved that tens of thousands were purged from the Uzbek Communist Party; and at least three thousand Uzbek police officers were fired as a result of Gdlyan's probe.[18]

Gdlyan's sensational disclosures of the "Uzbek mafia" made him unpopular in Uzbekistan, but a folk hero back home in Moscow; he was an easy winner in the elections of spring 1989 and served in the Congress of People's Deputies, the superparliament. By mid-1989, he and his co-investigator, Nikolai Ivanov, had the temerity to point an accusing finger at Yegor Ligachev, second in line in Gorbachev's Politburo, as being implicated in the Uzbek schemes. In his interview with me, Gdlyan mentioned Ligachev, four other former Politburo members, and several of Ligachev's aides, on whom he claimed to have evidence.

For months a hot controversy swirled: Ligachev thundered denials and vowed to have Gdlyan's head; people came forward charging that Gdlyan's investigative team had extracted confessions by brutal means. Gdlyan would not retreat. The Communist Party Central Committee eventually cleared Ligachev, and expelled Gdlyan and Ivanov from the Party. The state prosecutor and a commission of the Supreme Soviet said Gdlyan had not produced sufficient proof against Ligachev, but he stuck by his charges, infuriated that the prosecutor's office had broken up his investigative unit.

"Both East and West have criminal organizations," Gdlyan said to me philosophically. "But the nature of your *mafiosi* differs from ours. Your groups are purely criminal. Here, you cannot become an overnight millionaire without being part of the political power structure. To steal millions here, it's a must to have a state seal, a government position, and a limo, for official status."

SLAVERY AND THE STING OF SALT

Moscow's cotton colonialism not only corrupted Uzbek political life, but contaminated the Uzbek economy and the personal lives of Uzbeks as well. It ravaged the environment, adulterated the region's water supply, poisoned the health of millions, and blighted the lives of Uzbek farm workers, especially the women and children—more so than in any other large region that I visited in the Soviet Union.

"The cotton monoculture was a very convenient instrument for enslaving our people," said Abdur Rahim Pulatov, the Birlik leader. "You know, in Russian the term for cotton worker is cotton *rabochy—rab* for short. Well, there is another Russian word *rab*, which means slave. So a cotton worker is a cotton slave, and in Uzbekistan the cotton monoculture has also been the culture of cotton slavery."[19]

For years, Uzbek leaders and the Soviet press trumpeted cotton as the "gold" of Uzbekistan. But very little of that gold trickled down to Uzbek farm workers; by government statistics, 45 percent of Uzbekistan's workers—and farm workers are at the bottom of the heap—earn less than the Soviet subsistence wage of 75 rubles ($125) a month.[20] By the reckoning of Uzbek nationalists, Uzbek cotton farmers make only 16 kopeks (22 cents) an hour for their work, about one fourth as much as those who work on Soviet grain farms.[21] In addition to that level of poverty among farm workers, Uzbekistan has an estimated one million unemployed, and one of the highest unemployment rates in the country—22.8 percent, according to *Pravda*.[22]

Uzbeks insist that their farmers could do better financially if they could market cotton for themselves, at their own prices, rather than being forced to supply cotton to Moscow, at prices dictated by Moscow; or, they say, let us stop growing so much cotton and return to the farm crops for which Uzbekistan was renowned, a rich and profitable variety of tropical fruits and vegetables.

But the price of the cotton monoculture is reckoned in more than rubles; it is also reckoned in human and environmental terms. In the name of record cotton harvests, the ecology of Uzbekistan has been tragically destroyed. Cotton, constantly in need of irrigation, has literally been sucking the region dry. The water level of the republic's great rivers, the Amu Darya and the Syr Darya, has fallen dramatically. Not far from Urgench, I saw what was left of the Amu Darya River, once more than a quarter of a mile across and now several slender currents fifty and sixty yards wide, winding among the sandbars. Near Bukhara, I saw trucks driving in the riverbed; bridges ridiculously spanning great mud channels;

old riverbanks standing ten feet high, like out-of-place fortifications for peasant villages.

The greatest tragedy of all, however, is the Aral Sea, once a great inland saltwater body, now dying for lack of water from its emaciated tributaries. The Aral Sea is one of only a handful of places that Soviet authorities would not let us film, perhaps out of embarrassment over the ecological disaster. Once 25,676 square miles in size, more than the combined size of the states of Massachusetts, Connecticut, Rhode Island, and New Hampshire, it has lost 60 percent of its former size. Aralsk, the Urals' main fishing port, which used to provide one tenth of the entire Soviet fishing catch, now sits nearly forty miles from shore.[23] The new shores are vast salt beds. From the sky it looks as if a huge powdered doughnut encircles the shrunken sea. Winds lift the salt powder, and for hundreds of miles around, salt-filled air stings the eyes, clogs the lungs, and poisons the earth. Salt rains down, back into the shrunken rivers; river water, used for irrigation, salinates the soil; river water, used by humans for drinking, attacks the liver and corrodes the intestines.

In sum, the pernicious cotton monoculture has destroyed the precious working of the water cycle of Uzbekistan—and the normal healthy cycle of human life as well.

"The cotton monoculture is an evil thing for our people," Timur Pulatov, a popular Uzbek writer, said mournfully. "It has been killing us—first of all, killing our soil, weakening it. You know when you plant the same crop every year, the land, the earth, becomes exhausted. Cotton is a very powerful plant because it drains everything from the soil."[24]

The cotton monoculture has also been killing people, both through the relentless abdominal corrosion from salt in the water, and also through the pesticides and defoliants sprayed on the plants to fight the boll weevil and other borers. So much is infected by this toxic combination that at the hotel in Urgench, tourists are warned not only against drinking the water, but also against eating fresh fruits and vegetables; no matter how well they are washed, they have been contaminated by the irrigation water in which they have been grown.

Infants are the primary victims of this diseased ecology: Uzbekistan's infant mortality rate is one of the highest in the world. In Central Asia, most rural hospitals and clinics lack hot water; medical syringes are either nonexistent or used many times over; sanitation is abysmal and sewage stands stagnant. In the Karakalpak region, adjacent to the Aral Sea, more than one infant in ten dies; for Uzbekistan as a whole, the infant mortality rate is 43.3 percent, which puts it virtually on a par with Guatemala and Cameroon.[25]

Disease, like political corruption, is endemic. At the ancient city of Khiva, Mayor Bakhtiar Normetov told me that the health problem was so overwhelming, the Uzbek health system could not begin to cope with it. He said that as many as 70 percent of the adults and 80 percent of the children in the province were chronically ill.[26] That seemed hard to believe, but someone tipped me off to a massive survey that had just been completed in Khorezm Province, in which Khiva and Urgench are located. Several hundred medical workers had found that infectious diseases were rampant—typhus, dysentery, and hepatitis—not to mention gallstones, anemia, kidney problems of all kinds. The health teams checked 387,919 persons: 72 percent were sick—279,753 in all, including 101,216 children.

Years of exposure to foul air, water polluted with salt, sewage, and chemicals, the medical report said, have "exhausted the ability of the human organism to adapt. That is why we have a most unfavorable prognosis for the health of the people in this province, especially for women and children."[27]

FOR UZBEK WOMEN: SELF-IMMOLATION

"This is our rage, our protest. . . . We want to arouse our authorities and our people, to make them look at themselves as they really are, to make them rise up and say, 'We can't live like this anymore!' "[28]

Shukhrat Makhmudov is a forty-year-old Uzbek cameraman and film producer who has found new ways to promote Uzbek nationalism under Gorbachev's *glasnost.* Along with his wife, Raizeta, who is a film editor, he has worked for the official state documentary studio in Tashkent since his 1972 graduation from the State Film Institute in Moscow. For the first time in their lives, they feel liberated from the confines of official propaganda and able to show the truth to the Uzbek people.

"For many years, you see, they've only been shown how wonderful life was in Soviet Uzbekistan, how happily our women worked, how many doctors and engineers there were among them, how joyfully they picked that magnificent snow-white cotton," Shukhrat said sarcastically.[29]

Although not members of Birlik, Shukhrat and Raizeta are caught up in the burgeoning nationalist feelings of Uzbek intellectuals; they are using documentary films to help Uzbeks rediscover their cultural roots and face the terrible realities of their lives.

"We are not just critics; we feel strong compassion for our people's pain," said Shukhrat, a short, dark-haired, good-looking man with soft

Oriental features. "We do not make films with a cold eye and a cold heart. We feel with our people—it's *our* anguish too. We do not simply try to raise problems to be critical. We want our films to make people's lives better."

In the past two years, they have produced several powerful films on Uzbek life. In *Khudzhum,* they broke one taboo by exposing the exploitation of poor, uneducated women workers in a Samarkand textile factory. The film was named after a women's movement in the 1920s that aroused the Muslim women of Central Asia to cast off their veils, and the film was shot in the same factory where Khudzhum had held protests against exploitation under capitalism. Shukhrat's point was that seventy years of Soviet rule had not ended that exploitation. In a second film, *The Dignity and Mystery of a Smile,* the Makhmudovs shattered another taboo by portraying prostitution in Tashkent, and not just any prostitution, but prostitution of teenage girls.

"Raizeta and I make movie after movie of this kind because there are many people who are indifferent [to these things]," Shukhrat told me. "Somebody has to be involved, has to move. Somebody has to support *perestroika.* If everyone just keeps silent, just grumbles, who will act?"

Shukhrat and Raizeta took very seriously their social duty to forge a new outlook among Uzbeks. "You see, we ourselves create our people—by our social system, by our policy, by our morals," Shukhrat told me. "We created our people the way they are today—so obedient. I don't want to continue making this sort of people anymore. And doing the best we can, we'd like to create a new generation, with a new morality."[30]

I first saw Shukhrat and Raizeta at the Birlik rally in Lenin Square, arguing with the police, who were trying to stop them from filming. They were gathering footage for a new film on Uzbek nationalism, to be called *Point No. 5*—the place in a Soviet internal passport for a citizen's nationality: Russian, Ukrainian, Uzbek, Armenian, Jew, and so on.

Cotton figured prominently in their story, so our crew arranged to go and film with them at the Engels Collective Farm outside Samarkand. It was October—harvest time—but I saw no combines in the fields. Later on I would learn that the machinery was ineffective; its first harvesting run left so much cotton on the plants that the bulk of the work had to be done by hand, sometimes four and five times, as the crop matured. In the fields, I saw women (almost no men) slaving away in the blazing sun: doing ten or twelve hours of backbreaking labor, weeding the parched, dusty earth with a little hand-scythe, or, hunched over, dragging long harvest bags between their legs, plucking cotton from the plants, boll by boll.

At the farm's clinic we saw evidence of chronic sickness among cotton farmers. One woman, with an anemic infant, complained of stomach troubles and needed to be hospitalized, but she could not afford to miss work; so she and the sick child headed for the fields, with little medical relief. The doctors told us that toxic defoliants had been used too heavily, attacking the livers, kidneys, lungs, and other organs of the cotton pickers.

From there, Shukhrat headed for the primary school. In room after room, students said they would head for the cotton fields after school. All hands were needed; age was no barrier. At midday, as we filmed the smallest children having a school lunch of noodle soup under a portrait of a smiling Lenin, Shukhrat bent over one table of tots.

"Do you pick cotton too?" he asked a pretty little girl with bangs and no front teeth.

She nodded.

"How do you pick it? Show me."

She plucked an imaginary boll.

"Are you going after school to pick cotton?"

"Yes," she said.

"These little kids are already picking cotton and helping their parents at home," Raizeta told me.

"How old are they?" I asked.

"They're six years old," she replied, shaking her head. *"Six years old."*

Several hours later, in the fields, Shukhrat found a girl named Delfusa whom we had seen in school, a sturdy fifteen-year-old, toting a nearly full cotton bag. She had obviously been at work since school let out at two-thirty. By now, it was close to six.

"For how much longer are you going to work?" he asked her.

"Another half hour," she said. "Then I'll go home and I'll help my mother."

"And then what?" he asked.

"Then I'll do my homework," she said.

"Will there be time left to do homework?" he asked.

"Well," she said, "not much time."

"You're helping your parents," he observed. "You're not forced to pick, are you?"

Kneading her hands, she showed the tension. Clearly the money she made was crucial for her family, even at 7 cents a pound.

"Look," she said, "it's hard for our parents."[31]

With the others, she dragged her harvest bag over to the weighing machine. Her father, a truck driver, was weighing cotton for a group of

children. The sense of exploitation was overwhelming as these children
trudged home at dusk.

But if anything epitomizes the despair of the Uzbeks, it is the plight
of the women, which was captured in the most powerful of Shukhrat and
Raizeta's films, *The Flame.*

"The dirtiest, toughest jobs, the most difficult jobs in the Soviet Union
are always given to women," Raizeta declared with obvious anger. "And
that's true in Uzbekistan too. But here it's even much more extreme. The
situation is much worse here. . . . In our movie *The Flame,* we say that
everything starts with the woman, and when women are dying, a nation
is finished."[32]

In *The Flame,* Shukhrat and Raizeta tell a terrible story about Uzbek
women who commit suicide by setting themselves on fire out of despair
over their lives. It is a protest both against the exploitation and misery
foisted on the poorest, most defenseless elements of Uzbek society by
cotton colonialism, and against the conservative, male-chauvinistic ways
of Uzbek and Islamic culture. On the farm that we visited, the nurses in
the clinic told us that one twenty-four-year-old woman had burned herself
to death just two months earlier. Shukhrat said that in eighteen months,
more than 360 women in Uzbekistan chose to die in this horrible fashion—two every three days.

"They just pour kerosene on themselves and burn to death," Raizeta
said, "because their lives are unbearable, because of oppression, because
they can't live the way they want to. It's an extreme form of protest."[33]

Their movie is terrible to watch, young women still covering most of
their faces with veils, desperate eyes peering at the camera, marching to
work in the unbearable summer heat, flashing to scenes of ambulances,
and then female patients, arms and legs akimbo, rolled into the emergency
rooms, their bodies covered with burns.

"It's painful to realize that today, after so many years of the Soviet
regime's existence, practically nothing has changed," said Raizeta. "It's
very hard to watch, very hard to accept."

"You have two daughters," I said to them. "What is your dream for
them?"

"My dream," Shukhrat said simply, "is that neither my children nor
my grandchildren will ever have to make movies about the self-immola-
tion of women—ever!"

"EVERYONE SEEMS TO BLAME THE RUSSIANS"

The attacks of Uzbek nationalists on Moscow's cotton colonialism have fed a slow but steadily rising feeling against the Russians. Such frictions could become explosive in Tashkent, the Uzbek capital, which is a very Russified city. Back in the 1950s, Russians were a majority there, comprising 52 percent. By the 1970s, I found that Russians still outnumbered Uzbeks, though they had dropped to 40 percent of the population, as rural Uzbeks and other Central Asians came into the city[34]; and now their share is believed to be lower, but the exact figure is kept secret because the Russian presence is such a touchy issue.

In December 1986, anti-Russian feeling exploded in Kazakhstan after Dinmukhammed Kunyayev, the Kazakh Party boss for many years, was removed. Gorbachev replaced him with a Russian, Gennady Kolbin, violating an unwritten rule of Soviet politics—that the local Party leader in each republic must be of that republic's nationality. Moscow normally put a Russian in as second in command, the man generally regarded as the real boss, who ran things for the Kremlin. But the fiction of local leadership had to be maintained; when Gorbachev ignored that rule, the resulting riots in Alma-Ata, the capital of Kazakhstan, showed how close to the surface anti-Russian feelings were. Nothing so dramatic and violent happened in Uzbekistan, but anti-Russian sentiment has nonetheless been on the rise.

For years Russians prided themselves on having modernized Uzbekistan's educational system and economy, but even in the Brezhnev years, a few daring Uzbeks chided Moscow for exploiting the republic, extracting its wealth without plowing earnings back into local industry. They pointed out that 95 percent of the Uzbek cotton was shipped to textile plants outside Central Asia; only 5 percent was processed at home.[35] Uzbeks and other Central Asians resented the crude regional allocation of economic functions, with heavy industry located mainly in the European parts of the country, Siberia and the north exploited for their rich mineral deposits of gold, diamonds, oil, natural gas, iron, coal, and Central Asia for its cheap manpower. Under Gorbachev, some Uzbeks became more outspoken.

"Emotionally everyone seems to blame the Russians," said Abdur Rahim Pulatov. "I, for one, disagree with that, but I have to say that the anti-Russian mood is growing. And if we don't solve our problems, this mood will grow."[36]

In the seventies, I had come to know one Russian couple in Tashkent very well: a famous composer, Aleksei Kozlovsky, who, with his wife,

Galina, had been exiled there by Stalin in the 1930s. Like many thousands of Russians, the Kozlovskys had made Uzbekistan their home, never returning to Russia proper. Kozlovsky turned his exile into creative joy, training Uzbek musicians, conducting their orchestra, and composing symphonies that mixed Uzbek musical themes with classical European music. The Kozlovskys lived in a small home, surrounded by the kind of wild, unkempt garden that Russians love; their home became a haven for famous Russians, such as the poets Boris Pasternak and Anna Akhmatova, and also for many cultured Uzbeks. Kozlovsky died several years ago; when I went in 1989 to see Galina, white-haired and in her late seventies, she was losing her eyesight but still intellectually vigorous and creative. But she was feeling isolated and lonely.

"How is life, Galina?" I asked. "Has it changed much?"

"Frightfully," she said in her perfect English, learned as a diplomat's daughter.

"Yes, how?"

"Oh, Hedrick, it's difficult even to tell you," she said. "Very, very unhappy—the surroundings are not nice. I'm not used to such feelings, because all of my life that we lived here, my husband loved the people, and I also. They were very kind and very nice and good-natured."

"Do you still have Uzbek friends?" I asked. "People of your generation?"

"No," she said.

"What's happened?"

"They are unfriendly to Russians," she said. "They want us to go away. How can I go away if I have lived here forty-four years? They are dissatisfied, like everybody in this country. All the wrong things that were done by the government are ascribed to the Russians, because it was Moscow that dictated how they should live, what they should do, what they . . . how much cotton they must produce.

"There are whole regions that are absolutely poisoned. The mothers can't feed their newborn babies with their milk because the milk is full of salt. The salt comes from the dying great Aral Sea, one of the wonders of Central Asia. It's a pool now—no more a sea. All the salt is evaporating, and it's blown all about the country, and people are dying."[37]

DIFFIDENT NATIONALISM: NO SECESSION

For all the frustrations of the Uzbeks, their nationalist movement is fairly modest in size and ambition. Birlik's leaders claimed half a million followers out of twenty million people, but from my travels that seemed an exaggeration. The hard-core activists are the intellectuals, students, and a smattering of young workers who show up, five thousand or six thousand strong, at Birlik rallies. Their popular support is probably twenty times that number, but hardly half a million.

Politically, Uzbekistan is very conservative. Central Asia as a whole is reminiscent of the American Deep South on the racial issue in the early sixties: Throughout the eighties the hard-liners dominated the government; they tolerated some liberal protests, but kept pretty tight limits on activists; and so far, the great mass of people have not gotten swept up in the nationalist movement as people have in Armenia, Georgia, the Baltic republics, or Moldavia.

From Moscow's vantage point, Central Asia and its delegates to the People's Congress of Deputies are the hard-core Old Guard who solidly back Gorbachev against the radical reformers. The Uzbek intellectuals and journalists whom I met were very frustrated with their stand-pat deputies, who had won election the old way—unopposed—and who rarely bothered to take part in the political debates of the liberated all-union parliament. They sat silently, passively, taking their cue from the Party leader (Gorbachev) as they always have, voting with him even when he moved against their wishes. That is the tradition of Communist Party discipline.

At the local level, the liberal intelligentsia were even more frustrated by the rigidity of Uzbek leadership, its shying away from debate with the emerging democratic elements.

"The leaders of our republic, and of our province, and of our *raikom*, district Communist Party Committee, all have the Stalinist way of thinking," complained Kurambai Matrizayev, head of Urgench radio and television. "It's very hard for these people to change. It's very hard for Gorbachev to break their habits. They should watch Gorbachev on television and see how he allows deputies to disagree with him, to offer criticism. Our leaders should take a lesson from him. But they do not. They criticize the way I work as the local chairman of television and radio, because my nature is to be democratic, to talk with my people, to listen to those who work with me. But the Party bosses tell me: 'This is wrong. You are a weak leader. You've got to be tougher.' "[38]

Compared with the rest of the Soviet Union, Central Asia is so underdeveloped politically as well as economically that the new nationalists lapsed behind their counterparts in other regions. Their first objective was simply to stir a sense of nationhood among the Uzbeks, who had not been a separate nation before the Bolshevik Revolution; under the czars, they had been lumped with the rest of Central Asia in what was known as Turkestan. In the seventies and eighties, Uzbekistan was still a polyglot nation, an amalgam of Uzbeks, Russians, and other Central Asian peoples, especially Tadzhiks. So Uzbek nationalists tried to encourage a sense of Uzbek nationhood and pride. Their methods were fairly basic, with restoring the primacy of the Uzbek language as the first major step.

In Bukhara, Akhurnjan Safarov, an anthropologist at the local pedagogical institute, was doing his part by heading a drive to remove Communist names from city streets and restore prerevolutionary names or name streets for Central Asian folk heroes. "We had a national hero, Bukhana, who led our people against the Arab invaders in the eighth century, or Mahmoud Tarabin, who headed our people's uprising against the Mongol invaders," Safarov told me. "So why not name our streets after these national heroes—to educate our youth in the spirit of patriotism?"[39]

Even more politically daring was the effort to honor people such as Abdurauf Fitrat, an Uzbek writer, musician, historian, and revolutionary who had written works proclaiming pan-Turkic ideals in the 1920s. He had later collaborated with the Communists, but was arrested in 1938 during Stalin's purges, and shot in 1944. In the late 1950s, Fitrat was formally rehabilitated—declared innocent of any political crime; nonetheless, as a Turkic nationalist, he was still treated negatively in the Soviet press for the next thirty years.[40] Under Gorbachev, Professor Safarov and others have gotten a local high school renamed in Fitrat's honor and have made plans to publish two volumes of his works in 1991. Safarov had other projects too, such as reintroducing traditional Uzbek and Turkic fairy tales and children's games.

"Everyone is asking now, 'Who is the real me?' People are looking for their roots," Safarov said. "That's my personal reason for getting involved in these studies."

Another important revival movement is taking place among Muslims. In Samarkand, the mosque where I had seen two hundred or three hundred worshipers back in the seventies was filled with fifteen hundred worshipers at midday on a Friday in October 1989. There was an energetic new imam leading the prayers, though several worshipers told me it was still impossible for them to get the Koran and Islamic prayer books. And I saw only a sprinkling of young people in the sea of wizened graybeards bending in prayer to Mecca. The absence of the young embarrassed the mullah, Imam Mustafakhan Melikov, when I asked about it; a few moments later, in his sermon, he used the presence of our film crew to harangue the elders.

"You are being photographed by Americans," he told them. "Why don't you bring more children to our prayers? Why don't you bring those who are not working or in school? Bring them to the holy place and attract them to Islam."[41]

At the Islamic seminary in Bukhara, its graying rector, Haj Mukhtar Abdulayev, told me the number of his students had tripled from 40 to 125 in the years since Gorbachev had come to power, and that, within the past year, more than eighty mosques had been reopened in Uzbekistan[42] (Stalin had closed twenty-six thousand mosques[43]). From his description, the curriculum seemed limited to strict fundamentalist training. Both the imam in Samarkand and the rector at Bukhara struck me as men of extremely traditional views.[44]

In Tashkent, there was a push to shake up the Islamic Church establishment, widely regarded as a nest of Soviet puppets. In February 1989, a popular protest in Tashkent forced Moscow to remove the official head of Islamic affairs in Central Asia, Grand Mufti Babakhan. His replacement was slightly more progressive; still, the Islamic leaders whom I met knew little and cared less about the goals and activities of Uzbek nationalists and their secular cultural revival. The more liberal Birlik activists saw the reviving Islamic Church as a conservative rival rather than a partner in rekindling Uzbek nationalism and modernizing its culture.

Poets and writers such as Mohammed Salikh, tall and striking in his all-white tropical shirt and trousers, have stirred people with poetry readings on historic and nationalistic themes. His is a conservative, pro-Islamic kind of nationalism, playing on traditional themes, less secular and modern than that of Pulatov, the Birlik leader, or the Makhmudovs. In a region where the oral tradition is still important, especially in the countryside, it was typical of Salikh to remark that "poetry is still very influential—very useful for awakening people." And so were some new nationalist songs like those written by Dadhon Khassan. In the Uzbek Writers' Union, Salikh and Dadhon sang me a shy duet of several of Khassan's songs: "Turkestan, Koz Khamseh" ("Wake Up"), and "Usbegim" ("My Uzbek"), with the words *If you call yourself a son of your motherland, don't give away your language to others,* " and the refrain

> *Raise your head,*
> *Open your eyes . . .*
> *Join us in our ranks,*
> *Even if you must risk your life.* [45]

Initially, I took it as a sign of the relatively primitive stage of the Uzbek nationalist movement that Salikh and Dadhon had not seen the movies

of Shukhrat and Raizeta Makhmudov. In fact, the authorities were keeping the Makhmudovs' films from the public eye. *Khudzhum,* about the
exploitation of women factory workers, had been intended for an Uzbek
women's conference, but after Party officials previewed the film, they
barred it from being shown. Parts of the film about teenage prostitution
were broadcast on Moscow television, but not in Uzbekistan. *"The Flame*
has been shown only once on Tashkent television—at midnight," Shukhrat said, "and that was only a Russian-language version—not Uzbek.
There were thousands of letters sent to the station with demands to
rebroadcast *The Flame.* Tashkent television was going to show it again
this month [October 1989] but the new first secretary of the Uzbek
Communist Party, [Islam] Karimov, called the television officials and told
them, 'No more upsetting themes on television. They cause people anxiety. We want people in a good mood.' "[46] Shukhrat and Raizeta had to
resort to private showings to film clubs and interested groups; the Party's
ideologists kept their social criticism out of state-operated movie theaters.

Such restrictions checked the influence of Uzbekistan's new democratic activists, slowing their pace. As the Baltic nationalist movements
were winning elections, defying Moscow, and proclaiming independence,
the Uzbeks were pushing for reinstatement of their language. Other
republics were well ahead of the Uzbeks in demanding "economic sovereignty" in 1988 and 1989; the main Uzbek economic demand was a
reduction of the cotton quota and an opportunity to diversify agriculture.
It took three years, Mohammed Salikh told me, just to get Brezhnev's
fantasy target of 6 million tons of cotton reduced to 5 million, which was
what many Uzbeks assumed was the actual peak output. It was a genuine
triumph, then, in the fall of 1989, when Moscow agreed that the target
for 1990 would be 4.5 million tons.[47] Salikh was also encouraged by
Karimov's promise to give farm workers a pay raise and let them have
slightly larger private plots to farm.

Indeed, in the spring of 1990, the Uzbek leadership, especially the new
prime minister, Shukrulla Marsaidov, picked up the theme of "economic
independence" from Uzbek nationalists, angrily condemning Moscow's
"manipulation" of financial figures to make it look as though the Uzbek
economy were subsidized, whereas he claimed it provided three times as
much to the central economy as it got back.[48]

After Gorbachev declared his willingness in mid-June 1990 to tolerate
more regional autonomy and to renegotiate the 1922 treaty forming the
Soviet Union, the new Uzbek leadership began to try to catch up with
other republics. On June 20, Uzbekistan became the eighth Soviet republic, and the first in Central Asia, to declare its "sovereignty"—asserting

that its laws would take precedence over Soviet laws, though that seemed hopeful rhetoric, rather than a sign of secessionist intentions. Of more practical consequence was the economic alliance signed in late June by the five Central Asian republics, and aimed at gaining more regional and local control of the economy. At least initially, this was a brand of federalism that Gorbachev had indicated he could tolerate. Nor did it produce any dramatic confrontations. As Mohammed Salikh remarked, "We are doing all this without dramatizing the process, without playing to the crowds."[49]

Toward the radical wing of Birlik, the authorities became more repressive. Police used force to break up a rally of more than five thousand demonstrators in a suburb of Tashkent in March, brought charges against Abdur Rahim Pulatov, the head of Birlik, after the demonstrators burned some local office buildings, and issued emergency decrees banning further demonstrations. Periodically, there were terrible explosions of interethnic violence in Central Asia—in Fergana in Uzbekistan, in Kazakhstan, Tadzhikistan, and Kirghizia. But these seemed to burst suddenly out of economic despair, and then disappear. Aside from such random incidents, Central Asian nationalism was relatively diffident; it posed no great threat to Moscow.

"So long as the Communist Party is in power here, there are going to be only small changes," observed Anvar Shakirov, a well-traveled linguist at Samarkand University. "In Uzbekistan, there is a certain characteristic of people: They are yes-men, especially the leaders. It's a very Oriental trait. They watch for what people want up above them. They never say no to higher-ups. So that means for real changes we need a new type of leader, people elected from below, not appointed from above."[50]

Never, in my conversations with Uzbek activists, did I hear any talk of secession from the Soviet Union. For all their unhappiness with Moscow's "cotton colonialism," Uzbeks still felt dependent upon the Russians. They had not really broken out of the colonial mentality—as their peers had done in Georgia, Moldavia, or the Baltic republics. Central Asia was far more politically conservative than other regions. In the elections of March 1990, Uzbekistan's Communist establishment easily maintained its power, and Birlik split into two factions. More important, perhaps, many people became cynical about the practical impact of *glasnost* and the benefits of reform.

"The excitement over *glasnost* and democracy has dissipated," Raizeta Makhmudova told me during a visit to Washington in May 1990. "When it was new, people were in ecstasy at all the new things that were possible to say and do and see. But now, people notice that it has brought nothing new in their lives. People have become disenchanted and so they are not ready to defend *glasnost* and democracy. Public feeling coincides with the desire of the apparatus to maintain the old controls."[51]

CHAPTER 15

ARMENIA AND AZERBAIJAN: A SOVIET LEBANON

"In this country, we have only a single right—the right of territory. This is the sole right of the republic, of our nation. . . . So a fight over territory became a fight for our worth, our dignity as a people, as a nation."[1]
—Rufat Novrozov
Azerbaijani Economist
March 1990

"Today it is very important to understand . . . whether this city really belongs to us, whether this country really belongs to our people. All these things should become a reality at last. And for us, there is no turning back."[2]
—Ashot Manucharyan
Armenian Teacher
July 1989

In the Armenian capital of Yerevan, my first stop was to be School No. 183, but when we arrived, I was certain the driver had made a mistake. We were in a cul-de-sac of a high-rise ghetto. Before me stood what looked like a condemned building: a dismal, squat, two-story structure that had seen better days. It was in a canyon of dull, gray tenement apartments, faced with a mottled-gray stone that gave the entire district a melancholy appearance.

I had heard that School No. 183 was the most exciting and celebrated school in Armenia today, and I had expected something modern, something emblematic of the dramatic resurgence of nationalist spirit in Armenia. But this place looked bombed out, abandoned, dead.

Soviets make a fetish of official titles and name plates, but no plaque designated this building as a school. Several front windows were broken, and the sidewalk was littered with glass, loose rocks, and other debris. There was no hint of a playground, not a blade of grass.

"This doesn't look like a school," I said to the driver. "Are you sure this is the right place?"

An elderly Armenian and a man of few words, he merely nodded. To make his point, he turned off the engine, leaned back, pulled out a cigarette, and prepared to wait. Seeing my consternation, he flashed me a toothy grin.

I got out and approached the building but I could not open any door. It took considerable bellowing before someone finally came to let me and my companions in, even though the school principal and some teachers were supposedly expecting us. The main foyer had an eerie, lifeless feeling. It was summer, so the students were gone, but more than that, the place had been stripped clean, almost as if it had been vandalized.

Down the hall and around the corner, I finally detected some signs of life. Chairs and desks were stacked up against a wall; an electrician was replacing a ceiling light fixture. From one room came the sound of hammering: someone doing repairs. Apparently the front foyer was so naked because the school was undergoing what the Soviets call *remont,* a major repair job.

Farther on, I heard sounds of music, and upstairs I came across some teachers, Armenian women, dancing in a circle in the hallway, arms on each other's shoulders. They were following the directions of a slender, bearded male instructor, and moving to the rhythms of a simple, old-fashioned folk melody played on an ancient Armenian instrument that sounded like a recorder.

Like many Soviet facades, the exterior of School No. 183 had been misleading, but in a way that was the reverse of what is usually the case. Mostly, the facades of Soviet buildings exaggerate the importance and success of the institutions, but in this case, the dead exterior hid a dynamic interior: The school was a seedbed of ferment. Officials there had an intense commitment to the school that was highly unusual for Soviet teachers. They had close, proud ties with the neighborhood, and a democratic spirit that stimulated student activism. In a bare office with two desks and a broken phone, the young principal, Ashot Bleyan, explained how School No. 183 was revolutionizing the Armenian educational system by reviving ancient Armenian culture—music, folk art, language, dance; he and his staff were creating a startling new curriculum. In other republics, people dreamed about revamping their schools; here, people were doing it.

From past experience, I knew that in minority republics, the Soviet system provided two sets of schools: "Russian" schools, in which courses were all taught in the Russian language, and "national" schools, in which the main language was that of the local nationality, with Russian taught as well. School No. 183 was a national school; it had twenty-three hundred Armenian students and two hundred Russians. What bothered Bleyan was that even this "Armenian" school had been forced into a Russian mold.

"As you know, all over this country, schools have the same curriculum, the Soviet curriculum, which is created in Moscow," Bleyan told me. "It's the same program, same concepts, same textbooks, same courses. Nationality doesn't matter. In music, for example, the program is the same for Russia, the Ukraine, Moldavia, Armenia. The system allows for a few local idiosyncrasies—but minimal. The music taught is Russian. Our children have had to learn the music of composers of the past seventy years [the Soviet period]. Armenia has a musical tradition of two thousand years, which we feel our Armenian children should absorb—to understand what it is to be Armenian."[3]

To many Russians, this would sound brash and offensive. Rarely did a Russian travel with us, but that day, a Russian from the State Committee for Television and Radio in Moscow, German Solomatin, was with us. As Bleyan spoke, I could sense Solomatin's tension: He was irked by Bleyan's charge that Russians had suppressed Armenian culture. Solomatin was supposed to be a neutral, silent observer, but he could barely contain himself. Finally, he picked on Bleyan's manner of speech, trying to put him down as uncultured.

"You're a principal—why don't you speak better Russian?" Solomatin demanded.

Bleyan had been speaking in Russian as a courtesy to me, because I did not understand Armenian. His speech was clear and correct, though his choppy, singsong Armenian pronunciation was less than linguistically pure. Solomatin was pouncing on that flaw.

Bleyan bristled, conscious that he was being insulted in front of foreign guests.

"I don't think I speak Russian badly," he replied, barely suppressing his anger. "I *teach* Russian," he added, "as a *second* native language."

Solomatin started to take issue, because Russians think of their own language as first above all others, but he was shouted down by four or five other Armenian teachers in the room. The flash of anger on both sides reminded me how close to the surface nationalist feelings were. As voices rose, I cut in and asked the principal to go on with what he had been saying.

"We have redesigned the concept of the 'national' school," Bleyan resumed, coldly turning away from Solomatin. "We want to know who we are and where we are. This means reworking our school textbooks, and programs for literature, music, history, arithmetic, for everything. So our teachers have prepared two Armenian songbooks and two new musical textbooks. We are doing the same thing in literature. Our written literature starts from the fifth century. We have folklore, poetry, and literature, written in our classical language, Grabar, from which our modern regional dialects come. Now, with our new curriculum, our students can study Grabar starting in the fifth grade."

It sounded innocent enough. But I knew from my travels how radical it was to establish a genuine Armenian curriculum, and then to make the curriculum at School No. 183 a model for all of Armenia. Clearly, more was at stake here than mere academics; School No. 183 was stripping away the dominant Russian culture and endowing a new generation with a vibrant national consciousness. Only two or three other minority peoples—in the Baltics and Soviet Georgia—could rival the Armenians in forcefully asserting their national culture and identity.

Moreover, School No. 183 was more than a center of cultural renaissance—it was a hotbed of political rebellion. Its staff was perhaps the youngest in the whole U.S.S.R.: Bleyan, the principal, was only thirty-three, and the average age of the teachers was thirty. Moreover, they were almost all political activists. The teachers had gone on political strikes, and had rallied hundreds of high school students to join them. They were a vocal force in Yerevan.

Five of the school's staff had been arrested in the Soviet crackdown against Armenian nationalists in December 1988. Two were members of the now famous Karabakh Committee, eleven Armenian intellectuals who had spearheaded a popular movement demanding Armenian control over Nagorno-Karabakh, an enclave of Armenians located deep within the neighboring republic of Azerbaijan. But at School No. 183, they did not call it Nagorno-Karabakh; they gave it the ancient Armenian name—Artsakh.

The school was in fact an apt metaphor for Armenia itself. On the surface Armenia appeared to be destroyed, demoralized after the earthquake of December 1988, which had left 300,000 people homeless, and bloody anti-Armenian pogroms in Azerbaijan that had sent another 160,000 Armenians from their homes, fleeing for their lives. But physical appearances were misleading; Armenia—and the school—were full of democratic energy and expectation.

In the hallway outside the principal's office, I noticed a brightly colored wall mural, done in the style of Armenian folk art, not in the stilted style of Soviet socialist realism. The mural poked fun at an ugly green Soviet dragon, pictured as undulating through the hills of Armenia, its back crawling with Soviet army tanks and troops, symbolizing the military curfew and occupation after the mass protests over Karabakh. But standing over the dragon was a conqueror bigger than life: General Adranik Zorovar, a nineteenth-century Armenian hero, drawn with a dashing Armenian mustache. Still closer to heaven, beneath a rising, hopeful sun, loomed Armenia's sacred high ground, Mount Ararat, long ago annexed by Muslim Turkey. Except that in this mural, the painters had placed on its peak the Christian cross of the Armenian Orthodox Church.

"Extremists is what they call us," Bleyan said with a touch of pride. "That's what the Soviet press has nicknamed School No. 183—*extremists.*"

POLICE RAIDS AND DEATH THREATS

One of the least violent but most influential of the school's "extremists" is Ashot Manucharyan, the deputy principal, who, when I visited in June 1989, had just emerged from five months in a KGB prison in Moscow.

Ashot had been a prime mover in creating School No. 183's new curriculum. He had also been a prime mover on the Karabakh Committee. When he came out of jail, he was forbidden by Soviet authorities to continue his political activities and was ordered not to go outside Yerevan, but he quickly said he intended to violate his parole by going to address a political rally in the hill town of Hrazdan, about an hour's drive from Yerevan. He invited me and my colleagues Oren Jacoby and David Royle to come along.

"You may see me arrested again," he said matter-of-factly. "I have announced publicly that this restriction on me is a political measure, not a legal one, and I will not accept it."[4]

I found Ashot Manucharyan to be an unusually idealistic and public-spirited young man, outspoken but soft-spoken; not a firebrand, but firm and gently persuasive. Others told me that Ashot's quiet integrity and relentless devotion to ordinary people had inspired great popular trust. From his parents, both teachers, he had learned a strong commitment to public service. Years before, he had become an idealistic young member of the Communist Party, and in 1986 he was elected a deputy in the Armenian Supreme Soviet. His inspiration to public activism, he said, had come from his father.

"Until he was forty, my father was a very brave man, and very outspoken," Ashot said, adding with a soft smile: "He has only changed as he has gotten older.

"The KGB frightened him terribly last December, when I was arrested the first time [very briefly]. After my release, I went into hiding for nearly a month. Every night, they would come to our apartment at two or three A.M., to check for me, and it frightened my parents. After the second arrest—when I was in jail for a long time—my wife and my mother became fighters for my release; they became political activists. But my father . . . he never forbids me to go out, but he will ask me, 'Why do you give this speech?' or 'Must you go to that meeting?' He worries about me."

"How about you," I asked. "Do you worry?"

"Am I ever afraid? Yes, of course—I'm only human. Sometimes I feel fear. But less for myself. I really worry about my family."[5]

During his five months in Moscow's Butyrky Prison, Ashot was not mistreated, but he was kept incommunicado. No communication with the outside was permitted, except for one visit from his sister. He was put in a cell with a murderer, an armed robber, and an Uzbek official who had embezzled 300,000 rubles. What he found most unbearable was the ban on family contact. He had left his wife pregnant; his second son was born while he was in jail. At the public's urging, the child was named David, a symbolic Armenian David who would stand up against the Soviet Goliath.

The boy, now three, still stares at strangers with large, frightened brown eyes; Ashot's wife, Bibishan, bitterly remembers the police harassment.

"They would burst into our place after midnight and search the place," she recalled. "And we protested: 'Hey, you are Soviet people, not fascists. What right do you have to burst into our apartment on Sundays?' My father-in-law was very sick. We had to call the ambulance three or four times after these searches. He felt he was dying. I was on the verge of miscarriage. It was hysteria. I wouldn't wish anything like that on my worst enemy. Then [after they took Ashot] we were waiting. We were counting seconds, and then weeks. We wanted to have him back, especially the boy who wanted to hear his bedtime story and didn't want to go to bed without seeing his father. The boy became very nervous. That night [of his arrest], there was one soldier wearing a bulletproof vest and armed with a nightstick. The boy was half asleep when he suddenly saw these strangers, after midnight, and he kept saying: 'I hate them all, they took my daddy.' "

Ashot's face hardened as he listened. "You know, sometimes I felt moments of hatred—a desire to kill them all," he said. "Such a powerful hatred. They were subhumans, really. But I simply don't like to hate."

"He's just too honest, too sincere," his wife observed. "He wanted this freedom and *glasnost* so much, even during his student years. So when this fresh breeze started blowing, he couldn't keep away from politics."[6]

Ashot was constantly on the go, organizing relief for the earthquake victims, talking with students, putting pressure on the Yerevan City Council, negotiating privately with Party leaders, campaigning against them in public.

"I am not a soldier by nature," he told me, "but like all of my people today, I am a soldier in a political revolution. . . . We all want to become a country of free people, where human dignity is not a stranger, where the feeling of freedom is common. . . . My people were the first to raise their heads [under *perestroika*], and it purified them. People don't want to live the way they did, often doing things against their own will. And you know, the slave who is aware of his slave mentality is not a slave anymore."[7]

Ideas tumbled out of Ashot during our seventy-five-mile-an-hour drive up into the hills in a little car called a Zhiguli, a Soviet-model Fiat; the car shook terribly as it bounced over the bumpy roads.

Having been thrown out of the Communist Party for his independence, Ashot was deeply disillusioned with Soviet Communism. Though not an advocate of capitalism, he was a democrat to the core, more a democrat than a Karabakh fanatic. He believed the Soviet political and economic system was rotten, and was in favor of establishing a multiparty system, of giving land back to the peasants, and of fighting the corruption in Armenian politics—corruption not yet as bad as in Uzbekistan, but bad enough, he said, so that people paid bribes of 150,000 to 400,000 rubles to buy jobs as district Party leaders. He pointed out an Armenian teahouse along the highway; he said two political thugs had threatened to kill him there because he had been campaigning against a powerful Communist Party leader in the nearby town of Charensavan. They had told him never to show his face again in the town; Ashot had actually gone ahead and finished his campaigning, but after their threat, he said, "I told them I would be in the main square of Charensavan the next day at three o'clock, if they wanted to find me."

"What happened?" I asked.

"Nothing," he said with a shrug.[8]

For Ashot, it was just one of many little confrontations with the "mafia" of traditional Armenian Communist politics, an inevitable by-product of his challenge to the old political system.

When we reached Hrazdan, an industrial city of roughly fifty thousand, several hundred people had already gathered in an open field, mostly men in dark work clothes. Some militia officers stood in a huddle next to nearby apartment buildings, but they made no move to interfere. Ashot climbed a little ridge overlooking the field and was handed a microphone; at his appearance, the crowd chanted, "Artsakh! Artsakh! Artsakh!" punctuating each cry by hurling their right arms into the air. It was an Armenian ritual and rallying cry.

The crowd energized Ashot, who had been in a reflective mood. In the peaceful, slanting afternoon sun, the chants began to rise. Ashot was the teacher: He tutored and instructed them, patiently, thoughtfully, but powerfully. He spoke quietly, but his tone grew sharp when he talked of the injustice to Armenians in Karabakh, and, further, the political and economic corruption in Armenia itself. He reminded the people that not only had Armenians been arrested, but the Soviet army and national police had killed peaceful demonstrators in nearby Georgia. He attacked the Party and KGB for trying to silence the little people. As he warmed to his themes, the crowd responded. Moving among them, I could hear vows of revenge, muttered death threats to Azerbaijanis over the issue of Karabakh.

But Ashot did not play the demagogue; he did not pander to ethnic hatred. He warned against escalating violence, and tried to channel the passions of Armenian nationalism to the cause of democracy, justice, and reform.

"We must know why innocent people were killed in Georgia. Our authorities must answer. . . . We must decide who should have the power: the people or the Party Central Committee. . . . We must express every-thing that is in our hearts. We cannot keep it inside anymore. The time has come when we must act—and move forward. We all underwent great changes in this last year and a half. This period was more significant to our lives than the last one hundred years."9

"TERRITORY IS OUR SOLE RIGHT"

Karabakh, of course, was the issue that had galvanized Armenian nationalism from 1987 onward. It is what made the Armenians, as Ashot Manucharyan observed, the first of the Soviet peoples to explode, once Gorbachev's *glasnost* gave them freedom to speak. Karabakh became the lightning rod for all the discontent of the Armenians, discontent with economic misery, with the corruption and arrogance of their political leaders, with the pollution of their environment. For Armenia, Karabakh became what cotton was for Uzbekistan.

Except that Karabakh had roots deep in Armenian history; it was a long-suppressed territorial grievance that electrified the masses, and that instantly made it a cause célèbre for the entire nation of Armenians. And Karabakh was much more: It was an aching wound, a symbol of the injustice done to the Armenian nation by Soviet rulers and, before them, by the Turks; it was a holy cause for the Christian Armenians against the Islamic peoples that surrounded them; it was an icon of Armenian suffering through the centuries. In a very real sense, Karabakh is a microcosm of Armenia.

Karabakh is an Armenian island engulfed in a surrounding sea of Azerbaijanis, who are an ethnic blend of Persian and Turkic peoples, Islamic in their culture and religion. Armenia is an island of Christianity virtually surrounded by Islamic peoples: Turkey to the west, Iran to the south, Azerbaijan and all of Soviet Central Asia to the east. Only on the north is it bordered by another Christian nation, Soviet Georgia. In Armenia, there are about 3 million Armenians, and another 1.5 million are scattered around the U.S.S.R.; the Soviet Union has ten times as many Turkic people—42 million—plus another 54 million in Turkey itself.

Historically, this area of the Caucasus, the land bridge connecting Europe and Asia, has seen unending conflict. The Armenians have endured centuries of persecution. They lost about a million people in Turkey during the massacre of 1915, a mass slaughter that drove the Armenians into the arms of czarist Russia and then into alliance with the Bolshevik Revolution; Russia, under any banner, became Armenia's protector against the Turks.

Hanging at Etchmiadzin (the Vatican City of the Armenian Orthodox

Church) is a massive painting, a tapestry, that captures Armenia's view of itself. It depicts the heroic Armenian nation fighting off violent attacks from fierce soldiers on all sides, most of whom wield the characteristic curved swords of Turkish or Islamic warriors.

The Armenian church at Etchmiadzin is the cultural and emotional heart of the Armenian nation. The pageantry of its priests, celebrating mass in black hoods and purple robes, draws Armenians from all over the world, captivated by its rich ceremony and paying homage to the Catholicos, or Patriarch, of the world Armenian Church. Records and relics mark Armenia as the first Christian nation, converted in 303, several decades before the Emperor Constantine declared Christianity the official religion of the Roman Empire.

The Church survived for the past seventy-five years by accommodating to Communist rule and working out a live-and-let-live arrangement. When I visited Armenia in the seventies, I found that many Communist Party officials were clandestine believers whose relatives had church baptisms and weddings in defiance of official atheism. There were thirty thousand baptisms performed a year, I was told. In 1971, Catholicos Vasgen II claimed that nearly half the Armenian people were churchgoers, although others said that was an exaggeration.[10] When I saw him again in 1989, Vasgen II estimated that under the more open conditions of *glasnost,* 50–60 percent of the urban population and 80 percent of the rural population were Christian believers.[11]

With the church as the principal vessel of Armenian language, culture, and national cohesion, Armenians maintained a strong sense of national identity, even in the darkest years of Communist rule. Their republic is ethnically the purest of all fifteen major political regions of the U.S.S.R.: Ninety-four percent of Armenia's population are Armenians, according to the 1989 census. Its historical traditions have been well preserved; its national archive, the famous Matenadaran Library, is an unusually rich repository of chronicles and ancient manuscripts, all written in Armenia's distinct script, testimony to the people's pride in their long history.

By contrast, Azerbaijan is a relatively young nation that never enjoyed a clear and coherent history or a distinct national identity to match Armenia's. In what is now Azerbaijan, the ancient Greeks found a mingling of innumerable tribes; the region later became a province of Persia. The Arab conquest in the eighth century brought Islam; then came occupation by the Mongol invaders; later, after the rule of an independent khan, the region became the site of continual battle between Persians and Ottoman Turks. In 1829, czarist Russia annexed northern Azerbaijan, leaving the southern portion around Tabriz to Persia.

Paradoxically, perhaps, this checkerboard history and mixed heritage has left modern Azerbaijanis extraordinarily sensitive to what they see as the territorial integrity of their republic: their primary claim to nationhood. As one highly Russianized Azerbaijani, a young economist named Rufat Novrozov, explained to me, "In this country, we have only a single right—the right of territory. This is the sole right of the republic, of our nation." Stalin, he said, had stripped all the minority nationalities of everything else. "Territory was all we had left," he said. "They could not change our territory without our agreement. So a fight over territory became a fight for our worth, our dignity as a people, as a nation."[12]

Novrozov and other Azerbaijanis acknowledged their weak sense of nationhood. Said Novrozov: "When Azerbaijanis meet each other, they ask, 'Where are you from?' And people answer, 'I'm from Nakhichevan or Karabakh or Kazakh'—from provinces, not from Azerbaijan. They have stronger regional loyalty than national loyalty. In general, we thought of ourselves as Turks."

For many Azerbaijanis, then, the political—and eventually the military—struggle with Armenia over Karabakh has become a test of Azerbaijani national legitimacy; and also a catalyst for a developing Azerbaijani nationalism, a path to a new and stronger national identity. The Armenian challenge for control of Nagorno-Karabakh is both a threat and a stimulus. "The fight for Karabakh," Novrozov said, "is a fight for national [self-] determination, in the form of a fight for territory."

Azerbaijan had been awarded control over Nagorno-Karabakh by Stalin in July 1921, after a confusing period of revolution, civil war, and nationalist uprisings. In 1905 and again in 1918, the Armenians and Azerbaijanis had fought over Karabakh and Nakhichevan, another contested territory. By the early 1920s, the census showed Karabakh was 95 percent Armenian in population; but Azerbaijanis claim that it was originally dominated by their people through the eighteenth century, and that the Armenians arrived only in the nineteenth century.

To Armenians, Stalin's decision was a horror, a double cross; earlier in 1921, the regional Bolshevik leadership had decided to give Karabakh to Armenia. A few Armenians, and even some Russians, suspect Stalin of having acted with satanic purpose, knowing the Karabakh issue would rile the Armenians and keep these two nationalities forever at dagger points.

In a wider sense, the explosion over Karabakh in the 1980s was a natural consequence of the very concept of the Soviet multinational empire. During the Bolshevik Revolution, Lenin was looking for allies against the czarist regime, and he bargained for the support of the minority peoples on the fringes of czarist Russia by promising them autonomy and self-determination once the czar was overthrown. After the Revolution, first Lenin and later Stalin carved up the political map along ethnic lines, clustering Armenians together, Georgians, Ukrainians, Uzbeks, and so on. But inevitably, there were demographic pockets that did not fit a neat map; people who did not match their neighbors. And this was especially true in the Caucasus and Central Asia, where peoples and tribes had moved and mingled for centuries. Karabakh was one of those demographic pockets where the local population did not match its neighbors.

What made Armenians acutely sensitive to the fate of Karabakh in the 1980s was the painful example of Nakhichevan, another province that Stalin had awarded to Azerbaijan. Its population had also once been mainly Armenian, but over several decades of the twentieth century, Azerbaijanis had become the majority through a deliberate program of resettlement: Armenians left, Azerbaijanis moved in. Nowadays, Armenians point with alarm to a similar, though slower trend in Karabakh—the Armenian share of the population has fallen from 95 percent in 1921 to 75 percent in 1981. Armenians with whom I talked were deathly afraid that Karabakh would be forever lost through what they derisively termed "Azerbaijanization." Moreover, Armenians, from taxi drivers to the Communist Party leader Suren Arutunyan, accused the Azerbaijani government in Baku of deliberately letting Armenian towns and villages in Nagorno-Karabakh become run down, of refusing to spend money on schools, hospitals, housing, and other facilities, in hopes of provoking an Armenian exodus from Karabakh.

Periodically, the Armenians' frustration had erupted in the Brezhnev years; they made repeated efforts to get back their "lost territories" of Karabakh and Nakhichevan, through private appeals to Party leaders in Moscow, letter-writing campaigns, and public demonstrations. On April 24, 1965, the fiftieth anniversary of the Turkish massacres, one hundred thousand people demonstrated in Yerevan in what began as an officially sanctioned gathering and then grew into spontaneous demands for the "territories."[13] That same year, forty-five thousand Armenians in Karabakh signed a petition to the Soviet Council of Ministers, seeking reunification of Karabakh with Armenia. Years of Stalinist repression had not snuffed out nationalist passions; when Gorbachev's *glasnost* lifted the political lid, the Armenians were the first people to seize aggressively upon the new openness.

COLD-BLOODED MURDER

It was almost immediately after Gorbachev's accession to power in 1985 that Armenians began bombarding the new leadership with appeals to return Karabakh and Nakhichevan. In 1987, the Karabakh Committee was formed to lobby Moscow and organize public support in Armenia. That fall Armenia became the site of the first large public demonstrations of the Gorbachev era, the central issues being Karabakh and industrial pollution. But the real explosion of public protest came in early 1988, after the Armenians felt they had been deceived by Gorbachev, triggering a campaign that would force the ouster of Communist leaders in both Armenia and Azerbaijan and set Armenia once again on the path to war with its neighbors.

The Armenians had high hopes that Gorbachev, with his democratic approach, would let the Armenian majority in Karabakh determine its own destiny and rejoin Armenia. After lengthy private negotiations with the Communist Party Central Committee in Moscow, there was great excitement in Armenia at a December 1987 report in the French Communist newspaper *L'Humanité*. The paper quoted Armenian economist Abel Aganbegyan, an adviser to Gorbachev, as telling the Armenian community in Paris that Moscow—presumably meaning Gorbachev—had decided to settle the issue of the Nagorno-Karabakh situation, and to return the province to Armenia. Aganbegyan's statements, repeated in the Soviet press, hit like thunder in the Azerbaijani capital of Baku.

The Azerbaijani leadership warned Moscow that any change on Karabakh would not only bring hundreds of thousands of Azerbaijanis into the streets, but would inflame all of Soviet Central Asia. This was an ominous threat to the Kremlin, and many Soviet officials, for fear of opening up a Pandora's box, opposed any change in territorial arrangements in the Caucasus. Across the country, there were at least thirty-five significant territorial disputes; a change in one area was sure to invite pressures on other disputed territories, a nightmare for Moscow. Nonetheless, the Armenians were on the offensive, and on February 20, 1988, the regional soviet, or council, of Nagorno-Karabakh, dominated by Armenians, called for transferring the region to Armenian control. The Soviet Politburo immediately rejected and condemned this move as an "extremist" action. Yerevan reacted with an eruption of demonstrations more massive than the Soviet Union had seen since the Bolshevik Revolution. On February 25, between half a million and a million people assembled in downtown Yerevan, carrying banners that proclaimed KARABAKH IS PART OF AR-MENIA! and KARABAKH IS A TEST CASE FOR *PERESTROIKA*![14]

In Azerbaijan, emotions flamed out of control, and on February 27, a mob of young Azerbaijani toughs went on a bloody rampage against Armenians in Sumgait, a city about thirty miles from Baku. After three days of looting and murder, thirty-two people were dead, hundreds were wounded, and tens of thousands had fled for their lives.

When I visited Sumgait, Azerbaijani officials admitted to me that it is a breeding ground for violence—a tough industrial town with high unemployment, inadequate housing, terrible pollution from thirty-two chemical plants and other heavy industry, and what officials called "criminal elements"—meaning ex-convicts legally barred from living in Baku.[15]

On each of the three terrible days, Azerbaijani rallies charged with emotion had been held in Lenin Square, in front of Sumgait City Hall, and city leaders took part. Armenian refugees told me later that the mobs had been sent out by official leaders in Sumgait to hunt Armenians. After the violence, Sumgait's mayor and Party boss were fired for incompetence, but their successors insisted to me that the old officials had not fomented the violence. They acknowledged that those officials had been slow and ineffective in controlling police and city authorities; but they contended that emotions had been fired up, not by local officials, but by the accusations of Azerbaijanis, who had come to Sumgait with stories of having been chased out of Armenia and Karabakh.[16]

The bloodbath in Sumgait changed the dynamics of the Karabakh dispute: It was a nightmare, publicized worldwide, and, in sharpening hostilities on both sides, it propelled both into an escalating cycle of violence.

In Sumgait, I talked with Azerbaijanis who had given shelter to terrified Armenians, and outside Yerevan, I talked with Armenian survivors, who described the carnage. One young woman, Irina Melkunyan, who had hidden for hours in a neighbor's bathtub, told of hearing the mob breaking down doors, hurling furniture out the windows, starting bonfires. She had married into a family in which five people, including her husband, were murdered: mother, father, daughter, and two sons.[17] A middle-aged woman, Asya Arakelyan, told me how she had tried to escape into the apartment of a Russian woman across the hall, but had been chased down by a gang wielding bicycle chains, knives, and hatchets.

"The Azerbaijanis came, all dressed in black," she said, trying to control her terror as she relived the trauma. "They went through every building, looking for Armenians and shouting slogans—'Death to Armenians,' 'We'll annihilate all the Armenians. Get them out of here.'

"They broke down our apartment door and my husband and I escaped. Our Russian neighbor took us to her place. They smashed and burned everything in our place, and then came, with a bullhorn, and told us to come out in the name of the law. I was close to the door and they hit me first with their crowbar. They grabbed me and started pulling me downstairs, outside, to the courtyard. They threw me down, ripped my dress, and started wildly beating me with anything they could lay their hands on. And those axes and knives—it was terrible. They had a big knife and they threatened to cut my head off. When I looked up, I understood they were about to kill me. So I raised my arm in self-defense, and they slashed open my arm with their huge knife."[18]

She showed me how she had shielded her head, exposing a terrible scar, nearly a foot long, a slice all across the soft flesh of her underarm. We were sitting knee-to-knee in a tiny room, and I could feel her begin to cry. When I reached out to comfort her, she seized my hand, telling me through her tears that the Azerbaijani mob, taking her for dead, had thrown a rug over her.

"Then they dumped some gasoline over my body and burned me," she said. "I didn't know that, right next to me, they had gone at my husband. They hacked him with an ax and burned his body. Practically next to me. Only I did not know it then."

She glanced at a nearby dresser, where she had a framed portrait of her husband, a nice-looking man in his fifties, dressed in a business suit. The sight of him was too much to bear. She broke into sobs, her body throbbing.

"I was there for hours, losing consciousness," she went on haltingly. "Rain started. It stopped the fire. . . . When I came to, it was dark. I was bleeding. My back was all burned. . . . Finally, my younger son came to me. 'Mama, Mama, what happened to you?' I lifted my head with difficulty and told him to run: 'Go away or else they will kill you.' He asked me not to move and went for an ambulance. There were Azerbaijani cars all around. He asked them to take him to the ambulance, but they wouldn't help. . . . Later, much later, the boy came back with a truck."

Considering it a miracle that Asya Arakelyan was alive, the Armenians called her the "Madonna" of Sumgait.

For some, the bloodbath at Sumgait was a modern reenactment of the Turkish massacre of 1915. A journalist named Armen Oganesyan, a trim, steely, violently passionate Armenian nationalist, said:

"If you know Armenian history, you should know that Armenians were always victims—always paying with their lives, with their lands, with their possessions, going through endless genocides, endless manslaughters, endless bloodshed." As Armen spoke, his brown eyes were burning. "Right now you see a so-called minigenocide, because Azerbaijanis are like Turks, and their pan-Turkic ideology sees Armenia as the big obstacle to their unity, to achieving the goals of pan-Turkism. People want to present all this as Christians against Muslims and vice versa. I have nothing against Islam, but when someone wants to use religious fanaticism as a political weapon, causing the death of children and old people, it becomes a crime."[19]

I saw Armen several times; he took me to other groups of refugees, showed me his articles about Sumgait, explained his desperate attempts to see justice done, seethed with raw fury that only a few minor punishments had been meted out against the Azerbaijani perpetrators. His pain was understandable, but to me he seemed a fanatic who was nursing and spreading hatred. Ashot Manucharyan was trying to turn the pain and passion of Karabakh toward reform, whereas Armen Oganesyan was turning it toward revenge. He said to me that his ethic was Old Testament: an eye for an eye.

Sadly, it was easy to find victims on the other side. By the summer of 1989, when I reached the Caucasus, about 200,000 Armenians had fled from Azerbaijan, and about 160,000 Azerbaijanis had fled from Armenia. Most of these Azerbaijani refugees were concentrated in Baku, where their anger fueled the already heightened tensions. There were still about 200,000 Armenians living in Azerbaijan, but virtually all of the Azerbaijanis cleared out of Armenia as a result of waves of Armenian violence and intimidation, especially in October and November 1988.

In a very plain Baku apartment, I talked with an Azerbaijani family, the Guliyevs, whose twenty-eight-year-old son, Magaran, had been attacked by Armenians in Massis, a city about twenty miles from Yerevan, and not far from their former village of Zangiler, where there had been periodic violence. By the family's account, Magaran Guliyev's murder was as brutal, savage, and cold-blooded as that of Asya Arakelyan's husband.

As tensions had risen in Armenia through the summer of 1988, the Guliyev family, like many Azerbaijanis, had begun preparing to move to Baku. Coming back from Baku, their older son, Magaran, was set upon at the Massis railroad station by Armenians, who attacked him and his uncle with hammers, axes, and screwdrivers.

"They were hiding, a group of them," Mrs. Guliyev said she was told by the uncle, who somehow survived. "My son got off the train and they attacked him and my brother. My brother fell down; they thought he was dead. So they beat my son, hammered him several times, and threw his body in some water [near the station]. It was sort of a swamp. A soldier found him, saw him still breathing, and brought him to the hospital. In three days, they called us from the hospital and said: 'There's a dead man here. Come and take him.' "

The victim's body was buried immediately, but after a couple of weeks his family decided to take his body with them to Azerbaijan, and they had his body exhumed. "There were many Armenians around, including the heads of the local militia, Babahanyan and Iskandaryan, and many soldiers," said Mushtur Guliyev, the surviving son. "They were all saying, 'All the Turks should be killed. . . . All the Azerbaijanis should be caught and killed this way—have their heads cut off.' "

The family was sitting around a rough wooden table in the courtyard of their apartment building—mother, father, brother, two sisters, wife, and small child. Their grief hung in the summer air, thick and heavy. The father, a gray-haired workman, was crying openly, as were the women.

"When I went to get my son's body, there was a militiaman, named Makhachiyan, who asked me: 'Why are you crying? Is this not enough for you? We should have annihilated all of your kind, as we did this one.' "[20]

THE EROSION OF COMMUNIST POWER

Along with the spasms of violence in Armenia and Azerbaijan, the drumbeat of guerrilla war was rising in Nagorno-Karabakh through 1988 and 1989—the planting of land mines, arson, villages blockading each other, strikes, ambushes, shoot-outs like that between the Hatfields and the McCoys. In November 1988, the Soviet army imposed martial law and a curfew in Yerevan and Baku, but several thousand troops could not keep the peace in the mountains of Karabakh. The death toll mounted, building ineluctably toward civil war.

First Gorbachev tried to ban the Karabakh Committee, then he cracked down, arresting its leaders in December 1988 and January 1989, and at the same time arresting the most outspoken Azerbaijani nationalists. But by mid-1989, he let these activists free, and there was an upsurge in nationalist activity in Armenia and Azerbaijan. In both capitals, the cancer of Karabakh was sapping the strength of the Communist Party, undermining the foundations of its rule.

Alarmed by the massive unrest in early 1988, Gorbachev had fired Party leaders in both republics and installed his own choices; but as Moscow temporized, satisfying neither the Armenians nor the Azerbaijanis, populist leaders took politics into their own hands. Party leaders were driven by the need to keep up with the masses in the streets. Under popular pressure, the Armenian Supreme Soviet declared Karabakh part of Armenia; the Azerbaijani parliament angrily rejected that move. In each capital, Party leaders were caught between Moscow's demands to control "extremists" and somehow pacify the new democratic activists, and the pressures of mass demands for justice—and victory—on Karabakh.

"I find myself in a very difficult situation," Suren Arutunyan, first party secretary of Armenia, confessed to me. "I have no right to intervene in the internal affairs of a neighboring republic, Azerbaijan. On the other hand, I have no moral right to remain indifferent. . . . A constructive solution must be found. Postponing a solution will do no good. You cannot keep one hundred seventy-five thousand Armenians living in Nagorno-Karabakh [apart from Armenia] by force. For seventy years, they have felt oppression. They have been humiliated as a nationality, unable to learn the history of their people, to study their language, artifically separated from the rest of their nation."[21]

Hotheads like Armen Oganesyan kept the pot boiling, fueling the passions of conflict. Moderates like Ashot Manucharyan sought to use popular pressures to persuade the government to accept democratic reforms, to clean up political and economic corruption, to protect the environment, to help the poor.

In July 1989, when I was there, Yerevan was in turmoil over daily reports that Azerbaijanis had blocked all the roads into Nagorno-Karabakh, an act of civil war. Each day brought rumors and reports of new casualties. Ashot led a group from the Karabakh Committee and the Armenian Supreme Soviet to a Yerevan City Council meeting; although he was not a council member, his popular following gave him clout in the corridors of government. Ashot directed his team like a congressional floor leader, from a seat on the aisle halfway back in the hall; others checked with him before going up to the podium. One colleague arrived from Karabakh, and Ashot counseled him not to inflame emotions in the hall. Gradually, Ashot and his group took the political initiative away from the mayor and Party leaders, bargaining for a resolution appealing for immediate action from Moscow to lift the road blockade, and chiding the Communist Party for doing too little.

Suren Arutunyan, the Armenian Party leader, admitted to me that the Party faced a "crisis of trust" in Armenia; the damage had been done, he said, over many years. Arutunyan was Gorbachev's man, part of Gorbachev's new generation of reformers; for several years he had worked in Moscow under Aleksandr Yakovlev, a principal architect of Gorbachev's reforms.

"To be candid, in our republic, the Communist Party and Soviet bodies have lost a good part of their authority," Arutunyan conceded during a long conversation in his large, well-furnished office. "Our people have great doubts about our capabilities. . . . In the early stages of *perestroika*, we underestimated the severity of our interethnic problems. . . . I tell you honestly, the overwhelming majority of our political leaders were not prepared to meet the problems which we now face. Our personalities were formed under quite different conditions. Very abruptly, everything has changed."

Arutunyan echoed Gorbachev's impatience with the inability of the Party Old Guard to adapt. "I am especially indignant when Party officials, who are called to lead *perestroika*, drag behind events," he said. "I'm quite critical of my own performance. . . . It is hard to find new people. Each new appointment is real torture for me, because our resources are so limited."22

In his late forties, his hair prematurely silver, Arutunyan was a good deal more modern-minded than Party leaders in Central Asia. He was opening contacts with reformers and intellectuals; shortly before our get-together, he had gone for a meeting with Yerevan University students, and wound up enduring an unprecedented five-hour question-and-answer session. His own children were university age: His twenty-three-year-old daughter was studying at Yerevan University, and his nineteen-year-old son was doing his compulsory two years of military service with the KGB border troops. I asked Arutunyan if he had trouble keeping up with the thinking of the younger generation.

"My son's thinking is more modern, more flexible than mine," he replied. "When I talk with him, I can't help feeling like a conservative. And that's not easy for me to admit."

Very unusual for a Soviet Communist leader in his openness, he offered to introduce me to his family, and when I returned to Yerevan a month later, he invited me, my wife, Susan, and our film crew to dinner. He was living in an elaborate government guest house, guarded and behind walls. The family were very gracious; Arutunyan's wife and daughter were dressed for a party, while his son, more informal, wore slacks and a short-sleeved shirt. The boy had his father's self-confidence and directness.

I asked him if the student generation regarded the Karabakh Committee, an obvious challenge to his father, as important.

"Yes, very important," he said. "And the students trust them."

"More than you trust the older generation?" I asked. "More than you trust your parents?"

"You mean my father?" he asked, raising an eyebrow. "I can tell you that the chasm that opened during the [Brezhnev] period of stagnation between the leaders and the people is very hard to overcome. You see, there is *still* mistrust of the leadership."

"During the period of stagnation," Arutunyan interjected, trying to correct his son and deflect the criticism.

But the son stood his ground.

"Before, and now, over all these years," the young man insisted. "We cannot take for granted anything our leadership says. But the Karabakh Committee represents the people."

Arutunyan smiled gamely, and after his son's obvious put-down, he lectured the young man and me.

"Don't idealize the Karabakh Committee," he advised. "I don't fully share some of my children's views here. The committee people aren't always right, due to their political inexperience. . . . But we must engage in the widest possible dialogue with these informal organizations. We must cooperate with them and make compromises."

"You know, there's a member of the committee named Ashot Manucharyan," I said. "Can you work with him or not?"

"What do you mean, 'can or cannot'?" Arutunyan shot back. "We invited him [to meet with us], and he made a lot of remarks and proposals at our session. We have no choice. We have to work with him."[23]

The willingness of a Communist Party leader to work with a grass-roots leader, especially one recently released from a KGB prison, was an indication both of these extraordinary times in the Soviet Union, and also of how compelled Arutunyan felt to combine forces with genuine populists in order to regain the popular following the Communist Party had lost.

"For the first time in my professional life," he said to me, "I have discovered the genuine power of the masses. Sure, theoretically I knew it was there. I read Marx and Lenin and other theorists. But now I see that history is really only created by the masses."[24]

Arutunyan was pursuing an intelligent strategy: seeing Ashot Manucharyan as an ally against the escalation of violence. Even as the Yerevan City Council meeting was droning on that afternoon, emotions over the blockade of Karabakh spilled out into the streets. Thirty or forty thousand people gathered below the hilltop where the Matenadaran Library was situated. Other speakers whipped up popular feelings, but Ashot warned against being "dragged again into this dirty game of bloodshed.

"We are not talking about secession from the Soviet Union, about political separation," he told the crowd. "We are talking about our future as a nation. Today it is very important to understand whether our way is right, whether this city really belongs to us, whether this country really belongs to our people. All these things should become a reality at last. And for us, there is no turning back."²⁵

PRIVATE ARMS, PRIVATE ARMIES

Gorbachev, stuck between past policy and his present preachings, equivocated on Nagorno-Karabakh. He satisfied neither Armenia nor Azerbaijan nor Nagorno-Karabakh, thereby ensuring a steady crescendo of violence. Past policy dictated that no Soviet borders could be changed for fear of setting a dangerous precedent; Gorbachev's new politics of *glasnost* and democratization proclaimed the goal of self-government and self-determination, which is what the Armenians in Karabakh desperately wanted: a referendum to decide their own future. But it was also a step sure to inflame the Azerbaijanis.

Gorbachev took a middle course. In January 1989, on the advice of the famous physicist-democrat Andrei Sakharov, he suspended the powers of the two political bodies that had been at loggerheads in Karabakh—the Azerbaijan republic's overall control of Karabakh, and the local, Armenian-dominated provincial council—and he put the province of Nagorno-Karabakh under Moscow's direct rule. In the short run, that cooled Armenian hotheads, but as time dragged on, it placated no one. The Armenians still wanted Karabakh joined to their republic; the Azerbaijanis demanded its return to their control. Moscow was caught in between, fearful of disappointing the Armenians with their influential foreign communities in Paris, Los Angeles, and throughout the Middle East and Europe, but also afraid of angering the Azerbaijanis, and the Muslim peoples of Central Asia and the world at large.

"Applying self-determination would cause a bloody explosion in Azerbaijan—a great, bloody explosion," said Leonid Dobrokhotov, a Central Committee official familiar with the leadership's thinking. "In Armenia, the tension is also rising. There's no radical decision that can be taken. This problem is like Northern Ireland or Lebanon. These problems go on and on. If we satisfy one side, the other will explode."²⁶

The price for Gorbachev of neither resolving the problem nor halting the violence was terrible. There was a flow of almost daily casualties and unending criticism of Moscow; and people lost confidence in the central government's ability to protect its citizens. Gorbachev was leaving people to their own devices, implicitly encouraging Soviet citizens to take law and order into their own hands.

There was a wider, more dangerous lesson in the conflict in the Caucasus too: that in a multinational empire organized along the lines of ethnic republics, roughly sixty-three million Soviet citizens were living outside the frontiers of their own national republics; they were ethnic minorities, living in regions dominated by and legally under the control of other nationalities, who might turn on them. Roughly half of these people were Russians; the other half were Uzbeks living in Kirghizia, Meskhetians living in Uzbekistan and Kazakhstan, Armenians and Azerbaijanis living in each other's republics—in each case victims of mass violence during the Gorbachev years. From 1987 to 1990, the death toll from periodic violence by ethnic majorities against local minorities rose into the hundreds.

In recent years, the volume of arms in private hands has grown astonishingly in the Soviet Union. By one Soviet estimate, there were at least fifteen to seventeen million unregistered guns in the nation in 1989,[27] and Paul Goble, an American specialist on Soviet nationality problems, estimated the figure to be more like thirty to forty million.[28] According to another account, there is a black market in guns in almost every major Soviet city, with virtually any item from the Soviet military inventory on sale. In Odessa, "fifty to eighty rubles will buy a grenade, five hundred to eight hundred rubles will buy a pistol. Add two hundred rubles for ammunition." Ports and border areas are reported to offer foreign firearms. In Baku, a visiting American scholar was told that American M-16's were for sale at the city's "midnight market."[29] As the conflict escalated in the Caucasus in late 1989, whole carloads of weapons disappeared from military stocks into the hands of guerrilla armies.

Under the pressures of rising conflict and public tension, the unraveling of Communist authority was even more dramatic in Azerbaijan than in Armenia. When I was in Baku in mid-July 1989, an Azerbaijani Popular Front was just about to organize formally and to marshal mass support. Toward the end of 1988, a group of Baku intellectuals had started to set up a democratic-style popular front, similar to those in other republics, to promote Gorbachev's political and social reforms. A familiar combination of cultural and religious repression, economic discontent, environmental pollution, anger at a corrupt local leadership, and a sense of colonial exploitation [Moscow's buying oil from Baku at a small fraction of the world market price] all provided fertile soil for a grass-roots movement. In late June 1989, some of the most extreme nationalists, arrested six months earlier, were released from prison.[30] Close to 160,000 Azerbaijani refugees from Armenia had concentrated in and around Baku, many without jobs and adequate housing, a festering mass of discontent. Azerbaijani workers were riled by their own grievances, as well as by the Karabakh issue. These forces fused into an explosive combination once the Azerbaijani Popular Front was formally proclaimed on July 17, 1989.

Far more rapidly than any other mass movement in the Soviet Union, the Azerbaijani Popular Front shot from obscurity into having a hammer-lock on power. Within two months, it was dictating terms on Karabakh and on Azerbaijani sovereignty to the Communist Party hierarchy. Its leverage came from the emotional fission created by the Karabakh issue, the mass of unemployed refugees in Baku, and its declaration of an economic blockade of Armenia proper as well as of Nagorno-Karabakh. Initially, Communist Party leader Abdur Rahman Vezirov had refused to recognize the front, disparaging its leaders as hooligans and extremists and ignoring its demands—that the military curfew imposed by the Soviet army be lifted; that there be immediate general elections, economic sovereignty for the republic, and restoration of full Azerbaijani administrative control of Nagorno-Karabakh.[31]

"Moscow has to take a hard line against Armenians," a front leader, Abdulfaz Aliyev, declared. "They have not found a solution and are only trying to please the Armenians. Innocent people are suffering in that region [Karabakh] the way the situation is now."[32] Later, Aliyev added: "We simply will not relent on this issue. It is our land, and that is that."[33]

Beginning in late August, the front showed its muscle with a string of mass demonstrations and labor strikes; a two-day general strike in August closed sixty enterprises. But its most menacing display of raw power was the stranglehold it clamped on the entire republic of Armenia.

On September 4, 1989, the front announced that it was imposing a total road and railroad blockade on Armenia to force the national government to return Karabakh to Azerbaijani rule. Armenia was especially vulnerable: Its trunk lines from the rest of the country ran through Azerbaijan, bringing in 85 percent of its freight. My Armenian contacts said that rail traffic had been squeezed since mid-July, but the situation became acute in the fall. The Armenian economy nearly came to a halt: There was no gasoline for private cars, transport, or farming, and the fall harvesting came to a stop. Ambulances and the militia were put on minimum rations.

Because of the lack of grain, the bread shortage became acute; no outside food supplies were getting through. Armenian farmers were killing their livestock because they did not have enough fodder to keep the animals alive. All kinds of goods stacked up on the rail lines, even housing materials and supplies for the victims of the Armenian earthquake. The

Soviet press reported that about four hundred trains with sixty thousand cars were idle.[34]

By mid-September Gorbachev's hand-picked Communist Party leader Vezirov bowed to the front's pressures and agreed, in effect, to share power. On September 13, he signed a "protocol" with Azerbaijani Popular Front leaders, accepting most of their demands, including the demand for a special session of the Azerbaijani Supreme Soviet, to pass a law on sovereignty, in which the republic reserved the right to defy federal authority and reaffirmed its constitutional right to secede. The law was passed ten days later.

"We don't advocate leaving the Soviet Union," said one director of the front, Nadzhaf Nadzhafov. "Our position is that if the conditions are right, we can live in the Soviet Union. But if the conditions are not right, that clause on secession would be our last resort."[35]

In return for concessions, the front was supposed to lift the rail embargo, but it did not. At a critical Communist Party Central Committee meeting in Moscow on September 19, Gorbachev not only thundered his disapproval at Baltic talk of secession, but he gave the Azerbaijanis, without naming them, an ultimatum. "Where a threat has arisen to the safety and lives of the people, we will act decisively, using the full force of Soviet laws," he declared.[36] Effectively, the Kremlin gave the Azerbaijanis forty-eight hours to back down. But they were not intimated and, inexplicably, Gorbachev did not follow through on his threat. The rail blockade continued until October 11, when the Azerbaijanis suspended it on condition that Moscow dissolve its special government committee for Karabakh. Moscow did not act, and the blockade was immediately reimposed—and extended to Soviet Georgia, because the Georgians had refused to collaborate with the Azerbaijanis. The Armenians accused Moscow of intentionally letting the blockade continue so as to bring Armenia to its knees. But the rest of the country was suffering too: The Soviet press reported that more than one million tons of freight, food, and supplies transiting the Caucasus for other places in the country were blocked.

By early October, military combat in and around Karabakh had escalated to undeclared civil war, between what amounted to private armies on both sides, equipped with weaponry provided to them by blood brothers inside the Soviet army. One senior Soviet official called the conflict "a homemade Lebanon," a bitter communal war that was drawing increasingly on combat-tested veterans of the Soviet war in Afghanistan, no longer amateurs armed with hunting weapons but troops trained by Moscow for heavy combat.[37] When a civilian helicopter from Armenia landed at Gadrut in Nagorno-Karabakh, inspectors found that it was carrying grenades, explosives, detonators, rifles, hunting weapons, gunpowder, parts for anti-aircraft weapons, and instructions for operating heavier weapons. The two sides had graduated from rifles and land mines to machine guns, anti-tank weapons, helicopters, armored cars, anti-aircraft guns. In one very graphic report in mid-October, Moscow television showed railroad engines with great gaping holes or mangled by anti-tank weapons. The deputy prime minister of Armenia complained that bridges were being blown up and there was "continuous strafing of trains."

On November 28, 1989, the government in Moscow yielded to the bloody, costly Azerbaijani stranglehold: With Armenian deputies boycotting the session, the all-union Supreme Soviet voted to end Moscow's direct rule over Nagorno-Karabakh and to return the disputed province to Azerbaijani control.

Rather than easing the situation, that decision seemed to exacerbate tensions. Armenia's Supreme Soviet defiantly proclaimed a United Republic of Armenia, embracing Karabakh and even including it in the 1990 Armenian budget. The rail blockade eased, off and on, but killings, sabotage, and kidnappings continued sporadically until the next terrible explosion, on January 13, 1990, in Baku.

In a bloody echo of the carnage at Sumgait, mobs of Azerbaijanis, many of them the unemployed refugees massed in Baku, went on another anti-Armenian rampage. A state of emergency was declared, but Azerbaijanis told me that they saw violence take place in the presence of Soviet troops; apparently the force occupying Baku, eleven thousand army and national-police troops, did not intervene during the three days of the anti-Armenian pogrom.

Only a week later, *after* the violence had subsided because virtually all of the Armenians in the city had fled, did Gorbachev send twelve thousand more troops into Baku to quell the Azerbaijani nationalists. The films I saw of that operation, which took place overnight on January 19–20, showed a brutal, overpowering assault: tanks and armored personnel carriers spraying apartment buildings with gunfire, tracers fired back from Azerbaijani snipers on rooftops, civilian buses riddled with machine gunfire, rows of passengers slumped against the windows, forever motionless. Some top leaders of the Azerbaijani Popular Front were arrested. More than one hundred Azerbaijanis were killed, and a million people turned out two days later to mourn them and denounce Gorbachev.

Gorbachev's crackdown turned the rage of Azerbaijan against the Russians, for it was Russian troops who had invaded. Elmira Kafarova, chairman of the Azerbaijani Supreme Soviet, condemned the Soviet action as "a gross violation of Azerbaijani sovereignty" and vowed that "the Azerbaijani people will never forgive anyone for the tragic way their sons and daughters have been killed."[38] The Azerbaijani Supreme Soviet demanded the withdrawal of Soviet forces within forty-eight hours. In Moscow, demonstrators outside the Defense Ministry carried banners saying: GORBACHEV HANGMAN, STOP THE TERROR IN BAKU; NO—TO OCCUPATION. In Baku, Azerbaijanis held rallies to burn their Communist Party cards. Even in Moscow, at the Supreme Soviet, Gorbachev came under fire for sending in the troops without consulting the national parliament.

Defense Minister Dmitri Yazov belatedly gave a political justification for the operation: The troops, he said, were sent into Baku "to destroy the organizational structure" of the Azerbaijani Popular Front, which, according to Yazov, was running a network of forty thousand armed militants who had been on the verge of overthrowing Soviet authorities in the region.[39] Indeed, front members had seized control of the police station and city offices in Lenkoran, near the Iranian border on the Caspian Sea, on January 11, and two days later, a huge demonstration in Baku had called for the ouster of the republic's Communist Party boss, Vezirov.[40] Gorbachev's delay in ordering troops into Baku was taken as evidence by Azerbaijanis that he had acted not for what the world took as the humanitarian motive of saving the Armenians but for the political motive of saving the Communist regime in Baku.

"In Baku, I have seen two kinds of assassinations," said Azerbaijani economist Rufat Novrozov, who works closely with Russian scholars at a prestigious institute in Moscow, but was in Baku during the events of January. "I saw many things, and it was a horror. First, the assassination of Armenians, then the assassination of Azerbaijanis. It was personal terrorism, then it was state terrorism, government terrorism."[41]

In the aftermath of the invasion, sensational evidence surfaced that Party and police hard-liners in Moscow and Baku may have been plotting a provocation to bring on Gorbachev's crackdown. According to a detailed account pieced together by Bill Keller of *The New York Times,* the police and KGB had advance knowledge that an anti-Armenian pogrom was in the making, but they did nothing to stop it; local Communist Party officials initiated the creation in January of an Azerbaijani paramilitary organization, the so-called National Defense Committee, in order to discredit the Azerbaijani Popular Front by making it appear more violent than it was, and Viktor Polyanichko, the second-ranking Communist Party leader in Azerbaijan—a Ukrainian, and Moscow's most trusted agent in Baku—had for a year or more encouraged Azerbaijanis to form a popular front. Once it was formed, he had tried to turn it toward a militant, chauvinistic direction, hoping to provoke violence and thereby justify Moscow's intervention with force.[42]

Azerbaijanis with whom I talked scoffed at Yazov's charge that the front was bent on toppling Communist rule. They insisted that all they wanted was a change in Party leadership and a democratic chance to compete for power; that they did not want to stage a coup d'état.

"Now we have a coup d'état," commented Novrozov, who is from the moderate wing of Azerbaijani nationalists. "There is no Azerbaijani state, no Azerbaijani government, no Azerbaijani leadership. Now, there is military power. . . . The Soviet invasion showed the real attitude of Moscow toward Azerbaijanis. Gorbachev would never do the same thing in the Baltic republics. Gorbachev wants to look like a democrat in Europe, in the world, and the Baltic republics have very close relations with European countries. . . . Their [Moscow's] relationship with Muslims is not the same. They think the Muslims are not clever people, but foolish, stupid people, and only Russia can be the leader of this nation. . . . I think that Russia, the Soviet Union, has lost Azerbaijan forever. . . . People will never forget the crime in Baku."[43]

Huge Soviet occupying forces have settled into a long, sullen occupation to keep order in Baku and Yerevan, although there is periodic violence, especially in the hills of Nagorno-Karabakh. In late May 1990, Armenian nationalists clashed with a Soviet troop train arriving in Yerevan; the gun battle left twenty-two dead.[44] In late July, Gorbachev ordered all nationalist vigilante groups and armies to disband and surrender their arms within fifteen days; Vadim Bakatin, the Soviet minister for internal affairs, estimated that ten to twenty thousand Armenians were connected with illegally armed bands, and he said others had put the figure as high as one hundred thousand. Gorbachev's order met defiance from the Armenian Supreme Soviet, filled with nationalist supporters; the legislature rejected Gorbachev's proclamation on grounds that it "contradicts the Armenian people's natural right to self-defense," as well as the United Nations Charter.[45]

So the legacy of Gorbachev's policies in the Caucasus is a new hatred of the Russians and a turning away from Communist Party leaders. After the new nationalist coalition occupied public buildings in March, Suren Arutunyan was replaced as Armenian Party chief, evidently because the Kremlin felt he could not cope with the situation.[46] By August 1990, a forty-five-year-old leader of the Karabakh Committee, linguist Levan Ter-Petrosyan, was elected to the top post in the republic—chairman of the Armenian Supreme Soviet. Gorbachev agreed to turn over to Ter-Petrosyan the task of trying to collect arms from bands of armed Armenians—a sign of how far he had been forced to yield real power to grass-roots leaders.[47] For by the fall of 1990, Gorbachev was confronted with an Armenian government that had been elected on a platform of seeking independence. Nearly three years of frustrating protests had left the Armenian people suspicious that Mother Russia could no longer be counted on as Armenia's ultimate protector against the "Turks."

In Azerbaijan, only a few extremists had talked about secession in 1989 but a year later, well-educated, highly assimilated moderates such as Rufat Novrozov discussed it openly. Deep down, however, they seemed to want to stay in the Soviet Union, provided they were allowed to run Azerbaijan themselves, to revive their culture and their economy as they saw fit.

Only grudgingly did Gorbachev accede to demands for genuine home rule in Azerbaijan or Armenia. He refused to bend to the bloodletting of violent extremists on both sides, and it was unclear whether he would move far enough to satisfy more peaceful political radicals. Moreover, he dared not suspend martial law and military occupation in the Caucasus for fear that that would bring on full-fledged civil war.

CHAPTER 16

LITHUANIA: BREAKING THE TABOO OF SECESSION

"If the world accepts one country being oppressed by another country, using aggression to establish some unjust status quo, then violence will rule the world—not the principles of international law and justice."[1]

—Vytautas Landsbergis
Lithuanian Leader
July 1989

"There is no absolute freedom in this. We have embarked on this path, and I am the one who chose to go ahead with it. My own personal fate is linked to that choice. The two states [Lithuania and the U.S.S.R.] must live together."[2]

—Gorbachev, June 1990

The most insistent and menacing challenge to the unity and integrity of the Soviet state came, ironically, not from Central Asia with its fifty million Muslims, and not from the boiling civil war in the Caucasus, nor from the Ukraine, the second-largest of the Soviet republics. It came from tiny Lithuania.

It came not violently, but peacefully, and it came not from the implicit power of hundreds of thousands of people massing in the streets, nor from the terror of rampaging mobs, but from the very means that Gorbachev had chosen for political reform—the ballot box.

The confident, well-organized skill with which the Baltic national movements in Lithuania and neighboring Estonia and Latvia won elections not only demonstrated far greater political sophistication than that exhibited by national movements elsewhere in the Soviet Union, but gave political revolt in the Baltics a legitimacy that was impossible for Gorbachev to deny.

The first democratic victories in the Baltics actually produced what Gorbachev wanted: a dynamic new thrust for reform in the most economically and politically advanced region of the Soviet Union, the region he hoped would become the showcase and model for reform for the rest of the country. But the tempo of political change in the Baltics, sitting on the edge of Eastern Europe, was extremely swift, and soon the Baltic peoples, especially the Lithuanians, were pushing beyond the limits of Gorbachev's plans for reform. For in spite of preaching the gospel of democracy and self-determination, Gorbachev found the consequences unpalatable when Baltic nationalism veered toward independence, secession, and the breakup of the Soviet empire.

The first powerful jolt of the Baltic earthquake came in the election of March 26, 1989—the first free election in the Soviet Union in seven decades, and the first in the Baltic states since Stalin and the Red Army had annexed them in 1940. It was the nationwide election for Gorbachev's new parliament, the all-union Congress of People's Deputies.

With a camera crew, I watched the voting and interviewed people positively spilling over with enthusiasm for the new politics. For the first time in their lives, they were voting in elections that were not a charade. They had a choice, an alternative to the hand-picked Communist Party candidates: a slate of candidates from Sajudis, the Lithuanian nationalist movement.

"It is so different this time," one middle-aged worker told me. "Before, we voted just to get our names checked off. [Voting was compulsory.] I could cast [identical] ballots for my entire family, for my whole building. That's how it was before. But *today,* we're really electing. We're choosing the candidates we prefer."

Neither Lithuania nor any other part of the Soviet Union had electronic voting machines, so the ballot counting was slow. Preelection polling was unknown, and people were not even sure whether the count would be honest. In many parts of the country, the Party apparatus had blocked alternative candidates from running. But in Lithuania, Sajudis had developed a strong enough following to ensure a fair election. And besides, members of the Lithuanian media, many of them reformers, were watching the proceedings like hawks.

It was morning before the tally was complete, and a small crowd had gathered outside the modest old building in downtown Vilnius, the capital of Lithuania, where Sajudis had its second-story, walk-up office. The Baltic peoples, especially the Lithuanians, are cool and unflappable, accustomed to bearing disappointment and hardship stoically; they are rarely given to public exuberance. But this morning, there was excitement in the air.

When a Sajudis staff aide emerged to post the results of the election on a bulletin board, the crowd demanded that he call out the returns. And so, one by one, he read off the names of the Lithuanian government and Party officials who had always been rubber-stamped in past elections:

"Chairman of the Supreme Soviet—defeated."

The crowd let out a whoop.

"Chairman of the Council of Ministers—defeated."

Cries of "Look at that!"

"Secretary of the Communist Party—defeated."

More cheers.

"Another secretary of the Communist Party—defeated."

Shouts of approval.

And so on down the line: deputy prime ministers, the head of the Lithuanian Gosplan, the Communist leader of Vilnius, a particularly unpopular Stalinist leader of one city district, the head of a pro-Russian movement opposing Sajudis—one big name after another, beaten by political newcomers.

In an incredible sweep, Sajudis, which had held its founding congress only five months earlier, in October, had won thirty-one out of forty-two seats; eight were still to be contested in runoffs, and in that second round, Sajudis won all eight. So Sajudis finally emerged with thirty-nine out of Lithuania's forty-two deputies.

Because these elections were for seats in the new all-union parliament in Moscow, not for posts in the Lithuanian government itself, government and Party officials in Lithuania had not been literally thrown out of their jobs; the Communist Party still held official power.

But the Communist Party had been thoroughly rejected and discredited. Political upheaval in Lithuania was running *ahead* of what turned out to be the dramatic unraveling of Communist power in Eastern Europe that took place in the fall of 1989. The unofficial opposition—Sajudis— had overwhelmed the Soviet Communist Party in Lithuania as convincingly as Solidarity, the Polish labor movement, would defeat the Polish Communist Party three months later.

No one, not even the optimists in Sajudis, had expected such a stunning victory. Without actually controlling the Lithuanian government, Sajudis could now drive the political agenda as the recognized voice of the people in Lithuania.

The crowd on the sidewalk was jubilant beyond words, and incredulous.

"It's wonderful . . . it's wonderful," a man with a lush red beard kept repeating, like a small boy who has just opened a Christmas present that exceeds his wildest imagination.

"This means we will live with hope," said a broad-faced grandmother in a mohair hat, tears welling up in her eyes. "We trust Sajudis."

"Down with the Stalinists—that's what it means," said a burly man with a mustache.

"Sajudis stands for the sovereignty of Lithuania," the grandmother insisted, "for economic and political sovereignty—the end of occupation."[3]

THE TRADE SECRET OF A SOVIET EDITOR

In the Lithuanian language, *sajudis* means a spontaneous "coming together," a meeting of the minds as well as a social coalescing. That literally is what happened in the case of the Lithuanian nationalist movement.

Sajudis had emerged, in the summer of 1988, simultaneously with popular-front movements in the neighboring Baltic republics of Estonia and Latvia. All three had developed more swiftly than nationalist movements elsewhere in the Soviet Union. Their strategy had been shrewd: Forming themselves as broad umbrella organizations, they had invited all to join, welcoming Communists as well as anti-Communists, and all nationalities. They were also careful not to call themselves political parties or to define themselves as the official opposition, even though in time that is how they came to function. And the Baltic popular fronts had presented themselves as champions of *perestroika,* as allies of Gorbachev and Gorbachev-style reformers in the battle against the Party's Old Guard.

When I asked why politics were moving so much faster in the Baltics than elsewhere in the Soviet Union, people would say, "Because we're more European than the others."

Lithuanians, Latvians, and Estonians see themselves as part of Europe and of European culture. Not only are they geographically close to Germany, Poland, and Scandinavia, but they are more attuned to the politics of self-determination than are the Slavic peoples of Russia and the Ukraine, or the Turkic peoples of Central Asia. They are more inclined to look Westward than inward.

In the seventies, when my Moscow friends traveled to the Baltics, a favorite region for vacationing and shopping, they would say they were "going West," because the Baltics had a higher standard of living, more interesting art and fashions, and a Western feel to the architecture of their cities and to their manners and attitudes. In the Baltics, Muscovites felt they could escape the drabness of Soviet life; they could find an Old World charm in the cobbled streets of Tallinn in Estonia, Vilnius and Kaunas in Lithuania, and Riga in Latvia. The green, rolling countryside reminded me of the American Midwest: tree-lined fields dotted with solid, well-kept individual farms, or *khuttors,* as they are known in the region, instead of the clustered, log-cabin villages of the Russian heartland.

It is this European spirit, this European atmosphere, and this dream of being once again a part of Europe that has given special thrust to the Baltic movement for independence.

In politics and economics, the Balts look askance at the Russians, with their long centuries of authoritarian rule, their submission to the czar, to "the center," as the heart of Communist power in Moscow is colloquially known.

"The Russians do not understand what is happening here," Arvydas Juozaitis, a Lithuanian political scientist and a young leader in Sajudis, told me on Election Day. "We have information that Gorbachev and others in the Politburo think of Sajudis as a shadow of the Lithuanian Communist Party. They cannot conceive of a grass-roots movement actually starting from below. They see reform as coming from above. They have a primitive political culture."[4]

Intellectuals in the Baltic republics point with pride and nostalgia to their period of political independence, from 1918 to the Stalinist conquest in 1940. Lithuanians treat this period as a golden age of Baltic democracy, overlooking the fact that the final thirteen years of this period were characterized by single-party, hard-line, right-wing rule.

Through most of their history, Estonia and Latvia, often known together as Livonia, had fallen under foreign rule: by Denmark, by the Teutonic Knights from what became known as Prussia, then by Sweden, and finally by Russia's Peter the Great. Lithuania had a more independent tradition; in 1321, under Grand Duke Vytautas Gediminas, Lithuania conquered all of Byelorussia and half of the Ukraine, including Kiev and reaching down to the shores of the Black Sea. Gediminas's son linked

Lithuania to Poland, a union that lasted for three centuries. When Poland was carved up in 1795, Lithuania fell under czarist Russia. So Baltic independence has been episodic, but the last episode, the twenty-two years of independence between the world wars, has been a catalyst to the new nationalist fervor.

In the 1989 elections, Sajudis was the most dramatically successful of the three Baltic movements, partly because it was the most cohesive and best organized, but also because Lithuanians more clearly dominate their republic demographically than Estonians and Latvians do theirs.

After World War II, Stalin deliberately watered down the ethnic purity of the Baltics, sending in waves of ethnic Russian settlers, and two other Slavic peoples, Ukrainians and Byelorussians, to work in newly built Soviet factories there; the Baltic states sit astride a natural invasion route to Russia, and Stalin considered the Slavs more politically dependable than the Balts. By 1989, Latvians comprised only 52 percent of their republic's population of 2.7 million; Estonians 61 percent of Estonia's 1.6 million people; and Lithuanians 80 percent of Lithuania's 3.7 million.[5]

As small nationalities, the Balts felt especially vulnerable to this immigration of Russians and other Slavs, and feared extinction as peoples. And it was this fear that won their nationalist movements near-universal support among their own communities.

The Estonian Popular Front was the first in the Soviet Union to develop a master plan for its republic's economic autonomy. And in November 1988, it was the first to push a declaration of sovereignty through its parliament: Estonian laws were to take precedence over Soviet laws; no law passed in Moscow would have force unless it was confirmed by Estonia. By acceding to this daring measure, the Estonian Communist Party leadership maintained public credibility at a time of nationalist fervor, and that credibility helped it to contain the political challenge posed by the Estonian Popular Front.

In Lithuania, a parallel move was blocked and postponed by the Communist leadership under Algirdas Brazauskas. So there, the Communist Party won a temporary victory, but it cost the Party popularity, and would contribute to its downfall in the 1989 elections. And if Sajudis was temporarily defeated on this issue, it nevertheless won a string of other victories: the declaration of Lithuanian as the official language of the republic, the resurrection of the national flag and anthem from the independence period, and publication of a political program calling for a "neutral, independent, and demilitarized Lithuania," though acknowledging that secession was a theoretical goal.

In 1989, for the first time under Soviet rule, Lithuania openly celebrated the anniversary of its independence, February 16, 1918. Two hundred thousand people gathered in Kaunas to witness the restoration of the Liberty statue in Unity Square. Vincentas Cardinal Sladkevičius, who had been exiled from Kaunas for thirty-three years, made a radical call for Lithuanian independence, and Brazauskas, first secretary of the republic's Communist Party, had come around enough to declare that "Lithuania without sovereignty is Lithuania without a future."[6]

It was a far cry from the Lithuania of the seventies. Even in the Brezhnev era, there had been Lithuanian political protests: In 1972, when I was visiting, two young men had burned themselves to death and seventeen thousand Lithuanians had signed a petition to United Nations Secretary General Kurt Waldheim, charging religious repression by Soviet authorities. As always in Lithuania, religion and nationalism were intertwined, and the Communist press warned of the danger of "religious fanaticism."[7]

On a trip to Vilnius, I had wanted to attend and photograph a Sunday mass, to see who dared take part in religious services. I wondered whether it was only the old, or was it also younger people. The main cathedral was closed, but other churches were functioning, and I had inquired at my hotel about how to get to a service. Saturday evening, I went out to dinner, leaving my camera inside my locked suitcase. The next morning, I found the camera still inside the locked suitcase, but the lens had been smashed, hit with a blunt instrument in several places. Obviously, the authorities did not want more publicity about Catholic activism in Lithuania.

And now, in February 1989, the Communist Party leader was sharing the same platform with the long-exiled Catholic cardinal.

In addition to Sajudis's election sweep, what impressed me more than anything else, on my return to Lithuania in 1989, was the Sajudis newspaper: Its circulation was one hundred thousand. In a country where the Communist Party jealously controlled the press, I found it remarkable that any other political movement could have a weekly newspaper with such a large readership. The openness of the paper, the topics it raised, its defiance of Moscow and of local Communist Party leaders, indeed its continued existence, marked Sajudis apart from the other national movements I had seen.

"If we had enough newsprint, we could sell three hundred thousand," said the editor, Romouldas Ozolas. "But we can't get enough paper."[8]

By profession, Ozolas is a philosophy professor at Vilnius University. He was one of the founders of Sajudis, and is a member of its inner leadership, but he was quick to admit, "We are not politicians—we are amateurs. We still have to grow local politicians. So far we don't have any, because you cannot call [Communist] ideologues politicians."

Slender, angular, and outspoken, Ozolas is a quick-witted scholar who enjoys the game of politics. Experience editing a stuffy academic journal had won him the post of chief editor of what quickly became the most popular newspaper in Lithuania—*Atgimimas,* which means "Renaissance" or "Rebirth." Even its Russian-language edition had a circulation of thirty thousand; and all across the republic, it spawned fifty smaller, local imitations.

"Our movement could not exist without our newspaper," Ozolas told me. "Our one hour of Sajudis on television is a big help. But our people have great faith in the printed word, a strong tradition of reading, especially the older people. It is the press that really unites the people."[9]

When the first issue of *Atgimimas* appeared on September 16, 1988, the authorities did not bother to censor it. In the spirit of *glasnost* and Lithuanian nationalism, they let it have newsprint and access to the Communist Party printing plant. Two months later, after the paper had attacked the Lithuanian parliament as "an autocracy" that violated the new spirit of democracy by refusing to pass a declaration of Lithuanian sovereignty, the Communist leadership imposed censorship. Hard-liners began harassing the newspaper, denying it use of the Party printing plant (despite the fact that Ozolas was a member of the Politburo) and trying to cut off its paper supply. Conservatives in Moscow wanted *Atgimimas* shut down.

"They called all our suppliers, their paper factories in Russia, and now nobody wants to sell us paper, even though we are prepared to pay triple the normal price," Ozolas told me. "I do not know what we will do. Newsprint is their way of backing us into a corner."[10]

By July 1989, simply getting out each issue had become Ozolas's biggest headache. Printing the paper at a book-publishing house had become erratic; issues came out two and three weeks late, often stacked up one behind another. As Ozolas found new sources of newsprint, Moscow tracked them down and choked them off. It was political trench warfare.

Still, I saw people reading fresh issues of *Atgimimas;* and despite censorship, it was still raising the most explosive issues—Soviet military occupation, the secret protocols of the Hitler-Stalin pact under which Stalin occupied the Baltic states, questions of economic and political sovereignty.

Knowing the power of "the center" in this highly centralized economy, I asked Ozolas how he managed to get paper.

"We have so-called socialist entrepreneurship, which means the possibility for organizations to make direct barter deals," he replied. "We're ready to pay for paper with beef, or, let's say, with bricks."

An echo of the cooperatives: Bricks and beef were in short supply, and therefore worth more than money—worth enough to entice some Soviet paper factory into supplying contraband newsprint to political radicals in Lithuania.

"But," I asked, "where does an editor-in-chief lay his hands on beef or bricks to exchange for newsprint?"

A smile crossed Ozolas's face: "This is the trade secret of a Soviet editor-in-chief."[11]

DON'T CROSS THE "RED LINES"

The man who felt the brunt of the Sajudis political offensive, and who was reeling from the movement's election sweep in March 1989, was Algirdas Brazauskas, Lithuania's Communist Party leader, a Gorbachev-style reformer and an experienced Party official with a popular touch.

I found Brazauskas an unusually agile politician, especially for a Party leader. He had been installed by Gorbachev in October 1988 after he had dared to appear at nationalist rallies that his Old Guard predecessor had tried to suppress. Like Gorbachev in Moscow, Brazauskas was trying to readjust Party policy to the rapidly changing popular mood. In November 1988, he had blocked the parliamentary move to make Lithuanian laws supreme over Soviet laws; a few months later, he recognized this as a tactical mistake and shifted his position.

Brazauskas looks as immovable as a Notre Dame fullback. He is a handsome blond heavyweight who had been an Olympic sailor and a track athlete in his youth and is still athletic in his fifties. His personal warmth, easy approachability, willingness to admit the Party's past mistakes, and instinct for moderation made him popular among ordinary Lithuanians, and Russians living in Lithuania saw him as their protector. Moscow saw him as its anchor at a time of rapidly shifting tides. Ardent nationalists had no use for him, because he was a Communist, but the more pragmatic wing of Sajudis saw Brazauskas as a useful buffer, a go-between for them with the Kremlin, until they had built up enough strength to take over power, and negotiate for themselves.

I came to see the political evolution of Algirdas Brazauskas as symbolic of Lithuania's move toward independence.

I met Brazauskas on the morning after the Communist Party's electoral defeat in 1989. The leaders of Sajudis had cannily left Brazauskas and his like-minded deputy, Vladimir Beryozov, without challengers, sensing that if they were beaten, the Kremlin would replace them with hard-liners. So Brazauskas had been spared personal humiliation. Still, he was stung by the Party's defeat, and I was frankly impressed that in such circumstances he had enough grit and poise to do an on-camera interview with an American correspondent.

Months later, Brazauskas admitted to me that the election debacle had been his darkest moment, but on the morning after, he was gamely trying to maintain a facade of confidence, although he allowed that the pace of change baffled him.

"Just a year ago, it was difficult to imagine that such things could happen in our republic," he said. "It all started only eight months ago."

I asked him if the election had not indicated the Party's loss of public trust, its control of events.

"Yes," he replied candidly. "I would say it means *perestroika* should speed up its tempo. People want to see faster results. . . . We should speed the creation of a state governed by law. We should speed up economic reform."

At one point, Brazauskas tried to draw some comfort from the convenient fiction that Sajudis was not calling itself a political party. But later he conceded, "We do have a political opposition, but I don't see any tragedy in that. We have to learn democracy."

On the most crucial issues, however, Brazauskas sounded Moscow's line. I asked him what he had meant by his very nationalist-sounding comment a few weeks earlier that Lithuania without sovereignty was Lithuania without a future.

"I meant that as part of the Union family of republics, each republic should have its own political sovereignty, its own constitution, system of law, system of education, cultural life," he said. "Independence means that a self-sustaining republican [economic] system should be established, that our republic's economy should . . . [set our own] prices, system of payment, our national budget."

In short, he was in favor of Lithuanian autonomy *within* the Soviet Union. And he had limits—what he called "red lines"—that could not be crossed.

"We can join [Sajudis] up to a certain point," he said, "but if someone speaks about leaving the Soviet Union, that would be considered stepping over the line. . . . Sovereignty within the Soviet Union—this is the only realistic sovereignty we can think of, considering how our economy is integrated into the framework of the Soviet Union."

Other steps that he rejected, other red lines, were "an independent currency, or withdrawal of Soviet troops from the territory of Lithuania."[12]

Nonetheless, while Brazauskas held the formal reins of power, he clearly understood that Sajudis was setting the agenda, and pushing the pace of change. He saw that he could govern only by forging a partnership with the moderate wing of Sajudis, and in fact he had met with their leaders just before he saw me. He was being pulled along by events, but he was desperately trying to set limits, to slow the pace, to avoid a fateful collision with Moscow.

At that stage, even the leaders of Sajudis were being coy about their ultimate goals. Like Brazauskas, most of them talked about "sovereignty," implying autonomy within the Soviet Union, rather than about "independence," meaning secession. For some, this was a matter of conviction; for others, it was a tactical movement.

"Are you for staying in the union or are you against that?" I asked Ozolas.

"This question is like asking whether God exists or not," he parried.

"Oh my God," I groaned. "This is life, not metaphysics."

"Well," he answered, "what I am trying to say is that there is no nation in the world that would willingly give up its independence. But to call for that now, when one can be decapitated for that very comment, would be politically unwise."[13]

GUDRI LAPÉ—"THE CLEVER FOX"

When I returned to Vilnius three months later, in June, and again in July, the tempo had quickened; Lithuanian nationalism had gained new momentum. The democratic mood was so much further advanced than it was in other parts of the Soviet Union that coming to Lithuania was like coming to another country. Talk of independence was in the air; Ozolas was no longer worried about being "decapitated" for discussing secession. The Lithuanian parliament had passed a sovereignty law giving it veto power over Soviet laws; it had proclaimed that all property in its territory should be Lithuanian, not Soviet. In Moscow, people were still arguing over the one-party system, but in Lithuania there was already a Democratic party, a Peasant party, a Christian Democratic party, an Independence League.

In one of the most dramatic developments, the Lithuanian Komsomol, or Young Communist League, made up of young people from high school to age thirty-five, severed its ties with Moscow in mid-June and declared itself an independent organization. To Lithuanians, this was an important symbolic break, a harbinger of things to come. My contacts at Lithuanian television, Audrius Braukyla and Algis Jacobinas, said that, as the Communist Party's youth arm, the Komsomol would not have acted without some encouragement from the Party itself. In defiance of Moscow officials who had come to impose the Soviet line, the Lithuanian Komsomol had renounced Marxism-Leninism as its official doctrine, endorsed freedom of conscience, admitted Catholic believers, and passed a program calling for Lithuania's becoming an "independent democratic state outside the Soviet Union."

There were many other straws in the wind. The Catholic Church now had a regular Sunday-morning slot on weekly television and had won official recognition of twelve holidays. Schoolboys were quitting the Communist Young Pioneers to join the Boy Scouts, which had just been reestablished. Lithuanians had formed their own Olympic Committee, and wanted to send a separate team to the 1992 games.

In dozens of ways, large and small, Lithuanians celebrated the rebirth of their national spirit. On June 24, St. John's Eve, Lithuanians outside of Kaunas sang and danced the whole night through, around a bonfire in the traditional pagan Festival of the Dew; for four decades this celebration had been banned by Communist authorities as a dangerous public gathering. In major towns and cities, statues and monuments commemorating pre-Communist heroes were restored. On Bald Hill, overlooking Vilnius, Lithuanians restored the Monument of the Three Crosses, erected in 1916 to martyrs in Lithuania's past and clandestinely dynamited by Stalinists one night in 1950. They also restored the famous statuary ripped down from the pediment of the central cathedral by the Stalinist regime.

In moves full of political significance, Communist names were stripped off the main streets and replaced with the old pre-occupation names. The sixty-mile highway connecting Vilnius and Kaunas, called Red Army Avenue by the Soviets, once again became Volunteer Avenue, honoring the Lithuanian volunteers who had defended the country's independence in 1918. In downtown Vilnius, the main street was no longer Lenin Prospekt but Gediminas Street, for Lithuania's most renowned grand duke.

If one individual personified this nationalist revival, it was Vytautas Landsbergis, chairman of Sajudis. At first glance, Landsbergis seemed an unlikely rival to Brazauskas, and an even more unlikely challenger to Gorbachev, the champion of media-age politics. Gorbachev radiates power, and Brazauskas is a lion of a man, but Landsbergis is a classic intellectual: a slightly stooped and otherworldly fifty-eight-year-old music professor, an unremarkable-looking figure in glasses, rumpled suits, sensible shoes, wispy mustache, and goatee. He teaches musicology at Vilnius Conservatory; next door is the Lithuanian KGB, in an almost identical building, which students impishly nicknamed "Conservatory Number Two."

Landsbergis projects neither power nor charisma, but rather the quiet, serious, reflective manner of an academic who has written nine books and is an accomplished pianist. Even on his cherished topic of Lithuanian independence, his speeches are dry, thoughtful, didactic discourses, rather than passionate orations. Everything about him is understated—except his message.

"He is not Ronald Reagan, he is not handsome, he is not smooth, he is not especially articulate," Romouldas Ozolas conceded. "But he is principled, and firm in his convictions and morality. And right now we do not have the luxury to choose a [chairman] who can both put forth ideas and have a pretty face."[14]

Landsbergis's hallmarks are a deep and abiding patriotism, a lifelong commitment to Lithuanian identity and the renaissance of Lithuanian culture, a tenacious devotion to the cause of the republic's independence. He comes from a long line of Lithuanian patriots; both his grandfathers fought Russian domination during the nineteenth century. In his artistically furnished five-room apartment, ample by Soviet standards, Landsbergis has an oil portrait of his maternal grandfather, Jonas Jablonskis, a linguist who ardently defended the Lithuanian language after it was outlawed by the czars. His paternal grandfather, Gabrielus Landsbergis, a journalist and playwright, opposed czarist rule as a writer for an underground newspaper that was published in Lithuanian; he wound up imprisoned and deported for his nationalist activities. During World War II, his father, Vytautas Landsbergis, Sr., a prominent architect and public figure during the period of Lithuanian independence, fought in the underground against the Nazi invaders.

The Soviet occupation came first, in June 1940, and even now, half a century later, it remains a vivid memory to Landsbergis, though he was only eight years old at the time. He remembers how his older brother, Gabrielus, looked at the first Soviet units, which evidently included a large contingent of soldiers from Central Asia, and whispered: "Look—the Mongols have arrived."[15]

During the Soviet-occupation years, Landsbergis did not become an outspoken dissident, though friends such as Ozolas emphasize that, unlike many Lithuanian intellectuals, Landsbergis "never submitted to the Soviet yoke." In fact, Landsbergis devoted his academic life to the quiet defense of Lithuanian culture. To Landsbergis, as to many Soviet intellectuals, culture and politics have always been inextricably connected; protecting one's national culture became a substitute for political activity. Landsbergis was part of a small, private, inbred world of Lithuanian intellectuals, mostly Catholics (though he is Protestant), whose primary goal was to nourish the flame of Lithuanian culture in the face of relentless Russification and Sovietization. His speciality was the Impressionist symphonies and paintings of the turn-of-the-century Lithuanian composer and painter Mikalojus Čiurlionis.

"You have to understand that, for many years, cultural activity meant political activity," Landsbergis observed. "By protecting our culture, we also protected our national identity. Otherwise, we would have been Russified—first in language and later in thinking."[16]

That same fierce and unyielding spirit brought him to the fore in Sajudis in November 1988, when Moscow was bent on splitting Sajudis and undercutting its growing strength. Landsbergis, with his quiet manner and strong convictions, became a unifying influence. Others looked up to his skill as a conciliator among various factions. Moreover, his calm exterior hid inner forcefulness, a strong sense of purpose and direction, and a surprisingly canny feel for public opinion and political strategy. He soon earned the nickname Gudri Lapė, which in Lithuanian means "clever fox."

"Landsbergis is very clever; he is a cool thinker," conceded a political adversary, senior Communist Party official Justas Paleckis. "He plays chess very well. He can see a lot of moves ahead. On the negative side, maybe he is too caught up in Lithuania before the Second World War, that cultural framework, that way of thinking. Maybe his life as a musician and theoretician left him with too little contact with Moscow and politicians abroad. Because he seems not to take into consideration events outside Lithuania."[17]

It is true that Landsbergis has tunnel vision when it comes to his dreams for Lithuania. Yet my first encounter with him, late one evening in July 1989 at the Vilnius airport, was on his return from America, where he had talked with members of Congress and visited Western embassies, and shortly before he was to head off for Sweden to try to further develop foreign support. The next day, over a breakfast of tea and toast in his kitchen, I asked Landsbergis about his goals for Lithuania.

"We are looking for Lithuania as an independent state, as we were up until 1940," he said. "I'd like to see all of Eastern Europe evolving toward a community of free, independent countries, and I'd like to see Lithuania, Latvia, and Estonia finding their places within this community."

"But is it possible to secede?" I asked.

"We do not need to secede. We are not a part of the Soviet Union, under international law. The annexation of 1940 gives no legal grounds for our being in the Soviet Union. We are a part in some practical way; we are ruled from Moscow. But we do not feel ourselves part of the Soviet Union."[18]

In short, Landsbergis and Sajudis argued that the Hitler-Stalin pact of 1939, which carved up Eastern Europe and handed the Baltic republics to the U.S.S.R., was an act of piracy; that the puppet governments which supposedly appealed for Soviet intervention were artificial creations of Moscow; and that the Soviet army illegally annexed Lithuania by force. By that same logic, the United States refused for half a century to recognize the incorporation of the Baltic states into the Soviet Union. Such logic was crucial, moreover, to Lithuania's challenge to Gorbachev. Landsbergis and Sajudis felt they were righting a historical wrong: Since the Baltics were never freely joined to the Soviet Union, they did not need to secede legally, but merely reclaim their independence. To expect more of them, according to Landsbergis, was a travesty of history and international law.

"If the world accepts one country being oppressed by another country, using aggression to establish some unjust status quo," Landsbergis said to me, "then violence will rule the world—not the principles of international law and justice."

"What will you do about the Soviet troops in Lithuania?" I asked. "I have seen Sajudis demonstrations and petitions demanding, 'Occupiers, Go Home.' "

On this touchy issue, Landsbergis had devised a shrewd strategy for asserting Lithuanian sovereignty, without dismissing Moscow's defense concerns. He did not demand immediate withdrawal, pointing out to me that Poland was a sovereign nation, with Soviet forces on its territory—but by Polish consent. The first step, therefore, was to get Moscow to acknowledge that its forces were in Lithuania only by permission of a sovereign Lithuanian government.

"We are now planning a charter project that will define the presence of Soviet troops in Lithuania as temporary," he said, "and that will enable us to set the conditions for their presence here."

Lithuania's economic survival as an independent country was another big question mark. The republic was known for high-quality farm products, electronics, and other light industry, but as of 1989 its "exports" went overwhelmingly to the rest of the Soviet Union. I wondered how far Lithuania would go in cutting these economic ties. And how would little Lithuania survive economically in a world where West European countries were combining into Europe '92?

"As of now, Lithuania is only a colonial adjunct of the Soviet economy; it cannot administer its own economy," Landsbergis answered. "Lithuania can never be isolated from its neighbors. It was never our intention to cut all connections with the Soviet Union. We will use our natural resources, our normal economy, in connection with the Soviet Union, but we will also look for new avenues to widen our contacts with the West."

One major concern raised by the Kremlin was the fate of the Russians, Poles, and other nationalities who comprised 20 percent of Lithuania's population. I knew that Lithuanians resented longtime Russian residents who had never bothered to learn the Lithuanian language, and they wanted to stop further immigration. The Lithuanian parliament was considering a new law to confer citizenship and the right to vote only on ethnic Lithuanians, or residents of five years or more. On immigration, Sajudis advocated that enterprises pay a 20,000-ruble head tax for each new worker brought into the republic. My question was whether Landsbergis and Sajudis wanted the Russians to go home.

"We don't want to drive anybody out," Landsbergis said. "We're not trying to stop people from coming here, but we want to control our immigration. We want to know what is happening to our demography, to foresee the trends."

Finally, how did Landsbergis size up Brazauskas?

"I think he's a good person and his intentions are good," Landsbergis replied. "We see his outlook and his political line changing."

It was true that on some topics Brazauskas was shifting into line with Sajudis; he agreed with the head tax on new workers; he had accepted a de facto multiparty system; and he was discussing the idea of separating Lithuania's Communist Party from Moscow's. Moreover, he was now openly talking about partnership with Sajudis—"we listen to their advice; they're helpful to our government," he told me. But he was not ready to share power formally. There were still major differences.

When I saw Brazauskas at his summer vacation home near the Lithuanian port of Klaipėda in July 1989, he took sharp issue with Sajudis's petitions calling for the removal of Soviet troops. That was utterly "unrealistic," short of general disarmament in Europe, he said. In terms of the economy, he had shifted in favor of a separate Lithuanian currency, as a step toward greater financial autonomy, but he differed with Landsbergis about Lithuania's ability to survive economically as a separate nation. He accepted the Sajudis view that the "notorious" Hitler-Stalin pact of 1939 violated international law, but insisted Sajudis could not simply turn the clock back.

"We have to take the present reality into consideration, the existence of the Soviet Union," he said to me. "It is impossible to start from 1939 again." In short, eight months before Lithuania would declare its independence, Brazauskas was strongly opposed to secession. His strategy was to push for transformation of the Soviet Union into "a union of free republics, a union of free states."[19]

And Brazauskas was growing impatient with Moscow. The pressure of being pulled in opposite directions by Gorbachev and Sajudis was getting to him. He could feel the need to deliver tangible signs of autonomy, especially on the economy, in order to check the growing sentiment for independence. But Moscow was not moving fast enough, and he feared that Gorbachev and his advisers did not really grasp "the political importance" of their rigidity: how Moscow's refusal to relax tight central control was fueling nationalist impatience in Lithuania.

To me, Brazauskas sounded less hopeful of holding the line for Moscow and the Communist Party than he had in March. I took his mood as a measure of how rapidly he felt events were moving, and how little time he felt there was to prevent a fateful collision between Gorbachev and Lithuanian nationalism.

Other Lithuanians, I found, were watching Brazauskas closely. They were asking, "In the showdown, will Brazauskas be Moscow's man or ours?"

RUSSIAN ISLANDS IN A BALTIC SEA

As Landsbergis had indicated, an especially delicate problem for Baltic leaders was posed by the Russians living in their midst: their long-term future in the region and their political reaction to Baltic self-determination. They could disrupt the whole trend of events.

The problem was substantial: 2.6 million of the 8 million people living in the Baltic republics in 1989 were non-Baltic peoples—1.6 million Russians and a million Poles, Ukrainians, Byelorussians, and others.[20] The backbone of the region's work force in heavy industry, especially in Latvia, was Russian; Russian and Ukrainian directors and engineers ran the biggest plants. In general, the loyalties of these groups have run strongly to Moscow; drastic political change, let alone secession, threatened the good life these people enjoyed in the Baltic region, and that made them un-happy.

Baltic political activists were acutely sensitive to the dangerous conse-quences of violence between their peoples and Russians. Leaders of all three Baltic movements went to great lengths to avert, limit, and defuse physical clashes, fearing that any incident could be seized upon by hard-liners in the Kremlin as a pretext to order Soviet troops to crush Baltic nationalism, as Gorbachev had done with the Azerbaijanis in Baku. I heard of several cases where leaders of Sajudis or the Estonian Popular Front moved swiftly to keep small incidents from escalating, even per-suading their own people to drop charges in order to keep nasty sparks from spreading.

In fact, while it frequently angered Gorbachev that Baltic nationalists were challenging his pace of reform, threatening, as he saw it, not only the fate of *perestroika* but his own political survival, the Baltic movements spared him the bloody carnage of the Caucasus and Central Asia. For the politics of Baltic nationalism were cool, not hot, and cool politics kept political violence to a minimum.

Yet even without bloodshed, there were interethnic tensions: Some Russians spoke of encountering animosities on a personal level; large numbers were roiled by the sudden requirement that they learn Lithua-nian, Estonian, and Latvian as the new languages of government and commerce; many were fearful of being forced to leave the region, to give up good jobs and living conditions; others worried that if they stayed, they would be denied equality. The state-run media in Moscow, in making a case against Baltic sovereignty, portrayed Russians and other Slavic peo-ples in the Baltics as persecuted minorities. Russian workers, teachers, and industrial managers in the Baltics formed their own political organiza-tions—Interfront in Estonia and Edinstvo ("Unity") in Lithuania and Latvia.

In February 1989, Edinstvo held a rally of eighty thousand people in Vilnius to protest demands by Sajudis to have Lithuanian replace Russian as the republic's official language. A month later in the Estonian capital of Tallinn, Interfront turned out fifty thousand people against "creeping counterrevolution undermining socialism in Estonia and in the Baltic region."[21] By June, Edinstvo was urging Moscow to set up a commission to investigate Lithuanian steps toward establishing sovereignty, and in July, thousands of Russian factory and shipyard workers in Tallinn went on strike to protest Estonian demands for economic autonomy. Some of the protests only hardened Baltic feelings against Russians.

I came across a microcosm of these problems in the Lithuanian town of Snieckus, and at the nearby Ignalina nuclear reactor.

Situated seventy miles northeast of Vilnius, Snieckus is a little island of Russians in the heart of the most beautiful lake region in Lithuania—a huge open region nicknamed "Lithuanian Switzerland." With its massive trucks and huge highway signs in Cyrillic (differing from the normal Latin script on highway signs), Snieckus rises up out of nothing, a town created from scratch thirteen years ago, a product of Soviet industrialization and colonization. It has become a privileged enclave of the prestigious Ministry of Atomic Power—a special economic zone, one of the choicest residential areas in the Soviet Union. Its high-rise apartment blocks are well built, attractively laid out, and comfortably furnished; its stores are better stocked than those in normal cities; it has far more cars per capita than Vilnius, and a nearby lake with a beach; there is a huge fancy high-tech disco, and a $5 million Olympic-sized gym.

The *raison d'être* for Snieckus is the Ignalina nuclear reactor. Since 1977, some thirty-five thousand people have come there to build the reactor, work at the reactor, or support the work force—95 percent of them are Russians or Russian-speaking.[22]

All across the Soviet Union, there are literally hundreds of industrial projects like Ignalina. To Russians and to the "center" in Moscow, these are proud symbols of economic progress bestowed by the Kremlin on local regions. But to Lithuanians, Snieckus is an unwanted Russian colony, an ethnic invasion, and the Ignalina nuclear plant an ecological disaster, sullying one of the most unspoiled regions of all Lithuania. To them Snieckus is a symbol of precisely what they hate about Soviet control: a conquering power seizing the choicest terrain for its own purposes, without the consent of the local nationality.

After the nuclear accident at Chernobyl in April 1986, the plant at Ignalina, built on the Chernobyl model, became a target of the Lithuanian environmental movement, a core element of Sajudis. Initially, Moscow planned for four 1,500-megawatt reactors at Ignalina, to provide electric power for Lithuania, Latvia, and parts of Byelorussia. Two were in operation by the time of the Chernobyl accident, and a third was under construction. But grass-roots politics intervened: A string of protests climaxed on September 17, 1988, when six thousand Lithuanians formed a human ring around the entire facility. They demanded a halt in construction, and inspection of the two operating reactors, because of a recent fire and reported radiation leaks. Under this pressure, Moscow suspended construction of the third unit.[23]

By the time I visited Ignalina in July 1989, Anatoly Khromchenko, the plant director, doubted that the third and fourth reactor units would ever be built. Despite the privileges that Snieckus offered, Khromchenko said he was having trouble luring young atomic specialists from the top institutes in Moscow, Leningrad, and Sverdlovsk to work there, and some of his younger engineers were leaving. Lithuanians had practically stopped working at the plant; they comprised only 3 percent of the plant's two thousand workers.

"What's the problem?" I asked.

"Maybe they're scared," he replied, implying fear of radiation hazards.

"Isn't it also because of the political tensions?" I ventured.

"Well, certainly, the tension is there," Khromchenko conceded. "One can feel it in the press all around: Russians are called occupiers; other terms are also used. They suggest we get out. The tension is definitely there."[24]

Silver-haired and fifty-six, Khromchenko had been in Snieckus since 1977, but he said that he had never bothered to learn Lithuanian. Now, with Lithuanian become the official language, he had set up a course for his two hundred top managers and engineers, and he was studying the language himself—slowly and with great difficulty.

Other Russians told me that Snieckus had lost the once-optimistic morale of a high-prestige project.

"We're worried," said Aleksandr Zharik, a blond activist in Edinstvo who had denounced Lithuanian activism in a letter to the Soviet press. "There is a campaign against Russians here in Lithuania. We are accused of many things. . . .

"When I came here in 1986, local people came and talked to us as friends, as fellow citizens of the Soviet Union. They treated us as equals. But recently, as the national resurgence began, some 'comrades' began to feel superior to other nationalities, and they told us, 'The Russians should go.' . . . Once, there were leaflets here, calling for killing Russians, but we responded calmly. Nobody was worried. It happened on a weekend. Everyone went fishing. Nobody wanted to fight. Our people are very responsible. They have common sense. They can face a difficult situation. . . . So, we are going to stay. It remains to be seen what will happen in the long run, but so far we'll stay. We built this town and we're going to live here."[25]

Not only are Soviets much less accustomed than Americans to career mobility, but Snieckus is a good deal that is hard to match elsewhere.

"To leave this place means starting all over again from scratch," Valery

Antipyevt, another worker, pointed out. "It's not only a question of getting a job, but you have to arrange for an apartment, move all your possessions. It's not that simple.

"I've been working here twelve years. Where should I go? I don't have the slightest idea." He shook his head. "And to achieve such a high standard of living, it's not so simple. People have apartments here, *dachas*, garages. Everyone has his vegetable garden, a little orchard, a good harvest. It would be hard to give up this land. I'm afraid people won't give it up."

Like the reactor boss, Antipyevt was having trouble learning Lithuanian, and he clearly did not like it. "It's pretty hard," he said. "You have to have a lot of free time in the evening to prepare your homework. And still, two times a week are not enough to learn it."

For Russians, who are accustomed to setting the rules, to being at home anywhere in the Soviet Union and to expecting the locals to speak their language and to be grateful to them, it was a shock to be told that they had to adjust to local conditions. The new terms of life were not only abhorrent; they were also hard to comprehend. Suddenly the Russians felt like strangers, aliens in what they saw as their own country.

"Until recently," Antipyevt said, "we could never imagine that we could become some sort of a foreign body among the Lithuanian people."[26]

COLLISION COURSE

That same gulf of widening incomprehension separated Gorbachev and Moscow from the Baltic states, especially Lithuania, as 1989 wore on. The Russian leadership in Moscow—and Gorbachev's team was predominantly Russian—simply could not grasp that they were now viewed as foreigners by the overwhelming majority of people in the Baltic republics. They could not fathom how rapidly the desire for sovereignty had become a determination to achieve independence.

But there were ample signals of "independence fever" in the Baltics in the fall of 1989. The most powerful and dramatic was the massive demonstration on August 23—the fiftieth anniversary of the Hitler-Stalin pact.

For half a century, Moscow had denied the existence of any secret deal between Hitler and Stalin to divide up Eastern Europe and the Baltics. Throughout most of 1989, the three Baltic republics had been gathering documents from the German government, calling for an official Soviet investigation into the Hitler-Stalin pact, and issuing appeals for official renunciation of the secret protocol on the Baltics.

Five days before the demonstration, in an evident effort to placate Baltic nationalists, Politburo member Aleksandr Yakovlev told *Pravda* that "without a doubt," Hitler and Stalin had secretly and illegally divided up Eastern Europe, including the Baltics. But Yakovlev, who headed a parliamentary commission investigating the matter, contended that the secret pact had no significance for the future of the Baltic republics because, he claimed, the Baltic states had freely joined the Soviet Union.[27] He was alluding to the actions of puppet governments set up by the Soviets.

Six weeks later, twenty-two members of Yakovlev's twenty-six-member commission issued a report declaring the Hitler-Stalin pact "null and void" and asserting that the panel's findings had been "distorted" by the Party leadership, obviously meaning Yakovlev.[28]

On August 23, more than one million people formed a human chain 370 miles long: a "freedom chain" linking the three Baltic capitals. People joined hands and passed on the word "Freedom" until it had traveled, from one person to the next, the entire distance from Tallinn (Estonia) in the north, through Riga (Latvia) in the middle, to Vilnius (Lithuania) in the south. The participation of one million people meant virtually one out of every five Latvians, Lithuanians, and Estonians took part—someone from every family.

The Kremlin's reaction was thundering and abusive, an explosion of fury at Baltic "extremists," ignoring the fact that there was such mass participation in a peaceful event. In a long, stinging statement, the Communist Party Central Committee accused Baltic nationalists of exploiting "democracy and openness" in order to incite "the peoples of the Baltics to secede from the Soviet Union." And it added an ominous warning: "Things have gone far. . . . The fate of the Baltics is in serious danger. People should know into what abyss they are being pushed by nationalist leaders. The consequences could be disastrous . . . if the nationalists manage to achieve their goals. The very viability of the Baltic nations could be called into question." The Kremlin also knocked its own minions in the region—the Party and government leaders, who were accused of "losing heart" and "playing up to nationalist sentiments."[29]

The statement was an obvious throwback to the old-style Kremlin ideological denunciations, and since Gorbachev was out of Moscow on summer vacation, the initial temptation in the Baltics was to blame it on Yegor Ligachev, then leader of the hard-line Politburo faction. But within days, spokesmen announced that Gorbachev had personally approved the statement. At the time, Gorbachev was under fire from hard-liners, and he may have gone along to appease them; but he was also obviously angered at the Baltic challenge. In response, Baltic Communist leaders like Lithuania's Algirdas Brazauskas tried to find a middle position; nationalists like Vytautas Landsbergis held their ground.

"This statement was an attempt to frighten us with political terror and to ignite hostilities against us," Landsbergis said. "But we long ago decided that this is something we must do—fight for our independence. We're not extremist, and we are not violent, but we are determined."[30]

Other issues were pressing Brazauskas to align more closely with the nationalists. One was the military service of Baltic youth. Scores of young Lithuanian recruits, drafted into the Soviet army, were deserting: They were coming home with terrible stories of beatings and abuse by other soldiers, especially Central Asians, who took Moscow's anger out on individual Lithuanian recruits. In one sensational case, Arturo Sokolauskas, a young Lithuanian, had been forced by other soldiers to stand guard for seventy-two hours, without sleep; in addition, he had been beaten, abused, and gang-raped. Crazed by their hazing, Sokolauskas had shot all eight dead. In a case given national publicity, he had gone on trial and been committed to a mental institution; his father had declared that he would not let his younger son serve in the army. The incident had occurred in 1988, but the issue was kept alive by a documentary circulated in 1989 by Lithuanian filmmaker Algimantas Zukas.[31]

Sajudis and the Baltic popular fronts were demanding that Baltic recruits be given the right to serve on their home territory. Brazauskas took up the issue with Defense Minister Dmitri Yazov, but Yazov would not agree,[32] further roiling Lithuanian opinion.

On the economy, Brazauskas was moving closer to Sajudis, constantly pressing for economic autonomy, for each republic to control all property within its territory, for the power to make investment decisions and take administrative command of local industry away from the ministries in Moscow. Prices were another bugaboo: The Baltic republics felt that Moscow's pricing system worked to their disadvantage. Moreover, the Baltic peoples knew their standard of living was higher than that elsewhere in the country, they could see the Soviet economy sinking, and they did not want to be dragged down. Kazimiera Prunskiene, a Sajudis leader appointed by Brazauskas as Lithuania's deputy premier for economics, shared Lithuanian anxieties with Pavel Bunich, a reform economist in Moscow in the fall of 1989.

"If we knew that in two or three years the Soviet economy would turn around and we could live like real people, we would stay in the Soviet Union," Prunskiene told Bunich. "But we don't believe that you'll be able to get on your feet in two or three years. We think we will have to go independent, leave the Soviet Union. We understand that the first couple of years will be very hard for us. But after that, we will reorganize our economy and get on our feet. We'll be all right."[33]

All these pressures were working on Brazauskas. He was walking a tightrope between Lithuania's yearnings for independence and Moscow's fulminations against "nationalist hysteria" and "separatism." Through the fall of 1989, as Communist rule in Eastern Europe was crumbling, there was a steady flow of defectors from the Communist Party in Lithuania. Brazauskas kept trying to persuade Moscow to give the Baltics flexibility; Gorbachev was letting Eastern Europe go, but holding on tight to the Baltics. He summoned Brazauskas and the other two Baltic Communist Party leaders to a face-to-face session on September 14 and laid down the law: no split in the Soviet Communist Party.[34] Economic reforms proposed in the Supreme Soviet left the Baltics far from satisfied.

The final straw was the Communist Party Central Committee plenum on September 19–20. "Talk of secession is an irresponsible game," Gorbachev declared. "Those calling for it are no more than adventurists."[35]

Gorbachev used the occasion to spell out what the minority republics could *not* do, not what they could do. By scheduling the plenum, he had raised expectations of new liberal measures, especially for the Baltics; but now he dashed those hopes. He appeased Party hard-liners by making big concessions to the Russian republic, the bastion of Old Guard strength, at the expense of other republics. And he yielded to the arguments of Prime Minister Ryzhkov and his central planners, who opposed giving more autonomy and economic power to the Baltic republics and other minority regions. For Communist leaders in the Baltics, the session was an unmitigated disaster; it proved that Sajudis and the popular fronts had been right: It was impossible to trust Moscow. That plenum further radicalized opinion in the Baltics.

In the immediate aftermath, Brazauskas staved off the radical faction in his own party that wanted a split from Moscow. The Lithuanian Party was constantly under fire—for the repressions and deportations of Lithuanians after World War II, for the heavy hand of Soviet rule, for the Soviet military presence, for economic failures, for suppression of Lithuanian culture, for constantly bowing to Moscow's will. As pressures from below mounted, Politburo members were on the phone from Moscow hammering Brazauskas to stay in line; Gorbachev exhorted him to maintain Party unity.

"I can't give you the exact quote," Brazauskas told me later, "but everything led to the conclusion that the Party must be one, only unity; there can't be organizational changes. It would weaken our Party in Lithuania. We would lose authority."[36]

Brazauskas was on a knife edge, facing the most difficult and politically dangerous step of his career: crossing one of his own "red lines" by leading the Lithuanian Communist Party to declare its separation from the Communist Party of the Soviet Union. On December 20, he could hold out no longer, and led the breakaway from Moscow.

"We had to decide if we were going to depart from the trends among the people or move with them," Brazauskas explained. "And what else does the Party live for? It has to be for the people. We were deeply convinced that . . . only in this way could we become a political force that people could believe in. . . . You can't constantly answer [accusations] and feel guilty. At some point, you have to do something."

The morning after, the wrath of Moscow fell on Brazauskas. Gorbachev poured forth a string of public denunciations. The private phone calls, Brazauskas told me, were even more blistering—not only from Gorbachev but from other enraged members of the Politburo, who cursed Brazauskas as a traitor.

"I had to listen . . . to things that I had never heard before in my entire fifty-seven years," he told me. As he remembered those phone calls, his entire face and neck reddened.

It is easy for Westerners to underestimate the importance of the Lithuanian Communist Party's break with Moscow. But for many Lithuanians, that declaration of independence was a prelude, a springboard toward political independence for Lithuania as a whole.

Gorbachev understood the stakes, and after his fury had subsided, he flew to Lithuania in a bold and daring effort at personal persuasion. As Lithuanians pointed out, this was the first time a Soviet leader had visited the republic in fifty years. Gorbachev made a desperate plea against secession: "We must look for a solution together. If somebody succeeds in splitting us apart that means trouble. . . . You remember that."

In his topcoat, gray fedora, and scarf, and with his gray-faced wife, Raisa, always at his side, Gorbachev barnstormed across Lithuania like a Western politician, engaging in give-and-take with the street crowds. He prodded workers to think twice about their economic future alone in the world; he lectured people across the hood of his car, reminding them that their actions could upset his entire *perestroika*, even topple him from power.

"There is no absolute freedom in this," he cautioned. "We have embarked on this path, and I am the one who chose to go ahead with it. My own personal fate is linked to that choice. The two states must live together."[37]

But his jawboning did not seem to move the Lithuanian people, and by the end of his visit, Sajudis leaders thought Gorbachev and the Politburo were bending their way, preparing to accept independence. Yuri Maslyukov, a centrist in the Soviet Politburo, told factory workers that Lithuanians had the legal right to secede under the Soviet constitution, and that force would not be used to prevent them. In an interview with Swedish television, Yegor Ligachev, the leading Politburo hard-liner, ruled out the use of force. "Tanks cannot solve such problems," he said.[38] Gorbachev himself noted the emergence of multiple political parties in Lithuania, and while that was still not technically permitted, he dismissed it as no "tragedy." But he urged Lithuanians to wait for Moscow to pass a law outlining procedures for secession—a move denounced by Sajudis as "a propagandistic trap" designed to stall the process, and sure to be loaded with conditions that would make actual secession impossible.

"[Gorbachev] understood after being in Lithuania that Lithuania will not be part of the Soviet Union," Romouldas Ozolas told me later. "Before that, he thought it was the opinion of only a few people— 'extremist professors,' he called us. But after he was in Lithuania, and after he talked with the workers, he was convinced that Lithuania would behave only the way that we had said."[39]

In short, Gorbachev's mission seemed too little, too late. For Lithuanians, the question about independence was no longer "if," but "when."

Lithuania, like other republics, was due to elect a new parliament in February and March 1990. Sajudis, campaigning on a platform of swift independence, won seventy-two of the ninety races settled in this first round of balloting; the second-round races were staggered, but enough had been settled by March 10 for Sajudis to control 97 of the 141 seats in the parliament, and for the Brazauskas wing of the Communist Party to have twenty-five seats. What is more, Brazauskas had now crossed the final red line: He was now on record for independence. The die was cast.

On March 10, the day before the new parliament was to convene, Brazauskas and Landsbergis met with their partisans. Ideology seemed to have been stood on its head: The elite of the Vilnius Communist Party, summoned by Brazauskas to the city's modern, Scandinavian-style symphony hall, looked like prosperous, well-fed bourgeois businessmen in their well-cut suits; the Seimas, or council of Sajudis, meeting in a plainer auditorium, looked like a much less well-heeled collection of college professors and political upstarts. The proletariat was nowhere to be seen.

Brazauskas prepared his legions for a new role—giving up power and going into the opposition. "I would like to invite all not to be saddened, not to be depressed, but to feel that we are an honorable opposition, that there is room for honorable opposition," he told them.[40] He declared his own intention to vote, the next day, for independence.

But in a long and thoughtful interview, he told me that the prospect of an economic squeeze by Moscow worried him. "People are very upset, very nervous, high-strung," he said. "It's very dangerous for society, and people don't see their future. What's going to happen next? Where are we going? What are we going to get? What are our relations with our neighbors going to be? Is this going to elicit some countermeasures?"[41]

At a packed meeting of Sajudis, Landsbergis told the nationalists to be ready to govern and to hold together. He was, typically, calm and professorial.

That last day seemed unusually quiet for the eve of a revolution. I talked with Landsbergis; he was too exhausted, too busy with last-minute questions about parliamentary procedure to be elated. Amid other rumblings, there were reports that the Soviets were going to seize the port of Klaipėda on the Baltic Sea. Landsbergis went to the radio station to appeal for calm from all major communities, broadcasting first in Lithuanian, then in Russian and Polish; he was accomplished in all three languages.

Gorbachev had not used the two months since his visit to Vilnius to pass any law on secession, but there was strong likelihood that he would do so at the Congress of People's Deputies on March 12. The Lithuanians wanted to act first.

Lithuania's new Independence Day, March 11, went according to script. Crowds cheered Brazauskas and Landsbergis as they came for the opening session of the parliament. Both were nominated for the chairmanship, the new leader of Lithuania. It was a choice between experience in dealing with Moscow and a clean break with the past. By what amounted to a 91–38 party-line vote, Landsbergis was elected. As Landsbergis proceeded to the dais, Brazauskas looked oversized and out of place at his small desk, seven rows back. He blushed, gritted his teeth, and gamely applauded. It was a hard day for him.

Weeks later, Gorbachev insinuated that the Lithuanian declaration of independence was done in the dark of night, as if it were an act of stealth. That was not the case. The whole procedure was wide open, to the Soviet press as well as to Lithuanian and foreign journalists. The actual vote came at close to 11 P.M., not out of any clandestine motive but because the assembly, heavy with college professors, took forever with technicalities. Under Landsbergis's tutoring, the delegates were careful not simply to declare independence, but also to reassert Lithuania's former independence and to revive the 1938 constitution of the Republic of Lithuania.

At the climactic moment, the delegates broke into applause at their own daring—in defiance of Moscow, of Gorbachev, of Soviet might. As a red, yellow, and green Lithuanian flag was unfurled behind the dais, the entire hall rose and solemnly sang the old Lithuanian national anthem. Landsbergis shyly turned to hug the new vice chairmen of the assembly, and the hall broke into cheers of "Free Lithuania! Free Estonia! Free Latvia!"

Outside in the courtyard, where Lithuanian flags were snapping in a sharp Baltic wind, workmen removed the Soviet hammer-and-sickle seal from the main doorway of the parliament building, and a crowd of several hundred people, who had braved hours of cold for this moment, began stomping on the Soviet emblems. Landsbergis emerged into what seemed his first terrifying moment as the new leader of Lithuania. I saw his smile turn into a look of anxiety as the crowd surged forward to engulf him with applause and flowers. A ring of guards, who had wanted to ferry him through the crowd, gave up and ushered him into the building. Long into the night, people in the courtyard mobbed individual deputies with joy as they came out, and families hugged each other.

Gorbachev's reaction was not immediate; in Moscow, he was preoccupied with establishing the new office of the Soviet presidency and with getting himself elected. Then, on March 15, four days after the Lithuanian declaration, he pushed through the Congress of People's Deputies a secession law requiring a popular referendum, a five-year wait, and final approval by the all-union parliament, a condition that nationalists everywhere regarded as intolerable because it gave Moscow a veto over their right of self-determination.

Gorbachev demanded that Lithuania revoke its declaration of independence, and with that began the denunciations and the pressures that Brazauskas and Landsbergis had anticipated: Soviet tanks rumbling through the streets of Vilnius, leaflets dropped from Soviet army helicopters warning of disaster and telling Lithuanians to turn back, the bloody seizure of Lithuanian youths who had deserted the army and taken refuge in a hospital, the occupation of Communist Party buildings, and the seizure of a Lithuanian printing plant. Soviet guards were posted at industrial installations, which were ordered by Moscow not to obey the new Lithuanian government. On April 18, Moscow turned off Soviet oil supplies to Lithuania's only refinery at Mazeikiai, and on the next day it cut off 85 percent of Lithuania's supply of natural gas. As the economic embargo widened, Lithuanians took to riding bicycles, scrimping on fuel and supplies, and quietly working out barter trade for some supplies with the cities of Moscow, Leningrad, Lvov, and parts of Siberia where democratic groups had won control of local governments in the March 1990 elections.

At times, the siege teetered perilously close to a violent crackdown, which Gorbachev told the United States he was holding in check. Undoubtedly he was restraining some hard-liners, but the campaign of pressure against Lithuania was his policy. It had all the earmarks of his earlier damnation of the August 23 demonstration and the December 20 Communist Party break. Gorbachev has a temper; he has often reacted sharply to what he takes as a challenge to his personal authority and his own political timetable. His response to the Lithuanian crisis followed that pattern: He accused the Lithuanians of trapping him with a unilateral act and savaged them for not taking time to negotiate—although he had been reluctant to consider independence, let alone negotiate the terms for secession. He insisted that his law on secession, passed *ex post facto,* be followed.

Moreover, Gorbachev's public blustering evinced a sense of personal affront at Lithuania's action and Landsbergis, with his quiet defiance and stinging quip that "the spirit of Stalin is walking the Kremlin again"; this obviously enraged Gorbachev, and he was bent on both putting down this upstart and preventing Lithuania's political sedition from starting a chain reaction in other republics. He was determined not to allow a precedent.

The Lithuanian leaders had expected some such reaction from Gorbachev; where Landsbergis had miscalculated was in the reaction of the West. He had counted on diplomatic recognition from some countries, hopefully the United States. He had proven himself a master at marshaling the moral force of public opinion inside Lithuania, first against Brazauskas and then against Gorbachev. He understood that he was in an unequal fight against the might of the Kremlin, and he had counted on outside opinion—both in other Soviet republics and in the West—to offset that might. But he had not prepared the ground well enough. The other Baltic republics did not join or applaud the Lithuanians; instead, they initially criticized them for excessive haste. In the West, President Bush and other leaders offered neither recognition nor clear-cut support. The White House kept public pressure on Gorbachev not to use large-scale military force, although it tolerated lesser moves; and Landsbergis irked Western leaders by comparing their hesitancy to the appeasement of Hitler by the Western powers at Munich in 1938.

It was Kazimiera Prunskiene, newly installed as prime minister, who won some outside support when she was sent in mid-April on a mission abroad to secure foreign oil. Denmark received her as a head of government; Norway and Canada dickered with her about ways to supply oil; important committees in the United States Congress, where conservatives threatened to tie trade concessions for Gorbachev to an end of his Lithuanian embargo, gave her a prestigious reception. Finally, President Bush, trying to avoid angering Gorbachev, but needing some way to show his involvement, received Prunskiene as a private citizen.

She was submitted to the indignity of a personal search of her purse and belongings at the front gate, and Mr. Bush fended off her entreaty to act as a mediator between Moscow and Vilnius. Nonetheless, her long and widely reported hour with the president constituted a kind of de facto White House political recognition.[42] In London, Prime Minister Thatcher saw her too. Prunskiene, the epitome of competence and pragmatic pursuit of her goals, seemed to succeed where Landsbergis had not. She rose in popularity at home, and slowly Lithuania's isolation eased.

In May, the Baltic states revived their solid front, putting more pressure on Gorbachev. Estonia and Latvia made their own declarations of independence, though more cautiously than Lithuania, promising Moscow they would negotiate and take their time. Moldavia's parliament gave a vote of support to Lithuania. Then came endorsements from some Moscow and Leningrad political liberals. What finally turned the tide was the election on May 29 of Gorbachev's political nemesis, the radical populist Boris Yeltsin, as chairman of the parliament of the Russian republic. While Gorbachev was in Washington meeting with President Bush, Yeltsin met with Landsbergis and other Baltic national leaders, promising them support and trade, if necessary. Yeltsin wasted no time in pushing through the Russian republic parliament a declaration of Russian "sovereignty" that made the laws of the republic superior to the all-union laws passed by the federal parliament.

In short, what had begun as an isolated challenge from Lithuania had broadened so much that Gorbachev was forced to the bargaining table. Yeltsin's action threatened Gorbachev's base of power in the largest, most populous, most important republic in the union. Once again, Gorbachev showed his capacity to shift his position in the face of new realities.

On June 12, some ninety-three days after the Lithuanian declaration of independence, he sat down with his erstwhile challengers, Yeltsin and the three leaders of the Baltic republics, as well as with the leaders of the other eleven republics, and began to spell out plans for a much looser Soviet confederation. He softened his demands for Baltic political retractions. No longer did he insist that they revoke their declarations of independence; he would settle for temporary suspension of those declarations and the laws passed to implement them. And in a gesture toward Lithuania, Prime Minister Ryzhkov told Prunskiene that Moscow was allowing an increase of natural-gas supplies to a Lithuanian fertilizer plant.[43]

Gorbachev finally reopened the oil pipeline and ended his other trade sanctions against the rebellious Lithuanians on June 30, the day after their parliament had agreed to suspend their declaration of independence for one hundred days. They had acted after Gorbachev had pledged to start negotiations on independence.[44] Later, he tried to lure them into joining discussions on turning the Soviet Union into a looser federation, but all three Baltic republics refused to take part. They felt they had Gorbachev moving on the track toward their independence and they were not prepared to compromise, especially after Lithuania had faced down his embargo.[45]

Step by step, Gorbachev had been forced to give ground, but in the process he had made Lithuania an object lesson to other republics; they could not merely declare independence and expect to exit the Soviet Union. At least in the short run, his tactic worked; other republics issued declarations of "sovereignty" but not "independence," indicating that they wanted more freedom—but within the union. For the Baltics, Gorbachev seemed to be saying that if all his enticements failed, he was willing to make an exception and to break the taboo on secession.

CHAPTER 17

BACKLASH IN MOTHER RUSSIA

"Russophobia has spread into the Baltic countries and Georgia, and it is penetrating into other republics. . . . [W]e are tired of being the scapegoats, of enduring the slurs and the treachery. . . . Live with us or not, just as you like, but do not behave arrogantly toward us."[1]

—Valentin Rasputin
Russian Writer
June 1989

"We need a holy, dynamic Russia. . . . It is bad . . . to have a weak, lame Russia. A great country cannot have a weak center, a weak heart. Our culture is sick."[2]

—Stanislav Kunyayev
Russian Editor
September 1989

In Mother Russia, at the heart of the Soviet empire, the rising demands and aspirations of the minority republics in Central Asia, the Caucasus, and especially in the Baltics, have stirred a backlash of ethnic Russian nationalism.

Under some Newtonian law of politics, actions at the fringes of the

Russian empire have created a strong reaction at the core. In Moscow, and across the central Russian heartland, I encountered bitterness, an exaggerated sense of grievance among Russians that the Lilliputians were pushing the Russian Gulliver around, and that this was grossly unfair, because under Soviet rule, Russia proper had sacrificed and suffered more than all the others had.

Long before Gorbachev came to power, some Russians were working quietly at Russia's cultural revival. In the seventies under Brezhnev, I had seen the restoration of a few famous churches and historical monuments. Even Stalin, who destroyed so much of the Russian past, had preserved the Hermitage Museum and the czarist palaces in Leningrad. He was playing on the Russian autocratic tradition, resuscitating Peter the Great and even Ivan the Terrible to justify his own imperial tyranny. Later had come the Russian environmental movement, and the prose of the "village writers"— the *derevenshchiki,* who had celebrated the purity of life in the Russian countryside, writing in a natural prose style free of the cant of Soviet ideology. Under Gorbachev, these trends had accelerated. But by 1989, something new surfaced—a sharp edge of resentment among fervent Russian nationalists, a reaction against what they called "the little peoples." Since the seventies, a small band of writers, painters, filmmakers, and other intellectuals had from time to time insisted that a cultural, economic, and political injustice had been done to Russia. But political controls suppressed these feelings among the larger Russian public. Now these smoldering Russian grievances appeared quite openly among farmers, workers, and pensioners, in the military, and in the upper reaches of the Communist Party, where open Russian nationalism had previously been taboo.

One rainy Saturday morning in October 1989, I was interviewing Yuri Prokofyev, Moscow's Communist Party first secretary. We were discussing the difficulties of *perestroika.* When I mentioned that Russians were complaining that current political trends favored minority nationalities and were unfair to the Russian republic, the largest and most powerful of the fifteen union republics, Prokofyev suddenly became animated.

"It's not fair right now—I agree with that," he shot back. "If we take all of our history, then Russia has gotten less than the others from the country's internal development. If we take the Baltic republics, then all of the industry that they have now was built with the resources and funds of the union as a whole. If you look at the rural areas—agriculture in the Ukraine, the Baltic republics, and Central Asia—people there are on a higher level and better provided for than peasants in Russia.

"If we compare Russia, for example, with England as a colonial power—England squeezed everything out of the colonies and dominions to create a great empire . . . but it turns out Russia is far more backward. It put everything it could into the colonies, if you can call them that, and now they're talking about seceding. And Russia is left, if you'll excuse me, with a bare butt."[3]

The vehemence of Prokofyev's response surprised me, because he is not normally prone to political bluff and bluster; he is polite and business-like—a Party technocrat. Given the accusations that I had heard in Uzbekistan, Azerbaijan, Armenia, and Lithuania about Russian suppression of local cultures and exploitation of local economies, it was odd to hear a high Russian Party official complaining that the ruling majority was persecuted too. But I knew that Prokofyev was not just posturing; his comments reflected a feeling among ethnic Russians that they, too, had been victimized under Stalin, and now other nationalities were unjustly accusing them of imperial sins.

Perhaps no moment in the new Soviet politics captured their anger more vividly than a speech given by the extremely popular Siberian writer Valentin Rasputin at the first session of the Congress of People's Deputies in June 1989.

Rasputin is a gifted storyteller who writes of the Russian countryside and of the lives of simple people in Russian villages. In the seventies, he emerged at the forefront of the village writers, gaining both a popular following and a measure of official favor from Brezhnev, who was sympathetic to Russian nationalist feelings. Although not a Party member, Rasputin was especially admired by the conservative wing of the Party for writing books and stories that affirmed Russian virtues and values and rejected Western influences. By the mid-eighties, he had grown in stature and popularity, even among liberal urban intellectuals, who considered his politics right-wing and chauvinistic but loved his literature; his books sold as many as two million copies each.

Rasputin's voice came from deep in the Russian heartland, and he commanded a large audience, especially when he was given the platform of the nationally televised session of the new Soviet parliament.

He began by delivering a warning about the dangers of excessive democracy, and a powerful indictment of the moral decay brought on by the permissive sensationalism of modern mass culture, a refrain from his famous short novel *The Fire*. Published in 1985, the book portrayed Russia teetering on the edge of a cultural abyss.

Then Rasputin moved on to talk about how Russia was being unjustly attacked by upstart nationalists on the periphery.

"Russophobia has spread into the Baltic countries and Georgia, and it is penetrating into other republics," he declared. "Anti-Soviet slogans are being combined with anti-Russian ones. Emissaries from Lithuania and Estonia are carrying them to Georgia, creating a united front. From there, local agitators are being sent to Armenia and Azerbaijan. . . . The activities of the Baltic deputies, who are attempting to introduce, by parliamentary means, amendments to the constitution which would allow them to part from this country, are readily noticeable here at the Congress."[4]

Rasputin had a Russian riposte, dripping with sarcasm, to throw back at the Baltic secessionists—one that played to resounding applause among the conservative, and mainly ethnic Russian, majority at the Congress:

"Would it be better perhaps for *Russia to leave the union* [sharp applause in the hall], considering that you blame it for all of your misfortunes, and considering that its weak development and awkwardness are what are burdening your progressive aspirations? Perhaps that would be better?

"This, incidentally, would also help us solve many of our own problems, both present and future. [More applause.] We still have a few natural and human resources left—our power has not withered away. We could then utter the word 'Russian' and talk about national self-consciousness without the fear of being labeled 'nationalistic.' . . . [Warm applause.]

"Believe me when I say that we are tired of being the scapegoats, of enduring the slurs and the treachery. We are told that this is our cross to bear. But this cross is becoming increasingly unwieldy. . . . The blame for your misfortunes lies not with Russia but with that common burden of the administrative-industrial machine [created by Stalin], which turned out to be more terrible to all of us than the Mongolian yoke, and which has humiliated and plundered Russia as well, to the point of near suffocation. . . .

"Live with us or not, just as you like," Rasputin told the Baltic secessionists, "but do not behave arrogantly toward us. Do not harbor ill for those who have not earned it."[5]

Rasputin's message resonated profoundly among Russians, far beyond the halls of the Congress of People's Deputies. For many months, his speech was triumphantly echoed by Russian nationalists, especially his trump card: the taunt that Russia should go it alone, secede from the union. Russians saw this as more than a bitter joke; they saw it as a warning to the others. Russian secession, they felt, would knock the other nationalities flat, and the mere threat of it would bring them to their senses, and make them appreciate Russia's importance. For Russia comprises half the population and two thirds the landmass of the Soviet Union; it has been the center, the command point, the bridge, the glue that held the rest together, gave it a framework and a foundation. This was the Russia of Stalinist times—the "elder brother" to the "little peoples."

As Yuri Prokofyev remarked to me, the other republics were "tied hand and foot" to Russia; without Russia, he sniffed, they would be only a union of "dwarf governments."

At first glance, such lamentations seemed inappropriate, coming from the people who had for so long ruled the roost. The Russian people, Russian history, Russian culture, Russian politicians, government officials, engineers, scientists—they have dominated the entire country. This was especially true under Gorbachev. In Brezhnev's time, the Politburo had included several members from non-Slavic nationalities, but except for Foreign Minister Eduard Shevardnadze, who was from Georgia, the non-Slavic minorities had disappeared under Gorbachev. His Politburo was the most Russian since the Bolshevik Revolution, and so was his Council of Ministers.

Yet oddly enough, many Russians spoke with envy of Georgians, Lithuanians, Armenians, Estonians, or Ukrainians, because they all had the trappings of nationhood: their own parliaments, their own languages, their cultural traditions, national histories, their own academies of sciences, even their own Communist Parties. By contrast, the Russians complained that the Russian republic had no academy of sciences, no Russian encyclopedia, no Russian television network, no Communist Party to call its own. These Russians overlooked the fact that Pushkin and Tolstoy were the country's most revered writers; that schoolchildren of all nationalities had to learn the Russian language; that Russian culture and history were taught all over the country; that Moscow television, broadcast in Russian, was the medium of the entire country; that the whole economy and all the major political institutions were commanded by Russians.

Instead, unhappy Russians would point out to me that whenever there was a poster of children from the fifteen Soviet republics, the others all wore their national costumes but the Russian child wore the Soviet Komsomol uniform of blue suit and red scarf. For them, that epitomized how Russia had been forced to surrender its identity on the altar of the Soviet Communist state.

What Russian patriots were doing was drawing an important distinction between Russia and the Soviet Union, between Russian culture, history, and traditions and the culture, history, and values of the Soviet era, the Soviet regime. Under Lenin and especially under Stalin, Russia had been subsumed into the Soviet Union; the Soviet state had treated the two as one and the same for seventy years; for that matter, that is how most Russians had regarded themselves. Moscow television, the Academy of Sciences, and the Communist Party were assumed to serve Soviet and Russian interests simultaneously; the regime saw no distinctions, which is what the other nationalities had so long resented.

But now, under Gorbachev's new freedoms, the Russians, like the other nationalities, were saying that many decisions taken in the Soviet interest had worked against Russia and the Russians. They resented Stalin for having cast himself as a Great Russian nationalist, especially since he was born a Georgian; they hated his exploitation of Russian nationalism in the service of the Soviet state. The most sophisticated and liberal of them knew that Stalin's nationalism was a throwback to the dynastic creed of the conservative czars, a creed in which the nation and nationalism were identified with the state, with the ruler.

The new Russian nationalism of the eighties and nineties was radically different: It was anti-statist, romantic. The nation and nationalism were embodied in the people, in the Russian folk, their culture, and their beloved Russian countryside. Pure Russian nationalists, like nationalists in other regions, wanted to crack the Soviet facade, to break out of the statist mold, and they wanted to reassert Russian culture and Russian identity.

"GRAINS OF TRUTH"

For many Russian nationalists, their cause begins with grieving over what has been lost. And few have done that more movingly than Vladimir Soloukhin, who, like Valentin Rasputin, is a writer. Now in his middle sixties, Soloukhin grew up in a peasant hamlet outside of Vladimir, about 115 miles northeast of Moscow.

Vladimir is famous in the history of Old Russia, a city founded in 1108, as the power of Kiev was waning. The gently rolling meadows around Vladimir, the almost white skies of summertime, are a classic image of central Russia. Soloukhin has poetically evoked that countryside, its peasant life, and his own boyhood in a series of lyrical but candid accounts of the region, starting in 1962 with a work that he called *Vladimir Country Roads.*

In 1989, I found him summering in the village of his birth, at work at a simple wooden table in a corner of a plain, second-floor bedroom in his boyhood home. A two-story log cabin, it had bare floors, simple iron-frame beds, a lamp, no indoor plumbing, and a dirt road out front.

"I write by hand," Soloukhin told me, "and then give my manuscript to a typist."

Soloukhin is a large man of ample frame, broad face, slow speech, and kindly blue eyes; he has about him a comfortable lack of pretense. Long ago, he had moved to Moscow and become a prominent writer, but he still had little use for coat and tie. He wore old pants and a short-sleeved shirt as he slowly walked the paths of his village, gazing at the green fields or stopping by a small cemetery in the woods. He liked to sit, as country people do, on a bench in front of an *izba,* or log cabin, and visit with the neighbor ladies. Or he would stroll to the pond behind his home, watch the ducks paddle or the women kneel down on the opposite bank to do their washing by hand. In summertime, it was a tranquil pastoral scene, a relief from Moscow. But Soloukhin was angry; he found village life hard and dreary, and his hometown almost dead.

"You can't imagine how hard life has become for these people," his wife, Rosa, said. "The one country store only works two hours a day. They have nothing to sell."

"No meat, no fish, no chickens," Soloukhin said.

"Not even a bar of soap for the last six months!" his wife cut in. "No dresses, no clothes."

"They eat what they grow themselves," he said. "And when we come from Moscow, we bring a carload of groceries from the city. We're about out now."[6]

It was a wild idea—bringing food from the city to farm country. I pointed to a cow ambling along the village path, and Soloukhin told me there were only a couple of cows in the village, not enough to provide milk for everyone.

He pointed to a spot where his boyhood school had once stood. There was no replacement for the old school; there were not enough children. Homes were abandoned.

What was it about his writing that made it so popular? I asked. What were his millions of readers looking for?

"Grains of truth," he said.

"Read my books: *Letters from the Russian Museum,* or *Dart Boards on Icons,*" he went on. "My readers want somebody to tell them the truth about what is going on. Today it's easier. Everyone is talking. But when I started writing, in the sixties, seventies, nobody was talking about things. . . . People need the truth, the truth about our countryside. Nobody before had mentioned that our countryside is deserted, that there are eight hundred thousand abandoned homes [in central Russian villages]. Nobody ever mentioned that there were no peasants anymore, that the process of destruction of the peasantry was a success. Only the word 'peasant' exists. There are some agricultural workers who work on the collective farm for a salary, and that's it. . . .

"This is my home, my native village where I was born, and every year I see that less and less remains. It was destroyed by all those years of hunger, by all those Five-Year Plans, by the collectivization. . . . And my experience is typical. In my books, people see . . . themselves, their childhood, their villages, their homeland. They look for that and find it, because our experience is all the same. We are all Russia.

"The Soviets came. The Soviet Union is an international state. And the first governments of this country, in 1917, '18, '19, were decidedly non-Russian. They were multinational governments. The state banner was the world revolution; even our anthem was called 'The Internationale.' Everything Russian had to be suppressed. Why did they destroy ninety-two percent of our churches? Because they had to neutralize the national feelings of Russians. Why were all the towns and villages renamed? In order to weaken the national feelings of Russians. The new government and new state had one goal: to liquidate all these Russias and Georgias and Latvias and so on. And they began with the Russian nation.

"Let me quote Trotsky to you. He said: 'Russia is like a woodpile which we will add to the fire of the world revolution.' "[7]

It was this devastation, this rural poverty in central Russia, that Yuri Prokofyev had had in mind when he said that Russia had suffered more than the other republics, and that the farm regions of the Russian heartland were worse off than other regions.

But the desecration that offended Soloukhin most, even though he was not a religious believer, was the destruction of the village church next door to his home. Its walls were still standing, but it was a shell, in ruins: All the statuary and icons had been pillaged, the murals had been defaced and scraped off the walls, the floors were a dungeon of debris. Weeds towered over Soloukhin's head as he led me through what had once been a churchyard, and into the abandoned hull.

"Our village has existed since the twelfth century, and since the twelfth century we had our Church of the Holy Mother," he said. "This particular building was erected in 1847. It served our village and fourteen neighboring villages. I was baptized here. All my ancestors were baptized in this church, married here, buried here. This church was the fortress of our spiritual life. Around the church was the cemetery, with the graves of our fathers and grandfathers and great-grandfathers. . . ."

Soloukhin's parish church was first assaulted in the thirties, under Stalin.

"It was in 1931—I was small then, six years old, but I remember it," he recalled. "The women went on strike—they tried to blockade the road. But the workers went up to the bell tower and threw the bells down, and took them away. The church continued to be active. It was closed in 1961, under Khrushchev. By then, people didn't even bother to resist."

Soloukhin led us into the dim interior, dust rising through shafts of sunlight from the rubble on the floor. He gazed up at the naked, dingy, crumbling walls, and imagined this church as it had been: a vessel of Russian culture, art, history, and the embodiment of the town's spirit, its heritage, and the story of its people, their births, marriages, funerals.

"There were lots of monuments [here], wonderful marble monuments. There were icons from the sixteenth and seventeenth centuries, pieces of art for our village," he said. "It was like the Louvre . . . the Louvre museum, with ancient books and icons. And look at what has become of all that. This. . . . It's horrendous. It's a devastation. This is the disaster of today's Russia. . . . Film this, film *this*. It's a symbol of Russia today. Russia used to have thousands and thousands of churches, and they're all—ninety-two percent of them—like this."

Soloukhin saw it as his mission to tell this story of the Russia that once was, "to awaken Russian national self-awareness, to write books, to make speeches, to make people feel their own history. For years, we've been told that before 1917 we had nothing but misery and darkness. However, we had a great empire, a great culture, a rich country. So one must tell people the truth, that Russia wasn't poor. It was a rich country and the culture was great—Dostoyevsky, Tolstoy, Borodin, Mendeleyev, dozens of others."

As he talked, Soloukhin reminded me of Aleksandr Solzhenitsyn, whom I had met several times in the seventies, when he was still in Moscow. He, too, had preached the greatness of czarist Russia.

"I know him personally," Soloukhin said. "I esteem him highly as a writer. I like the firmness of his principles. I like his outlook. His position is firm and he is a monarchist."

"Do you agree with him?" I asked, knowing that Soloukhin had been a Communist Party member since 1952.

"Yes," he said. "I am a monarchist, and a vehement one."

"Why?" I asked.

"Because I think this is the best way of ruling this country."

NATIONALISM—AN IDEOLOGY FOR COUNTERREFORM?

Unlike the nationalist movements in most of the minority republics, Russian nationalism has no single unifying movement such as Sajudis in Lithuania, the Karabakh Committee in Armenia, the popular fronts in several republics, or the Ukrainian movement known as Rukh. Nor does it have a single policy focus, such as secession in Lithuania or recovering Nagorno-Karabakh in Armenia. In the minority republics, the unifying force of nationalism is an opposition to "the center"—a common antipathy toward Moscow's domination. But in Russia, nationalist feelings sprawl across the political spectrum, from left to right to extremist right. The nationalist cause is a divisive one.

In the minority republics, the general process of political liberalization and the urge for national self-renewal are mutually reinforcing. But in Russia, Gorbachev's drive for greater democracy has brought upheavals and disorder that grates against the most basic instinct of traditional Russian nationalists—for Russia to be ruled with an iron hand. So, as reform has progressed, divisions among Russian nationalists have sharpened.

There is a strong and ongoing conflict between liberal and moderate Russophiles, who seek a Russian cultural flowering under a new democratic system that is tolerant toward other nationalities, and the right wing of Russian nationalism, which is disdainful, even hostile, toward the minority nationalities and hankers for a dominant, authoritarian Russia. In elections and opinion polls, there is strong evidence that the moderates have far wider support among the populace, but the right wing is more vocal, more aggressive, more organized; despite its small numbers, it is the driving force of Russian nationalism, and in a volatile situation it is the more dangerous element.

Conservative Russian traditionalists like Solzhenitsyn, Rasputin, and Soloukhin are anti-Marxist; as Russian purists, they reject the Communist system. But like hard-line Communists, they have an urge for absolutism, for a strong hand at the top; they advocate a strongly centralized Russian state, with an emphasis on unity, cohesion, and order. Their politics are a throwback to the past; their grand dream is to put a czar back on the throne and reinstitute Russian Orthodoxy as the state religion, and if that is too impractical, at least to reimpose strong rule from the top. They reject Western-style pluralism, which Solzhenitsyn once derisively called "democracy run riot."[8]

The more moderate wing of Russian nationalists are anti-Stalinist; they seek a democratic Russia with a mixed market economy. Their primary interest is cultural, not political, and they advocate Russia's cultural revival, not its political domination of others. They want to revive their cultural heritage, to emphasize those elements of the Russian past (such as individual religious faith and the moral power of Russian art and literature) that strengthen Russian culture and would speed the downfall of Stalinist authoritarianism. And they support Gorbachev's drive for democracy. They are modern in their thinking, and open to the world at large; therefore, they oppose the political absolutism of the Russian Right, as well as its romantic urge to pull back into Holy Russia, away from the modern world.

For the moderates, nationalism raises dilemmas: They are torn between loyalty to the Soviet Union and loyalty to Russia. Other nationalities see aggressive Russian nationalism as a threat; it is offensive to moderates and liberals, who value pluralism and tolerance even as they pursue Russia's cultural revival. In fact, the moderates dislike the term "Russian nationalism"; they prefer to be called "patriots."

Dmitri Likhachev, the aging patron of the moderate wing, explained it this way: "For me, patriotism is the love of one's country, while nationalism is the hatred of other peoples."[9]

This attitude is typical of the moderates: They openly support the idea that other nationalities should assert their rights, whereas conservative Russian nationalists like Rasputin bitterly resent the new, self-assertive nationalism of minority republics and openly criticize "the little peoples."

Finally, the extremist wing of Russian nationalism, on the far right, stands against Gorbachev. It is reactionary, bent on imposing strong authoritarian order, and on finding villains and scapegoats for the present Soviet crisis. Extremist Russian nationalism veers into anti-Semitism and toward fascism.

For Gorbachev, the most serious political threat in Russian nationalism has been that, with the steady loss of popular faith in Communism, Russian nationalism might become a rallying cry for political hard-liners of all stripes. At a time of economic disintegration and political confusion, nationalism is a simple ideology capable of sweeping up millions of ordinary Russians in its undertow. The primary danger has been that right-wing Russian nationalists would form a reactionary alliance with neo-Stalinists in the Party, the army, and the police, each side dismayed by the chaos let loose by Gorbachev and determined to halt the process of reform in order to reimpose discipline. In this role, Russian nationalism could become what Alexander Yanov, an American specialist on the Soviet political Right, called "the ideology of counterreform."[10]

Gorbachev and his advisers are aware of this risk. Even before interethnic tensions rose sharply in 1989 and 1990, Gorbachev made an open bid for support among the natural constituency of Russian nationalism by fashioning alliances with its moderate intellectual leaders and by dramatic moves of cooperation with the Russian Orthodox Church.

With Gorbachev's blessing, Dmitri Likhachev, a revered academician with impeccable credentials as a Russian patriot and environmentalist, became chairman of the Soviet Cultural Foundation, and Gorbachev's wife took a seat on the board. One of the organization's main functions is the restoration of Russian historical monuments and buildings—a primary goal of many moderate nationalists.

Gorbachev also had another older moderate nationalist, the respected writer Sergei Zalygin, installed as chief editor of *Novy Mir*, the most prominent liberal literary magazine in Moscow. Like Likhachev, Zalygin was a strong advocate of protecting and preserving the Russian environment, and his writing celebrated the Russian countryside and the Russian past. Zalygin had been one of the leaders in a sacred Russian cause—the battle against a plan to reverse the northward flow of Siberian rivers so the water could be diverted to the hot, dry Islamic republics of Central Asia. In this battle, Zalygin had teamed not only with conservatives like Rasputin and Soloukhin, but also with liberal, anti-Stalinist writers like Andrei Voznesensky and Yevgeny Yevtushenko, who were opposed to the Russian Right.

Zalygin's democratic instincts made him a rival to the right-wing nationalists. At *Novy Mir*, he promptly moved to steal their thunder, publishing a series of articles on Russian philosophy during the nineteenth century, an important theme for cultural revivalists. He included the work of Nikolai Berdyayev, who favored a synthesis of Slavic and Western values.[11]

Zalygin also moved to publish the political icon of the Russian Right, Solzhenitsyn. Characteristic of a liberal, Zalygin began by publishing large portions of *The Gulag Archipelago*, Solzhenitsyn's biting indictment of Stalinist terror. Neither Zalygin nor Gorbachev could afford to leave Solzhenitsyn to right-wing nationalists to champion. It was a political coup for them both to publish Solzhenitsyn in a liberal journal, and not to leave the cause and the voice of Russian nationalism solely to the Right.

THE CHURCH: THE GOLDEN CUPOLAS

Gorbachev's most important and widely heralded gesture toward Russian nationalist sentiments was to declare an end to the Communist Party's ideological war against the Russian Orthodox Church, and to cast himself as an advocate of a religious revival in Mother Russia.

For the masses of ordinary Russians, especially those in rural areas, nationalism begins with love of country and reverence toward the Church. Throughout the Soviet period, the Orthodox Church survived by accepting a circumscribed existence, occasionally exploited by political leaders; Stalin even used the Church in World War II as a force to rally Russian patriotism. But generally the Church has been under siege from the atheistic propaganda of the Party. Publicly, at least, it was long relegated to tokenism, and left to *babushkas*, old women; to clerics; and to appearances at international peace conclaves, where its prelates proclaimed Soviet goodwill. Gorbachev, whose mother and grandmother were believers, altered the atmosphere, gave the Church new legitimacy, and opened up new opportunities. In doing so, he was going after the heart and soul of Russian nationalism.

In April 1988, Gorbachev held an important symbolic meeting with the late Patriarch Pimen and other leaders of the Church, an encounter that was widely publicized as the first meeting of a Communist Party leader with the Church hierarchy since World War II. Gorbachev gave his political blessing to the reopening of hundreds of Orthodox churches, and to the return of other sanctuaries, such as Moscow's Danilov Monastery and Kiev's Pechersky Monastery, which had been seized by the state under Stalin, Khrushchev, and Brezhnev. The Kremlin museum also turned religious relics over to the Orthodox Church, in ceremonies shown on *Vremya*, the main evening newscast, to 150 million viewers. And finally, in June 1988, Gorbachev allowed a week of celebrations of the millennium of the Orthodox Church. While he himself did not take part, his wife, Raisa, was a conspicuous participant at the main opening ceremonies, which were held on June 10 at Moscow's Bolshoi Theater. Orthodox believers, not only in Russia but also in the Ukraine and Byelorussia, where the Orthodox Church is strong, came to regard Gorbachev as their advocate and protector.

"We understand *perestroika* as the means of our spiritual resurrection as well as our economic development and our cultural reawakening," Metropolitan Filaret, head of the Orthodox Church in Kiev, told me. "The Church has ceased to be considered an obstacle to the development of socialist society. It has become a facilitator of this development."[12]

In 1988 and 1989, the metropolitan said, the Orthodox Church had opened two thousand parish churches all over the Soviet Union; eighteen hundred of them were old churches like the one in Soloukhin's village, and two hundred were brand new. This was the first big addition in many years to the eighty-five hundred functioning Orthodox churches already in existence. The rapid expansion, which cost the Church tens of millions of rubles in repairs and renovations of old sanctuaries, had caused a shortage of priests; and so, Filaret said, the Church was adding new religious seminaries in Minsk and Kiev, to the three that were already operating, as well as religious academies for choral singers, psalm readers, and others.

Beyond that, Filaret said, there was a widening of the Church's sphere of public activity: Church leaders were permitted to be elected to the Congress of People's Deputies, to appear on television, to meet with scholars, to expand Church publications; they could engage in such social activities as running charitable organizations, working in hospitals, joining campaigns against illiteracy and alcohol abuse. Even under more difficult conditions, Filaret said, the Church had baptized thirty million people from 1971 to 1988; and he was confident of an even stronger surge now, especially since the Soviet people were suffering from "a spiritual vacuum."

Moreover, in a not-so-subtle promotion of the Church's role in support of Mother Russia's imperial ambitions, Metropolitan Filaret emphasized that the Church had strength in several republics besides Russia—in the Ukraine, Byelorussia, Moldavia, Estonia, and Latvia, among others. (In fact, I remembered Lithuanian friends complaining that even in Vilnius, there were more Orthodox than Catholic churches.) The bonding promoted by the Church was particularly strong among the three Slavic nationalities, Filaret said. "We have mutual roots in ancient *Rus*—Russians, Byelorussians, and Ukrainians all drink from the same source," he observed. "Our church is truly multinational. The role of the Russian Orthodox Church as a unifying factor is characteristic throughout our one-thousand-year history."

For many nonbelievers, the Russian Orthodox Church is the embodiment of Russian history and culture, a repository of art, music, and architecture as well as religion. For me, too, one of the treasures of driving through Old Russia, near Vladimir, Suzdal, Rostov, and Yaroslavl, was to see the gentle, onion-shaped cupolas of Orthodox churches, blue, green, or gold, rising over the open fields and villages below. I could understand why people happily dedicated their labor to restoring old churches.

On the southwestern edge of Moscow, in what used to be the village of Zolotaryova and what is now a sea of fifteen-story tenement apartments, I found a crew of ten workmen restoring the Church of the Archangel Michael, built in 1740. In the seventies, Zolotaryova had been a mere cluster of peasant homes. Now it looked as overpopulated as Cairo or Calcutta. The red-brick church, with its five cupolas, had long been used to store grain, and later as a metal workshop. In the eighties, as Moscow's housing blocks swallowed up the region, the church was spared, because the metro system ran underneath it; otherwise, it probably would have been demolished to make room for yet another apartment block.

"Look at all those deformities, those ugly boxes," said Vladimir Galitsky, gesturing at the apartments. "I dislike them intensely."

Galitsky was an engineer by training, an architect by avocation, formerly a specialist on architectural theory at the Institute of History. By mid-1989, he was a government administrator, but his passion was restoring churches. He spent his spare time supervising the restoration of the Church of the Archangel Michael, his jewel among the "junky boxes" of modern Moscow.

He studied old books on church architecture, obtained money from the Orthodox Church for gold plating for the cupolas, shouted to the workmen high on the scaffolding, instructing them on how to place the cross once again on the highest cupola.

"It is important to me personally to restore such beauty," he said, "and to know that after our work is done, people can enjoy this beauty." His young daughter was excited just to see the golden cupolas reappear. His mother, a believer, had made him promise, virtually on her deathbed, that he would work to restore the church.

"It is important to me because I love history—the history of the Russian people, of other nations," Galitsky said. "I feel great respect for historic landmarks. So it was very important to me to help restore it. It was created by the people and the people need it back. This history will help people to be educated, to develop their morality, their culture. . . .

"And when you look at this shrine, it's beautiful. It's like the music of Beethoven or Bach."[13]

In the heart of Moscow, others were at work trying to revive the old, prerevolutionary face of the city, which had been largely destroyed by Stalin, Khrushchev, and Viktor Grishin, the Moscow Party boss of the Brezhnev era. One of the most popular grass-roots movements in Russia is the All-Russian Society for the Preservation of Historical and Cultural Monuments; its Moscow branch alone claims eight hundred thousand dues-paying members. It was a far larger body than similar groups I ran across in Uzbekistan, Armenia, Georgia, the Ukraine, Lithuania, and Estonia. And yet, Aleksandr Trefimov, the chairman of the preservation society's Moscow branch and a professor at the Moscow Art Institute, told me that the other republics are far ahead of the Russians in restoration.

"Unfortunately, we only began to follow their example recently," Trefimov said. "Previously, the trend in Moscow, and in Russia as a whole, was to get rid of these landmarks."

We were strolling through an old section of Moscow called Staraya Sloboda, near the home of wealthy prerevolutionary textile magnate Sava

Morozov. Trefimov told me how the preservation society had privately raised funds and gotten city permission to restore the classical residences of Morozov and other prerevolutionary merchants and aristocrats along Old Aleksei Street (still called that by local people, although it had been renamed Communist Street by the Bolsheviks). Farther on, we came to Malaya Vorona, Little Crow Street, where Trefimov and his organization were trying to revive some of the former charm of the city by renovating a run-down warren into a renovated quarter of cafés, ateliers, artistic workshops.

Trefimov was infuriated that Party leaders had ordered the demolition of old sections of Moscow. For more than twenty years, he had been fighting the encroachment of cheap modern buildings, such as the concrete-slab worker dormitories that loomed overhead. He was fighting a rearguard battle.

"Destruction of the old architecture was a terrible thing." A middle-aged academic, Trefimov suddenly turned emotional as he described the cultural crudeness of Communist leaders. "Ancient Moscow cannot be restored. It cannot regain the urban landscape that London or Paris has today. Those cities all have their national faces, while Moscow does not. . . . This disturbs our people, and so masses of people have come to our organization, because there is a certain instinct for self-preservation in people."

Trefimov was a moderate nationalist; like other liberals, he supported the cultural renaissance of other nationalities. "First you must respect other cultures and then you will respect your own," he told me. But his passion for preservation of things Russian was desperate.

"For us, it has really become a matter of life and death," he said. "Let me give you an example: Why did the Mongolians, who were so strong militarily and had a large population, why did they suddenly cease to matter as a nation? The reason is that the Mongolians were much lower in their cultural level than the nations they conquered. So these Mongolians were actually absorbed by the cultures of the nations they conquered in war."

"As a Russian, are you really worried that this could happen to your culture?" I asked.

"Yes, as a Russian, I am afraid of this possibility," he answered. "If our national culture is alive, we can sleep peacefully. But if it is not, our nation will disappear. If the progress of our cultural restoration remains as slow as it has been, we will risk, if not total disappearance, then the loss of our national cultural face. And eventually it will disappear in toto."[14]

"WE NEED A GREAT RUSSIA"

These relatively modest concerns of the moderate nationalists—restoring historic Moscow, protecting the Russian environment, reviving old writings, giving religious believers new freedom—fitted in easily with Gorbachev's attempts to create a more democratic Soviet socialism. But such limited aims did not satisfy the angry Russian Right, the more combative, fundamentalist wing of Russian nationalism. Deep down, the right wing would like to halt reform, turn back the clock, and bring back an iron fist at the top.

The Russian Right sees itself as battling not merely against the devastations of the past, but the moral depredations of the present. As Eastern Europe has thrown off the Communist yoke, it has moved to borrow from the politics and economics of the West; but as Russian nationalists anticipated the collapse of Communism at home, they went the other way—not Westward, but inward. They were at war not only with Bolshevism, but with the whole process of modernization: urbanization, industrialism, twentieth-century technology, the influence of the West. In Siberia, some of their Luddite supporters have gone about smashing computers.

Self-pity is the engine that drives this brand of Russian nationalism, a self-pity that lays the blame for Russia's apocalypse on others: on the Soviet system, on Gorbachev's reforms, on the pernicious influence of Western mass culture, on minority nationalities, on Jews. Russian nationalists reject the charge that Russians, ruling the empire, are responsible for their own fate. Paradoxically, even as the Russophiles berate the Soviet system for their misery, some are defensive about Stalin, as if blaming Stalin were blaming Russia too—because Stalin is so widely regarded as the quintessential Russian despot.

In the eyes of Russian nationalists, seven decades of Communism have left Russia not only materially impoverished but poorer in spirit as well. The heart of Russia became a wasteland—tens of thousands of villages abandoned, Russia's natural riches of oil, gas, timber, and gold plundered by economic ignoramuses running the Kremlin, and sold off to foreigners for a pottage, its churches desecrated, its treasury depleted, its monarch executed, and its once great intelligentsia scattered all across the globe. It has had to endure the trauma of almost mindless industrialization and urbanization, a plummeting birth rate, rampant alcoholism (about forty bottles of vodka a year for every man, woman, and child), a rising crime rate, and one of the highest abortion rates in the world—an average of six abortions for every adult woman.[15]

This catalog of suffering has left the Russian Right not only feeling victimized but searching for a new faith. Its sense of crisis has spawned a slew of new Russian organizations whose very names reflect the hunger for a new belief in Russia: Fatherland, Memory, Patriot, Fidelity, Renewal. In their street rallies, they fly the flag of the patron saint of Old Russia, Saint George slaying the dragon. On November 7, 1989, in the west Siberian oil city of Tyumen, Russian nationalist demonstrators mocked the political turmoil set loose by Gorbachev's *perestroika:* The huge red banner they carried quoted the hard-line czarist minister Pyotr Stolypin: THEY NEED GREAT UPHEAVALS, BUT WE NEED A GREAT RUSSIA![16]

Right-wing nationalists nurse the concept of Holy Russia, a nation with a special historic mission: a Third Rome, after Rome and Constantinople, called in the modern era to propound a Third Way, a Russian way between capitalism and communism. One of the most romantic statements of the Russian credo was Aleksandr Solzhenitsyn's *Letter to the Supreme Leaders,* in which he invoked a mystical celebration of Holy Russia. Written in 1973, before he was exiled to the West (which he termed "spiritual castration"), Solzhenitsyn's open epistle to the leadership urged Russians to cast off the false god of modern technology and "the dark, un-Russian whirlwind" of Marxist ideology, to shed Moscow's East European empire and its non-Russian republics, and to turn inward, away from Europe, to develop the Russian hinterland. Invoking the soul-soothing silences, the human scale, and the moral goodness of the Russian villages, Solzhenitsyn urged the Kremlin leaders to turn away from industrial mass production and to reduce the economy to small-scale; to reduce all dwellings to two stories—"the most pleasant height for human habitation."[17]

The cultural leaders of the Russian Right today yearn for Solzhenitsyn's return from his exile in Cavendish, Vermont. They openly admire him as a prophet of Russian fundamentalism. *Nash Sovremennik,* the literary bible of the right wing, proudly ran his essay "Live but Do Not Lie" in the fall of 1989.

Echoing Solzhenitsyn, Stanislav Kunyayev, the editor of *Nash Sovremennik,* told me: "We need a holy, dynamic Russia. If we achieve that, our other republics will be better off. It is bad for them to have a weak, lame Russia. A great country cannot have a weak center, a weak heart. Our culture is sick. Our young people have been pulled away from their roots. Now they are attracted to a cosmopolitan culture in which America, with its rock and roll, plays a very large part."[18]

Characteristically, the Russian Right is better at lashing out at what it is against, than at spelling out what it is for. Generally, it is against a market economy, against the enrichment of speculators, against joint ventures with Western businesses, against free-trade zones, which nationalists fear will be exploited by multinational corporations. "Our essayists say a free market will not work," Kunyayev said. "It will lead to mass unemployment and turmoil. We must go very slowly, by stages. In the meantime, we must maintain the firm state structure." The one Gorbachev economic reform that wins applause from the Russian Right is returning land to the peasants; nationalists see that as a way of reviving the Russian heartland.

But they view Gorbachev's venture in democratization with fear and disdain. Their spokesmen use the Soviet parliament to broadcast their cause, but they are ill at ease in such a Western institution as a legislature. On an evening in September 1989, in honor of Sergei Vikulov, who retired after twenty-one years as chief editor of *Nash Sovremennik,* the outspoken nationalist writer Vasily Belov drew fervent applause from several hundred well-heeled sympathizers by flailing the new Soviet democrats:

"The prophets of democracy are telling us again and again that the Russian people are fools in everything. Oh, you fly-by-night democrats, Mother Russia is so tired of you all! We are so tired of your screams, of the wailing and whining from foreigners. We do not need any of it. We will make it on our own."[19]

As Kunyayev and Belov indicated, nothing causes more profound dismay among right-wing nationalists than what they see as the loss of moral values in Russia, and the invasion of materialism and mass culture from the West: Western music videos, jeans, television, rock and roll, American cigarettes, and explicit sex in movies.

"Before the advent of television, our people were the vehicles of their own culture," Sergei Vikulov, then still editor of *Nash Sovremennik,* told me in mid-1989. "They had it in the depth of their souls. . . . Now I can see enormous contrasts from ten years ago. Before, when I went to my home village in the Russian north, I could see the people singing folk songs, dancing folk dances in the village club, playing roles in some folk plays. Now everyone sits by the TV and stares at it. They watch what they are shown, and even when they can't sit any longer, they still watch TV. And what are they shown?"

This man in his mid-sixties, in a dark suit and dull tie, gave me a look of disgust, slouched his hips suggestively, then put one hand on his pelvis and reached out the other as if holding an imaginary guitar:

"They are shown those crazy guitars producing that strange sound. . . . *Ah-uh-ah-uh-ahhhhhhh!* And those crazy dancers who are dancing barefoot on tables. Can you understand it? Our poor old women clutch at their heads in frustration and ask: 'What is this? Who are these people and why do they display such behavior?' They can't understand what they are being offered."[20]

Valentin Rasputin was even more hostile toward Western influences, complaining about "the moral permissiveness and lustfulness, the unscrupulousness and sensationalism of the mass media.

"Our young people perished senselessly in Afghanistan, and they are being maimed just as senselessly in the undeclared war against morality," he fumed. "We are observing almost open propaganda of sex, violence, and liberation from all moral norms. . . . Have you noticed? . . . Just as the voice of the announcer fades away, after reporting human misfortunes and sacrifices, the television screen becomes filled with the cacophony of frenzied music. . . . Where does it go from here? A children's sex encyclopedia containing pictures which would make even an adult uncomfortable. . . ."

Russia, Rasputin warned, was in danger of repeating the fall of the Roman Empire.[21]

A NEW BATTLE OF STALINGRAD

In their fury and frustration, the right-wing nationalists launched a campaign against Gorbachev's most liberal economic advisers and reform economists, such as Tatyana Zaslavskaya, Abel Aganbegyan, Leonid Abalkin, and Nikolai Shmelyov. And they went after the most progressive elements of the Soviet media. Since early 1987, cultural warfare has raged between Right and Left—a surrogate battle reflecting internal fights in the upper reaches of the Party hierarchy.

War was declared in March 1987 at a meeting of the Writers' Union of the Russian republic, a stronghold of the Russian Right. The two top officials of the union, the writer Sergei Mikhalkov and the writer and filmmaker Yuri Bondarev, threatened to unleash "a new Battle of Stalingrad" against liberal editors, who were publishing negative works about the Russian past and present.[22] With Stalingrad, Bondarev was evoking not only the old dictator's name (the city is now called Volgograd) but the battle in which the Russians, backed against the wall, repulsed the Nazi invaders.

Carrying out their threat, the Russian Right lashed out at Soviet television, and went after liberal newspapers such as *Moscow News* and *Sovetskaya Kultura*. But their primary targets were Vitaly Korotich, chief editor of *Ogonek* (the liberal flagship of Gorbachev's *glasnost*), and Anatoly

Anayev, who had turned the monthly *Oktyabr* into a hotbed of liberal attacks on the Soviet system. Right-wingers tried endlessly to get those two editors fired, without success—presumably because both were protected by Aleksandr Yakovlev, Gorbachev's chief ally in the Politburo for cultural affairs.[23] Yakovlev has long been a bête noire of the Russian nationalists; in 1972, he lost a high Central Committee post because of an article warning against the dangers of Russian nationalism. More recently, in his rebuttal to the neo-Stalinist Nina Andreyeva, he derided crude peasant patriotism as *"kvas* patriotism" (named for a favorite Russian peasant brew).[24]

But the Russian Right, too, had powerful allies in the hierarchy. Many high-ranking Russian officers in the Soviet military are widely regarded as their silent partners, and even patrons. The ability of right-wing organizations like Pamyat ("Memory") to get permission for demonstrations near the Kremlin is widely taken as evidence of support for the right wing within the police and KGB. But it was Yegor Ligachev, the most durable right-wing antagonist in Gorbachev's Politburo, who gave his blessing to some of the pet concerns of the Russian Writers' Union in mid-1987. He endorsed the group's battle against the liberal press, especially its resistance to attacks on Soviet classics, as well as its concern that the West was attempting to foist bourgeois mass culture on the Soviet Union.[25] Since that time, the Russian Right, especially the right-wing writers, have been widely seen as surrogates for Ligachev and more reactionary members of the Party's Old Guard.

In ideological terms, this is a strange political alliance; Russian nationalists and neo-Stalinists begin as polar opposites. Russian nationalists are angry at the Soviet system for its destruction of their homeland; the Orthodox Church is their ideological anchor and they hang religious icons in their homes. Many of them openly praise the czarist regime overthrown by the Bolsheviks, and they hold special admiration for the czarist prime minister Pyotr Stolypin. For neo-Stalinists, believing Communists, not only czarism, but Stolypin in particular, are anathema, and the Church their ideological enemy.

What has created this marriage of convenience is a shared disgust and alarm at the chaos that has followed in the wake of Gorbachev's democratic reforms; the urge to restore order and bring Russia back under strongman rule; mutual distaste for market economics; common mistrust or rejection of the West; powerful patriotism; and mutual determination to see Russia and the Soviet Union prevail against the threat of disintegration. In this alloy, the two most important elements that forge unity among hard-liners in the army and KGB, neo-Stalinists in the Party, and the new Russian Right are the instinct for order and the Imperial Russian urge to hang on to every scrap of territory within the U.S.S.R.[26]

The Russian Right has poured forth the ideology of counterreform from a handful of publications, including two controlled by the Writers' Union: the newspaper *Literaturnaya Rossiya* and the literary monthly *Nash Sovremennik* (which means "Our Contemporary," its nineteenth-century name). Aligned with them have been two neo-Stalinist publications, *Sovetskaya Rossiya*, the Communist Party newspaper that printed the neo-Stalinist attack on Gorbachev by Nina Andreyeva; and *Molodaya Gvardiya* (*Young Guard*), which runs a steady screed against the liberal press and such liberal leaders as Aleksandr Yakovlev.

Nash Sovremennik has gathered together such village writers as Valentin Rasputin, Vasily Belov, Vladimir Soloukhin, and Viktor Astafyev, most of whom are enormously popular with the Russian reading public. Astafyev's novel *The Sad Detective* had a print run of 2.75 million; it viewed Russia's cultural decline with alarm. Belov's polemical novel *Everything Is Still to Come* had a similar massive printing; it depicted the Western-oriented Soviet intelligentsia as being in the clutches of an insidious Jewish-Masonic conspiracy. By comparison, Gorbachev's book *Perestroika* sold about 300,000 copies in the Soviet Union.

There is a similar mass response to the exhibitions of the Russian nationalist painter Ilya Glazunov, who is a vain, garrulous, chain-smoking painter who effusively advertises prerevolutionary family connections with the St. Petersburg aristocracy and crams his apartment with imperial artifacts. Two million people saw Glazunov's month-long exhibition in Moscow in June 1986; one and a half million more attended when it moved to Leningrad that October. What draws the crowds are Glazunov's realistic portrayal of themes of eternal Russia: churches, Russian princes battling invaders, poor village women, and such works as *Return of the Prodigal Son,* a portrait of a young Russian in Western jeans returning to his home in Russia, where there are icons on the walls. In the summer of 1988, Yegor Ligachev showed up at one of Glazunov's exhibits, in a gesture of endorsement for the artist's nationalistic work.

ANTI-SEMITISM AND PAMYAT

Right-wing Russian nationalists are obsessed, as their writings and conversations testify, with what they see as the excessive influence of Jews in Soviet society. Despite their denials, anti-Semitism lurks barely beneath the surface of the Russian Right. It is another element of their politics that allies them with such Communist Party neo-Stalinists as Nina Andreyeva.

In terms of Soviet history, however, the Russian nationalists have their own special viewpoint. Both Soloukhin and Vikulov suggested to me that the Bolshevik Revolution was not really a Russian revolution at all but rather the work of a multinational cabal led by Jews, mainly Trotsky; and, of course, it was based on a theory by another Jew, Marx. Some Russian nationalists have even offered the fantastic theory that Lenin's grandfather was Jewish; many make the incorrect claim that Jews dominated the Bolshevik Party leadership in its early years. Stanislav Kunyayev suggested to me that Trotsky was really the evil genius behind Stalin's terror of the thirties, even though Trotsky was then in exile.

"Stalin did not invent the concepts of rigid dictatorship, forced collectivization, and enslavery of the peasantry," Kunyayev said emphatically. "He got those ideas from Trotsky."[27]

Others, disregarding the fact that Jews were prime targets of Stalin's purges, have come up with the incredible theory that Stalin was duped by those around him, and that the purges were really the work of Stalin's sinister lieutenant Lazar Kaganovich, a Jew.

"I think today that Jews here should feel responsible for the sin of having carried out the Revolution, and for the shape that it took," Valentin Rasputin asserted. "They should feel responsible for the terror. For the terror that existed during the Revolution and especially after the Revolution. They played a large role, and their guilt is great. . . . In this country, those are Jewish sins because many Jewish leaders took part in the terror, in the repression of the kulaks, of the peasants, and so on."[28]

Nowadays, Russian nationalists hold Jews responsible for many problems. In a polemic so popular with Russian nationalists that it has been reproduced and spread all across Russia, Igor Shafarevich, a prominent mathematician and Russophile, accused the Soviet Jews in mid-1989 of stirring up a current wave of Russophobia.[29] A few months later, in December 1989, the Russian Writers' Union debated whether to withdraw recognition of its Leningrad branch because it had too many Jewish members, and to admit a much smaller rump group of Russian nationalists.[30] In March 1990, a group of Russian nationalists, including Stanislav Kunyayev, published a letter in the right-wing newspaper *Literaturnaya Rossiya* that asserted Jews were deliberately stirring up anti-Semitism in the Soviet Union in order to make it easier for them to emigrate.[31]

It is a short step from these accusations to the activities of Pamyat, the extremist right-wing splinter group that has been most openly associated with anti-Semitic protests and has stirred fears of incipient Soviet fascism.

Pamyat developed in 1979 as an informal group within the moderate All-Russian Society for the Preservation of Historical and Cultural Monuments. But it turned extremist under Dmitri Vasiliyev, a photographer and a minor actor in Soviet movies, who is a powerful, bombastic speaker. Starting in 1986, Vasiliyev made a series of violently angry, reactionary, often anti-Semitic speeches, which were recorded and circulated around the country. He brought Pamyat into public view as an independent entity with a demonstration in May 1987.[32] Soon, the organization invited comparison with German Fascism because its members wore black T-shirts and military greatcoats, and carried a banner with the double eagle of the Romanov dynasty and zigzag bolts of lightning that evoked Nazi swastikas.

I found Vasiliyev a more truculent, vitriolic version of the Russian Right intellectuals. He is a bullish, barrel-chested Russian, who affects collarless peasant blouses; a natural street demagogue, he speaks at a high decibel level and knows how to arouse a crowd to passion. It would have been easy to dismiss Vasiliyev—except for his message; except for the hundreds of people at Pamyat street demonstrations; except for periodic incidents of violence perpetrated in Pamyat's name.

Every charge Vasiliyev made was more shrill than anyone else's. Others spoke of Russian suffering; Vasiliyev told me Russians have suffered "the most cruel political genocide." The Bolshevik Revolution was, to him, a Jewish conspiracy; the czarist regime was "a million times better." He agreed, seriously, with Rasputin that Russia should secede from the Soviet Union. Despite Russian dominance of the leadership, he complained, "We have no Russian ruling Party organ, no Central Committee. We are deprived of our own anthem, our banner, our national seal. Even the word *Russia* is not in use today."[33] He told others that the Communist Party Central Committee, the Soviet legal system, and the media were controlled by Jews, "who are masterminding the systematic destruction of Russian culture."[34]

In late 1989, on Soviet television, Vasiliyev called for the restoration of the monarchy and said that he would not mind being the new czar.[35]

However outlandish, he worried both liberals and the Soviet police—although some Jews feared that he had a tie-in with the police and that was how he escaped arrest. In January 1989, Vitaly Korotich, the liberal editor of *Ogonek,* told me, a group of young toughs shouting the name *Pamyat* and rabid anti-Semitic slogans broke up an election meeting that was preparing to nominate Korotich for people's deputy. In fisticuffs that broke out between Korotich's supporters and the intruders, the invaders called Korotich a "kike" and called out, "Korotich, you Jew, give back your silver coins."[36] (Korotich is not Jewish.)

Periodically, Soviet authorities warned Vasiliyev that he and Pamyat risked prosecution under Article 74 of the Russian republic's criminal code that bars "incitement to national discord." The city government ignored Vasiliyev's efforts to have Pamyat registered as a legal organization, though that did not halt the activities of Pamyat or other groups, liberal or right-wing. And hate incidents continued to occur intermittently; Sasha Kuprin, a young documentary producer who works for *Ogonek*'s television unit, told me he had been beaten up one night by four men who said they were from Pamyat. They left him with a concussion. He thought the attack was prompted by a film he had made about right-wing violence. At a Jewish restaurant, Chez Youssef, Russian nationalists had staged noisy, disruptive fights and insulted the owner; its outdoor buffet stand was burned down and the restaurant was forced to close.[37] Vasiliyev denied any Pamyat connection with the fire; in fact, he denied that Pamyat was in any way anti-Semitic.

There were new spasms of violence in early 1990, and panic spread among Moscow Jews after a Pamyat raid on a group of liberal writers, the so-called April Committee, as they were meeting at the Soviet Writers' Union building on January 18, 1990. About three dozen young thugs, wearing Pamyat badges and chanting anti-Semitic slogans through megaphones, stormed into the meeting and attacked and seriously wounded several older writers. Then, threatening a pogrom on May 5, the Feast of Saint George, they stalked out, shouting: "Next time, we'll come with submachine guns, not megaphones!" Outside, police hustled the gang away, but made no arrests, according to witnesses.[38] However, the incident was widely condemned by high authorities, and warnings against any anti-Semitic violence were issued by the KGB, the prosecutor's office, and many media outlets. No pogrom took place on May 5.

Pamyat's mass support has always been a mystery. Its demonstrations have usually drawn only hundreds or at best a few thousand people, never any massive crowd. In early 1988, Vasiliyev claimed that the organization had twenty thousand members in Moscow, with chapters in thirty other Russian cities.[39] KGB security officers have called that a wild exaggeration; in early 1990, a top KGB officer put Pamyat's membership at "no more than two hundred members in Moscow and only about one thousand in the whole country."[40] It is said to be organized in secretive cells, making its membership hard to calculate. Liberal Russophiles like Dmitri Likhachev have advised against underestimating the danger of a small, clandestine, violent minority. In the spring of 1990, as Gorbachev was striving to get himself elected to the new Soviet presidency, Likhachev warned of the dangerous alternative on the right. He called it "the party of Pamyat" but he meant much more than Vasiliyev and his band of thugs. Likhachev was referring to a wider alliance that embraced the broader Russian Right, and the right wing in the Communist Party, including not only Yegor Ligachev, but rising new figures as well.

"In our country now, the most powerful organization is the Communist Party, and then 'the party of Pamyat,' " he said. "It's an insignificant percentage, but they are very vociferous people. And we know that the [German] Fascist party was also vociferous and represented a minority. . . . Nevertheless, they can seize power because they are organized."[41]

I asked Aleksandr Yakovlev, whom Vasiliyev had marked as enemy number one of Pamyat, whether it was a dangerous group.

"I think to some extent, yes," he replied. "Not Pamyat itself, alone. I think most responsible people there are concerned with monuments, alcoholism, ecology—so, fine. There is also a group of leaders who want to push their activities into the political sphere; they are looking for guilty people. But that's alien to a true Russian. Anti-Semitism, nationalism— that's alien to Russians, especially the intelligentsia."[42]

THE HIGH-STAKES POLITICS OF NATIONALISM

Even so, the political power of the angry Russian Right, and its not-so-hidden allies within the Soviet power structure, became dangerous enough for Gorbachev, during the stormy fall of 1989 through the spring of 1990, to feel the need to outflank and co-opt Russian nationalism. Spurred on by Russian nationalists, provincial Communist Party leaders such as Boris Gidaspov in Leningrad, Leonid Bobykin in Sverdlovsk, and former Moscow Party boss Lev Zaikov were pressing for a separate Communist Party organization for the Russian republic—a demand that Gorbachev understood not only as a reflection of the poisonous political frustration of the Russian masses, but also as a tactical threat to his personal power.[43]

In 1988 and early 1989, the reformist, liberal wing of Soviet politics had been on the upsurge; late 1989 brought the right-wing reaction.

New organizations sprouted up and mushroomed: Edinstvo ("Unity"), with Nina Andreyeva as its figurehead leader; Otechestvo ("Fatherland"), a more respectable version of Pamyat; the United Front of Russian Workers, which sought to organize the Russian blue-collar workers as a mass base of the Russian Right and to mobilize them against Gorbachev's economic reforms. In October 1989, a group of twenty-eight Russian nationalist deputies from the Supreme Soviet met in Tyumen, in west Siberia, to form a parliamentary caucus to fight "reverse discrimination" by other nationalities against Russia. Their main grievances were that Russia's oil, gold, and other natural resources were being exploited by other parts of the country, and that Russians were becoming a minority in the Soviet Union because of rapid birth rates in Central Asia and elsewhere. The Tyumen group issued a declaration that directly attacked Gorbachev's policies—criticizing him for letting the army be discredited; for lowering the level of "state patriotism"; and for dismantling strong executive rule, a bulwark of the Russian state for centuries.[44]

Gorbachev catered to these growing pressures. He might not have understood the power of nationalism in the minority republics, but as a Russian, he understood that nationalism had a powerful pull on his own, discontented people, who were looking for someone to blame and something new to believe in. He could not afford to let the power of Russian nationalism be turned against him personally, as Party rivals seemed determined to do.

Gorbachev made his move in September 1989, at the often-postponed Communist Party Central Committee meeting on nationality issues. He stole the thunder from the right wing by taking a strongly pro-Russian slant. In his opening speech, he promised to set up a "Russian Bureau" in the Communist Party to appease the nationalists; he made a concession to the demands of the Siberian lobby, which wanted more power granted to regional authorities; and he pledged other changes in the "state structure" of the Russian republic. Most of all, in a clear effort to defuse Russian discontent, Gorbachev woefully detailed the sacrifices made by Russia for the sake of the union.

He reminded all the minority republics that economic integration had brought benefits to all.

And then, typical of his style, Gorbachev warned the Communist Party regulars not to carry the lamentations about Russia's misfortunes too far! "If somebody claims that . . . Soviet power has not wrought essential changes, as compared to prerevolutionary Russia, he is engaged in dishonest distortion of reality, intended to whip up nationalist passions and to motivate various extremist demands."[45]

Having made his bow to the right, Gorbachev put himself in charge of the Party's new Russian Bureau, and he got three conservatives purged from the Politburo, including the former KGB chief, Viktor Chebrikov, who sympathized with hard-line Russian nationalists. At the end of 1989 he also indicated willingness to start setting up a Russian Academy of

Sciences, a Russian Ministry of Internal Affairs, Russian trade unions and publishing houses.

The Russian Right was not placated. Its appetite was whetted, its politics made more brazen. Economic recession, and Gorbachev's ending the Communist Party's constitutional monopoly on power in early February 1990, served to further cement the alliance between the nationalists and the Communist Party neo-Stalinists. In late February, just ten days before elections all across Russia, several thousand right-wingers jammed a hockey stadium outside Moscow and jeered Zionists, "foreign exploiters"—and Gorbachev. Members of Pamyat peddled their creed; vendors sold czarist symbols and booklets decrying the exploitation of Russia by other Soviet republics, liberals, Jews, and the current Soviet leadership. And the main speaker, Nina Andreyeva, accused the West of "infecting" the "Russian motherland" with AIDS and pornography. Then she declared that the Communist Party should have demanded Gorbachev's resignation, and the ouster from the Politburo of his allies Aleksandr Yakovlev and Eduard Shevardnadze, at its latest meeting.[46]

Still, Gorbachev continued to court the Russian Right. After he engineered his own election to the presidency in March 1990, he took the astonishing step of bringing two Russian nationalists into his new, powerful, ten-member presidential council. In the company of such official heavyweights as Yakovlev and Shevardnadze, Prime Minister Nikolai Ryzhkov, the heads of the KGB and Defense Ministry, no self-proclaimed nationalist had enough rank to serve on the council. Nonetheless, either as a concession to nationalist strength or as a maneuver to co-opt the Right, Gorbachev put on his council two particularly tart-tongued nationalists: Valentin Rasputin (the only non-Party member on the council); and Veniamin Yarin, a worker from Sverdlovsk, who as a Supreme Soviet deputy had become an aggressive right-wing critic of reform.[47]

Ironically, however, the noisier the Russian Right became and the more Gorbachev appeased it, the worse it did with the voters in Soviet elections. Its mass support, always a question mark, turned out to be very thin— perhaps because many ordinary Russians hear echoes of Stalinism in the rhetoric of hard-line Russian nationalists.

In 1989, candidates from Pamyat and the Russian Right fared badly in the first nationwide parliamentary elections; none of their prominent candidates had been elected. In the March 1990 elections, their weakness among the masses was once again exposed. The fulminating right-wing Writers' Union leader Yuri Bondarev lost a race for people's deputy in the Russian republic on his favorite battleground—Stalingrad (Volgograd). In the Moscow city elections, *Nash Sovremennik* editor Stanislav

Kunyayev and the Russian nationalist painter Ilya Glazunov were also beaten. Right-wing nationalists won only 10 out of 460 seats in the city council; they did no better in Leningrad.

The new democratic Soviet Left outmaneuvered both the Right and Gorbachev's Communist Party. Sensing the powerful populist pull of Russianism, social democratic reformers organized a bloc that they called Democratic Russia, shrewdly playing to the two opposite populist tendencies among Russian voters—the urge for democracy and Russian nationalist feelings. And they swept into power in cities such as Moscow, Leningrad, Sverdlovsk, Gorky, and Volgograd. Thus, by stealing Russophile rhetoric to attack the Communist Party and by promising more local rule, the democratic Left turned the politics of Russian nationalism against its creators.

The final irony was that Boris Yeltsin, not Mikhail Gorbachev, stole the Russian nationalist thunder. After the March 1990 elections, Yeltsin emerged as the populist champion of the "underdog" Russians—the defender of Russian sovereignty against Gorbachev and the hated Soviet Party apparat.

Running for election to the Supreme Soviet of the Russian republic, Yeltsin won 80 percent of the vote against eleven rivals in his home city of Sverdlovsk, in the Ural Mountains—deep in the Russian interior. (Soviet law permits running where you choose and holding elected office at two levels.) Yeltsin had once again demonstrated more popular support than any other figure in Soviet politics. By comparison, Gorbachev has never entered a contested popular election.

After his Sverdlovsk victory, Yeltsin was set on becoming elected the leader of the Russian republic. He ran for the post on a program of more rapid reform, greater autonomy for the Russian republic, a renegotiation of Russia's relations with the central government and other elements of the Soviet Union, the creation of a separate, convertible Russian currency, the establishment of a Russian KGB independent of the Soviet KGB, and the closing of nuclear test sites in the Russian republic. This was heady brew for Russians, who had watched six other republics race ahead of them in demanding sovereignty and autonomy from "the center."

For this most dramatic stage of his political comeback, after a year's work in the new politics, Yeltsin had a host of allies in the Russian parliament, more than two hundred deputies from the Bloc of Democratic Russia, one third of the assembly.

Gorbachev now suddenly saw the power of Russian nationalism coming at him from Yeltsin's democratic, pro-market Left instead of the authoritarian, anti-reform Right. He moved to squelch the challenge, to block

Yeltsin's election as chairman of the Russian parliament. He lashed out at Yeltsin as a "political swindler," who put forth phony claims of being able to solve the country's problems and was guilty of ideological heresy. Among Party members, the overwhelming majority in the parliament, Gorbachev tried to discredit Yeltsin by accusing him of peddling the "corrosive acid" of separatism and "anti-socialist" politics.

"A serious analysis will show that what he [Yeltsin] is offering under the banner of restoring Russia's sovereignty is a call for the breakup of the union," Gorbachev told the deputies. "[This is] an attempt to separate Russia from socialism, which is not mentioned once in Comrade Yeltsin's speech. . . . Socialism hasn't even found a place in the title of the Russian Soviet Federated Socialist Republic. . . . He suggested that from now on it be called the Russian Republic. There's no longer any 'socialism' or 'Soviet' power there."[48]

Against Yeltsin, Gorbachev used a right-winger and Russian nationalist as a stalking horse—Ivan Polozkov, the hard-line Party chief of Krasnodar Territory, who had previously attacked Gorbachev's economic cooperatives as a "malignant tumor."[49]

But Yeltsin's popular pull was too strong. After two deadlocked votes, pro-Yeltsin telegrams from the people flooded the deputies, tipping the balance narrowly in Yeltsin's favor. On May 29, 1990, Yeltsin became the chairman of the Russian parliament, the top-ranking elected official in a domain that stretches from Leningrad to Vladivostok. That made him, next to Gorbachev, the second most potent political figure in the country. Yeltsin wasted no time in getting the Russian parliament to declare its sovereignty.

For a moment, it seemed as though Yeltsin's election had turned the politics of Russian nationalism on its head by putting the nationalist cause in the hands of moderates and liberals. But the Russian Right was not to be denied.

Right-wing Communists, relentlessly pushing for the revival of a separate Russian Communist Party, were no longer appeased by Gorbachev's token gestures. They outmaneuvered him while he overextended himself with the new Soviet presidency, with economic problems, with globetrotting diplomacy. The right-wingers called a founding congress of the Russian Communist Party in Leningrad in June 1990, and Gorbachev was forced to attend or risk surrendering the field to his conservative critics. As it was, Gorbachev had to endure a thunder of criticism—charges that he was introducing capitalism, catering to the West, and had squandered Russia's victory in World War II by giving away Eastern Europe. And then he acquiesced while the right-wing elected its new darling, the feisty, bantam-sized Polozkov, to be the leader of the Russian Communist Party.

Gorbachev was now confronted on both sides by newly elected rivals, each flying the banner of resurgent Russian nationalism, and using it for contrary purposes. He was being pulled in opposite directions.

With a revived Russian Communist Party, the right wing had gained an organizational power base of national dimensions. Its mass support was limited; its political muscle was in the Party apparatus and among senior army generals who were increasingly critical of Gorbachev in public. And in Polozkov, it had an aggressive new leader, an advocate of slowing reform and consolidating strong, centralized rule at the top.

On Gorbachev's left was Boris Yeltsin, a liberal nationalist—indeed, more liberal than nationalist—who was determined to use Russian nationalism for the liberal objective of weakening the Kremlin and centralized economic controls, and also for challenging the grip of the right-wing apparatus.

As soon as he was elected the leader of the Russian republic, Yeltsin reached out to forge links with the leaders of the Baltic republics. This had a powerful impact on Gorbachev, putting new pressure on him to accommodate the centrifugal forces of nationalism tearing at the very fabric of the Soviet Union.

On June 12, 1990, Gorbachev was finally forced, belatedly and reluctantly, to sit down with the leaders of all fifteen republics and begin the serious reallocation of power between the central government and its constituent republics. Seven decades after Lenin had promised the minorities self-determination, Gorbachev was being dragged into putting that promise into practice. His policy of *glasnost* had set free the powerful urges of ethnic nationalism; and now the power of nationalism, in Russia and around the periphery, was compelling Gorbachev to reshape the very structure of the Soviet state in a desperate effort to prevent its total disintegration.

PART FIVE

The Taste of Democracy

*I*n politics, Gorbachev was far bolder than in economics or in dealing with the rising challenge of minority nationalities. To modernize his country, he knew that he had to break up the Stalinist power structure that still ruled with an iron grip. He had to move the Soviet Union from dictatorship toward democracy.

In this arena, Gorbachev was the opposite of Deng Xiaoping in China; Deng believed it was possible to have economic reforms, to modernize his country by giving regions, enterprises, and individual peasant farmers more economic freedom and flexibility, without granting political freedoms.

Gorbachev, urged onward by Aleksandr Yakovlev, concluded that political and economic reforms went hand in hand. If he was to energize his people and to engage them in rejuvenating their country, he had to give them a stake, a voice, and a role in making policy. Gorbachev did not promise full democracy; his slogan was "democratization."

Without understanding initially how far he would have to go, Gorbachev knew he needed a housecleaning in the Communist Party and an end to the Party's diktat over every facet of Soviet life. His purpose was to disperse power.

Yakovlev and other Party reformers understood that this approach would inevitably require stripping the Communist Party of its monopoly on political life and opening the way to a multiparty system. As Gorbachev embarked on his reforms, he did not intend to go that far, and indeed for close to five years he shied away from that. Only when confronted by the swift overthrow of hollow Communist regimes in Eastern Europe and by the democratic pressures within his society, was he finally persuaded.

Democratization came slowly; except for the Party, Soviet society was a political vacuum. It lacked the institutional framework for democracy. It lacked even the basic building blocks for what John Stuart Mill and John Locke called a "civil society"—a multitude of self-generated, self-sustaining voluntary associations representing various popular interests. What Russians called the "Party state" dominated everything.

So Gorbachev had to stimulate popular initiative and engagement—first with informal groups, then with elections, next with a rejuvenated parliament that genuinely debated and ratified or rejected policy, and finally by forcing the Party to give up its legally guaranteed supremacy.

Yet even though Gorbachev was the catalyst of a massive political change, he had only a general notion of where he was going; by the admissions of his closest advisers, he had no stage-by-stage blueprint for political reform. His lurches first this way and then that way were evidence that he was improvising as he went along.

Several times he initiated reforms only to resist their natural consequences. Repeatedly, he was overtaken by the forces that he let loose and the process that he had initiated. More radical reformers outflanked him, impatient with his conservatism and constantly pressing him to go faster than he wanted.

Quite deliberately, he placed himself in the political center—between the radical reformers who were pressing him to go faster, and the hard-line Party *apparatchiki,* who controlled the organs of state security as well as the government ministries and regional Party committees, and who did not want to let go of their power. He tried to reform the Party from within, but ultimately discouraged, he created the new Soviet presidency and forced the Party to relinquish its control at the pinnacle of power.

CHAPTER 18

GRASS-ROOTS ACTIVISM: REINVENTING POLITICS

"*Perestroika* is not manna from
heaven. Instead of waiting for it
to be brought in from somewhere,
it must be brought about by the
people themselves."[1]
—Gorbachev, June 1988

"We found out that our opinion
counts. You see, Gorbachev gave us
some sort of belief in ourselves.
A belief that *we* could do it."[2]
—Viktor Zakharov
Carpenter
March 1989

Ivanovo is a rough industrial city in central Russia, a seedbed of revolt among the Russian blue-collar proletariat under the czars, and a provincial bastion of hard-line Communist orthodoxy even in the nineties.

When I arrived in Ivanovo in 1989, Party leaders still ruled like feudal lords. They opposed Gorbachev's push for change, tenaciously clinging to power and, in open defiance of Moscow, they resisted the new politics of pluralism.

Ivanovo's political traditions favored the Communist status quo. Even though the city was only about 150 miles northeast of Moscow, people in the capital thought of it as a provincial center in the silent depths of Russia, largely untouched and uninfluenced by the outside world. It was a hard, self-contained nugget of Stalinism.

Party bosses still preached the catechism of Ivanovo's revolutionary past, the city's long ties to the industrial workers' movement. It is the kind of city Marx had in mind when he summoned the workers of the world to unite and to throw off their chains. A century ago, Ivanovo became the Russian Manchester, an industrial sweatshop, the core of the Russian textile industry. During seven decades of Soviet power, its industrial muscle grew: Its population tripled to more than half a million, and its industry expanded, adding manufacturing and machine building.

With a large industrial work force, Ivanovo was one of the first Russian cities to spawn a Marxist proletariat, and thus was a natural stronghold of the Communist Party. In the 1880s, Ivanovo seethed with industrial discontent and labor activism. More than a decade before the Russian Revolution, workers there formed trade unions; during the 1905 uprising against czarist rule, Ivanovo's workers dared to establish some of Russia's first *soviets*, or workers' councils, which operated much like union strike committees defending Ivanovo's textile workers.

So, both before and during the 1917 Revolution, Ivanovo was in the vanguard of the Bolshevik movement. In the Soviet era, the city was a paradigm of iron-fisted Stalinist rule, tolerating neither deviation nor dissent. Even in the Gorbachev years, the city lays proud claim to the Bolvshevik title "Motherland of the First Soviets," and its schoolchildren, wearing the blue uniforms and red scarves of Communist Young Pioneers and standing rigidly at attention, take turns as the honor guard at an eternal flame and other monuments to the Revolution.

"Because the Party hailed this as 'the city of the first soviets,' they beat us down, beat our independence out of us," observed Leonid Slychkov, a slender intellectual in his forties who specializes in Russian literature and restoration of old Russian buildings. "In the 1930s, Ivanovo was a center of Stalinism."[3]

I went to Ivanovo with a film crew in March 1989, two days before the first nationwide elections under Gorbachev, precisely because Ivanovo was such an Old Guard stronghold. I was curious to see if Gorbachev's political reforms had pushed out into the conservative Russian hinterland. And I stumbled onto something entirely unexpected, something that the Party bosses desperately did not want me and my camera crew to film.

"THERE'S A BIG FREEZE HERE"

As we headed out to observe election campaigning in the rural regions around Ivanovo, a young man tipped us off that there was a hunger strike going on at a local church. When we returned at day's end, the city was pitch black, but we noticed a crowd outside the fence of a large, brick church building. I asked our Soviet driver to stop, but he ignored me. At our hotel, I asked to be taken back, but the driver refused. The Ivanovo television official escorting us pointedly advised that we had only a couple of hours for dinner before our night train left for Moscow; he dismissed the crowd as merely people waiting for trolleys. Our Moscow television escort, Eddie Baranov, said we had a right to go look, but he warned that local authorities would take great offense, since our announced plan was to cover the elections. I insisted nonetheless, but the driver, who may have been working for the police, again refused to take us to the church. It took twenty minutes of haggling before he relented.

From the seventies, I knew that reaction well. Whenever there was a public protest, the reflexive instinct of police and Party, especially in the provinces, was to cover it up, deny its existence, and stonewall.

It was after 9 P.M., late for a sidewalk gathering in a provincial Soviet city in March. But a couple of hundred people were still there—agitated, milling about, talking in low voices, peering through the iron railing of the fence that surrounded the church. Gray-uniformed militiamen moved among the crowd, keeping people from spilling into the streets, but making no arrests. The church gates were all closed, the church itself was closed, but when trolleys paused at the intersection of Friedrich Engels Avenue and Sarmento Street (named for a Mexican revolutionary), almost no one got on. People were drawn to the hunger strike; the mere existence of a spontaneous democratic protest was unprecedented and exciting for Ivanovo.

Young people quickly informed me that four hunger strikers, all women, were lying on the church steps; they were demanding that this Russian Orthodox church, closed for half a century, be reopened. Seventy feet away in the darkness, the women were hard to make out, let alone film. Marty Smith and I decided to spend the night and film in the morning. Our Ivanovo hosts were furious. They made strenuous efforts to get us out of town, insisting that there were no hotel rooms, no transportation to Moscow the next day, and that we were exceeding our original plans. I filibustered past the time of our train departure, and then miraculously the hotel found first one bed, then three, then enough for all six of us. My fear, harking back to the seventies, was that the KGB would arrest the hunger strikers and they would be gone by morning.

Shortly after 7 A.M. we were at the church. It was a tall, imposing shrine made of dark-red brick; its five green cupolas loomed against a turbulent El Greco sky, dominating the downtown landscape. Officially, this was known as the Church of the Presentation, but everyone called it the Red Church. At one time, the Red Church had obviously been the main Russian Orthodox church in Ivanovo; but Stalin had nationalized it in 1938. For the last four decades, it had housed local-government archives. In all, people told me, Ivanovo had once had twenty-eight working churches; now it had only one—on the outskirts, eight miles from downtown.

To avoid the scrutiny of militia patrols, I went around to the far side of the church to climb over the fence, and made my way to the portico, where four women were lying under coats and blankets, half dozing. They looked pale and immobile. One was reciting Psalm 17. Another woman nearby, who was relaying messages to the hunger strikers and circulating a petition on their behalf, told me the hunger strike was in its fourth day.

On the church doors over the four women hung a handwritten banner: ANNOUNCING A HUNGER STRIKE. FROM THE 21ST OF MARCH, WE WILL NEITHER EAT NOR DRINK UNTIL THE OPENING OF THE RED CHURCH. WE ARE PREPARED TO DIE IN THE MOTHERLAND OF THE FIRST SOVIETS.

The women were Larissa Kholina, a fifty-year-old dentist; her twenty-eight-year-old daughter, Rita Pilenkova, a philologist who was working as a hospital aide; Valeriya Savchenko, a forty-six-year-old jurist, who said that she was forced to work as a cleaning woman because, due to her beliefs, authorities would not let her practice law; and Galina Yakhukov-skaya, a fifty-year-old sympathizer from the distant Kuban region.

Under Gorbachev's new policies, such churches were to be returned to believers, but Ivanovo Party leaders were resisting, and the hunger strikers were forcing the issue. They told me that five months of appeals to local officials had yielded nothing, although the Council for Religious Affairs in Moscow had agreed that the Red Church should be given to a newly formed congregation.

"Did you personally go to Moscow?" I asked.

"Yes, we were in Moscow—last November twenty-third," said Larissa Kholina, a sturdy woman whose oval face was wrapped in a soft gray scarf.

"And they promised you they would reopen this church?"

"They registered our request and gave us an official certificate."

"And what did the local authorities say?"

"They said we should stop even dreaming about it," she said. "We think this church should be given to the people, and if our death would speed the decision, it will be all right. We thought that only death would bring the authorities to their senses."

"Russia itself will die without its faith, its religion," her daughter, Rita, added.

"The authorities told us that if we choose to die, that's our right," said Valeriya Savchenko, in a weak voice.

"What about Gorbachev?" I asked.

"Well, we are thankful to him," Larissa said, "because he started all of this. He said actually there is a need to reopen churches."

"Did you send him a letter?" I asked.

"Yes, we did," Larissa answered.

"Did you get an answer?"

"Unfortunately, nothing," she said. "Our letters probably never reached him. You know this bureaucratic machinery stands between him and us."4

I could understand their frustration but I also saw it as a mark of Gorbachev's new liberalism that this act of religious and political defiance against local authorities was allowed to continue—and that we were not blocked from filming it. Fifteen years earlier, I'd seen small political protests in Moscow, but they were quickly shut down and the demonstrators exiled to Siberia.

Local officials refused to see me that day, and I left Ivanovo shortly thereafter. I was caught up in the national elections and their aftermath, and the Moscow press printed nothing about the outcome in Ivanovo. In May, we tried again to contact the Ivanovo political leadership, but they would not even deal with us.

"These people are afraid of everything and they are embarrassed, so they get aggressive," explained Nikolai Shishlin, a Gorbachev spokesman and speech writer at the Communist Party Central Committee in Moscow. "They don't know how to handle these poor women who want the church, and they don't know how to handle you."5

Through the Central Committee staff, Ivanovo's Communist Party leaders sent word for me and my crew to stay out of Ivanovo and warned that we would be arrested if we returned. I went back anyway with the film crew in May.

Larissa Kholina, her daughter, Rita, and Valeriya Savchenko told me that their hunger strike had ended after sixteen days, but only after promises of action from city officials.

"A representative of the city executive committee came and talked to us for four hours," Larissa said. "He was trying to convince us to give up the hunger strike, saying the question would be resolved in the course of the month."

"And so you ended it?" I asked.

"Yes, we believed him. . . . After all, he is a *Communist,*" Larissa said sarcastically, mocking the Communist claim to honesty. "So we stopped the hunger strike and that was announced in the local newspaper, *Leninist.*"

Larissa had lost twenty-eight pounds and Rita twenty-four during the hunger strike; it had taken them a month to recover.

But the impasse over the Red Church remained. The women said that a compromise had been vetoed by the top Party boss of Ivanovo, a crusty hard-liner named Mikhail Knyazyuk, and his circle of Party apparatchiks.

"They gave us nothing, even though they had to, under the law," Larissa snorted. "They were supposed to provide us with at least a temporary building."

"These people were brought up in the atmosphere of Stalinism," Rita interjected, "and of course, they cannot change their mentality. They cannot 'restructure' themselves."

"So *perestroika* isn't working out here?" I suggested.

"Oh, *perestroika* is stuck in the mud here," Larissa said, shaking her head.

Rita grimaced, as if in pain. "All four wheels—stuck," she said.[6]

The local church hierarchy, having survived decades of Communist rule by avoiding confrontation, offered no comfort. The bishop, who had been in Ivanovo for thirty-eight years, was reluctant to pressure the Party leaders over the Red Church. Other priests said at least four new churches were desperately needed to accommodate several thousand believers, but Bishop Amvrosi, a staunch conservative, was cautious.

"To resort to extremism would be unwise," he told me. "We advised our parishioners just to wait. This is not a fast process. One should really be patient."

He had filed a petition for reopening the church but was opposed to public protests and hunger strikes.

"This hunger strike surprised us here in the Church very much," said the bishop, a large man in his sixties in flowing purple robes and with wispy white hair and goatee. "Maybe in secular life it has become trendy in the twentieth century—a hunger strike here, a hunger strike there. But I personally wouldn't bless a hunger strike as the means to achieve their goals. That is not exactly compatible with our Orthodox faith. And I was worried about their health."[7]

A young priest, whose name happened also to be Amvrosi but was no relation to the bishop, had backed the hunger strike. For that, he had been denounced in the press and falsely accused of sexual improprieties; hecklers had repeatedly appeared outside his home. Father Amvrosi suggested that Party leaders found it hard to accept reopening the Red Church because it would be such a prominent symbol of their political failure.

"Inevitably young people will go to church and it will become their gathering place, which will nullify seventy years of the Party's atheistic propaganda," he said. "Their goal has been to close churches, not open them. And, you see, the spirit of Stalinism is still with us. . . . There is a big freeze here. These local leaders want to violate the spirit of *perestroika*. They cannot comprehend the new trend."[8]

Moreover, their defiance was a classic illustration of the difficulties Gorbachev was having in implementing his reforms. Ivanovo's Party chiefs had no fear of retribution for refusing to carry out Gorbachev's policy; they evidently had protectors in Moscow. In fact, that summer Konstantin Kharchev was forced out after five years as head of the Council for Religious Affairs in Moscow, because Party hard-liners considered him too liberal. Kharchev told the Moscow press that some KGB and Communist Party Central Committee officials were sabotaging Gorbachev's policy on religion; he specifically accused Ivanovo's Party bosses of applying a vindictive policy in violation of the law.

"The members of the apparat don't forget their defeats," Kharchev said, evidently alluding to Gorbachev's support for religion. "This is plainly vengeance against believers and all people who have supported their just demands."[9]

Nonetheless, the hunger strike had been a spark; people told me that it had awakened Ivanovo politically. Local newspapers had become more daring, and began writing articles openly critical of the Party leadership, though one reporter was afraid to meet me for fear of official retaliation. A factory newspaper published a poll showing a majority favored reopening the church; three of Ivanovo's eleven deputies to the national congress supported the hunger strikers. A few informal groups were organized to push other issues, such as protecting the environment, restoring old buildings, and making local government more democratic. These became the nucleus for a popular-front movement.

"Suddenly people started to take an interest in the public life of the city," said the philologist and restorer Leonid Slychkov. "It was the hunger strike that awakened people."

Despite this trend, Ivanovo's officials were still in a truculent mood six months after the hunger strike, although Moscow's Council for Religious Affairs had once again agreed to return the Red Church. Mayor Anatoly

Golovkov, finally agreeing to see our team, admitted how much the hunger strike had upset the apparatus.

"Frankly speaking, I would say that it was very unpleasant and very unexpected," said Golovkov, a self-confident man in his early forties with close-cropped hair and cold blue eyes. "They caught us unaware. This is the first time that it happened in our city. We didn't know what to do. We didn't know how to talk to these women. The Party committee decided that their method was simply unacceptable. We tried to persuade them to take other approaches, but they didn't agree."

The central question, of course, was not tactics but policy: Why hadn't Ivanovo authorities simply turned over the church?

"That's not a simple question," Golovkov replied. "I would say there are three reasons. The first is my own personal attitude. I was raised an atheist. It is my deep conviction. And we have to be careful about the current trends going on in the Soviet Union. The second reason is that there is now a state archive located in the church, and it isn't possible to move the books for a year or more. And the third reason is that the church is located on one of the busiest city streets. We think it would not be acceptable to open this church on this very busy street. . . . I don't know what it's like in your country, but here, it's not always the best people who gather around a church. There are all sorts of wretched people who come and hang around by the fence or in the courtyard. It's simply not possible . . . not acceptable in the center of the city to have that kind of service going on."[10]

The word "power" was never used, but as the interview wore on, it became clear that power was the real issue. The Party hierarchy objected to surrendering its monopoly on power. It objected to bowing so obviously to grass-roots pressure, and it regarded the prospect of open ideological competition with the Church as distasteful.

The predicament of the Party apparatchiks in Ivanovo was a microcosm of the country as a whole. In the end, the Party bosses in Ivanovo had to give way to the squeeze from Gorbachev above and the popular pressures from below.

Mayor Golovkov squirmed and stalled in the fall of 1989, a time when the Party was lashing back at its foes; he said it would take a couple of more years before the archives could be moved.

Yet in March 1990, when I returned again to Ivanovo, I found that an important change had taken place: A priest and a group of worshipers, including Larissa Kholina and Rita Pilenkova, had been allowed to convert part of a building on the grounds of the Red Church into a small chapel for services. The archives were still in the church, and the worshipers were impatient to get their hands on the church proper. The priest, himself an artist, was already preparing new icons for the Red Church, and it was clear that the spontaneous public protest that I had witnessed a year earlier had gathered enough public support to force the old system to give way, however slowly.

FREEDOM OR ANARCHY?

Ivanovo's experience was typical of political evolution under Gorbachev. As he began his reforms, the country as a whole was virtually a political vacuum. It lacked political institutions independent of the Communist Party. The Party was the guiding force for everything: In Ivanovo it ran the city government, dictated religious policy, used what were essentially "company trade unions" to manipulate the proletariat, turned the city soviet into an empty showcase, a tool of the Party apparat instead of a people's forum.

The contrast between the Soviet Union and Poland, for example, is stunning. For decades, Poland has had a Catholic Church that was an ideological refuge and a base for political activism as well as a countervailing force to the Communist regime. Poland had a small private economic sector in farming and services. And most important, the independent Solidarity trade-union movement had a decade to develop as an alternative power base to the Communist Party—*before* Solidarity won the elections of 1989.

Soviet society lacked an independent political infrastructure, and so it had to begin virtually from scratch. Except for tiny bands of dissidents, religious believers, or would-be Jewish emigrants, the Soviet people were politically passive—and Russians were particularly so. They accepted politics as the province of the *vlasti*, the powerful; it was practiced in secret and then perpetrated on the masses. People at large never dreamed of participating.

"Politics is like the weather—it comes from on high," one of my Russian friends remarked during the seventies. "There's nothing that we can do about the weather except adjust—bundle up on cold days, wear raincoats when it rains, and wear light clothes when it's warm. The same with politics. *They* make the politics," he said, raising his eyebrows and tossing his jaw upward, to indicate the higher-ups, "and *we* adapt."

That resistance to democracy, even mistrust of democracy, as I commented before, has been embedded in the Russian psyche by a long history of absolutism under both czars and commissars. Russians have known precious little of such essential ingredients of democracy as moderation, constitutionalism, division of powers, rule of law, or restraint either by rulers or by revolutionaries. Political tolerance is not a typical Russian trait. Their politics has been given to extremes: iron rule or bloody revolt. This experience has left them with an abiding fear of chaos, disorder, of things careening wildly out of control, and therefore a strongly felt need for Authority to maintain order and to protect the people from violence and upheaval. As David Shipler, an experienced and talented observer of Russia, commented, there is "no authority without authoritarianism, no order without oppression, no change without upheaval."[11]

Many Russians have inherited from their turbulent and bloody past an inbred fear of freedom. Older Russians shudder, for example, at the twentieth century, which has brought them revolution, civil war, famine, massive purges, and two wars fought on Russian soil. A study of their own history has also taught Russians that pushing protests, taking liberties as it were, can provoke a violent crackdown from on high. Moral: Too much freedom has terrifying consequences.

Fear of freedom also arises from the fact that Russians sense that they are all anarchists in their souls. Democracy requires responsibility, the rule of law, a sense of compromise, a sense of self-restraint coming from within the individual, whether ruler or ruled. But history has not taught Russians the habits of compromise or restraint; theirs has been winner-take-all politics. And so they have a gut anxiety that others will use freedom against them; they find it hard to trust each other to use it responsibly.

So to a greater extent than Westerners, Russians have been relieved when order was imposed on them; and in the great mass of Russians, authoritarianism has bred passivity. It has made them submissive, unaccustomed to exercising individual liberties, and accustomed instead to a system of rules decreed from on high. As anyone who has lived among them knows, they delight in breaking those rules; despite surface appearances, they are not by nature a disciplined, Teutonic people. But their instinct for petty, clandestine defiance of authority is sometimes mistaken by outsiders for a suppressed democratic spirit. In a few people, perhaps; but more frequently it is something else—almost a child's game against powerful parents, a safety valve, a personal struggle to get away with an infraction by covertly bending the rules, rather than an open, democratic assertion that the people are sovereign.

Take seat belts: Traffic rules in Moscow require wearing them in private cars, though not in taxis. Even though a private motorist can be fined 5 rubles on the spot for failing to use his seat belt, practically no one uses them. To avoid fines, people simply pull the belts across their chests and let them dangle. Whenever I attached my belt and suggested that they were useful safety devices, Muscovites laughed me off. Not just a few people—everybody. All of them regarded seat belts as one more bureaucratic gimmick to plague their miserable lives. They never stopped to consider whether the belts made sense.

One day, I was with Sasha Lyubimov, a well-known TV personality from the show *Vzglyad,* and he hitched a ride for both of us from a woman designer. She was awed by his presence. We chatted in a mixture of Russian and English so that by the time he got out, the woman knew I was a foreigner. As I slid into the front seat vacated by Sasha, I threw the seat belt over me without connecting it. She looked over at me with a laugh and remarked, "Ah, I see you are a real Muscovite already. You don't bother to fasten your seat belt. You know our customs."

I laughed too, and then I noticed that her car was missing the bottom connector for the seat belt.

"Most people have the proper equipment," I said. "You don't even have all the equipment."

She laughed again.

"It's not necessary," she said. "Who needs it? We prefer to have our seat belts unattached. We like to pretend we're using them whenever the police are watching us. It's our little game with the authorities. We Russians love to play such tricks on the authorities."

It was a typical Soviet attitude: Rules are made to be broken, if you can get away with it. Life is a game: we and they. They make the rules and we break them. It is a game of absolutist politics, not of democracy—the individual cheating the system, instead of confronting the powers-that-be to demand reform or a better life. That is the traditional way of Soviet politics—breaking rules, not changing them or relaxing them.

In a democracy, people demand and expect greater freedoms, but if the citizenry does not have an inbred sense of responsibility and self-restraint, the system breaks down and freedom leads to anarchy. I recall seeing a sign at the border of Franco's Spain back in the 1950s: THERE CAN BE NO FREEDOM WITHOUT ORDER. Reading this, as I was, in a fascist dictatorship, I considered it a slippery pretext for totalitarian rule: Dictatorships use the demand for law and order to justify repression. To me, Franco's slogan was offensive, and alien, because in fact his regime—like Stalinist Russia—set order in opposition to freedom. Yet actually, in Western society, we take both order and freedom for granted and feel little need to make a fundamental choice between them.

Except for the Civil War more than a century ago, we Americans have not known war on our own soil. We have not experienced mass civic conflict in which cities have been demolished and millions of people have perished. In our bones, we do not know the price of such disorder. Our system is stable, and a structure of social order exists, despite periodic eruptions of racial violence or mass demonstrations over such issues as the Vietnam War. We have learned that these events do not threaten the fundamental stability of our institutions and the essential security of our society. And after centuries of Anglo-Saxon and Roman legal traditions, we have an internal sense of restraint.

For the most part, we are a law-abiding people, whose infractions of the rules come at the margins—traffic speeding, cheating on income taxes, using the office phones for personal calls. Only the mass drug problem carries the threat of real social disorder, of the unraveling of our social structure. It causes panic because it is a dark, menacing force, unpredictable and uncontrollable. We feel vulnerable because we cannot guarantee our own safety or, worse, that of our children. It is at this point that we come closest to an instinctive understanding of the Russian panic about social chaos, and of their wariness toward democracy. Given the choice between order and a freedom that risks chaos, vast masses of Russians choose order—and they have done so for centuries.

Prior to Gorbachev, the episodes of democracy in Russian history were few, limited, and ultimately unsuccessful. In 1825, there was an abortive uprising of czarist officers, known as the Decembrists, who were pressing for the abolition of serfdom, and the creation of a constitutional monarchy and an elected legislature. They wound up hanged or in exile. Another period of reforms took place under Czar Alexander II, who freed the serfs in 1861; but he was assassinated on the day he signed a decree approving a representative assembly. From 1906 to 1917, under the popularly elected legislative Dumas, there was a period of economic and political pluralism, of independent farmers and a flourishing press, but this attempt at constitutional government was so fragile that it crumbled under the assault of the Bolsheviks.

So Gorbachev's political reforms were not only challenging a power structure determined to defend itself, they were bucking the accumulated weight of Russian history. As the hunger strikers in Ivanovo discovered, reformers had to fight not only a powerful institutional enemy but also deeply embedded conservative attitudes and popular inertia.

"Democracy is something you learn gradually," Vladimir Pozner said to me. "It's a process. It cannot be decreed. I mean we, the Soviet people, are not a democratic people. We have not had a democratic heritage. You look back in Russian history—what democracy? It's something you have to learn to use. Some people in our country are more democratic than others. But if you look at our reaction when we don't like something—say we don't like a movie, people will say, 'You should ban that movie.' When they don't like what someone is saying on television, they will say, 'He shouldn't be allowed to say that.' Such a reaction is spontaneous."[12]

Given my own experience with Soviet political passivity in the seventies, what surprised me in the eighties was how many people quickly grasped at the new freedom that Gorbachev offered—not to overturn the system, but to assert some basic demands.

Before Gorbachev, there had been a spontaneous, unofficial environmental movement to save Siberia's famous Lake Baikal from industrial pollution; there had been a few groups devoted to restoring Russian historical monuments. And there were tiny clusters of dissidents operating at the fringes of society, whose sympathizers in the Soviet mainstream shunned them for fear of police reprisals.

As a result, many Western experts, and Soviets themselves, were astonished by how rapidly political initiative crystallized under Gorbachev. His call for political pluralism clearly tapped into a hunger for independent activity at the grass roots that almost no one had anticipated. In his first year or two, most new political activity was either at the dissident fringe or still modest and devoted to such politically safe goals as historical or environmental preservation.

But from 1987 onward, all kinds of unofficial, informal groups mushroomed almost overnight—the most sensational being the popular-front movements in the Baltic republics and other minority regions. In the mainstream of Soviet life there were suddenly hundreds of new groups: the *afghantsi*, Afghan war veterans lobbying for proper health care, for preferred treatment as consumers, and for understanding from the home folks; in the Ukraine, a group called Zelenni Svet ("Green World"), protesting pollution and nuclear-power stations in populated areas; Memorial, a nationwide network dedicated to rehabilitating and aiding victims of Stalinism and raising money to build them a national memorial; a Leningrad group called Spaseniye, or "Salvation," whose proclaimed goals were to preserve monuments of history and culture and to democratize public life; in Moscow, groups like Civic Dignity, the Club of Social Initiatives, People's Action, Democratic Perestroika. Later came groups like the Union of Lawyers, independent associations of cooperatives or peasant farmers, and some upstart reformers among military officers who formed a group called Shield.

In April 1987, Boris Yeltsin, then Communist Party boss of Moscow, allowed members of 148 different groups to meet in Moscow's famous Hall of Columns, site of some of Stalin's show trials. The nonstop, sophomoric debates of these suddenly liberated Russians were called a "kinder-garten for democracy" by one organizer.[13] A year later, a similar meeting of about 100 different groups led to the formation of the Democratic Union, which openly declared itself an opposition party, even though opposition parties were still illegal.

By early February 1988, *Pravda* estimated that the Soviet Union had about thirty thousand unofficial or informal groups, or *neformalny*, in Soviet shorthand.[14] That statistic was misleading because it included vast numbers of tiny little rock-music fan clubs and clubs of sports fans. Nonetheless, by the end of 1988 there were probably several thousand microgroups concerned with social, political, religious, environmental, and nationalistic issues. The most potent new grass-roots movement to emerge in 1989 was that of striking coal miners in Siberia, the Ukraine, Vorkuta, and Karaganda. The massive walkout by some 150,000 miners in July—the first truly large-scale labor strike since the Bolshevik Revolu-tion—brought the government to its knees, forcing promises of higher pay, better working and living conditions, and more rapid economic reform. Some of the strike leaders used their new muscle in regional politics and talked of forming an independent trade union.

Initially, the national Communist leadership was not only tolerant but approving of grass-roots activism; as a response to Gorbachev's program of democratization, it was evidence of popular engagement in public life. From the Party's perspective, the more the merrier. Proliferation of mi-crogroups meant less of a threat to the Party, because in the early phases, none of the groups was large or extensively organized; moreover, as tiny atoms of political action, all competing with one another, they were vulnerable to domination by the Party or manipulation by the KGB.

Yet the longer-term implications of these embryonic cells of democracy were more threatening to the Party apparat. This was Gorbachev's pur-pose: to use these new "informals" as a populist force to pressure and cow the hard-line apparatchiks. Indeed, as the groups became bolder, and as some, like the popular fronts and striking miners, began to merge into larger coalitions, to reach for wider mass appeal and challenge the Party frontally, hard-liners—not only in Ivanovo, but in Moscow and around the country—began sounding the alarm.

By February 1989, things had moved so far that former KGB chief and Politburo member Viktor Chebrikov could no longer contain his worries. On a visit to Moldavia, where a popular front had begun to rival the Party, Chebrikov lashed out at grass-roots activism.

"Individual, so-called informal associations are doing considerable harm," he declared. "While demagogically declaring their support for *perestroika,* they hinder it by their actions. There are outright anti-socialist elements who are trying to create political structures opposed to the Communist Party of the Soviet Union. We must, of course, react to such attempts and actions. . . . We must deal a sharp, public rebuff, from a Marxist-Leninist position, to the leaders of informal groups which seek to push the masses on the road to anarchy and lawlessness, on the road to destabilization, on the road to creating legal and illegal structures opposed to the party."[15]

BRATEYEVO: NO GRASS GROWS

Gorbachev was on the opposite tack, encouraging people to demand better government and become politically active, and never more ardently than at the Nineteenth Communist Party Conference in June 1988. In the immediate wake of that conference, one of the most dramatic battlegrounds between the Party and grass-roots activists was an ugly, polluted district known as Brateyevo on the southern outskirts of Moscow.

In Brateyevo, I encountered a citizens' grass-roots movement that reminded me of neighborhood politics in New York City—but to see it in Russia was astonishing, because it seemed to flare into the open, out of nowhere. The residents, provoked by the arrogant disdain of city authorities and the Party apparat, coalesced into an unprecedented "Self-governing Committee." They waged tenacious trench warfare that was ultimately much more dangerous to the Communist Party apparat than were Ivanovo's hunger strikers.

The four women of Ivanovo had the limited objective of trying to reclaim a church. In Brateyevo, the people were after control over development of their "microdistrict" of sixty thousand residents and they were after long-term political influence. And their movement became a model for scores of other Moscow districts and for people in many other cities.

The issue in Brateyevo was the environment, a pressing concern all across the country, an issue almost as widespread and powerfully felt as the urge for religious revival. As in Western countries, environmental concerns have spawned some of the largest and most successful popular protests in the Soviet Union, blocking industrial development and construction of nuclear plants.

Brateyevo is a natural target—and breeding ground—for grass-roots activists. It epitomizes the worst in the Soviet urban landscape. It is a massive, cheerless, twenty-story tenement project choked by the pollution of the heavy industry that surrounds it: a huge petrochemical refinery that supplies half of Moscow's gasoline; an enormous coking plant that converts coal to industrial coke; and half a dozen other large factories that poison the air with acid fumes and billowing gray smoke. The area is a kind of instant slum: barren of greenery, prefab tenements aging and cracking before they are occupied, large metal power stanchions marching right through the residential area, their wires humming and snapping. Industrial silt has piled up on the banks of a nearby river, which is too filthy for swimming and exudes a swampy, malodorous stench.

After dinner in Brateyevo late one evening, I stepped out on my hosts' balcony to look at the exhaust flame from the tower of the petrochemical plant about half a mile away. I began coughing and my eyes watered. My Soviet friends were less afflicted only because they had adjusted to the sting in the air and the foul odor. My host, Haik Zulumyan, a philosophy professor, who is a beautiful classical pianist as well as a fan of American jazz pianist Oscar Peterson, told me that many people in Brateyevo, especially the elderly, are constantly sick and dizzy from the industrial pollution.

"We exist here, but you can't call it life in the normal sense," a group of 192 high school students wrote in an appeal to the local district council. "Grass doesn't grow in this area. Trees are dying. The air smells like a chemical laboratory. Gas exhaust from the oil refinery causes headaches, dizziness, loss of attention. It is hard to exercise here. Many gasp for air even after light exercise. We have no place for leisure. Brateyevo has no public facilities. The neighborhood cinema is ten bus stops away."[16]

Brateyevo was originally planned as an industrial zone; the Moscow city health department ruled in the early 1980s that it was unfit for human habitation because of surrounding industry and a water table just below the land's surface. But Party leaders and city bureaucrats, desperate for new housing space, ignored the health warning and ordered a huge apartment region built; they began moving thousands of people into the area in 1985.

"There was not enough housing space, no place to build," Yuri Prokofyev, who became Moscow Party leader after Brateyevo was built, told me in self-defense. "We used to have only five or six air-monitoring stations for such a large city. The officials simply didn't pay attention to this sort of thing in the past."[17]

To make matters worse, city planners saved money by scrimping on stores, service shops, schools, kindergartens, and clinics in Brateyevo. So the few facilities provided have been hopelessly overcrowded. School No. 27 in Brateyevo has the largest student body in Moscow—but not by plan.

"It was designed for eleven hundred seventy-six students, but we have twenty-three hundred students and by 1991 we will have thirty-two hundred students," said Tatyana Sivilna, the principal. "We have to use three shifts, and still the average number of students per class is forty-five. The school cafeteria cannot service all the students, so our kids cannot eat normally. There is no fresh air in the school. There is no point in talking about the quality of our education in these conditions. . . . Our region has twenty-three thousand children but it doesn't have any sports facilities. No playgrounds."[18]

Muscovites could have easily foreseen this overcrowding. But because of the terrible housing shortage, many people—especially those who had been living elsewhere in cramped communal apartments with several small children—grabbed at the chance to move to Brateyevo.

"We were seven years on the waiting list, and when our turn came they named Brateyevo," explained Nina Shchedrina, a school librarian. "We came to look around and didn't like it very much, but we didn't have any choice."[19]

"WE STARTED FEELING LIKE HUMAN BEINGS"

Public patience in Brateyevo boiled over when the Moscow city government began in May 1988 to implement plans for twenty-one more industrial projects within Brateyevo's already smog-choked district. They were to include the largest printing plant in all of Europe; a huge warehouse for bulk raw materials; a regional depot for subway trains; a large park for trolley buses; a transportation terminal for handling millions of passengers from city subway and bus lines bound for Moscow's most heavily used domestic airport at Domodyedovo; plus a collection of light-industrial plants and major scientific and research institutes.

"Suddenly I began to realize that I was in a very dangerous place," Nina Shchedrina recalled. "I have a son. I'm trying to raise him to be strong and healthy. I was worried about his health and the health of my husband. So I started making phone calls. I called the district executive committee and the district council. They kept saying, 'Oh, there's nothing terrible here. Everything will get better.' But things got worse. I came to the conclusion that the authorities were simply not defending my interests. . . . And I saw an announcement over by the store saying that whoever was interested in improving the ecological situation should come to a meeting. So I decided to go and I took a girlfriend."[20]

That first meeting, on July 12, 1988, led to organized protests. But instead of heeding the citizens' complaints, local authorities pressed ahead with construction and switched to what Nina called "a strategy of silence." As she said, "They figured the less we knew, the better. Everything was done secretly, done very quickly. They worked at night, on three shifts, so that people would not notice what was going on. But we noticed, and we took more steps."

On July 27, the activist group in Brateyevo called for picketing the construction sites. In a country where democracy has never taken root and where citizens normally bow before the might of the state, it was a daring and unprecedented step. Even in cosmopolitan Moscow, citizens are not easily roused to political causes. Decades of repression have conditioned them to be passive and cynical. But in Brateyevo, people were so angry at intolerable living conditions, and their committee so well organized, that they ran picket lines around the clock for five days. In all, several hundred people took part, many using their bodies to block trucks from bringing in materials for construction. The picketers had a guitar and cooked food at night. A young law professor, Sergei Druganov, coached them on how to avoid arrest and helped keep the militia at bay.

The Brateyevo protest quickly attracted attention from local Moscow television, the national TV show *Vzglyad,* and such liberal newspapers as *Moscow News, Komsomolskaya Pravda,* and the weekly *Ogonek.* Nina Shchedrina, who has the classic blond good looks of a Russian worker-heroine cast at Mosfilm Studios, was shown on television blocking the path of huge dump trucks.

"We can't put up with any more," she declared. "We want to recall our formally elected deputies and nominate deputies who live here and breathe this air. We want them to understand all our problems and our pain."[21]

Publicity helped the cause, and construction was temporarily suspended. It was a stunning moral victory. Druganov and other leaders took Brateyevo's case to the Moscow City Council and to local officials in the Red Guard District, where Brateyevo is located. Brateyevo's Self-governing Committee demanded a permanent halt to the construction; it developed an alternative plan for a green belt of parks, playgrounds, and athletic facilities around the apartment complex; and it called for the removal of the petrochemical and coking plants, the worst offenders in terms of pollution.

A series of angry meetings ensued with the Red Guard District leaders. "There were some very tense moments, because truly this was breaking the old stereotypes [of Soviet politics]," Yevgeny Pavlov, chairman of the district council, told me. "We thought they were not raising the issue properly, and they thought the executive committee and the district Party committee . . . should move more quickly."

Sergei Druganov accused the Party of ducking the problem and hiding behind the district council and its executive committee, though under the Soviet system these official bodies traditionally take orders from the district Party boss—in this case an old-fashioned apparatchik, Vyacheslav Zheltov. Months later, Nikolai Pilyayev, a Party secretary, admitted to me that Druganov was right.

"This was the first time we had to deal with these kinds of questions," Pilyayev said. "When the people talked of a bad ecological situation and objected to construction, it was new for us. We had never come up against it before. . . . We were somewhat passive at first. We just ignored those people."[22]

To step up the pressure, the Brateyevo Self-governing Committee called for a public referendum to put Brateyevo's residents on record— choosing between the city's industrial zone and Brateyevo's plan for a green belt. The committee was breaking new ground; Soviet law had no provision for public initiatives or referendums. For maximum participation, the committee wanted to hold the referendum on March 26, 1989— the national Election Day. The local bosses were in an uproar; in a sternly worded private letter to Druganov, they banned the referendum and warned that the militia would be called out to maintain order.

This angered Druganov and the Brateyevo Self-governing Committee, who had been careful to keep their protests peaceful and orderly. When I attended their meeting three days before the election, they were furious at local officials.

"They painted us as a band of extremists," Druganov fumed.

"There are lots of people coming to warn us and make dirty hints," added philosophy professor Haik Zulumyan, who was a co-chair.

"They spat in our face," said a balding, goateed plumber, a bit of a Lenin look-alike. "What kind of *perestroika* is this?"[23]

At this point, Gorbachev's political reforms were just beginning to take root, and I found the willingness at that meeting to confront the powers-that-be quite remarkable. These were ordinary people—a plumber, a carpenter, a driver, a woman pensioner, a teacher, a librarian, some rank-and-file Communist Party members—so emboldened by Gorbachev that they were talking about taking power away from local Party overlords.

"Somehow we started feeling like human beings," said Viktor Za-kharov, a carpenter with thoughtful eyes and a great mane of white hair.

"We are not a crowd anymore—we're individuals. We're a group united by mutual interests."

"And we have gotten some self-respect, which is very important," injected Pyotr Kolesnikov, the goateed plumber.

"We found out that our opinion counts," Zakharov said to me. "You see, Gorbachev gave us some sort of belief in ourselves. A belief that *we* could do it."

"He gave us some sort of feeling that we are free to say whatever we think," said Vyacheslav Lomkain, a mechanic. "Before, we said only what they wanted us to say. We were cautious. Now we have a feeling that somebody is really listening to us, taking us into consideration."

The problem was that the "somebody" was Gorbachev, not the local bosses who had just banned the referendum. So the committee drafted a new protest against the ban and demanded that "this discriminatory decision be changed, since it violates the basic human rights of the sixty thousand Brateyevo residents."

Eventually, the local authorities agreed to a referendum—not on Election Day, as residents wanted, but a week later; they were counting on a low turnout once the novelty had worn off. On referendum day, Haik Zulumyan made the rounds of the apartment development with a bullhorn, summoning the voters; people trooped in a light snowfall to School No. 998. The turnout was high and the vote overwhelmingly for the committee.

Unfortunately, the results had no legal power, only the force of a recommendation. As Sergei Druganov complained, "Now we have many laws which are either not enforced or laws ratified stillborn, or simply an absence of laws. All this means that our social relations, our civic life, function very poorly." But to press their cause, the Brateyevo activists demanded a hearing before the district council, a local assembly with 315 members representing the six hundred thousand people in the Red Guard District. Brateyevo comprised 10 percent of that population, but the council—elected before the Gorbachev reforms—included not a single deputy living in Brateyevo.

Moreover, district officials had lined up a barrage of experts from ministries, from the airline Aeroflot, from the city transportation network, from the Moscow architect's office—all of whom pushed for the industrial projects. Nikolai Borisevich, head of the city architectural office that had mapped out the Brateyevo industrial zone, argued that industry would bring jobs (though there was a shortage of labor in the district) and that, as a concession, one industrial site had been moved five hundred yards farther from the apartment area. A health official asserted that the city had no hard scientific evidence that Brateyevo's health problems were worse than in other regions, though he conceded all were in bad shape. Transportation experts insisted that the subway depot, trolley-bus park, and transfer terminal were vital to the city.

Haik Zulumyan protested that the debate was stacked because there were so many powerful state interests trying to drown out the will of the people. "Their budgets consist of billions of rubles and this power gives rise to their self-righteous mentality, which disregards the interests of individuals," he complained. He quoted scientists as saying that there were cancer-causing agents in the Brateyevo air; and finally, he read off the results of Brateyevo's referendum: 21,972 in favor of the green belt, only 38 for industrial development. But Sergei Druganov was denied a chance to speak for several hours and, though normally phlegmatic, he sharply chided the chair. Others from Brateyevo burst out in frustration that only two of their leaders got to speak.

"Comrade deputies," shouted Pyotr Kolesnikov, the outspoken plumber with the goatee, "we are sitting here listening only to those who were registered to speak. Please, listen to us, listen to the public. There were only two people who spoke from our committee."

"Please relax, comrade," the chair replied. "There are fifty people on the list."

"I'm also on the list!" Kolesnikov snapped back, and he turned to his colleagues. "They are not going to let us speak."[24]

What most angered the Brateyevo activists was that district leaders had manipulated the agenda so that the projects were voted on one by one and not as a package, as they wanted. They left the session grumbling.

"Nothing has changed—unbelievable!" blurted out one activist. "The one with the power wins."

"With one-party rule, nothing will change," echoed another. "There used to be repressions and the repressions continue. This blah, blah, blah can go on for another five years."

I talked later with Pavlov, the chairman of the district council. "In the council," I said, "the residents of Brateyevo asked for a simple vote for or against the industrial zone. Why wasn't that possible?"

"You're right that the vast majority of residents expressed their desire not to build these industrial developments," said Pavlov, who had gained experience in deflecting pointed questions. "The council shared that viewpoint. But we had to take into account the opinion of all the deputies. And the deputies thought that this was not only in the interest of the area but in the interest of all of Moscow."[25]

In the end, Brateyevo residents had to settle for less than they wanted.

Some projects, such as the mammoth printing plant and the industrial warehouse, were killed; but the subway depot and the trolley-bus park were given the go-ahead. The local district government pledged to spend 2 million rubles to develop recreational facilities and plant trees; another 1 million rubles was given to Brateyevo's Self-governing Committee to administer. What is more, self-governing committees sprang up quickly in thirty-eight other districts in Moscow, and in many other cities.

Across the country, Soviet environmental protests have scored many local and regional victories over the past three or four years. Russian activists have blocked a scheme to reverse the northern flow of several Siberian rivers for industrial purposes. By Gorbachev's count, environmentalists have shut down roughly one thousand industrial enterprises that manufacture everything from chemicals and metals to pencils, paper, and pharmaceuticals.[26] Environmentalists have been especially effective in fighting the nuclear-power industry, where the government has felt on the defensive.

Since the Chernobyl accident in April 1986, anti-nuclear protests have forced the shutdown of the Metsamor atomic plant in Armenia and halted expansion of reactors at Chernobyl and Khmelnitsky in the Ukraine and Ignalina in Lithuania. They have forced the government to abandon plans to build new reactors at Odessa, Kharkov, Chigirin, and the Crimea in the Ukraine; near the Russian cities of Volgograd and Krasnodar; and near the Byelorussian capital of Minsk. Overall, some 30,000 megawatts of planned nuclear capacity has been abandoned or postponed since Chernobyl; public protests have also interrupted nuclear-weapons testing at Semipalatinsk in Kazakhstan.[27]

Local Green movements have been operating all over the country, and a Green party has been formed in the Ukraine. And while a well-organized national environmental movement has been slow to take shape, Gorbachev's reforms have clearly empowered activists on this issue probably more than any other. In terms of mass support, the Greens rival or surpass the striking coal miners and their demands for economic reforms and independent trade unions, though environmentalists have won fewer sensational headlines than have the miners.

Brateyevo is a good example of how grass-roots environmental protest can affect Soviet political life. Its Self-governing Committee was an excellent political training ground. In fact, the longer-term *political* consequences of the struggle over Brateyevo's industrial pollution were perhaps more significant than the *environmental* gains won for this woefully polluted community.

Old-style Soviet politicians lost out; the district Party boss, Vyacheslav

Zheltov, and Nikolai Pilyayev, the district Party secretary whom I met, were fired. Yuri Prokofyev, who as Moscow Party leader was their overseer, told me bluntly: "There are some people who are used to the administrative method—giving commands or carrying out orders—and they can't give it up. They simply can't work another way. We have to find work for them outside the Party."[28] Yevgeny Pavlov, the district council chairman, ran for reelection in 1990, but lost.

On the other side, the citizen-amateurs succeeded as politicians: Nina Shchedrina, the librarian, won election to the district council in March 1990; Haik Zulumyan, the philosopher, was elected to the Moscow City Council, where he became chairman of the committee on self-government; and Sergei Druganov, the lawyer, won a seat in the Supreme Soviet of the Russian republic.

As Druganov observed, these political results and the psychological changes among people in Brateyevo were probably the most important consequences of the grass-roots revolt against the new industrial zone once planned for Brateyevo.

"What's going on is a radical restructuring of people's way of thinking, a radical *perestroika* of a person's relationship to society," Druganov asserted.

"People are beginning to comprehend that things depend on every individual. If everyone does not participate in *perestroika*, then nothing will happen in the end. . . .

"We understand that we have to fight. We have to stand up for our rights."[29]

CHAPTER 19

ELECTIONS: CROSSING OUT PARTY BOSSES

"Press on, comrades—we from above, you from below. This is the only way *perestroika* can happen. Just like a vise. If there's pressure from only one side, it won't work."[1]
—Gorbachev, February 1989

"Everyone was pessimistic. . . . They thought, Nothing will come of this. It was all unknown territory for us. Our first task was to battle the apparatus. Our second task was to activate the population."[2]
—Yelena Zelinskaya
Leningrad Campaign Organizer
April 1989

The election of March 1989 was a watershed for Soviet society, a historical divide that marked the beginning of a new political era and Gorbachev's move toward a new political order.

That election was the single most powerful catalyst of change in political *perestroika*. By starting the shift of power away from the Communist Party, it launched the transformation of the Soviet political system.

By world standards, the election process was unfair and imperfect. It was intended by Gorbachev as a modest, controlled, incremental step *toward* democracy; it was not truly democratic. Out of 2,250 new deputies, 750 were reserved for the Communist Party, the Komsomol youth organization, trade unions, and other professional groups. The election procedures were manipulated by the Communist Party apparat to protect its power and cripple embryonic democratic forces. In 399 districts, Party officials ran unopposed, and in many regions, such as Armenia and Central Asia, the elections were run the old way. In fact, the great majority of those elected to the new Congress of People's Deputies were Party regulars and loyalists trained by a lifetime of discipline to follow the leader.

Still, the election of March 1989 was like lightning crackling across a long-darkened sky. It struck the foundations of the Soviet power structure like thunder, sending shock waves through the Party establishment.

It was the first election in seven decades with a choice. There were 1,101 election districts that had competition, and 2,895 candidates in all.[3] After years of fabricated unity, of meaningless elections for the Party's designated candidates, the novelty of choice galvanized people from Leningrad to the Pacific Far East. To a far greater degree than anyone, including Gorbachev, anticipated, the chance to reject Party bosses was a powerful magnet; it pulled together democratic movements in the Soviet Union's most important political centers—Moscow, Leningrad, Kiev, Minsk, the Baltic republics. It spawned television debates; it heard calls for a multiparty system; it unearthed army colonels and lieutenants who openly opposed the older generation of generals and called for the end of the Soviet military draft (and in self-defense, some generals advocated student deferments). It forced high officials for the first time to lay out their views, answer questions about how they got cars and apartments, and whether they believed in God.

In the end, the election demonstrated that even when the process was stacked in favor of the Party, it was possible to defeat high Party officials around the country and elect a new wave of radical reformers. The election left the public incredulous, exhilarated, and astonished by its own power.

In the wake of that election began the real shift of power away from the Communist Party and the slow development of a national parliament to challenge the Party's monopoly on control. By lifting a new coterie of reformers and political amateurs to the national stage, the election was the genesis of a political opposition, unsteady and disorganized at first, and certainly no match for the Party machine, but increasingly challenging and purposeful.

In time, the forces set loose by Gorbachev in that election outraced him and his designs for reform. His political offspring harangued him for being too timid and too tied to the Party's Old Guard, and they pressed him toward bolder and more ambitious measures. He was dragged along, repeatedly, reluctantly, by the forces legitimized by the election he had called.

That election, and the first session of the Congress of People's Deputies that followed it, made it all but impossible for Party diehards to halt the momentum of reform or to turn back the path of Soviet history. Short of someone's repeating Stalin's bloody murder of millions, that election and its political consequences made *perestroika* permanent.

That had been Gorbachev's intention, not from the start of his reign but by mid-1988: to use competitive elections to shake up the Party apparatus, open up avenues for new blood to flow into the political system, and at the same time build public support for economic reform by drawing masses of people into public life and giving them a stake in *perestroika*. On the economic side, he did not succeed; but on the political side, he succeeded more than he intended.

As the election approached, Gorbachev traveled the country, preaching his cause, spurring people on to new activism. In a nationally televised encounter on the sidewalks of Kiev, the Ukrainian capital, he invited ordinary people to help him break the yoke of the entrenched bureaucracy.

"Press on, comrades—we from above, you from below," Gorbachev declared. "This is the only way *perestroika* can happen. Just like a vise. If there's pressure from only one side, it won't work."

"The old officials should be replaced!" people shouted.

"Officials should develop from the process of *perestroika,*" Gorbachev shot back. "We should replace the old ones. But where will we get new ones?"

Then he added with a shrug and a grin, "If only we could bake them, like pancakes."[4]

PLAYING THE "GAME OF DEMOCRACY" FOR REAL

Nowhere in all of Russia was Gorbachev's call to action more eagerly or effectively answered than in Leningrad, probably because its politics were so polarized. The city had a long tradition of hard-line Party leaders—from Stalin's henchman Andrei Zhdanov to Gorbachev's onetime Politburo rival Grigory Romanov. Over the decades, crude, iron-fisted rule had bred a festering discontent among a proud but suppressed intelligentsia, many of whom saw themselves as heirs to the European intellectual traditions of czarist St. Petersburg. On the political Right were the neo-Stalinist legions represented by Nina Andreyeva, the teacher whose manifesto had denounced *perestroika;* on the Left were people such as the feisty, independent-minded television producer Bella Kurkova.

In early 1989, feelings were particularly raw because the city government under Mayor Vladimir Khodyrev had decided to raze some old buildings, including the famous Hotel Astoria, once known as the Angleterre. In a city that nurses memories of its imperial past, people considered it a sacrilege to destroy one of the favorite landmarks of old St. Petersburg, still a popular symbol with Leningraders. Khodyrev's decision, backed by the regional Party boss Yuri Solovyov, had provoked the first spontaneous demonstrations in Leningrad in early 1988 and, when he ignored popular feelings, new outbursts in 1989.

"We knew that feelings against the apparatus were extremely powerful; we knew the whole city hated Solovyov," said Yelena Zelinskaya, a soft-spoken writer in her mid-thirties and one of the main organizers of the anti-Party campaign in the spring of 1989. "I hate Khodyrev—he's my personal enemy for what he did to the Hotel Angleterre. We knew the city hated him. Never have we lived so badly in Leningrad. Our living standards under Solovyov are lower than under Romanov and the others before him. Sugar is rationed. Can you imagine—my baby cannot get enough sugar? Our air is worse than ever. Our water is dirtier. Our job [in the election] was to channel the rage of the people against the apparatus.

"So we decided to take part in the election—without hope," Zelinskaya admitted to me. "Everyone was pessimistic. People were frightened. They thought, Nothing will come of this. It was all unknown territory for us. Our first task was to battle the apparatus. Our second task was to activate the population. We had to talk people into taking part in the election. People did not normally participate. I myself had never voted before. But the election campaign was a way to mobilize people, a way to advertise our democratic movement, a way to develop our political muscles."[5]

By that spring, Leningrad was burgeoning with informal groups, from environmental coalitions like Epicenter, Delta, and the Council for Ecological Culture, to historical groups like Salvation and Peterburg, and political organizations like the Leningrad branch of the International League of Human Rights and Club Perestroika. In January 1989, several hundred activists from these various groups met at the House of Writers and formed a democratic coalition that called itself Election '89. They began to draw up a list of candidates, and they formed several committees

to manage the campaign: a legal advisory group to help candidates overcome the obstacles of getting nominated, a "psychological" group to
coach candidates on how to conduct a campaign, a third group to draft
a common program, a fourth group on mobilizing voters and instructing
them how to vote for the first time in a multiple-choice election.

In Leningrad, as elsewhere, the provincial Party leadership resorted to
tricks and maneuvers to block the nominations of rival candidates. Gorbachev's procedures required a two-stage process—first, nomination by factories, institutes, hospitals, farms, and then approval at district meetings
run by the Party or governmental apparatus. Several top officials, including Leningrad Province Party boss Yuri Solovyov, a junior member of the
Politburo, managed to stymie all would-be rivals, and to run unopposed.
Nonetheless, there was still a chance to defeat them: The election law
required the winner to get at least 50 percent of the vote, and it gave
voters the right not only to vote *for*—but also *against*—a candidate. If
enough people crossed out a candidate's name so that he sank below 50
percent, he lost.

Leningrad's Election '89 coalition targeted the Party's unopposed leaders just as vigorously as it pushed its own nominees in contested races.
Yelena Zelinskaya, with her relentless determination and fervent distaste
of the Party apparat, had built an extensive network of friends and contacts from her university years, and from living at the fringe of dissident
politics in the Brezhnev era. Out of her high-ceilinged apartment near one
of Leningrad's canals, Zelinskaya ran a precinct-by-precinct get-out-the-
vote operation that would have done her credit at the Iowa caucuses in
an American presidential campaign. For a nation that had not known a
democratic election for seventy-two years, hers was a very sophisticated
nuts-and-bolts political operation.

On Election Day, March 26, 1989, Zelinskaya had controllers at every
precinct and district, checking the flow of voters; at night, after the polls
closed, these controllers monitored the vote count, and kept her informed
by phone—a sheer miracle given the vagaries of the Soviet phone system.
The regional and city Party leadership, never having faced a challenge of
any kind before, were confident of victory. Soundings by Party organizations at the district and precinct level assured Yuri Solovyov of at least
60 percent of the vote.[6] But by 1 A.M., well before the Party had a full
count, Yelena Zelinskaya knew that even though Solovyov had no opponent, he had fallen!

Two days later, the Party's own newspaper, *Leningradskaya Pravda*, ran
the results: Solovyov had gotten just 45 percent of the vote. There had
been 109,000 people for him, but 133,000 others had gone to the trouble

of crossing out his name—a real testimony to public anger at the Party apparat.[7]

What is more, the voters rejected the entire slate of high Party and city officials, seven in all: Solovyov and his deputy; city Party leader Anatoly Gerasimov and Mayor Vladimir Khodyrev; the leader of the provincial government and his deputy; and the Leningrad regional military commander. After the May 14 runoffs, the anti-Party coalition had elected a slate of reformers, including Anatoly Sobchak, a Leningrad University law professor; Yuri Boldyrev, an outspoken twenty-eight-year-old engineer; Boris Nikolsky, editor of the literary magazine *Neva*, which in January 1989 had printed a scathing attack on the Communist Party, even faulting Gorbachev; and Nikolai Ivanov, a federal investigator who had accused Politburo member Yegor Ligachev of corruption.

Leningrad Party leaders were stunned. As the Soviet press reported, "Literally to the last hour they believed they would win."[8] Some Party officials blamed the press and Leningrad television for biased coverage. Gerasimov admitted the Party had been complacent and had ignored the public's desires when making policy decisions. Solovyov said that the Party "didn't take into account the psychological conditions of the population," especially the need to improve living conditions. Khodyrev blamed everyone but himself.

It was the most stunning blow to the Party's prestige since the Bolshevik Revolution. "I believe it will have a very long-term impact," Boris Nikolsky told me. "Before the election, people thought that this was a 'game of democracy' put on by the leaders. They thought it would come out as elections used to come out, all arranged by the bosses. Now people realize that they have the power to express their opinions and to have an impact."[9]

It was, in Zelinskaya's words, "a real revolution"—the first in Leningrad since the Bolshevik assault on the czar's Winter Palace in 1917.

MOSCOW: COMEBACK FOR BORIS YELTSIN

The elections were also devastating for the Party in Moscow; not only did the hand-picked mayor and some high officials lose, but the Party failed to stop the irrepressible voice of populism—Boris Yeltsin, the hard-driving provincial Party boss who had first been brought to Moscow and promoted into the Politburo by Gorbachev in 1985, and then had been broken by Gorbachev in 1987 for being too brash, too outspoken, too radical a reformer.

To Westerners, Yeltsin might seem a raw, bullish demagogue, but to the Russian man in the street, Yeltsin is a natural for the new politics of *glasnost.* He is a rough-talking, hard-drinking, no-nonsense construction engineer–turned–Party boss, a strapping man with a beefy Russian face, a sharp tongue, and a talent for self-promotion. He has a way of voicing, and igniting, the civic rage of the Russian masses.

Born in a village near the Ural Mountain city of Sverdlovsk in 1931—the same year Gorbachev was born—Yeltsin has had a rebellious streak since childhood. Now silver-haired, he can be charming as well as boorish. He is bright, tireless, and undaunted, a demanding boss and a dangerous foe. At important government and Party meetings, he seems to thrive on confrontation; he will slash at an opponent, and then flash a tight grin and arch an eyebrow at his victim.

By his own account, Yeltsin is prickly, sharp-tongued, and difficult; he appropriately titled his autobiography *Against the Grain.* At Politburo meetings, he felt like an alien, an outsider, and he would provoke the two top men, Ligachev and Gorbachev, with his combative ways. At one session, on September 12, 1987, Yeltsin reported, he made twenty separate criticisms of Gorbachev's proposed speech for Revolution Day—"which caused [Gorbachev] to explode. . . . I was amazed that anyone could react so hysterically to criticism."[10] Gorbachev's aides tried to cast Yeltsin as primarily a foe of Ligachev, with Gorbachev in the center. But Yeltsin's primary challenge was directed at Gorbachev, both publicly and privately.

Yeltsin pushed Gorbachev beyond the breaking point at a Central Committee meeting in October 1987; this was a moment of Party self-congratulation, and Yeltsin was the skunk at the tea party. He rose to tell the Party bosses that "in the eyes of the people the Party's authority has drastically fallen," to chastise the Party for going slow on *perestroika,* and to warn against leaving Gorbachev "totally immune from criticism," because such adulation could bring a new "cult of personality"—a chilling echo of the euphemism once used to describe Stalin's dictatorship. Yeltsin anticipated the onslaught against him—stinging accusations and political excommunication.

Overnight, Yeltsin had become a folk hero. Fired from his high posts but spared a Stalinist execution or exile, he had been given a sinecure post in the Ministry of Construction, and now in the election of March 1989, he was attempting his political comeback. He was running as the voice of the people for the post of at-large deputy from the entire city of Moscow, the single largest election district in the country.

Better than any other politician of the Gorbachev era, Yeltsin had found how to turn earthy barrages against the privileged arrogance and bureaucratic incompetence of the Party elite into vote-getting appeal. Yeltsin's platform called for the Party to be subordinate to the new, popularly elected Congress of People's Deputies, for an end to privileges for Party members, for direct elections at all levels, including head of government, for the rule of law, for popular referendums, for abolition of many ministries, for cancellation of big industrial projects, and for postponement of the space program. Yeltsin cast himself as the people's David against the Party's Goliath.

The Party apparat did everything it could to destroy Yeltsin, and each step backfired, only making him more popular. When the Party threw red tape at his candidacy, he outfoxed them. When the Central Committee accused him of violating Party rules and appointed a commission to investigate, he turned his candidacy into a referendum on the Party establishment. During a televised debate, all the hostile questions were targeted at Yeltsin; one of his backers found out that the questions had been stacked and written not by ordinary listeners but by Party apparatchiks, and he went on another television show to expose the fraudulent debate. When the police, under Party orders, tried to block a Yeltsin rally in Gorky Park, the crowd swelled and marched on city hall, carrying signs that demanded, HANDS OFF YELTSIN!

Each obstacle thrown in Yeltsin's path only served to inflame public opinion; the Party dug its own grave, building up Yeltsin as the people's champion. Valentin Chikin, the anti-Yeltsin editor of the hard-line *Sovetskaya Rossiya*, told me an amusing anecdote about his eighty-four-year-old mother, who was confused by having to make a choice for the first time in her life. Chikin coached her to vote against Yeltsin; but to keep it simple, he instructed her simply to leave the first line—for Yevgeny Brakov, the general director of the Zil automobile factory—and to cross out the second line, Yeltsin; this would count as a vote for Brakov.

A couple of days after the election, Chikin saw his mother.

"Did you vote, Mama?" he asked.

"Yes, certainly," she said, grinning proudly.

"Did you do what I told you?"

"I crossed out the first line and left the second name," she said, grinning again.

"Oh, Mama," Chikin groaned, "that's the opposite of what I told you. Why did you do that?"

"I talked with the people in my building," she chirped. "They were all for Yeltsin. He's for the people. So I decided to vote for Yeltsin too."[11]

Under his political umbrella, Yeltsin brought together forces that intellectual reformers have always had trouble combining: blue-collar workers and the intelligentsia, pensioners and students.

"I'm voting for Yeltsin," said Eddie Baranov, a veteran of Moscow television, "because he's the first one in sixty years to raise his voice and shout out what he thinks. I need *him*, against *them.*"[12]

Yeltsin touched off an avalanche of public rage that buried the Party. He got five million votes—89.44 percent of the total—a stinging rebuff to the Party leadership, Gorbachev included.

"The Party Central Committee did not expect these results," commented Roy Medvedev, the dissident historian who had written about Stalin's terror, and had emerged from the twilight zone to win election himself. "There are people elected whom they did not want—Yeltsin, for example. He's a problem for Gorbachev. He's had a great triumph."[13]

For all its imperfections, the election of March 1989 was the most democratic ever held in the Soviet era up to that point. As Roy Medvedev said, there were stunning upsets all across the country. Some 399 candidates, mostly Party and government officials, had run unopposed, and 195 of them were rejected. In the debris of that election lay the political ruins of three dozen regional Party bosses in Russia, the Ukraine, and Byelorussia, plus the mayors of Moscow and Leningrad, and city leaders in Kiev, Minsk, Kishinev, and Alma-Ata. Sajudis, the national front in Lithuania, swept to victory over the Party; popular fronts scored powerfully in Latvia, Estonia, and Moldavia, as did anti-Party coalitions in Russian cities such as Yaroslavl, Sverdlovsk, and Kuibyshev.[14]

The Party's image of invincibility had been shattered, despite the roadblocks it threw at its new opponents. Many people called the election a referendum against the Party, but Gorbachev's circle construed it more narrowly—as a vote against the Old Guard apparat.

"It's very good they weren't elected," asserted Aleksandr Yakovlev, referring to the Party bosses who had been beaten. With Gorbachev, Yakovlev had co-authored the strategy of using elections to purge the Party from below.

"I know [the losers] and it's great, a terrific example of people voting correctly," he exulted. "Out of the thirty-six, to be honest, I only felt a bit bad for two of them."[15]

Gorbachev seems to have been as surprised as others by the force of the populist vote, but he seized on it as evidence that his revolution from above had now been met by a popular upsurge. "The elections demonstrated that *perestroika* has ceased to be a cause mostly for enthusiasts and trailblazers," he asserted. "We can say that today it has become a truly nationwide movement."[16]

Gorbachev was right: Literally tens of millions of people had taken part in a Soviet election for the first time in decades with some sense that their vote counted for something. And the election had vaulted many new reformers from around the country onto the national stage. Leningrad had a strong slate, as did Moscow: people such as economist Oleg Bogomolov, criminal investigator Telman Gdlyan, political scientist Sergei Stankevich, historian Yuri Afanasyev, and scientific technician Arkady Murashev, an advocate of a multiparty system. The Academy of Sciences elected the world-famous dissident physicist Andrei Sakharov, sociologist Tatyana Zaslavskaya, space scientist Roald Sagdeyev, radical economists Nikolai Shmelyov, Nikolai Petrakov, and Pavel Bunich. From other regions and organizations came radical editors such as Yegor Yakovlev of *Moscow News* and Vitaly Korotich of *Ogonek,* poet Yevgeny Yevtushenko, and economist Gavril Popov, the future mayor of Moscow.

No one could be sure in advance, because no one outside the Communist Party was organized enough to take a nose count, but some reformers guessed they had more than 300, perhaps as many as 400, like-minded deputies in the new Congress—a minority among 2,250, but a large enough group of activists to affect the course of debate and to have a strong impact on the national television audience.

"The big surprise for Gorbachev is that there was such a grass-roots upheaval," commented Boris Kurashvili, a scholar at the Institute of State and Law and a daring exponent of reform under Brezhnev. "There will be independent, unmanageable deputies in the new People's Congress—I figure twenty percent.

"Ten percent is enough to have an opposition that can be heard," Kurashvili emphasized. "There will be enough to form an opposition, an independent bloc."[17]

CHAPTER 20
CONGRESS: GENESIS OF AN OPPOSITION

"Gorbachev is justifiably regarded
as the man who launched *perestroika,*
. . . [but] he finds it difficult to
understand that he is no longer the
only leader of *perestroika.* They are
cropping up all around the country."[1]

—Yuri Afanasyev
Congress Deputy
July 1989

"This is not *real* democracy. The
atmosphere was very different from
previous Supreme Soviet sessions. . . .
The delegates . . . put tough questions to
Gorbachev and he had to reply. They had
their own proposals. . . . So that is . . .
significant democracy, but not *real* democracy."[2]

—Roy Medvedev
Supreme Soviet Deputy
May 1989

Virtually on the eve of the new superparliament, the Congress of People's
Deputies, one hundred thousand people held a rally near Moscow's Lenin
Stadium to support the new liberal deputies and to listen to their ringing
denunciations of the Party apparatus. The speakers included many of the

most influential reformers elected to the Congress: members of the Moscow group, the Leningrad slate, popular-front deputies from the Baltic republics, radicals from the Ukraine, the Ural Mountains, and Siberia.

Heady with victory, they were gearing up for the Congress, demanding more radical change, more power to the people. For seventy years, the Supreme Soviet had been among the world's most supine legislative bodies—no one casting a negative vote, except for a rare smattering in mid-1988. The reformers were now intent on putting life and spine into this moribund institution.

"*Perestroika* in the old sense is ended—the reform from above is ended," said Boris Kagarlitsky, a leader of Moscow's popular front, which had organized the rally. "We are coming to the beginning of the popular revolution. But it will be a dangerous process, and that can also end tragically."

"Why is it dangerous?" my colleague Louis Menashe asked.

"Because we are now seeing . . . the people beginning to show their teeth to the bureaucracy. Still, the bureaucracy has more teeth. It's still much stronger."[3]

The thirteen-day Congress—unprecedented in Soviet history—was an open clash of two contending forces, two casts of mind: a loose, disorganized collection of newly elected radicals bent on challenging the old system and forcing reform, and the loyalist Old Guard, derisively nicknamed by the reformers "the aggressively obedient majority," determined to protect its power and to contain what it saw as an upstart rabble. Between them, playing one force off against the other, using the Left to prod the Right to change, activating the Right to hold the Left in check, and always steering a conservative majority to follow his lead, was the ringmaster—Mikhail Gorbachev.

The Congress opened on May 25, 1989. At a minimum, liberals and radicals wanted democratic procedures, especially open debate and an open agenda. The old power establishment had other designs. It wanted the Congress merely to perform the perfunctory chores of electing Gorbachev as the legislative chairman, in effect Soviet president, and of selecting 542 of its own members to serve in the Supreme Soviet, as the permanent legislature to enact laws and approve policy. (The Congress was a special body, sitting only twice a year.) Over the objections of reformers, who wanted a testing examination of Gorbachev's policies before any vote, Gorbachev rammed through his agenda; debate was put off until the end.

No sooner was the vote taken than the reformers were protesting; their moral leader, physicist Andrei Sakharov, was on his feet, demanding to be heard. Sakharov was even more stooped than I had remembered from the seventies, when I used to watch him at his kitchen table sipping tea from a saucer and nibbling little sour green apples, or when I listened to his vibrant defense of human rights against some new repression by Brezhnev and Andropov. In those days, Sakharov's podium had been his small apartment on Chkalova Street, KGB cars down on the road, agents watching who came and went, his wife, Yelena Bonner, interrogated day after day, his stepchildren harassed. He was then ostracized by other academicians, and shunned by his own children and his former wife. Sakharov had braved it all—the cheap slanders and the vicious hypocrisy—remarkably without bitterness. I had marveled at him; he was a saint—fearless, untiring, always prepared to sacrifice himself for others. His manner was gentle, but he was morally uncompromising. In time, I came to admire Andrei Sakharov more than any other human being I had ever met.

Now, his appearance as spokesman for a budding, still inchoate democratic opposition at the Congress signaled the political transformation taking place. It was incredible to see him in this setting, a massive ceremonial hall with thousands of red seats, and a presidium of two dozen members sitting in polished wooden benches stretching across an opera-sized stage, which was dominated by a huge white plaster statue of Lenin.

There stood Sakharov, once defiled and exiled, now a revered public figure, clearly respected—by Gorbachev, among others—as a voice of reason and conscience. Sakharov's shoulders were hunched, his head rimmed by a wispy fringe of hair, his hearing weak, and his step unsteady. He was a heroic but frail figure; now sixty-eight, he had aged badly during nearly seven years of brutal exile in Gorky, where he and his wife were cut off from almost all human contact and had to stage a hunger strike to get decent medical treatment. His wife later told me how suffocating it had been to have guards accompany them to the bread store and keep people away, or to have doctors force-feed them in the hospital. Through it all, Sakharov's independent spirit remained unbroken, and even if his voice now quavered, his message was clear. On this day of days, he supported Gorbachev, but for Sakharov, free, democratic debate was not a matter of majority approval of an agenda—it was a point of principle.

"I think we *must* have a discussion," Sakharov said with direct simplicity. "We would *disgrace ourselves* before our entire people if we did otherwise. *We cannot do otherwise.* This is my profound conviction. . . . We cannot allow elections to be held in a formal manner. In these conditions, I do not consider it possible to participate in this election."[4]

WHAT ABOUT YOUR WIFE?

As Sakharov finished and before the chairman could curtail discussion, a dozen other reform deputies had crowded to the front of the chamber, shouting to be recognized. Gorbachev, sitting beside the temporary chairman, seemed to acquiesce momentarily. Seizing the instant, they began to barrage him with questions.

Marju Lauristan, outspoken leader of the Estonian popular front, said she saw no alternative to Gorbachev but had several tough questions "which I would like answered before I can vote with peace of mind":

What political and legal guarantees for self-determination by minority republics would Gorbachev put into the Soviet constitution? When had he personally found out that army troops with trenching shovels and gas were being used against peaceful demonstrators in Tbilisi on the night of April 8?

And finally: "Do you personally consider the use of the army for punitive operations against civilians to be compatible with democracy and the rule of law in our country?"[5]

Other questions were more personal.

"There has been a great deal of talk about your building a country *dacha* in the Crimea," asserted Aleksandr Shchelkanov, a fifty-year-old deputy from Leningrad. "Millions now watching on TV should be given a straight answer, and only you can give it."[6]

Leonid Sukhov, a motor-pool driver from Kharkov, stunned the entire hall by asking what was on many lips—a question about the influence of Gorbachev's wife, Raisa.

"I compare you not to Lenin or Stalin but to the great Napoleon, who . . . led his people to victory, but owing to sycophants and his wife, transformed the republic into an empire," Sukhov said. "Apparently you are unable to avoid the adulation and influence of your wife. I am willing to vote for you—but just heed these critical comments."[7]

A whole string of delegates, especially younger ones from Moscow, Sverdlovsk, Leningrad, and Ivanovo, pressed Gorbachev to give up his post as general secretary of the Communist Party, if he wished to serve as head of government.

"I cannot understand how it is possible to combine the two functions," complained Sergei Zvonov, a twenty-six-year-old Komsomol leader from Ivanovo. "That concentrates too much power in the hands of one man, which is contrary to democracy."[8]

As I watched from the press gallery, I knew that no other Soviet leader since Lenin would have brooked such a public challenge. But Gorbachev had obviously decided to allow his critics and questioners their day, to let his openness to challenge serve as an example to other government and Party officials, to let it serve as a school in democracy for the nation at large.

At one point, Gorbachev—who had simply assumed the chairmanship of the session without election—was abruptly reminded that in a society of laws, power and privilege have their limits. As he was addressing the presidium, Aleksei Levashov, a young political scientist from Leningrad, strode to the podium and interrupted Gorbachev, refusing to recognize his authority to head the proceedings.

Gorbachev (to the presidium): "Don't worry, we agreed that all presidium members will preside in turn . . ."

Levashov: "Comrade deputies, according to the constitution . . ."

Gorbachev (to Levashov): "Just a minute—I haven't given you the floor."

Levashov: "It's the [election] commission chairman who should give me the floor."

Gorbachev: "Just a minute. I'll give you the floor, but just the same you should ask for it first. You should show respect to the Congress and the presidium. Please go on, introduce yourself."

Levashov: "Comrade deputies, according to the constitution . . ."

Finally, after a couple of hours, Gorbachev left the chairman's seat, came down to the lectern, and gave an impromptu twenty-three-minute speech, answering some questions, ignoring others.

"I am in favor of dialogue," he said. "All of us today are just learning democracy. We are just now shaping our political culture."

He launched into a general defense of *perestroika,* but acknowledged that it was "moving with difficulty." He said the Communist Party should get out of trying to run the economy, spoke in favor of giving republics more sovereignty, but also urged interethnic harmony. Then he turned to the personal items.

"I accept your businesslike criticism as comradely remarks—I am open to that," Gorbachev said. "The *dacha* question, since it has been raised directly that way, I have said already that in my life, in my whole life, neither I nor members of my family have ever had, or now have, any personal country homes. As far as state *dacha*s are concerned, they are made available to the government leadership . . . and the Party has built retreats for high officials. Perks exist everywhere, comrades. . . . Let's set up a Supreme Soviet commission; let's make an inventory. . . ."

On the "painful" question of bloodshed in Georgia, Gorbachev equivocated. "The army should do the army's job," he declared, but he added that that job was to maintain stability, not to "pacify the people." He disavowed personal responsibility, claiming that he had learned about the army's violent use of force only the morning after it had occurred, a reply that met with some audible skepticism.

Gorbachev sidestepped the question about Raisa, made no concession to demands that he relinquish his Party post, and did not address fears that he would have too much power. His only gesture was the assurance that "I will not exploit my present [Party] position or my future [government] position. . . . I will fight . . . to prevent what has happened in our country from ever happening again."9

This scenario was far short of the general policy debate demanded by radical reformers. Still, Gorbachev's willingness to allow for Q-and-A was a gesture to them and a symbolic bow to the concept that the nation's leadership had to answer to the elected parliament—an important precedent used later by the liberals.

When it came to selecting a chairman for the new Supreme Soviet, Boris Yeltsin was nominated along with Gorbachev, but Yeltsin tactfully withdrew. Then, to great surprise, Aleksandr Obolensky, an unknown construction engineer from Apatita, a town north of Leningrad, nominated himself as an alternative to Gorbachev. Amid murmuring in the hall, Obolensky laid out a progressive program calling for an independent judiciary, a constitutional court, cutting the power of ministries, firing the finance minister because of his hostility to cooperatives, and making the soviets, or regional assemblies, superior to the Communist Party and executive authority all across the country. Obolensky, feeling all elections should be contested, offered his nomination as a matter of principle.

"I am well aware I have no chance of winning," Obolensky said, "but I want us to have a precedent for holding elections. The voters who elected me demand this."10

Obolensky caught everyone off guard. His speech brought spontaneous applause from liberals, and uncomfortable chatter from the claque of conservatives Gorbachev had installed near the front of the hall.

The ensuing debate and the vote on whether to allow Obolensky's candidacy led to the first real test of sentiment in the Congress. When it was over, 689 deputies voted for the principle of competition; 1,415 deputies voted against even allowing a rival to run against Gorbachev.

So Gorbachev ran unopposed and got 96 percent of the vote (2,133 in favor, 87 opposed). Liberals grumbled about looking like rubber-stamp assemblies of the past.

In fact, once Gorbachev was installed, he railroaded through his agenda, ensuring the election of hand-picked lieutenants to all the key leadership posts in the Congress and the Supreme Soviet. He used the obedient majority to block any challengers; all races were uncontested.

So the die was cast by Gorbachev's alliance with the impregnable conservative majority. Even if they sometimes disagreed with Gorbachev, the loyalists understood that their only hope for holding power was to maintain unity and discipline behind Gorbachev. Radicals could debate, could score points against Gorbachev, against government policy, against the system—and their use of that opportunity was important for shaping public opinion and for firmly establishing the practice of open disagreement. But Gorbachev held the high cards; anytime that he wanted to swing the tide, he could signal his wish and manipulate the obedient majority. The solid regiments of Party loyalists and careerists were ready to do his bidding, as they always had been, from Lenin to Stalin to Brezhnev and Chernenko.

"This is not *real* democracy," the historian-now-deputy Roy Medvedev commented to me that afternoon. "The atmosphere was very different from previous Supreme Soviet sessions, where all people did was listen. The delegates today put tough questions to Gorbachev and he had to reply. They had their own proposals and positions, and the country could see that. So that is a significant change for us—it's *significant* democracy, but not *real* democracy."[11]

THE SOVIET NEW BREED

Sergei Stankevich, one of the sharp, new activist Moscow radicals, agreed with Medvedev. "We have no chance to change the general course of events during this Congress . . . because we are in a minority," he told me during an afternoon recess. "We would like to have more profound changes, deeper changes. But we are in the minority now. And our main task now is not to become a majority. That's unrealistic. [Better] to show our people a real alternative."[12]

Stankevich is typical of the Soviet new-breed politicians. Whatever his frustrations, for him the politics of summer 1989 were a dream come true. Slender, clean-cut, and serious, Stankevich looks twenty-three, but he is in his upper thirties. As a political scientist, he had been studying parliamentary government, mainly the U.S. Congress, for fifteen years in dusty archives, most recently at the Institute of History. But in all that time, he had never been to America, never seen a live, functioning Western parliament. Suddenly, Gorbachev's new politics gave Stankevich the wholly unexpected opportunity of becoming a real politician, of testing his skills as a power player.

As a student at Moscow State University, Stankevich had steered clear of the Communist Party. He was skeptical of Communist orthodoxy, turned off by the corruption of the Brezhnev era, and disillusioned by the Soviet invasion of Afghanistan. As a teenager, he admired many things in the West and considered himself part of the Beatles generation. "I learned English so I could understand the Beatles' songs," he told me with a shy grin. In 1987, Stankevich had been drawn into the Communist Party as part of the "Gorbachev wave," his idealism excited by the prospect of reform. He soon joined other radical Communists in a group called Inter-Club, which wanted to reform the Party from within.

Only in January 1989 did Stankevich decide belatedly to run for the Congress of People's Deputies; he was one of many academics and political amateurs who came out of the woodwork. Angered by attacks on Boris Yeltsin by the Party apparatus, Stankevich organized—and publicized—a telegram of support to Yeltsin from several young reform candidates. Back then, climbing on Yeltsin's bandwagon was an act of some courage for such a junior Party member; in fact, his district Party organization considered expelling Stankevich for his generally liberal, Westernized politics. Stankevich was running against the Party hierarchy, as a strong advocate of making the popularly elected legislatures, the soviets, more powerful than the Party.[13]

As Stankevich had expected, his defense of Yeltsin and his own positions were very popular moves. They marked him apart from rivals in a multicandidate race in Cheremushkinsky District, a sprawl of urban housing on the south side of Moscow. To his own surprise, he made it through the first round into a runoff, and then he won the second round to gain a precious seat in the Congress. Suddenly he had become a celebrity, appearing on television, addressing large crowds. Now, with his knowledge of parliamentary procedure and a certain poise bred from facing down competition, Stankevich was a rising young comer among the Moscow radicals.

He felt that if the reformers were too small a minority to compete for high posts, they should make the session a public test of Gorbachev's commitment to democratization. Like other reformers, he wanted Gorbachev to repeal anti-democratic laws, such as a decree that put restrictions on public meetings and rallies; it had been approved in July 1988 by the old Supreme Soviet. In the provinces, and sometimes in Moscow and Leningrad, hard-line bosses and police chiefs had used the decree to ban democratic rallies and to arrest organizers; liberals wanted the decree suspended. On the first day, they demanded a vote but Gorbachev, who had a way of ignoring unwelcome proposals, refused.

During a recess, I caught up with Yeltsin to ask his reactions to the session so far. He was unhappy. I asked him whether he thought ordinary people in Moscow would be satisfied.

"No, they will be deeply dissatisfied," Yeltsin retorted, eyes flashing, head bobbing over a whirl of reporters who were crushing in on both of us. "I think you will have a chance to see on the Moscow streets. There is a good reason why the authorities decided to refrain from making any decisions during the Congress on the issue of street demonstrations. They are pretty well aware that there are lots of Muscovites ready to go out and demonstrate."[14]

Late that evening, as the session was ending, Stankevich tipped me off that two thousand of his supporters were holding a rally near Pushkin Square in the heart of Moscow, and he was going to meet with them. Together, we walked fifteen blocks from the Kremlin up Gorky Street. "My voters came to me and said we must go there immediately," Stankevich told me. "There is a real possibility for bloody conflict. We should try to help these people."

When we got there, we could hear the crowd, but in the darkness, all we could see at first were clouds of rising dust and several rings of police, some in riot gear, with helmets and billy clubs. One group of demonstrators had planned to march on the Kremlin, but the police had surrounded them. Now, they were penned inside the police rings.

As we approached, I could hear shouts.

"Long live freedom of assembly!" someone cried.

"Respected citizens, please roll up your flags and leave the square," commanded a police officer over a bullhorn. "Your meeting is over. Stop violating public order."

"Never, comrades!" came back the retort. "We'll hold to the last man. We won't stand for it."

Once Stankevich showed his deputy's badge, the police cordon opened to let us through. A few yards farther on, the crowd engulfed us, pressing in like a vise, chanting rhythmically, "Stan-kay-vich! Stan-kay-vich!" Then a babel of shouts, angry accusations, and a melee over a megaphone that was being passed to Stankevich. Fearful that the first sign of a scuffle would be used by the police as a pretext to make arrests, he used it to try to calm the crowd.

"I ask you . . . be calm, if possible," he shouted through the megaphone. "Don't get hurt or do anything rash."

Above the din, Stankevich gave a shouting report to his voters. He told of reform proposals, of the voting, of the demands made, of the reformers' frustration at the rigidity of the hard-line majority.

"They spat in our faces," he declared.

A plump woman, obviously a rally leader, took back the megaphone and tongue-lashed Stankevich for the reformers' failure to wring concessions from Gorbachev. It was obvious from her comments, and those of others, that these people had followed the live telecast of the Congress in detail, with the fresh enthusiasm of people long denied that privilege and hungry to use it well. It was also obvious that these people saw the Congress as the voice of the people and they were angry that it was being manipulated by Gorbachev and the hard-liners.[15]

The demonstration lasted until 3 A.M. The police were not violent, but they made a few arrests. The menacing atmosphere was enough to prompt Stankevich and other liberals to take the issue of free assembly and the anti-rally decree back to the Congress floor the next day. But when Stankevich went to the rostrum to make his report, conservative deputies drowned him out with rhythmic applause, a typical Soviet harassment tactic.

Like all the new Soviet breed, Stankevich speaks with a refreshing and almost naïve candor that lacks the polished platitudes of many American politicians. He is unvarnished, direct, thoughtful, rather resembling Jimmy Carter, though instead of singsong, he is given to a matter-of-fact monotone that would worry an American media adviser. Yet beneath Stankevich's academic exterior, there is a hard self-confidence that rises to a challenge. On that morning, he bristled when he sensed that his political manhood was being rudely tested.

"They were trying to dump me," he recalled later. "I was very angry at that moment. I understood that besides these two thousand delegates in this hall, millions of people were in front of their TV sets and they [would] judge me by my every word and gesture. It was an unforgettable feeling. I knew I had to defend my position, that I could not lose face in this situation, this real conflict. I understood: If I lose face, I cannot be a real politician. People will not trust me."[16]

Facing down his challengers, Stankevich turned to Gorbachev, demanding that he bring order to the hall.

"I am asking that respect be shown to deputies," Stankevich said.

Gorbachev backed him. "We're going to go very slowly if you keep interrupting," he warned the other deputies.

"This anti-democratic tendency of drowning out speakers at the Congress is impermissible," declared Stankevich, his voice rising toward a shout.

One of the old-line deputies, sitting in the front row, shot back: "He's too young—too young to teach us."

Stankevich heard the taunt; it was a spur, a stimulus to counterattack.

"Excuse me—are you talking to me?" he retorted. "I ask the chairman to stop the anti-democratic actions that unfortunately are becoming fashionable here. It's a disgrace. I have been sent here by three hundred and eighty thousand voters, and you have no right to shut me up."

Stankevich was not only protecting himself; he was also trying to force Gorbachev to stop the conservative majority from doing what it had done the first day: clap and talk in order to rattle liberal speakers and drown them out.

"I will try to conduct this Congress in an organized fashion so it doesn't degenerate into a farce," Gorbachev declared.

"I didn't see the police dispersing the rally," said Stankevich. "Still, some actions must be taken. Some space in Moscow must be set aside for the people to gather, to learn the news and meet with deputies. It's absolutely essential for the normal functioning of the Congress."

On the heels of his report, reform delegates made another push to put the rally decree to a vote. Gorbachev relented, knowing full well that the conservative majority would not overturn a decree that gave large discretion to local authorities—that is, to themselves and their allies in the apparat. And he signaled his own desire to see the decree sustained, and it was.

After the vote, Gorbachev tried to put a good face on it, to be conciliatory to the radicals by giving a soft interpretation of the decree. "The question is decided, but what does that mean?" he said. "We don't suspend the decree, but the decree does not prevent rallies."[17]

The reformers had hoped for much more from Gorbachev; they had hoped that in promoting the new politics of mass participation, Gorbachev would come out against the decree himself and see it stricken. Many reformers had assumed that since Gorbachev had called the elections in March and had convened the Congress, he would be in their camp most of the time. But the first two days of the Congress had shown just the opposite.

"Gorbachev's mind is unclear to us," Stankevich said, not wanting to write him off completely so early in the session. "He is not fully predictable in his actions. We anticipated that his behavior during this Congress would be more in support of the democratic line, the democratic group."[18]

As the Congress wore on, Stankevich found himself repeatedly on the opposite side from his mentor and hero. His seat was in the sixth row, not far from Gorbachev, and he found that the Soviet president often spotted him voting against his position; he could overhear Gorbachev commenting to aides on the dais, "Well, look, Sergei is against us once again."

After the Congress was over, one national magazine ran a photograph of the two of them, Stankevich and Gorbachev, standing toe-to-toe on the empty dais, talking intently during one of the breaks. Gorbachev had beckoned to Stankevich to come up to the dais for a personal chat; Stankevich had clearly been flattered by such personal attention, especially when Gorbachev showed that he knew something about Stankevich personally, that he had studied the American Congress.

From his reading, Stankevich knew about the charm treatment. He understood that Gorbachev was lobbying him the way that Lyndon Johnson, as president, had shrewdly massaged the egos of younger members of Congress by taking them aside to talk, man to man. Gorbachev was "working" Stankevich, trying to soften his radicalism, trying to win him over to a more centrist position.

"What did he say to you?" I asked Stankevich.

"He said, 'Well, I understand your aims. I understand that you are sincere in your activity. But please don't accelerate the process. Don't push . . . don't push, because maybe we should go steadily. . . . So you should be more moderate, in order to avoid sharp conflict during this Congress.' "

"What was your reply?" I asked.

"Well, my words [were], 'If we stop our activity, the whole Congress will go in the old way and we can lose the trust of our voters. So that if we would like to have really new decisions, we should insist on some radical proposals. They should be heard, at least. They should be heard. They should be taken into account . . . in order to demonstrate the whole spectrum of positions, in order to have more freedom of choice.' "[19]

BRINGING THE GENERAL TO HEEL

All across the nation the reformers were heard, day after day. The Congress was such a hot running political soap opera, providing six or eight hours of live television programming daily, that part of the country simply stopped working. There, before their eyes, people could see the brash young deputies daring to challenge the most powerful figures in the land, Party leaders, ministers, army generals, those accustomed to giving orders and never having to answer for their actions. People were glued to their television sets, and government officials estimated that production nation-wide fell off 20–40 percent during the two weeks of the Congress. For a nation that had never seen real political debate, this was a festival of free expression. And it was the radical reformers who provided the fireworks.

By the second week, they had begun to work together informally as a loose grouping based around the Moscow and Leningrad delegations. They took their cues from people such as Andrei Sakharov, Boris Yeltsin, the radical economist Gavril Popov, and Yuri Afanasyev, a former Party activist and Komsomol apparatchik who now headed a historical institute and was the most tart-tongued radical speaker. It was Afanasyev, hand-some, with close-cropped hair, and powerfully built, who taunted the conservatives for being an "aggressively obedient majority" still mired in a "Stalinist-Brezhnevite mentality" that was "out of step with the times and the needs of the country."

In all, something close to four hundred deputies were part of the loose cluster of reformers, but they were far from an opposition bloc. It was too soon for formal organization; these new deputies were too ill acquainted with each other and with the changing political system to be ready to organize that way. And they had many diverse interests. There was one cluster of nationalist democrats from the three Baltic republics, and some like-minded nationalists from Moldavia, Georgia, the Ukraine, and else-where. There was an even larger group of Russian democrats interested in economic reform, environmental protection, seeing more power given to the soviets or legislatures at all levels of Soviet society, and determined to reduce the power of the Party apparatus and the centralized state.

Some radicals, like Yuri Afanasyev, wanted to pressure Gorbachev, to break with him if need be, to force big changes that would seize power from the Party. Others, such as Stankevich, were more pragmatic, liberal rather than radical; even when Gorbachev blocked them, they saw them-selves as Gorbachev's shock troops against the diehard Right, eager to push him further, faster, but hesitant to treat him as an adversary. They were all moving to open up the Soviet political system and wrest power from the Party-state apparat. Day by day, from the Congress podium, they set about shattering old taboos while the conservative Old Guard cringed in their seats.

In one stinging speech, former Olympic weight-lifting champion Yuri Vlasov savaged the KGB as "a threat to democracy," condemning it for a history of torture, murder, and misuse of psychiatric hospitals to intimi-date free-thinkers. Today, Vlasov said, the KGB was "not a service but a real underground empire which has not yet surrendered its secrets."

Vlasov's father, a committed Communist and diplomat in China, had disappeared in 1953 at the hands of state security. "We must honor the memories of our fellow citizens who were victims of excesses and executions," Vlasov said solemnly.

The strapping former athlete, who was now in his fifties, got a standing ovation from hundreds of deputies when he called for the removal of KGB headquarters from Dzerzhinsky Square in downtown Moscow because of the "unforgettable bloody history of the building." Gorbachev joined the applause briefly when Vlasov said the KGB chairman should be approved by the Congress; but Vladimir Kryuchkov, the head of the KGB, and other members of the Politburo sat with blank stares through his shocking address. It was the sharpest public attack on the KGB in memory.[20]

In a similar vein, Boris Yeltsin called for a new Soviet constitution that would bring the Communist Party under the rule of law, transfer primary power from the Party to the Supreme Soviet and Congress, eliminate the Party's control of the mass media, and provide for direct election of the chief of state. Yeltsin had already been the focus of controversy in the Congress; the Gorbachev-controlled presidium had maneuvered the conservative majority to exclude Yeltsin and Stankevich from membership in the Supreme Soviet, an obviously outrageous move given the fact that Yeltsin represented the largest constituency in the country. The liberals created an uproar, and after another deputy offered to give up his seat in favor of Yeltsin, Gorbachev belatedly sanctioned the move.

Yeltsin's speech was a manifesto for reformers, but the poet Yevgeny Yevtushenko—ever theatrical, in a bright white suit to match the white plaster statue of Lenin—upstaged Yeltsin. Yevtushenko explicitly demanded what was unthinkable to Gorbachev and the Old Guard. He reminded the hall (87.6 percent of the deputies were Communists[21]) that he was *not* a Party member and then called for repeal of Article VI of the Soviet constitution, which enshrined the Party's "vanguard role" in Soviet society and guaranteed its monopoly on power. And he advocated a new amendment to ensure that all citizens—"Party member or non-Party member—have . . . complete equality when being nominated to fill any Soviet state positions, including the highest ones." This struck at the heart of the Party's control of the entire country through its system of *nomenklatura*—the secret appointment of all government officials, heads of industrial enterprises, farms, and top leaders in the army and security services.[22]

One sacred cow after another was skewered. The radicals' irreverence was epitomized by publicist Yuri Chernichenko and historian Yuri Karyakin. Chernichenko had the cheek to publicly mock Politburo member

Yegor Ligachev, whose responsibilities had recently been shifted from ideology to agriculture. "I merely want to ask, as I was asked a hundred and sixty-eight times," Chernichenko demanded to snickering in the hall, "why in a politically essential sector have they placed a man who understands nothing of [agriculture], and who has failed in ideology?"[23] Karyakin called for restoring Soviet citizenship to the exiled writer Aleksandr Solzhenitsyn and then assaulted the holy of holies: He appealed for the removal of Lenin's body from the mausoleum on Red Square, the shrine built by Stalin to glorify the Party dictatorship.

"Lenin himself wanted to be buried beside the grave of his mother at the Volkon Cemetery in St. Petersburg," Karyakin reminded the deputies, but his wishes were ignored, as Karyakin sarcastically recalled—"of course, in the name of Lenin."[24]

But the reformers wanted more than rhetorical victories; their own power rested on mass public support, and their greatest fear was that the power of the army, KGB, and special security troops under the Ministry of Internal Affairs would be used to crush democratic protests and to suffocate the entire reform movement. Fresh in their minds was the brutal crackdown in Tbilisi, Georgia, during the wee hours of April 9, less than seven weeks before the opening of the Congress. They demanded guarantees that troops would never again be used against peaceful rallies and that high officials would be held accountable for such acts of repression.

Protesting the violence in Georgia became the reformers' most successful cause. From the very first moments of the Congress, on May 25, when a Latvian delegate called for a minute of silence to honor the victims of the "Tbilisi massacre," that tragedy became a primary issue. Gorbachev had been asked about his role, and when he disclaimed any advance knowledge of the crackdown, one deputy asked what the point was of having a national leader who could be ignorant of such actions. Eldar Shengelaya, secretary of the Georgian Filmmakers' Union, circulated an amateur videotape that showed tanks and armored cars running down people in the streets; the corpses of women and children, their heads and bodies bloodied, reportedly by troops wielding trenching shovels; and other victims asphyxiated by poison gas.

A Georgian deputy, T. V. Gankrelidze, described the events to the Congress: how at 4 A.M. on "bloody Sunday," after demonstrators had gone to sleep in the central square, troops had sealed off the exits and then staged a brutal assault. "The Tbilisi tragedy revealed the utter bankruptcy of the U.S.S.R. legal mechanism," the deputy declared. He called for the expulsion from the Congress of Colonel General Igor Rodionov, who had commanded the troops in that operation. (As military commander for

Georgia, Rodionov had been elected a deputy from the Georgian district of Borzhomi two weeks before the massacre.)

"Only complete *glasnost* and punishment of those responsible can prevent the catastrophic effect of this tragedy on the moral state of our fellow citizens," Gankrelidze asserted. "Colonel General Rodionov has neither the moral nor legal right to remain a people's deputy for the U.S.S.R. from Georgia."[25]

The charges brought one of the most dramatic showdowns of the Congress: Rodionov, in uniform and with a chestful of medals, made his way to the rostrum, demanding the right to reply. He is an imposing man, with a strong, deep voice and a commanding presence. It was obvious that it rankled him to be called to account before this assembly.

"It is necessary to give a political evaluation of what happened in Tbilisi," he declared. "The deputy who spoke before me said the rally was peaceful . . . [but] there were vile appeals for physical violence against Communists, and anti-Russian and nationalist attitudes were being fanned. . . . All measures of persuasion and appeal to reason [had] been exhausted and there remained the extreme measure—to apply force. . . ."

A voice from the audience shouted: "We have witnesses among the deputies, so you'd better . . ."

The chair cut in: "Just a minute—we have given over the floor. Let him say what he has to say. . . ."

Rodionov: "The situation was very complex. I am sure that the person who spoke here was not present there on the street. I was there from three A.M. . . . and stayed as long as necessary. I saw it all with my own eyes.

"There were mistakes on our side. We were in a hurry. . . . Incidentally, comrades, according to official information, sixteen people died at the site of the tragedy. . . . Not a single one of those who were picked up, and the square was clear by six A.M., not a single one had a cut or a stab wound. Not one of the sixteen."

There was a commotion in the hall and some protests.

Rodionov: "Do not interrupt me! The investigative agencies have gone into this. . . . I am especially disturbed, comrades, by discussion of the use of chemical agents. . . . People talk here about how bad it was in 1937 [at the peak of Stalin's purges], but I think it is worse now than in 1937. Now, people can talk about you on television, write about you in newspapers, and the mass media can defame you, however they wish and without justification."[26]

When Rodionov finished, there was prolonged applause from the obedient majority. But the reaction was far different across the country, and

Gorbachev sensed it. Suspicions had been raised about the Kremlin's role, and Gorbachev sent out a deputy, Politburo member Anatoly Lukianov, to read to the Congress the texts of cables between Party headquarters in Moscow and Tbilisi; these exculpated Gorbachev and put the blame on Georgian Communist Party leaders. The wrangle broadened, in full public view, when the Georgian Party leader, Dzhumber Patiashvili, accused General Rodionov of giving him exaggerated reports of the danger from demonstrators, which tricked him into approving the use of force.

Roald Sagdeyev, a deputy who was Gorbachev's leading space scientist, called the Georgian mess "our Irangate, and General Rodionov is our Colonel Ollie North."[27]

The radicals were on the hunt for a smoking gun, and Gorbachev felt compelled to bow to their demand for a parliamentary investigation. He named Sagdeyev and other reformers to a commission headed by Anatoly Sobchak, a law professor and one of Leningrad's leading radicals. Rodionov was quickly relieved of his command and named head of the General Staff military academy, but his career had clearly been damaged. It was a powerful lesson to the army.

As the parliamentary investigation proceeded, it contradicted the Kremlin's previous denials of Politburo involvement in the events of "bloody Sunday." The radicals had a powerful ally inside Gorbachev's inner circle—Foreign Minister Eduard Shevardnadze, who was also the former Georgian Party chief. Shevardnadze had flown to Georgia to investigate, arriving just as the plans to crack down were unfolding, but evidently he was not informed of the intention to use force until after the fact. *Moscow News* carried an article on September 10, 1989, revealing that Defense Minister Dmitri Yazov had given Rodionov orders for the Soviet troops to use force and that authority had come from Victor Chebrikov, former head of the KGB, who was described as the Politburo "duty man" on the fateful night. Yegor Yakovlev, the editor of *Moscow News*, told me that Shevardnadze had provided information for that article and given it political protection. Ten days later, Chebrikov was thrown out of the Politburo.

The parliamentary inquiry also pointed to Yegor Ligachev, who, while Gorbachev was visiting Britain and Cuba, had chaired a Politburo session on April 7, authorizing the use of troops. Ligachev charged that Gorbachev and Shevardnadze had been at the April 7 meeting—and Anatoly Sobchak publicly accused Ligachev of lying. Nonetheless, Ligachev and Yazov had somehow both survived; Chebrikov and Rodionov became the fall guys.

The radicals could count the Tbilisi affair as their biggest single victory at the Congress. It would take months for the political drama to play out, but the plot line was clear before the Congress closed: High officials were being brought to account by the new political system, and in the end, heads rolled. The reformers had taken Gorbachev literally when he preached the gospel of a new "law-governed state." And on the issue of "bloody Sunday" they had clearly established the vital principle of parliamentary oversight of the government. For a fledgling democratic parliament, that was no mean feat.

THE SOLEMN TREAD OF THE LOSERS

The hard-liners, largely a silent majority during the first week, took out their vengeance later in the Congress session. Their pent-up frustration at the radicals boiled over on June 2 at the most distinguished dissident in the assembly, Andrei Sakharov, for his accusations against Soviet forces in Afghanistan. The humbling of Sakharov was an emotional but calculated display of the power and passion of the right wing. The Old Guard was intent on humbling the reformers on national television and undercutting their power by casting them in the public's eyes as anti-patriotic.

Sergei Chervonopisky, a thirty-two-year-old former major in the Soviet airborne troops who had lost both legs in the war, and one of 120 Afghan war veterans in the Congress, was the first to savage Sakharov. A hand-picked Komsomol delegate from the Ukraine, Chervonopisky lashed out at Sakharov for his charge, in an interview with the Canadian newspaper *Ottawa Citizen*, that Soviet pilots had sometimes fired on Soviet soldiers to prevent them from being taken alive by Afghan rebels.

"To the depths of our souls we are indignant over this irresponsible, provocative trick by a well-known scientist," Chervonopisky declared. He accused Sakharov of trying to discredit the Soviet armed forces and attempting "to breach the sacred unity of the army, the Party, and the people."

Gorbachev and the entire Politburo joined in a standing ovation for Chervonopisky's censure of Sakharov, and again when he concluded with a paean to Communism, a word that he said had not been used enough at the Congress. "The three words for which I feel we must all fight," declared the thundering Afghan veteran, "are *state, motherland,* and *Communism.*"[28]

Gorbachev gave the hard-liners free rein, and speaker after speaker heaped opprobrium on Sakharov. "Who gave him the right to insult our children?" demanded a fifty-year-old farm worker.

"Not a single order or anything like it was issued at the General Staff and the Ministry of Defense, nor did we receive any such savage instructions from the political leadership of our nation," declared Marshal Sergei Akhromeyev, former chief of the General Staff. "All of this is a pure lie, a deliberate untruth, and Academician Sakharov will not find any documents to substantiate it."[29]

A twenty-five-year-old teacher from outside Tashkent told Sakharov: "You have insulted the entire army, the entire people. . . . I have nothing but contempt."

When Sakharov rose to make his own defense, he had to shout to be heard above the boos and catcalls. Just as he had done in the seventies, he faced the angry chorus alone, and he did not flinch or retreat.

"The Afghan war was a criminal adventure . . . a terrible sin," he asserted. "I came out against sending troops to Afghanistan and for this I was exiled to Gorky. I am proud of this exile to Gorky, as a decoration which I received. . . . I have not apologized to the Soviet army, for I have not insulted it. I have insulted those who gave criminal orders to send troops to Afghanistan."

He insisted that no one could accuse him of false accusations until there was a full investigation of his charges.[30]

Gorbachev and Sakharov clashed more directly on June 9. These were the final moments of the Congress, and Gorbachev was putting a favorable gloss on its work, indulging in his characteristic fence-straddling between radicals and regulars. He began by welcoming the "critical spirit, fresh thinking," and "constructive opposition" of the reformers; but he concluded by categorically rejecting their broadside attacks on the Communist Party and warning them against "a struggle against the apparatus."

The conservatives did not even want to let Sakharov speak, but Gorbachev gave him five minutes. And his final assessment was gloomier; he worried that the Congress had failed to achieve a real transfer of power from the self-perpetuating Party-state apparat to the elected parliament, and he warned that concentrating great power in one man, Gorbachev, was "extremely dangerous." As Sakharov laid out a program to halt the KGB's domestic operations, strip the Party of its legal supremacy, and make all high state officials subject to recall by the Congress, Gorbachev told him his time had run out.

Sakharov tried to go on.

"Finish up," Gorbachev scolded.

"I am finishing," Sakharov pleaded. "I have left out a great deal."

"That's all!" Gorbachev chided. "Your time, two time allotments, has run out."

Sakharov mumbled something more.

"All!" commanded Gorbachev. And he cut off Sakharov's microphone.[31]

These two confrontations with Sakharov captured the anger of the Right and Gorbachev's impatience with the reformers. What is more, they displayed the sharp ideological cleavage at the Congress, and in the country as a whole.

But these episodes could not obscure the larger meaning of the Congress. For in spite of Sakharov's anxieties and the obvious limitations of a parliament controlled by a stacked majority of regulars with a vested interest in the status quo, in two short weeks the Congress had altered the political landscape of the Soviet Union.

By letting liberal and radical reformers debate freely, Gorbachev had given the entire nation a schooling in the new politics, via television. He had also begun reshaping the institutional structure of the political system. Admittedly he had held the reins tightly; still, he had begun to shift power away from the closed sanctuaries of the Communist Party hierarchy to the open arena of the new superparliament.

Regardless of what Gorbachev said or of his manipulative tactics, he had conveyed a change in the flow of power by his very presence. There, before the nation, he sat every day for thirteen days, from gavel to gavel, watching, listening every moment, commenting, responding, guiding the whole process. It was a personal tour de force. The picture of Gorbachev with his headphones, his arm gestures, his quick flashes of temper, or his gestures of conciliation all carried a message to ordinary people, and to the Party apparat, that this process, this body, was significant enough for the nation's leader—indeed, almost the entire national leadership—to devote full time to it.

Russians are careful readers of visual symbols. The physical picture of Gorbachev's commitment to the Congress was indelible; it took attention—and power—away from the Party. The Party regulars felt the loss, and eventually came to make this theft of power a major point of contention with Gorbachev.

At a minimum, he had sanctioned the idea of legislative oversight and had shifted the arena of debate, and hence that of policy-making, out of the Party's hands. His move was not direct and complete enough to satisfy Sakharov and the radicals, but it was palpable enough for the Old Guard to feel it.

An episode at the end of the second week of the Congress sticks in my mind. I came out of the Kremlin's Hall of Congresses quickly after the session and found myself among the members of the Politburo and senior

Party officials as they were walking across the Kremlin grounds. Black limousines rumbled over the Kremlin cobblestones, like so many power boats idling up to a dock, ready to ferry the Party VIPs to a Communist Party Central Committee plenum gathering that night. But the leaders kept walking, their security men fending off my efforts to talk to them.

Gorbachev was far ahead, so I could not see his face, but the mood of the others was somber, funereal; there was no animated conversation, no exchange of pleasantries, just a low mutter. Their silent, sober mood spoke volumes. It suggested that the power barons of the Communist Party had been chastened, and irked, by the challenging tone of the reformers; it had been a wholly new experience for them, and now they were walking across the Kremlin grounds with their tails figuratively between their legs. Their whole way of life had come under fire, and they understood from Gorbachev's sanction of the political free-for-all that things could never be the same again.

THE OPPOSITION TAKES SHAPE

Their political nightmares only increased. No sooner did the Congress end its session, than the new Supreme Soviet went to work—the very next day, June 10, 1989—and despite reformers' fears that it would be an old-fashioned captive assembly, it immediately shocked the government. The Supreme Soviet was a 542-member miniature version of the Congress, operating as the permanent legislature, whereas the Congress met briefly twice a year as a constitutional assembly.

As the Supreme Soviet convened, the legislative battle over the Tbilisi affair was fresh in everyone's mind; it set the tone for advice and consent in the Supreme Soviet. The deputies heeded Sakharov's advice that confirmation of government ministers was the legislature's responsibility. Gorbachev had maneuvered approval of Prime Minister Nikolai Ryzhkov from the Congress, but his cabinet faced the Supreme Soviet. Its grilling of Ryzhkov's ministers was so aggressive that eventually three ministers— including one deputy prime minister—were rejected, the nominations of six more were withdrawn by Ryzhkov because of opposition by legislative committees, and two others quit in the face of likely defeat.

No one was more sharply interrogated than Defense Minister Dmitri Yazov. During a five-hour debate broadcast on national television, Soviet viewers saw the extraordinary spectacle of one of the nation's most intimidating figures being subjected to a bold and unrelenting parliamentary inquisition.

Deputies grilled the graying, heavy-set, and slow-moving Yazov about military corruption, discipline problems, violent hazing of new recruits, and poor living conditions for career officers and sergeants. They pressed him to apply student draft exemptions, and to consider ending the draft in favor of a professional army, and they inquired about combat readiness and the size of military forces.

Genrikh Borovik, head of the Soviet Peace Committee, tried to get Yazov on record as opposing further nuclear-weapons testing and acknowledging the dangers of radioactivity. Yazov tried to duck, more than once, and Gorbachev had to prod him to answer directly; eventually Yazov said: "We have to develop weapons; otherwise we will lag behind the U.S."

Among four hundred written questions were several about the size of the armed forces—a figure never publicly revealed. Yazov, hesitating, eyed Gorbachev for guidance.

"Well, I don't think it will be a secret, Mikhail Sergeyevich . . ."

"Go on," Gorbachev nudged.

Yazov said the figure would be 3.7 million after Gorbachev's promised reductions of 500,000 were completed.

Adapting to the new rules of Soviet politics, Yazov said the size of the military budget was for the Supreme Soviet to decide, but he went on record in favor of cutbacks. "I think that is appropriate," he said. "You see, in the end you have so many weapons, mountains of weapons, and you can become a prisoner of those weapons. . . . Naturally, this [reduction] will to a certain extent reduce the combat readiness of the armed forces, but we must perceive combat readiness not in an abstract way but in comparison with other states and blocs."[32]

Nonetheless, Yazov staunchly opposed the demands of Baltic deputies that non-Russian recruits be allowed to serve in their home republics— and they announced that they would vote against him. He also rejected proposals for a professional army. He claimed widespread reports of hazing in the military were exaggerated, but he admitted that the army lacked housing for sixty thousand career officers and sergeants soon due to be mustered out. And he refused to go along with a call from university educators for the release of 176,000 university-level draftees; six days later the Supreme Soviet overruled him and discharged the students.

Several deputies in uniform were among Yazov's sharpest critics. Lieutenant Colonel Viktor Podziruk, a military reformer from the Ivanovo region, accused Yazov of granting the top brass too many perks and cushy retirement, and permitting a system of political patronage. He called for cutting deadwood and chastised Yazov for reducing technical training while protecting political indoctrination units and sports regiments. Lieutenant Nikolai Tutov, a twenty-eight-year-old pilot from Orenburg in western Siberia, was even more outspoken. He said the army was in a quagmire because "Dmitri Timofeyevich Yazov has no real conception of *perestroika* in the armed forces," and he called for Yazov's replacement. Other deputies argued that Yazov was too old, too inflexible, too stuck in the past, and the country needed a younger, more modern-minded chief.

Gorbachev, sensing danger, stepped into the argument; the defeat of his own hand-picked defense minister would be devastating. Trying to save Yazov, Gorbachev admitted shortcomings in the military and endorsed some of the deputies' demands for change. But in an effort to take Yazov off the hook, he asserted that Yazov had inherited a bad state of affairs when he took over in May 1987, and had made improvements; he also pointed out that defense policy was formulated not by Yazov alone, but by the National Defense Council headed by Gorbachev himself.

Only this personal intervention rescued Yazov—and even then Gorbachev had to bend the rules. Confirmation requires a majority of at least 272 votes; Yazov got only 256 yes votes, with 77 against and 66 abstentions. Because there were so many absentees, Gorbachev persuaded the Supreme Soviet to amend its rules and accept a plurality instead of the required majority. But the Supreme Soviet, put on guard, set up a new committee to oversee the Ministry of Defense and KGB.

Victorious, Gorbachev flew off to France, and on the very next day, with Prime Minister Ryzhkov in the chair, the Supreme Soviet rejected Deputy Premier Vladimir Kamentsev, chairman of the Foreign Economic Commission and a key figure in Ryzhkov's plans for reinvigorating the economy through foreign economic projects. Deputies accused Kamentsev of nepotism and squandering the country's raw materials.

The Supreme Soviet sessions attracted so much public interest that the government decided to delay the televised broadcasts until evening, to get people back to work. Wherever I traveled, I found everyone, from scholars and Party officials to hotel maids, with their chairs pulled up in front of television sets until 2 A.M., still incredulously watching the new politics. And then they dragged to work the next morning.

Over the summer months and then in the fall session of the Supreme Soviet, the radicals began to use committees to advance their causes and to critique government policy. The great bulk of policy initiative and legislation still came from the government, but the Supreme Soviet shaped a new pension law and passed its own bill for reducing taxes on cooperatives from 90 percent to 35 percent. In the spring of 1990, it rejected the unpopular bread and food price increases proposed by Ryzh-kov and forced more liberal provisions into his economic reform bill. More significant, it passed two crucially important initiatives of the radicals: a law banning censorship and permitting any individual or group to operate a newspaper or television station; and a law granting wide powers to local governments, including control of property within their jurisdiction.

By the fall of 1990, the Supreme Soviet was not yet a Western-style legislature, but it was gradually accumulating power at the expense of the Party apparatus and the executive branch.

Equally important, the 1989 summer Supreme Soviet session brought the formation of an organized opposition. In mid-July, Boris Yeltsin called for formation of a "leftist-radical" group to push for more rapid reform; he said more than 300 deputies from the larger Congress had expressed interest. Frustration was forcing the radicals to organize; their demands for constitutional reforms had been ignored, and they felt at a disadvantage on other issues. So on the weekend of July 29–30, 1989, what became known as the Inter-Regional Group took shape; some 316 Congress deputies attended its founding session in Moscow, including 90 from the Supreme Soviet. Another 119 deputies, unable to attend, signified that they would join.[33] At that stage, they avoided declaring themselves a party or picking an ideological label; a certain vagueness helped preserve unity among this diverse group.

The Inter-Regional Group had two main bases of support. One nucleus was from the Baltic republics, where the national drive for self-determination was the primary interest and rallying cry. It was reinforced by other nationalist deputies from Moldavia, Georgia, and the Ukraine, who favored republican sovereignty, but were less assertive and less cohesive than the Baltic delegations. Its second main base was the Russian reformers, mainly from Moscow, Leningrad, and provincial centers such as Sverdlovsk, Yaroslavl, Novosibirsk, and Volgograd. This element included economists and budding entrepreneurs whose primary goal was to reduce the power of ministries and to push market economics; political reformers whose priority was to build the effective power of the Congress, Supreme Soviet, and local soviets; journalists who were after legislation that would end censorship; environmentalists who wanted most of all to fight industrial pollution and the hazards of nuclear power. The Russian reformers were tolerant of minority nationalists, but they did not support total independence; and the Balts supported the dispersal of power in Moscow, but their real interest was regional. So there was common ground among the constituent groups, but the coalition had its limits.

Equally important, the reformers were divided among radicals and pragmatists. The more fiery radicals like Yuri Afanasyev accused Gorbachev of being paralyzed by fear and of failing to take bold action; they urged the Inter-Regional Group to declare itself an opposition to Gorbachev.

"Gorbachev is justifiably regarded as the man who launched *perestroika* but is no longer capable of being the leader of both the reform and the *nomenklatura* [the Party-state apparat]," declared Afanasyev. "He has to make a choice. He finds it difficult to understand that he is no longer the only leader of *perestroika*. They are cropping up all around the country."[34]

In the same vein, Yeltsin proposed that the Inter-Regional Group demand local, regional, and republican elections in the fall of 1989, to give a new impulse to the democratic movement. (The Party apparat was trying to cancel local elections; Gorbachev leaned toward putting them off until 1990.) Yeltsin asserted that the coal miners' strikes in the Ukraine and Siberia signaled that the public was fed up with talk and wanted faster action for reform. "The people have been disappointed by the Congress and the Supreme Soviet," Yeltsin declared; the miners' strike committees were "embryos of real people's power."[35]

Pragmatic liberals, such as Sergei Stankevich, argued that it was unrealistic for the Inter-Regional Group to force a confrontation with Gorbachev at this stage. Other deputies disagreed with Yeltsin on the issues. The pragmatists saw the role of the Inter-Regional Group not as Gorbachev's opposition, but as a liberal force backing *perestroika* but pressing Gorbachev to move more boldly and to ignore right-wing foot-dragging.

Typical of its diversity, the Inter-Regional Group could not settle on a single leader. It chose five co-chairmen: Yeltsin, Sakharov, Afanasyev, the economist Gavril Popov, a shrewd, low-key strategist, and Viktor Palm, an Estonian scholar who represented the Baltic delegations.

What united these diverse elements most was common hostility to the Party apparatus; their determination to break up the centralized, dictatorial structure of Soviet power and to curb the arbitrary power of the army, KGB, and national police; and their insistence on free assembly, rule of law, and the authority of elected legislatures as guarantees for the pluralistic, democratic politics that Gorbachev had promised.

The more assertive they became, the more warily Gorbachev reacted. As the Supreme Soviet closed its session on August 4, Gorbachev warned the new Inter-Regional Group not to divide the Supreme Soviet nor to create artificial confrontations. The conflict grew sharper in late September. After two days of heated debate on September 23–24, the Inter-Regional Group adopted a platform calling for movement toward a multiparty system, a mixed economy, a free press, and a popularly elected head of government. The platform specifically demanded the abolition of the Communist Party's monopoly on power, and Sergei Stankevich drafted a law to legalize alternative political parties. Having now organized formally, the reform coalition demanded that Gorbachev recognize them as a parliamentary opposition and grant them their own staff, offices, bank account, and newspaper.

Gorbachev had swung to the right that fall, under heavy pressure from Politburo conservatives, and now he lashed back at the radicals. Through aides, he flatly refused their demands for formal recognition and the organizational trappings of an opposition. Stung by their criticism, Gorbachev denounced the radicals on the first day of the fall session of the Supreme Soviet, September 25. Without naming the Inter-Regional Group, he condemned any interference with the efficiency of the Supreme Soviet and warned them against making trouble. And he chastised the reformers for speeches with "too little content and too much harshness, and even simply a disrespectful attitude toward the Supreme Soviet."[36] At a stormy meeting with editors and cultural leaders on October 13, Gorbachev was more vitriolic; he lashed out at the reform deputies, calling them "a gangster group."[37]

Even moderates like Stankevich were dismayed to have their patron turn on them so sharply. Stankevich suggested to me that Gorbachev was exhausted from nearly five years of reform, and that he was so much a prisoner of his own past that he was incapable of moving much further, especially to surrender the Party's guaranteed political supremacy.[38]

So Gorbachev had been overtaken by the forces he had let loose and was now trying to check them, and they were fighting him more openly. They were still a legislative minority, but public pressures were mounting in their favor—the nationalist movements all over the country, and other populist movements, such as environmental protesters and the coal miners' strike committees. Through the fall of 1989, Gorbachev acquiesced in the crumbling of Communist regimes across Eastern Europe, but he grew harsher at home, resisting the nationalists, spurning the Inter-Regional Group. But come the spring of 1990, he responded to the pressure for yet another momentous shift of power away from the Party to the new institutions of government.

ANARCHY OR THE "IRON FIST"?

It was the radical reformers Yeltsin and Sakharov, in speeches to the first Congress, and then collectively in the September 1989 platform of the

Inter-Regional Group, who first proposed a popularly elected president. The reformers saw the presidency as a vehicle for taking power away from the Party, as a counterweight to the Politburo, a means for weaning Gorbachev from the influence of the Old Guard apparat. Amid periodic rumors about the dangers of a military coup or a right-wing plot to oust Gorbachev, moderate reformers saw the presidency as a way of protecting Gorbachev's survival by giving him a legally impregnable base of power.

For months Gorbachev rejected the idea, probably because he knew that the Politburo and other strongholds of Party power would never accept such a surrender of their authority. In a speech to the Supreme Soviet on October 23, 1989, Gorbachev argued against "starting off along the path of switching to presidential power" on grounds that the country's democratic processes were still too feeble to invest such a concentration of power in the hands of one man. That would undermine the effort to build up the authority of the legislature, he said, and divert energies from engaging the people in grass-roots politics.[39]

A little over three months later, in February 1990, Gorbachev had flip-flopped: He seized the idea of a strong presidency and was ramming it through the Supreme Soviet; he called for a special session of the Congress of People's Deputies to pass the necessary constitutional amendments.

The motives for Gorbachev's turnaround were complex. Central Committee officials told me that he was increasingly frustrated by seeing his economic and political reforms blocked by Yegor Ligachev and Party conservatives; a presidency would free him of that albatross. Undoubtedly, too, Gorbachev had in mind the precedent of Nikita Khrushchev; in the early 1960s, Khrushchev had alienated the Party hierarchy by attacking its lines of power, and the Politburo barons had thrown him out on October 14, 1964. Gorbachev had been far bolder than Khrushchev in bringing the Party under assault, and he had faced dangerous rumblings through the fall and winter of 1989–90; Moscow was full of coup talk. So a popularly elected presidency offered him a safer power base.

Most important, however, was the sense of chaos and disintegration in Soviet society: rising crime, the breakdown of the economy, and the widespread disenchantment with *perestroika*. There was a sense that things were falling apart. Nationalist movements were growing more powerful and more willing to challenge Moscow. Generals complained about thousands of Soviet youth ducking the draft, and of thousands more deserting in the republics. The killing of Armenians by mobs of Azerbaijanis in January 1990 had been followed by new outbursts of interethnic violence across Central Asia. Gorbachev himself had complained of "a kind of chain reaction accompanied by an orgy of violence."[40]

That fall and winter, Moscow intellectuals whom I knew talked darkly of the dangers of "civil war" or a violent repression by the army, KGB, and Party right-wingers, a crackdown that they feared would snatch away the precious new freedoms of *glasnost* and democratization. I heard less of this as I traveled out across the country, except in places where there was actual ethnic strife. Nonetheless, the overall sense of social and economic collapse had awakened the desperate Russian fear of disorder—of anarchy—and the reflexive response of the right wing, using what Russians call the "iron fist" to impose order from above.

At the center, in the Central Committee and the Kremlin, officials spoke of a paralysis of power, and the need to fill the power vacuum. "Central power is now much too weak," complained Gorbachev's alter ego, Aleksandr Yakovlev. "We need to strengthen it."[41] No one rival then threatened Gorbachev, but with the economy in such terrible shape, his prestige had fallen. He had lost power in practical terms; his orders were not being carried out—no one's were. The old system of top-down commands had been deliberately shattered, so that the nation's economic structure and the Party hierarchy were no longer functioning effectively, though they still stifled individual initiative; and the new system of democratic self-interest and legislative power had not yet taken hold, to spark spontaneous economic growth and enterprise.

The final straw for Gorbachev was the anti-Armenian violence in Baku. Before he sent in eleven thousand Soviet troops, Gorbachev claimed to have been hamstrung by legal requirements that he first gain the consent of Azerbaijani authorities and of the presidium of the Supreme Soviet, a process that took three or four days. With a strong presidency, Gorbachev's team argued, he could have taken firm action more swiftly. The Baku episode seems to have tipped the balance in Gorbachev's mind and also enabled him to win endorsement of a strong new Soviet presidency from the Communist Party Central Committee and the Party regulars who still dominated the Supreme Soviet.

But Gorbachev, eager to shore up his power and free himself from the constraints of both the Politburo and the legislature, had a serious problem. Legally establishing a presidency required amending the Soviet constitution, and only the Congress of People's Deputies could do that. It was convened on March 12, 1990. Gorbachev wanted swift action, but he could not be sure that he had enough votes. He was handicapped by the changing arithmetic and politics of the Congress. Amending the constitution required a two-thirds vote; in a body with 2,250 members, the magic number was 1,497. But with deaths and absentees, only 2,021 deputies registered for the session. Every single missing deputy made Gorbachev's task harder, because it subtracted from his potential total. Moreover, the deputies from Lithuania—which had just declared its independence on March 11—were attending as observers and were boycotting the vote.

What is more, Gorbachev could not count on support from the Inter-Regional Group, because he had turned their democratic presidency into an office with dictatorial powers, and they were by now very wary of Gorbachev's intentions. One of Sakharov's final warnings had been not to give one leader too much power. With that in mind, the liberals accused Gorbachev of trying to rush through the new presidency without time for proper consideration and careful drafting of the necessary constitutional amendments.

"We can still feel the great totalitarian tradition in this country," protested Sergei Stankevich, after Gorbachev railroaded his presidential bill through a preliminary vote in the Supreme Soviet. "If the law is adopted [by the constitutional Congress] in its present form, the president can do almost everything."[42]

At the Congress, the Inter-Regional Group was split between the "aggressive opposition" and the "constructive opposition"—Stankevich's terms. The aggressive faction, led by Yuri Afanasyev, advocated uncompromising opposition to Gorbachev's proposal; the pragmatic faction, represented by Stankevich, wanted to modify the proposal to make it more reasonable. Stankevich warned the radical caucus that Afanasyev's strategy was impractical and doomed, given the mood of the country. "It is not possible for us to stop it," he told me. "We must try to make it more acceptable. We must save Gorbachev from himself, oppose him and force compromise."[43]

Gorbachev's strategy was to sweeten his package for the radicals by combining it with two measures of great interest to the Inter-Regional Group: new constitutional language on permissible forms of economic property; and the elimination of Article VI, the constitutional guarantee of the Communist Party's political monopoly. He was coupling the presidency with constitutional sanction of a multiparty system. He had already won approval of that package from the Party's Central Committee.

To get his way on the presidency, Gorbachev engaged in more blatant manipulation of the Congress than ever before. When reformers were pressing him too hard, he ignored their requests to speak; if they already had the podium, he would cut off the mikes; more than once, he closed the microphones in the entire hall to lecture the deputies; and he simply refused to allow votes on proposals that did not suit him.

His parliamentary sleight-of-hand—more slippery, as one reporter said, than the tricks of the legendary American House Speaker Sam Rayburn or Senate Majority Leader Lyndon Johnson—reached a climax when Gorbachev duped the Inter-Regional Group on the critical vote to establish the presidency, *before* they had a chance to offer amendments to his proposal from the floor. Gorbachev stood normal parliamentary procedure on its head, and even ignored the rules of the Congress. Under normal procedure, amendments to a proposal are considered first, and then it is voted on as amended. When Gorbachev first put his presidential proposal to a vote on March 13, the reformers thought it was a vote in principle and that there would be a second reading later, after amendments were attached. But Gorbachev whisked the proposal through—it carried easily by a vote of 1,771 in favor, 164 opposed, and 74 abstentions—and then pronounced it adopted as part of the Soviet constitution.[44]

The radicals were outraged when they learned that Gorbachev had hoodwinked them, and that their amendments would now require a two-thirds vote, instead of a simple majority, as the rules required. A stream of radicals vehemently protested Gorbachev's chicanery and demanded another vote.

"This is a parliamentary abomination," Stankevich exploded. "We have violated all the classic parliamentary rules and several of our own rules of procedure."

"It's a circus," fumed Arkady Murashev, a Moscow radical who had voted for Gorbachev's package. "We were manipulated. We didn't know what we were voting for."

Gorbachev, unmoved, coldly cut them off. "This is normal procedure in parliaments all over the world," he said. "The discussion is closed."[45]

The radical reformers were crestfallen. Their only comfort was that Stankevich, with his skill in the intricacies of bill drafting, had been meeting privately with Gorbachev's aides to work out changes in the proposal. And on the night before the vote, he had won acceptance of limitations on the most egregious excesses of Gorbachev's proposal. So those provisions were included in the version approved by the Congress and were now part of the constitution.

Stankevich had a list of amendments aimed at making the Soviet president legally accountable and at curbing his dictatorial powers. Of his list, about half of the key amendments had been accepted. Most important were the inclusion of the legislature's power of impeachment, by a two-thirds vote of the Congress, for presidential violation of laws or the constitution; and also significant limits on the president's powers to issue decrees and to declare a state of emergency.

Gorbachev's draft had granted the president virtually unlimited power to issue decrees and to declare a state of emergency, and then impose direct presidential rule in any region of the country. These provisions legally made the president a czar or dictator, and alarmed the reformers. Stankevich had insisted on language that allowed presidential decrees only "on the basis, and in fulfillment, of the constitution . . . and the laws of the U.S.S.R." On declaration of a state of emergency, Stankevich inserted the requirement that the president must receive a request or gain approval from the local government, or else obtain immediate confirmation of his action by a two-thirds vote of the Supreme Soviet. One exception was made for declaring martial law in the event of a foreign military attack on the Soviet Union.

Other inroads on Gorbachev's draft were accomplished by the liberals. One made it less cumbersome for the legislature to override a presidential veto; another took the authority to appoint a Constitutional Control Commission away from the president and gave it to the chairman of the Supreme Soviet. The Baltic delegates from Estonia and Latvia, whose votes Gorbachev needed badly, bargained for language pledging that the new presidency "does not change the legal position or entail any restriction on the competence of union and autonomous republics," obviously including their constitutional right to secede.

In short, there had been the real politics of compromise. Stankevich was especially pleased with the changes on presidential decrees and the state of emergency. "Those are real limitations on the president," he told me. "They make [Gorbachev's proposal] almost acceptable to me." But progress was fitful; rights won on paper did not always work out in practice. Stankevich was smarting at Gorbachev's high-handed floor tactics, and with other reformers, he was determined to fight for still further restrictions.

The reformers got one important floor amendment through—a provision protecting the chairman of the Supreme Court from removal by the president; but they failed on others because they were boxed in by Gorbachev's procedural trick. A proposal to strike any mention of the Communist Party in the constitution got a vote of 1,067 to 906—positive but not a two-thirds majority.

The most important effort, and the most painful defeat, was a proposal that would have forced Gorbachev to give up his post as general secretary of the Communist Party; the amendment prohibited the president from serving as an official of any party, but again, while the vote was 1,303 to 607, a solid margin of victory, it was short of two thirds (1,497). That so angered the radicals that they demanded a new vote on the original proposal for the presidency. Gorbachev, sensing conservative impatience, shrewdly called for a vote on whether to vote again. That idea went down to resounding defeat.

Stankevich's final effort was a bid to limit Gorbachev to an initial term of two to three years. The new constitutional change provided for a five-year term and popular elections. But with the polls showing a severe drop in his public support, Gorbachev evidently feared a popular vote and wanted his first election made by the 2,250-member Congress. Stankevich and other reformers were willing to vote for him—but only on condition that Gorbachev agree to a short, transitional first term.

"I sent Gorbachev a note saying, 'If the idea of a transitional presidency of two or three years is adopted, then everything will be okay, and a lot of radicals will vote for you,' " Stankevich recalled later. "I stood near the microphone at the front, trying to get recognized. But Gorbachev ignored me. It was a real risk for Gorbachev not to let our proposal come to a vote. He made a big choice: five years or nothing!"[46]

Gorbachev was gambling that he had drawn a stark choice for the Congress: either back him all the way or face anarchy and chaos. It was a typical Gorbachev tactic to force his critics into a predicament where they felt they had no alternative but to side with him, despite strong differences with him.

As reinforcement, just before the vote on whether the Congress should elect the president, Gorbachev sent to the podium two of the most influential voices with the liberals: his Politburo ally Aleksandr Yakovlev and Dmitri Likhachev, the elderly academician with impeccable anti-Stalinist credentials, who is known as a voice of reason. Both made the argument that the country was in too deep a crisis to afford the delay and the divisive turmoil of a popular presidential election.

"The idea of a popular vote is attractive, correct, and legal," Yakovlev conceded, "but any delay can throw us back. . . . I am afraid of a miscalculation that will cost our country and our people dearly."[47]

Likhachev drew a parallel between the situation in 1990 and the situation after February 1917, when Russia's prerevolutionary experiment in constitutional government was undermined by civil turmoil. Sitting in the gallery, I could feel a chill silence descending on the hall as the tall, distinguished, aging scholar spoke.

"I remember perfectly well the February Revolution," said Likhachev, who was a boy of eleven at that time. "I know what people's emotions are like, and I have to tell you that at the present time our country is swept with emotions. In these conditions the direct election of a president would lead to a civil war. Believe me. Trust my experience. I am opposed to a direct election. The election should be held here and without delay."[48]

The stage was set for Gorbachev, and he came perilously close to losing. Everyone watched the electronic voting teller attentively: 1,542 for, 360 against, 76 abstentions. Gorbachev's margin of victory was only 45 votes.

Now he had to go through the actual balloting for president. Two other candidates were nominated by conservatives: Prime Minister Ryzhkov and Interior Minister Vadim Bakatin; both withdrew in favor of Gorbachev, but not before there were several blistering speeches attacking him, from both left and right, the liberals worried about Gorbachev's enshrining one-man rule, and the conservatives condemning him for a country in ruins.

"We live in a nightmarish situation, in a nightmarish country, under a nightmarish system of doing things," protested a bemedaled military officer.

"Every minute he is losing votes of deputies," Vladimir Tikhonov, a leading reformer, commented to me during a smoke break. "More and more people are unhappy with the machinery of changing the constitution. Have you ever seen a legislature amend and pass a constitution orally—with oral amendments? And in just three days? No civilized country operates this way."[49]

I asked Dmitri Likhachev how he thought the people would vote, if given a chance.

"I doubt Gorbachev would win," he replied. "People are upset about food. They would vote for someone else—a negative vote in protest against the government."[50]

That sentiment was palpable in the hall too, and the secret ballot for the president gave Gorbachev's critics and enemies, including those in the Party apparatus and the military, a hidden chance to vote against him.

By law, Gorbachev needed votes from at least 50 percent of the total membership of the Congress. A year before, in the first Congress, Gorbachev had received 96 percent; but as Tikhonov said, support seemed to be ebbing by the hour.

When the final tally came in, Gorbachev had just 59 percent, an embarrassingly small majority from this establishment assembly. Out of 2,250 deputies, only 2,000 took ballots—and not taking a ballot was one way of opposing Gorbachev; 54 ballots were invalid, and 122 did not use their ballots (again, votes against Gorbachev). Of the ballots cast, 1,329 votes were for Gorbachev, 495 against. But counting the unused ballots, the negative vote was really somewhere between 600 and 800. Obviously, both right-wingers and radicals had opposed him in significant numbers.

The next day, Gorbachev administered the oath of office to himself, promising to uphold the Soviet constitution and pledging a new surge of radical reforms. But the final action of the Congress, a Gorbachev-engineered denunciation of Lithuania's declaration of independence, was hardly a promising beginning: It was a stream of invective, a charade of parliamentary procedure, a throwback to the old obsequious Supreme Soviets of the Stalin and Brezhnev eras; it embarrassed and infuriated my Moscow intellectual friends.

In the immediate aftermath, the reformers were disappointed with the whole process, and fearful that the legislature was still the pliable tool of Gorbachev, on whom almost everything depended. Stankevich, Tikhonov, and others, such as Roy Medvedev and the writer Aleksandr Gelman, openly decried the shortcomings of both the Congress and the Supreme Soviet; Gorbachev and the government had the political initiative, controlled the budget, could manipulate the conservative majority, and the new democrats had only a skeleton staff, an infant newspaper, and the bare framework of organization.

It was, as Medvedev repeated to me, "not real democracy." But as he also observed, the changes were significant.

In a year, from the elections of March 1989 to the Congress of March 1990, Gorbachev had overseen the establishment of a new parliamentary system and a new presidency. In a country where kings and dictators had ruled for life or until some cabal dethroned them, there was now an elected president, with a fixed term of office, a line of succession (the chairman of the Supreme Soviet and the prime minister), and a two-term limit. There were provisions for impeaching the ruler, for passing legislation against his will, and for overriding his veto.

However imperfectly it worked, the Supreme Soviet had shown that it dared to reject government policy and throw out government ministers, and it now had the constitutional power to topple a government— through a vote of no-confidence.

Of course, the system looks better on paper than in reality; Soviet leaders are experts at nice-sounding proposals, but bad at putting them into practice, especially when they cut across the interests of the rulers. Gorbachev was no exception, as he had shown in the Congress. As Stankevich observed to me, "Gorbachev is not a democrat—he is a democratic autocrat."

Still, for a society that has never heeded the rule of law, the changes in the structure and functioning of the government have been momentous.

This was hardly a Western-style democracy, but Gorbachev could no longer exercise power in isolation, like Stalin; he had to operate more like a Western leader, dealing and bargaining with a variety of forces. In May 1990, for example, the Supreme Soviet rejected the price increases and the economic-reform program put together by Gorbachev and Ryzhkov. The Communist Party had no say in the matter—it was losing its grip on power.

The Politburo and the Central Committee were being superseded by the new mechanisms of elected government, a presidency and the Supreme Soviet. Gorbachev had shifted the primary power for ruling the country out of the hands of the Party, and he had tolerated, however reluctantly, the rise of a political opposition.

CHAPTER 21

COMMUNISM: "KNEE-DEEP IN GASOLINE"

"When people see the elated tone . . . in our press about how bourgeois leaders praise *perestroika,* it raises questions in their minds. They remember Lenin's advice: 'Think twice anytime your class enemy praises you.' "[1]

—Ratmir Bobovikov
Provincial Party Boss
April 1989

"How is it possible to have a situation where life is humming all around, and where vital problems are being discussed by the people out in city squares, but certain Party organizations are still chewing stale gum?"[2]

—Gorbachev, July 1989

No institution in Soviet society had more to lose from Gorbachev's reforms than the Communist Party apparat, what the Russians call the *nomenklatura:* the self-selecting, self-perpetuating hierarchy of the Party, and the inner core of government officials and economic executives who are named to their posts by the Party. In a famous book, the maverick Yugoslav Communist Milovan Djilas called this *The New Class.*

These are not rank-and-file Communists, the nineteen million members of the Soviet Communist Party. These are the Party's inner hierarchy, its power elite: the Politburo, the Central Committee, and their staffs, as powerful as the Office of the Presidency in Washington combined with the apparatus of the congressional leadership; the power barons who rule all the republics, provinces, cities, districts, and villages; their legions of apparatchiks; the Party secretaries and Party committees in every farm, factory, coal mine, university, TV station, army unit, KGB detachment; the staffs of hundreds of Party newspapers at every level of society, from *Pravda* to industrial shop-floor leaflets; as well as thousands of Party lecturers, propagandists, speech writers, and instructors constantly agitating on the Party's behalf.

It is a formidable political machine—217,700 full-time employees with an annual budget of more than 2.7 billion rubles (officially $4.5 billion).[3] Add the interlocking echelons of key leaders in the government and in all facets of the economy, all of whom are dependent on the Party's patronage, and you have the *nomenklatura*. Add, too, another million part-time Party workers and lecturers. This is more than any normal political party; it is what the New Left of American politics calls "the power structure," an entire web of power. It is the Party integrated into the governmental and economic structure of the Soviet state, at every level of society. That is what makes the Party-state apparat so difficult to dislodge.

To break the Party's grip on power in the Soviet Union was different from overthrowing Communist rule in Eastern Europe. For one thing, the Communist parties in Poland, Hungary, East Germany, and Czechoslovakia were imposed by the Soviet army, whereas in Russia, the Party came to power out of a homegrown revolution. In Eastern Europe, the Communist Party was an agent of alien rule, a tool of an occupying army, so that when the power force of local nationalism was released, the mass of the nation turned against the Party. That also happened in the minority regions of the Soviet Union; Lithuanians, Armenians, Ukrainians, and others turned against the Party. But Russia was different; for all the grievances of Russian nationalists, a strong Communist Party had meant a powerful Russia, dominating a huge empire. Stalin had played that theme, especially during World War II. Party and nation had been linked; so nationalism was not a force that reformers could use to turn the masses of Russians against the Party.

With the natural instinct for survival of politicians and bureaucrats everywhere, the *nomenklatura* intuitively understood just how much of a threat was posed by Gorbachev's drive to shake up the Soviet system and to bring in new blood. Most of them mistrusted his ulterior motives, despite what he said, and they fought him every time he chipped away at their edifice, or shook the foundations of their power.

But as Gorbachev geared up *perestroika,* the Party was no longer a Stalinist monolith. Since Khrushchev's time, it had included three factions: a small minority of anti-Stalinist reformers, another minority of neo-Stalinist counterreformers, and a majority of conservatives committed to protecting the status quo.[4] Under Gorbachev, the different tendencies multiplied. Party liberals backed reform, convinced it was vital to save the Party; a small radical minority wanted more sweeping reforms. Some conservatives endorsed economic reform only and opposed political changes. The bulk of the *nomenklatura,* politically to the right of Gorbachev, paid lip service to *perestroika* because it was the Party line, but they dug in their heels against assaults on the Party's supremacy and control. They were strongest among the Party machine in the provinces, in the military and the KGB, in the right-wing Party press, in some ministries, and in the Politburo faction led by Yegor Ligachev.

Gorbachev's well-nigh impossible task was to persuade the *nomenklatura* that what was clearly against their individual and collective self-interest in the short run was in the higher interest of the Party over the long run. He tapped into their lifelong habits of unity, discipline, following orders from the top, to try to get them to do what troubled them in the marrow of their bones: to change their ways and gradually surrender some of their power.

Initially, Gorbachev's strategy was to reform the Party from within by drumming out the Brezhnevite Old Guard, by gradually replacing other officials bit by bit, and by carrying out minor periodic purges and cutbacks. But there were so many layers that he could not scrape away the Old Guard fast enough; a new layer replaced the old one. By 1987, pursuing "socialist pluralism," he allowed formation of rival groups, of informal grass-roots organizations, but he wanted to restrict them to the role of junior partners, protecting the Party as the dominant force in Soviet society. Nevertheless, over time, his aides told me, the intransigence of the apparat gradually "radicalized" Gorbachev, and his assaults on its entrenched power became more frontal.

The first real jolt to the apparat's power was the election of 1989.

Before that, Gorbachev had been whittling away at the old structure through press articles that jabbed constantly at Stalinist terror and Stalinist thinking, and through the Nineteenth Party Conference in mid-1988, where he made the *nomenklatura* endure the open challenge of free-thinking reformers. Then, in October 1988, he really cut into their power, with a swift, surgical behind-the-scenes coup at a Party Central Committee meeting. He forced President Andrei Gromyko and three other senior Brezhnev holdovers into retirement; he stripped hard-liner Yegor Ligachev of the ideology portfolio—responsibility over the press and media; he disbanded the Party Secretariat (until then, Ligachev's stronghold); and he began to lop off Central Committee staff departments that dealt with economic management.[5]

Still, these were modest blows compared to the March 1989 elections, which shattered the Party's image of invincibility. With the defeat of several dozen high Party and government officials across the country, the Party had lost face, and the apparat stood in jeopardy of losing their jobs.

"I am convinced that for us the moment of truth has come," conceded Ivan Saly, a burly district Party leader in Kiev, who had fallen victim in the elections and was scrambling to adjust to the new democratic mood. "We can no longer entertain illusions. We have suffered a major political defeat."[6]

At the top, Gorbachev had insulated all but one full member of the Politburo (Vitaly Vorotnikov) from having to face public elections. One hundred VIPs, led by the Politburo, were awarded the Party's "golden seats" in the Congress, though they had to go through the formality of election by the Party Central Committee. Yet even that sanctuary of Party orthodoxy was infected by dissent: Out of a few hundred votes, Gorbachev got twelve negative votes, Aleksandr Yakovlev fifty-nine, and Yegor Ligachev seventy-eight.

But that was nothing compared to the stinging personal humiliation of less exalted, but still important, Party officials who were rejected by the voters. These provincial czars, the *obkom* bosses, as Russians call them—leaders of the *oblast* or provincial Party committees—were publicly humbled. These big shots, used to riding around in limousines, to sitting behind huge desks and giving orders, were suddenly shorn of moral authority, of their pretense of ruling in the name of the people.

"The Party is losing its role as vanguard of the people," Leonid Dobrokhotov candidly admitted to me. Dobrokhotov works as a liberal, reformist supporter of Gorbachev in the Central Committee staff. "The constitution says the Party is the vanguard, but that means nothing. The Party is only the vanguard in the minds of people. Either it has authority, or it doesn't. Either people believe in it, or they don't. That's the Party's problem. We've lost that, and now we have to get it back. . . ."[7]

"There's a real division within the Party between the old mentality and the new mentality, between Right and Left," Dobrokhotov remarked to me on a different occasion. "The election result has sharpened this division. The Old Guard, the Right, sees the election as bad, the outcome as grave. The Left sees the election as good, favoring progressive forces that support *perestroika*. Gorbachev is now using a purge from below, rather than forcing people out by a purge from the top."[8]

AN APPARATCHIK TASTES DEFEAT

In Moscow, the highest-ranking Party official to feel the sting of defeat was Yuri Prokofyev, then number two in Moscow, second secretary of the city Party committee. Prokofyev ran in the Kuibyshev District, where he had formerly been the Party leader; he came in third in a three-man race, with just 13.5 percent of the vote. I tried to interview him after the elections, but he kept ducking me; his Party colleagues said he was in a state of shock and depression. When I finally saw him in the fall, he was still bitter about being rejected by his old Party district.

"I worked, I tried, I thought I worked decently, and then when people started to wipe out what was done by the Party in years past, it made me very bitter," Prokofyev told me.

"I was hurt because I had worked in this district for eight years, put all of my efforts into it, to develop it. Some things worked out, not everything, but right now we're finishing the subway station. We've built Houses of Culture for Young Pioneers. We've fixed up many streets, built a new housing development. . . . And of course, the people did not think so highly of it. That was insulting to me. But it taught me how to get used to real political struggle."

When I asked Prokofyev why the public rejected him if he had done so much, he cited their rage over economic shortages, their anger at his taking the Party line against Yeltsin, and the Party's terrible loss of authority, something that hit him the instant he entered the campaign.

"I had low expectations because I had an early sense of the attitude toward Party officials," he said. "To be honest, I didn't expect such strong criticism and such a strong battle against me. After the second or third meeting [with the voters], I sensed that I wasn't going to win. . . . All of the problems in the district—housing, transportation, food—all of that was directed at me. . . . As a Party secretary, I had to justify the situation, rather than criticize it. People wanted me to criticize the Council of Ministers or Gorbachev or the Central Committee. Had I done that, I would have been elected easily."

"What about the privileges of the Party elite that Yeltsin mentioned in his campaign?" I asked.

"What kind of Party privileges do I have?" Prokofyev retorted. "I have a two-room apartment of thirty-five square meters with my wife. Our son lives in a two-room apartment with twenty-nine square meters with his wife and child. What other privileges? I rent a government *dacha* for about five hundred rubles [$833] a year. And I have a car."9

The apartments were hardly Park Avenue–style; yet in a city of tight housing, they were very ample. Many families of five live in less space than Prokofyev shares with his wife. And the idea of a car and a country *dacha* smacks of luxury to Russian workers.

Even though Yeltsin was not a direct rival, he figured prominently in Prokofyev's campaign because the Party had tried so hard to crush Yeltsin.

"People often asked me questions about Yeltsin," Prokofyev said. "I have a negative attitude toward him, because I worked with him shoulder to shoulder for three months in the Moscow Party committee and city council, and I don't think he's democratic. If he comes to power, to the leadership, it would be a repeat of Stalinism, because by nature he's a boss. He likes people to be subordinate to him. He is democratic only in words. When I explained that to people, they didn't accept it. People like what he says. They don't know his essence."

Prokofyev, a man in his early fifties, was a Party career man, a traditional apparatchik. But he was also a new-style leader in the Gorbachev mold; he had gotten the Soviet equivalent of a Ph.D. in economics, and his manner was hardly that of a hard-line Party boss: He was businesslike and thoughtful; short and unimposing—not a desk-pounding ideologue or a right-wing martinet.

In fact, Prokofyev was something of a weather vane among the apparat. He was accustomed to a certain political compass, and he was disconcerted that it no longer guided him. Not only had the election left him scarred, but Gorbachev's *perestroika* had confused him and left him disoriented, as it had many apparatchiks.

"The Party began *perestroika* and decided on several priorities, but in my view, a well-worked-out political and economic platform doesn't exist," Prokofyev complained. "Democracy, *glasnost,* a market economic system—these are only theses right now. So it's hard. Everyone understands *perestroika* in his own way. . . . I think the most important thing is for the Party leaders to decide what they want, what kind of society they want, so that everyone understands. Then we can know who's who: who are the enemies, and who are our supporters."

Prokofyev's personal destiny was uncertain and precarious after the election, though defeat did not require him to surrender his Party post just because he had lost a race for the Congress of People's Deputies. The only body that could dismiss him was the Moscow city Party committee (or a signal from the Politburo bosses, who had kicked Yeltsin out in late 1987). Prokofyev was not fighting Gorbachev or blaming reform for his defeat, and probably for those reasons, he survived his election debacle. By the time I saw him in the fall, he still had his job; but he was defensive when I asked him whom he—and the Party—now claimed to represent.

"In the system that exists, I can say that I represent one-point-two million Communists in this city," he replied.

The bigger issue, it seemed to me, was the legitimacy of the Party itself. As Dobrokhotov had said, the Party had to find ways to win back its claim as the political vanguard.

"Will you run again in local elections?" I asked.

"I don't think so." Prokofyev shook his head. "The chances of winning are pretty slim for Party officials. That will change only if the economic situation changes. If people's lives get better, and they feel some results, then their attitudes will change. Right now, things aren't getting better— unfortunately. It's a very difficult situation for the Party right now."

GETTING RID OF "DEAD SOULS"

The 1989 elections made clear for the first time that Gorbachev's goal was to move power—not all power, but some—from the Communist Party to the government, to the Congress of People's Deputies and the all-union Supreme Soviet. It was a delicate operation, requiring tactical zigzags. The Party was still his own power base, and it was still too formidable a force simply to ignore and leave to its own devices. He could not allow it to slip out of his control and become a solid phalanx opposed to him and to *perestroika.* If he could not bend the apparat to his will, at least he had to immobilize it, neutralize it. So periodically, like any political leader in the West, he had to tend to his power base, hear out his angry constituents, defend their interests until he had decided whether to try to strip them of still more power.

As part of his general strategy, he decided to open up the workings of the Party apparat to public scrutiny as one way of keeping on the pressure for internal Party reform. Sometimes that tactic worked, and sometimes it backfired, which then allowed the apparat to put pressure on Gorbachev and force him to retreat.

Traditionally, the Communist Party has kept its internal feuds private, thus maintaining the facade of unity. From 1985 well into 1989, for example, Gorbachev and Ligachev went to great lengths to claim that they were in harmony, even though a simple reading of their speeches revealed their conflicts. But after the March 1989 elections, there was such a fractious explosion inside the Party that it could no longer be hidden. Gorbachev suddenly released, in the pages of *Pravda*, what had hitherto been the secret speeches of closed Party Central Committee meetings—in this case the plenum of April 25, 1989—so that the public could see how the provincial bosses had screamed in protest over the elections.

One defeated Party candidate after another took to the podium to heap blame on "political extremists" for leveling scurrilous charges against the Party and for pandering to the public; on the central press for sensationalizing the issue of Party privileges; on the way the Party leadership was allowing the infiltration of Western values and political methods; and on Gorbachev's economic reforms for failing to produce. Several speakers warned Gorbachev that he was pushing democracy too far, opening the door to "anarchy and total license"; they demanded a crackdown against the informal democratic groups that had toppled the Party barons.

"In our province and in Moscow, it has become fashionable to distribute leaflets, posters, and all kind of appeals," said the Moscow Province Party chief, Valentin Mesyats, who lost his election bid. "Let me tell you: These are no childish pranks. These are political slogans which call for the overthrow of Soviet power and the overthrow of the Party. . . . The main thing now is not to retreat."[10]

"Events in the last few years and especially in recent months in the Baltic republics, the Caucasus, Moscow, Leningrad, Moldavia, and other regions, and the slogans now openly printed in our press [by] informal associations, give us no grounds for passivity or peace of mind," warned Ivan Polozkov, the Party chief in Krasnodar Territory, who would be elected a year later as Party leader for the entire Russian republic. "When people . . . call for the entire party to be blamed for Stalin's crimes and hold rallies for the breakup of the U.S.S.R. and the elimination of the Communist Party, when there are calls to hang Communists, not to fulfill government decisions, and to sabotage Soviet laws, and there is no official reaction, then let's honestly admit that we have already gone a bit too far!"[11]

"We must stop trying to pin the mistakes and crimes of individual Communists, leaders included, on the entire Party and its policy . . . stop the discrediting of the elected Party *aktiv* and the groundless censuring of the management apparatus," declared Ratmir Bobovikov, the regional boss in Vladimir Province. "When people see the elated tone of articles in our press about how bourgeois leaders praise *perestroika*, it raises questions in their minds. They remember Lenin's advice: 'Think twice any-time your class enemy praises you.' "[12]

In their anger, the defeated Party leaders made the Soviet press their whipping boy. Azerbaijani Party chief Abdur Rahman Vezirov stooped to accuse "independent periodicals" of fostering "a kind of ideological AIDS in our people."[13] Others picked up his chant.

Vladimir Melnikov, the Party boss in the Komi republic, candidly admitted that sugar rationing, the shortage of soap, the erratic supply of meat, and the lack of modern appliances, children's clothing, and shoes had contributed to Party losses in his area. There were now mass work stoppages, hunger strikes, unsanctioned rallies and demonstrations, he said, some pushed by "extremist-minded elements . . . who come to us from the center [Moscow]". Then, with an alarm typical of the Party apparat, Melnikov pointed an accusing finger at the media.

"Was the outcome of the elections not influenced by the well-targeted salvos that the press and television fired at the first secretaries of provincial Party committees?" he demanded. "Comrades, look at the movies, look at our magazines. What has become of patriotism and civic-mindedness? How are we going to educate our young people? We are raising them in a totally different spirit. Can this really not worry the ideological staff of the Central Committee and the Politburo?"[14]

Yuri Solovyov, the Leningrad Province chief and junior member of the Politburo, who had led the entire Party slate in Leningrad to ignominious defeat, admitted to his colleagues: "For understandable reasons, it is not easy for me to speak today."

Right after his defeat, Solovyov had taken personal responsibility, a theme he now touched on only lightly. The undercurrent of his remarks blamed Gorbachev's policies. While Solovyov never mentioned Gorbachev, he said the Soviet president's policy on cooperatives had legalized speculation and unearned income, "which has gotten out of control." He said Gorbachev's plan to have workers elect their managers had produced plant directors "who willy-nilly pander to . . . the syndrome of consumer-ism, greed, and freeloading." He charged that an "ideological spineless-ness has infiltrated the Party ranks" and that reformers were trying "to turn a party of action into a party of debating clubs." And he warned that the young now saw the Communist Party as "a party of mistakes and crimes."

Finally, Solovyov invited the right-wing apparat to do battle. As an alternative to Gorbachev's Congress of People's Deputies, Solovyov pro-posed "an all-union congress of workers' delegates" with regional rallies to arouse the masses. It was an invitation to a new political class struggle, a rallying cry for hard-liners to mobilize a blue-collar counterforce to combat the grass-roots groups of urban intellectuals.[15]

Gorbachev was undeterred—he gave the bleating Party barons a scolding. He took some responsibility for the economic mess, but he also pinned blame on them for the public's anger over disastrous housing, transport, and other consumer services, and he admonished them that it was time to "change their style of work to be closer to the people."

Perestroika, he advised them, would take iron nerves and a steady stomach. Just as his reforms were generating "a powerful movement from underneath," he said, some Party leaders "are beginning to panic and very nearly perceive a threat to socialism." Instead, Gorbachev told them to learn how to work in democratic conditions and to get into "the thick of life"; and he slapped back at Solovyov's dig about the Party becoming a weak-kneed "debating club."

"The party's dialogue with the working people is not weakness or making the Party a discussion club," Gorbachev retorted. "If it is weakness to conduct a dialogue with all segments of the society, then I do not know what courage is."

Gorbachev dismissed the apparat's complaints as "nostalgic yearning for authoritarian methods."[16]

In case they did not get the message, Gorbachev carried out a purge of Old Guard holdovers on the Central Committee—"lame ducks," or, in Russian lingo, "dead souls." These were former Party officials whom Gorbachev had previously fired or demoted from important posts; under Party rules, they kept their seats on the Central Committee until the next Party Congress replaced them—and Party Congresses occurred only every five years.

Gorbachev wanted them off the committee because they were a nuisance, and also a threat; technically, the Central Committee had to approve his policies and it could remove him from his post. In 1985, he had inherited what was essentially Brezhnev's Central Committee; in February 1986, at the Twenty-seventh Party Congress, Gorbachev replaced roughly 40 percent of the Brezhnev holdovers, but close to 60 percent were still around.[17] They were a drag on Gorbachev's reforms and he wanted them out; at that April 1989 Party plenum, he got rid of 110 "dead souls" by "persuading" them to retire.

Since Gorbachev was cutting deadwood, it seemed strange that he did not also purge the Party hard-liners who had lost elections. Aides said that Gorbachev wanted the purge to come from the Party's rank and file; and in a few places that happened. By and large, however, Gorbachev let the defeated barons stay on, including those who had attacked his policies.

Some, such as Yuri Prokofyev, figured out how to work the new, democratic style of politics to their advantage; Prokofyev got promoted to Moscow Party chief when Gorbachev moved out Lev Zaikov, a Politburo conservative, in late 1989.

But Leningrad remained a thorn in Gorbachev's side, and eventually he had to deal with it; Leningrad was far too important a power base, and the defeat of its entire Party slate had been far too visible for Gorbachev to ignore. Moreover, Leningrad Party boss Yuri Solovyov had hardly been contrite at the Party meeting, and he had been even more truculent since then. When I visited Leningrad in June 1989, I heard repeated speculation that Solovyov was on his way out. Instead, he became more defiant; he was reviving Leningrad as a hotbed of hard-line opposition to *perestroika*. Finally, Gorbachev could brook no more. On July 12, he showed up in Leningrad for a Party meeting that fired Solovyov and appointed a successor, Boris Gidaspov, a fifty-six-year-old science administrator, who had won a seat in the March 1989 elections, and whom everyone presumed to be less hard-line than Solovyov.

Gorbachev made Solovyov endure the indignity of sitting beside him during a joint television appearance with Gidaspov, while Gorbachev ran down the failings of the Leningrad Party apparatus and sarcastically derided Solovyov's outdated style of leadership.

His voice heavy with sarcasm, Gorbachev asked how it was possible, in a city such as Leningrad, to have a situation where life was brimming with action and public debate on city squares, "but certain Party organizations are still chewing stale gum?"[18]

THE DANGERS OF "DUAL POWER"

Within the Party, Gorbachev was riding high after the March elections. His political reform was on track, his personal power at a peak. The right wing of the Party apparat was on the defensive, nursing its wounds; it was angry, but cowed.

Power is rarely static, however, and reform never moves in a straight line; it has fits and starts. The power that flows, also ebbs. The tide within the Party turned against Gorbachev in the summer of 1989—and it had been reversed in good measure by events. The entire nation was in upheaval. The *nomenklatura*, which had been shaken in the spring, was now alarmed that the Party was losing control.

The most stunning blow was the wave of mass strikes by coal miners in western Siberia, the Ukraine, around Vorkuta in the north, and near

Karaganda in Central Asia. In mid-July 1989, several hundred thousand miners walked off the job, the first massive strike since the 1920s—with the ominous potential of touching off a popular revolution because of widespread economic despair. The walkout struck fear into the government, which was already anxious to keep the germ of worker unrest from spreading.

Until the strike, the apparat could blame political ferment on the press and the intellectuals, but now the proletariat was lashing out at the Party. The miners were in fury that after seventy years, the Party had failed to deliver on the promises of the Bolshevik Revolution, and that in four years, Gorbachev's *perestroika* had delivered them nothing. With their walkout paralyzing much of Soviet heavy industry, Gorbachev quickly sided with their demands. Prime Minister Ryzhkov promised almost anything—higher pay, fringe benefits, better working conditions, housing, meat, soap—to get the miners back to work.

At the same time, nationalist violence was on the rise between Armenia and Azerbaijan; there were outbreaks in the Ferghana Valley of Uzbekistan; and Baltic nationalists were stepping up their drive toward secession. From the center, it looked as though the Soviet Union were beginning to tear apart.

Closer to home, the *nomenklatura* saw another threat: the danger of what Yuri Prokofyev and others called "dual power"—a rival power base, paralleling the Party, with members free of Party control. The Congress of People's Deputies and the Supreme Soviet were asserting real power, invading the Party's domain, usurping its prerogatives. The legislature was appointing and rejecting government ministers, it was seriously debating policy—and it was doing all this without any guidance from the Party. Only three Politburo members and very few other top apparatchiks were in the Supreme Soviet; obviously Gorbachev was keeping them out.[19] Control was the heart of the *nomenklatura* system—unity under a single central command—and the Party's control of all major political decisions, appointments, policies, was slipping away.

By actually starting to apply Lenin's slogan "All Power to the Soviets," Gorbachev was undermining the essence of the dictatorship of the *nomenklatura*. The nerve endings of Party regulars told them this erosion could be as fatal as the strike of a cobra.

"We say that we're passing over power to the soviets, and that is happening," Yuri Prokofyev snorted. "But then we have to think of what the role and place of the Party is, because two kinds of power can't exist, right? We have to deal with the question of the Party itself so that it does not lose its authority."[20]

Technically, all Supreme Soviet deputies who were Party members (85 percent) were expected to follow the Party's orders. But there was a breakdown in Party discipline: The deputies were defying the Party; they were going their own way—even to the point of demanding removal of the constitutional guarantee of the Party's supremacy in all walks of Soviet life. The apparat found this breach of discipline especially intolerable.

These concerns were gnawing at the apparat when Gorbachev met on July 18, 1989, with the Politburo and 150 regional Party first secretaries. The atmosphere was charged. The anger that had percolated among the regional bosses at the Central Committee meeting in April was now boiling at a higher and more dangerous level—among Politburo members, including Gorbachev's supposed partner in reform, Prime Minister Nikolai Ryzhkov.

Up in arms, Gorbachev's colleagues ganged up on him, citing the nation's political chaos and the erosion of Party power. The chorus of discontent on all major issues had the ominous ring of an incipient cabal:

Lev Zaikov, Moscow Party chief: "[M]any Party committees are losing control of the situation. . . . Wherever you look, there is relentless propaganda of Western values. The news from 'over there' is about luxury cars and villas, shop windows and so on. And our news? Perpetual shortages, law breaking, drug addiction. It is as if *perestroika* had changed nothing, as if we could find no other color except black to paint our own picture."[21]

Vitaly Vorotnikov, leader of the Russian republic: "The point is that *perestroika* is not going the way we want it to and there is mounting criticism among the people. . . . The time has come to change the whole range of [our] precepts."[22]

Yegor Ligachev, ranking Politburo conservative: "Recently there have been calls for a multiparty system. In a federated state, such as the Soviet Union, this is simply fatal. A multiparty system would mean the disintegration of the Soviet federation. . . . [The] Communist Party is the only real political force that rallies and unites all the country's peoples into a union of republics."[23]

Leonid Bobykin, the Sverdlovsk regional secretary, cut close to Gorbachev himself, without naming him. There was "no firm line on ideological questions," he said. "The role of the Central Committee Secretariat has been weakened recently. Obviously we need a Central Committee second secretary."[24]

Bobykin's was the voice of the apparat, alarmed at how Gorbachev had emasculated the very core of its power by disbanding the Secretariat and cutting the Central Committee staff. Bobykin was a hard-line Party veteran who was very close to Prime Minister Ryzhkov. By proposing a new

Party number two, he was raising a direct threat to Gorbachev; it meant Gorbachev's letting go of some power and allowing a pretender to his throne. Gorbachev had moved Ligachev out of that post in October 1988 and had allowed no one to step into his shoes.

Ryzhkov picked up Bobykin's theme, accusing Gorbachev of neglecting the Party; he did not hesitate to lecture Gorbachev under the guise of addressing the Party elite.

"We must do everything to help ensure that [Gorbachev] devotes more attention to his Party duties," Ryzhkov told the gathering. "We must free him from trivial questions, which are bogging him down."[25]

As if Gorbachev had been indulging in trivia; no matter, Ryzhkov was warning Gorbachev—if the Party was going to be saved, and if Gorbachev was going to save himself, he had better defend the citadel, and stop playing around with democratic institutions. Even more pointedly, Ryzhkov, as prime minister, seemed to be telling Gorbachev, as president, to get off his back and stick to Party business.

Ryzhkov's salvo was all the more stunning because he was usually an ally, not a critic, of Gorbachev, although during that summer they had exchanged barbs in public. Gorbachev had invited the Supreme Soviet to rake Ryzhkov over the coals, and the prime minister was paying him back. He had emerged at the moment as Gorbachev's chief antagonist.

The picture Ryzhkov painted was stark: a Party "reduced to self-flagellation and often to open castigation" of its own apparat; a Party blindly stumbling along without a clear strategy; a Party gone soft and losing power; a Party whose leaders were foolishly acting as if nothing had gone wrong.

"So many accusations have been brought against the Party both in our country and abroad—more than ever before in its entire history—that it is in fact losing authority," Ryzhkov declared. "[Yet] despite the loss of authority and of influence over all that is happening in society, willingly or not, we have continued to maintain the illusion that nothing out of the ordinary has happened, that as before the main levers remain in our hands and that using them, we can, as before, with the very same methods, govern . . . the country."

Ryzhkov was alluding not only to the coal mines and minority republics careening out of control, but to power slipping away right under the Party's nose in the Supreme Soviet. It was ironic that the Politburo member in charge of the government was the one to rise to the Party's defense. But Ryzhkov was especially sensitive on this issue because he personally had been humiliated by the Supreme Soviet. His policy had been ripped apart, and his ministers; and he was obviously furious.

"Things are reaching the point where the Party is being relegated to a backseat in public life—this was shown by the elections," Ryzhkov argued.

"In my view, we must acknowledge that the assessment made after the elections is not quite accurate. We overestimated statistics, citing the fact that 85 percent of the elected deputies are Communists. But this quantitative majority means little," he pointed out. "They [have] literally forced their way to the rostrum with their own platforms, programs, proposals, and accusations, often including insinuations against the Party. And the Politburo found itself on the sidelines, in an isolated position, as if it had fallen under seige. . . .

"We need now to find new approaches, new methods, new principles to govern relations among the triangle of power that has emerged today in our system of government—the [Party] Central Committee, the Supreme Soviet, and the U.S.S.R. Council of Ministers. . . . A real and mighty power has appeared in the form of the Congress of People's Deputies and the U.S.S.R. Supreme Soviet. If the Party does not find a way out of this, then it may lose influence over state government.

"Things have not yet reached the point where the slogan 'Party in Danger' is justified. But if we face the truth, we must clearly see that this possibility exists. . . ."[26]

It was a powerful indictment of Gorbachev's policy, coming from the man who was second in power in fact, if not by formal designation. Not only was Ryzhkov prime minister, but opinion polls showed him second to Gorbachev in mass popularity, and his stock was soaring among the *nomenklatura*.

In spite of all this, my Party contacts denied that Ryzhkov was setting himself up as the point man of a political coup against Gorbachev; they said that Ryzhkov, as an economic manager, did not see himself becoming political number one.

Perhaps. I found it hard to gauge from a distance. Most politicians who get close to the top have the ambition to become number one, but the chemistry of Ryzhkov's relations with Gorbachev, who had appointed him and brought him along, might have forced Ryzhkov to suppress that ambition.

If Gorbachev was bothered by this onslaught from his Politburo colleagues, he did not show it. With the supreme self-confidence that has been his most effective armor when he is challenged, Gorbachev took the offensive.

"There will be no return to 'the good old days,' " he bluntly told the hard-liners who wanted to roll back *perestroika*. "It is impossible to decree the Party's authority. . . . Today, authority can only be 'won' " by progressive action.

Gorbachev conceded that it was irresponsible not to worry about the destiny of the Party, but he insisted it was equally irresponsible to become mired in pessimism. He admitted that the turmoil caused by *perestroika* was painful, but he justified that as a necessary by-product of reform aimed at real change.

"This creates extra tension," he said, "but this is what makes these revolutionary years." And he admonished the conservatives that others were able to seize the initiative whenever the Party fell behind the pace of change in society; he exhorted them to bring in new blood. "A renewal of cadres is needed, an influx of fresh forces," he said.

Gorbachev was blunt and unflinching, not even bothering to respond to Bobykin's proposal for a deputy and bypassing most of Ryzhkov's unhappy litany. With sheer force of conviction and personality, he overrode his critics and laid the blame for the Party's predicament squarely at the feet of the apparat.

"How can it happen that a party organization with many thousands of Communists, which possesses its own newspapers, its own professional workers, which possesses everything—suddenly begins to lose the initiative?" Gorbachev asked.

"There is only one reason for this: It means that we are lagging behind. It means that among us somewhere, there's a gap between words and deeds, between the masses and the Party, which—as a vanguard—ought to be out front."[27]

Gorbachev and the apparat had reached a standoff. The *nomenklatura* could not make him halt or reverse his democratic and press reforms; he could not force them to make real political changes. They could not keep him from shifting power to the Congress, but he could not get them to stop blocking his economic program. He was frustrated by their rigidity, but he lacked the power or the will to conduct a wholesale Party purge. They disliked his strategy, but they could not remove him because of his mass support, his power base in the legislature, and because they had no real alternative to his program except a return to Stalinism, which would lead to mass bloodshed.

With neither side content, the battle was bound to resume.

A PLOT AGAINST GORBACHEV?

Something happened between the summer and fall of 1989 to turn Gorbachev around. His rhetoric and his actions swung to the right; retrenchment replaced reform. He became the Party's defender instead of its attacker. It was not wholly surprising for Gorbachev; his path was a series of zigzags, a living testament to Lenin's dictum that revolution is "two steps forward, one step back."

Through that fall, Gorbachev showed personal strain more transparently than ever before. At times, he acted as if he felt he was losing control of events, that the country's social, political, and economic disintegration was overwhelming him. When challenged, he snarled and snapped. He seemed under intolerable pressure from the Party's right wing. At times, he acted like a dictator: He flew off the handle at the leaders of Baltic nationalism; he thundered his outrageous charge that the Inter-Regional Group deputies were "a gangster group"; he called for the resignation of Vladislav Starkov, editor of *Argumenty i Fakty*, for printing a public-opinion poll that made Gorbachev look bad.

At an angry session with senior newspaper editors, Gorbachev spluttered: "Reading the press, you get the feeling that you are standing knee-deep in gasoline. The only thing lacking is a spark."[28]

Anxiety about an impending explosion hung over Moscow in the fall and winter of 1989–90. The city was periodically swept by rumors of an imminent coup against Gorbachev by the Party right wing and the military. In a televised speech at the Congress of People's Deputies the previous June, Gorbachev himself had brought up such rumors, and he had laughed them off, joking that according to rumors, over the past four years "I have died seven times and my family has already been slain three times."[29]

The coup speculation was more insistent in the fall; it broke into print, in mid-August, when *Moscow News* ran an article headlined IS OCTOBER 1964 POSSIBLE TODAY? (alluding to the Party coup that threw out Khrushchev). And its answer was yes. On September 8, the television show *Vzglyad (View)* ran a piece on the political power struggle in the Kremlin. Other articles about the dangers of a coup or a violent explosion between "the upper echelons" of power, meaning the army, and the "grass roots," meaning the masses, appeared in the popular weekly *Ogonek* and the Moscow daily, *Moskovskaya Pravda*. Speaking in Vienna, Georgy Smirnov, a Central Committee official, confirmed "rumors according to which some people in the U.S.S.R. are thinking aloud about overthrowing state and Party chief M. S. Gorbachev."[30]

Because of my experiences in the seventies, when so many Moscow rumors had proven false, I had long been skeptical of such speculation. Now, in the late eighties, there was so much turmoil in the country that people were inclined to believe and say anything. Still, *Moscow News* and *Ogonek* had excellent connections with the liberal faction of the Party leadership—Yakovlev, Shevardnadze, and Party officials who worked under them. The fact that these publications printed such stories was an indication that Gorbachev's liberal allies seriously feared a coup. Printing coup stories was supposed to be prophylactic.

A ranking Baltic Communist Party official, whose chief was very close to Gorbachev and who met with Gorbachev several times in September 1989, told me that there had actually been an attempt by the right-wing faction of the Politburo to oust Gorbachev. He had gone off on a five-week vacation in the Crimea during August; while he was away, Politburo conservatives and the neo-Stalinist Right were particularly outspoken. Leningrad's citizen activist Nina Andreyeva went further than ever before—attacking Gorbachev by name for the first time and calling him a "bourgeois," who was out to destroy socialism. On September 1, Viktor Chebrikov, the Politburo hard-liner who had formerly headed the KGB, delivered a very tough law-and-order speech demanding crackdowns on many fronts. Yegor Ligachev, too, called for repression against "those people who are forever attacking the Party, the Soviet Union, our glorious army, and the security organs."

According to this Baltic Communist contact, who said his information came indirectly from Gorbachev himself, Gorbachev had planned to return from vacation on Sunday, September 10, but he was tipped off by allies in Moscow that a right-wing cabal was afoot, and he came home two days early, on Friday. Everything was prepared for his ouster, my source said, and on either that Friday or Saturday, at a rump meeting of the Politburo, the hard-liners confronted Gorbachev. According to my source, "They said to him bluntly, 'It's time to change,' "—meaning change leadership.

In this version of events, Ligachev was the real power behind the cabal, but Chebrikov took the lead in attacking Gorbachev to his face and demanding a change. The two had been emboldened by Ryzhkov's switch in July, supposedly feeling for the first time that the balance in the Politburo had tipped in their favor. Somehow, Gorbachev managed to face them down—the account is sketchy at best—but personal chemistry is often crucial in those situations. For waverers, Gorbachev was the establishment leader. Nonetheless, during the next fortnight, he was under intense pressure, as each side maneuvered behind the scenes to marshal its forces for a showdown at the scheduled Central Committee plenum on nationalities issues, September 19–20. In the middle of the month, Ligachev supposedly told visiting French Communists that he was confident of an imminent change at the helm.

I never got confirmation of the story that Gorbachev had been pressed to resign by Politburo hard-liners on September 8 or 9, but on September 19, one of Gorbachev's speech writers, Nikolai Shishlin, told me cryptically: "This is a very dangerous time for my boss." Shishlin was tense— awaiting the outcome of the Central Committee session. Gorbachev himself had been quoted on September 16 by Vaino Väljas, the Estonian Communist Party leader, as having said: "*Perestroika* is experiencing one of its most serious and difficult periods, with extremist forces consolidating, and with the conservative wing consolidating."[31] My Baltic contact told me that Gorbachev had indicated to Väljas, an old Party friend, that not just *perestroika*, but he himself was in trouble.

My source reminded me that Gorbachev had made a speech to the nation on September 9, which he called "an open cry to the public for support."

I remembered that speech well. I was in Sverdlovsk and had been so struck by how bad Gorbachev looked—strange for a man coming back from a five-week vacation—that I had pointed it out to my wife, Susan, who agreed. His tone was so alarmist that we were both riveted to the television set. He had an air about him of catastrophe.

"Everything is bound up in a tight knot," he said, ticking off nationality conflicts, economic shortages, public despair—and he saw malicious hands at work.

"We are seeing how attempts to discredit *perestroika* are being made from both the conservative and ultraleftist positions," he told the Soviet people. "From the midst of this discordant choir, scare stories of imminent chaos and arguments about the danger of a coup, or even civil war, may be heard. . . .

"Some would like to create an atmosphere of alarm, of uncertainty. It is difficult to rid oneself of the impression that this is all to someone's advantage. . . .

"In effect, an attempt is being made from conservative positions to impose assessments of the situation that would prompt counteraction against *perestroika*. . . . They call for return to the old command methods; otherwise, they say, there will be chaos."[32]

Gorbachev also disapproved, as before, of what he saw as the excessive zeal of ultraprogressives, whom he accused of demanding a breakthrough "at one gallop, at one stroke."

But the main threat in his mind clearly came from the Right; and to meet it, Gorbachev himself moved to the right. He stole the right wing's thunder by making a very tough law-and-order speech, using almost the identical language that Chebrikov and Ligachev had been using during his vacation.

"We cannot tolerate violations of state, labor, and technological discipline. . . . We cannot tolerate the fact that the national economy is in a feverish state because of interruptions in transportation. . . . I cannot disregard the question of crime. . . . The Supreme Soviet has considered it necessary . . . to increase the number of internal security troops."

What was most striking was his about-face on the Party. After hounding the Party apparat in mid-July to change its ways and bluntly telling it that the Party had to earn authority, here he was, eight weeks later, trumpeting the Party's importance and defending its power.

"The role of the Party, as the uniting, vanguard force of society, is indispensable," Gorbachev declared. "Those who are . . . attempting to undermine the Party's influence, must know that this will not work. We are confident that despite all the criticism directed at the activity of various Party committees and various Communists, the working people have a good understanding of the importance of Lenin's Party for the destiny of socialism."[33]

This was the line Gorbachev took all fall; he sounded like Ligachev. After meeting with the Communist leaders of the Baltic states, where local parties were on the verge of splitting from Moscow, Gorbachev declared: "It would be a grave historical mistake to weaken such a powerful political organism as the Communist Party of the Soviet Union."[34] At the Central Committee session on September 19–20, he preached the gospel of patriotism, scolded aggressive nationalists, and catered to Party conservatives by making concessions to Russian nationalism.

Nonetheless, having survived, he quickly settled scores with the right-wing faction in the Politburo. He purged his enemies—three of five Politburo conservatives: the dangerous Chebrikov; Vladimir Shcherbitsky, the iron-fisted boss of the Ukraine; and Viktor Nikonov, an economic right-winger. Many read Chebrikov's ouster as punishment for ordering the army crackdown in Tbilisi, Georgia; but others insisted it had to be something more, since the whole Politburo, even Gorbachev, was tainted with the Tbilisi episode. My Baltic contact suggested Chebrikov was axed for daring to challenge Gorbachev directly. Ligachev survived, but shorn of his clique.

Even with that tactical victory, Gorbachev showed the strain on a visit to Kiev in late September. During one of his sidewalk conversations with people, someone asked if he wasn't afraid to leave Moscow for fear of a coup. "No, this is . . ." Gorbachev began, but quickly changed the subject. Yet when a woman asked how he managed "to bear a country of so many millions on your shoulders," her worrying reminded him of his mother.

"During the Congress of People's Deputies my mother was listening, and she said, 'Why is he doing all this? . . . He ought to come home to me and drop it all.' "

People all laughed. Gorbachev then turned to the woman, and in an echo of Robert Frost's famous couplet "And miles to go before I sleep,/ And miles to go before I sleep," Gorbachev said with tired reverie and resignation:

"So your words sound to me like my mother's. But you can't [stop], you know. The country believes; people now believe. . . . So it's all the way . . . all the way."[35]

The intense pressure from the right wing pushed Gorbachev to retrench. Many a Party leader has purged rivals, only to adopt their policies. Alarmed by events, Gorbachev aligned himself with the loyalist apparat. His response to challenge was a tough fist, epitomized by his decision to send twelve thousand Soviet troops into Baku in January 1990, not so much to save the Armenian victims of a pogrom, but, as Defense Minister Dmitri Yazov said, to save the Communist Party from being thrown out by the Azerbaijani Popular Front.

That fall and early winter were a gloomy season for radical reformers in the Supreme Soviet. They were appalled by Gorbachev's swing to the right; they despaired of his ever breaking the Party's lock on power. Several told me that they feared Gorbachev was too much a prisoner of his own past, too wedded in his bones to the Party apparat, ever to try for a full democratic reform that would strip the Party of its power monopoly.

CHAPTER 22

THE PARTY: LOSING POWER, LOSING PEOPLE

"The organs of power are so
irresolute. . . . The state, as it were,
belongs to no one. . . . We need a conductor."[1]
—Ivan Polozkov
Provincial Party Chief
March 1990

"If you want to bury the Party,
split the Party, then continue on
this way. Think hard. Think hard."[2]
—Gorbachev, July 1990

"They don't believe the Party is
still the party of the working class.
. . . A certain part is leaving because of
disappointment with the Party
over *perestroika*. The working class has
gotten nothing but empty shelves and inflation."[3]
—Yuri Prokofyev
Moscow Party Chief
June 1990

Gorbachev is restless. He rarely sticks with one approach for long. For he is powerfully influenced by events.

In the fall of 1989, he clearly felt besieged; his political horizon was dominated by domestic turmoil, and his reflexive response was to retrench and get tough. But by early 1990, another reality filled the horizon—the nightmarish collapse of Communism in Eastern Europe. Gorbachev had let one Communist regime after another crumble, and this had confirmed his view that survival required staying close to the people. His response was to return to the path of reform.

He had seen that where the Communist Party had been rigid, arrogant, aloof, where it could not flow with the tides of history, it was swept away. And he could hardly have failed to ponder the personal fate of such Party leaders as Erich Honecker in East Germany and Nicolae Ceauşescu in Romania, one arrested, the other executed, without realizing that the Soviet Party apparat could drag him down too.

At home in the Soviet Union, the clamor against the Party was rising again as 1989 was ending. In early December, the parliaments of Lithuania and Estonia formally sanctioned multiparty political systems. Simultaneously, forty thousand people held a rally in Leningrad and voted in a mass show of hands to revoke Article VI of the constitution, the one protecting the Party's political supremacy over all Soviet institutions, including the government. In Moscow, Andrei Sakharov called for a two-hour workers' strike on December 10 to demand a vote on Article VI at the upcoming Congress of People's Deputies.

"I think [the Party's] constitutionally fixed exclusiveness is inadmissible, undemocratic, and, judging by everything, undermining the Party's prestige," Sakharov declared.[4]

When the Congress convened on December 12, Sakharov made his move, but Gorbachev blocked him.

Sakharov went to the podium with a sack of mail to demonstrate public support for stripping the Party of its constitutionally guaranteed monopoly of power. At the climax of Sakharov's speech, Gorbachev interrupted, ringing the bell to end Sakharov's time.

Sakharov: "Then I . . . then I . . . I will get telegrams which I have received."

Gorbachev: "Come to me and I'll give you three files containing thousands of telegrams."

Sakharov: *"There are sixty thousand here!"*

Gorbachev (ordering): "That's all."

Sakharov (continuing): ". . . sixty thousand signatures."

Derisive clapping drowns out Sakharov.

Gorbachev: "So let's not press each other, resting on and manipulating the view of the people. Let's not."[5]

Gorbachev, testy and temperamental, wheeled out the obedient conservative majority and put down Sakharov's appeal for a vote on Article VI.

"We don't need to rush things," Gorbachev had said earlier to a Party meeting.

But, tragically, time ran out on Sakharov, two days after their confrontation. On the morning of December 14, he worked with the Inter-Regional Group on issues of reform; that evening, he died of heart failure. Democratic reform had lost its most authentic voice, the reformers their most unifying leader. Gorbachev joined in honoring Sakharov at the Congress.

Most of the time, however, Gorbachev was still sounding and acting like right-winger Yegor Ligachev. Only later did it become clear that he was not so much rejecting fundamental political change as he was jealously asserting his prerogative to control the process, to decide personally when and how he would let certain steps be taken. Eventually, he developed a scheme: If the Party was going to lose power, he would take advantage of that moment to buttress his personal power. He would couple the change in the Party's status with a proposal to establish a new, more powerful presidency.

So, even as he was stifling Sakharov's final attempt to sweep away the Party's legal crutch, Gorbachev was laying the political groundwork to make such a move himself, if he chose. Once again, he was warning the Party that it could afford to ignore the popular will only at its own peril. In a speech on December 10, Gorbachev pointed to the fall of the East European Communists as a fate that awaited the Soviet Party unless it mended its ways.

"Fraternal parties are no longer ruling in Poland and Hungary," he said, and the Communist regimes in East Germany and Czechoslovakia "have largely lost their positions. . . . The Soviet people do not want to put up with the fact that at a time when the normal rhythm of life has been broken, their local and national leaders are often doing nothing."[6]

Under the pull of these new realities, Gorbachev kept shifting. A month later, on January 12, 1990, he flew to Lithuania to try to head off secession, and he was confronted with a multiparty system already in existence, though the Soviet constitution still barred it. He personally met with two Communist parties, the pro-Moscow loyalists and the much larger pro-independence Lithuanian Communist Party. Lithuania also had the powerful nationalist movement, Sajudis, and smaller parties. Although Gorbachev had again rejected a multiparty system as recently as a month before, and had once called it "rubbish," he closed out his two-day Lithuania visit by remarking that he did "not see anything tragic about a multiparty system." A day later, he added, "We should not be afraid of a multiparty system the way the devil is afraid of incense."[7]

Gorbachev tried to make it sound offhand, but it was his first public sanction of a momentous change. Before long, he was pushing this policy as his own.

In early February, Gorbachev summoned the Party Central Committee into session, and once again the conservatives were fuming. On the eve of the session, Moscow saw its largest demonstration since the Revolution—two hundred thousand people just off Red Square, calling for the Party to surrender its constitutional monopoly. Radicals had organized the rally, but held it so near the Kremlin that it had to have Gorbachev's blessing; there was no police interference. What is more, the Party press blossomed with articles favoring a transition to a multiparty system—which suggested political choreography by Mikhail S. Gorbachev.

What Gorbachev was asking the Party itself to revoke was Article VI of the Soviet constitution. It states:

> The Communist Party of the Soviet Union (CPSU) is the leading and guiding force of Soviet society and the nucleus of its political system, of all state and public organizations. The CPSU exists for the people and serves the people.
>
> Armed with the Marxist-Leninist teaching, the Communist Party shall determine the general prospects of society's development and the line of domestic and foreign policy of the USSR, give guidance to the great creative activity of the Soviet people, and place its struggle for the victory of Communism on a planned, scientific basis.
>
> All Party organizations shall function within the framework of the Constitution of the USSR.[8]

When the Central Committee convened on February 5, 1990, Gorbachev proposed that the Party agree to strike Article VI, and to approve a new, strong presidency as a way to ensure centralized order.

The battle was joined along familiar lines; the hard-liners immediately counterattacked.

Ligachev had drawn a different lesson from the nightmare in Eastern Europe. He stressed the loss of empire and the imminent danger of a resurgent Germany, the threat of a "new Munich," which would redraft the postwar frontiers and see East Germany swallowed up by the West. Boris Gidaspov, personally installed by Gorbachev as the Leningrad Party leader and now quickly establishing himself as a new champion of conservatives, defended the apparat. The Party was the only force, Gidaspov said, that "can act as a constructive, consolidating base of our state and as guarantor of a socialist path of development."[9] Valentin Mesyats, the

Moscow Province chief, accused Gorbachev of leading the country down the road to anarchy and voiced outrage that the Soviet leader was assaulting the apparat. "Why is the Central Committee to assume a defensive position?" Mesyats demanded. "The Party began *perestroika*, has led it, and should proceed as its vanguard."[10]

But this was a rearguard effort. Having stripped Ligachev of support in the Politburo, Gorbachev had the big guns on his side this time.

Vadim Medvedev, the ideology secretary, said that unless the Party opened up democratic channels to let the public voice its discontent, the Soviet Party would follow those in Eastern Europe. Foreign Minister Eduard Shevardnadze declared that "a viable party doesn't need a monopoly on power. . . . The power monopoly has played a bad joke on us."[11] Nikolai Ryzhkov, who had swung over to Gorbachev, advised the apparatchiks that "no party has a perpetual monopoly on power." The Soviet Party, he warned, "has lost the combative qualities which are organically inherent in any leading force." To succeed, he said, the Party should get rid of Article VI and fight for popular support.[12] Aleksandr Yakovlev, who more than anyone in the leadership had been the advocate of this change, said simply: "Society itself will decide whether it wishes to adopt our politics."[13]

That was Gorbachev's point. "The Party," he declared, "can exist and play its role as the vanguard—only as a democratically recognized force. This means that its status should not be imposed through constitutional endorsement."[14]

To Party hard-liners, this was the suicidal step they had instinctively refused to take. But at that moment, the Party apparat was reeling, on the defensive from a string of scandals exposing the corruption of the Party bosses that had led from Leningrad to Volgograd, Kiev, Tyumen in western Siberia, and Chernigov in the Ukraine. In Leningrad, the final indignity had been heaped on the former Party boss Yuri Solovyov; he had been expelled from the Party after an investigation disclosed his use of Party influence to buy a Mercedes at a cut-rate price.[15]

So the apparat was on the defensive. Not only was it being goaded by Gorbachev, but it was demoralized by evidence of its waning support among the Party rank and file. Moreover, it was trapped by its own rules and traditions. It operated under Lenin's principle of "democratic centralism," which had the ring of rule from below but the reality of rule from above, and the requirement that the Party faithful follow discipline. In this case, Gorbachev had come to the Central Committee not just with his own policy, but with the collectively approved policy of the Politburo. The Central Committee was discipline-bound to follow the Politburo line and vote for its own funeral. Grudgingly, unhappily, it voted as it was told. Only one vote in the 249-member Central Committee was cast against stripping the Party of its monopoly power—and that was cast by Boris Yeltsin. His complaint was that Gorbachev had not gone far enough.

"We have taken a step of exceptional magnitude," Aleksandr Yakovlev said after the vote. "Power is being transferred from the Party to the soviets."16

The Party's surrender of its dominion over every facet of Soviet life was a watershed, but it had not vanished into thin air; it was merely accepting the principle of competition. It was not surrendering actual power, except where rivals were popular and organized enough to win it, and clever enough to dislodge the Party bureaucracy from all the places where it had implanted itself over the decades. A new principle had been established, but an old reality still existed. Theoretically, the state machinery was now liberated from the Party's grip, but the apparatus of the Party was still so tightly intermingled with the apparatus of the state, especially in the army and KGB, that it would take years to disentangle them.

Nonetheless, Gorbachev had achieved a quite remarkable personal victory. As leader of both Party and government, he had been a captive of each. Both the Party and the new Congress and Supreme Soviet hemmed him in politically, from opposite sides, limiting his ability to maneuver. By lifting the Party's dictate from all Soviet institutions and by simultaneously winning the Party's approval for a new presidency (later voted into law by the Congress of People's Deputies), Gorbachev was getting the better of both rivals. As president, he was no longer constitutionally subservient to the Party, and he had greater power to act independently of the Supreme Soviet. So the Party's loss was his gain; he had strengthened his power base apart from the Party, and had put more distance between himself and the increasingly unpopular apparat.

WILL THE PARTY SPLIT?

As the decisive Central Committee session came to a close in early February, Gorbachev's new worry was the polarizing trend of Party politics: Ligachev's right wing versus the left-wing radicals led by Boris Yeltsin. As a catalyst of change, Gorbachev welcomed ferment and debate; it helped him keep pressure on the apparat. But as a centrist and a Leninist, Gorbachev wanted to prevent a split. He might want to reduce the Party's power, but he still saw it as an important institution of stability and cohesion, a check on the radical reformers, ballast against ethnic strife. So Gorbachev warned the Party faithful: "We must all stand together [and] not start dividing into clans and groupings. That way we will ruin the Party and the country."[17]

Gorbachev's words came too late. There were already identifiable factions taking organizational form. In January, the radical reformers in the Party had formed Democratic Platform, a group dedicated to forcing the Communist Party to become more democratic internally and to give up its legally guaranteed dominance in Soviet politics.

In the apparat, radical reformers had limited support—though among the leadership, they regarded Aleksandr Yakovlev as their philosophical patron. But from the Party rank and file, they claimed a mass following, especially among the urban intelligentsia, and that claim seemed legitimate. A senior Central Committee official, Aleksandr Lebedev, told me that the Party's own polling data indicated that 30–40 percent of the rank and file shared the views of Democratic Platform and might side with it if the Party were to split.[18] In June 1990, the weekly newspaper *Argumenty i Fakty* published a poll of 5,326 Party members (probably parts of the same poll) taken by the Central Committee's sociology section, which showed that more ordinary Communists shared the views of Democratic Platform than of the Party's right-wingers. Roughly half indicated their liberal leanings by saying the Party should reject conservatism; only one third took the conservative view that the Party should reject liberal reformers.[19]

At Democratic Platform's organizational session in Moscow on January 20–21, the leadership included the most prominent deputies in the Congress and Supreme Soviet—Boris Yeltsin, Gavril Popov, Yuri Afanasyev, Sergei Stankevich, and Ilya Zaslavsky. In all, the meeting attracted about 450 delegates from reformist political clubs in more than seventy-eight Soviet cities.[20]

The program adopted by Democratic Platform called for drastic changes. First, it demanded internal democracy within the Party: scrapping the Leninist rule of "democratic centralism," revoking Lenin's 1921 ban against organized factions within the Party, requiring multicandidate elections for all Party posts, and barring privileges for Party higher-ups. More broadly, Democratic Platform went beyond advocating a multiparty political system to pressing for the abolition of the *nomenklatura* system and for dissolving all Party organizations in factories, farms, and other institutions, including the armed forces, the KGB, and the police. Its overall goal was to convert a totalitarian party into a parliamentary party, allowing internal competition and then competing with other parties for elected office.[21]

One irony is that this radical reform movement took root in the Higher Party School, organized by Stalin, and for decades the purveyor of Stalinist orthodoxy for Party "cadres"—officials of the apparat. Since Stalin's time, it had been the special educational training ground for promising midcareer Party officials in their thirties and forties, especially those marked by early success for higher leadership posts. In 1990, it had thirty-seven hundred students and four hundred teachers. Ligachev had attended the Moscow Higher Party School; Gorbachev had gone through one of the fifteen branches scattered across the country.

The school's rector, Vyacheslav Shostakovsky, was an ardent advocate of reforming the Communist Party; he cashiered some of the old-line Stalinist faculty and encouraged debate and experimentation. When I made a visit there, the evidence of Shostakovsky's free spirit was everywhere: not only "students" arguing over the destiny of the Party and the tactics of reform, but computer experts doing "after hours" research for foreign joint ventures, and a sociologist working as a consultant for several new Soviet cooperative enterprises. Shostakovsky himself was out making speeches and organizing meetings on behalf of radical change.

Initially, Sergei Stankevich told me, the idealists in Democratic Platform had hopes of getting the Soviet Communist Party to follow the model of the Hungarian Party: to cast off the Old Guard apparat, take a new name, and adopt the policies of European social democrats. Yuri Afanasyev was bluntly skeptical: "My conviction is the Party cannot be reformed." His plan was to lead the organization out of the Communist Party and set up a new party.[22] Vladimir Lysenko, another leader of Democratic Platform, rather cheerfully embraced the idea of a splinter movement. The Party's Central Committee, he declared, is "an empire full of mummies. . . . The dead are overtaking the living. A schism is necessary and inevitable."[23]

Communist Party hard-liners were quite happy to accommodate people of Afanasyev's ilk. In April, the Central Committee issued an open letter to the Party's nineteen million members denouncing Democratic Platform and urging its members to resign, unless they pledged to conform to Party policies. Some Party organizations began throwing out reformers. Although Gorbachev denied there was a purge, he came down hard on Party members who disagreed with the Party's position; he said they should quit, but of their own accord. It was an important moment, because he was siding with the right wing against the liberals, who wanted to do what he had proclaimed as his own goal: reform the Party from within. Afanasyev took Gorbachev's hint and turned in his Party card in mid-April.

Democratic Platform's most prominent deputies, Yeltsin, Popov, Stankevich, Zaslavsky, and others, were elected to city government or to the Supreme Soviet of the Russian republic in March 1990, and they drifted away from the organization. So in the crucial election of delegates to the Twenty-eighth Communist Party Congress, Democratic Platform could not use its best voices to rally support. With the Party apparat controlling the elections, Democratic Platform wound up with only 125 of the 5,000 Congress delegates, a proportion far short of what its mass support would have promised.

THE REVENGE OF THE RIGHT

More menacing to Gorbachev was the resurgence of the right wing; he seriously misjudged its power and purpose after having beaten or seduced it into submission so many times. Each beating and each seduction seemed only to sharpen the apparat's lust for vengeance and for a power base to advance its cause. The chosen vehicle of the regional power barons was a new Russian Communist Party. They had been demanding it ever since their public humiliation in the 1989 elections; after suffering more setbacks in the 1990 elections at the hands of the new democratic radicals, they became more insistent. As their popularity fell, their anxiety and anger grew.

In late 1989, Gorbachev had tried to appease them with token gestures, such as setting up a Russian Party Bureau, but typically, he kept that bureau under his own thumb. He had promised new authority and new institutions to the Russian republic, but the apparat saw that citadel slip through its fingers into the hands of its nemesis, the renegade Boris Yeltsin. Though its own new champion, the provincial Party leader Ivan Polozkov, had run neck and neck with Yeltsin on two ballots for the top position in the republic, Gorbachev had withdrawn him on the third ballot, only to see Yeltsin beat someone more moderate. In the process, however, the Right had shown its strength.

And while Gorbachev was preoccupied with his new presidency, with the economy, and with world diplomacy, the right wing set out to capture the machinery of the Party and challenge Gorbachev's control. Stealing a page from his book, the hard-liners intended to undermine him from below. Their first step was to stack and control elections for the five thousand delegates to the all-union Party Congress; they wanted a majority in order to dictate terms to Gorbachev. Then, before the *all-union*

Party Congress, they planned to found their cherished new *Russian* Communist Party and show their power.

The Leningrad Party organization took the lead in this campaign—Leningrad, shamed by the 1989 elections and publicly humiliated by Gorbachev's quip about a Party organization whose functionaries were still "chewing stale gum." Gorbachev thought he had an ally in Boris Gidaspov, the new Leningrad leader, but he had miscalculated, or else he had been hoodwinked by Ligachev, who still had well-placed agents making appointments under Gorbachev's nose. Gidaspov, an ambitious opportunist, quickly catered to the right wing. Under his protection, and in tandem with the reactionary United Front of Russian Workers, the Leningrad Party apparat organized an "action conference" for the new Russian Communist Party in April; in June, it called the founding Congress.

These machinations got a sudden, unwitting boost from a classic political gaffe by Gorbachev and Ryzhkov. The massive public panic in response to the food-price increases and other economic measures announced by Ryzhkov in late May played directly into the hands of the right wing. Ryzhkov's announcement that bread prices would triple in July and other prices would shoot up in early 1991 gave the apparatchiks the opening they had longed for. Heretofore, not much of the public had been moved by their attacks on Gorbachev's reforms. Now, overnight, people all over the country were aflame with fear over talk of free-market economics; the right-wing apparat, so long a target of the popular mistrust, could pose as the defenders of little people by opposing the Gorbachev-Ryzhkov plan for a "regulated market economy."

Belatedly, Gorbachev woke up, and, sensing the danger of a new Party organization controlled by his opponents, he tried to stop the Right from forming the Russian Party. But he was too late. The process had too much momentum. In order not to let the right-wingers have things all their way, Gorbachev was forced into attending the founding Congress. Hoping to outwit the right-wing apparat, Gorbachev got himself named presiding officer and insisted that the delegates be those elected to the all-union Party Congress. But the apparatchiks had done their spadework while he was neglecting the Party, and they were ready for him. The delegates were in their pocket; out of roughly twenty-seven hundred delegates, more than forty percent were from the apparat.[24] It was, as the disconsolate liberals later lamented, "the apparat Congress."

Even before the Russian Party Congress opened on June 19, 1990, it was clear Gorbachev was in for a siege. Yegor Ligachev had dropped all

pretense of unity, and was shrilly attacking Gorbachev on every policy—
Eastern Europe, nationalities, market economics, and the role of the
Party. At a conference of farm officials, he accused Gorbachev of making
"concession after concession" that could lead to the breakup of the Soviet
Union and the Party; Gorbachev was in danger of becoming a "president
without territory."[25] To halt Gorbachev's move toward market econom-
ics, Ligachev demanded a national referendum—socialism or capitalism.
He had sounded the keynote.

Like sharks, the right wing relentlessly savaged Gorbachev throughout
the five-day Congress. Their invective had never been sharper or more
personal. No sooner had Gorbachev made his routine opening statement
than the first speaker, Ivan Osadchy, a Congress organizer, accused Gorbachev of pushing the Party toward "suicide." Under his leadership,
Osadchy declared, the once-mighty Party had been "reduced to crouching
unarmed in the trenches, under massive shelling by anti-socialist
forces."[26]

Viktor Tyulkin, Party secretary at Leningrad's Kirov Factory, said Gorbachev's *perestroika* had done so little for the proletariat that there was
"a mass exodus of workers" from the Party—seven hundred from his own
plant had already quit, and four hundred more had signaled their intention to do so. Tyulkin charged that the Gorbachev-Ryzhkov package
would lower the people's standard of living still further. And in what was
widely taken as an anti-Semitic slur (Russian nationalists claim Jews have
trouble rolling their Russian *R*), Tyulkin mocked reformers such as Democratic Platform leader Vladimir Lysenko as "comrades who have trouble
pronouncing the word 'Russian' and frankly have no wish to pronounce
the word 'Communist.' "[27]

To an unprecedented degree, military officers, angry over the loss of
Eastern Europe, joined the harangue against Gorbachev. Colonel General
D. A. Volkogonov bemoaned the lack of a clear strategy to Gorbachev's
reforms and the nation's uncertain leadership. Far more harshly, General
Albert Makashov gave vent to the anxieties of troop commanders that the
Soviet Union was sinking as a world power.

"Germany is reuniting and will probably become a member of NATO,
Japan is becoming the decisive force in the Pacific. Only our wise peacocks
are crowing that no one is going to attack us," the general declared. He
decried the policy of withdrawing Soviet troops from Eastern Europe—
"countries that our fathers liberated from Fascism"—and then, to waves
of applause from this conclave of hard-liners and self-proclaimed Russian
patriots, General Makashov added: "Comrades, the army and navy will
be needed yet by the Soviet Union."[28]

When Ligachev's turn came, he sided with the military in denouncing "the collapse of the socialist commonwealth." Then he leveled the grievous charge that Gorbachev had made policy on economic reform, the German question, and Eastern Europe without consulting the Politburo, thus letting policy control slip out of the Party's hands. And he hinted that Gorbachev ought to give up his top Party position. Tongue-lashing the reformers of Democratic Platform, Ligachev warned that "the main danger to the Party today is the destruction of the Party from within."[29]

On several previous occasions when stung by critics, Gorbachev had peremptorily threatened to resign. It was an extreme ploy, designed to get his way and warn his accusers not to go too far lest they lose a leader whom most people considered indispensable. Ligachev had pushed this button. Gorbachev rose to advise his taunters: "I think, comrades, that people are not taking the general secretary of the Party, the president of this country, very seriously. It is not a question of me personally; tomorrow, or in ten or twelve days [at the all-union Party Congress], someone else might be general secretary or Party chairman. To condemn and make accusations, you ought to understand a great deal more."[30]

Gorbachev won a strong round of applause, but little else. In the end, the apparat elected one of its own, Ivan Polozkov, the fifty-five-year-old Party leader in Krasnodar Territory, as leader of the new Russian Communist Party. He was certainly not Gorbachev's choice, but Gorbachev seemed either powerless or too demoralized to stop Polozkov.

Back in mid-March, in a speech laced with stiletto innuendos, Polozkov had made a biting attack on Gorbachev's weak leadership: "The organs of power are so irresolute. . . . The state, as it were, belongs to no one. . . . We need a conductor."[31] Later, Polozkov, a pint-sized true believer with charcoal hair and blunt candor, had needled Gorbachev for lack of ideological conviction. "Gorbachev is too tolerant, too slow. He thinks too much," Polozkov told reporters. "He's too careful."[32]

Now, in June, he reminded the Congress that in the late seventies, when Gorbachev had been the Party leader in Stavropol, he himself had been Gorbachev's overseer from the Central Committee's organizational department, the section that supervised the work of provincial Party organizations. With patronizing approval, he recalled Gorbachev's introduction of reform measures, as if he, Polozkov, had been the tutor. Then he turned on the Gorbachev of today, chiding him for "inconsistency and concessions." And lest anyone misunderstand, Polozkov traced the nation's current problems to a "crisis of leadership."[33]

The apparat's obvious triumph sent Gorbachev's Party supporters into a tailspin and set the radical Democratic Platform group to talking about a mass walkout from the Twenty-eighth Party Congress. Some radicals did not wait. The Leningrad television producer Bella Kurkova and six of her Communist colleagues at *Fifth Wheel* turned in their Party cards right after Polozkov's election. "I could not stand to be in a party that picked Polozkov," Bella told me.[34]

The very thing that Gorbachev had wanted to prevent—the polarization of the Party into left-wing and right-wing factions—had now taken concrete form, and Gorbachev's partisans in the apparat blamed him directly. I found Party centrists such as Moscow Party leader Yuri Prokofyev and liberal Central Committee officials such as Aleksandr Lebedev furious at Gorbachev for having let himself be so outmaneuvered.

"Gorbachev paid little attention to preparations for the Russian Party Congress," Prokofyev spluttered. "No one is paying attention to the Party. Gorbachev went to the United States, Gorbachev met with Thatcher, he was preoccupied with other business, and meanwhile. . . ."[35]

"He was too busy being a global statesman," Lebedev echoed bitterly. "He is not good at organizational politics. He left it to others, and they did a terrible job. It's as if 'his people' were working for someone else. He neglected the very thing he should have done first of all. And now look at the problems we have."[36]

Gorbachev himself was so worried by the resurgence of the right wing and the threat to his own leadership that, according to Lebedev, he tried to get Party leaders to postpone the forthcoming all-union Communist Party Congress. Boris Yeltsin backed postponement, but Gorbachev ran into resistance from other leaders. The right wing was riding high and was not going to let Gorbachev off the hook.

THE POLITBURO'S LAST HURRAH

Gorbachev was right to brace for a blow at the Twenty-eighth Communist Party Congress, but the Party's problems were more serious than the ups and downs of factional infighting. In the country, the Party's prestige had fallen disastrously; it was losing members by the tens of thousands. As the elections of 1989 and 1990 showed, millions of ordinary people—including millions of rank-and-file Communists—were turning their backs on Party leaders; they no longer looked to the Party for national leadership.

In terms of public trust, the Communist Party ranked seventh behind the army, the Russian Orthodox Church, the Supreme Soviet, and even behind the KGB, government ministries, and trade unions, according to an opinion poll taken for the weekly newsmagazine *Ogonek* in May 1990.

Only the police and the Party's unpopular youth arm, the Komsomol, ranked lower. Nearly 60 percent blamed the Party for slowing the country's growth; half held the Party responsible for the current situation being out of control; one third said the Party no longer played a significant role in Soviet life.[37] Another poll, taken by sociologist Yuri Levada's team to measure political tendencies, found that if the country actually had a multiparty system, less than 19 percent would vote for the Communist Party, 11 percent for the Democratic Platform, nearly 10 percent for a workers' party, and 7 percent each for the Greens and for social democrats—all this without any organized parties in opposition. But half of the people could not state any preference, a sign of mass ambivalence about the Party: neither total rejection nor loyal support.[38]

Even more worrisome to Party officials were the rising defections. Since the 1988 euphoric high point over Gorbachev's reforms, the Party had been losing members—at least 259,605 by its own admission in 1989. The exodus was worst in Moscow, Leningrad, the Baltic republics, and the Siberian mining and industrial areas of Kemerovo, Chelyabinsk, and Krasnoyarsk.[39]

Pravda carried letters from defectors. There were old-timers fed up with reform, or the lack of it; liberal intellectuals angry at the Old Guard or Gorbachev; workers feeling cheated. Coal miners held a nationwide congress in the Ukrainian mining city of Donetsk in mid-June 1990 to begin setting up an independent union. And one of their resolutions, passed by a vote of 308–116, showed their disillusionment with the Party, which many workers felt was abandoning its proclaimed blue-collar constituency in favor of apparatchiks, intellectuals, and white-collar workers.

"We do not consider the Communist Party our party," the miners declared. "We call for a mass exit from the Party."[40]

Worker defections alarmed Party officials such as Yuri Prokofyev. In the first half of 1990, he told me, the Moscow Party had lost twenty thousand members—half of them workers. "They don't believe the Party is still the party of the working class," Prokofyev explained. "They don't believe in the Party's social and economic policies. A certain part is leaving because of disappointment with the Party over *perestroika*. The working class has gotten nothing but empty shelves and inflation."[41]

Prokofyev had been in a watch factory that morning; I asked him how the workers reacted to Gorbachev's battle with the right-wing apparat.

"The workers jumped all over me about that," Prokofyev reported. "They said that if the Party is only going to be concerned with its internal problems, and is not worried about society, then why do we need such a party?"

That was an echo of things I had heard and read; in a Siberian newspaper, *Sibirskaya Gazeta,* readers were asked whose interest the Party promoted; 85 percent said the interests of Party functionaries.[42] And in fact, at the Twenty-eighth Communist Party Congress in Moscow, the apparat had stacked the deck—it comprised 48 percent of the delegates; 20 percent were government officials and factory or farm directors and the like; only 7 percent workers and peasants.[43] Party officials tried to make the best of this, calling it a "party of all classes"—precisely what made the blue-collar workers angry.

Gorbachev's aides knew that it would be a miracle if the Party Congress did not produce a new stream of defections, if not an open split. The radicals of Democratic Platform were threatening to quit unless they won drastic changes in the Party rules. Gorbachev was striving to prevent a split, to win a general mandate for his policies, to limit the damage from the right wing, and to bring new blood into the upper echelons. The right wing simply wanted blood; it was after the scalps of the Gorbachev team.

As the Congress convened on July 2, 1990, the tone was set in the opening minutes when Vladimir Bludov, a delegate from the Soviet Far East, called for the immediate removal of the entire Politburo. His proposal was rejected, but the delegates won the right to examine the performances of individual Politburo members, one by one; their grilling was merciless. Prime Minister Ryzhkov and ideology chief Vadim Medvedev were jeered; boos and hisses rained on Leonid Abalkin, the economist; Yuri Prokofyev was so inundated with angry clapping as he tried to defend Gorbachev that he had to start his speech over four times. Several of Gorbachev's allies, Medvedev, Aleksandr Yakovlev, and Eduard Shevardnadze, announced they were resigning from the Politburo, but that did not calm the fury.

Yakovlev sailed more boldly into the right-wing storm than did Gorbachev. "Shaking from our feet the mud of enmity and suspicion that has built up over decades, it is time [for us] to end the [ideological] civil war," he told the hard-liners. "A misfortune happened, for a Party based on a revolutionary idea has turned into a Party of power, . . . a Party of unquestioning obedience, Communist arrogance, and Communist lordliness. . . . It is precisely the backbone of the authoritarian organism that *perestroika* is striving to break, and for precisely that reason it provokes seething hatred among certain strata. . . .

"One can defend dogma for a certain period of time, but no one has yet succeeded in stopping life. . . . Let us remember that not only empty shelves but also empty souls brought about *perestroika* and the demand for revolutionary changes."[44]

Yakovlev's daring speech won strong applause from liberals and moderates but did not halt the right-wingers. On the fifth day, the right-wing scapegoating became so heated that Gorbachev stepped in. "If you want to bury the Party, split the Party, then continue on this way," he remonstrated. "Think hard. Think hard."[45] His firm hand prevented a political lynching on the spot.

As a Westerner, wary of military influence on civilian politics, I found it eerie to see the military so much in evidence—ranks of army generals and colonels in the balcony in their khaki uniforms; the ivory-yellow shirts of naval officers in solid rows; KGB officers with their telltale blue shoulder boards; Major General Ivan Nikulin raking the leadership over the coals for losing Eastern Europe. Aleksandr Yakovlev defiantly faced down the hard-liners, telling them it was popular will that had toppled the Eastern European regimes. "We cannot repeal the fact that the volume of labor production in South Korea is ten times higher than in the North, and that people in West Germany live better than in the East," he declared.[46] Foreign Minister Shevardnadze, accused of being an architect of retreat, told the hall that the armed forces had squandered 700 billion rubles ($1.2 trillion) on excessive military spending, and that arms agreements with the West would net a peace dividend of 250 billion rubles ($400 billion) over the next five years.[47]

Gorbachev could not restrain himself. "Do you want tanks again?" he demanded of the military. "Shall we teach them how to live?" And then, insisting that the military high command had agreed with his policies, he issued a warning to the dissident generals and colonels: "All officials must be loyal to the government. And if they are decent people and they disagree, they must resign."[48]

The politics of the military and the KGB produced one of the most sensitive conflicts of the Party Congress, a debate that cut to the bone of Party power. With 1.1 million Communists in the military and security services, the Party has long used a network of Party committees to ensure political reliability of the armed forces. Radicals from Democratic Platform demanded those ties be cut; they argued that in a law-governed, multiparty state, the military and KGB should be "depoliticized" and Party committees shut down. Their demands had become more insistent after a recently retired KGB officer, Major General Oleg Kalugin, who had once been acting chief of KGB operations in the United States, caused a sensation by asserting in several press interviews that despite efforts to assume a more democratic image, the KGB had been virtually untouched by five years of *perestroika* and was continuing its efforts to penetrate new Soviet political organizations.[49] Kalugin had called for "depoliticization" of the KGB—that is, elimination of the Party network throughout the secret police—and Democratic Platform had taken up its cry, forcing the issue at the Congress.

In full uniform and wearing their medals, Defense Minister Dmitri Yazov and KGB Chief Vladimir Kryuchkov trooped to the rostrum to squelch the idea of eliminating the Party's political network in the armed forces and KGB as a menace to national security. On this litmus issue, Gorbachev opposed reform. Before the Congress, he had signed an order stripping General Kalugin of all his KGB medals and honors. At the Congress, he signaled in his opening speech that he sided with the right wing against the reformers; he would keep the Party and the army bonded.

This underscored a crucial element of Gorbachev's political strategy. Reformers wanted him to quit as Party leader and to concentrate on the presidency, but he refused, and presumably one reason was to have under his thumb the mechanisms that kept check on the army and KGB. For amid national turmoil, a military freed of political restraint was arguably the greatest threat to Gorbachev's survival. Moreover, the military itself was torn by interethnic tensions, and Gorbachev may have seen the Party as the one element of cohesive glue.

But on the flash point of market economics, Gorbachev clashed with the right wing. On the first day, the conservatives had demanded—and won—a vote to have the word "market" stricken from the name of the economic commission of the Congress. Yegor Ligachev lashed out at Gorbachev's economic policies, savaging him for five years of "mindless radicalism."[50] Even Kryuchkov, the KGB chief, warned: "It would be a fatal mistake to thrust the country into the embrace of the elemental forces of the market."[51] Gorbachev chided them all for churlish alarm, and then offered the sop to a swirl of reporters that the leadership should resign in two years if the economy did not improve.

It was Boris Yeltsin, not surprisingly, who had the temerity to walk into the lion's den and tell the right wing that they were "bankrupt," to urge Gorbachev and the Party's moderates to join in "a center-left alliance of all socialist forces to prevent a schism that will otherwise lead to the Party's total defeat." He laid out Democratic Platform's manifesto— liberalize the Party rules, get its cells out of the military and KGB, transform itself from an "apparatus" party to a "parliamentary" party, and change its name to the Party of Democratic Socialism. If the leadership rejected this "one last chance," Yeltsin warned, the Soviet Communist Party would, like those in Eastern Europe, be "left by the roadside." Sheer force of personality won Yeltsin an attentive audience and light applause.[52]

But everyone knew that this was not a serious challenge. Significantly, Gorbachev had already slammed the door shut on all the internal reforms advocated by the radicals. Over their objections, he had reinstituted Lenin's "democratic centralism," and the right wing had backed him solidly. From the outset he had sided with the right wing on all the crucial issues of the Party's internal operation, and privately he had won a fair amount of right-wing support in return.

By the second week, Gorbachev had weathered the worst of the right-wing storm. There was a solid, silent middle at the Congress that had not taken sides in the noisy clashes of the first week; after the first few days, Gorbachev and Yakovlev had lobbied them effectively to keep them solidly behind Gorbachev. Moreover, even the right-wingers understood that they could not afford a power showdown with Gorbachev. He had given them a lot of what they wanted, by protecting the Party's top-down controls and the Party's network in the army, and by rejecting reforms. A pitched battle against Gorbachev would not only unite the Party's Center and Left against the Right, but a nasty internal fight would probably hasten the flow of defections among the rank and file. Gorbachev might be unpopular with the apparat, but he was also irreplaceable for them. His ouster—or, worse yet, an open and unsuccessful attempt to oust him—would only hasten the Party's demise.

So the right wing did not offer a candidate for Party chairman; they might applaud Ligachev's sallies, but they understood that rhetoric was one thing and supreme power was another. So Gorbachev was reelected general secretary without serious opposition.

The real test came on the choice of deputy general secretary: Yegor Ligachev saw one last chance to grab for the Party machinery, and made a lunge; Gorbachev's candidate was his hand-picked Ukrainian leader, Vladimir Ivashko, a Party loyalist with some appeal to the right wing. Gorbachev's team lobbied hard for Ivashko. Said Georgy Shakhnazarov, Gorbachev's aide: "If Ligachev is elected, there will be a collapse."[53] But with Gorbachev once again secure, the Party readily bowed to his will; Ligachev, nearly seventy, was a nostalgic figure, a voice of the past. When the tally was counted, he had been swamped—only 776 were for him, 3,642 against.

In defeat, Ligachev left the field, announcing his retirement to Siberia. And that helped clear the way for an expanded but much less powerful Politburo, with new faces such as right-winger Ivan Polozkov and the centrist Yuri Prokofyev. This was what Gorbachev had wanted—a major change at the upper echelons of the Party. Both the Politburo and the policy-approving Central Committee were virtually all new; out of more than four hundred old Central Committee members and candidate members, fewer than fifty remained. Gorbachev had finally gotten the fresh blood that he wanted, though it would take time to tell how much policy leeway this new body would give him. He had shuffled faces in the past, only to be surprised how little change that had brought.

In any case, Gorbachev had faced down the angry apparat, and had prevailed. As the Congress began, the apparatchiks were full of confidence from their victory in the Russian Party Congress. But this time they were big losers. Gorbachev had conquered them once again, but he had not tamed them once and for all. On the issue of reforming the inner workings of the Party, he had bowed to the Right, not even trying to reform the Party rules to make the Party more democratic. He had brought new blood into the central Party machinery, but the recalcitrant apparat remained entrenched in many bastions of provincial power, in the Russian republic, and also in the Ukraine, Byelorussia, and Central Asia. And their chosen leader, Ivan Polozkov, was not only in charge of the Russian Party apparatus but sitting in the new Politburo.

At the Twenty-eighth Party Congress, Gorbachev also lost the most dynamic and popular wing of the Party. As the Congress ended, he shouted out the Leninist slogan "The Party Lives and the Party Will Live!" But it was a hollow cheer; the Party was already losing its lifeblood. Gorbachev had been unable to preserve unity, to reconcile the irreconcilables within the Party. He had given so much to the Right that he lost the Left, an outcome to which he seemed resigned in advance. He knew the liberals would be disillusioned by how much ground he gave to the right wing, and their reaction was not long in coming.

On July 12, the second-to-last day, Boris Yeltsin strode into the Congress in a dark suit, a written statement in hand. He had given fair warning that he would quit if the Party did not change; still, it was a thunderbolt when he announced his resignation.

To cries of "Shame! Shame!" Yeltsin said that as head of the Russian republic and "in connection with the move toward a multiparty system, I cannot fulfill only the instructions of the Communist Party. As the highest elected figure in the republic, I have to bow to the will of the people."[54] The next day Leningrad Mayor Anatoly Sobchak and Moscow Mayor Gavril Popov followed suit; and then, quickly, prominent radicals such as Moscow Deputy Mayor Sergei Stankevich; Yeltsin's economic adviser, Mikhail Bocharev; and the leaders of Democratic Platform, Vyacheslav Shostakovsky and Vladimir Lysenko, who announced plans to form a new "democratic coalition."

The numbers were not immediately dramatic; but the Party was losing the most effective vote-getters in its ranks, the most energetic reformers, and in some cases the very people whom Gorbachev himself had attracted two or three years before. There were hundreds of others, I knew, from excited conversations I had had before and during the Congress with liberal activists in Leningrad and Moscow and with people from other parts of the country. The comments of Andrei Kortunov, a thirty-three-year-old foreign-policy analyst at Moscow's Institute of the U.S.A. and Canada, were typical and telling.

"Many of us had previously refused to join the Party because we felt our nation's politics were dirty, but we decided in 1987 or 1988 that Gorbachev was making a serious effort to reform our society, and that we should help him," Kortunov told me. "We saw he was threatened from the right. We had a feeling that deep in his soul, Gorbachev was a real liberal, that he was one of us, but he had to hide his real face, he had to play by the rules, or the system would crush him.

"But in the last year, it became clear to us that Gorbachev was not a liberal. Many of us expected him to resign as general secretary of the Party and to separate himself from the Party bureaucracy. But he has not wanted to do that. He is always a consensus seeker; he wanted approval from all sectors of society.

"So, many of us were disillusioned. I have felt a sense of personal betrayal. Yakovlev is more like what I thought Gorbachev would be like. But Gorbachev is trying for a consensus where there is none. It turned out that the Party apparatus today is just like the apparatus five years ago, just like fifty years ago. It puts its interests ahead of the people's interests. Our apparatchiks are like the Bourbons: They forgot nothing because they learned nothing. There's no use dealing with these people. The only way is to fight them from another party—to confront them in political battle."[55]

This disillusionment among the reformers whom Gorbachev had drawn into the Party earlier in his tenure was the price he paid for preventing his own schism with the apparat.

His great achievement at the Party Congress, and one with significance for the future course of reform and the ultimate fate of the Communist Party itself, was stripping the once-almighty Politburo of real power over the government. This had obviously been carefully planned and engineered in private before the Congress opened; Gorbachev's closest Politburo allies were to quit, setting an example for others. The only threat was an effective right-wing revolt and victory by Ligachev. But Ligachev's defeat ensured the success of Gorbachev's plan. For with his retirement, the way was cleared for the entire old leadership, except for Gorbachev, to leave the Politburo.

This meant that at the top of the power pyramid, the Siamese connection between Party and state—the heart of the Party's power—had finally been severed.

When Gorbachev had set up his new presidency in March 1990, he had taken the first major step in moving supreme power out of the Party's hands. But then he had appointed a presidential council as his inner cabinet, and it included half a dozen key figures from the Party Politburo—Prime Minister Ryzhkov, Foreign Minister Shevardnadze, Defense Minister Yazov, KGB Chief Kryuchkov, and his personal adviser, Aleksandr Yakovlev. So even with the presidency in place, there had still been an intimate overlap between Party and state at the highest policy-making level. With that link retained, Ligachev and the rest of the Politburo could demand their say before government decisions were taken.

At the Twenty-eighth Party Congress, with the five key members of Gorbachev's government leaving the Politburo, except for Gorbachev himself, there was no longer any overlap. And there was no reason to consult the Politburo beforehand on government policy; it was left to deal with Party affairs. Moreover, Gorbachev was much less vulnerable to being overthrown by an unhappy Politburo once its power had been reduced.

In sum, the Party Congress was the culmination of an effort Gorbachev had begun with the elections of March 1989, the Congress of People's Deputies that summer, and the presidency set up in March 1990—to shift policy-making power out of the Party into the new institutions of government. The final step was the separation of Party and state at the highest level.

For the Party, already losing mass support among the rank and file, that was an irreparable and potentially fatal loss of power.

CHAPTER 23

CITY HALL: THE NEW POLITICAL ENTREPRENEURS

"The big leaders are too preoccupied with the
fight for power within the Party, so they
don't pay attention to the city level,
they do not consider it a real danger
so far. But I think they make a real mistake."[1]
—Sergei Stankevich
Deputy Mayor of Moscow
June 1990

"This is Leningrad city property. The
running water, sewage, electricity for
Smolny [Party headquarters] are all provided
by the city. If we are not respected,
we can cut off all of the above. Then let
them see how they can get along in that building."[2]
—Anatoly Sobchak
Mayor of Leningrad
June 1990

Many of the leading radicals who quit the Communist Party in the summer of 1990 had found a promising new arena for actually wielding power—city hall.

Even before establishing a national political party that could challenge the fading but still entrenched Communist Party, the reformers could win majority control of city councils and take charge of an important segment of the political system. As power at the center fragmented, this was an important opening to seize.

At the city level, they could build the infrastructure of democracy and develop new national parties, even a democratic coalition, from the bottom up. City hall was an excellent place to learn the nuts and bolts of making policy, exercising power, and battling the Party apparat for day-to-day authority. It was an ideal stepping-stone for the wave of political newcomers who had flowed into the system after the 1989 election, who had learned to confront Gorbachev, Ryzhkov, and government ministers in the Supreme Soviet, but who were still woefully short of experience in running government themselves.

These reformers were desperate to accomplish something at the local level, instead of merely debating points in the Supreme Soviet and the Congress of People's Deputies, or being outvoted by Gorbachev's obedient majority. Given the feuding and posturing between Gorbachev and the Party's right wing, and the policy stalemate at the top, the radicals wanted to show that a more flexible approach could produce authentic change and improve people's daily lives.

They could chip away at the Party's control of the press and television by bringing out newspapers of their own, or by organizing independent television outlets. While Gorbachev and Ryzhkov wallowed in ideological uncertainty or tried half measures on economic reform, the radicals could use city governments to push free-market economics. They could take practical steps: authorize the sale of unprofitable state enterprises; improve operating conditions for cooperatives; sign deals for foreign joint ventures; encourage private Soviet entrepreneurs by throwing lucrative city contracts their way.

The most canny reform politicians took advantage of Soviet electoral law, which allowed anyone to hold office at two levels of government simultaneously. So they sat in the Supreme Soviet, where they drafted laws that passed power to local governments, and then they got themselves elected to local governments, to carry out the laws that they themselves had written.

Their dream of actually exercising power turned into reality with the elections of the spring of 1990. It was these elections, at the republic, province, city, and district levels, that the apparat had wanted to prevent, and that Gorbachev had agreed to postpone for six months, because the Party bosses knew that they would take another beating.

Some Party officials, such as Yuri Prokofyev, the centrist Party leader in Moscow, and Mikhail Knyazyuk, the hard-line Party boss in Ivanovo, caught on to ways of beating the new democratic election process. They ran as candidates from rural villages, where the Party's machine-style politics still worked among the peasantry. Prokofyev, needing a seat in the Moscow City Council, picked a country town called Butovo, which had only recently been brought within the city limits, and showered it with minor "pork barrel" improvements during the election campaign. So despite his fears about running as a Party boss, Prokofyev managed to win a council seat.

In Ivanovo, Knyazyuk also picked a rural district, from which to get elected to the Russian-republic parliament; on the other hand, Anatoly Golovkov, the Ivanovo mayor who had callously dismissed the hunger strikers trying to reopen the Red Church, was thrown out of office by urban voters. On the morning after the election, he complained to me, choking down his bitterness, that Gorbachev was pushing democracy too fast.[3]

This was a typical result: Party bosses maneuvering to hold power in the countryside, but decimated once again in the heart of the bigger cities. This time, however, the defeat hit home.

In 1989, the race had been for the optional prestige of a seat in the distant national legislature. This time, the stakes were control of local government.

In Moscow, radical reformers from the Inter-Regional Group pulled together a political coalition that united the Moscow Popular Front, the anti-Stalinist association called Memorial, the Moscow Association of Voters, and various ecological groups and democratic political clubs. They shrewdly named their coalition the Bloc of Democratic Russia. As Sergei Stankevich explained, opinion polls had shown that the most powerful trends in Russian politics were pushing people to the left and to the right: toward democratic populism opposed to the power "mafia"; and toward Russian nationalism, which the right wing was trying to appropriate. And so the reformers in Moscow cannily crafted the name "Democratic Russia" to appeal to those two contrary trends.

To build a coalition in the Moscow city government, Stankevich and two other well-known deputies, economist Gavril Popov and Nikolai Travkin, a mathematical physicist, worked Western-style political techniques. All three had become celebrities from their frequent televised appearances at the national Congress and Supreme Soviet; during the 1990 election campaign they made the rounds of Moscow political rallies as media heavyweights. They publicized the Bloc of Democratic Russia; they made speeches for younger allies; they circulated campaign leaflets endorsing less prominent candidates.

What was especially fascinating was the fast learning curve of these new Soviet politicians. On one of my trips to Moscow, Stankevich had asked me how to get American political books about coalition building; he despaired of the Russian penchant for windy philosophizing, and the absence of a knack for the give-and-take of compromise and political organizing. Then he had visited Washington; he had gone around Capitol Hill getting pointers from American politicians such as New Jersey Senator Bill Bradley. Now, only a little more than a year after having emerged from his institute's archives, he was using the coalition-building techniques of the American power game; and he was consulting opinion polls, by then commercially available from Soviet sociologists such as Boris Grushin, one of Yuri Levada's colleagues.

In Leningrad, the precinct-by-precinct operation run so successfully by Yelena Zelinskaya in the 1989 campaign was revived under the banner of Democratic Election '90, which played openly on the growth of anti-Party feeling during the year since the 1989 election. Several candidates from the democratic coalition told me that they survived only by playing down their Party membership. One coalition candidate, a bright forty-year-old ecologist named Konstantin Yarukhin, described the problems he encountered at political rallies.

"People reacted to my being a member of the Party," Yarukhin told me. "They said it was no use talking to me, because I was a Communist. But when I explained to them my ideas of reform, they were pleased and surprised. Other times, people talked with me first, liked my views, and then were astonished when they discovered I was a Party member. It made me think twice about why I am staying in the Party."[4]

As in Moscow, many of the lesser-known candidates in Leningrad rode the coattails of nationally known Supreme Soviet deputies like electrical engineer Yuri Boldyrev and fifty-three-year-old law professor Anatoly Sobchak, who was rated in one opinion poll as the third-most-popular figure in the country, behind Gorbachev and Yeltsin.

In the big industrial city of Sverdlovsk, the slate from Democratic Russia got a shot in the arm from Yeltsin, who had gone home to his birthplace and the region where he had once been the Party leader to run for the parliament of the Russian republic. Sverdlovsk had an active popular front, a very liberal film studio, a thriving youth movement, and a strong team of democratic-minded deputies in the national legislature, led by Gennady Burbulis, a management specialist, and Valdimir Volkov, a Party secretary in a huge machine-tool plant, who had thumbed his nose at the apparat and sided with Yeltsin.

In coal-mining cities such as Kemerovo in western Siberia and Donetsk in the Ukraine, the network of miners' strike committees gave the democratic, anti-Party activists a powerful political base for the election. In other major Russian cities such as Gorky, Volgograd, Tyumen, and Kuibyshev, popular protests against the corrupt practices of local Party bosses in the winter-spring of 1990 fueled the drive of democratic outsiders for control of city hall. In Volgograd, even the new Party leaders who came to power were radicals who aligned with non-Party reformers.

In the Ukrainian capital of Kiev and the ardently nationalistic city of Lvov in the western Ukraine, the rising Ukrainian national movement Rukh, after lagging for a long time behind similar movements in other republics, became a force in the local elections. In the Moldavian capital of Kishinev and the Byelorussian capital of Minsk, popular-front movements organized slates of opposition candidates. And of course in the Baltic republics, the powerful national movements were waiting to pounce on the 1990 elections, to gain control of local and republic governments.

The 1990 election campaign changed the political map of the country. Insurgents scored well in the republican elections throughout the Baltics, in Russia, the Ukraine, Byelorussia, and Moldavia, although only in Lithuania did they win an absolute majority in the national legislature.

But their upset victories at the city level, from Siberia to Leningrad, were stunning.

In Moscow, city government in the capital of world Communism passed into alien hands on April 20, 1990. The Bloc of Democratic Russia, led by Popov and Stankevich, captured 281 of the 442 seats in the city soviet, or city council. The Communist Party was reduced to holding 90 seats, so few that Party boss Yuri Prokofyev admitted to me later that he found it embarrassing to sit in the minority section. The radicals, with more than 60 percent of the seats, elected the pudgy, tousle-haired economist Popov, as the new mayor of Moscow. And they chose Stankevich, the serious-minded young political scientist, as deputy mayor.

In Leningrad, the cradle of the Bolshevik Revolution, Democratic Election '90 won 68 percent of the four hundred seats in the city soviet, and then elected Anatoly Sobchak as mayor. "We were overcome with a feeling of euphoria when we occupied Marinsky Palace [city-council chambers]," Yelena Zelinskaya told me. At first, it was practically like a holiday. "For three days, our deputies all wore their jeans and sweaters," Zelinskaya said. "Then, after three days, they changed into suits and ties and became more businesslike."[5]

In Kiev, the third-largest Soviet city, the insurgents claimed the largest group of deputies, but the balance was so even, between the new forces of democratic nationalism and the more traditional Party regulars, that

it took forty days for the city council to pick a compromise mayor—
Arnold Nazarchuk, the fifty-seven-year-old chief of a local electronics
complex, and his progressive deputy, Aleksandr Mosiyuk, a thirty-five-
year-old professor of physics and mathematics. But the experience of
having to bargain for power and office softened the old battle lines; as one
Kiev editor put it, the independents were radicalizing the Communists.[6]

The central press in Moscow never bothered to publish election returns
from around the country. No political organization save the Communist
Party had a good enough information network to ferret out the results
across the country; and the Party had no desire to publicize its defeats.
Even three months after the 1990 election, the democratic radicals in
Moscow and Leningrad still had only sketchy information, but by their
count, democratic insurgents now dominated city councils in fifteen to
twenty cities—not only Moscow, Leningrad, and Kiev, but also such
major Russian cities as Sverdlovsk, Gorky, Volgograd, Kemerovo, Tyumen, and Kuibyshev. Though still in the minority, independents had also
elected solid blocks of delegates in other places, such as Omsk, Novgorod,
Arkhangelsk, and Krasnoyarsk.[7]

In the Ukraine, the Lvov City Hall fell to an anti-Party coalition, which
elected Vyacheslav Chernovil, a former dissident jailed in the seventies,
as mayor; in Donetsk, the miners won at least 40 percent of the seats;
democrats supposedly prevailed in the major industrial city of Kharkov.
In the Baltics, popular fronts had strong influence in the main cities, as
they did in other republic capitals such as Minsk and Kishinev, where local
Party leaders were rejected by the voters.

There was a fairly consistent pattern. Except in Central Asia, where
little changed, the Party apparat clung to elected power in the outlying
provinces, but in urban areas Party officials either were turned out of city
councils or were confronted with strong new activist minorities of democratic delegates and had to bend to these new political pressures. It was
a sea change; Gorbachev and the Party apparat very quickly began to feel
its effects.

DEFYING GORBACHEV, RIGHT UNDER HIS NOSE

Almost as soon as the first of these new insurgent city councils took office
in April 1990, they showed their independence and their muscle—by
defying the trade embargo that Gorbachev invoked on April 19 in his
attempt to crush Lithuania's bid for independence.

Ironically, Gorbachev's blockade forced the Lithuanians, and the new independent city governments in central Russia, Siberia, the Ukraine, and elsewhere, to make deals behind the Kremlin's back. The embargo had the unintended effect of helping to break down the Kremlin's highly centralized control of the Soviet economy.

The Lithuanians were desperate for Russian oil, gas, and raw materials, as well as for spare parts and industrial goods from the Ukraine, Byelorussia, and Moldavia. So they sent trade delegations to the city governments in Moscow, Leningrad, Lvov in the Ukraine, Kishinev in Moldavia, Minsk in Byelorussia, and as far away as Sverdlovsk in the Ural Mountains and Omsk and Tyumen in western Siberia. And they found that the new democratic-led governments in these places were eager to barter for Lithuanian textiles, clothing, fabrics, bricks, and a variety of services.

Initially, the trade began with private black-market deals on a small scale, but it mushroomed quickly. Before long, as one Lithuanian legislator disclosed, the Lithuanians were sending truck convoys with food to an automobile plant in the Urals and a tractor plant in Minsk, in return for spare parts; and to sawmills in Siberia in return for lumber needed by Lithuanian furniture factories. Another barter arrangement saw newsprint brought to Lithuania from the Komi region of northern Russia, in exchange for Lithuanian publication of Komi's uncensored newspapers.[8] The Lithuanian government cut off its normal food shipments to Soviet military bases and to Soviet contractors, if they abided by Gorbachev's embargo; and they took those supplies and diverted them to friendly business partners. Before long, Lithuanian officials said, they had deals to ship eight thousand tons of meat a month to the new Moscow City Council, and four thousand tons a month to Leningrad, plus deals for substantial supplies of dairy products for both cities.[9]

The new Moscow and Leningrad city councils had been quick to pass resolutions condemning Gorbachev's trade embargo. The Leningrad council had denounced the blockade as an act of aggression that violated international law, and called upon Gorbachev to lift the blockade. In Moscow, democratic-minded deputies had seen the embargo not only as an effort to crush a democratically elected government in Lithuania, but also as an ominous sign of autocratic rule from the Kremlin and an implicit threat to the budding democratic city governments in Russia as well.

Leningrad, as the major Russian city closest to Lithuania (it is within four hundred miles of Vilnius), had been the most anxious to protect the normal flow of commerce with Lithuania. The city council set up the Committee for the Defense of Lithuania and in early April sent one of its members, Aleksandr Seryakov, a tall, wiry physicist who specialized in molecular spectroscopy, to Vilnius to establish trade and political relations with the self-proclaimed independent Republic of Lithuania.

Soon after Gorbachev's embargo had been imposed, Seryakov and Professor Julius Juzelionas, a Lithuanian academic-turned-politician, had swapped lists of goods for barter, because initially Gorbachev's embargo against Lithuania had caused a backlash in Leningrad. For example, Lithuania had stopped supplying fabric to Leningrad textile factories, and production had suddenly dropped. To avoid having its factories shut down, Leningrad had to help the Lithuanians obtain their primary need— fuel—denied them when Gorbachev cut off supplies of oil and natural gas.

In open defiance of Gorbachev's embargo, the Leningrad City Council declared its moral support of Lithuania, and openly authorized Lithuanians with private cars and trucks to buy gasoline in Leningrad. And a larger volume of industrial trade developed privately. City-council deputy Seryakov frequently acted as the middleman to get new barter deals started. Two or three times a week, he told me, he was approached by Lithuanian contacts eager to open up channels of supply in Leningrad.

"Lithuanians came to me because I was part of the delegation that went to Lithuania and addressed their national council, and my speech was televised. So they knew me," Seryakov explained. "Usually, the Lithuanians coming to me were factory managers and collective-farm directors who were asking for gasoline and diesel fuel. Even though we have shortages in Leningrad, I would always try to find them some enterprises which could help them. Normally some kind of deal was struck between an enterprise in Leningrad and the Lithuanian farms. What they trade is their business. I just help them to find each other."[10]

Illicit trade during the Lithuanian embargo had a more important, long-term consequence: It prompted the Leningrad City Council to set up regular trade missions in all three Baltic republics, anticipating the day when they would secede from the U.S.S.R. and become independent states. Leningraders had no question that enduring trade relationships with the independent Baltic states were in their self-interest, and they were not about to let Gorbachev's objections interfere.

"Now, the Leningrad City Council has the right to go into business directly, according to a recently adopted law on local self-government," Seryakov informed me. "On the business side, enterprises buy their products and trade directly with Lithuania on a barter basis. Hopefully that will be more efficient and we can trade on a larger scale, beneficial to the whole city and not just to a handful of factories."

To Seryakov, and to Mayor Sobchak, with whom I talked later, the main point was that Leningrad was asserting its right to establish its own trade relations, as well as protecting the rights of its local enterprises, without getting permission from the Kremlin.

"The Leningrad City Council assumes the power and responsibility," Seryakov said. "Unlike previously, when Moscow governed everything, we are going to run the city ourselves, and establish ties with other regions of the country, directly, without going through the central authorities in Moscow."

His comments sounded as if the democratic reformers were bent on establishing something like the old Hanseatic League, the mercantile association of German and Scandinavian towns and cities that had operated around the shores of the Baltic Sea from the thirteenth century onward.

Those comments were echoed by the radical reformers who took over the Moscow City Council. They had long chafed under what they saw as Gorbachev's excessively centralized control of both the economy and relations with minority republics. And so, like the Leningraders, the Muscovites plunged into trade with Lithuania, in violation of Gorbachev's embargo.

At one point, they had the audacity to run a whole trainload of fuel from Moscow to Lithuania—right under the Kremlin's nose. Sergei Stankevich told me about it late one evening in his city-council office; at the time, the embargo was still in force, so he was reporting about contraband deals.

"We received meat from [the Lithuanians] and we gave them some fuel and some machinery goods," Stankevich said. "We made up a special train with fuel barrels and we sent it to Leningrad. And they redirected the train to Lithuania."

"Where does the fuel come from?" I asked.

"From a Moscow oil-processing plant," he said.

"Which one?"

"Oh, I'm afraid you can't receive such information," he said, a knowing smile creasing the corners of his eyes.[11]

At that point, the radicals were keeping the scope and details of their trade secret, to avoid Kremlin reprisals. But as soon as the embargo was lifted, on June 29, the Lithuanians proudly disclosed their trade with a host of cities: Moscow, Leningrad, Omsk, Smolensk, Saratov, Arkhangelsk, Pskov, Tyumen, Minsk, and even faraway Uzbekistan, not to mention individual factories or enterprises elsewhere. The Lithuanian government claimed that through barter deals with parts of the Soviet Union, and not counting old Soviet contracts, it had imported 892 million rubles' (nearly $1.5 billion) worth of goods during the embargo, and had shipped back an equal volume.[12] If correct, those figures signified a staggering breakdown of centralized economic control, and defiance of Gorbachev—mainly by the new city governments.

"ALL POWER TO THE SOVIETS"

This bold new brand of urban politics had its roots in Leninism; it had been legitimized seven decades earlier by Vladimir Ilyich Lenin himself. In the summer of 1917, during the crescendo that produced the Bolshevik Revolution, Lenin had seen the popularly elected city soviets in Petrograd and across Russia as a crucial springboard to the Bolsheviks' ultimate seizure of power; and he canonized the slogan "All Power to the Soviets." When the provisional government of Prime Minister Aleksandr Kerensky objected, Lenin protested: "Such opposition means nothing but renouncing democracy!"[13] Of course, once Communist control was firmly established, Lenin emasculated the soviets as independent power bases, and ever since, the Party had used them as the window dressing of the "workers' state."

As part of his political strategy, Gorbachev had decided to invest real power once again in popularly elected soviets—first of all, in the Congress of People's Deputies and the Supreme Soviet; and then in soviets all across the country. Gorbachev was repeating Lenin's tactic, using the soviets as vehicles for an assault on the centralized power structure of his day. Lenin used them to fight Kerensky and the remnants of the czarist state; Gorbachev was using them to humble the Party apparat and to fashion a countervailing power to oppose it.

The democratic-minded radicals were quite happy to adapt the tactics of both Lenin and Gorbachev and to use the hallowed scripture of Soviet Communism's patron saint against his own party. Months before the spring elections of 1990, I began seeing radicals and young people wearing T-shirts and sweatshirts emblazoned with ALL POWER TO THE SOVIETS. It had now become a rallying cry for foes of the Party apparatus.

Before the 1990 elections, city soviets had been tools of the Party bosses—in effect, mere puppets. Theoretically, the city Party committee and the city soviet shared power; they often shared office buildings, newspapers, special rest homes, and cafeterias, as well as responsibility and authority. But, in fact, the Party pulled the strings.

The prospect of genuine independence in city hall alarmed the Party apparat, and in several cities it moved to preempt the new reformers. Even

Gorbachev acted alarmed—he immediately stripped the new Moscow City Council of control over street demonstrations and rallies, asserting his personal control on the grounds that "supreme state and government institutions are situated in the Kremlin and other places in the center of the city."[14] Once in office, the new city council protested, immediately appealing to the newly established Soviet Constitutional Oversight Commission to revoke the order, asserting that direct presidential rule was permissible only in the wake of palpable danger to public order.

Gorbachev's move, and other actions by local Party officials, immediately sharpened a sense of confrontation. Moreover, the radicals came into office with the natural instincts of political winners everywhere: They reached for the spoils of victory and fought for control of very practical instruments of power—real estate, the machinery of local government, control of the Party press and television.

In Moscow, the first battle was over the loyalties of the newly elected city deputies themselves. Since the great bulk of them were Communist Party members, the immediate question was whether they would stick with the Bloc of Democratic Russia, which had helped them get elected, or submit to Party discipline.

"It was a real confrontation from the very beginning," Stankevich told me. "Our local Party chief [Yuri Prokofyev] tried to press the Communists [in the city council] but they rejected this attempt. And so we succeeded in consolidating our democratic coalition."

The election of Gavril Popov as mayor of Moscow on April 20 had sealed the psychological break from the Party for the independent-minded deputies, 90 percent of whom were political novices.

Popov immediately became embroiled in the next battle, over the most important buildings in the city of Moscow—buildings that were symbols of political power.

"The Party tried to capture the administrative buildings in Moscow," Stankevich told me. "We have thirty-three districts in the city, and each district has an administrative building. Normally, you can find there the offices of the district council, the district Party organization, and the district Komsomol. The Party made the former city council adopt a decision to transfer these buildings from the soviets to the Party. So we had to counterattack at once. We reversed the old decision. The Party tried to appeal to the courts, but the court didn't accept their suit. So now we are the proprietors."[15]

Prokofyev, the Party boss, had a different version: He claimed that the Party had put up one third of the funds for those buildings, 23 million rubles in all, and that its investment entitled the Party to keep its offices in those buildings. He accused the radical reformers of picking fights with the Party.

"Mossoviet [the Moscow City Council] clearly has an anti-Party stance," Prokofyev said. "They are trying to show the supremacy of the city council and the district councils over the Party in this city."[16]

Stankevich said that it was up to the thirty-three individual district councils to collect rent from their district Party committees, but he voiced confidence that the Party would pay up in 1991, as the Moscow city government began to exercise its new taxing power, under a law passed earlier in 1990 by the Supreme Soviet.

"They will pay rent to the district councils," Stankevich insisted. "Previously, they didn't pay anything—not a single ruble. They will start paying in 1991. For them, it's a very serious situation—because we have new tax authority at the beginning of 1991. We can tax any enterprise, up to a forty-percent rate, and that includes Party enterprises, Party newspapers and printing plants. The Party wants tax credits, favorable treatment, so I think they will agree to pay rent."[17]

The next confrontation came over control of the newspapers. For years, the Moscow Party Committee had jointly controlled two newspapers, the more official morning *Moscow Pravda (Moskovskaya Pravda)*, with a circulation of 725,000, and the more informal and readable afternoon daily, *Evening Moscow (Vechernaya Moskva)*, with a circulation of 625,000. Just before the reformers took over city hall, the Party seized exclusive control of *Moscow Pravda* by simply erasing the city council's name from the newspaper's masthead. Even though the Party offered to continue sharing *Evening Moscow,* the democrats in the city council were furious at the Party's power grab. But initially the Party was unmoved.

"*Moskovskaya Pravda* was always a Party paper," asserted its editor, Valery Lysenko, a staunch Party man. "All the main decisions, on personnel, finances, were made by the Party, even when technically they were joint decisions with Mossoviet. The role of Mossoviet was a formality. Mossoviet itself was a formality."[18]

Mayor Popov decided to insist on either having joint control of the morning paper restored or having the Party pay some compensation. Popov, a short, portly, rumpled professor, likes behind-the-scenes negotiations. He makes tough demands, but he is a bargainer. In this case, he had his eye on setting up an entirely new newspaper, independent of Party influence, to break the Party's dominance of the media. Similar efforts were mounted by democratic city councils in Volgograd, Tyumen, and Sverdlovsk. In Leningrad, the city council had won outright control of one of two daily newspapers formerly controlled jointly with the Party. Volgograd was also ahead of Moscow; both the local province and the local city government started publishing their own independent newspapers in June and July 1990.[19]

In Moscow, as elsewhere, one major problem was that the Party controlled not only the newspapers but the printing plant and the supply of newsprint as well. Prokofyev, a relatively moderate Party leader, decided to make concessions to the new city council, rather than harden the lines of confrontation.

"We will reduce the circulation of our paper by two hundred thousand, to make it possible for Mossoviet to put out its own newspaper," he told me in late June 1990. "We will take this paper from *Evening Moscow*— not from *Moscow Pravda,* which remains the organ of the Party. And we have offered Mossoviet services—our printing plant, office space, and so on—so they can create their own newspaper."

Popov and his people made plans to bring out not one, but two new publications—first, by the fall of 1990, a newspaper called *Stolitsa (Capital),* starting as a weekly and eventually becoming a daily; and second, in early 1991, a weekly magazine called *Kurant,* an old Russian word meaning "bell chimes," or "time," and evoking the name of one of the oldest newspapers in Russian history, published in the early eighteenth century under Peter the Great.

The breakthrough had taken place. Given the chance to launch its own paper, the city council quickly negotiated and signed preliminary agreements with Western publishing interests (Robert Maxwell of England and Robert Hersant of France) to set up two new printing plants. They began dickering for major Western investments in a new Moscow broadcast center as well. So within four months of organizing itself, the new city government of Moscow had moved swiftly to establish its independence from the Party and the national government in the field of communications. And it put the Party on notice that it was no longer the master, but merely a tenant, in the halls of Moscow city government.

LENINGRAD: WHO OBEYS WHOM?

In Leningrad, the confrontation between the new city council and the Party was sharper and more hostile. Both of the main protagonists, provincial Party leader Boris Gidaspov and Mayor Anatoly Sobchak, were fighters; neither was inclined to yield an inch on the central definition of power in the confusing situation that Gorbachev had created: Who obeys whom?

Gidaspov, unexpectedly put into the top Party job in the summer of 1989, quickly established himself as a proud and ambitious opportunist who was quite ready to side with the Party's right wing against Gorbachev in order to gain influence. He was a promoter of the Russian Communist Party Congress, which Leningrad hosted; and while he was no ironclad conservative, he was a strong Party loyalist. Even though his career had been as a scientist and administrator, not as an apparatchik, when he assumed command of the hard-line Leningrad regional Party hierarchy, he became its spokesman; and in the spring of 1990, he put down a liberal challenge from a Democratic Platform faction within the Leningrad Party.

Before being elected mayor that same May, Sobchak had won a reputation in the Supreme Soviet as a legislator capable of cold logic, fierce independence, and a polemical manner. Debating on national television came naturally to the Leningrad law professor. Powerful people did not intimidate him; he had publicly taken on Gorbachev, Ryzhkov, and Ligachev, individually and collectively, to argue for individual rights, to insist on the rule of law and fair procedures, to oppose the repressive use of force, to attack official corruption. Rather quickly, Sobchak became known as the most effective parliamentarian among the Inter-Regional Group. He led the attack that caused the first minister in Ryzhkov's government to be rejected; he came within two votes of pushing the Supreme Soviet to revoke the Party's monopoly on power—several months before Gorbachev was ready for that step; he ferried a tough report on the army's crackdown in Tbilisi, Georgia, through a committee and then accused Ligachev of lying to the committee; and several times, his crisp debating points caused Gorbachev to send government proposals back to be redrafted, or to drop devious parliamentary tactics.

"I have been a mountain climber and I know there are no absolutely smooth or impenetrable walls in nature," Sobchak once observed. "It's impossible to sit tight when it comes to the life or death of just one person, or the life or death of an entire society."[20]

It was his striking presence—fearless candor, legislative agility, and telegenic good looks—that gave Sobchak national recognition and a popularity that ranked behind only Gorbachev and Yeltsin, within a few months of his arrival on the national political stage in early 1989.

In person, or on television, Sobchak seems too cerebral, too educated, too fast-talking, and too high-pitched in voice to have natural appeal for the Russian masses. Instead of Boris Yeltsin's earthy charisma, Sobchak projects the cooler, blue-eyed, blond appeal of suburban gentry. With his new prominence, he now travels frequently to the West (he was in

Portland, Oregon, getting an honorary degree a couple of days after his election as mayor). Sitting in the baroque and gilded grandeur of his spacious chambers in a former czarist palace, Sobchak looks more Western than Russian in his tweed sport coat, rep tie, and gray flannel slacks. And with the poise and self-confidence of a Speaker of the House at home with Robert's rules of order, he corrals the freewheeling Leningrad City Council, which looks—and is—about as large and as self-absorbed as the U.S. House of Representatives.

Sobchak never had been a deeply committed Communist; he had joined the Party only in 1989, after the government promised to withdraw Soviet troops from Afghanistan. In July 1990, he was one of the first prominent reformers to quit the Party at the close of the Twenty-eighth Party Congress. Well before that he had made it clear that in Leningrad he was ready for a head-to-head fight to bring the Party to heel and to assert the supremacy of the popularly elected city council.

"We will not share power with anyone," he declared shortly after his election. "After we start working we shall see which affairs Party bodies will meddle in. . . . I hope our cooperation with the [Leningrad] Party committee will be fruitful. The main thing is that all power belongs to the soviet. Anyone who would fancy opposing this power should remember the fate of all those who have ever opposed soviet power."[21]

It was characteristic of Sobchak to strike quickly—only a month after assuming office—at the most sensitive nerve: to protest that the KGB was delivering daily reports on Leningrad's internal-security matters to Gidaspov, the Party chief, but not to him as mayor. Sobchak condemned this as a Stalinist legacy and warned the Leningrad KGB to heed the power of the city soviet.

"For decades the army, the MVD [Ministry of Internal Affairs], and KGB were led not by the state, but by the Party," Sobchak complained. "This is one of the most 'fruitful' Stalinist ideas, which enabled Stalin to create 'his' state. Now the point is to restore the state to its original form. . . . For a month already I have occupied the post of chairman of the Leningrad city soviet [mayor], but the daily reports on what is happening in the city are put on the table of Boris Gidaspov. The heads of the administrative bodies do not consider it necessary to supply me with the corresponding information. I informed these comrades that the city soviet will confirm them in their posts and, therefore, they need to make a choice about who governs them—the state or the CPSU [Party]."[22]

Mirroring what had happened in Moscow, Sobchak and the Leningrad City Council immediately got into a fight with the regional Party leadership over control of real estate and other property claimed by the Party through some eleventh-hour finagling by the outgoing city council, which had transferred about fifty major pieces of real estate to other organizations. The reform city council immediately froze those transfers; Sobchak said these were city properties. He demanded control—and in most cases occupancy—of thirty-nine district administrative centers; several czarist palaces and other historic buildings; Lenizdat, the Party's publishing house and the largest printing plant in the city; the Party's hotel and meeting center; its dairy farm, with four hundred head of cattle, which supplied meat and milk to Party cafeterias and to high officials; a sanitarium and several country *dachas* for the Party elite; a fleet of cars and trucks that had long been at the Party's beck and call.

The sharpest confrontation came over the headquarters of the Leningrad Province Party Committee at Smolny, once a nineteenth-century private school, which had been taken over by Lenin during the Bolshevik Revolution as his headquarters. Ever since, the Leningrad Party had occupied Smolny; in fact, to Leningraders, the word Smolny had become synonymous with Party power.

I was told that Gidaspov had had the effrontery to show up at the first city-council sessions, acting like a powerful uncle patronizing his nephews; he had told Sobchak that there was no way the Party could be evicted from Smolny, because the Party had earned the building with the blood of the Revolution. Sobchak retorted: "Those workers and sailors seized Smolny to establish soviet power, not to give it to the Communist Party."[23]

Sobchak was perhaps better able than anyone else to make the city's claim to Smolny and the rest of those properties; he had been one of the architects in the Supreme Soviet of a law that transferred all but certain designated categories of property to local governments, effective June 30, 1990. This law was central to the property claims of city councils in Moscow, Leningrad, and elsewhere.

Cornered and outmaneuvered, Gidaspov escalated the issue to the Kremlin, trying to get Gorbachev to save Leningrad Party headquarters. Finally, just before the June 30 deadline for the transfer of properties, Prime Minister Ryzhkov issued a decree nationalizing all property in the Soviet Union historically linked to Lenin—specifically Smolny and several other Leningrad buildings.

Sobchak threatened reprisal. "This decree is illegal," he argued. "I reject this action. This is Leningrad city property. The running water, sewage, electricity for Smolny are all provided by the city. If we are not respected, we can cut off all of the above. Then let them see how they can get along in that building."[24]

Later, Sobchak tried to pass off his threat as "a joke," but he reasserted his determination to use every measure to establish the contested buildings as city property. "These buildings cannot be considered state property," he told me. "According to the Law on Property, only industries and organizations necessary for the functioning of the nation can be regarded as state property—communications, mass media, central television, defense industries. We are going to fight this decree. We'll hold a referendum, and on the basis of its result, we will appeal to the Russian government [Yeltsin]."

The feisty Leningrad City Council had already shown readiness to take matters directly into its own hands. During a fight with Moscow Central Television over a controversial broadcast, about two dozen deputies had gone to the Leningrad branch of state television and physically asserted the city's authority. Like other institutions, Leningrad television was caught between two masters: the State Committee for Television and Radio, headquartered in Moscow, and traditionally subordinate to the Party, and the city council, which technically had to consent to any appointments of senior Leningrad television officials. Until the reformers took office, that had been a formality. In practice, the ideology department of the Leningrad Party apparat set the policy line for Leningrad television.

What had provoked the showdown was a broadcast scheduled for April 5, 1990: a scripted interview with Nikolai Ivanov, a federal investigator and people's deputy, who had prepared a series of sensational charges of high-level economic corruption that included Gorbachev and his wife.

According to Bella Kurkova, executive producer of *Fifth Wheel*, the Kremlin's television bosses had wanted none of this information on the air, and had given orders to Boris Petrov, chairman of the Leningrad branch of the State Committee for Television and Radio, to block the show. The Leningrad City Council, for whom Ivanov was a hero, had then passed a resolution ordering that the show go on the air, but Petrov had followed Moscow's orders. Despite advance publicity, Ivanov was not allowed in the studio.

The next day, the Leningrad City Council had suspended Petrov from his post and appointed his deputy, Viktor Senin, to replace him; Senin was a member of the city soviet. That evening, about twenty deputies went to the television station with the order to ensure that Ivanov was allowed to broadcast. Petrov fled the station after the deputies confronted him, Senin signed off on the show, and Ivanov went on the air and made his charges.

The episode was not one of the city council's proudest victories; Petrov claimed that the deputies had messed up papers and bodily ejected him. Moscow authorities accused the city council of an illegal seizure of the television station. Nearly three months later, Petrov was still coming to work, because the Kremlin and the city council could not agree on a replacement for him. But the council had made its point; it had broken the Party's and Moscow's control of Leningrad television.

As Bella Kurkova put it, "The Party is losing its tribune and, therefore, the possibility of influencing people. Nowadays, it is the democrats who can influence the people of Leningrad on television."[25]

"SHOW PEOPLE A DIFFERENCE"

The ambitions of the urban democrats went well beyond trench warfare with the Party apparat. In most cities where the insurgents took control, the reformers were bent on moving more rapidly than the national government into a market economy. Worried by the deteriorating economic situation, Sobchak, Popov, Stankevich, and others came into office aware that they had precious little time to demonstrate results before popular disillusionment would engulf them, along with Gorbachev. The more sophisticated understood that their role as critics had spared them responsibility for a year, but that taking control of a part of government made them accountable too.

The Party had lost power because of its dismal record; the reformers had to do better. Like a Western politician, Stankevich remarked shortly after his election to city hall: "My main motto is: Show our people the difference."[26] And he meant basic things such as stopping industrial construction, using funds for better housing, building more schools and health clinics, cleaning up the city, paving streets.

Mayor Popov, a fifty-three-year-old economist whose career had been teaching at Moscow State University and editing an academic journal, also had an unusual streak of pragmatism for a scholar-theoretician. Some Russian colleagues joked that perhaps he was more of a realist than most Russians, because he is of Greek descent. In an early interview as mayor, Popov ticked off five practical priorities: ecology, medicine, housing, city economy, and philanthropy. All of this assumed market economics and encouragement of private enterprise.[27]

In its first three months, the Popov administration moved quickly: It halted the construction of a huge new power station that was unpopular with environmental groups; it hired outside contractors to repave the worst of the city's streets; and, in a grand gesture of municipal largesse, it issued a decree transferring ownership of all state-owned apartments to the renters who occupied them—Muscovites could now legally buy and sell apartments without resorting to black-market subterfuges to evade state regulations.28

The most immediately visible project was the repair of the city's ubiquitous and treacherous potholes. Because state construction trusts were notorious for crawling inefficiency, the new city council decided on an innovation: It turned to private cooperatives—not only to get quicker results but to show skeptics the benefits of private enterprise. It set the cooperatives in competition with each other and with state construction gangs on various small projects, and it held out as the prize for best performance a 30-million-ruble contract to repair Moscow's seventy-mile circumferential highway, known as the Ring Road.

The winner of the competition was Stroitel ("Builder"), a private firm run by a tough, cunning, hard-driving, sixty-one-year-old contractor named Vadim Tumanov, a veteran of Stalin's Siberian labor camps. As a teenager in the 1940s, he had gotten into trouble for political dissent, and he had compounded his difficulties by fighting with other prisoners and rifling the camp safe. But after Stalin's death, he was pardoned and released. In the camp, Tumanov had developed a gang of laborers willing to work hard for extra pay, and when he got out, he went into what amounted to private construction for thirty-five years, dodging the state by operating in rural, far-off regions, where, because he got things done, local officials turned a blind eye to his capitalistic ways of doing business. Under Gorbachev, Tumanov came out into the open and become known for good, fast construction work in the Karelia region, north of Leningrad along the Finnish border.

The Moscow City Council lured Tumanov into doing a four-mile stretch of the Ring Road, as a tryout. State construction firms normally completely ignore deadlines, but Tumanov drove his crew of 130 men around the clock for two months, an unheard-of pace for Soviet construction, in order to finish on time. The men worked twelve-hour days and pulled down pay up to 1,200 rubles a month, four times the Soviet average. Tumanov even brought in floodlights for night work; and the city fathers allocated thirty-five trucks and the output of one Moscow asphalt plant to keep the operation going at full speed.

"I am accused of knowing how to make a profit," Tumanov told Francis Clines of The New York Times. "There is no secret [to it]. You get organized and you keep initiative alive. . . . Only productivity can save this country—all other talk is garbage."29

Tumanov's performance, which drew astonished stares from truckers on the Ring Road, was a classic lesson in free-market productivity. His results were far better, faster, and cheaper than those of state firms—and the work was done on time. It was a showcase for the new city council.

The council's housing giveaway, decreed in late June 1990, did not enjoy such immediate success. Gorbachev's government had previously announced plans to sell people their apartments, in order to sop up billions of rubles of private cash and help close the federal deficit. They were chagrined at being upstaged by Moscow's decision to give away those apartments. Yet simple as that sounded, the mechanics were difficult.

In the interests of fairness, Stankevich told me, the original blanket offer of free apartments was qualified: Up to 120 square feet per person would be free, but surplus footage would have to be paid for. Weeks later, the city had not figured out the correct price, or how to compensate more than one million people who were living in communal apartments with much less than 120 square feet per person. Clearly, the giveaway was a bonanza for most of Moscow's 9.5 million residents; but there was the potential for political backlash if too many others wound up dissatisfied. Many people were complaining that suddenly they were responsible for maintenance.

The most dramatic—and controversial—early action by the Moscow City Council came in the wake of Prime Minister Ryzhkov's announcement in late May 1990 that bread and other food prices were going to rise fast. To control the ensuing panic-buying and the mass influx of frantic out-of-town shoppers, the city council quickly passed a regulation barring outsiders from shopping in Moscow stores. Store clerks were to require shoppers to show Moscow passports. City dwellers were relieved, but the regulation provoked a horrendous outcry from the surrounding countryside. People had long been accustomed to traveling to Moscow to shop, even for staples, because the capital was so much better supplied than their home regions. Traditionally, as many as two million people streamed through the city daily, and panic had multiplied that number. Moscow's action triggered threats to retaliate from nearby farm regions, and other agricultural regions all the way to Uzbekistan—regions from which Moscow got its food. The reformers had unwittingly aroused traditional provincial animosities against Moscow as an elite city, and had put Moscow's winter food supplies in jeopardy.

But disaster turned into opportunity. Forced by the uproar into sitting down face-to-face with angry provincial leaders, the new city council saw a chance to move into business in a big way, bypassing the central planners. For hectic days and nights, Popov, Stankevich, and others negotiated furiously with regional officials from twenty-seven central Russian provinces, including Yaroslavl, Tula, Vladimir, Ryazan, and Kalinin (renamed Tver). They swapped shopping lists that laid out an exchange: machinery, cars, appliances, and manufactured goods from Moscow, in exchange for meat, milk, and farm produce from the surrounding regions.

Then the city council leaders persuaded Prime Minister Ryzhkov to let the council have control over 12.5 percent of the total output of the factories and enterprises located in the city.[30] In the past, those goods had been earmarked by Gosplan and Gossnab for nationwide allocation; Moscow now needed them for its barter deals.

Starting in 1991, the city council had plans to take some of its corporate taxes in the form of goods—trucks, refrigerators, television sets, and the like—and use them to barter with its regional trading partners for food supplies. As Stankevich explained, the city had to resort to barter in goods, because "our money is no good."

So just as Gorbachev's trade embargo of Lithuania had stimulated new trading relations, the crisis over Ryzhkov's proposed increase in bread prices spurred Moscow and its neighbors to develop direct new avenues of commerce. Their trade deal was only an intermediary step toward a market economy, but it helped loosen the grip of the central state apparatus.

This was just the beginning of the Moscow City Council's business ventures. By the fall of 1990, Moscow sent 2,000 city-owned trucks to the Orenburg region in western Siberia to help transport the grain from the harvest, and another 750 trucks to Astrakhan. The old city government had done similar things, but the new city council had a commercial twist: It made Orenburg promise to pay with Siberian grain for the use of trucks. It also got a pledge from Astrakhan to supply vegetables, tomatoes, and melons. Similar deals were made with farming areas just outside Moscow: The city council promised to arrange for factory workers to help gather the harvest, in exchange for a payoff in meat and produce.

On another front, city reformers began to challenge the commercial monopolies of government ministries. They had two goals: to get their hands on hard-currency earnings for the city's treasury, and to provide new openings for private cooperatives or state enterprises capable of adapting to market economics. One target was Moscow's four major airports, which the council wanted to take over with the idea of setting up a municipal agency like the New York Port Authority, and then encouraging the start of smaller, private airlines. When the Ministry of Aviation snubbed the upstart reformers, the Popov-Stankevich team reminded the ministry that the airports were sitting on city land and getting vital city services such as water, electricity, and sewage, and that these services could be withheld unless the ministry turned over the airports, or agreed to heavy user fees in hard currency. That started negotiations in earnest.

"We would like to exploit the airports in a commercial way," Stankevich explained. "It's good business for the city. Why not?"[31]

Another prime target was Intourist, the national tourist monopoly and the bête noire of foreign travelers in the Soviet Union. Its practice was to charge foreign tourists steep hard-currency rates and then pay its Moscow subcontractors in cheap rubles for their work, such as transport, repairs, hotel services. The city council wanted a share of those hard-currency earnings, for itself and for Moscow businesses. As leverage, the council passed a regulation requiring that Intourist pay in hard currency for all services, and that all basic deals be sanctioned by the council. It also made plans to help put other private and state firms into competition with Intourist.

The Moscow reformers came into office with the overall objective of stimulating entrepreneurship. One of the first actions of the city council—echoed in Leningrad, Volgograd, Sverdlovsk, and other big cities—was to make it much easier for Soviet private cooperatives to get started and to operate. Mark Masarsky, the Novgorod house builder, told me in midsummer 1990 that new city governments, even the one in Novgorod, had drastically eased restrictions on cooperatives. What is more, these cities were ready to give business to private firms, unlike their old, hard-line predecessors. Masarsky had come to Moscow looking for a big city contract for renovating old housing.[32]

With the national government bogged down in endless debate about economic reform in mid-1990, the Moscow City Council took on the role of midwife for market economics. The reformers conceived of having the city, with its control of land and property, stimulate the creation of businesses by going into partnership with foreign investors, or with Soviet private firms, acting not only as co-owner and sponsor but also as a political protector for the fragile new market sector. Typical was the role Deputy Mayor Stankevich played in bringing Soviet firms together with Ikea, the Swedish furniture maker, to promote a joint enterprise under the aegis of the city council, which was eager to ease the severe furniture shortage in Moscow.

"Of course, it is not absolutely normal for us to operate in such a way, but since we have almost no economic activity independent of the state, our democratic city councils have to start this activity," Stankevich explained to me. "So in Moscow, we are establishing what we call the House of Trade. It is an incubator for joint ventures, for stock companies, for new independent enterprises. We help create them and give them a legal basis and full opportunity for independent activity. And they give us part of their profits, or part of their product—things the city badly needs—for example, meals for our schoolchildren."

More broadly, Mayor Popov moved to develop an infrastructure for business. The city council set up an employment agency and authorized the opening of a very simple wholesale barter market, to let Soviet enterprises make money from the stocks of spare parts and raw materials they had been hoarding for years. Stankevich traveled to Washington and several European capitals to try to negotiate Western investments for a Moscow Bank for Reconstruction and Development, to help finance the city's ambitious projects and to underwrite mixed Soviet public-and-private companies.

"You see the same kinds of things going on in other cities where democrats are in power—in Sverdlovsk, Kuibyshev, Leningrad, Gorky, Donetsk," Stankevich said. "They try to control the administrative buildings. They try to control local newspapers and establish radio stations. And also they are trying to become real entrepreneurs in their cities, because it is a real life-and-death situation for them."[33]

In Leningrad, the new city council was behind Moscow but moving in the same direction.

Mayor Sobchak told me of Leningrad's efforts to privatize the economy by selling off unprofitable state enterprises, by promoting cooperatives, by making conditions attractive for foreign joint ventures. Sobchak was particularly eager to exploit Leningrad as a tourist center. He was angered that so much of the city's profits from tourism were skimmed off by Intourist and sent to the national government, rather than being kept by the Leningraders who earned them and reinvested in the city. His goal was to develop local competition for Intourist.

Sobchak's big dream was to turn the entire Leningrad region into an economic free zone—to free Leningrad's economy from national regulations, taxes, customs controls, and, above all, the dead hand of Soviet ministries and central planning. The base had been laid: A modest industrial free zone had been established in Vyborg, a city in Leningrad Province on the border with Finland; a dozen foreign firms were already building plants. Sobchak wanted a massive expansion, and on August 1 he got the go-ahead from Boris Yeltsin's Russian republic for setting up banks, stock companies, joint enterprises, and other deals. Nonetheless, he still needed Gorbachev's blanket approval for Leningrad enterprises to market products abroad without deal-by-deal permission from Moscow ministries; and for the city to sell land to foreigners, and set up its own customs zone.[34]

Sobchak told me that in spite of his feuding with the Party apparatus and the ministries, his free-zone concept could succeed. He insisted that it had the ardent backing of Gorbachev's main new economic advisers, Nikolai Petrakov and Stanislav Shatalin.

Nonetheless, reformers like Sobchak, Popov, and Stankevich acknowledge that for all their energy, new ideas, and noble objectives, city radicals have an uphill road. As Popov has warned repeatedly, they must deliver widespread benefits quickly before rank-and-file workers turn against their market reforms as simply a means to line the pockets of a new Soviet bourgeoisie. They confront the ingrained conservatism of the Russians; Sobchak's initial offers to sell off unprofitable state stores and enterprises had very few takers. In the tough world of Soviet bureaucratic infighting and international finance, the radicals are still innocents. They need quick, large infusions of Western capital to show some movement. It is hard to see how they can carve out economic enclaves in the cities independent of the rest of the Soviet economy, without provoking an economic war with the countryside.

What the radicals had going for them in 1990—their first year in power—was the political initiative and popular support. They were the most dynamic element in Soviet society and in the political system; with the disintegration of authority and control at the center, they had wide openings to exploit. Moreover, with the nation's economy in crisis and little prospect of a turnaround, it was in Gorbachev's interest to promote some brights spots to help persuade a skeptical population that market economics has a payoff.

"Gorbachev needs us to succeed," Sobchak asserted. "The country is more interested in this than we are, because it needs a showcase for the benefits of a market economy."[35]

PART SIX

CONCLUSION

CHAPTER 24

THE OUTLOOK: WILL IT COLLAPSE OR WILL IT ENDURE?

"[E]xperience teaches that the most critical moment for bad governments is the one which witnesses their first steps toward reform."[1]
—Alexis de Tocqueville, 1856

QUESTION: What's the difference between the Soviet Union and the United States?

ANSWER: Gorbachev could probably get elected president in the United States.
—Soviet political joke, March 1990

From afar the Soviet Union seems so stricken by tumult, chaos, and uncertainty, that it is easy to discount the profound transformation that has taken place, or to worry that it will all end in disaster and be wiped away. That view misses the magnitude of what has already occurred.

What we have been watching is no less than the most extraordinary peaceful revolution of the twentieth century.

In human history, there have been years of surpassing consequence for the future course of events: the popular revolts of 1848 against the old order of Europe; the Russian Revolution of 1917; the defeat of Hitler and the onset of the Cold War in 1945.

The years 1989–90 are of similar historical significance. In 1989, in what seemed like barely an instant, Eastern Europe threw off Soviet rule and the alien system of Communist power imposed by the Soviet army. In that same bright year and in 1990, the old order was shattered inside the Soviet Union, and Gorbachev set in place political changes of enduring importance, not only for Soviets but for the destiny of mankind.

An era has ended—not simply the era of the Cold War, but the era of Soviet totalitarianism. It has been felled like a rotting oak. The Communist Party has been stripped of its domination over the entire life of the nation. The *nomenklatura,* the inner priesthood of the Party-state, has lost its immunity; it still clings to certain strongholds, but it is in decline. After popular rejection in two elections, it now sees the Party rank and file draining away. The Politburo, once the pinnacle of power under Stalin, Khrushchev, and Brezhnev, has lost its preeminent authority to new governmental institutions: the presidency, the Congress of People's Deputies, and the Supreme Soviet, where suddenly, for the first time, debates and votes count for something.

With the choke hold of fear broken and dissent now tolerated, Russians are no longer politically passive. They have plunged into election campaigns, mass demonstrations, environmental protests, miners' strikes—all evidence of a hunger for participation that could not have been predicted even as late as 1987, two years *after* Gorbachev took power. The breathtaking pace of popular self-emancipation and the growth of grass-roots activism has outstripped what Gorbachev had intended. Change, initially decreed from above, now rises more insistently from below. One after another, eleven republics have declared their sovereignty over the center—though their actions constitute pressure on Gorbachev rather than their assumption of governing power. The people have chosen fresh, iconoclastic voices to represent them: Boris Yeltsin, Lithuania's Vytautas Landsbergis, the new reform mayors, scores of people's deputies, and hundreds more at the local level. These new populist advocates have dared to challenge every facet of Soviet power, and in the fall of 1990, they initiated the first serious stirrings of a multiparty system.

What the world had come to know as the Communist credo lies discredited. The Soviet leadership has abandoned the messianic dream of remaking the world according to the gospel of Marxism-Leninism; and at home, it has admitted the failure of Communism's gossamer promise of Utopia. Gorbachev has talked of resuscitating Communism in a new form—as a humane Leninism that to Western ears sounds like democratic socialism. But since the crash of the old credo, no new ideology has taken hold. Nationalism has moved powerfully into the vacuum—a centrifugal and explosive force, not a source of unity or cohesion. That portion of Soviet society, mainly the intelligentsia, for whom the democratic ideal is a sufficient ideology, is still precariously small.

Nonetheless, the free market of ideas is now at work in the Soviet press and on television, and it has spilled into the streets; the police state still functions but it no longer chills ordinary people into silence, nor muffles poets, pundits, or playwrights. Free expression is alive and vibrant; and it has belatedly gained legal anchor and protection from a new law that permits anyone or any group to start a newspaper or to operate a television station, though as a practical matter the Party still controls paper supplies and the only national television channels.

The notion of a "law-governed state," now a refrain of Gorbachev's political catechism, has slowly begun to take practical form. The institutional instruments of democracy—independent courts, an unfettered legal profession, a free press, elections, a two-term limit on the presidency, the process of legislating—all these are in their infancy, and therefore inevitably fragile. But the chances for their survival and growth have been improved by the practical dispersal of authority among contending power centers—the presidency, the legislature, the Party apparat, the new leadership in republic and city governments, the military and the KGB, even masses of striking workers.

In short, these two years have given birth to a rough system of political checks and balances that impose real limits on the exercise of power, by Gorbachev or any would-be successor. As the feudal barons in the Soviet provinces have come to understand, it is no longer possible to move the Soviet people by fiat and fear alone; as Gorbachev has also painfully learned, the new Soviet politics require compromise and collaboration. The old order has been dismantled, even if the new order has not yet taken shape.

THE ECONOMY: THE PRICE OF AMBIVALENCE

Where *perestroika* has conspicuously failed to achieve the most rudimentary and essential transformation is the place where it began—the economy. The rhetoric of reform has filled the air for more than three years, but the old economic mechanism has been little altered. The old channels of central control, the old industrial ministries and their state monopolies, the old inefficiencies of featherbedding, fixed prices, and false accounting, the old habits of Soviet workers, have resisted change.

The Stalinist command system has been damaged but not dislodged. With each passing year, it has functioned less effectively; but nothing has been fashioned to replace it. Cooperatives are in operation, but they are unpopular, especially those that provide services rather than produce goods. Individual property has been written into law, but most people are not yet accustomed to its commercial potential. The language of the market—competition, profits, free prices, and productivity—has come into vogue among urban intellectuals and government circles, but so far these concepts inspire fear, not confidence, among the masses; they cut against the grain of deep-set attitudes.

"The conservativism that has eaten into everyone and into society, like rust, has turned out to be more durable than we expected," Aleksandr Yakovlev confessed to me one afternoon. "Resistance to change has turned out to be very strong. A person gets his two hundred rubles [pay] without really working, and today he's told to work, and he'll get one hundred rubles more. He knows he'll have to *earn* not only those one hundred rubles but the first two hundred, which he used to get without working. To get people to work, economically, democratically, is very hard."[2]

What is more, the tenacity and guile of the bureaucracy have been greater than Gorbachev anticipated, as has the difficulty of purging people of their Stalinist mind-set, their Stalinist habits.

Without question, the task of economic reform is monumental. But Gorbachev himself is considerably to blame for not attacking it more directly at the outset. He missed his best opportunity—during his first two or three years, a time of popular faith in and tolerance toward the new leadership, and the period of his greatest popularity, before public passions had been let loose by *glasnost.* He squandered that precious time trying to find his way. For in his quest for a "more humane socialism," Gorbachev has been crippled by his own ambivalence. In the economy, the realm of policy most critical to his ultimate success, Gorbachev was operating without a blueprint. He knew what he was against, without being certain enough about what he was for, or how to get it.

Gorbachev has changed direction several times. He began in 1985–86 with a conservative drive to strengthen discipline, to fight alcoholism, to set up huge new central agencies, to look to science and technology to produce modernization. He fanned popular expectations of a dramatic turnaround, with sloganeering about economic "acceleration" (us-

koreniye) and hopeful talk of competing on the world market within a few years. Unlike Deng Xiaoping in China, Gorbachev did not move quickly to build a mass constituency for economic reform by generating pocket-book results—by giving peasants freedom to earn more and by putting more food on the table for people in the cities.

By 1987, he had shifted from organizational shuffling and demands for discipline to a wholly different tack, the more liberal prescription that he had once advocated as Party leader in Stavropol: decentralization of economic control, more autonomy for industrial enterprises and for regional authorities. Only gradually, in 1988 and 1989, did he edge further toward market economics. But he was moving without the clarity and conviction that he needed to persuade his Politburo colleagues or his people.

He was constantly at pains to reassure both the masses and the Party elite that he would not demand heavy sacrifices or radically alter the status quo. Somehow, magically, life would improve—without pain. In 1987, in his book *Perestroika,* Gorbachev proclaimed with typical buoyant self-confidence that he was "looking within socialism . . . for the answers," and the West should not expect him to adopt capitalism.[3] Later, as he tried more daring experiments, Yegor Ligachev's conservative faction in the Politburo and the Party apparat held him back. But even with the Soviet economy in deep decline, Gorbachev made it clear through 1989 and 1990, in speech after speech, that he himself was shying away from the unpredictable world of supply and demand. He raged at the inefficiencies of central planning; he wanted it to work better, he wanted more flexibility, but he was not ready to scrap it for something radically different.

The parallel drawn by his close friend and colleague Eduard Shevardnadze was to Franklin Roosevelt's drive to lift America out of the Depression with the New Deal, a program to save capitalism by grafting on elements of socialism.[4] Gorbachev's notion of "grafting" on something new was to take half steps, to make piecemeal changes. As late as April 1990, after five years in office, he refused to follow Eastern Europe's plunge into market economics—"shock therapy," his economic advisers called it; he publicly promised the workers that he would not agree to measures that would cost them jobs or shut down plants. He seemed paralyzed by fear of a popular backlash. Gorbachev was discovering that the institutions of democracy could make economic reform harder; the Supreme Soviet, responding to public outcry, swiftly killed badly overdue consumer price increases in late May. So Gorbachev retreated. Only in the fall, worried about being upstaged by Boris Yeltsin, did he begin to redefine his notion of socialism to allow for a transition to genuine markets, free prices, stock companies, and the kind of competitive environment that would lead sometime in the early nineties to a mixed socialist-capitalist economy.

In politics, Gorbachev could bypass the recalcitrant apparat by creating new institutions and by inviting mass involvement in *glasnost* and in the new politics of elections. In economics, he could not bypass the economic apparatus, because he was reluctant to risk setting people free with the new institutions of market economics. In politics, the public was eager for change and he played to its eagerness; in economics, the people were wary of changes and he bowed to their caution.

At each turn, Gorbachev was hampered by the fundamental paradox that *perestroika* is an assault on the state, and its leader is the head of state. He was held back not only by his own ideological ambivalence but also by his dual roles—by trying to play both Luther and the pope, both Master Architect of reform and Father Protector of the system.

TURNING A WEAK HAND INTO GRAND STRATEGY

In spite of all the obvious problems, Gorbachev has already established himself as one of a handful of twentieth-century leaders who have galvanized and transformed their nations, and thereby affected the larger course of history. In terms of his impact on the world, he has put himself in the class of such paramount figures as Roosevelt, Lenin, Churchill, Gandhi, Stalin, Mao, and Adenauer.

Forces of change were gathering within Soviet society before he came to power, but Gorbachev was the indispensable catalyst. He set them loose and thereby transformed the Soviet Union, Eastern Europe, and the world beyond.

Gorbachev was following the Russian tradition of the reformer-czars who created what Russians call "revolutions from above": Peter the Great, who westernized Imperial Russia at the turn of the eighteenth century, or Aleksandr II, the "Czar Liberator," who freed the serfs and initiated the period of "great reforms" late in the nineteenth century.

Yet contrary to Gorbachev's claims that he took over the Kremlin with a clear vision and a well-developed concept for *perestroika*, he was constantly experimenting, defining his path along the way, much as Franklin Roosevelt had proceeded with the New Deal. Both men seized grand opportunities and then nimbly responded to the quixotic course of events. Gorbachev began *perestroika* with a general sense of direction, and then zigzagged his way through history; he had no master plan.

One day, talking with Aleksandr Yakovlev, who was closer to Gorbachev's thinking than any other colleague, I had a chance to put to him the question of whether Gorbachev and his inner circle had begun *perestroika* with an overall plan.

"No," Yakovlev replied. "Yes, and no. There was a clear-cut understanding that what had existed had to be overturned—the authoritarianism, the command-bureaucratic economic system. It was clear that democracy had to be developed, but in what amounts or how? That plan didn't exist. It was clear that we had to return to Lenin's theory that people should rule their affairs. But how could that be done, in what stages? That, of course, wasn't there at the beginning. There was one thing, and the most important: that society would have to radically change its nature—what we call 'renewal.' But we had to find the instruments along the way, in the process of transformation: in politics, the economy, culture, the law, *glasnost,* and democracy. And it turns out that those instruments are very important—no less important than the overall concept."[5]

Gorbachev is propelled by a brimming self-confidence that he can ride over realities that would daunt lesser men, but in his intrepid resolve there is a not-so-obvious and perhaps essential element of naïveté. I have heard his aides describe him as so optimistic and so convinced of his own reasoning that he is naïve about the darker motives of others, a poor judge of how the Russian man in the street will react. At times, they say, he simply shuts out words of caution, not wanting to hear of the obstacles. Yakovlev described to me how innocent he and Gorbachev were, starting out on the road to *perestroika*.

"In 1984, 1985, I had moments of romanticism. I thought that the ideas of *glasnost,* renewal, democracy, would grab the masses," Yakovlev confessed. "But when you think more about those ideas, you see that it couldn't have happened that way. You have to stand on the soil of reality. Over more than sixty years so much conformity appeared in our economy, public life, politics, that you can't break it in one year, or two years, or five."

So Gorbachev's genius is not strategy, but improvisation. He is a brilliant improviser, an instinctive tactician, far quicker on his feet than his rivals, foreign or domestic. His skill is not so much in imposing his will on history as in discerning its flow, guiding it when he can, more often riding the tide.

To say this is not to denigrate Gorbachev. According to historians, some of the modern world's "great visionaries" have operated in the same way. The British historian A.J.P. Taylor, in his biography of Otto von

Bismarck, Germany's nineteenth-century "Iron Chancellor," has suggested that while Bismarck was a genius at political maneuvering, he was often driven by events rather than being their guiding force.[6] My colleague Simon Serfaty of the Johns Hopkins Foreign Policy Institute draws a parallel between Gorbachev and the late President De Gaulle of France, whom Serfaty has described as a masterful opportunist who took advantage of situations inherited from others. "It is precisely such ability to seize the opportunities opened by any new conjuncture which made him a true revolutionary," Serfaty wrote.[7]

Gorbachev, like all great leaders, has gotten credit in hindsight for being a visionary when he was clever enough to abandon those policies that did not work and to play up those that did. In fact, the longer *perestroika* has gone on, the more frequently Gorbachev has had to react to the flow of events rather than dictating their course, the more he has been propelled by the forces he himself released and been forced to catch up, merely to survive. Certainly one of Gorbachev's greatest assets is his personal capacity for change, for learning. He is forever trying something new, ever evolving. In every arena of policy, he has miscalculated, blundered badly, and had to reverse course. What is remarkable is his willingness to cast off failed policies without apology, to cut his political losses, and then to treat the inevitable as if it had been his design.

He is a master of retreat as well as of attack; examples of this ability are legion.

He failed entirely to anticipate that his own policies would release powerful forces of nationalism in the minority republics that would threaten the entire fate of reform. He treated local nationalists with benign neglect, patronizing approval, token appeasement, stinging denunciation, and finally, in Lithuania and Azerbaijan, he tried to crush them with either military force or economic embargo. But when those failed to stem the tide of nationalism, Gorbachev finally made a virtue out of offering other nationalities more of the autonomy they were demanding, and out of negotiating independence for the Baltic republics.

Boris Yeltsin has provided another litmus of Gorbachev. Gorbachev tried to banish and excommunicate Yeltsin, to beat him down; but ultimately, when Yeltsin bounced back with mass support and when Gorbachev needed that popularity to help sell economic reform to a reluctant populace, he allied himself with Yeltsin.

For a long time, Gorbachev treated a multiparty system as political anathema. The persistent pressures of the Inter-Regional Group to strip the Communist Party of its political monopoly provoked him into temperamental outbursts. But in the end, the logic of events forced him to make a 180-degree turn: He adopted the view of the opposition and then became the master persuader who induced the Party to bless this heresy.

Or again, on Eastern Europe, Gorbachev was more realistic and daring than his predecessors in the Kremlin; he saw the region less as a proud empire than as an economic albatross, and so to cut the Kremlin's financial losses and political liabilities, he let it go. But the swiftness of the Communist collapse caught him by surprise, and he vehemently opposed a reunified Germany, and even more adamantly vetoed its membership in NATO. Yet eventually, with West German Chancellor Helmut Kohl by his side, Gorbachev acquiesced both in German unification and NATO membership, and he made it sound as though that were the outcome he had secretly favored all along, if only he had been given the right assurances and some financial aid.

Gorbachev even managed to convert Soviet defeat and withdrawal from Afghanistan into a public-relations triumph at home. Again and again, he has demonstrated that he is an expert at turning a weak hand into grand strategy.

Perestroika could never have advanced so far without Gorbachev's single-minded determination, his will to succeed, his daring, his relentless energy. But it also would have failed without his political agility, his flexibility, his uncanny capacity for survival.

Gorbachev has seemed perpetually in trouble, but he is a master escape artist—a political Houdini, as Bill Keller of *The New York Times* put it—who has not only foiled political rivals but has also confounded the Western Kremlinologists who were too quick to count him down and out. The headlines on their punditry tell the story: GORBACHEV'S LAST SUMMIT (May 1990), GORBACHEV: GOVERNING ON THE RAZOR'S EDGE (December 1989), LIFE AFTER GORBACHEV: THE SOVIETS' GRIM FUTURE (November 1989). But Gorbachev has more political lives than a cat. He defies the political laws of gravity, or to quote *Time* magazine's portrait: "he hang-glides across the abyss."[8]

But not without cost. For all his victories, Gorbachev is no longer the colossus among his own people that he was in the heyday of *perestroika*, mid-1988. Now, like an American president or a West European prime minister who has led his nation through nearly six years of rough times, he has paid a price: The luster is gone, his popularity has plummeted. The right wing blames him for the breakdown of the old order at home and the loss of Eastern Europe. The radical and progressive reformers have been disillusioned by his moderation. And the great mass of ordinary people, seeing no more food in the stores than when he began, have grown cynical toward Gorbachev's promises of a better life. It is a source of wry humor in Moscow, as well as in New York and London and Paris, that Gorbachev is more popular in the West than he is at home.

His fall in popularity should come as no surprise; for more than five years, Gorbachev alone has borne the burden of accountability for the upheaval in people's lives. Both Left and Right were free to finger-point and criticize; only when Yeltsin took over as the leader of the Russian republic, and Popov and Sobchak were elected the mayors of Moscow and Leningrad, did anyone independent of Gorbachev share responsibility for making government work.

By the fall of 1989, I heard people in Moscow suggesting that the Gorbachev era of reform was over; they spoke of Gorbachev as a transitional figure. No longer did they put him on a par with Lenin, whom they saw as an authentic revolutionary, the creator of a new political and economic order. They had begun to call Gorbachev a "Kerensky"—comparing him to Aleksandr Kerensky, the prime minister of the provisional government of 1917, the precursor to Lenin, the leader whose modest tremors of reform prepared the way for the real political earthquake. After five years, these people suggested, Gorbachev was a spent force: He had done much, but he had exhausted his own potential and he was incapable of going further, because he was a prisoner of attitudes drawn from a lifetime under Stalin, Khrushchev, and Brezhnev. It would take someone with a new cast of mind to finish the job, the reformers said, and they had successors in mind—Yeltsin, Sobchak, or Popov. The Right, too, had its new champion, the Russian Party first secretary, Ivan Polozkov.

DARK SCENARIOS

With so much still in flux and so many contradictions in Soviet society, it is impossible to predict how *perestroika* will play out. The disintegration of the old system has gone so far, social turmoil is so widespread, and the economic situation is so precarious that in Moscow, a city of Cassandras, the most articulate people are pessimistic. They are full of dark scenarios—ethnic civil war, an economic crash, a total breakdown of law and order, the emergence of a new right-wing dictator, furious anti-Semitic pogroms, Russian nationalist revanchism lashing out at the world.

At every step of the way, there has been the potential of catastrophic violence—civil war or a bloody revolution. In nearly six years, there have been numerous instances of communal bloodshed and hundreds have been killed. But given the enormity of the changes under way and the passion of the forces unleashed, what is remarkable is not how much but how little mass violence there has been.

It is impossible to dismiss the possibility of mass ethnic bloodshed. Only occupation by twenty-five thousand Soviet army troops has kept Armenia and Azerbaijan from renewing civil war. As president, Gorbachev has commanded the private armies and guerrilla forces in these republics to disband and surrender their arms, but they have defied him, as have guerrilla forces in other republics. Vadim Bakatin, the minister of internal affairs, reported in mid-1990 that there were armed bands operating in Georgia, Moldavia, Latvia, Lithuania, and Estonia, and in Central Asia among Uzbeks, Kirghiz, and Kazakhs.[9] Significantly, Bakatin did not mention Russia, or the Ukraine, the second-largest republic and the only one capable of posing a serious armed challenge to Russia proper.

In terms of governmental stability, what is important is that the violence so far has taken place far from Moscow, outside the Russian republic; and street revolutions rarely topple governments unless they rise within the nation's capital and engage a nation's dominant people.

In Moscow, Gorbachev has allowed large political demonstrations but, with a sizable military garrison in reserve nearby, he has kept order. Even the largest Moscow rallies have been much smaller than the mass marches in East European capitals, and they have never approached the passion of the frenzied mobs that toppled Nicolae Ceauşescu. Nor has Gorbachev tempted fate, as Ceauşescu did when he summoned the masses to the central square of Bucharest to address them, and thereby set the stage for the rampage that led to his own overthrow.

Out across the Soviet Union, violence has been sporadic. The combustion of ethnic tensions has suddenly exploded in some distant region and then died down; in Central Asia, it has sometimes burst into flames and skipped, once, twice, three times, to other places, flaring briefly in each place, but not setting off a general conflagration. Significantly, that kind of violence has broken out almost exclusively in Central Asia and the Caucasus. By comparison, even the viciously anti-Semitic hate-mongering of the right-wing Pamyat group has led to very little actual bloodshed. In most of the country—the Baltics, the Ukraine, Byelorussia, Moldavia, the vast Russian republic—nationalist leaders have explicitly eschewed violence, preaching instead peaceful change. So that while spasms of violence and local conflict will probably continue, it seems unlikely that ethnic tensions will trigger a general civil war.

War or not, the Soviet Union is in the process of disintegration, though that scenario will probably be less drastic than many Westerners imagine. The Baltic republics, with a total population of 8 million, are determined to secede, and Gorbachev is committed in principle to allowing their independence. Other republics where there is widespread sentiment for secession include Georgia (5.4 million) and Moldavia (4.3 million), plus the western Ukraine around the once-Polish city of Lvov, and the Azerbaijani province of Nakhichevan, bordering Iran. It is hard to imagine that Gorbachev would allow all these regions to secede, but even if he did, that would involve no more than 25 million people out of a nation of 290 million.

Many a Western scholar has voiced the view of Timothy Garton Ash that "if history is any guide the decline of empires does not stop halfway,"[10] but it is conceivable that Gorbachev could get away with a partial, peaceful dissolution and still keep the bulk of what is now known as the Soviet Union intact, though with power decentralized.

At present, the prevailing demand of local people in most parts of the country is for their own sovereignty, primarily in economic affairs; almost every republic has been pressing Gorbachev to surrender central power to a looser confederation. Once again, Gorbachev seems to be bowing to the inevitable by negotiating ways to revise the Soviet federal structure. If he not only is willing to make sufficient concessions to reach agreement but succeeds in actually making it function, he could wind up with a new confederation of 265 million people (the Russian republic, the Ukraine, Byelorussia, Central Asia, Armenia, and perhaps others). Smaller than the current Soviet Union, it would still be a continental giant of superpower size.

More menacing to Gorbachev and the fate of his reform movement would be mass civil unrest growing out of an economic breakdown: social outrage turning to anarchy—a general strike crippling the nation's factories and transport system, massive refusal by farmers to deliver crops to the cities, food riots in Moscow and other urban areas, economic uprisings in the Russian heartland that the army could not, or would not, quell.

As the crucial 1990 fall harvest began, the government braced for rising social tensions. Prime Minister Nikolai Ryzhkov sounded the alarm that despite one of the most bountiful growing seasons in recent years, grain deliveries to the government from state and collective farms had fallen behind those in 1989. Such a trend, he warned, could lead to serious food shortages through the winter of 1990–91, possibly sparking civil unrest. Ryzhkov also disclosed a drastic worsening in the supply of consumer goods in the western regions because East European visitors were buying cheaper Soviet goods on the Soviet black market. Industrial plants, Ryzhkov complained, were refusing to abide by state economic plans.[11] And he warned that the country was running out of hard currency and could not import even as much food as in 1989, to make up for any shortfall in the 1990 harvest. In short, the economic crisis was worsening.

For Ryzhkov, schooled in central planning and responsible for making it work, those were disastrous indicators. But in terms of the long-range prospects for reform, aspects of his gloomy report may have pointed to precisely the trends that reform has needed—a further erosion of the old economic order to make way for market economics. As the Lithuanians and the new city governments discovered in the spring of 1990, they could do business with each other, bypassing the central government; now, it seemed, farms, industrial plants, other regions, and republics were pursuing that path too. Ryzhkov's open puzzlement over the odd disappearance of the bountiful grain harvest suggested that many food suppliers were making their own deals and not telling the government.

Unquestionably, food shortages are the tinder of revolution. Lenin's fiery slogan in 1917 was "Peace, Bread, and Land." It was a potentially dangerous moment in September 1990 when Moscow began reporting bread shortages for the first time. But as the past two years have shown, acute shortages of many consumer goods in the Soviet Union do not necessarily trigger revolt. Soviet economic production is down, but not as disastrously as the barren shelves in Soviet stores indicate. The explanation of many Russians is that more and more goods are disappearing from state shops and reappearing in the underground economy. In the seventies, the black market was illegal, but even then it was so vast that I called it a countereconomy. In the nineties, it borders on the legal and is even more massive, perhaps 10–20 percent of the national output. People at all levels are ingenious at finding goods that are "nonexistent." Massive hoarding and under-the-table sales are a fact of life; some people have surprising private stocks. Whenever hard-to-get items appear unpredictably in stores, the lucky shoppers on hand buy out the supply, regardless of their own needs. That has been standard operating procedure for years, accentuated by the latest economic hardships.

A Moscow intellectual told Jim Hoagland of *The Washington Post* in mid-1990 that he had five refrigerators in his apartment, so that whenever perishable goods appeared on the market, he could hoard them. A senior Kremlin official told a Western businessman that one of his civil servants had stockpiled a five-year supply of soap. Some Western economic specialists believe that a twenty-million-ton shortfall of harvested grain that never made it into official channels in 1989 was sold in private trade by Soviet farmers.[12]

That does not relieve the desperate circumstances of the millions of people at the bottom, the pensioners, the rural poor, and unskilled workers. But by world standards, Russians are extraordinarily patient, willing to endure conditions that Westerners, or even Poles, would find intolerable. Moreover, Americans, convinced that the current Soviet economic agony cannot go on for much longer without a social explosion, sometimes forget how long America lay in the grip of the Great Depression: twelve years from the stock-market crash of 1929 until the beginning of World War II in 1941, with the numbers of unemployed ranging as high as sixteen million. Soviet society may be in the midst of such a long and severe stretch of hardship, and the level of political instability that goes with it.

Inevitably, the question arises whether Gorbachev can survive, or whether chaos will produce a new dictator who will turn the clock back to Stalinism.

For the outside world, the worst prospect would probably be the rise of a hard-line Russian nationalist fascism bred of economic chaos, military and political humiliation, and anger at the world's exploiting Soviet weakness—a parallel to Hitler's rise in Germany.

Yet paradoxically, as Gorbachev's mass popularity has fallen, he has become more secure in his position as chief of state. A cabal of Old Guard conservatives in the Politburo seems less threatening; his old Party rivals have been dispersed. Ivan Polozkov, the new Russian Communist Party chief, is a potential point man for a political coup by the right wing, but he does not yet have the stature to challenge Gorbachev, especially after the political rout of the Party's right wing at the Twenty-eighth Communist Party Congress. Moreover, Gorbachev's election to a five-year term as president has put him beyond the Party's power of removal.

Another black scenario that has worried Moscow intellectuals is that senior army generals, alarmed by mass civil unrest, would move against Gorbachev to install one of their own or a hard-line Party figure. Gorbachev has been careful to court the army, by including Defense Minister Dmitri Yazov on his presidential council; and he has kept the Party's political network in the army, as a check on its reliability. Gorbachev is reported to have even more carefully cultivated the KGB, long an institutional rival to the army, so that neither agency could be certain where the other would stand in a power struggle.

But most important, as several knowledgeable civilian politicians told me, the armed forces are no more a monolith than the Communist Party or Soviet society as a whole. The senior generals, the generation among whom the hard-line sentiments seem the strongest, are indoctrinated in the tradition of loyalty to the Party leader—Gorbachev. Among junior and field-grade officers, Party loyalty has less pull, but at these ranks there is a strong and active movement of political democrats and progressives, many of whom think the army should stay out of politics entirely. Another complication stems from the ethnic divisions that tear at the unity of the army as well as at Soviet society in general.

Anatoly Sobchak, who as the reform mayor of Leningrad would presumably be among the first officials arrested in a military takeover, scoffed at the idea of a military coup. His argument to me was that even desperate hard-liners dared not move because of internal political divisions in the armed forces—because they could not count on others to support a move against Gorbachev. I asked about repeated rumors that Colonel General Boris Gromov, former Soviet army commander in Afghanistan and more recently commander of the Kiev military district, was a potential focal point of army plotting. More senior generals, Sobchak told me, dismiss Gromov, who is in his forties, as "a mere boy."

"We have no one in the army strong enough and popular enough to try it," Sobchak said. "To take over the government, you have to have some idea of what to do. You have to be popular with the masses. I know the mood of our people. They would never accept it. The army leaders know that if they tried such a thing, the people would be out in the streets protesting. No, I do not think it will happen."[13]

If the military were tempted, they know that Gorbachev would be a formidable and cunning foe, especially hard to dislodge because of his election as president. Nor is it likely that he would allow civil unrest to reach a point where the army felt compelled to take over in order to preserve law and order. In Azerbaijan, Gorbachev showed willingness to use troops to put down civil strife, and presumably he would not hesitate to do so again, especially if he sensed that riots in the streets were putting his own survival—and the fate of his reforms—in jeopardy.

But assuming for a moment that Sobchak is wrong and a hard-liner did seize power, I cannot imagine a new Stalinist dictatorship. The Soviet system has already changed too much; too many people around the country in the institutions of government and the press now control elements of power for one man to gather all the strings of control. The new populists, Boris Yeltsin in the lead, have demanded that the military stay out of politics and that the Party break its ties with the military, and there is wide popular sympathy for those views. The breakdown of the economy, the erosion of discipline, the power of striking workers—all these are impediments to dictatorial rule. In one republic after another, a would-be dictator would meet mass discontent and resistance. Restoring right-wing totalitarian rule would take years of relentless purges—and I am skeptical that even what remains of the Communist Party, let alone the rest of Soviet society, would stomach that.

REFORM CAN OUTLIVE GORBACHEV

"The politics of the right has no future. Our future is left radicalism. The politics of our country has nowhere to go except to the left."[14]

That was the assessment given me by Interior Minister Vadim Bakatin on July 4, 1990, at the very moment when the right wing was riding high at the Communist Party Congress. I found this judgment especially significant, coming from Bakatin. He is the Soviet Union's top cop, a veteran Party boss from the provinces but more sophisticated than most, a moderate Communist leader who has won favor with both the Party's right wing and Gorbachev centrists.

In Soviet shorthand, Bakatin's term "left radicalism" was the direction staked out by Boris Yeltsin. It was also the direction in which Gorbachev felt pulled by events and by necessity toward the conclusion of his sixth year. Although he had helped bring the left-wing reformers into being and had sometimes blessed their politics, he had long resisted an open alliance.

Nonetheless, by the second half of 1990, Gorbachev was drawn to Yeltsin's politics. Instinct taught him to neutralize his most serious rivals by joining forces; and after Yeltsin's election as the political leader of the Russian republic, people all over the country talked of Yeltsin as a rival and potential successor to Gorbachev. That was something Gorbachev had to take seriously.

After all the Party's efforts to crush Yeltsin, his reemergence at the national leadership level made Gorbachev look, for the first time, less indispensable to the future of reform. And yet Gorbachev and Yeltsin were natural allies; they needed each other, and needed to overcome the bad personal chemistry of their past. As president, Yeltsin would lack something vital that Gorbachev had—the acceptance of the apparat and the military, the Party conservatives who so mistrusted and loathed Yeltsin. Facing such hostility as president, Yeltsin would dangerously polarize Soviet politics.

But Yeltsin had what Gorbachev most desperately lacked—a popular mandate. Yeltsin had risked what Gorbachev had not dared: testing his popularity with the voters. Yeltsin had run twice and come home with millions of votes; he had a mass following and legitimacy that Gorbachev needed. So a Yeltsin-Gorbachev alliance combined populism with establishment power; it was potentially the central symbol of the next phase of *perestroika*.

What is more, Yeltsin had a fresh dynamism that sometimes ebbed in Gorbachev. He had become the primary advocate for nationalist leaders around the country who were pressing for a looser confederation. Yeltsin had accepted Lithuania's bid for independence; he had provided the final straw that broke the blockade against that republic in early June 1990, announcing that Russia would not honor Gorbachev's embargo. Yeltsin had given his blessing to an economic free zone in Leningrad, and to a new independent television network. He had unveiled a plan for a five-hundred-day transition to a market economy: first, legalizing private property, then abolishing government subsidies and selling off state enterprises and stalled construction projects. Only toward the end, when other essential elements were in place, did Yeltsin intend to take the most controversial step—lifting government controls on prices.[15] Yeltsin employed other unconventional maneuvers: To give incentive to Russian farmers to bring in the fall harvest, he offered special coupons that guaranteed purchase of scarce consumer goods.[16]

On virtually every point, Gorbachev had been pushed to accommodate the positions taken by Yeltsin.

In fact, barring a massive upheaval brought on by economic depression, most of the prevailing trends of Soviet politics, as Gorbachev neared the end of his sixth year, pointed not toward retreat, as anxious Moscow intellectuals feared, but toward still further, bolder reforms.

The rudiments of a multiparty system were becoming visible; political pluralism was on the rise all around the country, while the Communist Party was losing mass support. The pressures for political decentralization were more insistent than ever, and Gorbachev was bending to them. The radical reformers in charge of city governments had seized the political initiative, and Gorbachev himself had moved to the left to make common cause with the radical reformers on many issues. One major danger was that they, like Gorbachev, might not be able to deliver economic results fast enough to satisfy the masses; another was that their market economics would produce such inequalities that a backlash would be provoked among ordinary workers who were still stuck in the mentality of "equal poverty for all."[17]

What was most significant was that the entire process of reform had gained a momentum of its own, a momentum that would outlive Gorbachev, whatever his personal fate might be. For the first time, there were political leaders who were committed to democratic reforms and who could be considered potential successors to Gorbachev—either in the near future (Yeltsin) or later on (Popov, Sobchak)—if he managed to finish out his presidential term to 1995. And the odds of Gorbachev's surviving that long politically seemed strong, certainly better than 50-50.

In 1988, I had gone to Moscow wondering whether Gorbachev could make *perestroika* work in the coming two or three years. I left thinking it would take five or ten years. After another two trips, I saw such an enormous social transformation under way that I understood it was bound to take two or three decades at least—a time frame far beyond the reach of any one leader.

Over that long a period, reform was bound to ebb and flow. I could conceive of a conservative retreat, especially in the face of economic disaster and social upheavals; Gorbachev himself might backtrack once again. But if there was a reversal, my sense was that it would be a temporary interruption in the long process of reform. Retreat could last for several years. But if so, my expectation would be that a new, younger generation of reformers—the Stankevich generation, perhaps—would be ready to resume reform's forward thrust. In sum, though the path was certain to be rocky, I came to feel that *perestroika* had a dynamism that assured its own permanence.

Gorbachev has changed our world more definitively than he has changed his own. The transformation that has taken place beyond Soviet borders is irreversible. Eastern Europe's economic future is uncertain, but its political future outside the Soviet empire is not in doubt. Gorbachev's acquiescence in the reunification of Germany and its membership in NATO cannot be revoked by a successor in the Kremlin. A political and historic divide has been crossed.

Given the turmoil inside the Soviet Union, the Soviet army cannot pose a credible military threat to the West or the United States in the years directly ahead. In both Moscow and Washington, the powerful economic demands to reduce military spending will only hasten the process of arms control and cutbacks in nuclear arsenals, and that is a self-reinforcing process. The popular hunger to seal the end of the Cold War cannot be resisted by leaders anywhere.

As if to prove that his intent was global, Gorbachev has not only relinquished the Kremlin's East European empire, but he has also changed its politics in the Third World. Most dramatically, he has withdrawn Soviet troops from Afghanistan. And in the wake of Iraq's invasion of Kuwait, he cut off Soviet arms sales to Iraqi dictator Saddam Hussein.

In all of his foreign-policy moves, and above all, in changing the nature of the Soviet system, what Gorbachev has done for us is change our national agenda. Thanks to Gorbachev's "new thinking," we have been allowed to move from a world dominated by the stark calculus of the arms race and the nuclear first strike, to one concerned primarily with the economics of world trade and competition, and to the issues of human poverty, global warming, the quality of life, and the care of the environment.

The process of change within the Soviet Union is primarily a matter for Soviets themselves; outside influence can only be marginal. But given the delicate balance in the Soviet economy today, the West has a stake—in its own self-interest—in seeing the process of *perestroika* carried forward. Under the new Soviet conditions, that does not mean that the West must ensure Gorbachev's survival or provide aid only to the national government. The rise to power of democratic reformers in the cities, in the Russian republic, in the Baltic republics, and in other regions provides new channels for Western aid and engagement for years to come. These may be more effective avenues in the early nineties for promoting democratic pluralism and market economics than the national government; and the success of regional leaders may determine the national leadership of the next generation. In the interim, Gorbachev still provides a vital protective umbrella for these emerging figures and their reforms.

Gorbachev's dominance of world affairs over the past six years is astonishing, given the weak hand he has had to play. For it is worth remembering that Gorbachev is the leader of a country whose supposed allies were quick to desert the moment they were given a chance; whose diverse nationalities challenge the national government and the fabric of national unity; whose single powerful Party elite constantly menaces the national leader; and whose economy is a disaster.

In spite of all these handicaps, to a remarkable degree Gorbachev has managed to command the political initiative not only in his own country but in the world at large. He has kept our attention riveted on the unfolding drama in the Soviet Union. And he has done it, I believe, by being willing to confront the most fundamental problems that trouble his people and that hold back his nation.

Facing the truth and publicly debating the nation's most acute and vexing difficulties is supposed to be the strength of democracies. Isn't it extraordinary that today this is being done not in the West but in the land of Stalin and Ivan the Terrible?

That is a point worth pondering in democratic societies, where political leaders have not been nearly so candid with their people, nor so daring in their politics.

What Gorbachev is attempting—on a grand scale and in the incredibly short span of one decade—is something genuinely new on this planet, and that explains both the uncertainty of the process and its compelling fascination.

History is full of men on horseback trampling fragile democracies underfoot. But there is no precedent for a single leader attempting the peaceful transition from a dictatorship to democracy.

BOOKS

Aslund, Anders. *Gorbachev's Struggle for Economic Reform.* Ithaca, N.Y.: Cornell University Press, 1989.

Bialer, Seweryn. *The Soviet Paradox: External Expansion & Internal Decline.* New York: Alfred A. Knopf, 1986.

———, ed. *Inside Gorbachev's Russia.* Boulder, Col.: Westview Press, 1989.

Brown, Archie, ed. *Political Leadership in the Soviet Union.* Bloomington, Ind.: Indiana University Press, 1989.

Brzezinski, Zbigniew. *The Grand Failure.* New York: Charles Scribner's Sons, 1989.

Cohen, Stephen F., and Katrina vanden Heuvel. *Voices of Glasnost.* New York: W. W. Norton, 1989.

Directory of Soviet "Informal" Political Organizations and Samizdat Publications. Chicago: Soviet-American Review, 1988.

Doder, Dusko. *Shadows and Whispers.* New York: Random House, 1986.

——— and Louise Branson. *Gorbachev: Heretic in the Kremlin.* New York: Viking, 1990.

Goldman, Marshall I. *Gorbachev's Challenge.* New York: W. W. Norton, 1987.

———. *U.S.S.R. in Crisis.* New York: W. W. Norton, 1983.

Gorbachev, Mikhail S. *Perestroika.* New York: Harper & Row, 1987.

Grossman, Vasily. *Forever Flowing.* New York: Harper & Row, 1972.

Guroff, Greg. *Entrepreneurship and Economic Innovation in Imperial and Soviet Russia.* Princeton, N.J.: Princeton University Press, 1983.

Hewett, Ed A. *Reforming the Soviet Economy: Equality Versus Efficiency.* Washington, D.C.: Brookings, 1988.

Hosking, Geoffrey. *The Awakening of the Soviet Union.* Cambridge, Mass.: Harvard University Press, 1990.

Lenin, Vladimir I. *Collected Works,* Vol. XXX. Moscow: Progress Publishers, 1965.

————. *Collected Works*, Vol. XXV. Moscow: Progress Publishers, 1964.

Lewin, Moshe. *The Gorbachev Phenomenon*. Berkeley, Cal.: University of California Press, 1988.

Mandelstam, Nadezhda. *Hope Against Hope*. New York: Atheneum, 1970.

Marx, Karl, and Friedrich Engels. *Collected Works*, Vol. I. New York: International Publishers, 1975.

Medvedev, Roy. *Let History Judge: The Origins and Consequences of Stalinism* (revised and expanded edition). New York: Columbia University Press, 1989.

————. *On Stalin and Stalinism*. Oxford: Oxford University Press, 1973.

Medvedev, Zhores. *Soviet Agriculture*. New York: W. W. Norton, 1987.

————. *Gorbachev*. New York: W. W. Norton, 1986.

————. *Nuclear Disaster in the Urals*. New York: W. W. Norton, 1979.

Mickiewicz, Ellen. *Split Signals: Television and Politics in the Soviet Union*. New York: Oxford University Press, 1988.

Mirsky, D. S. *A History of Russian Literature*. New York: Vintage Russian Library, 1958.

Morrison, Donald, ed. *Mikhail S. Gorbachev: An Intimate Biography*. New York: Time, Inc., 1988.

Nagel. *Nagel's Encyclopedic Guide: U.S.S.R.* Geneva: Nagel, 1970.

Nahaylo, Bogdan, and Victor Swoboda. *Soviet Disunion: A History of the Nationalities Problem in the USSR*. New York: The Free Press, 1990.

Nove,Alec.*Glasnost in Action: Cultural Renaissance in Russia*. Boston: Unwin Hyman, 1989.

————. *An Economic History of the U.S.S.R.* (2nd revised edition). Middlesex, England: Penguin, 1982.

Popov, Gavril. *Upravleniye Ekonomikoi—Ekonomicheskiye Metody*. Moscow: Ekonomika, 1985.

Pozner, Vladimir. *Parting with Illusions*. New York: Atlantic Monthly Press, 1990.

Remington, Thomas F. *The Truth of Authority: Ideology and Communication in the Soviet Union*. Pittsburgh: University of Pittsburgh Press, 1988.

Robinson, Geroid Tanquary. *Rural Russia Under the Old Regime*. Berkeley, Cal.: University of California Press, 1969.

Sel'skokhozaistvennoye Provisvodstvo v Lichnikh Podsovnikh Khozaistvakh Naseleniya. Moscow: Goskomstat, 1989.

Serfaty, Simon. *France, DeGaulle, & Europe*. Baltimore: Johns Hopkins University Press, 1968.

Shelton, Judy. *The Coming of the Soviet Crash*. New York: The Free Press, 1989.

Shmelyov, Nikolai, and Vladimir Popov. *The Turning Point: Revitalizing the Soviet Economy*. New York: Doubleday, 1989.

Simis, Konstantin. *USSR: The Corrupt Society*. New York: Simon and Schuster, 1982.

Smith, Hedrick. *The Russians* (revised edition). New York: Ballantine, 1984.

Solzhenitsyn, Aleksandr I. *Letter to the Supreme Leaders*. New York: Harper & Row, 1974.

Sumner, B. H. *A Short History of Russia*. New York: Harcourt, Brace, 1949.

Tocqueville, Alexis de. *The Old Regime and the Revolution*. New York: Harper & Brothers, 1856.

Utechin, S. V. *A Concise Encyclopedia of Russia*. New York: E. P. Dutton, 1964.

Vernadsky, George. *A History of Russia*. New Haven, Conn.: Yale University Press, 1954.

Walker, Martin. *The Harper Independent Traveler: The Soviet Union.* New York: Harper & Row, 1989.
———. *The Waking Giant.* New York: Pantheon Books, 1986.
Yanov, Alexander. *The Russian Challenge.* Oxford: Basil Blackwell, 1987.
Yeltsin, Boris. *Against the Grain.* New York: Summit Books, 1990.

ARTICLES

Abalkin, Leonid. "Not Sharing, but Earning." *Ogonek,* Oct. 7–14, 1989.
Andreyev, Sergei. "The Power Structure and Problems of Society." *Neva,* No. 1, Jan. 1989.
Andreyeva, Nina. "I Cannot Forsake Principles." *Sovetskaya Rossiya,* Mar. 13, 1988.
Aslund, Anders. "Gorbachev: Governing on the Razor's Edge." *The Washington Post,* Jan. 28, 1990, pp. C1–C2.
Berdyayev, Nikolai. "Man's Fate in the Modern World." *Novy Mir,* No. 1, 1989.
Bialer, Seweryn, and Joan Afferica. "The Genesis of Gorbachev's World." *Foreign Affairs,* Vol. 64, No. 3, America and the World, 1985.
Borovik, Artyom. "Diary of a Reporter." *Ogonek,* Nos. 28, 29, and 30, Jul. 1987.
Breslauer, George W. "Evaluating Gorbachev as a Leader." *Soviet Economy,* Vol. 5, No. 4, Oct.–Dec. 1989.
Brown, Archie. "Political Change in the Soviet Union: Movement Toward Democracy." *The World Policy Journal,* Vol. 6, No. 3, Summer 1989.
———. "Gorbachev: New Man in the Kremlin." *Problems of Communism,* May–June 1985.
Brumberg, Abraham. "Moscow: The Struggle for Reform." *New York Review of Books,* Mar. 30, 1989.
Brzezinski, Zbigniew. "Post-Communist Nationalism." *Foreign Affairs,* Vol. 68, No. 5, Winter 1989–90.
Condee, Nancy, and Vladimir Padunov. "The Frontiers of Soviet Culture: Reaching the Limits?" *The Harriman Institute Forum,* Vol. 1, No. 5, May 1988.
Dobbs, Michael. "*Perestroika* at a Crossroads in the Soviet Heartland." *The Washington Post,* Jul. 1, 1990, pp. A1, A30.
———. "Gorbachev's Other Face: Lenin Heir and Savior of Soviet Communism." *The International Herald Tribune,* Sept. 22, 1989, pp. 1, 8.
———. "Separatism in Azerbaijan Growing Since Crackdown." *The Washington Post,* Feb. 16, 1989, pp. A1, A36–37.
Dunlop, John B. "The Contemporary Russian Nationalist Spectrum." *Radio Liberty Research Bulletin: Russian Nationalism Today,* Dec. 19, 1988.
———. "Soviet Cultural Politics." *Problems of Communism,* Nov.–Dec. 1987.
Fairbanks, Charles H., Jr. "Gorbachev's Cultural Revolution." *Commentary,* Aug. 1989.
———. "The Soviet Elections in Gorbachev's Political Strategy." Unpublished paper, Summer 1989.
Feshbach, Murray. "Demographic Trends in the Soviet Union: Serious Implications for the Soviet Military." *NATO Review,* Oct. 1989.
———. *Soviet Military Health Issues.* Washington, D.C.: Joint Economic Committee of the U.S. Congress, Fall 1987.

———. "The Age Structure of Soviet Population." *Soviet Economy,* Vol. 1, No. 2, Apr.–June 1985.

———. *Population Trends and Dilemmas.* Washington, D.C.: The Population Reference Bureau, Inc., Aug. 1982.

Fierman, William. "*Glasnost* in Practice: The Uzbek Experience." *Central Asian Survey,* Vol. 8, No. 2, 1989.

Fukuyama, Francis. "The End of History." *The National Interest,* No. 16, Summer 1989.

Goble, Paul. "Gorbachev: Facing the Nationality Nightmare." *The Washington Post,* Mar. 25, 1990, pp. C1, C2.

———. "Soviet Ethnic Politics." *Problems of Communism,* Jul.–Aug. 1989.

———. "The End of the 'National Question': Ideological Decay and Ethnic Relations in the U.S.S.R." Unpublished paper, 1989.

———. "Three Realities in Search of a Theory: Nationalities and the Soviet Future." Unpublished paper, 1989.

Gorbachev, Mikhail S. "Merakh Pseldovataln'novo Osyushesvleniya Agrarnoi Politiki KPSS na Sovremennom Etape." *Izbranniye, rechy i stat'i,* Moscow, 1987.

Hammer, Darrell P. " '*Glasnost*' and 'The Russian Idea.' " *Radio Liberty Research Bulletin: Russian Nationalism Today,* Dec. 19, 1988.

Hewett, Ed A. "Is Soviet Socialism Reformable?" *SAIS Review,* Vol. 10, No. 2, Summer/Fall 1990.

———. "American and Western European Approaches to the Soviet Union: Economic Issues." Lecture for the Aspen Institute Conference on U.S.-Soviet Relations, Dubrovnik, Yugoslavia, Aug. 27–31, 1989.

———. "The Dynamics of Economic Reform." Remarks at the conference "Soviet Domestic Change and Geopolitical Strategy Under Gorbachev," Johns Hopkins School of Advanced International Studies, Washington, D.C., Feb. 16–17, 1989.

———. "*Perestroyka* and the Congress of People's Deputies." *Soviet Economy,* Vol. 5, No. 1, Jan.–Mar. 1989.

———. "Gorbachev's Economic Strategy: A Preliminary Assessment." *Soviet Economy,* Vol. 1, No. 4, Oct.–Dec. 1985.

Hough, Jerry F. "Why Gorby is Defying the Pundits' Predictions." *The Washington Post,* Feb. 11, 1990, pp. C1, C4.

———. "Gorbachev's Politics." *Foreign Affairs,* Winter 1989–90.

———. "The Politics of Successful Economic Reform." *Soviet Economy,* Vol. 5, No. 1, Jan.–Mar. 1989.

———. "The Politics of the 19th Party Conference." *Soviet Economy,* Vol. 4, No. 2, Apr.–June 1988.

Jones, Anthony, and William Moskoff. "New Cooperatives in the USSR." *Problems of Communism,* Nov.–Dec., 1989.

Kaiser, Robert G. "Red Intrigue: How Gorbachev Outfoxed His Kremlin Rivals." *The Washington Post,* June 12, 1988, pp. C1, C2.

Keller, Bill. "How Gorbachev Rejected Plan to 'Shock Treat' the Economy." *The New York Times,* May 14, 1990, pp. A1, A10.

———. "Soviet Economy: A Shattered Dream." *The New York Times,* May 13, 1990, pp. A1, A12.

———. "Did Moscow Incite Azerbaijanis? Some See a Plot." *The New York Times,* Feb. 19, 1990, p. A8.

———. "Russian Nationalists: Yearning for an Iron Hand." *The New York Times Magazine,* Jan. 28, 1990.

Klyamkin, Igor. "Why It Is Difficult to Speak the Truth." *Novy Mir,* No. 2, Feb. 1989.

Lapidus, Gail W. "Gorbachev and the National Question." *Soviet Economy,* Vol. 5, No. 3, Jul.–Sept. 1989.

———. "Gorbachev and Reform of the Soviet System." *Daedalus,* Spring 1987.

Legvold, Robert. "The Revolution in Soviet Foreign Policy." *Foreign Affairs,* Vol. 68, No. 1, America and the World, 1988–89.

Menashe, Louis. "Tinker on the Roof." *Tikkun,* Vol. 3, No. 5, Sept.–Oct. 1988.

———. "Repentance." *Cineaste,* Vol. XVI, No. 3, 1988.

———. "*Glasnost* in Soviet Cinema." *Cineaste,* Vol. XVI, No. 2, 1987–88.

Morrow, Lance. "The Unlikely Patron of Change." *Time,* Jan. 1, 1990.

Nitze, Paul H. "Gorbachev's Plan for a Communist Comeback." *The Washington Post,* Jan. 10, 1990.

Parrott, Bruce. "Gorbachev's Gamble: Political, Economic, and Ethnic Challenges to Soviet Reform." *SAIS Review,* Vol. 10, No. 2, Summer/Fall 1990.

———. "Soviet National Security Under Gorbachev." *Problems of Communism,* Nov.–Dec. 1988.

Reddaway, Peter. "Life After Gorbachev: The Soviets' Grim Future." *The Washington Post,* Nov. 26, 1989, pp. C1–C2.

———. "The Threat to Gorbachev." *New York Review of Books,* Aug. 17, 1989.

Remington, Thomas F. "Intellectuals, the 'Middle Class,' and the Drive for Reform." Paper presented to the conference "Soviet Domestic Change and Geopolitical Strategy Under Gorbachev," Johns Hopkins School of Advanced International Studies, Washington, D.C., Feb. 16–17, 1989.

Remnick, David. "Gorbachev: The Glow Is Gone." *The Washington Post,* May 27, 1990, pp. B1, B4.

———. "Comrade Personality." *Esquire,* Feb. 1990.

———. "The Cultivation of Young Gorbachev." *The Washington Post,* Dec. 1, 1989, p. B8.

Ruble, Blair. "The Social Dimensions of *Perestroika.*" *Soviet Economy,* Vol. 3, No. 2, Apr.–June 1987.

Schmemann, Serge. "The Emergence of Gorbachev." *The New York Times Magazine,* Mar. 3, 1985.

Schroeder, Gertrude E. "The Role of Property in Communist Countries: Past, Present, and Future." Unpublished paper, University of Virginia, Aug. 1988.

———. "Anatomy of Gorbachev's Economic Reform." *Soviet Economy,* Vol. 3, No. 3, Jul.–Sept. 1987.

———. "Gorbachev: 'Radically' Implementing Brezhnev's Reforms." *Soviet Economy,* Vol. 2, No. 4, Oct.–Dec. 1986.

Selyunin, Vasily. "Sources." *Novy Mir,* No. 5, May 1988.

Semyonov, V. "Ukrepleniye Ekonomiki Kolkhozov i Sovkhozov." *Finansy SSSR,* No. 9, 1985.

Sheehy, Gail. "Gorbachev, Red Star: The Shaping of the Man Who Managed the World." *Vanity Fair,* Feb. 1990.

Sherlock, Thomas. "Politics and History Under Gorbachev." *Problems of Communism,* May–Aug. 1988.

Shipler, David. "Between Dictatorship and Anarchy." *The New Yorker,* June 25, 1990.

Shmelyov, Nikolai. "New Anxieties." *Novy Mir,* No. 4, Apr. 1988.
———. "Advances and Debts." *Novy Mir,* No. 6, June 1987.
Sinyavsky, Andrei. "Russian Nationalism." *Radio Liberty Research Bulletin: Russian Nationalism Today,* Dec. 19, 1988.
Starr, S. Frederick. "Party Animals." *The New Republic,* June 26, 1989.
———. "A Usable Past." *The New Republic,* May 15, 1989.
———. "Soviet Union: A Civil Society." *Foreign Policy,* No. 70, Spring 1988.
Teague, Elizabeth, and Dawn Mann. "Gorbachev's Dual Role." *Problems of Communism,* Jan.–Feb. 1990.
Tolz, Vera. "Informal Groups and Soviet Politics in 1989." *Radio Liberty Report on the USSR,* Nov. 24, 1989.
———. "Informal Groups in the USSR." *Washington Quarterly,* Winter 1988.
Treml, Vladimir G. "The Most Recent Input-Output Table: A Milestone in Soviet Statistics." *Soviet Economy,* Vol. 5, No. 4, Oct.–Dec. 1989.
Tsipko, Aleksandr. "We Should Not Fear the Truth." *Nauka i Zhizn,* No. 2, Feb. 1989.
———. "Egotism of Dreamers." *Nauka i Zhizn,* No. 1, Jan. 1989.
———. "Perversities of Socialism." *Nauka i Zhizn,* No. 12, Dec. 1988.
———. "The Roots of Stalinism." *Nauka i Zhizn,* No. 11, Nov. 1988.
Van Atta, Don. " 'Full-Scale, Like Collectivization, but Without Collectivization's Excesses': The Campaign to Introduce the Family and Lease Contract in Soviet Agriculture." Revised version of paper prepared for annual meeting of American Association for the Advancement of Slavic Studies, Chicago, Nov. 2–5, 1989.
———. "Theorists of Agrarian *Perestroika.*" *Soviet Economy,* Vol. 5, No. 1, Jan.–Mar. 1989.
Woll, Josephine. " *'Glasnost'* and Soviet Culture." *Problems of Communism,* Nov.–Dec. 1989.
Yakovlev, Yegor. "To Halt the Pendulum Is to Stop the Clock." *Moscow News,* Oct. 29–Nov. 5, 1989.
Yanov, Alexander. "Russian Nationalism as the Ideology of Counterreform." *Radio Liberty Research Bulletin: Russian Nationalism Today,* Dec. 19, 1988.
Z. "To the Stalin Mausoleum." *Daedalus,* Winter 1990.
Zavslavskaya, Tatyana. "The Novosibirsk Report." *Survey,* Vol. 28, No. 1, Spring 1984.

NOTES

Author's Note: While many of the translations are my own, I have relied extensively on the *Foreign Broadcast Information Service* and the *Current Digest of the Soviet Press,* referred to in the notes as *FBIS* and *CDSP.* To clarify the distinction between *interviews* and *conversations* in citations: In my *interviews,* I used video or audio recording devices and worked from transcripts; in *conversations,* I took handwritten notes. If the citation refers to *interview* or *conversation,* it is with the author, unless otherwise specified.

INTRODUCTION: AFTER THE WALL CAME DOWN

1. Zinovy Yuryev, conversation with the author, May 27, 1988.

1. THE HIDDEN WELLSPRINGS OF REFORM

1. Mikhail Gorbachev, *Perestroika* (New York: Harper & Row, 1987), pp. 23–24.
2. Tatyana Zaslavskaya, interview with the author, Sept. 26, 1989.
3. Abel Aganbegyan and Timur Timofeyev, director of the Institute of International Labor Studies, interviews with the author, Mar. 7–9, 1988.
4. Zaslavskaya, *op. cit.*
5. "The Novosibirsk Report," in *Survey,* Vol. 28, No. 1 (Spring 1984), pp. 83–108. The formal title of the paper, according to Zaslavskaya, was "The Improvement of Productive Relations and the Social Mechanism of Economic Development."
6. Dusko Doder, *Shadows and Whispers* (New York: Random House, 1986), pp. 169–70, 186–90.
7. "The Novosibirsk Report," *op. cit.*
8. Zaslavskaya, *op. cit.*

2. THE BREZHNEV GENERATION: SLIDE INTO CYNICISM

1. See Marshall I. Goldman, *U.S.S.R. in Crisis* (New York: W. W. Norton, 1983), pp. 109–11. Also, interviews with the author, Jan. 1984.
2. Moshe Lewin, *The Gorbachev Phenomenon* (Berkeley: University of California Press, 1988), p. 49.

3. *Ibid.*, pp. 86, 89, 91, 93, 95.

4. Martin Walker, *The Waking Giant* (New York: Pantheon Books, 1986), pp. xx–xxi.

5. Leonid Dobrokhotov, interview with the author, Sept. 28, 1989.

6. *Ibid.*, Jan. 8, 1990.

7. Hedrick Smith, *The Russians*, rev. ed. (New York: Ballantine, 1984), pp. 684–98.

8. Roy Medvedev, interview with the author, Oct. 9, 1989.

9. Sergei Stankevich, interview with the author, Jan. 8, 1990.

10. Aleksandr Yakovlev, interview with the author, Oct. 9, 1989.

11. Dobrokhotov, interview, Sept. 28, 1989.

12. Vadim Medvedev, *The Administration of Socialist Production: Problems of Theory and Practice* (Moscow: Publishing House of Political Literature, 1983).

13. Anders Aslund, *Gorbachev's Struggle for Economic Reform* (Ithaca, New York: Cornell University Press, 1989), pp. 35–36.

14. Dobrokhotov, interview, Sept. 28, 1989.

15. Yakovlev, *op. cit.*

3. GORBACHEV AND THE KHRUSHCHEV GENERATION

1. Vadimir Tikhonov, interview with the author, Sept. 26, 1989.

2. This account of the Gorbachev family comes from the author's interviews with Gorbachev's uncle Sergei Gopkolo and several elderly residents of Privolnoye, Nikolai Lubenko, Pavel Ignatenko, and Aleksandr Yakovenko, on Dec. 6, 1988; and with a close family friend, Grigory Gorlov, on Dec. 7, 1988.

3. Gorlov, interview with the author, Sept. 8, 1989.

4. Gopkolo, *op. cit.*

5. Zhores A. Medvedev, *Gorbachev* (New York: W. W. Norton, 1986), pp. 22–28.

6. *Ibid.*, p. 26.

7. Antonina Shcherbakova, interview with the author, May 30, 1989.

8. Gorlov, interview with the author, Dec. 8, 1988.

9. Yakovenko, interview with the author, May 30, 1989.

10. *Ibid.*, Dec. 6, 1988.

11. Lyubov Grudchenko, interview with the author, May 30, 1989.

12. Mariya Grevtsova, interview with the author, Dec. 6, 1988.

13. David Remnick, "Comrade Personality," *Esquire*, Feb. 1990, p. 78.

14. *Ibid.*, "The Cultivation of Young Gorbachev," *The Washington Post*, Dec. 1, 1989, p. B8.

15. Ivan Manuilov, conversation with Louis Menashe, Dec. 6, 1988.

16. Mikhail Gorbachev, interview with *Unita*, May 20, 1987, *FBIS*, May 20, 1987, p. R5.

17. Gopkolo, interview, Dec. 6, 1988.

18. Gorlov, interview, Dec. 7, 1988.

19. This description of university life comes from the author's group interview with several of Gorbachev's classmates, Nadezhda Mikhailova, Vladimir Lieberman, Rudolf Kulchanov, Vladimir Kuzmin, and Natalya Rimachevskaya, May 23, 1989; and from a separate interview with Zdenek Mlynar, Mar. 29, 1989.

20. Kulchanov, *op. cit.*

21. Mlynar, *op. cit.*

22. Lieberman and Kulchanov, interview, May 24, 1989.

23. Lieberman, interview, May 24, 1989.

24. Mlynar, *op. cit.*

25. Fridrikh Neznansky, participant in discussion in *Possev*, Nov. 4, 1985, p. 22.

26. Lev Yudovich, in "Gorbachev, New Chief of Russia, May Make a Tougher Adversary," *The Wall Street Journal*, Mar. 12, 1985, p. 1.

27. Mikhailova, Kulchanov, Kuzmin, interview, May 24, 1989.

28. Mlynar, *op. cit.*
29. Neznansky, *op. cit.*
30. Mlynar, *op. cit.*
31. Nikolai Shishlin, conversation with the author, Apr. 30, 1990.
32. Dusko Doder and Louise Branson, *Gorbachev: Heretic in the Kremlin* (New York: Viking, 1990), pp. 2–4.
33. Gorbachev, *FBIS*, Nov. 3, 1987, p. 44.
34. Aleksandr Yakovlev, interview with the author, Oct. 9, 1989.
35. Roy Medvedev, interview with the author, Oct. 9, 1989.
36. Kulchanov, interview, May 24, 1989.

4. HOW DID GORBACHEV MAKE IT TO THE TOP?

1. Zinovy Yuryev, conversation with the author, June 6, 1988.
2. Vladimir and Lydiya Kolodichuk, interview with the author, Dec. 5, 1988.
3. Grigory Gorlov, conversation with the author, Dec. 7, 1988.
4. Viktor Nikitin and Valentina Brelova, interview with the author, Dec. 7, 1988.
5. Gorlov, conversation with the author, Mar. 14, 1990.
6. Brelova, *op. cit.*
7. Zdenek Mlynar, interview with the author, Mar. 29, 1989.
8. Mikhail Novikov, interview with Joyce Barnathan, spring 1988, as research for the author's documentary films on Gorbachev and *perestroika.*
9. Valentin Mezin, interviews with the author, Dec. 6–8, 1988.
10. Konstantin Nikitin, interview with the author, Dec. 6, 1988; and Vsvelod Mukakhovsky and Aleksandr Nikonov, interviews with the author, Apr. 13, 1989.
11. Viktor Postnikov, interview with the author, Dec. 5, 1988.
12. *Ibid.*, Sept. 26, 1989.
13. Gorbachev, "Merakh Psledovateln'novo Osyushesvleniya Agrarnoi Politiki KPSS na Sovremennom Etape," *Izbranniye, rechy i stat'i* (Moscow, 1987), pp. 180–200.
14. *Ibid.*, p. 200.
15. *Ibid.*, p. 199.
16. Postnikov, interview, Sept. 26, 1989.
17. Donald Morrison, ed., *Mikhail S. Gorbachev: An Intimate Biography* (New York: Time, Inc., 1988), p. 103.
18. Yulian Semyonov, interview with the author, Oct. 18, 1989.
19. Sasha Gelman, interview with the author, Sept. 18, 1989.
20. Nikolai Shishlin, interview with the author, Nov. 30, 1988.
21. Vladimir Tikhonov, interview with the author, Sept. 29, 1989.
22. Tatyana Zaslavskaya, interview with the author, Sept. 26, 1989. She said the six were Nikolai Federenko, Aleksandr Nikonov, Vladimir Mozhen, Ivan Lukianov, Tikhonov, and herself.
23. Zaslavskaya, interview, Sept. 26, 1989.
24. Postnikov, interview, Sept. 26, 1989.
25. Roald Sagdeyev, interview with the author, Dec. 15, 1988.
26. Yevgeny Velikhov, conversation with the author, June 6, 1988.
27. Valentin Lazutkin, conversation with the author, Dec. 14, 1988.
28. Aleksandr Yakovlev, interview with the author, Oct. 9, 1989.
29. Gorbachev, speech to scientific and cultural leaders, Jan. 6, 1989, *FBIS*, Jan. 9, 1989, p. 53.
30. Dusko Doder, *Shadows and Whispers* (New York: Random House, 1986), p. 267.
31. Mikhail Gorbachev, *Perestroika* (New York: Harper & Row, 1987), p. 13.
32. Gorbachev, speech, Jan. 6, 1989, *FBIS*, Jan. 9, 1989, p. 52.

5. "WHAT DO YOU THINK?"

1. Yuri Levada, conversation with the author, Mar. 15, 1990.
2. Leonid Sedov, interview with the author, Sept. 25, 1989.
3. Vladimir Shlyapentokh, conversation with the author, Mar. 23, 1990.
4. Levada, *op. cit.*
5. Levada, Alex Levinson, Lev Gudkov, Aleksandr Golov, Sedov, Boris Dubin, and Nadya Zorlaya, interview with the author, Sept. 25, 1989.
6. Levada, conversation, Mar. 15, 1990.
7. Nadezhda Mandelstam, *Hope Against Hope* (New York: Atheneum, 1970), p. 13.
8. These polling figures were provided to me by Gudkov, Levinson, and Levada, of the Center for the Study of Public Opinion on Social and Economic Issues, on Apr. 11, 1989, and were later updated.
9. Actually, the Institute of Sociological Research had conducted a poll of 940 Muscovites in May 1988 for *The New York Times* and CBS News, and found that three of four wanted multicandidate elections and doubted that the Soviet one-party system would permit Gorbachev's promised democratization. See *The New York Times*, May 26, 1988, p. A1.

6. *GLASNOST:* A MARRIAGE OF POLITICAL CONVENIENCE

1. Gorbachev, speech to Nineteenth All-Union Conference of the Communist Party of the Soviet Union, June 28, 1988, *Pravda*, June 29, 1988, p. 4.
2. Vladimir Pozner, conversation with the author, June 6, 1988.
3. Karl Marx, "Debates on Freedom of the Press and Publication of Proceedings of the Assembly of the States," *Karl Marx: 1835–43*, pp. 167–68, Vol. I of Karl Marx and Frederick Engels, *Collected Works* (New York: International Publishers, 1975).
4. *The New York Times*, May 22, 1990, p. A10.
5. Gorbachev, speech, Dec. 10, 1984, *FBIS*, Dec. 11, 1984, p. R6.

7. TROUBADOURS OF TRUTH

1. Tankred Golenpolsky, conversation with the author, June 5, 1988.
2. See Louis Menashe, "Tinker on the Roof," *Tikkun*, Vol. 3, No. 5, Sept.–Oct. 1988; "Repentance," *Cineaste*, Vol. XVI, No. 3, 1988; and *"Glasnost* in Soviet Cinema," *Cineaste*, Vol. XVI, No. 2, 1987–88, pp. 28–33.
3. *The Washington Post*, May 25, 1990, p. D2.
4. Vasily Grossman, *Forever Flowing* (New York: Harper & Row, 1972), p. 203.
5. Artyom Borovik, "Diary of a Reporter," *Ogonek*, Nos. 28, 29, 30, Jul. 1987.
6. *Ibid.*
7. Vitaly Korotich, conversation with the author, June 7, 1988.
8. *Izvestia Ts.K. KPSS*, No. 1, 1989, pp. 138–39.
9. Vasily Selyunin, "Sources," *Novy Mir*, No. 5, May 1988, p. 169.
10. Aleksandr Tsipko, "The Roots of Stalinism," *Nauka i Zhizn*, No. 11, Nov. 1988, in *Current Digest of the Soviet Press*, Vol. XLI, No. 10, Apr. 5, 1989, p. 3.
11. Eduard Shevardnadze, conversation with the author, Dec. 7, 1987.
12. Vasily Pichul, interview with the author, Apr. 29, 1989.
13. Arkady Ruderman, remarks at Yaroslavl Film Club, Sept. 10, 1989.
14. *Ibid.*
15. *Ibid.*, interview with Sherry Jones, Sept. 13, 1989.
16. *The New York Times*, June 30, 1988, p. A1.
17. Gorbachev, June 28, 1988, *Pravda*, June 29, 1988, p. 2.
18. *The New York Times*, June 30, 1988, p. A13.

8. STALINISM: THE OPEN WOUND

1. Andrei Smirnov, conversation with the author, Mar. 15, 1990.

2. Nina Soboleva, conversation with the author, Apr. 24, 1989.

3. Zenon Poznyak, interview with the author, Apr. 23, 1989.

4. *Ibid.*, Sept. 16, 1989.

5. *Ibid.*, Apr. 23, 1989.

6. Maya Klishtornaya, interview with the author, Sept. 17, 1989.

7. Poznyak, interview, Sept. 16, 1989.

8. *Ibid.*

9. *Ibid.*, Apr. 23, 1989.

10. *Ibid.*

11. *Ibid.*, Sept. 16, 1989.

12. *Ibid.*, Apr. 23, 1989.

13. Yuri Solomonov, conversation with the author, Apr. 27, 1989.

14. Andrei Borovik-Romanov, conversation with the author, June 2, 1988.

15. Soboleva, *op. cit.*

16. Alla Nikitina, conversation with the author, Apr. 21, 1989.

17. Genrikh Borovik, conversation with the author, June 6, 1988.

18. This polling was done through "Project Understanding," a Soviet-American effort jointly run by the Institute of Sociology, Moscow, and Marttila & Kiley, Inc., of Boston. John Marttila shared the results with the author, Apr. 14, 1989.

19. Vadim Andreyenkov, conversation with the author, Apr. 23, 1989.

20. Nina Andreyeva, "I Cannot Forsake Principles," *Sovetskaya Rossiya,* Mar. 13, 1988, in *CDSP,* Apr. 27, 1988, pp. 1, 3.

21. *Ibid.*, p. 4.

22. Valentin Chikin, interview with the author, Apr. 29, 1989.

23. For an excellent early account of this maneuvering, see Robert Kaiser, "Red Intrigue: How Gorbachev Outfoxed His Kremlin Rivals," *The Washington Post,* June 12, 1988, p. C1.

24. Solomonov, conversation with the author, Apr. 29, 1989.

25. Vitaly Korotich, conversation with the author, June 7, 1988.

26. Roy Medvedev, conversation with the author, Dec. 14, 1988.

27. "The Principles of Restructuring: The Revolutionary Nature of Thinking and Acting," *Pravda,* Apr. 5, 1988, p. 2, *CDSP,* Vol. XL, No. 14, May 4, 1988, pp. 1–5.

28. Vladimir Krushin, interview with the author, Sept. 23, 1989.

29. David Remnick, "Gorbachev's Furious Critic," *The Washington Post,* Jul. 28, 1989, p. C1.

30. Andreyeva and Krushin, interview with the author, Sept. 23, 1989.

31. Galina Klokova, interview with the author, Sept. 15, 1989.

32. Oleg Voloboyev, interview with the author, Sept. 15, 1989.

33. Roy Medvedev, author of the most authoritative Soviet study of Stalinism, *Let History Judge* (New York: Knopf, 1972), updated his work in 1989 and recently estimated the Stalinist death toll at forty million. See *Argumenty i Fakty,* No. 5, 1989.

34. Viktoriya Kulikova, interview with the author, May 3, 1989.

35. *Ibid.*, interview with Sherry Jones, Sept. 9, 1989.

36. Leonid Milgram, interview with the author, Sept. 26, 1989.

37. *Ibid.*, interview with Sherry Jones, Sept. 14, 1989.

38. Milgram and students, filmed by Foster Wiley, Sept. 28, 1989.

9. THE MEDIA VERSUS THE APPARAT

1. Bella Kurkova, interview with the author, Sept. 22, 1989.

2. *Ibid.*, conversation with the author, Apr. 4, 1989.

3. *Leningradskaya Pravda,* Apr. 6, 1989.

4. Kurkova, interview, Sept. 22, 1989.

5. Officially at that time, 800 rubles was $1,333, unofficially $133, more than three times a good worker's salary.

6. Kurkova, conversation with the author, Apr. 5, 1989.

7. Zoya Belyayeva, Sasha Krivonos, Natasha Sereva, Tatyana Smorodinskaya, interview with Sherry Jones and Louis Menashe, Sept. 20, 1989.

8. Aleksandr Nevzorov, conversation with the author, Sept. 22, 1989.

9. Tamara Maksimova and Vladimir Maksimov, conversation with the author, Apr. 4, 1989.

10. *Fifth Wheel* footage shown the author, Apr. 4–5, 1989.

11. Kurkova, interview, Sept. 22, 1989.

12. *Ibid.*

13. *Ibid.*

14. Viktor Senin and Kurkova, interview with the author, Sept. 22, 1989.

15. Aleksandr Melnikov, interview with the author, Sept. 5, 1989.

16. Gennady Metyakhin, conversations with the author, Sept. 3–5, 1989.

17. Aleksandr Tsvetkov, Valentina Kurikalova, Dmitri Pushkar, and Yevgeny Kovalev, conversations with the author, May 5 and 11, 1989.

18. Valentin Lazuktin, conversation with the author, Dec. 5, 1988.

19. See Ellen Mickiewicz, *Split Signals: Television and Politics in the Soviet Union* (New York: Oxford University Press, 1988), pp. 89–98.

20. "Dissident Yelena Bonner and the Road to Change," *The Washington Post,* Nov. 16, 1989, p. C16.

21. Anatoly Lysenko, conversation with the author, Nov. 30, 1988.

22. Dmitri Zakharov, conversation with the author, Mar. 15, 1990.

23. DDT, "Revolution," translation by Michele Berdy and Anne Lawrence.

24. *Vzglyad,* June 15, 1989, *FBIS,* June 22, 1989, pp. 73–74.

25. *Vzglyad* footage shown the author, Dec. 12, 1988.

26. *The New York Times,* May 17, 1989, p. A9.

27. Sasha Lyubimov, conversation with the author, Oct. 10, 1989.

28. Zakharov, conversation, Mar. 15, 1990.

29. Yegor Yakovlev, interview with the author, Sept. 27, 1989.

PART THREE: LOOKING FOR *PERESTROIKA*

1. Gorbachev, *Izbrannye rechy i stati* (Moscow: Politizdat, 1987), Vol. 2, p. 86.

2. *Ibid.,* speech to the Twenty-seventh Communist Party Congress, Feb. 26, 1986, *CDSP,* Mar. 26, 1986, p. 12.

10. THE CULTURE OF ENVY

1. Vladimir Pozner, conversation with the author, June 6, 1988.

2. Tatyana Tolstaya, interview with David Royle, Jul. 30, 1989.

3. Andrei Voznesensky, interview with the author, Mar. 13, 1990.

4. Pavel Bunich, conversation with the author, Nov. 2, 1989.

5. Vladimir Kabaidze, speech to Nineteenth All-Union Conference of the Communist Party of the Soviet Union, June 29, 1988, *CDSP,* Aug. 24, 1988, p. 22.

6. Tatyana Zaslavskaya, "The Novosibirsk Report," *Survey,* Vol. 28, No. 1 (Spring 1984), pp. 90ff.

7. Nikolai Shmelyov, "Advances and Debts," *Novy Mir,* June 1987, p. 145.

8. Pozner, *op. cit.*

9. Vladimir Yadov, conversation with the author, Apr. 11, 1989.

10. Igor Beshev, conversation with the author, Sept. 14, 1989.

11. *PlanEcon Report*, Vol. 6, Nos. 7, 8, Feb. 21, 1990, p. 13.

12. Nikolai Y. Petrakov, *Rabochaya Tribuna*, Apr. 24, 1990.

13. Otto Latsis, *Rabochaya Tribuna*, Mar. 27, 1990.

14. "Person Without a Job," *Pravda*, Oct. 31, 1989.

15. Andrei Smirnov, conversation with the author, Mar. 15, 1990.

16. *Ibid.*, Oct. 10, 1989.

17. Rair Simonyan, conversation with the author, Jul. 5, 1989.

18. Leonid Abalkin, "Not Sharing, but Earning," *Ogonek*, Oct. 7–14, 1989, pp. 1–2, 25–27, translated in *Joint Publications Research Service*, Nov. 17, 1989, p. 7.

19. Aleksandr Yakovlev, interview with the author, Oct. 9, 1989.

20. Vladimir Mayakovsky, *Vladimir Ilyich Lenin* (Moscow: Sovetskaya Rossiya, 1981), pp. 42–43.

21. Aleksandr Kuzmin, conversation with the author, Apr. 26, 1989.

22. Galya Zhirnova, conversation with the author, Sept. 11, 1989.

23. Volodya Konoplanikov, conversation with the author, Sept. 12, 1989.

24. Roy Medvedev, *On Stalin and Stalinism* (Oxford: Oxford University Press, 1973), p. 190.

25. See Geroid Tanquary Robinson, *Rural Russia Under the Old Regime* (Berkeley: University of California Press, 1969), pp. 10–11, 64–75, 117–28.

26. Felicity Barringer, Chautauqua at Pitt: The Fifth General Chautauqua Conference on U.S. and Soviet Relations, 1989, Oct. 30, 1989.

27. Dmitri Zakharov, conversation with the author, Mar. 15, 1990.

28. Anatoly Sobchak, conversation with the author, Sept. 23, 1989.

29. Pozner, conversation with the author, Sept. 30, 1989.

30. Nikolai Shmelyov, speech to Third Congress of People's Deputies, Mar. 12, 1990, *FBIS*, Mar. 14, 1990, p. 74.

31. *Ibid.*, "New Anxieties," *Novy Mir*, Apr. 1988, p. 175.

32. Mikhail Gorbachev, speech in Sverdlovsk, Apr. 26, 1990, *Radio Liberty Daily Report*, Apr. 27, 1990, p. 2.

11. WHY THE RELUCTANT FARMERS?

1. Gorbachev, speech to Fourth All-Union Congress of Collective Farmers, Mar. 23, 1988, *CDSP*, Apr. 20, 1988, p. 1.

2. Dmitri Starodubtsev, interview with the author, Sept. 14, 1989.

3. Doak Barnett, conversation with the author, May 2, 1990.

4. Alec Nove, *An Economic History of the U.S.S.R.*, rev. ed. (Middlesex, England: Penguin, 1976), p. 106.

5. Gavril Popov, *Upravleniye Ekonomikoi—Ekonomicheskiye Metody* (Moscow: Ekonomika, 1985), p. 280.

6. See pp. 11, 14, 32, and 33, *Sel'skokhozaistvennoye Provisvodtsvo v Lichnikh Podsobnikh Khozaistvakh Naseleniya* (Moscow, Goskomstat, 1989).

7. *The New York Times*, Mar. 16, 1989, pp. A1, A6.

8. Zhores Medvedev, *Soviet Agriculture* (New York: W. W. Norton, 1987), p. 403.

9. Gorbachev, speech to Twenty-seventh Communist Party Congress, Feb. 25, 1986, *CDSP*, Mar. 26, 1988, p. 15.

10. V. Semyonov, "Ukrepleniye Ekonomiki Kolkhozov i Sovkhozov," *Finansy SSSR*, No. 9, 1985, pp. 3–11.

11. *Ibid.*, *Prodovolstvennaia Programmai Finansy* (Moscow, 1985), p. 113.

12. Georgy Shakhnazarov, conversation with the author, Dec. 15, 1988.

13. Gorbachev, speech to Fourth All-Union Congress of Collective Farmers, *op. cit.*

14. Vladimir Tikhonov, interview with the author, Sept. 29, 1989.

15. *Ibid.*
16. Abel Aganbegyan, conversation with the author, Feb. 27, 1988.
17. M. Vagin, *Sovetskaya Rossiya*, Sept. 29, 1987.
18. Valery N. Romanov, conversation with the author, Jul. 29, 1989.
19. Yevgeny Sokolov, "A Vexatious Fact—Lack of Realism," *Izvestia*, Jan. 28, 1990, p. 2.
20. Zhores Medvedev, *op. cit.*, pp. 16, 42–55, 73–81.
21. V. I. Lenin, *Collected Works* (Moscow: Progress Publishers, 1965), Vol. XXX, p. 113.
22. Roy Medvedev, *Let History Judge*, rev. ed. (New York: Columbia University Press, 1989), p. 230.
23. Nikolai Shmelyov, "New Anxieties," *Novy Mir*, Apr. 1988, p. 165.
24. Nikolai Sivkov, "This Is My Job," *Moscow News*, Jan. 21–28, 1990, p. 6.
25. "To Sivkov's Farmstead," *Izvestia*, Jan. 14, 1990.
26. Semyon Sharetsky, *Sovetskaya Rossiya*, Dec. 30, 1989, p. 6.
27. Shmelyov, "Advances and Debts," *Novy Mir*, June 1987, p. 147.
28. Gorbachev, *Pravda*, June 29, 1989, p. 2.
29. *Ibid.*, Oct. 14, 1988, p. 2.
30. *Ibid.*, *Krasnaya Zvezda*, Feb. 24, 1989, pp. 1–3, *FBIS*, Feb. 24, 1989, p. 59.
31. Yegor Ligachev, *Pravda*, Mar. 3, 1989, p. 2.
32. *The Washington Post*, Mar. 13, 1989, p. A26.
33. *Ibid.*, Mar. 17, 1989, p. A1.
34. Vladimir Dorofeyev, interview with the author, Sept. 13, 1989.
35. Starodubtsev, conversation with the author, May 4, 1989.
36. Lydiya Popova and Starodubtsev, interview with the author, Sept. 13, 1989.
37. Aleksandr F. Orlov, interview with the author, Sept. 13, 1989.
38. Orlov family, group interview with the author, Sept. 13, 1989.
39. Starodubtsev, interview, Sept. 14, 1989.
40. Gorbachev, speech to Fourth All-Union Congress of Collective Farmers, *op. cit.*, p. 6.
41. See V. Bashmachnikov, in group discussion, "The Land Awaits a Proprietor: How We See the Law on Leasing," *Izvestia*, Feb. 14, 1990, p. 1.
42. "The Owner and the Land: The Population's Attitude Toward the Draft Law on Land," *Izvestia*, Feb. 28, 1990, p. 2.
43. Aleksandr P. Vladislavlev, *Moscow Domestic Service*, Apr. 5, 1990, *FBIS*, Apr. 19, 1990, p. 60.

12. THE CAPTIVE CAPTAINS OF SOVIET INDUSTRY

1. Worker, Uralmash Machine Works, interview with Marian Marzynski, Sept. 7, 1989.
2. Mikhail Gorbachev, "On the Party's Tasks in the Fundamental Restructuring of Economic Management," speech to Central Committee plenum, June 25, 1987 (Moscow: Novosti Press Agency Publishing House, 1987), p. 42.
3. President Tito, in Seweryn Bialer, *Inside Gorbachev's Russia* (Boulder, Colo.: Westview Press, 1989), p. 218.
4. Nikolai Shmelyov and Vladimir Popov, *The Turning Point: Revitalizing the Soviet Economy* (New York: Doubleday, 1989), p. 114.
5. "The Uralmash Incident," *Izvestia*, Mar. 23, 1988, p. 3.
6. "A Matter of Chance: What Uralmash Achieved," *Izvestia*, Dec. 15, 1988, p. 2.
7. Igor Stroganov, conversation with the author, Jul. 26, 1989.
8. Gorbachev, *Perestroika* (New York: Harper & Row, 1987), p. 33.
9. *Ibid.*, p. 23.
10. Gorbachev, "On the Party's Tasks," *op. cit.*, p. 47.
11. *Ibid.*, p. 50.
12. Nikolai I. Ryzhkov, *Pravda*, June 30, 1987.

13. Gorbachev, speech in Murmansk, Oct. 1, 1987, *FBIS,* Oct. 2, 1987, p. 29.

14. Stefan Pachikov, conversation with the author, Apr. 18, 1989.

15. Shmelyov, "Advances and Debts," *Novy Mir,* June 1987, p. 144.

16. See Alec Nove, "The Problems of *Perestroika,"* *Dissent,* Vol. 36, No. 4, Fall 1989, p. 463.

17. Shmelyov, "Advances and Debts," *op. cit.*

18. Gorbachev, "On the Party's Tasks," *op. cit.,* p. 46.

19. *Ibid.,* p. 45.

20. *Ibid.,* p. 49.

21. Ryzhkov, quoted in Gertrude E. Schroeder, "Anatomy of Gorbachev's Economic Reform," *Soviet Economy,* Vol. 3, No. 3, Jul.–Sept. 1987, p. 226.

22. Gorbachev, "On the Party's Tasks," *op. cit.,* p. 51.

23. For an excellent analysis of the role and views of Prime Minister Nikolai Ryzhkov, see Anders Aslund, *Gorbachev's Struggle for Economic Reform* (Ithaca, N.Y.: Cornell University Press, 1989), pp. 39–43, 62.

24. Zhores Medvedev, *Nuclear Disaster in the Urals* (New York: W. W. Norton, 1979), pp. 4, 16, 22, 164–69.

25. Stroganov, interview with the author, Sept. 8, 1989.

26. Uralmash exit interview, filmed by Jean de Segonzac, Sept. 7, 1989.

27. Georgy Pospelov, conversation with the author, Sept. 7, 1989.

28. Stroganov and working woman, interview with the author, Sept. 9, 1989.

29. Stroganov, interview, Sept. 8, 1989.

30. *Ibid.,* conversation with the author, Jul. 27, 1989.

31. *Ibid.,* interview with the author, Sept. 7, 1989.

32. *Ibid.,* conversation, Jul. 26, 1989.

33. *Ibid.,* conversation with the author, Sept. 8, 1989.

34. *Ibid.,* interview, Sept. 7, 1989.

35. Vladislav Grammatin, Uralmash staff meeting, filmed by Jean de Segonzac, Sept. 8, 1989.

36. Anatoly Osintsev, conversations with the author, Jul. 27 and Sept. 8, 1989.

37. Stroganov, conversation with the author, Sept. 9, 1989.

38. *Ibid.,* conversation with the author, Sept. 7, 1989.

39. Leonid Abalkin, interview with the author, Sept. 21, 1989.

40. *Ibid.,* conversation with the author, Jul. 7, 1989.

41. Grigory Yarlinsky, Gennady Melikyan, Yuri Ivanovich, discussion with Abalkin, Sept. 25, 1989.

42. Abalkin, interview, Sept. 21, 1989.

43. Anders Aslund, "Gorbachev: Governing on the Razor's Edge," *The Washington Post,* Jan. 28, 1990, p. C1.

44. Bill Keller, "How Gorbachev Rejected Plan to 'Shock Treat' the Economy," *The New York Times,* May 14, 1990, p. A1.

45. Gorbachev, speech at Nizhny Tagil, Apr. 27, 1990, *FBIS,* Apr. 30, 1990, p. 114.

46. *Ibid.,* speech in Sverdlovsk, Apr. 26, 1990, *FBIS,* Apr. 30, 1990, p. 117.

47. *Ibid.,* quoted by Tass, May 23, 1990, *FBIS,* May 24, 1990, p. 101.

48. Ryzhkov, speech to the Supreme Soviet, May 24, 1990, *FBIS,* May 25, 1990, pp. 37–57.

49. Stanislav Shatalin and Vladen Martynov, press conference, Washington, D.C., June 1, 1990.

50. Yuri Prokofyev, interview with the author, June 27, 1990.

51. Pavel Bunich, in *Izvestia,* May 29, 1990, *FBIS,* May 31, 1990, p. 57.

13. THE NEW ENTREPRENEURS: TRYING OUT CAPITALISM

1. Oleg Smirnoff, conversation with the author, Apr. 16, 1989.

2. Gleb Orlikhovsky, conversation with the author, Mar. 3, 1990.

3. Aleksandr Yakovlev, interview with the author, Oct. 9, 1989.

4. The Law on Individual Labor Activity, enacted Nov. 19, 1986, was the first general legislation,

later followed by individual decrees on certain areas. See Anders Aslund, *Gorbachev's Struggle for Economic Reform* (Ithaca, N.Y.: Cornell University Press, 1989), pp. 153–54.

5. Gorbachev, speech at Fourth All-Union Congress of Collective Farmers, Mar. 23, 1988, *Pravda*, Mar. 24, 1988, pp. 1–3.

6. *Ibid.*, *CDSP*, Apr. 20, 1988, p. 4.

7. See Aslund, *op. cit.*, pp. 163–67, and Anthony Jones and William Moskoff, "New Cooperatives in the U.S.S.R.," *Problems of Communism*, Nov.–Dec. 1989, p. 29.

8. Gorbachev, speech, March 23, 1988, *CDSP*, Apr. 20, 1988, p. 2.

9. See Alec Nove, *An Economic History of the U.S.S.R.*, rev. ed. (Middlesex, England: Penguin, 1982), pp. 83–92, 102–13.

10. Professor Grossman kindly shared with me findings from Gregory Grossman and Vladimir Treml, Berkeley-Duke Project on the Second Economy of the U.S.S.R., May 20, 1990.

11. Nikolai Shmelyov and Vladimir Popov, *The Turning Point: Revitalizing the Soviet Economy* (New York: Doubleday, 1989), p. 199.

12. *Ibid.* Also see articles in *Izvestia*, Aug. 18, 1985, and *Pravda*, Sept. 5, 1987.

13. Aleksandr Borin, "Podmena," *Literaturnaya Gazeta*, Jul. 15, 1987, p. 11.

14. Hedrick Smith, *The Russians*, rev. (New York: Ballantine Books, 1984), pp. 124–25.

15. *Ibid.*, pp. 125–30.

16. Konstantin Simis, *U.S.S.R.: The Corrupt Society* (New York: Simon and Schuster, 1982), pp. 86–87.

17. Abel Aganbegyan, conversation with the author, Apr. 12, 1989.

18. Sergei Vladov, conversation with the author, Dec. 18, 1989.

19. Igor Stroganov, conversation with the author, Jul. 26, 1989.

20. Stanislav Dailitko, conversations with the author, Jul. 26 and Sept. 6, 1989.

21. Aleksandr Smolensky, conversation with the author, Sept. 19, 1989.

22. Aleksandr Friedman, conversation with the author, Sept. 18, 1989.

23. Smolensky, conversation with the author, Sept. 18, 1989.

24. Valentin Pavlov and Leonid Abalkin, conversation with the author, Sept. 21, 1989.

25. Smolensky, conversation, Sept. 19, 1989.

26. Mark Masarsky, conversation with the author, Sept. 1, 1989.

27. *Ibid.*, Sept. 3, 1989.

28. Yuri Kaplan, conversation with the author, Sept. 3, 1989.

29. Aleksandr Bokhan and Masarsky, interview with the author, Sept. 19, 1989.

30. Masarsky, interview with the author, Sept. 19, 1989.

31. *Ibid.*, Sept. 20, 1989.

32. U.S.S.R. State Committee for Statistics, cited in "Cooperation-89," *Moscow News*, Apr. 1, 1990, p. 10.

33. "Hurdle Race," *Moscow News*, Apr. 1, 1990, p. 10.

34. *Ekonomika i Zhizn*, Jan. 1990, p. 11, *CDSP*, Vol. XLII, No. 3, 1990, p. 23.

35. "Cooperator's Profile," *Moscow News*, Dec. 26, 1989, No. 52, p. 12.

36. Vadim Kirichenko, chairman, State Committee for Statistics, *Moscow News*, Apr. 1, 1990.

37. Andrei Smirnov, conversation with the author, Mar. 15, 1990.

38. Tankred Golenpolsky, conversation with the author, Sept. 19, 1988.

39. *The New York Times*, Mar. 5, 1989, p. 3.

40. Yevgeny Chazov, interview with the author, Aug. 3, 1989.

41. "Hurdle Race," *Moscow News*, Apr. 1, 1990, p. 10.

42. Smirnoff, conversation, Apr. 16, 1989.

43. L. Kislinskaya, "Barrier Against Racketeering," *Sovetskaya Rossiya*, Jan. 26, 1989, p. 4.

44. "Cooperatives: Let Us Explain the System Again," *Izvestia*, Mar. 3, 1990, p. 2.

45. Leonid Dobrokhotov, conversation with the author, Dec. 2, 1988.

46. Vladimir Tikhonov, conversation with the author, Aug. 3, 1989.

47. "A Case Involving Millions," *Moscow News*, Mar. 5–12, 1989, p. 12; and *Trud*, June 13, 1989, p. 2.

48. Orlikhovsky, conversation, Mar. 3, 1990.

49. *Moscow News*, Oct. 1, 1989, p. 5.

50. *Ibid.*

51. Moscow television, Mar. 13, 1990, *FBIS*, Mar. 14, 1990, pp. 51–52.

52. Tikhonov, conversation with the author, Mar. 14, 1990.

53. *The New York Times*, Mar. 7, 1990, p. A1.

54. "Decree of the President of the U.S.S.R.: On New Approaches to the Solution of the Housing Problem in the Country and Measures for Their Practical Implementation," *Pravda*, May 20, 1990, p. 1.

55. *The New York Times*, May 21, 1990, p. A1.

56. Masarsky, conversation, Sept. 1, 1989.

57. Yakovlev, *op. cit.*

PART FOUR: THE EMPIRE TEARING APART

1. Gorbachev, speech to Russian Communist Party Congress, June 19, 1990, *FBIS*, June 20, 1990, p. 90.

14. UZBEKISTAN: "OUR LANGUAGE IS OUR HEART AND OUR SOUL"

1. Abdur Rahim Pulatov, interview with the author, Oct. 1, 1989.

2. Shukhrat Makhmudov, interview with the author, Oct. 5, 1989.

3. Pulatov, Birlik rally, Oct. 1, 1989.

4. Nuraly Kabul, conversation with the author, June 8, 1989.

5. Makhmudov, conversation with the author, Oct. 4, 1989.

6. Mohammed Salikh, conversation with the author, June 12, 1989.

7. Rafik Nishanov, *Pravda Vostoka*, June 17, 1989, p. 2.

8. William Fierman, *"Glasnost* in Practice: The Uzbek Experience," *Central Asian Survey*, Vol. 8, No. 2, 1989, p. 33.

9. Pulatov, interview, Oct. 1, 1989.

10. *Narodnoye khozaistvo SSSR* (Moscow: Financy i statistiki, 1989), pp. 19, 26.

11. Hedrick Smith, "Islam Retaining a Strong Grip on Uzbeks," *The New York Times*, Nov. 22, 1972, p. 8.

12. Bogdan Nahaylo and Victor Swoboda, *Soviet Disunion: A History of the Nationalities Problem in the U.S.S.R.* (New York: Free Press, 1990), p. 217.

13. Fierman, *op.cit.*

14. Telman Gdlyan, interview with the author, Oct. 7, 1989.

15. "Verdict Announced, Problems Remain," *Moscow News*, Jan. 15–22, 1989, p. 5.

16. Gdlyan, *op. cit.*

17. James Critchlow, "Further Repercussions of 'The Uzbek Affair,'" *Radio Liberty Report on the USSR*, May 4, 1990, p. 1.

18. *Ibid.*, p. 20.

19. Pulatov, interview, Oct. 1, 1989.

20. Islam Karimov, *Pravda*, Sept. 22, 1989.

21. Salikh, conversation, June 12, 1989.

22. "Person Without a Job," *Pravda*, Oct. 31, 1989, p. 2.

23. Martin Walker, *The Harper Independent Traveler: The Soviet Union* (New York: Harper & Row, 1989), p. 270.

24. Timur Pulatov, conversation with the author, June 8, 1989.

25. Esther Fein, "In Soviet Asia Backwater, Infancy's a Rite of Survival," *The New York Times*, Aug. 14, 1989, pp. A1, A6.

26. Bakhtiar Normetov, conversation with the author, June 10, 1989.

27. "Sick People—72%; That's What a Medical Study Showed," *Khorezmskaya Pravda*, May 23, 1989, p. 3; see also "Let's Talk About Health," *Khorezmskaya Pravda*, May 18, 1989, p. 3.

28. Makhmudov, interview, Oct. 5, 1989.

29. *Ibid.*, Oct. 2, 1989.

30. *Ibid.*, Oct, 5, 1989.

31. *Ibid.*, field dialogue filmed by Jean de Segonzac, Oct. 15, 1989.

32. Raizeta Makhmudova, interview with the author, Oct. 2, 1989.

33. Shukhrat Makhmudov and Raizeta Makhmudova, interview with the author, Oct. 3, 1989.

34. Smith, *op. cit.*

35. Nahaylo and Swoboda, *op. cit.*, pp. 215–16.

36. Pulatov, interview, Oct. 1, 1989.

37. Galina Kozlovskaya, interview with the author, Oct. 1, 1989.

38. Kurambai Matrizayev, conversation with the author, June 11, 1989.

39. Akhurnjan Safarov, conversation with the author, Oct. 3, 1989.

40. Fierman, *op. cit.*, p. 13.

41. Imam Mustafakhan Melikov, sermon, Samarkand mosque, Oct. 5, 1989.

42. Haj Mukhtar Abdulayev, interview with the author, Oct. 3, 1989.

43. "Islam Regains Its Voice," *Time*, Apr. 10, 1989, p. 99.

44. Melikov, interview with the author, Oct. 5, 1989; Abdulayev, *op. cit.*

45. Salikh and Dadhon Khassan, conversation with the author, Oct. 2, 1989.

46. Shukhrat Makhmudov, conversation with the author, Oct. 4, 1989.

47. Salikh, conversation, Oct. 2, 1989.

48. *Pravda Vostoka*, Mar. 29, 1990, pp. 2–3.

49. Francis X. Clines, "Defiance of Kremlin's Control Is Accelerating in Soviet Asia," *The New York Times*, June 29, 1990, pp. A1, A6.

50. Anvar Shakirov, conversation with the author, Oct. 4, 1989.

51. Raizeta Makhmudova, conversation with the author, May 14, 1990.

15. ARMENIA AND AZERBAIJAN: A SOVIET LEBANON

1. Rufat Novrozov, interview with the author, Mar. 7, 1990.

2. Ashot Manucharyan, speech in Yerevan, Jul. 12, 1989.

3. Ashot Bleyan, conversation with the author, June 17, 1989.

4. Manucharyan, conversation with the author, June 18, 1989.

5. *Ibid.*, interview with the author, Jul. 12, 1989.

6. Ashot and Bibishan Manucharyan, interview with Oren Jacoby, Jul. 11, 1989.

7. Ashot Manucharyan, interview, Jul. 12, 1989.

8. *Ibid.*, conversation, June 18, 1989.

9. Manucharyan, filmed by Oren Jacoby, June 18, 1989.

10. Hedrick Smith, "Soviet Armenian Church Is Confident and Strong," *The New York Times*, Dec. 18, 1971, p. 6.

11. Vasgen II, interview with the author, Jul. 9, 1989.

12. Novrozov, *op. cit.*

13. Mary Matossian, "The Armenians," *Problems of Communism*, Vol. XVI, No. 5, Sept.–Oct. 1967, p. 68.

14. *The Sunday Times* (London), Feb. 28, 1988, p. 1.

15. Afrend Dezhdamerov, Azerbaijan Communist Party Central Committee, interview with the author, Jul. 13, 1989.

16. Sumgait Deputy Mayor Ali Sasanov and Eldar Ismailov, third city Party secretary, interview with the author, Jul. 13, 1989.

17. Irina Melkunyan, conversation with the author, June 20, 1989.

18. Asya Arakelyan, interview with the author, Jul. 9, 1989.

19. Armen Oganesyan, interview with the author, Jul. 9, 1989.

20. Guliyev family, interview with the author, Jul. 15, 1989.

21. Suren Arutunyan, interview with the author, Jul. 10, 1989.

22. *Ibid.*, June 18, 1989.

23. Arutunyan and son, interview with the author, Jul. 10, 1989.

24. Arutunyan, interview, June 18, 1989.

25. Ashot Manucharyan, speech in Yerevan, *op. cit.*

26. Leonid Dobrokhotov, conversation with the author, Sept. 25, 1989.

27. "Vokrug ruzhya . . . ," *Kazakhstanskaya Pravda*, Sept. 18, 1987.

28. Paul Goble, conversations with the author, Oct. 18, 1989, and Nov. 17, 1989.

29. Stephen Sestanovich, "Soviet Chaos: Gunplay," *The Washington Post*, Jul. 23, 1989, p. C1.

30. Aydin Ambertov, Azerbaijani Popular Front spokesman, conversation with the author, Jul. 14, 1989.

31. Mirza Michaeli and William Reese, "The Popular Front in Azerbaijan and Its Program," *Radio Liberty Report on the USSR*, Aug. 25, 1989, p. 30.

32. *The Washington Post*, Sept. 3, 1989, p. A22.

33. *Argumenty i Fakty*, Oct. 1, 1989.

34. "Azerbaijanis End Strike, Let Supplies into Armenia," *The Washington Post*, Oct. 11, 1989, p. A34.

35. Bill Keller, "Nationalists in Azerbaijan Win Big Concessions from Party Chief," *The New York Times*, Oct. 12, 1989, p. A1.

36. Mikhail Gorbachev, speech to Communist Party Central Committee, Sept. 19, 1989, *FBIS*, Sept. 20, 1989, p. 38.

37. *The Washington Post*, Oct. 2, 1989, p. A23.

38. *Ibid.*, Jan. 21, 1990, p. A30.

39. *Izvestia*, Jan. 27, 1990, pp. 1–2.

40. See Elizabeth Fuller, "Gorbachev's Dilemma in Azerbaijan," *RL Report on the USSR*, Feb. 2, 1990, p. 14.

41. Novrozov, *op. cit.*

42. Keller, "Did Moscow Incite Azerbaijanis? Some See a Plot," *The New York Times*, Feb. 19, 1990, p. A8.

43. Novrozov, *op. cit.*

44. *The Washington Post*, May 29, 1990, p. A17.

45. *Ibid.*, Jul. 31, 1990, p. A17.

46. Arutunyan, conversation with the author, Jul. 5, 1990.

47. *The New York Times*, Aug. 10, 1990, p. A3.

16. LITHUANIA: BREAKING THE TABOO OF SECESSION

1. Vytautas Landsbergis, interview with the author, Jul. 24, 1989.

2. Esther Fein, "Gorbachev Urges Lithuania to Stay with Soviet Union," *The New York Times*, Jan. 13, 1990, p. A1; and David Remnick, "Gorbachev Urges Lithuanians Not to Press for Independence," *The Washington Post*, Jan. 12, 1990, p. A1.

3. Lithuanian voters, interviews with the author filmed by Maryse Alberti, Mar. 26–27, 1989.

4. Arvydas Juozaitis, conversation with the author, Mar. 26, 1989.

5. Map, "Ethnicity and Political Boundaries in the Soviet Union," Office of the Geographer, U.S. Department of State, based on preliminary data from 1989 U.S.S.R. census.

6. Algirdas Brazauskas, speech in Kaunas, Feb. 16, 1989, *FBIS*, Feb. 17, 1989, p. 63.

7. Hedrick Smith, "Lithuania Warns of Religious Backlash," *The New York Times*, Aug. 15, 1972, p. 5.

8. Romouldas Ozolas, interview with the author, Mar. 27, 1989.

9. *Ibid.*, conversation with the author, June 21, 1989.

10. *Ibid.*, interview with the author, Jul. 21, 1989.

11. *Ibid.*

12. Brazauskas, interview with the author, Mar. 27, 1989.

13. Ozolas, interview, Mar. 27, 1989.

14. Fein, "Lithuanian to the Core," *The New York Times*, Mar. 26, 1990, p. A8.

15. Landsbergis, conversation with the author, Jul. 23, 1989.

16. Michael Dobbs, "Unlikely Revolutionary Leads Lithuanian Drive," *The Washington Post*, May 7, 1990, p. A13.

17. Justas Paleckis, conversation with the author, Mar. 10, 1990.

18. Landsbergis, interview, Jul. 24, 1989.

19. Brazauskas, interview with the author, Jul. 22, 1989.

20. The Russian populations are drawn from the 1989 census; see *Nationalny sostav naceleniye*, State Committee for Statistics (Moscow: Information Publications Center, 1989).

21. *The New York Times*, Mar. 15, 1989, p. A10.

22. Mayor Rimantas Kumbis, conversation with the author, June 22, 1989.

23. Bill Keller, "Public Mistrust Curbs Soviet Nuclear Power Efforts," *The New York Times*, Oct. 12, 1988, p. A1.

24. Anatoly Khromchenko, interview with the author, Jul. 24, 1989.

25. Aleksandr Zharik and Valery Antipyevt, interview with Oren Jacoby, Jul. 24, 1989.

26. *Ibid.*

27. *Pravda*, Aug. 18, 1989, pp. 1–2.

28. *The Washington Post*, Sept. 30, 1989, p. A16.

29. *Pravda*, Aug. 27, 1989, p. 1.

30. *The New York Times*, Aug. 28, 1989, p. A1.

31. Algimantas Zukas, conversation with the author, June 24, 1989.

32. Brazauskas, conversation with the author, Jul. 24, 1989.

33. Pavel Bunich, conversation with the author, Nov. 1, 1989.

34. *FBIS*, Sept. 15, 1989, p. 26.

35. Gorbachev, *FBIS*, Sept. 19, 1989, p. 38.

36. Brazauskas, interview with the author, Mar. 10, 1990.

37. Fein, "Gorbachev Urges Lithuania to Stay with Soviet Union," *The New York Times*, Jan. 13, 1990, p. A1; and Remnick, "Gorbachev Urges Lithuanians Not to Press for Independence," *The Washington Post*, Jan. 12, 1990, p. A1.

38. Keller, "Buying Time in Lithuania," *The New York Times*, Jan. 13, 1990, p. A1.

39. Ozolas, interview with the author, Mar. 9, 1990.

40. Brazauskas, speech to Vilnius Communist Party, Mar. 10, 1990.

41. Brazauskas, interview, Mar. 10, 1990.

42. Kazimiera Prunskiene, meeting with Washington reporters, May 3, 1990.

43. *The New York Times*, June 13, 1990, p. A18; and *The Washington Post*, June 13, 1990, p. A1.

44. *The New York Times*, June 30, 1990, p. A1.

45. *The Washington Post*, Jul. 29, 1990, p. A19.

17. BACKLASH IN MOTHER RUSSIA

1. Valentin Rasputin, speech to Congress of People's Deputies, June 6, 1989, *FBIS*, Aug. 9, 1989, p. 27.

2. Stanislav Kunyayev, conversation with the author, Sept. 15, 1989.

3. Yuri Prokofyev, interview with the author, Oct. 7, 1989.

4. Rasputin, *op. cit.*

5. *Ibid.*, pp. 27–28.

6. Vladimir Soloukhin and Rosa Soloukhina, conversation with the author, Jul. 18, 1989.

7. Soloukhin, interview with the author, Jul. 18, 1989.

8. See Aleksandr Solzhenitsyn, "Letter to the Supreme Leaders," in Hedrick Smith, *The Russians* (New York: Ballantine Books, 1984), pp. 568–69.

9. Dmitri Likhachev, *Le Nouvel Observateur*, May 8–14, 1987, quoted in John B. Dunlop, "The Contemporary Russian Nationalist Spectrum," *Radio Liberty Research Bulletin, Russian Nationalism Today*, Dec. 19, 1988, p. 4.

10. See Alexander Yanov, "Russian Nationalism as the Ideology of Counterreform," in *RL Research Bulletin, Russian Nationalism Today*, Dec. 19, 1988, pp. 43ff.

11. Nikolai Berdyayev, "Man's Fate in the Modern World," *Novy Mir*, No. 1, 1989.

12. Metropolitan Filaret, interview with the author, Jul. 19, 1989.

13. Vladimir Galitsky, interview with the author, Jul. 17, 1989.

14. Aleksandr Trefimov, interview with the author, Jan. 17, 1989.

15. Alex Alexiev, "Life-Death Struggle for the Soul and Center of Soviet Union," *Los Angeles Times*, Mar. 25, 1990, p. M2.

16. See Bill Keller, "Russian Nationalists: Yearning for an Iron Hand," *The New York Times Magazine*, Jan. 28, 1990, p. 50.

17. Aleksandr I. Solzhenitsyn, *Letter to the Supreme Leaders* (New York: Harper & Row, 1974).

18. Kunyayev, *op. cit.*

19. Vasily Belov, speech in Moscow, Sept. 28, 1989, filmed by Foster Wiley.

20. Sergei Vikulov, interview with the author, Apr. 26, 1989.

21. Rasputin, *op. cit.*, p. 26.

22. Julia Wishnevsky, *"Nash Sovremennik* Provides Focus for 'Opposition Party,' " *Radio Liberty Report on the USSR*, Jan. 20, 1989, pp. 1–3.

23. Even after October 1988, when Vadim Medvedev became the Politburo's nominal chief for press affairs, Korotich told me that he maintained close and regular contact with Yakovlev; other liberals made it clear that Yakovlev was their main protector in the Politburo.

24. Aleksandr Yakovlev, *Literaturnaya Gazeta*, Nov. 15, 1972; and the main rebuttal to Andreyeva in *Pravda*, Apr. 5, 1988, p. 2. Yakovlev subsequently identified himself as the author of the *Pravda* editorial.

25. Yegor Ligachev, quoted in John Dunlop, "Soviet Cultural Politics," *Problems of Communism*, Nov.–Dec. 1987, pp. 51–52.

26. Roman Szporluk, in "Dilemmas of Russian Nationalism," *Problems of Communism*, Jul.–Aug. 1989, pp. 15–35, divides Russian nationalists into two groups: "nation-builders," eager to restore Russia and willing to tolerate separatism among other nationalities, and "empire-savers," determined to hold on to "all of Russia," which they define as the territory of the U.S.S.R.

27. Kunyayev, conversation with the author, Sept. 12, 1989.

28. Rasputin, quoted in Keller, "Russian Nationalists," *op cit.*, p. 48.

29. Igor Shafarevich, "Russophobia," *Nash Sovremennik*, June 1989, pp. 167–92, *CDSP*, Vol. XLI, No. 46, pp. 16–19.

30. *Literaturnaya Rossiya*, Dec. 1, 1989, pp. 2–13.

31. Kunyayev, quoted in *The New York Times*, Apr. 18, 1990, p. A10.

32. Darrell P. Hammer, *"Glasnost* and 'The Russian Idea,' " *RL Research Bulletin, Russian Nationalism Today*, Dec. 19, 1988, pp. 14–15.

33. Dmitri Vasiliyev, interview with the author, Jul. 20, 1990.

34. "Gorbachev's Dead Rival," *The Washington Post*, May 17, 1988, p. A18.

35. Vasiliyev, Moscow television, Nov. 18, 1989, *Radio Free Europe/Radio Liberty Daily Report*, Nov. 27, 1989, p. 7.

36. Vitaly Korotich, conversation with the author, Jan. 15, 1989.

37. Sasha Kuprin, conversations with the author, Jul. 7 and 19, 1989.

38. *Komsomolskaya Pravda*, Jan. 21, 1990; *RFE/RL Daily Report*, Jan. 26, 1990, p. 6.

39. Vasiliyev, interview, *Moscow News*, Nov. 7, 1988, p. 4.
40. KGB Major General Aleksandr Karbainov, quoted in *RFE/RL Daily Report*, Feb. 20, 1990, p. 5.
41. Likhachev, interview with the author, Mar. 4, 1990.
42. Yakovlev, interview with the author, Oct. 9, 1989.
43. Conversations at Central Committee with Nikolai Shishlin and Leonid Dobrokhotov, Sept. 1989, and Anatoly Afanasyev, Moscow Party Committee, Sept. 1989.
44. *The Washington Post*, Nov. 23, 1989, p. A23.
45. Gorbachev, speech to Communist Party plenum, Sept. 19, 1989, *FBIS*, Sept. 20, 1989, p. 32.
46. *The New York Times*, Feb. 24, 1990, p. A6; *The Washington Post*, Feb. 24, 1990, p. A24.
47. *The New York Times*, Mar. 25, 1990, p. 16.
48. Gorbachev, speech, May 23, 1990, *FBIS*, May 24, 1990, p. 105.
49. *The Washington Post*, June 24, 1990, p. A1.

18. GRASS-ROOTS ACTIVISM: REINVENTING POLITICS

1. Gorbachev, speech to Nineteenth Communist Party Conference, June 28, 1988, *Pravda*, June 29, 1988, p. 2.
2. Viktor Zakharov, interview with the author, Mar. 23, 1989.
3. Leonid Slychkov, conversation with the author, May 27, 1989.
4. Larissa Kholina, Rita Pilenkova, and Valeriya Savchenko, interview with the author, Mar. 25, 1989.
5. Nikolai Shishlin, conversation with the author, May 26, 1989.
6. Kholina, Pilenkova, and Savchenko, interview with the author, May 27, 1989.
7. Bishop Amvrosi, interview with the author, May 27, 1989.
8. Father Amvrosi, interview with the author, May 28, 1989.
9. Konstantin Kharchev, interview, *Ogonek*, No. 44, 1989, pp. 17–21.
10. Anatoly Golovkov, interview with Martin Smith, Sept. 26, 1989.
11. See David K. Shipler, "Between Dictatorship and Anarchy," *The New Yorker*, June 25, 1990, p. 43.
12. Vladimir Pozner, interview with the author, June 6, 1988.
13. S. Frederick Starr, "Party Animals," *The New Republic*, June 26, 1989, p. 19.
14. *Pravda*, Feb. 5, 1988, *FBIS*, Feb. 12, 1988, p. 59.
15. Viktor Chebrikov, speech in Kishinev, Moldavia, Feb. 10, 1989, *Pravda*, Feb. 11, 1989, p. 2.
16. Andrei Martinov, delivering petition to Red Guard District Council, Apr. 26, 1989.
17. Yuri Prokofyev, interview with the author, Oct. 7, 1989.
18. Tatyana Sivilna, report to Red Guard District Soviet, Apr. 26, 1989.
19. Nina Shchedrina, interview with the author, Apr. 2, 1989.
20. *Ibid.*, interview with Martin Smith, Sept. 26, 1989.
21. Shchedrina, on *Good Evening, Moscow*, Jul. 29, 1989.
22. Yevgeny Pavlov and Nikolai Pilyayev, interview with the author, Sept. 28, 1989.
23. Sergei Druganov, Haik Zulumyan, Shchedrina, and others, Brateyovo Self-governing Committee, Mar. 23, 1989.
24. Red Guard District Council session, Apr. 26, 1989.
25. Pavlov, interview, Sept. 28, 1989.
26. See D. J. Peterson, "A Wave of Environmentalism Shakes the Soviet Union," *Radio Liberty Report on the USSR*, June 22, 1990, p. 8.
27. *Ibid.*; David Marples, "Growing Influence of Antinuclear Movement in Ukraine," *RL Report on the USSR*, June 22, 1990, p. 18; and Bill Keller, "Public Mistrust Curbs Soviet Nuclear Power Efforts," *The New York Times*, Oct. 13, 1988, p. A1.
28. Prokofyev, *op. cit.*
29. Druganov, interview with Martin Smith, Sept. 27, 1989.

19. ELECTIONS: CROSSING OUT PARTY BOSSES

1. Gorbachev, campaigning in Kiev, Feb. 20, 1989, *FBIS*, Feb. 20, 1989.
2. Yelena Zelinskaya, conversation with the author, Apr. 5, 1989.
3. *Izvestia*, Apr. 26, 1989.
4. Gorbachev, *op. cit.*
5. Zelinskaya, *op. cit.*
6. *Pravda*, Apr. 20, 1989, *FBIS*, Apr. 21, 1989, p. 60.
7. *Leningradskaya Pravda*, Mar. 28, 1989, p. 1.
8. *Sovetsyaka Rossiya*, Apr. 6, 1989.
9. Boris Nikolsky, conversation with the author, Apr. 5, 1989.
10. Boris Yeltsin, *Against the Grain* (New York: Summit Books, 1990), pp. 177–204, especially p. 182.
11. Valentin Chikin, conversation with the author, Apr. 29, 1989.
12. Eddie Baranov, conversation with the author, Mar. 25, 1989.
13. Roy Medvedev, conversation with the author, Apr. 10, 1989.
14. *Izvestia*, Apr. 24, 1989, reported thirty-one *oblast* secretaries defeated, but Aleksandr Yakovlev, in an interview with the author, Oct. 9, 1989, put the figure at thirty-six.
15. Aleksandr Yakovlev, interview with the author, Oct. 7, 1989. Jerry F. Hough, "The Politics of Successful Economic Reform," *Soviet Economy*, Vol. 5, No. 1, Jan.–Mar. 1989, p. 14, reports that thirty-eight *obkom* first secretaries were defeated.
16. Gorbachev, Apr. 25, 1989, *Pravda*, Apr. 27, 1989, p. 1.
17. Boris Kurashvili, conversation with the author, Apr. 13, 1989.

20. CONGRESS: GENESIS OF AN OPPOSITION

1. *FBIS*, Jul. 31, 1989, p. 51.
2. Roy Medvedev, conversation with the author, May 25, 1989.
3. Boris Kagarlitsky, interview with Louis Menashe, May 21, 1989.
4. Andrei Sakharov, Congress, May 25, 1989, *FBIS*, June 13, 1989, pp. 4, 24.
5. Marju Lauristan, Congress, May 25, 1989, *FBIS*, June 13, 1989, p. 23.
6. Aleksandr Shchelkanov, Congress, May 25, 1989, *FBIS*, June 13, 1989, p. 24.
7. Leonid Sukhov, Moscow television, May 25, 1989.
8. Sergei Zvonov, Moscow television, May 25, 1989.
9. Gorbachev, Congress, Moscow television, May 25, 1989, *FBIS*, May 26, 1989, pp. 10, 18–20.
10. Aleksandr Obolensky, Congress, May 25, 1989, *FBIS*, June 13, 1989, p. 13.
11. Medvedev, *op. cit.*
12. Sergei Stankevich, interview with the author, May 25, 1989.
13. *Ibid.*, Sept. 28, 1989.
14. Boris Yeltsin, interview with the author, May 25, 1989.
15. Demonstration, filmed by Jean de Segonzac, sound man Scott Breindel, May 25, 1989.
16. Stankevich, interview, Sept. 28, 1989.
17. Stankevich and Gorbachev, Congress, Moscow television, May 26, 1989.
18. Stankevich, interview with the author, May 26, 1989.
19. *Ibid.*, Sept. 28, 1989.
20. Yuri Vlasov, Congress, May 31, 1989, *FBIS*, Jul. 5, 1989, pp. 33–34.
21. Tass, Apr. 4, 1989.
22. Yevgeny Yevtushenko, Congress, Moscow television, June 1, 1989, *FBIS*, Jul. 14, 1989, pp. 40–42.
23. Yuri Chernichenko, Congress, June 1, 1989, *FBIS*, Jul. 14, 1989, pp. 18–21.
24. Yuri Karyakin, Congress, June 2, 1989, *FBIS*, Jul. 26, 1989, p. 10.
25. T. V. Gankrelidze, Congress, Moscow television, May 30, 1989, *FBIS*, June 3, 1989, pp. 2–5.

26. Col. Gen. Igor Rodionov, Congress, Moscow television, May 30, 1989, *FBIS*, June 30, 1989, pp. 5–9.

27. Roald Sagdeyev, conversation with the author, June 2, 1989.

28. Sergei Chervonopisky, Congress, June 2, 1989, *FBIS*, Jul. 26, 1989, pp. 1–3.

29. Sergei Akhromeyev, Congress, June 2, 1989, *FBIS*, Jul. 26, 1989, p. 4.

30. Sakharov, Congress, June 2, 1989, *FBIS*, Jul. 26, 1989, pp. 3–4.

31. Sakharov and Gorbachev Congress, June 9, 1989, *FBIS*, Aug. 29, 1989, pp. 40–41.

32. Dmitri Yazov, Supreme Soviet, Jul. 5, 1989, *FBIS*, Jul. 6, 1989, p. 43.

33. Tass, Jul. 31, 1989.

34. *FBIS*, Jul. 31, 1989, p. 51.

35. *Ibid.*, pp. 51, 53.

36. Gorbachev, Supreme Soviet, Sept. 25, 1989, *FBIS*, Sept. 25, 1989, p. 49.

37. *Ibid.*, in *The Washington Post*, Oct. 19, 1989, pp. A1, A42.

38. Stankevich, conversation with the author, Sept. 30, 1989.

39. Gorbachev, Supreme Soviet, Oct. 23, 1989, *FBIS*, Oct. 24, 1989, pp. 40–41.

40. *Ibid.*, Supreme Soviet, Feb. 14, 1990, *The New York Times*, Feb. 15, 1990, p. A20.

41. *The Washington Post*, Feb. 28, 1990, p. A19.

42. *The New York Times*, Feb. 28, 1990, p. A1.

43. Stankevich, conversation with the author, Mar. 13, 1990.

44. For an excellent, detailed account, see David K. Shipler, "Between Dictatorship and Anarchy," *The New Yorker*, June 25, 1990, pp. 42–70.

45. Michael Dobbs, "Gorbachev's Tactics Confound Critics of His Proposals," *The Washington Post*, Mar. 14, 1990, p. A22.

46. Stankevich, conversation with the author, June 25, 1990.

47. Aleksandr Yakovlev, Congress, Moscow television, Mar. 14, 1990.

48. Dmitri Likhachev, Congress, Moscow television, Mar. 14, 1990.

49. Vladimir Tikhonov, conversation with the author, Mar. 14, 1990.

50. Likhachev, conversation with the author, Mar. 14, 1989.

21. COMMUNISM: "KNEE-DEEP IN GASOLINE"

1. Ratmir Bobovikov, *Pravda*, Apr. 27, 1989, p. 7.

2. Gorbachev, Moscow television, Jul. 12, 1989.

3. Communist Party Central Auditing Commission Report, Congress, Jul. 5, 1990, *FBIS*, Jul. 5, 1990, pp. 26, 31.

4. See Stephen F. Cohen and Katrina vanden Heuvel, *Voices of Glasnost* (New York: W. W. Norton, 1989), p. 31.

5. See Peter Reddaway, "The Threat to Gorbachev," *New York Review of Books*, Aug. 17, 1989, pp. 19ff.

6. Ivan Saly, *Vechirny Kyiv*, Apr. 10, 1989, *Radio Liberty Report on the USSR*, Aug. 4, 1989, p. 29.

7. Leonid Dobrokhotov, interview with the author, Sept. 28, 1989.

8. *Ibid.*, conversation with the author, Mar. 31, 1989.

9. Yuri Prokofyev, interview with the author, Oct. 7, 1989.

10. Valentin Mesyats, *Pravda*, Apr. 27, 1989, p. 7.

11. Ivan Polozkov, *Pravda*, Apr. 27, 1989, pp. 3–4.

12. Bobovikov, *op. cit.*

13. Abdur Rahman Vezirov, *Pravda*, Apr. 27, 1989, p. 6.

14. Vladimir Melnikov, *Pravda*, Apr. 27, 1989, p. 7.

15. Yuri Solovyov, *Pravda*, Apr. 27, 1989, p. 4.

16. Gorbachev, *Pravda*, Apr. 27, 1989, pp. 1–2, *FBIS*, Apr. 27, 1989, pp. 34–48.

17. See Jerry F. Hough, "The Politics of Successful Economic Reform," *Soviet Economy,* Vol. 5, No. 1, Jan.–Mar. 1989, p. 6.

18. Gorbachev, Moscow television, *op. cit.*

19. See Elizabeth Teague and Dawn Mann, "Gorbachev's Dual Role," *Problems of Communism,* Jan.–Feb. 1990, p. 5.

20. Prokofyev, interview, Oct. 7, 1989.

21. Lev Zaikov, Jul. 18, 1989, *Pravda,* Jul. 21, 1989, pp. 1–4.

22. Vitaly Vorotnikov, Jul. 18, 1989, *Pravda,* Jul. 21, 1989, p. 4.

23. Yegor Ligachev, Jul. 18, 1989, *FBIS,* Jul. 21, 1989, p. 63.

24. Leonid Bobykin, Jul. 18, 1989, *FBIS,* Jul. 21, 1989, pp. 58–59.

25. Nikolai Ryzhkov, Jul. 18, 1989, *FBIS,* Jul. 21, 1989, p. 67.

26. *Ibid.,* pp. 65–68.

27. Gorbachev, *Pravda,* Jul. 18, 1989, p. 1.

28. Gorbachev, in *Moscow News,* Oct. 29, 1989, p. 3.

29. Gorbachev, Congress of People's Deputies, June 9, 1989, *FBIS,* June 12, 1989, p. 53.

30. *FBIS,* Sept. 18, 1989, p. 72.

31. Vaino Väljas, *FBIS,* Sept. 15, 1989, p. 26.

32. Gorbachev, Moscow television, Sept. 9, 1989, *FBIS,* Sept. 11, 1989, pp. 27–29; *CDSP,* Oct. 4, 1989, p. 1.

33. *Ibid.,* p. 27.

34. Gorbachev, *Pravda,* Sept. 16, 1989, *FBIS,* Sept. 18, 1989, p. 39.

35. *Ibid.,* in Kiev, Sept. 28, 1989, *FBIS,* Sept. 29, 1989, pp. 52–53.

22. THE PARTY: LOSING POWER, LOSING PEOPLE

1. Ivan Polozkov, *FBIS,* Mar. 14, 1990, pp. 52, 65.

2. Gorbachev, Twenty-eighth Congress of the Communist Party of the Soviet Union, *The Washington Post,* Jul. 8, 1990, p. A24.

3. Yuri Prokofyev, interview with the author, June 27, 1990.

4. Andrei Sakharov, *FBIS,* Nov. 27, 1989, p. 80.

5. Gorbachev and Sakharov, Congress, Dec. 12, 1989, *FBIS,* Dec. 13, 1989, p. 55.

6. Gorbachev, *Pravda,* Dec. 1, 1989, pp. 1–5; *FBIS,* Dec. 11, 1989, p. 52.

7. *The Washington Post,* Jan. 14, 1990, p. A9; Jan 15, 1989, p. A1.

8. *Keesing's Contemporary Archives,* Dec. 9, 1977, p. 28,702.

9. Boris Gidaspov, Feb. 6, 1990, *FBIS,* Feb. 8, 1990, p. 87.

10. Valentin Mesyats, Feb. 6, 1990, *FBIS,* Feb. 6, 1990, p. 65.

11. Eduard Shevardnadze, Feb. 6, 1990, *FBIS,* Feb. 8, 1990, pp. 55–56.

12. Nikolai Ryzhkov, Feb. 5, 1990, *FBIS,* Feb. 8, 1990, p. 79.

13. *The New York Times,* Feb. 8, 1990, p. 1.

14. Gorbachev, *FBIS,* Feb. 6, 1990, p. 45.

15. *The New York Times,* Feb. 4, 1990, p. A21.

16. *The Washington Post,* Feb. 8, 1990, p. A1.

17. Gorbachev, Feb. 9, 1990, *FBIS,* Feb. 9, 1990, p. 45.

18. Aleksandr Lebedev, conversation with the author, June 27, 1990.

19. *Argumenty i Fakty,* June 23, 1990, p. 2.

20. Francis X. Clines, "In Moscow, Heated Cry for an Opposition," *The New York Times,* Jan. 21, 1990, p. A14.

21. Dawn Mann, "Cracks in the CPSU Monolith," *Radio Free Europe/Radio Liberty Report on the USSR,* June 15, 1990, p. 2.

22. Yuri Afanasyev, *FBIS,* Jan. 30, 1990, p. 62.

23. Vladimir Lysenko, *FBIS,* Apr. 3, 1990, p. 47.

24. Julia Wishnevsky, "Two RSFSR Congresses: A Diarchy?" *RFE/RL Report on the USSR*, July. 6, 1990, p. 2.

25. Yegor Ligachev, *FBIS*, June 18, 1990, p. 55.

26. Ivan Osadchy, *FBIS*, June 19, 1990, p. 88.

27. Viktor Tyulkin, *FBIS*, Jul. 2, 1990, p. 93.

28. Gen. Albert Makashov, *The Washington Post*, June 20, 1990, pp. A31, A36.

29. Ligachev, *The Washington Post*, June 21, 1990, p. A1.

30. Gorbachev, *FBIS*, June 20, 1990, p. 79.

31. Polozkov, *op. cit.*

32. *The Washington Post*, June 24, 1990, p. A30.

33. *Ibid.*, June 23, 1990, p. A24.

34. Bella Kurkova, conversation with the author, June 28, 1990.

35. Prokofyev, *op. cit.*

36. Lebedev, *op. cit.*

37. *Ogonek*, June 16–23, 1990, No. 25, p. 1.

38. *Moscow News*, Jul. 8, 1990, p. 5.

39. *Izvestia Tsk KPSS*, No. 3, 1990, pp. 124–25, cited in *Radio Free Europe/Radio Liberty Report on the USSR*, May 18, 1990, pp. 1–3.

40. *The Washington Post*, June 16, 1990, p. A16.

41. Prokofyev, *op. cit.*

42. *Moscow News*, June 24, 1990, p. 8.

43. *Ibid.*, p. 9.

44. Aleksandr Yakovlev, Jul. 2, 1990, Moscow television, *FBIS*, Jul. 3, 1990, pp. 28–30.

45. Gorbachev, Congress, *op. cit.*

46. Yakovlev, Congress, Jul. 7, 1990, *FBIS*, Jul. 9, 1990, p. 41.

47. Shevardnadze, Congress, Jul. 3, 1990, *FBIS*, Jul. 5, 1990, pp. 7, 9.

48. Gorbachev, Congress, Jul. 10, 1990, *FBIS*, Jul. 11, 1990, p. 8.

49. See *Moscow News*, Jul. 1, 1990, p. 13.

50. Ligachev, Moscow television, Jul. 5, 1990.

51. Vladimir Kryuchkov, Congress, Jul. 3, 1990, *FBIS*, Jul. 5, 1990, p. 16.

52. Boris Yeltsin, Congress, Jul. 6, 1990, *FBIS*, Jul. 10, 1990, p. 1.

53. *The New York Times*, Jul. 12, 1990, p. A12.

54. *The New York Times*, Jul. 13, 1990, pp. A1, A6.

55. Andrei Kortunov, conversation with the author, Jul. 4, 1990.

23. CITY HALL: THE NEW POLITICAL ENTREPRENEURS

1. Sergei Stankevich, interview with the author, June 26, 1990.

2. Anatoly Sobchak, Leningrad radio, June 27, 1990, interview with the author, June 29, 1990.

3. Anatoly Golovkov, interview with the author, Mar. 5, 1990.

4. Konstantin Yarukhin, conversation with the author, June 28, 1990.

5. Yelena Zelinskaya, conversation with the author, June 28, 1990.

6. David Broder, "Home Rule for Kiev," *The Washington Post*, Jul. 15, 1990, p. A23.

7. Conversations with Stankevich, June 26, 1990, Sobchak, June 29, 1990.

8. *The Washington Post*, Apr. 26, 1990, p. A34.

9. *The New York Times*, Apr. 26, 1990, p. A12.

10. Aleksandr Seryakov, interview with the author, June 28, 1990.

11. Stankevich, interview, June 26, 1990.

12. Lithuanian Department of Statistics, "Lithuanian Barter of Lithuanian Products and Goods with the U.S.S.R. during the Blockade," Jul. 12, 1990.

13. V. I. Lenin, *Collected Works* (Moscow: Progress Publishers, 1964), Vol. XXV, p. 154.

14. *The New York Times*, Apr. 21, 1990, p. A1.

15. Stankevich, interview, June 26, 1990.

16. Yuri Prokofyev, interview with the author, June 27, 1990.

17. Stankevich, conversation with the author, Aug. 2, 1990.

18. Celestine Bohlen, "Amid Soviets' Changes, Who Owns the Papers?" *The New York Times,* June 6, 1990, p. A12.

19. Moscow radio, June 23, 1990, *FBIS,* Jul. 6, 1990, p. 64.

20. Sobchak, interview, *Moscow News,* June 10, 1990, p. 5.

21. *Ibid.,* interview, *New Times,* May 29–June 4, 1990, p. 7.

22. *Ibid.,* "Who Obeys Whom?" *Moscow News,* Jul. 8, 1990, p. 5.

23. Bill Keller, "Party, Facing Eviction, Clings to Its Properties," *The New York Times,* June 29, 1990, p. A4.

24. Sobchak, Leningrad radio, June 27, 1990, interview with the author, June 29, 1990.

25. Bella Kurkova, interview with the author, June 28, 1990.

26. Stankevich, conversation with the author, Mar. 12, 1990.

27. Gavril Popov, interview, *Rabochaya Tribuna,* Apr. 22, 1990, p. 5; *FBIS,* Apr. 27, 1990, p. 95.

28. *The New York Times,* Jul. 8, 1990, p. 1.

29. Francis X. Clines, "Private Lesson on Moscow Potholes," *The New York Times,* Jul. 28, 1990, p. A6.

30. Stankevich, conversation, Aug. 2, 1990.

31. *Ibid.,* interview, June 26, 1990.

32. Mark Masarsky, conversation with the author, Jul. 3, 1990.

33. Stankevich, interview, June 26, 1990.

34. Sobchak, conversation with the author, Aug. 8, 1990.

35. *Ibid.,* June 29, 1990.

24. THE OUTLOOK: WILL IT COLLAPSE OR WILL IT ENDURE?

1. Alexis de Tocqueville, *The Old Regime and the Revolution* (New York: Harper and Brothers, 1856), p. 214.

2. Aleksandr Yakovlev, interview with the author, Oct. 9, 1989.

3. Gorbachev, *Perestroika* (New York: Harper & Row, 1987), p. 36.

4. Eduard Shevardnadze, speech to Foreign Policy Association of New York, Oct. 2, 1989.

5. Yakovlev, *op. cit.*

6. A.J.P. Taylor, *Bismarck: The Man and The Statesman* (London: H. Hamilton, 1955), pp. 255–58.

7. Simon Serfaty, *France, DeGaulle, & Europe* (Baltimore: Johns Hopkins University Press, 1968), p. 163–64.

8. Lance Morrow, "The Unlikely Patron of Change," *Time,* Jan. 1, 1990, p. 44.

9. *The Washington Post,* Jul. 31, 1990, p. A17.

10. Timothy Garton Ash, "Ten Thoughts on the New Europe," *The New York Review of Books,* June 14, 1990, p. 22.

11. *The New York Times,* June 23, 1990, p. A6.

12. Jim Hoagland, "The Real Soviet Economy—Underground," *The Washington Post,* June 15, 1990, p. A25.

13. Anatoly Sobchak, conversation with the author, Aug. 7, 1990.

14. Vadim Bakatin, conversation with the author, Jul. 4, 1990.

15. *The Washington Post,* Jul. 21, 1990, p. A1.

16. *The New York Times,* Jul. 27, 1990, p. A6.

17. See Gavril Popov, "Dangers of Democracy," *The New York Review of Books,* Aug. 16, 1990, pp. 27–28.

INDEX

ABOUT THE AUTHOR

HEDRICK SMITH's twenty-six-year career with *The New York Times* took him to Vietnam, Cairo, Paris, and Washington, as well as Moscow, where his reporting from 1971 to 1974 won him a Pulitzer Prize. His books include the best-sellers *The Russians* and *The Power Game.* He is a fellow of the Foreign Policy Institute at the Johns Hopkins School of Advanced International Studies. He was chief correspondent of the four-part PBS miniseries *Inside Gorbachev's USSR*, and is a regular panelist on PBS's *Washington Week in Review.* He lives in Maryland with his wife, Susan.